JavaScript

for Web Warriors

Seventh Edition

Patrick Carey

Sasha Vodnik

Australia • Brazil • Canada • Mexico • Singapore • United Kingdom • United States

JavaScript for Web Warriors, Seventh Edition
Patrick Carey / Sasha Vodnik

SVP, Higher Education & Skills Product: Erin Joyner

VP, Higher Education & Skills Product: Thais Alencar

Product Director: Mark Santee

Associate Product Manager: Tran Pham

Product Assistant: Tom Benedetto

Learning Designer: Mary Convertino

Senior Content Manager: Michelle Ruelos Cannistraci

Digital Delivery Lead: David O'Connor

Technical Editor: Danielle Shaw

Developmental Editor: Deb Kaufmann

Vice President, Product Marketing: Jason Sakos

Director, Marketing: Danae April

Marketing Manager: Mackenzie Paine

IP Analyst: Ashley Maynard

IP Project Manager: Nick Barrows

Production Service: SPi Global

Designer: Erin Griffin

Cover Image Source: NesaCera/ShutterStock.com

Library of Congress Control Number: 2021909896

ISBN: 978-0-357-63800-2

Cengage
200 Pier 4 Boulevard
Boston, MA 02210
USA

Cengage is a leading provider of customized learning solutions with employees residing in nearly 40 different countries and sales in more than 125 countries around the world. Find your local representative at **www.cengage.com.**

To learn more about Cengage platforms and services, register or access your online learning solution, or purchase materials for your course, visit **www.cengage.com.**

Printed at CLDPC, USA, 06-21

BRIEF CONTENTS

CONTENTS

PREFACE

JavaScript is a client-side scripting language that allows web page authors to develop interactive web pages and sites. Although JavaScript is considered a programming language, it is also a critical part of web page design and authoring. This is because the JavaScript language enables web developers to add functionality directly to a web page's elements. The language is relatively easy to learn, allowing non-programmers to quickly incorporate JavaScript functionality into a web page. In fact, because it is used extensively in the countless web pages that are available on the World Wide Web, JavaScript is arguably the most widely used programming language in the world.

JavaScript, Seventh Edition, teaches web page development with JavaScript for students with little programming experience. Although it starts with an overview of the components of web page development, students using this book should have basic knowledge of web page creation, including familiarity with commonly used HTML elements and CSS properties. This book covers the basics of ECMAScript Edition 11 (June, 2020), which is supported by all modern browsers. This book also covers advanced topics including object-oriented programming, the Document Object Model (DOM), touch and mobile interfaces, and Fetch. The HTML documents in this book are written to HTML5 standards, with some XHTML-compatible element syntax. After completing this course, you will be able to use JavaScript to build professional quality web applications.

The Approach

This book introduces a variety of techniques, focusing on what you need to know to start writing JavaScript programs. In each chapter, you perform tasks that let you use a particular technique to build JavaScript programs. The step-by-step tasks are guided activities that reinforce the skills you learn in the chapter and build on your learning experience by providing additional ways to apply your knowledge in new situations. In addition to step-by-step tasks, each chapter includes objectives, short quizzes, a summary, key terms with definitions, review questions, and reinforcement exercises that highlight major concepts and let you practice the techniques you've learned.

Course Overview

The examples and exercises in this book will help you achieve the following objectives:

- Use JavaScript with HTML elements
- Work with JavaScript variables and data types and learn how to use the operations that can be performed on them
- Add functions and control flow within your JavaScript programs
- Trace and resolve errors in JavaScript programs
- Write JavaScript code that controls the web browser through the browser object model
- Use JavaScript to make sure data was entered properly into form fields and to perform other types of preprocessing before form data is sent to a server
- Create JavaScript applications that use object-oriented programming techniques
- Manipulate data in strings and arrays
- Save state information using hidden form fields, query strings, cookies, and Web Storage
- Incorporate touchscreen support and mobile capabilities in web applications
- Dynamically update web applications with Ajax and Fetch
- Build a web application using the jQuery library

JavaScript, Seventh Edition, presents twelve chapters that cover specific aspects of JavaScript programming. **Chapter 1** discusses basic concepts of the World Wide Web, reviews HTML documents, and covers the basics of how to add JavaScript to web pages. How to write basic JavaScript code, including how to use variables, data types, expressions, operators, and events, is also discussed in Chapter 1. This early introduction of key JavaScript concepts gives you a framework for better understanding more advanced concepts and techniques later in this book, and allows you to work on more comprehensive projects from the start. **Chapter 2** covers functions, data types, and how to build expressions. **Chapter 3** explains how to store data in arrays and how to use structured logic in control structures and statements. **Chapter 4** provides a thorough discussion of debugging techniques, including how to use the browser consoles integrated into all modern browsers. **Chapter 5** teaches how to manipulate the structure of a web document by creating element nodes and web page overlays. **Chapter 6** explains how to use JavaScript to make sure data was entered properly into form fields and how to perform other types of preprocessing before form data is sent to a server. **Chapter 7** covers advanced topics in manipulating data in text strings, arrays, and JSON. **Chapter 8** presents object-oriented programming concepts, including coverage of object classes and closures. **Chapter 9** explains how to save state information using hidden form fields, query strings, cookies, and Web Storage, and also briefly discusses JavaScript security issues. **Chapter 10** covers supporting touch and pointer events in a web application, as well as using data provided by mobile device hardware and optimizing a web app for mobile users. **Chapter 11** introduces the basics of how to use Ajax and Fetch to dynamically update portions of a web page with server-side data. **Chapter 12** introduces using the jQuery library to simplify common programming tasks in JavaScript. **Appendix A** provides detailed instructions on installing the XAMPP web server on a local machine. **Appendix B** gives a brief refresher on the basics of HTML, XHTML, and CSS. **Appendix C**, which is online, lists answers for all Quick Checks.

What's New in This Edition?

The seventh edition includes the following important new features:

- New coverage of JavaScript topics from ES6 including the `let` and `const` keywords, template literals, and arrow function syntax.
- Expanded coverage of important programming topics including regular expressions, multidimensional arrays, closures, function expressions, array functions, and sorting callback functions.
- Expanded coverage of object-oriented programming techniques, including the creation of object classes, object prototypes, and prototype chains.
- New and expanded coverage of the Event model, event bubbling and capturing, event objects, pointer events, keyboard events, and the Drag and Drop API.
- New coverage of the Fetch API and JavaScript promises.
- Expanded coverage of jQuery coding techniques and using the jQuery UI library.
- Twelve new chapter cases with code written to the latest JavaScript standards and covering such tasks as creating a Lightbox Slideshow, developing an interactive Poker Game, using JavaScript string methods to create a Word Cloud app, creating an interactive route map with the Google Maps API, and retrieving newsfeed data for an online blog.
- Four new case projects with each chapter and a fifth debugging project that tests the student's ability to locate and fix programming errors.
- Expanded coverage of browser developer tools for debugging and managing network connections and data.
- Updated page design makes it easier to follow steps and locate important information to use as a study guide or reference book.

Features

Each chapter in *JavaScript, Seventh Edition*, includes the following features:

- **Chapter Objectives:** Each chapter begins with a list of the important concepts presented in the chapter. This list provides you with a quick reference to the contents of the chapter as well as a useful study aid.

- **Figures and Tables:** Plentiful full-color screenshots allow you to check your screen after each change. Tables consolidate important material for easy reference.
- **Code Examples:** Numerous code examples throughout each chapter are presented in any easy-to-read font.
- **Key Terms:** The first use of key terms are printed in bold and orange font to draw your attention to important definitions.

Note | These elements provide additional helpful information on specific techniques and concepts.

Common Mistakes | These notes highlight common mistakes that a new programmer might make with the tasks and concepts introduced in the chapter and provide suggestions for locating and fixing those errors.

Skills at Work

These boxes provide guidance for navigating the world of work.

Best Practices

These boxes highlight guidelines for real- world implementation of various topics.

Programming Concepts

These boxes explain principles underlying the subject of each chapter or section.

- **Quick Check:** Several Quick Checks are included in each chapter. These Quick Checks, consisting of two to five questions, help ensure you understand the major points introduced in the chapter. Appendix C (provided online) gives answers to each chapter's Quick Check questions.
- **Summary:** These brief overviews revisit the ideas covered in each chapter, providing you with a helpful study guide.
- **Key Terms List:** These lists compile all new terms introduced in the chapter, creating a convenient reference covering a chapter's important concepts.
- **Review Questions:** At the end of each chapter, a set of twenty review questions reinforces the main ideas introduced in the chapter. These questions help you determine whether you have mastered the concepts presented in the chapter.
- **Hands-On Projects:** Although it is important to understand the concepts behind every technology, no amount of theory can improve on real-world experience. To this end, each chapter includes four detailed Hands-On Projects that provide you with practice implementing technology skills in real-world situations. Each project is a standalone project, giving you a wide variety of topics and difficulty levels.

- **Debugging Challenge:** Each chapter includes one Debugging Challenge project in which you are given code that contains errors preventing it from running or running correctly. Here you can practice the important skill of interpreting other people's code and repairing it.
- **Case Projects:** These end-of-chapter projects are designed to help you apply what you have learned to open-ended situations, both individually and as a member of a team. They give you the opportunity to independently synthesize and evaluate information, examine potential solutions, and make decisions about the best way to solve a problem.

MindTap

In addition to the readings, the MindTap includes the following:

- **Course Orientation:** Custom videos and readings prepare students for the material and coding experiences they will encounter in their course.
- **Coding Snippets:** These short, ungraded coding activities are embedded in the MindTap Reader and provide students an opportunity to practice new programming concepts "in-the-moment". The coding Snippets help transition the student from conceptual understanding to application of JavaScript code.

Instructor and Student Resources

Additional instructor and student resources for this product are available online. Instructor assets include an Instructor's Manual, Solutions and Answer Guide, Solutions Files, Teaching Online Guide, PowerPoint® slides, and a test bank powered by Cognero®. Student assets include data sets for the Hands-On Projects and Case Projects. Sign up or sign in at **www.cengage.com** to search for and access this product and its online resources.

Read This Before You Begin

The following information will help you prepare to use this textbook.

Data Files

To complete the steps, exercises, and projects in this book, you will need data files that have been created specifically for this book. The data files are available in the Student Resources. Note that you can use a computer in your school lab or your own computer to complete the steps, exercises, and projects in this book.

Using Your Own Computer

You can use a computer in your school lab or your own computer to complete the chapters. To use your own computer, you will need the following:

- **A modern web browser**, including the current versions of Chrome, Edge, Firefox, or Safari.
- **A code-based HTML editor**, such as Aptana Studio, Visual Studio Code, Notepad++, Eclipse, Adobe Dreamweaver, or Atom.
- **A web server** (for Chapter 11) such as Apache HTTP Server or Microsoft Internet Information Services and PHP. Appendix A contains instructions on how to install a web server and PHP.

Acknowledgements

Creating the Seventh Edition of JavaScript has truly been a team effort. Special thanks to Michelle Ruelos Cannistraci, Mary Convertino, Tran Pham, Erin Griffin, and Troy Dundas at Cengage, to developmental editor Deb Kaufmann, and to quality assurance and technical editor Danielle Shaw. Thanks also to the production team of copyeditors, proofreaders, and compositors at SPi Global.

And many thanks to the reviewers who provided valuable feedback: Thomas Brown, Forsyth Technical Community College; Tonya Melvin Bryant, Coastal Carolina University; and Pranshu Gupta, DeSales University.

(Patrick): This book is dedicated to my special girls: Abbey, Nicola, Sonia, Catherine, and most of all, Joan.

CHAPTER 1

Introduction to JavaScript

When you complete this chapter, you will be able to:

- Explain the history of JavaScript and scripting languages and how each has been developed for its current use
- Write content into a web page using JavaScript
- Add JavaScript code to a web page
- Create and apply JavaScript variables
- Work with event handlers within a web page
- Connect to an external JavaScript File

JavaScript is a programming language that adds complex interactive features to a website. Among its many applications, JavaScript can be used to validate data on web forms, generate new content in response to user actions, and store data that will persist from one web session to the next. JavaScript is an increasingly important tool for the website designer and programmer to create useful and powerful web applications.

This chapter introduces the basics of JavaScript and its role in developing interactive websites. You will create a JavaScript program for use in a web page and explore browser tools for evaluating your code.

Exploring the JavaScript Language

Before discussing the details of JavaScript, this chapter will examine how JavaScript fits in with the development of the web as the primary source of sharing content and commerce across the globe. JavaScript had its origins in the mid-1990s with the creation of the World Wide Web or web, which was developed to share data across a network of linked documents. In its early years, the web was primarily used for academic research and did not require much more than the ability to share text and graphic images between researchers.

The business world quickly recognized that the web could be a powerful tool for online commerce including the process of validating customer data. When JavaScript first appeared in 1995, it was used to handle as much of that validation as possible to speed up customer transactions. But what is JavaScript and how does it compare to other languages?

Introducing Scripting Languages

In discussing computer languages, especially those associated with website design, this book focuses on three general types of languages: programming languages, scripting languages, and markup languages.

A programming language is a set of instructions directing the actions of the computer or computer device. Before these instructions can be performed, they need to be compiled, a process by which those instructions are transformed into machine code that can be understood by the computer or computer device. The compiling is done by a program called a compiler. Thus, before you can work with a programming language, you need to have a working environment to build the code, test the code, and compile it. Examples of programming language include Java, C, C++, and C#. The browser that interacts with the web was created and compiled using a programming language like C++. This book will not examine those languages except in terms of how they might interact with JavaScript.

A scripting language belongs to a subcategory of programming languages that do not require compiling but instead are run directly from a program or script. Scripting languages need to be *interpreted*, in which the code is read line-by-line by an interpreter that scans the code for errors even as it runs. A JavaScript interpreter is built into every web browser, so to create a JavaScript program you only need a text editor to write the code and a web browser to run it. Examples of scripting languages include JavaScript, PHP, Perl, and Python.

Finally, a markup language is a language that defines the content, structure, and appearance of a document. Common markup languages include HTML (Hypertext Markup Language) used to define the content and structure of your web page and CSS (Cascading Style Sheets) used to define how that web page will appear on a specified device. This book focuses on the connections between HTML and CSS, which define the content and appearance of your web pages, and JavaScript, which provides tools for interacting with those pages (see **Figure 1-1**). These chapters assume that you already possess a basic knowledge of HTML and CSS.

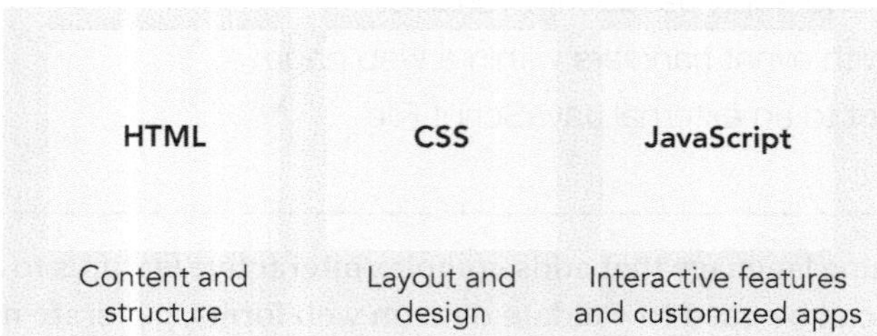

Figure 1-1 The roles of HTML, CSS, and JavaScript in web development

JavaScript and ECMAScript

The version of JavaScript discussed in this book is not the same as the one introduced in 1995. Over the years the scope and power of the language has grown to meet the needs of an ever-changing market that includes an increasing variety of devices from desktop computers to mobile phones. Who determines what JavaScript is and how it will develop is an important part of its story.

In the beginning, JavaScript was developed for the Netscape browser by the Netscape developer Brendan Eich. Shortly thereafter, JavaScript was supported by Microsoft's Internet Explorer browser in a slightly different form called JScript. One major headache for developers in the late 1990s was reconciling the differences between JavaScript and JScript as well as keeping up with the changes to the language as each browser sought to add features and tools the other browser lacked. Unlike a programming language such as C, at the time there was no single set of governing standards for JavaScript. Its growth was as unpredictable as the web itself.

Therefore in 1997, JavaScript was submitted to the European Computer Manufacturers Association (ECMA) as a proposal for a standardized scripting language that would work across a wide range of devices and browsers. A technical committee composed of developers from the major browser manufacturers was tasked with the goal of developing a set of standards for the language. The specification for this scripting language is called ECMAScript or ECMA-262. JavaScript is just one implementation of the ECMAScript standard, but it is the most important.

Every year a different version or edition of ECMAScript is released. Within a few years of release, most browsers will implement the changes in that edition, so while web programmers need to keep apprised of the changes in the most recent ECMAScript edition, they also need to write their code to conform to current browsers *and* older browser versions. **Figure 1-2** describes the most recent editions of ECMAScript at the time of this writing.

ECMASCRIPT EDITION	DATE ISSUED	FEATURES
6th Edition (ES6)	June 2015	Added new syntax for complex applications, included iterators and for . . . of loops, arrow functions, variable declarations using let and const
7th Edition (ES7)	June 2016	Added block-scoping of variables, exponentiation operator, and support for asynchronous execution
8th Edition (ES8)	June 2017	Added support for async/await constructions
9th Edition (ES9)	June 2018	Included rest/spread operators for variables, asynchronous iteration, and additions to regular expressions
10th Edition (ES10)	June 2019	Added features to object prototypes and changes to Array sorting
11th Edition (ES11)	June 2020	Added an optional object chaining operator for array and functions

Figure 1-2 Editions of ECMAScript

Note You can do a search on the web for the current support of different ECMAScript editions by desktop and mobile browsers.

The DOM and the BOM

Though they are often talked about as being identical, JavaScript is more than just ECMAScript. ECMAScript is the scripting language, but it does not tell you how to interact with the contents of a website or the browser. The full implementation of JavaScript is built on three foundations:

- ECMAScript, which is the core of the programming language, providing the syntax, keywords, properties, methods, and general structure for writing code.
- The Document Object Model (DOM), which describes how to access the contents of the web page and user actions within that page.
- The Browser Object Model (BOM), which describes how to access the features and behaviors of the browser itself.

The Document Object Model and the Browser Object Model are examples of an Application Programming Interface (API), which is a set of procedures that access an application such as a web page or a web browser. Just as the specifications for ECMAScript have developed and changed through the years, the specifications for the DOM and the BOM have also grown in response to the need for a robust and powerful scripting language for the web.

The specifications for the DOM are managed by the World Wide Web Consortium (W3C), the same group managing the development of HTML and CSS. **Figure 1-3** describes the different versions of the DOM that have been released over the years. Note that the DOM is used by programming languages other than JavaScript.

Unlike the Document Object Model, there is no formal set of standards for the Browser Object Model. Each browser is different and implements its own version of the BOM, but the BOM is largely the same from one browser to the next because it is to everyone's advantage to adhere to a common standard.

Now that you have had a short overview of JavaScript and its history, let's turn to how JavaScript works with your computer or mobile device and the computers that host the sites on the web you frequently visit.

DOM	DATE	FEATURES
DOM Level 0	1995	Provided a basic interface to access the contents of a web page using the initial version of JavaScript
DOM Level 1	October 1998	Added a way of mapping the content of a web page to JavaScript keywords, functions, properties, and methods
DOM Level 2	December 2000	Added an interface to events occurring within the web page, the contents of CSS style sheets, and the ability to transverse and manipulate the hierarchical structure of the web page content
DOM Level 3	April 2004	Added support for methods to load and save web documents, validate web forms, and provides the ability to work with keyboard objects and events
DOM Level 4	November 2015	An ongoing "living standard" that is updated to reflect the events and actions occurring within the document model based on the evolving needs of the market and mobile devices

Figure 1-3 Versions of the Document Object Model

Understanding Client/Server Architecture

To be successful in web development, you need to understand the basics of client/server architecture. There are many definitions of the terms "client" and "server". In traditional client/server architecture, the server is a device or application from which a client requests information. A server fulfills a request for information by managing the request or serving the requested information to the client—hence the term, "client/server." A system consisting of a client and a server is known as a two-tier system.

One of the primary roles of the client, or front end, in a two-tier system is the presentation of an interface to the user. The user interface gathers information from the user, submits it to a server, or back end, then receives, formats, and presents the results returned from the server. The main responsibilities of a server are usually data storage, management, and communicating with external services. On client/server systems, heavy processing, such as calculations, usually takes place on the server. As devices that are used to access web pages—such as computers, tablets, and mobile phones—have become increasingly powerful, however, many client/server systems have placed increasing amounts of the processing responsibilities on the client. In a typical client/server system, a client computer might contain a front end that is used for requesting information from a database on a server. The server locates records that meet the client request, performs some sort of processing, such as calculations on the data, and then returns the information to the client. The client computer can also perform some processing, such as building the queries that are sent to the server or formatting and presenting the returned data. **Figure 1-4** illustrates the design of a two-tier client/server system.

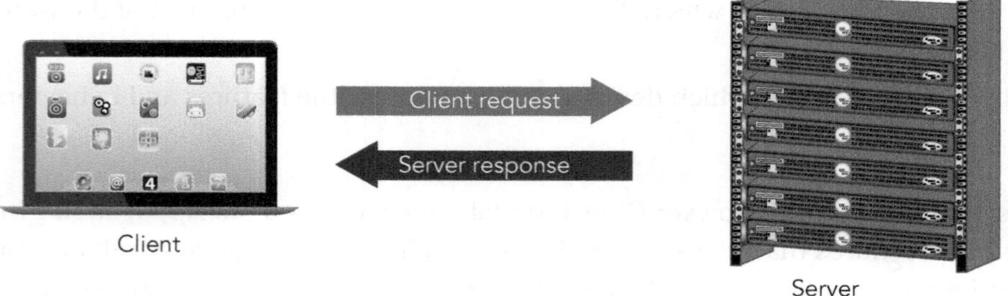

Figure 1-4 A two-tier client/server system

The web is built on a two-tier client/server system, in which a web browser (the client) requests documents from a web server. The web browser is the client user interface. You can think of the web server as a repository for web pages. After a web server returns the requested document, the web browser (as the client user interface) is responsible for formatting and presenting the document to the user. The requests and responses through which a web browser and web server communicate occur via Hypertext Transfer Protocol (HTTP), which is the main system used on the web for exchanging data. For example, if a web browser requests the URL *http://www.cengage.com*, the request is made with HTTP because the URL specifies the HTTP protocol. The web server then returns to the web browser an HTTP response containing the response header and the HTML for the Cengage home page.

After you start adding databases and other types of applications to a web server, the client/ server system evolves into what is known as a three-tier client architecture. A three-tier client/server system—also known as a multitier client/ server system or *n*-tier client/server system—consists of three distinct pieces: the client tier, the processing tier, and the data storage tier. The client tier, or user interface tier, is still the web browser. However, the database portion of the two-tier client/server system is split into a processing tier and the data storage tier. The processing tier, or middle tier, handles the interaction between the web browser client and the data storage tier. (The processing tier is also sometimes called the processing bridge.) Essentially, the client tier makes a request of a database on a web server. The processing tier performs any necessary processing or calculations based on the request from the client tier, and then reads information from or writes information to the data storage tier. The processing tier also handles the return of any information to the client tier. Note that the processing tier is not the only place where processing can occur. The web browser (client tier) still renders web page documents (which requires processing), and the database or application in the data storage tier might also perform some processing.

Note Two-tier client/server architecture is a physical arrangement in which the client and server are two separate computers. Three-tier client/server architecture is more conceptual than physical, because the storage tier can be located on the same server.

Figure 1-5 illustrates the design of a three-tier client/server system.

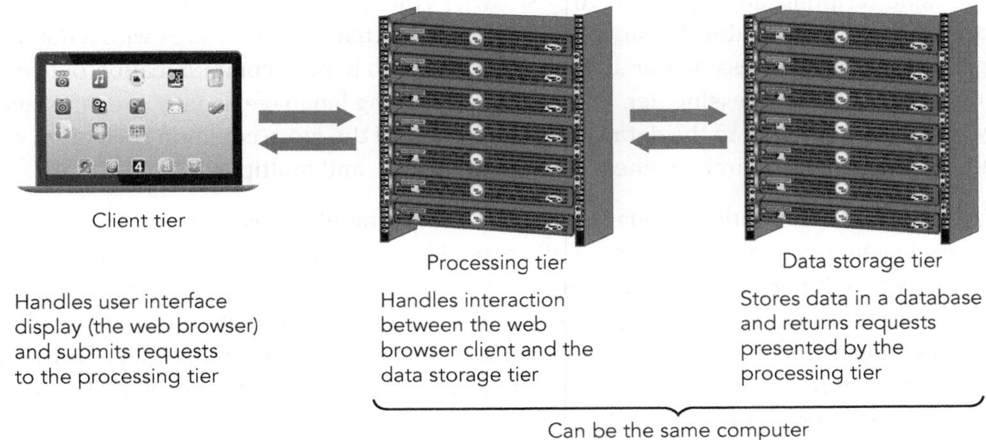
Client tier
Processing tier
Data storage tier
Handles user interface display (the web browser) and submits requests to the processing tier
Handles interaction between the web browser client and the data storage tier
Stores data in a database and returns requests presented by the processing tier
Can be the same computer

Figure 1-5 A three-tier client/server system

JavaScript and Client-Side Scripting

HTML was not originally intended to control the appearance of pages in a web browser. When HTML was first developed, web pages were static—that is, they couldn't change after the browser rendered them. However, after the web grew beyond a small academic and scientific community, people began to recognize that greater interactivity and better visual design would make the web more useful. As commercial applications of the web grew, the demand for more interactive and visually appealing websites also grew.

HTML could be used to produce only static documents. You can think of a static web page written in HTML as being approximately equivalent to a printed book; you can read it or move around in it, but the content is fixed.

What JavaScript provides that HTML needed is client-side scripting in which the scripting language runs on a local browser (on the client tier) instead of on a web server (on the processing tier). In this way, web pages can respond dynamically to user actions without putting extra strain on the operations of the server.

Note

Many people think that JavaScript is a simplified version of the Java programming language, or is related to Java in some other way. However, the languages are entirely different. Java is an advanced programming language that was created by Sun Microsystems and is considerably more difficult to master than JavaScript. Although Java can be used to create programs that can run from a web page, Java programs are usually external programs that execute independently of a browser. In contrast, JavaScript programs always run within a web page and control the browser.

For security reasons, the JavaScript programming language cannot be used outside of specific environments. The most common environment where JavaScript is run is a web browser. For example, to prevent malicious scripts from stealing information, such as your email address or the credit card information you use for an online transaction, or from causing damage by changing or deleting files, JavaScript allows manipulation only of select files associated with the browser, and then with strict limitations. Another helpful limitation is the fact that JavaScript cannot run system commands or execute programs on a client. The ability to read and write cookies and a few other types of browser storage is the only type of access to a client that JavaScript has. Web browsers, however, strictly govern their storage and do not allow access to stored information from outside the domain that created it. This security also means that you cannot use JavaScript to interact directly with web servers that operate at the processing tier. Although programmers can employ a few tricks (such as forms and query strings) to allow JavaScript to interact indirectly with a web server, if you want true control over what's happening on the server, you need to use a server-side scripting language.

Understanding Server-Side Scripting

Server-side scripting refers to programming using a scripting language that is executed from a web server. Some of the more popular server-side scripting languages are PHP, ASP.NET, Python, and Ruby. One of the primary reasons for using a server-side scripting language is to develop an interactive website that communicates with a database. Server-side scripting languages work in the processing tier and have the ability to handle communication between the client tier and the data storage tier. At the processing tier, a server-side scripting language usually prepares and processes the data in some way before submitting it to the data storage tier. Some of the more common uses of server-side scripting languages include shopping carts, search engines, discussion forums, and multiplayer games.

Without JavaScript, a server-side scripting language can't access or manipulate the user's web browser. In fact, a server-side scripting language cannot run on a client tier at all. Instead, a server-side scripting language exists and executes solely on a web server, where it performs various types of processing or accesses databases. When a client requests a server-side script, the script is interpreted and executed by the scripting engine within the web server software. After the script finishes executing, the web server software translates the results of the script (such as the result of a calculation or the records returned from a database) into HTML, which it then returns to the client. In other words, a client will never see the serverside script, only the HTML that the web server software returns from the script. **Figure 1-6** illustrates how a web server processes a server-side script.

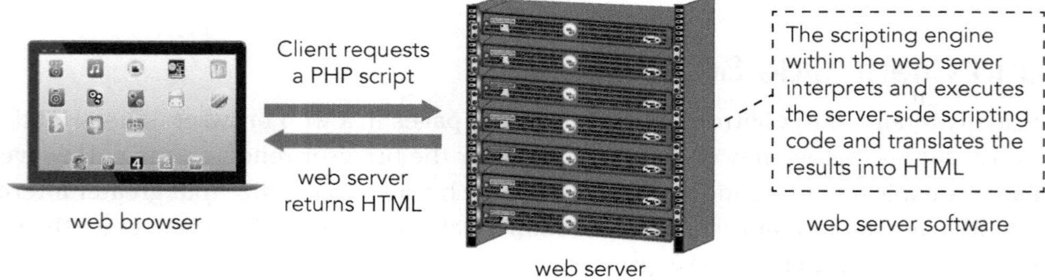

Figure 1-6 How a web server processes a server-side script

Should You Use Client-Side or Server-Side Scripting?

An important question in the design of any client/server system is deciding how much processing to place on the client and how much to place on the server. In the context of website development, you must decide whether to use client-side JavaScript or a server-side script. This is an important consideration that can greatly affect the performance of your program. In some cases, the decision is simple. If you want to control the web browser, you must use JavaScript. If you want to access a database on a web server, you must use a server-side script. However, there are tasks that both languages can accomplish, such as validating forms and manipulating cookies. Furthermore, both languages can perform the same types of calculations and data processing.

A general rule of thumb is to allow the client to handle the user interface processing and light processing, such as data validation, but have the web server perform intensive calculations and data storage. This division of labor is especially important when dealing with clients and servers over the web. Unlike with clients on a private network, it's not possible to know in advance the computing capabilities of each client on the web. You cannot assume that each client (browser) that accesses your client/server application (website) has the necessary power to perform the processing required by an application. For this reason, intensive processing should be performed on the server.

Because servers are usually much more powerful than client computers, your first instinct might be to let the server handle all processing and only use the client to display a user interface. Although you do not want to overwhelm clients with processing they cannot handle, it is important to perform as much processing as possible on the client for several reasons:

- Distributing processing among multiple clients creates applications that are more powerful, because the processing power is not limited to the capabilities of a single computer. Client devices—including computers, tablets, and smartphones—become more powerful every day. Thus, it makes sense to use a web application to harness some of this power and capability. A web application is a program that is executed on a server but is accessed through a web page loaded in a client browser.
- Local processing on client computers minimizes transfer times across the Internet and creates faster applications. If a client had to wait for all processing to be performed on the server, a web application could be painfully slow over a low-bandwidth Internet connection.
- Performing processing on client computers decreases the amount of server resources needed by application providers, decreasing costs for infrastructure and power use.

Now that you have seen how JavaScript fits within the client/server structure, in the next section you will explore how to start applying JavaScript to your own web pages.

Quick Check 1

1. How does a scripting language like JavaScript differ from a programming language like C#?
2. What are the three core foundations upon which JavaScript is built?
3. In client/server architecture, what is a client? What is a server?

Writing a JavaScript Program

Before you start writing JavaScript you must first choose an application in which to create your programs. You can work with IDEs or code editors.

IDEs and Code Editors

You have a lot of choices for creating your own JavaScript programs. Like HTML and CSS, writing JavaScript code requires only a basic text editor but you can also use an Integrated Development Environment (IDE) to manage all of the facets of website development, including the writing and testing of JavaScript code. Popular IDEs include the following:

- Microsoft Visual Studio (*https://visualstudio.microsoft.com*)
- Komodo IDE (*https://www.activestate.com/products/komodo-ide*)
- Aptana Studio (*http://www.aptana.com*)
- NetBeans (*https://netbeans.org*)

If you find an IDE to be either too expensive (though there are very good free IDEs available on the web) or containing too much overhead for your projects, you might be better suited with a code editor that simply manages the writing of HTML, CSS, and JavaScript code within a graphical interface. These editors include a number of features that make coding easier, including numbering the lines of code in a document and color coding text based on meaning—for instance, displaying JavaScript keywords in one color and user-defined text and values in another. Several good free code editors are available online, including the following:

- Visual Studio Code (*https://code.visualstudio.com*)
- Notepad++ (*https://notepad-plus-plus.org*)
- Brackets (*http://brackets.io*)
- Atom (*https://atom.io*)

The HTML, CSS, and JavaScript code samples displayed in this book are based on a code editor that uses color to distinguish different parts of the code. Your code editor might use a different coloring scheme, but that will not affect the code because HTML, CSS, and JavaScript are saved as basic text.

In this chapter, you will add JavaScript code to a web page for Tinley Xeriscapes, a landscaping company that specializes in plants that need minimal watering. A designer has created a new layout for the company's website, and they would like you to incorporate JavaScript to enhance the functionality of one of the site's pages. **Figure 1-7** shows a preview of the completed web page incorporating the functionality you will create in this chapter.

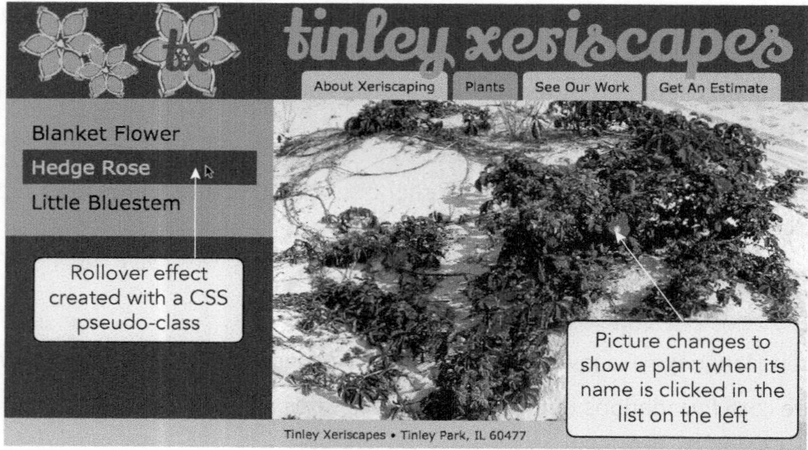

Figure 1-7 Completed Tinley Xeriscapes Plants page using JavaScript

U.S. Department of Agriculture

Open the HTML file for this web page now.

To open the Tinley Xeriscapes page:

1. Use your code editor to go to the js01 ▶ chapter folder of your data files.
2. Open the **js01_txt.html** file in your code editor.
3. Within the head section of the HTML file, enter your name and the date in the Author and Date lines.
4. Save the file as **js01.html**.

Next, begin writing the code of your first JavaScript program.

The `script` Element

JavaScript can be added to a web page by embedding the code within the following `script` element:

```
<script>
   statements
</script>
```

where *statements* are the individual lines of code in the JavaScript program. The following `script` element contains a single JavaScript statement displaying an alert window with the text message "Hello World":

```
<script>
   window.alert("Hello World");
</script>
```

When the browser encounters a `script` element, it stops loading the page and processes the statements enclosed within the script. In this case, the browser would stop loading the page to display the "Hello World" message. Once the script is run, the browser continues to process the remaining content in the HTML file. Add a `script` element now within the opening and closing `<figcaption>` tags in the HTML file for the Tinley Xeriscapes page.

To add the `script` element to the page:

1. Scroll down to the `article` element in the js01.html file within your code editor.
2. After the opening `<figcaption>` tag, type:

```
<script>
</script>
```

indenting the opening and closing tags to make your code easier to read. See **Figure 1-8**.

```
<article>
   <figure>
      <img src="#" alt="" title="" id="plantImg" />
      <figcaption id="imgCaption">
         <script>
         </script>
      </figcaption>
   </figure>
</article>
```

The script element encloses JavaScript code within an HTML file

Figure 1-8 Adding a `script` element

3. Save your changes to the file.

Next you will learn general rules for writing statements in JavaScript.

JavaScript Statements

The individual lines of code, or statements, that make up a JavaScript program in a document are contained within the `script` element. The following script contains a single statement that writes the text "Plant choices" to a web browser window, using the `write()` method of the `Document` object, which you will study shortly:

```
document.write("<p>Plant choices</p>");
```

Notice that the preceding statement ends in a semicolon. Many programming languages, including C++ and Java, require you to end all statements with a semicolon. JavaScript statements are not required to end in semicolons. Semicolons are strictly necessary only when you want to separate statements that are written on a single line. However, it is considered good JavaScript programming practice to end every statement with a semicolon whether strictly required or not. This is the convention that will be used in this book.

Understanding JavaScript Objects

Before you can use `script` elements to create a JavaScript program, you need to learn some basic terminology that is commonly used in JavaScript programming in particular, and in other programming languages in general. In addition to being an interpreted scripting language, JavaScript is considered an object-based programming language. An object is programming code and data that can be treated as an individual unit or component. For example, you might create a `carLoan` object that calculates the number of payments required to pay off a car loan. The `carLoan` object may also store information such as the principal loan amount and the interest rate. Individual statements used in a computer program are often grouped into logical units called procedures, which perform specific tasks. For example, a procedure may contain a group of statements that calculate the sales tax based on the sales total. The procedures associated with an object are called methods. A property is a piece of data, such as a color or a name, which is associated with an object. In the `carLoan` object example, the programming code that calculates the number of payments required to pay off the loan is a method. The principal loan amount and the interest rate are properties of the `carLoan` object.

To incorporate an object and an associated method in JavaScript code, type the object's name, followed by a period, followed by the method. For example, the following code references the `carLoan` object, followed by a period, followed by a method named `calcPayments()`, which calculates the number of payments required to pay off the loan:

```
carLoan.calcPayments();
```

For many methods, you also need to provide some more specific information, called an argument, between the parentheses. Some methods require numerous arguments, whereas others don't require any. Providing one or more arguments for a method is referred to as passing arguments. For example, the `calcPayments()` method may require an argument that specifies the number of months until the loan is paid off. In that case, the JavaScript statement would look like this:

```
carLoan.calcPayments(60);
```

You use an object's properties in much the same way you use a method, by appending the property name to the object with a period. However, a property name is not followed by parentheses. One of the biggest differences between methods and properties is that a property does not actually do anything; you only use properties to store data. You assign a value to a property using an equal sign, as in the following example:

```
carLoan.interest = .0349;
```

Programming Concepts | Objects, Properties, and Methods

Objects are one of the fundamental building blocks of JavaScript, as well as many other programming languages. You can think of an object as anything you want to be able to work with in your programs. Some objects, such as the `Document` object, are part of a document by definition. You can also create other objects that are necessary for the programs you want to create. Every object can have methods, which are actions that can be performed on it. Every object also has properties; each property is a different piece of information about the object. Understanding the relationship between objects, properties, and methods is an important part of building a strong foundation in JavaScript.

The next part of this chapter focuses on the `write()` method as a way of helping you understand how to program with JavaScript.

Using the `write()` Method

Almost everything within the web page and the web browser is an object and is thus part of the Document Object Model or the Browser Object Model. One of the most commonly used objects in the Document Object Model is the `Document` object, which represents the entire content of the web page. Any text, graphics, or other information displayed in the page is part of the Document object. You can write new content to the web page with the write() method of the Document object. For example, you could use the write() method to write content containing custom information such as a user's name or address.

Understand that the only reason to use the write() method is to add new text to a web page while it is being loaded by the browser. For example, if your web page incorporates constantly changing data such as stock quotes from a web server, you might use the write() method to add the stock data to the page. If you simply want to display text in a web browser when the document is first rendered, there is no need to use anything but standard HTML elements. The procedures for dynamically gathering information are a little too complicated for this introductory chapter. However, in this chapter you will use the write() method to display text in a web browser when the document is first rendered in order to learn the basics of JavaScript programming.

Different methods require different kinds of arguments. For example, the write() method of the Document object requires a text string as an argument. A text string, or literal string, is text that is contained within double or single quotation marks. The text string argument of the write() method specifies the text that the Document object uses to create new text on a web page. For example, document.write("Plant choices"); writes the text "Plant choices" in the web page (without the quotation marks). Note that you must place literal strings on a single line. If you include a line break within a literal string, you receive an error message.

Common Mistakes

By convention, the first letter of the name of a built-in object is capitalized when writing about the language, but typed in all lowercase in actual JavaScript code. For this reason, it is the Document object, but the document.write() and document.writeln() methods in JavaScript code. Be sure to enter object names in all lowercase in your programs.

The write() method performs essentially the same function that you perform when you manually add text to the body of a standard web document. Whether you add text to a document by using standard elements, such as the p element, or by using the write() method, the text is added according to the order in which the statements appear in the HTML file.

Note

Programmers often talk about code that "writes to" or "prints to" a web browser window. For example, you might say that a piece of code writes a text string to the web browser window. This is just another way of saying that the code displays the text string in the web browser window.

The following code contains a script that prints some text in a web browser by using the write() method of the Document object.

```
<script>
   document.write("<p>Plant choices<br />");
   document.write("for <a href=↵
      'http://planthardiness.ars.usda.gov'>↵
      hardiness zones</a> 5a-6b</p>");
</script>
```

Note

The bent arrow symbol (↵) at the end of a line of code indicates the code is broken in this book because of space limitations. When you enter code in your editor from code samples in this book, you should not press the Enter or Return keys at the end of a line that finishes with ↵. You must continue typing the code that follows on the same line.

Use the document.write() method now to write content to the Tinley Xeriscapes web page. To make the text easier to enter, you will use several document.write() statements. Pay close attention to the use of both single and double quotes within the text strings.

To apply the `document.write()` method:

1. Return to the **js01.html** file in your code editor.
2. Between the opening and closing `<script>` tags, add the following statements as shown in **Figure 1-9**:

```
document.write("<p>Plant choices for ");
document.write("<a href='http://planthardiness.ars.usda.gov'>");
document.write("hardiness zones</a>");
document.write(" 5a - 6b </p>");
```

The `document.write()` method writes content into the web page

```
<article>
   <figure>
      <img src="#" alt="" title="" id="plantImg" />
      <figcaption id="imgCaption">
        <script>
           document.write("<p>Plant choices for ");
           document.write("<a href='http://planthardiness.ars.usda.gov'>");
           document.write("hardiness zones</a>");
           document.write(" 5a - 6b </p>");
        </script>
     </figcaption>
   </figure>
</article>
```

HTML tags and content written to the web page

Figure 1-9 Applying the `document.write()` method

3. Save your changes to the file and then refresh or reload the **s01.html** file in your web browser. As shown in **Figure 1-10**, the page should now display the content created by the four `document.write()` statements.

Figure 1-10 Content generated using the `document.write()` method

4. Click the **hardiness zones** link from the inserted content and verify that your browser loads a Plant Hardiness Zone map.
5. Return to the **js01.html** file in your browser.

Best Practices | Using the `document.write()` Method

The `document.write()` method is a quick and easy way of writing content in your web page; however it is not without its problems. In general, using `document.write()` slows down your system's performance and load time as the browser must recreate the entire Document Object Model to incorporate the new content. **NEVER use the `document.write()` method after the browser has finished loading the web page because it will overwrite the entire web page.** A good rule of thumb is to use `document.write()` only for small snippets of content and only placed within a script embedded in the HTML file itself.

Case Sensitivity in JavaScript

JavaScript is a case-sensitive language, interpreting differences in capitalization as differences in meaning. Within JavaScript code, object names must always be all lowercase. This can be a source of some confusion, because in written explanations about JavaScript, the names of objects are sometimes referred to with an initial capital letter. For example, the `Document` object referred to with an uppercase *D*. However, you must use a lowercase *d* when referring to the `Document` object in a script, as in the code `document.write("Plant choices");`. Using a capital *D*, as in the statement `Document.write("Plant choices");`, causes an error message because the JavaScript interpreter cannot recognize an object named `Document` with an uppercase *D*.

Similarly, the following statements will also cause errors:

```
DOCUMENT.write("Plant choices");
Document.Write("Plant choices");
document.WRITE("Plant choices");
```

Note | Although HTML5 is not technically a case-sensitive language, it's considered good coding practice to write all HTML5 code in lowercase as well.

Adding Comments to a JavaScript Program

Just like in an HTML document, it's considered a good programming practice to add comments to any JavaScript code you write. Comments are lines of code that are not processed by browsers, which you use to add notes about your code. Comments are commonly used for specifying the name of the program, your name and the date you created the program, notes to yourself, or instructions to future programmers who may need to modify your work. When you are working with long scripts, comments make it easier to decipher how a program is structured.

JavaScript supports two kinds of comments: line comments and block comments. A line comment occupies only a single line or part of a line. To create a line comment, you add two slashes (//) before the text you want to use as a comment. The // characters instruct JavaScript interpreters to ignore all text following the slashes on the same line. You can place a line comment either at the end of a line of code or on its own line. Block comments hide multiple lines of code. You create a block comment by adding /* to the first line that you want included in the block, and you close a comment block by typing */ after the last character in the block. Any text or lines between the opening /* characters and the closing */ characters are ignored by JavaScript interpreters.

Note | A JavaScript block comment uses the same syntax as a comment in CSS, as well as in other programming languages including C++ and Java.

Next, you will add comments to the js01.html file.

To add JavaScript comments to the js01.html file:

1. Return to the **js01.html** file in your code editor.
2. Add the following block comment directly after the opening `<script>` tag:

```
/*
   Information on available plants
   including link to USDA website
*/
```

3. Position the insertion pointer after the semicolon at the end of the last statement containing the `document.write()` method, and type the following line comment:

```
// hardiness zones for Chicago and surrounding area
```

   See **Figure 1-11**.

```
<script>
  /*
     Information on available plants
     including link to USDA website
  */
  document.write("<p>Plant choices for ");
  document.write("<a href='http://planthardiness.ars.usda.gov'>");
  document.write("hardiness zones</a>");
  document.write(" 5a - 6b </p>"); // hardiness zones for Chicago and surrounding area
</script>
```


Figure 1-11 Adding JavaScript comments

4. Save your changes to the file and then reopen **js01.html** in your web browser. Verify that the JavaScript comments are not displayed in the browser and that the content generated by the `document.write()` statements has not changed.

Skills at Work | Using Comments for Team Projects

JavaScript programmers generally work in teams with other programmers, especially on larger projects. This means that as a programmer, you'll be regularly reading and making changes to code that other programmers wrote; in addition, other team members will be changing and extending code that you created. When working as part of a team of programmers, it's important to use comments to document the code you write. Including a comment before each section of code to explain its purpose can help other team members understand the structure of your code. In addition, including comments makes it easier for everyone on the team to find and fix bugs, because they can compare the explanation of what a section should do, found in the comment, with the code that follows.

Quick Check 2

1. What HTML element is used to embed JavaScript code within an HTML file?
2. Provide the JavaScript command to write the HTML content `<h1>Plant Types</h1>` to the web page document.
3. Provide the code to write the text, "Major Page Heading" as JavaScript block comment.
4. Provide the code to write the text, "Major Page Heading" as a JavaScript line comment.

Writing Basic JavaScript Code

So far, you've created a basic JavaScript program that stores comments and writes text to a web page. By incorporating a few additional JavaScript concepts into your program, you can make it flexible enough to apply to different situations, and responsive to user interaction.

Using Variables

The values a program stores in computer memory are commonly called variables. Technically speaking, though, a variable is actually a specific location in the computer's memory. Data stored in a specific variable often changes. You can think of a variable as similar to a storage locker—a program can put any value into it and then retrieve the value later for use in calculations. To use a variable in a program, you first write a statement that creates the variable and assigns it a name. For example, you may have a program that creates a variable named `curTime` and then stores the current time in that variable. Each time the program runs, the current time is different, so the value varies.

Programmers often talk about "assigning a value to a variable," which is the same as storing a value in a variable. For example, a shopping cart program might include variables that store customer names and purchase totals. Each variable will contain different values at different times, depending on the name of the customer and the items that customer is purchasing.

Assigning Variable Names

The name you assign to a variable is called an identifier. You must observe the following rules and conventions when naming a variable in JavaScript:

- Identifiers must begin with an uppercase or lowercase ASCII letter, dollar sign ($), or underscore (_).
- You can use numbers in an identifier but not as the first character.
- You cannot include spaces in an identifier.
- You cannot use reserved words for identifiers.

Reserved words (also called keywords) are special words that are part of the JavaScript language syntax. As just noted, reserved words cannot be used for identifiers. **Figure 1-12** lists some of the JavaScript reserved words.

abstract	char	double	finally	in	null	super	try
arguments	class	else	float	instanceof	package	switch	typeof
await	const	enum	for	int	private	synchronized	var
boolean	continue	eval	function	interface	protected	this	void
break	debugger	export	goto	let	public	throw	volatile
byte	default	extends	if	long	return	throws	while
case	delete	FALSE	implements	native	short	transient	with
catch	do	final	import	new	static	TRUE	yield

Figure 1-12 JavaScript reserved keywords

Variable names, like JavaScript keywords are case sensitive. Therefore, the variable name `curTime` is a completely different variable name than `curtime`, `CurTime`, or `CURTIME`. If a script doesn't perform as you expect, be sure you are using the correct case when referring to any variables in your code.

Note It's best practice to use camel case, which is a method of capitalization that uses a lowercase letter for the first letter of the first word in a variable name, with subsequent words starting with an initial cap, as in `myVariableName`.

Declaring and Initializing Variables

Before you can use a variable, you should declare it, which creates the variable for storing data and objects. Optionally, the variable can be initialized, which assigns it an initial value. Variables are declared and initialized using either the `let` keyword or the `var` keyword in the following statements:

```
let variable = value;
var variable = value;
```

where *variable* is the name of the variable and *value* is the initial value of the variable. The equal sign in the declaration statement is called an assignment operator because it assigns the value on the right side of the expression to the variable on the left side of the expression. The value you assign to a variable can be a literal string enclosed within quotation marks or a numeric value. The following statements use the `let` keyword to create variables named `taxRate` and `taxClass` with initial values of 0.05 and "sales".

```
let taxRate = 0.05;
let taxClass = "sales";
```

The difference between `let` and `var` lies with the scope of the variable being declared. Scope is a topic that will be discussed in the next chapter. The `var` keyword is the older standard; `let` was not introduced until ES6 in 2015.

Another way of declaring a variable is with the following `const` keyword:

```
const variable = value;
```

Unlike variables declared with `var` and `let`, variables declared with `const` store a constant value that cannot be changed.

In addition to assigning literal strings and numeric values to a variable, you can also assign the value of one variable to another. In the following code, the first statement declares the `salesTotal` variable without assigning it an initial value, the second statement declares the `curOrder` variable with an initial value of 47.58, and the third statement assigns the value of the `curOrder` variable to the `salesTotal` variable.

```
let salesTotal;
let curOrder = 47.58;
salesTotal = curOrder;
```

You can declare multiple variables in a statement using a single `let`, `var`, or `const` keyword followed by a series of variable names and assigned values separated by commas. The following statement creates three variables using a single `let` keyword:

```
let orderNumber = "R0218", salesTotal = 47.58, curOrder;
```

Notice that both the `orderNumber` and `salesTotal` variables are declared and initialized, while the `curOrder` variable is only declared with no initial value.

The main section of the Tinley Xeriscapes Plants page should display an image that changes depending on which plant name is clicked from a list of names on the page's left margin. To begin creating this effect, you will add JavaScript statements declaring three variables storing the file names of three images matching the plant names on the list.

To declare variables for three plant images:

1. Return to the **js01.html** file in your code editor.
2. Directly before the closing `</script>` tag, press **Enter** and type the following JavaScript statements containing the file names of three plant images:

```
//define variables containing plant file names
let blanket = "blanket.jpg";
let bluestem = "bluestem.jpg";
let rugosa = "rugosa.jpg";
```

See **Figure 1-13**.

Inline image that will display plant images

id of the plant image

Variables containing the file names of three plant images

```
<article>
   <figure>
      <img src="#" alt="" title="" id="plantImg" />
      <figcaption id="imgCaption">
        <script>
           /*
              Information on available plants
              including link to USDA website
           */
           document.write("<p>Plant choices for ");
           document.write("<a href='http://planthardiness.ars.usda.gov'>");
           document.write("hardiness zones</a>");
           document.write(" 5a - 6b </p>"); // hardiness zones for Chicago and surrounding area

           //define variables containing plant file names
           let blanket = "blanket.jpg";
           let bluestem = "bluestem.jpg";
           let rugosa = "rugosa.jpg";
         </script>
      </figcaption>
   </figure>
</article>
```

Figure 1-13 Declaring JavaScript variables

3. Save your changes to the file.

The default HTML code for the page has an `img` element to display plant images, but it sets the `src` attribute to # so that the default is to not display any image. Later you will write JavaScript statements to replace the `src` attribute value with one of the variable values you defined in this script so that the image changes in response to user actions.

Building Expressions with Variables

Just as with any text string or numeric value, the value of a variable can be written into a web page using the `document.write()` method. For example, the following statement displays the value of the `salesTotal` variable:

```
document.write(salesTotal);
```

Thus, if a value 47.58 has been stored in the `salesTotal` variable, that value will be written to the page.

Building an Expression

You can combine variables with text strings or numeric values using expressions. An expression is a literal value or variable, or a combination of literal values, variables, operators, and other expressions, that can be evaluated by a JavaScript interpreter to produce a result. Expressions are written using operands and operators.

Operands are the variables and literals contained in the expression. A literal is a value such as a text string or a number. Operators, such as the addition operator (+) and multiplication operator (*), are symbols used in expressions to manipulate operands. You have already seen several simple expressions that combine operators and operands as in the following statement:

```
salesTotal = 47.58;
```

which uses the assignment operator (=) to equate the `salesTotal` variable with a value of 47.58.

Note To assign a value to a variable, the value must be on the right side of the assignment operator and the variable on the left, as in the expression `firstName = "Graham";`. Reversing the order, as in the code `"Graham" = firstName;`, could produce an error in your script.

You can use the addition operator (+) with the `document.write()` method to combine a literal text string with a variable containing a numeric value. For instance, to give some context to the `salesTotal` value, you could modify the `document.write()` statement to place the variable within an HTML paragraph using the expression:

```
document.write("<p>Your sales total is $" + salesTotal +".</p>");
```

resulting in the following HTML code written to the web page:

```
<p>Your sales total is $47.58.</p>
```

You can also use the addition operator to perform arithmetic operations involving variables that contain numeric values. The following code declares two variables, assigning them numeric values. The third statement declares another variable and assigns to it the sum of the two variables.

```
let salesTotal = 47.58;
let shippingCost = 10;
let totalCost = salesTotal + shippingCost;
document.write("<p>Your total cost is $" + totalCost + "</p>";
```

The result is the generation of the following HTML code:

```
<p>Your total cost is $57.58</p>
```

Notice that this script uses the addition operator (+) to both add numeric values and to combine text strings. If you combine a text string and numeric value, JavaScript will treat both values as strings and will combine them rather than adding them. The following expression:

```
5 + "2"
```

will return the text string "52" and *not* the value 7.

Modifying Variables

You can change a variable's value at any point in a script by using an expression to assign it a new value. The following code declares a variable named `totalSales`, assigns it an initial value of 0 and then uses the addition operator to increase by the sum of the `item1Sales`, `item2Sales`, and `item3Sales` variables.

```
let totalSales = 0;
let item1Sales = 50, item2Sales = 75, item3Sales = 40;
totalSales = item1Sales + item2Sales + item3Sales;
document.write("<p>Total sales = $" + totalSales + "</p>");
```

The following HTML code is then written to the web page:

```
<p>Total sales = $165</p>
```

It is only necessary to declare the `salesTotal` variable once using either the `var` or `let` keywords. If you declare the variable using the `const` keyword, you cannot modify it after its initial value is set.

Understanding Events

By default, scripts are executed when the code is encountered by the browser as it loads the page content. You can choose other events to initiate the execution of a script. An event is a specific circumstance (such as an action performed by a user or an action performed by the browser) that is monitored by JavaScript and that your script can respond to in some way. JavaScript events allow users to interact with your web pages. The most common events are actions that users perform. For example, when a user clicks a form button, a `click` event is generated. You can think of an event as a trigger that runs specific JavaScript code in response to a given situation. User-generated events, however, are not the only kinds of events monitored by JavaScript. Events that are not direct results of user actions, such as the `load` event, are also monitored. The `load` event, which is triggered automatically by a web browser, occurs when a document finishes loading in a web browser. **Figure 1-14** lists some JavaScript events and explains what triggers them.

EVENT	KEYBOARD TRIGGER	MOUSE TRIGGER	TOUCHSCREEN TRIGGER
`blur`	An element, such as a radio button, becomes inactive		
`change`	The value of an element, such as a text box, changes		
`click`	A user presses a key when an element is selected	A user clicks an element once	A user touches an element and then stops touching it
`error`	An error occurs when a document or image is being loaded		
`focus`	An element, such as a command button, becomes active		
`keydown`	A user presses a key		
`keyup`	A user releases a key		
`load`	A document or image loads		
`mouseout`		A user moves the mouse pointer off an element	A user stops touching an element
`mouseover`		A user moves the mouse pointer over an element	A user touches an element
`reset`	A form's fields are reset to its default values		
`select`	A user selects text		
`submit`	A user submits a form		
`touchend`			A user removes finger or stylus from the screen
`touchmove`			A finger or stylus already touching the screen moves on the screen
`touchstart`			A user touches a finger or stylus to the screen
`unload`	A document unloads		

Figure 1-14 JavaScript events

Note that not all events happen with all devices. For instance, `keydown` and `keyup` are triggered only by a keyboard, and `touchend`, `touchmove`, and `touchstart` take place only on a touchscreen device. For this reason, it's important to choose trigger events that make your scripts available to users on all devices. You'll explore different methods of doing this as you build your JavaScript skills.

Working with Elements and Events

Events are associated with HTML elements. The events that are available to an element vary. The `click` event, for example, is available for a number of elements, including the `a` element and form controls created with the `input` element. In comparison, the `body` element does not have a `click` event, but it does have a `load` event, which occurs when a web page finishes loading, and an `unload` event, which occurs when a user goes to a different web page.

When an event occurs, your script executes any code that responds to that specific event on that specific element. This code is known as the event handler. There are a few different ways to specify an event handler for a particular event. One way is to include event handler code as an attribute of the element that initiates the event. For example, you can add an attribute that listens for a click to an `li` element in the navigation bar, and specify JavaScript code as the attribute value, such as code that changes the `display` attribute of the related submenu so it's visible. The syntax of an event handler within an opening tag is as follows:

```
<element onevent="JavaScript code">
```

The attribute name you use to specify an event handler combines the prefix `on` with the name of the event itself. For example, the attribute name for the `click` event is `onclick`, and the attribute name for the `load` event is `onload`. **Figure 1-15** various HTML elements and some of their associated event-related attributes.

ELEMENT	EVENT-RELATED ATTRIBUTES
a	onfocus, onblur, onclick, ondblclick, onmousedown, onmouseup, onmouseover, onmousemove, onmouseout, onkeypress, onkeydown, onkeyup, ontouchstart, ontouchend
img	onclick, ondblclick, onmousedown, onmouseup, onmouseover, onmousemove, onmouseout, onkeypress, onkeydown, onkeyup, ontouchstart, ontouchmove, ontouchend
body	onload, onunload, onclick, ondblclick, onmousedown, onmouseup, onmouseover, onmousemove, onmouseout, onkeypress, onkeydown, onkeyup
form	onsubmit, onreset, onclick, ondblclick, onmousedown, onmouseup, onmouseover, onmousemove, onmouseout, onkeypress, onkeydown, onkeyup
input	tabindex, accesskey, onfocus, onblur, onselect, onchange, onclick, ondblclick, onmousedown, onmouseup, onmouseover, onmousemove, onmouseout, onkeypress, onkeydown, onkeyup, ontouchstart, ontouchmove, ontouchend
textarea	onfocus, onblur, onselect, onchange, onclick, ondblclick, onmousedown, onmouseup, onmouseover, onmousemove, onmouseout, onkeypress, onkeydown, onkeyup, ontouchstart, ontouchmove, ontouchend
select	onfocus, onblur, onchange, ontouchstart, ontouchend

Figure 1-15 HTML elements and some of their associated events

The JavaScript code for an event handler attribute is contained within the quotation marks following the attribute name. The following code uses the `input` element to create a submit button.

```
<input type="submit" onclick="window.alert('Thanks for your↵
   order! We appreciate your business.')" />
```

This `input` element includes an `onclick` attribute that executes an event handler using the JavaScript `window.alert()` method, in response to a `click` event (which occurs when the mouse button is clicked or a user touches a touchscreen). The `window.alert()` method displays a dialog box with an OK button. You pass the `window.alert()` method a literal string containing the text you want to display. The syntax for the `alert()` method is `window.alert(`*`message`*`);`. The value of the literal string or variable is then displayed in the alert dialog box, as shown in **Figure 1-16**.

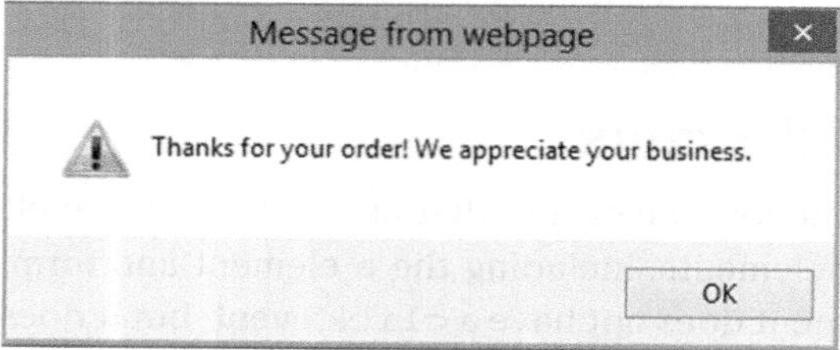

Figure 1-16 Alert dialog box

Source: © Microsoft Corporation

Notice that the event handler code specified as an attribute value—the `window.alert()` method—is contained within double quotation marks. Also notice that the literal string being passed is contained in single quotation marks. This is because the `window.alert()` method itself is already enclosed in double quotation marks. To ensure that browsers don't mistake the opening quote for the literal string as the closing quote for the value of the `onclick` event handler, JavaScript requires single quotes around the literal string.

The `window.alert()` method is the only statement being executed in the preceding event handler code. You can, however, include multiple JavaScript statements in event handler code, as long as semicolons separate the statements. For example, to include two statements in the event handler example—a statement that creates a variable and another statement that uses the `window.alert()` method to display the variable—you would type the following:

```
<input type="submit"
   onclick = "let msg = 'Thanks for your order! We appreciate your business.';
              window.alert(msg);" />
```

Referencing Web Page Elements

The Document Object Model allows you to reference any element on a web page by its `id` assigned using the HTML `id` attribute. For instance, the following HTML code creates an `input` element with the `id` value `firstName`:

```
<input type="text" id="firstName" />
```

To look up an element by its `id` value in your JavaScript code, use the `getElementById()` method of the `Document` object. For instance, to create a variable named `fName` that references the element with the `id` value `firstName`, use

```
let fName = document.getElementById("firstName");
```

Specific properties of an element can then be appended to the element reference. This allows you to retrieve information about an element or change the values assigned to its attributes. For example, suppose you have a web page that contains an `input` element with the `id` value `firstName`. You could change the value of the `input` element using this statement:

```
document.getElementById("firstName").value = value;
```

As an alternative, using the `fName` variable created above to reference the element with the `id` value `firstName`, you could use this code:

```
fName.value = value;
```

Next, you will add event handlers to the three `li` elements containing plant names in the `aside` element of the js01.html file. When a user's mouse pointer moves over one of these `li` elements, the `src` value of the `img` element with the `id` value `plantImg` will change to display the image of the plant.

To add event handlers to the plants.htm file:

1. Return to the **js01.html** file in your code editor.
2. Within the `aside` element, in the opening tag for the first `li` element, add the following event handler:

```
onclick="document.getElementById('plantImg').src = blanket"
```

3. In the opening tag for the second `li` element, add the following event handler:

```
onclick="document.getElementById('plantImg').src = rugosa"
```

4. In the opening tag for the third `li` element, add the following event handler:

```
onclick="document.getElementById('plantImg').src = bluestem"
```

Figure 1-17 shows the revised code in the file.

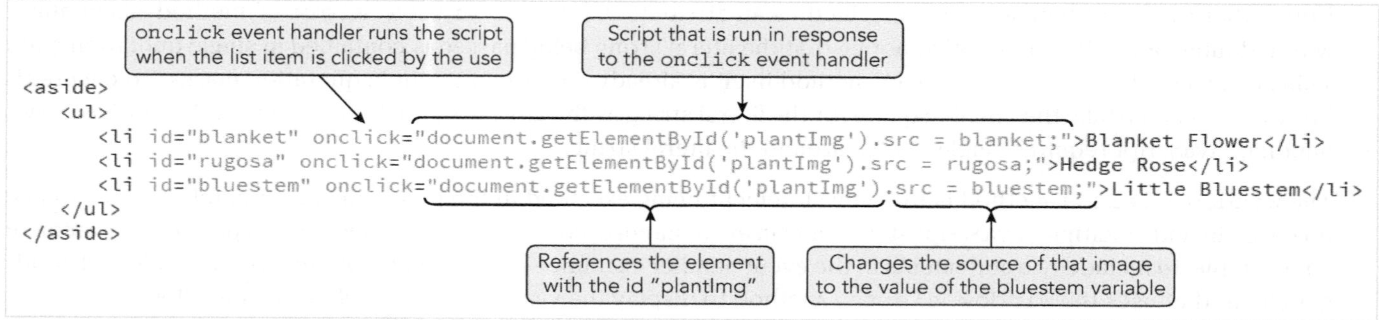

Figure 1-17 Changing the source of an inline image using JavaScript

5. Save the file, refresh or reload it in your web browser, and then click each plant name on the left side of the page. The picture of each flower should be displayed in the main section of the web page when you click its name. If the page doesn't load, or if you receive error messages, make sure that you typed all the JavaScript code in the correct case. (Remember that JavaScript is case sensitive.) **Figure 1-18** shows the web page after clicking Hedge Rose.

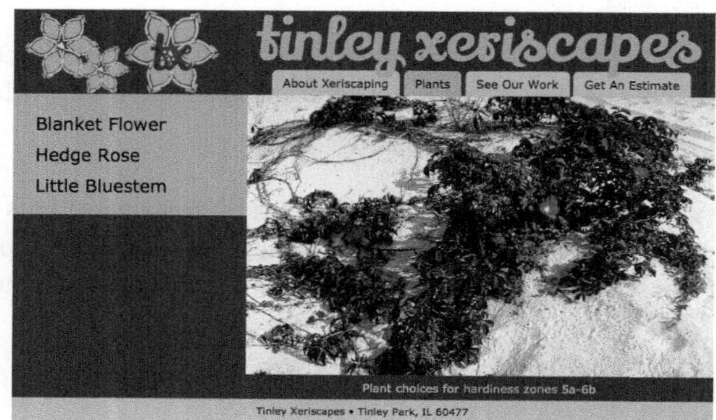

Figure 1-18 Web page after clicking Hedge Rose

U.S. Department of Agriculture

Quick Check 3

1. What are the three JavaScript keywords for declaring a variable?
2. What is the difference between declaring and initializing a variable?
3. What is returned by expression "100" + 10?
4. What is an event handler for?

Structuring JavaScript Code

You can place the `script` element just about anywhere in a document. However, there are a number of factors to consider in deciding the best location for the `script` element. In addition, there are rules to keep in mind regarding the organization of that code.

Including a `script` Element for Each Code Section

A single HTML file can contain several `script` elements. The following document fragment includes two separate script sections. The script sections create the information that is displayed beneath the `h2` heading elements.

```
<h2>Sales Total</h2>
<script>
   let salesTotal = 47.58;
   document.write("<p>Your sales total is $" + salesTotal + "</p>");
</script>
<h2>Sales Total with Shipping</h2>
<script>
   let shipping = 10;
   let totalCost = salesTotal + shipping;
   document.write("<p>Your sales total plus shipping is $" ↵
                  + totalCost + "</p>");
</script>
```

Figure 1-19 shows the output.

Sales Total
Your sales total is $47.58.
Sales Total with Shipping
Your sales total plus shipping is $57.58.

Figure 1-19 Output of a document with two script sections

Statements in one script section are accessible to subsequent script sections. For example, the `salesTotal` variable was declared in the first script, but its value was still accessible to the second script. For the purposes of your programs, you can think of the two scripts as being "connected" even if they are separated by HTML code.

Placing the `script` Element

Because of this connected nature, scripts can be placed anywhere within the HTML file. However, if the script contains the `document.write()` method, it should be placed where that content is to be written. You must use care when placing the script. Remember that part of loading the page is creating the Document Object Model that maps the entire page content. If your script references a part of the page that has not yet been loaded, an error will result. Thus, many developers will place scripts at the end of the document to ensure that the entirety of the page has been loaded into the DOM. You cannot use the `document.getElementById()` method to reference a page object until *after* that page object has been loaded into the DOM; otherwise, your browser will report an error.

All of this assumes that you are embedding your JavaScript commands within the HTML file. There is another option: placing your JavaScript statements in an external file.

Creating a JavaScript Source File

As you develop larger and more complex applications, you will want to move your code out of the HTML file into its own separate file known as a JavaScript source file. Like HTML and CSS files, a JavaScript source file is a text file that can be created using a basic text editor, though a code editor is often preferred. JavaScript source files are saved with a .js extension. They contain only JavaScript code and do not contain any HTML or CSS code unless that content is written using JavaScript statements like the `document.write()` method.

Referencing an External File

To attach a web page to a JavaScript source file, insert the following `script` element within the HTML file:

```
<script src="url"></script>
```

where *`url`* is the file name and location of the JavaScript file. The following `script` element loads the code contained within the report.js file into the web page:

```
<script src="report.js"></script>
```

The `script` element can be used either for embedding JavaScript code or accessing external JavaScript code, but it cannot do both at the same time. If you wish to embed some JavaScript commands to supplement commands stored in a JavaScript source file, you will need to insert a second `script` element for that purpose.

Using the `async` and `defer` Keywords

As with an embedded script, commands stored in an external file are loaded when the browser initially encounters the `script` element in the HTML file. Once again, this can cause errors if commands in the script reference page content that has not yet been loaded by the browser. You can modify when the external script file is accessed and loaded by adding the `async` or `defer` attribute to the opening `<script>` tag. The `async` attribute tells the browser to parse the HTML and JavaScript code together, only pausing to process the script before returning to the HTML file. The `defer` attribute tells the browser to hold off processing the script until after the page has been completely parsed and loaded. See **Figure 1-20**.

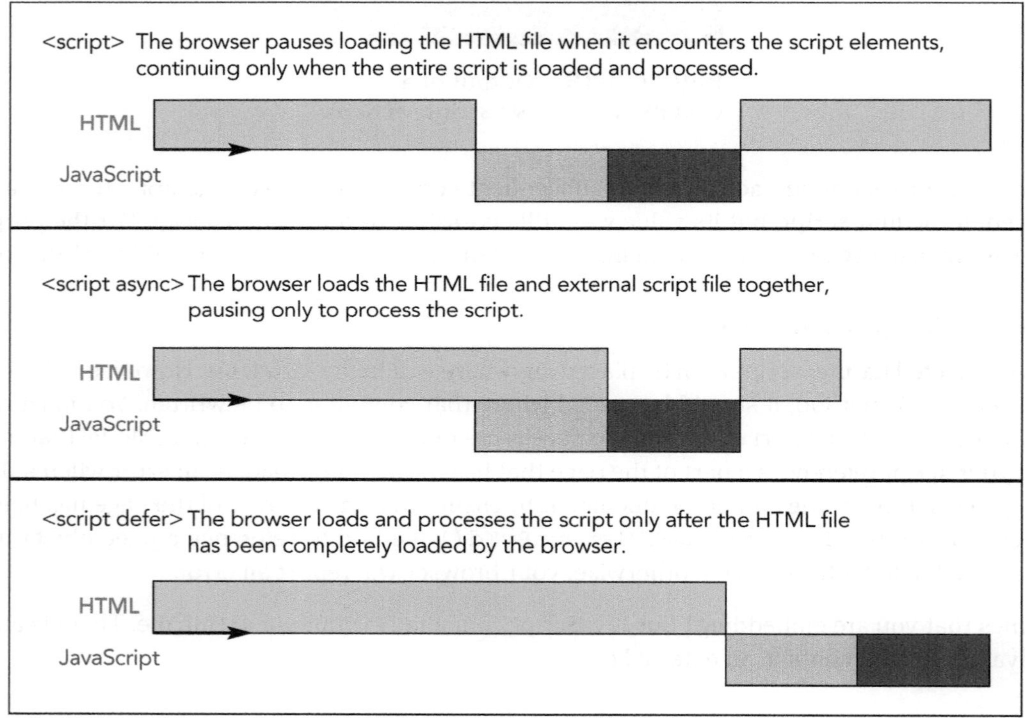

Figure 1-20 Loading HTML and JavaScript code

The `async` and `defer` attributes are ignored for embedded scripts so that any JavaScript code embedded within the HTML file will always be read and executed as soon as it is encountered within the HTML file.

As you grow in your understanding and mastery of JavaScript, you will put your code in an external file as opposed to embedding that code within the HTML file. There are several reasons for this:

- The code can be shared among multiple pages.
- Because the code is shared among multiple pages, it only needs to be downloaded once, which is a great benefit for users on mobile connections.
- Team members can more easily share code for joint projects.
- The HTML file will be neater and cleaner because your HTML elements will not be combined with JavaScript codes.
- It is easier to manage your website if each file focuses on a single task: HTML files for document content and structure, CSS files for page design and layout, and JavaScript files for interactive features and specialized tasks. Team members would then be responsible only for those files within their area of expertise.

Future chapters of this book will rely more on external JavaScript files and less on embedded code.

Connecting to a JavaScript File

To see how an external JavaScript file can be used to create the effects shown in this chapter, you will connect to a file containing commands to write page content and add `onclick` event handlers to the list items on the page. The content of this file is shown in **Figure 1-21**.

```
//define variables containing plant file names
let blanket = "blanket.jpg";
let rugosa = "rugosa.jpg";
let bluestem = "bluestem.jpg";

//add event handlers to the list items
document.getElementById("blanket").onclick = function() {
   document.getElementById("plantImg").src = blanket;
}
document.getElementById("rugosa").onclick = function() {
   document.getElementById("plantImg").src = rugosa;
}
document.getElementById("bluestem").onclick = function() {
   document.getElementById("plantImg").src = bluestem;
}

/*
   Information on available plants
   including link to USDA website
*/

let captionText = "<p>Plant choices for " +
                  "<a href='http://planthardiness.ars.usda.gov'>" +
                  "hardiness zones</a>" +
                  " 5a - 6b </p>";

document.getElementById("imgCaption").innerHTML = captionText;
```

Commands declaring JavaScript variables

Commands to apply event handlers to three web page elements

Commands to add HTML code to a page element

Figure 1-21 An external JavaScript file

Some of the statements in this file will be familiar to you, such as the first three statements to declare the blanket, rugosa, and bluestem variables. The rest of the file uses commands that will be new to you to create event handlers and write page content. Do not worry about completely understanding the code at this point. The next chapter will discuss these new commands and concepts in more detail.

Create a connection to this JavaScript file now.

To connect to an external JavaScript file:

1. Open the **js01_txt.html** file in your code editor. Enter ***your name*** and ***the date*** in the head section of the file.
2. Directly above the closing `</head>` tag insert the following `<script>` tag to connect the page to the js01b.js file as shown in **Figure 1-22**.

```
<script src="js01b.js" defer></script>
```

```
    <meta charset="utf-8" />
    <meta name="viewport" content="width=device-width,initial-scale=1.0">
    <title>Tinley Xeriscapes</title>
    <link rel="stylesheet" media="screen and (max-device-width: 999px)" href="tinleyhand.css" />
    <link rel="stylesheet" media="screen and (min-device-width: 1000px)" href="tinley.css" />
    <link href="http://fonts.googleapis.com/css?family=Lily+Script+One" rel="stylesheet" type="text/css">
    <script src="js01b.js" defer></script>
</head>
```

Name of external JavaScript file

Defer loading the JavaScript file until after the HTML file is loaded

Figure 1-22 Connecting to an external JavaScript file

3. Save the file as **js01b.html** and close your code editor.
4. Open **js01b.html** in your web browser.
5. Verify that the hyperlink for hardiness zones appears on the page and that clicking the hardiness zones links opens the appropriate page.
6. Return to the **js01b.html** file in your browser and verify that clicking the list of plants on the left margin displays the corresponding plant time.

Once you have created a link to an external JavaScript file, you should not have to modify the HTML file again unless you need to change the content or structure of the document. However, all future programming changes can be made in JavaScript file.

Working with Libraries

In addition to storing scripts for multiple pages in the same website, sometimes JavaScript source files store especially useful generic scripts used on many different websites. These files, known as libraries, are often developed by a single programmer or a team of programmers and distributed online. Many libraries are developed to solve a problem on one website and turn out to be useful for other sites as well. Programmers often make libraries available for free reuse.

After downloading a .js file containing a library that you want to use on a web page, you incorporate it into your HTML code just as you would any other JavaScript source file: by creating a `script` element in the head section and using the `src` attribute to specify the file name of the library.

A handful of libraries are commonly used to perform a variety of functions on large, complex websites. For instance, Node.js and jQuery contain tools for creating and managing large web applications. Another library, Modernizr, is widely used to enable web authors to deliver a consistent design and functionality across different browsers, browser versions, and platforms.

> **Note** Libraries can contain massive amounts of code. Because every extra line of code increases the amount of time a web page takes to download, web developers generally create customized versions of libraries that they use, so a library file downloaded for a site contains only those parts of the library that the site actually uses.

Validating Web Pages

When you use a web browser to open an HTML document that does not conform to the rules and requirements of the language, the browser simply ignores the errors and renders the web page as best it can. A document that conforms to these rules is said to be well formed. A web browser cannot tell whether an HTML document is well formed; instead, to ensure that a web page is well formed and that its elements are valid, you need to use a validating parser. A validating parser is a program that checks whether a web page is well formed and whether the document conforms to a specific language definition known as a DTD. The term validation refers to the process of verifying that your document is well formed and checking that the elements in your document are correctly written according to the element definitions in a specific DTD. If you do not validate a document and it contains errors, most web browsers will probably ignore the errors and render the page anyway. However, validation can help you spot errors in your code. Even the most experienced web page authors frequently introduce typos or some other types of errors into a document that prevent the document from being well formed.

Various web development tools, including Dreamweaver, offer validation capabilities. In addition, several validating services can be found online. One of the best available is W3C Markup Validation Service, a free service that validates HTML as well as other markup languages. The W3C Markup Validation Service is located at *http://validator.w3.org/*. The service allows you to validate a web page by entering its URL, by uploading a document from your computer, or by copying and pasting code.

If you're working with XHTML instead of HTML, JavaScript can present a challenge to creating valid documents. This is because some JavaScript statements contain symbols such as the less-than symbol (<) symbol, the greater-than symbol (>), and the ampersand (&). This is not a problem with HTML documents, because the statements in a `script` element are interpreted as character data instead of as markup. A section of a document that is not interpreted as markup is referred to as character data, or CDATA. If you were to validate an HTML document containing a script section, the document would validate successfully because the validator would ignore the script section and not attempt to interpret the text and symbols in the JavaScript statements as HTML elements or attributes. By contrast, in XHTML documents, the statements in `script` elements are treated as parsed character data, or PCDATA, which identifies a section of a document that is interpreted as markup. Because JavaScript code in an XHTML document is treated as PCDATA, if you attempt to validate an XHTML document that contains a script section, it will fail the validation. To avoid this problem, you can do one of two things. One option is to move your code into a source file, which prevents the validator from attempting to parse the JavaScript statements. Alternatively, if you prefer to keep the JavaScript code within the document, you can enclose the code within a `script` element within a CDATA section, which marks sections of a document as CDATA. The syntax for including a CDATA section on a web page is as follows:

```
<![CDATA[
statements to mark as CDATA
]]>
```

For instance, the following code snippet shows the body section of a web document containing JavaScript code that is enclosed within a CDATA section.

```
<body>
   <script type="text/javascript">
   <![CDATA[
      document.write("<h1>Order Confirmation</h1>");
      document.write("<p>Your order has been received.</p>");
      document.write("<p>Thank you for your business!</p>");
   ]]>
   </script>
</body>
```

Though you can make XHTML documents valid using a CDATA section, the simplest and most direct option is to put all your JavaScript in an external file. Website apps constructed in this way can work with both HTML and XHTML documents with little or no modification.

Quick Check 4

1. Why should you place scripts at the end of an HTML document's body section?
2. How do you incorporate the contents of a JavaScript source file into an HTML document?

Summary

- A programming language needs to be compiled to transform program code into machine code. A scripting language does not require a compiler but instead is read line-by-line by an interpreter that scans the code for errors even as it runs. A markup language is a language that defines the content, structure, and appearance of a document.
- JavaScript is a scripting language based on the standards of ECMAScript, which is constantly developed and adapted to meet the needs of modern browsers and devices.
- JavaScript is built on three foundations: the scripting language ECMAScript, the Document Object Model (DOM) that describes how to access the contents and actions within a web page, and the Browser Object Model (BOM) that describes how to access the features and behaviors of the browser.
- The specifications of the DOM are maintained by the World Wide Web Consortium (W3C), which also is responsible for the development of standards for HTML and CSS. The specifications of the BOM are determined by each browser, but a common set of standards have been adopted by all browsers to make coding more accessible.
- JavaScript programs can be created by a basic text editor or by a code editor for more sophisticated applications.
- In traditional client/server architecture, the server is usually some sort of database from which a client requests information. A system consisting of a client and a server is known as a two-tier system. The web is built on a two-tier client/server system, in which a web browser (the client) requests documents from a web server. A three-tier, or multitier, client/server system consists of three distinct pieces: the client tier, the processing tier, and the data storage tier.
- JavaScript is a client-side scripting language that allows web page authors to develop interactive web pages and sites. Client-side scripting refers to a scripting language that runs on a local browser (on the client tier) instead of on a web server (on the processing tier).
- Server-side scripting refers to a scripting language that is executed from a web server.
- A general rule of thumb is to allow the client to handle the user interface processing and light processing, such as data validation, but have the web server perform intensive calculations and data storage.
- The `script` element tells a web browser that the scripting engine must interpret the commands it contains. The individual lines of code, or statements, that make up a JavaScript program in a document are contained within the `script` element.
- An object is programming code and data that can be treated as an individual unit or component. The procedures associated with an object are called methods. A property is a piece of data, such as a color or a name, which is associated with an object.
- You can write content to a web page with the `write()` method of the `Document` object.
- JavaScript is a case-sensitive language, meaning that it interprets differences in capitalization as differences in meaning.

- Comments are nonprinting lines that you place in your code to contain various types of remarks, including the name of the program, your name, and the date you created the program, notes to yourself, or instructions to future programmers who may need to modify your work.
- The values a program stores in computer memory are commonly called variables.
- Reserved words (also called keywords) are special words that are part of the JavaScript language syntax.
- An expression is a literal value or variable or a combination of literal values, variables, operators, and other expressions that can be evaluated by the JavaScript interpreter to produce a result.
- An event is a specific circumstance (such as an action performed by a user, or an action performed by the browser) that is monitored by JavaScript and that your script can respond to in some way. Code that executes in response to a specific event is called an event handler.
- The `script` element can be placed anywhere within an HTML document. The loading and parsing of the HTML is interrupted to load and parse JavaScript commands unless the `defer` or `async` attribute is added to the `<script>` tag (for external JavaScript files).
- You can save JavaScript code in an external file called a JavaScript source file.

Key Terms

Application Programming Interface (API)
argument
assignment operator
back end
block comment
Browser Object Model (BOM)
camel case
Cascading Style Sheets (CSS)
character data (CDATA)
client
client-side scripting
code editor
comments
compiled
compiler
declare
Document Object Model (DOM)
ECMA-262
ECMAScript
European Computer Manufacturers Association (ECMA)
event
event handler
expression
front end
Hypertext Markup Language (HTML)
Hypertext Transfer Protocol (HTTP)
identifier
initialize
Integrated Development Environment (IDE)
interpreter
JavaScript
JavaScript source file
JScript
keywords
library
line comment
literal
literal string
machine code
markup language
method
middle tier
multitier client/server system
n-tier client/server system
object
operand
operator
parsed character data (PCDATA)
passing arguments
procedure
processing tier
programming language
property
reserved words
script
scripting language
server
server-side scripting
statement
static
text string
three-tier client/server system
two-tier system
validating parser
validation
variables
web
web application
well formed
World Wide Web
World Wide Web Consortium (W3C)

Review Questions

1. A programming language like Java requires a(n) ______________.
   a. interpreter
   b. Document Object Model
   c. compiler
   d. Browser Object Model
2. HTML is an example of a ______________.
   a. programming language
   b. machine language
   c. scripting language
   d. markup language
3. The syntax specifications for JavaScript are defined in ______________.
   a. HTML
   b. the Document Object Model
   c. the Browser Object Model
   d. ECMAScript
4. JavaScript is built upon ______________.
   a. ECMAScript
   b. the Document Object Model
   c. the Browser Object Model
   d. ECMAScript, the Document Object Model, and the Browser Object Model
5. The specifications for the Document Object Model are determined by ______________.
   a. each browser alone
   b. each device alone
   c. the World Wide Web Consortium (W3C)
   d. the European Computer Manufacturers Association (ECMA)
6. Which of the following is not a language used by web developers?
   a. JavaScript
   b. HTML
   c. CSS
   d. machine code
7. A system consisting of a client and a server is known as a ______________.
   a. mainframe topology
   b. double-system architecture
   c. two-tier system
   d. wide area network
8. What is usually the primary role of a client?
   a. locating records that match a request
   b. heavy processing, such as calculations
   c. data storage
   d. the presentation of an interface to the user
9. Which of the following functions does the processing tier *not* handle in a three-tier client/server system?
   a. processing and calculations
   b. reading and writing of information to the data storage tier
   c. the return of any information to the client tier
   d. data storage
10. Which of the following uses the correct case?
    a. `Document.write()`
    b. `document.write()`
    c. `document.Write()`
    d. `Document.Write()`
11. Which of the following is *not* a valid identifier?
    a. $InterestRate
    b. 2QInterest Rate
    c. interestRate
    d. _interestRate
12. When you assign a specific value to a variable on its creation, you ______________ it.
    a. declare
    b. call
    c. assign
    d. initialize
13. Code that tells a browser what to do in response to a specific event on a specific element is called a(n) ______________.
    a. method
    b. event handler
    c. response
    d. procedure
14. Which method displays a dialog box with an OK button?
    a. `document.write()`
    b. `document.writeln()`
    c. `window.alert()`
    d. `window.popup()`
15. Which of the following is not a JavaScript keyword used to declare a variable?
    a. `variable`
    b. `var`
    c. `let`
    d. `const`
16. What potential problems can occur if you load a script prior to the page being entirely loaded by the browser?

17. How can you make the browser not parse and load an external script file until *after* the page has loaded?

18. When should you use an external JavaScript file instead of embedding your JavaScript code within the HTML file?

19. Provide the JavaScript code to write the text "Copyright 2023" as a line comment. Provide the code to write the same text as a block comment.

20. What is a library?

Hands-On Projects

Hands-On Project 1-1

In this project you will use `document.write()` statements in a script section to add financial planning tips to a web page, creating the web page shown in **Figure 1-23**.

Hands-on Project 1-1

Financial Planning Tips

1. Reduce spending on non-necessities.
2. Use extra money to pay off debt,starting with highest-interest credit cards.
3. Continue paying off debts until you are debt free.
4. Put a fixed percent of your pay aside every payday.

Figure 1-23 Completed Project 1-1

Do the following:

1. Use your code editor to open **project01-01_txt.html** from the js01 ▶ project01 folder. Enter your name and the date in the comment section of the document head.
2. Save the file as **project01-01.html**.
3. Within the `article` element, directly below the `h2` element, enter the opening and closing tags of a `script` element on separate lines.
4. Within the script insert a JavaScript line comment containing the text **create ordered list**.
5. Below the line comment, insert multiple `document.write()` commands to write the following HTML code for an ordered list:

```
<ol>
   <li>Reduce spending on non-necessities.</li>
   <li>Use extra money to pay off debt,
      starting with highest-interest credit cards.</li>
   <li>Continue paying off debts until you are debt free.</li>
   <li>Put a fixed percent of your pay aside every payday.</li>
</ol>
```

6. Save your work and open **project01-01.html** in your web browser. Verify the content of the page resembles that shown in Figure 1-23.

Hands-On Project 1-2

In this project, you will create a web page that uses variables to display information about high-speed Internet plans offered by an Internet service provider. The completed page is shown in **Figure 1-24**.

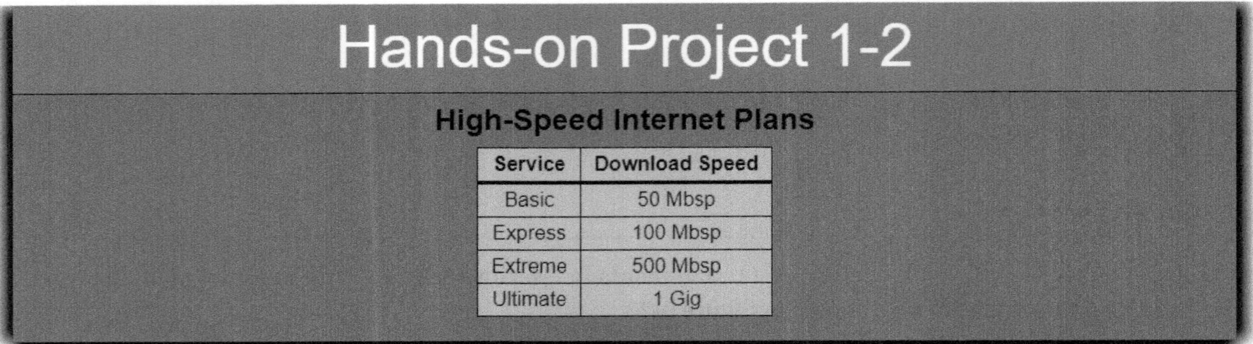

Figure 1-24 Completed Project 1-2

Do the following:

1. Use your code editor to open **project01-02_txt.html** and **project01-02_txt.js** from the js01 ▶ project02 folder. Enter your name and the date in the comment section of each document and save them as **project01-02.html** and **project01-02.js,** respectively.
2. Below the comment section in the project01-02.js file, declare the following variables with indicated initial values: `service1Name` = “Basic”, `service2Name` = “Express”, `service3Name` = “Extreme”, `service4Name` = “Ultimate”, `service1Speed` = “0 Mbps”, `service2Speed` = “100 Mbps”, `service3Speed` = “500 Mbps”, and `service4Speed` = “1 Gig”.
3. Save your changes to the file.
4. Return to the **project01-02.html** file in your code editor. Directly above the closing `</head>` tag, insert a `script` element to load the project01-02.js source file. Do not add either the `async` or `defer` attributes to the script so that the code in the external file is loaded immediately as the web page is parsed by the browser.
5. Go to the first table row of the `tbody` section of the web table. Within the first `<td>` tag, insert a script to write the value of the `service1Name` variable. Within the second `<td>` tag, insert another script to write the value of the `service1Speed` variable.
6. Repeat Step 5 for the two cells in each of the next three table rows in the `tbody` section, writing the values of `service2Name` and `service2Speed` variables through the `service4Name` and `service4Speed` variables.
7. Save your work and then open **project01-02.html** in your web browser. Verify that the content of the page resembles that shown in Figure 1-24.

Hands-On Project 1-3

In this project, you will explore how to write text to a specific element in your web page in response to the `onclick` event handler. To complete the exercise, you will apply the following JavaScript expression:

```
document.getElementById('id').innerHTML = 'text';
```

where *`id`* is the value of the *`id`* attribute for the page element and *`text`* is the text of the content to be written into the element. You will use this expression to enhance a web form by displaying the message “Thank you for your order” when the user clicks the Submit button. **Figure 1-25** shows the completed web page.

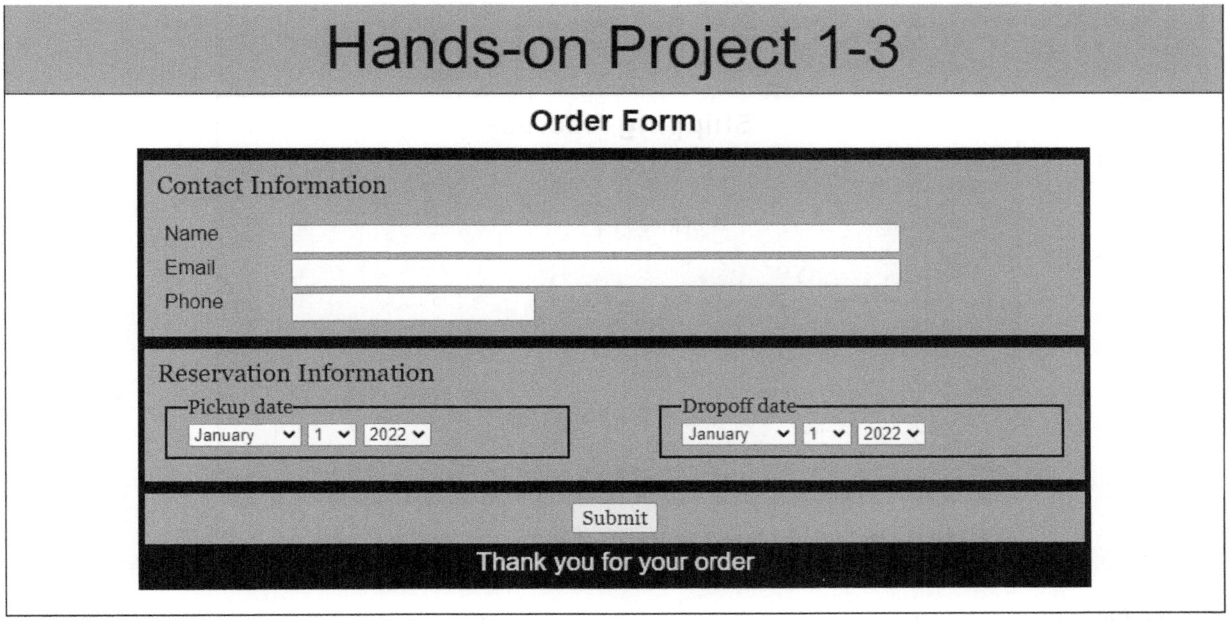

Figure 1-25 Completed Project 1-3

Do the following:

1. Use your code editor to open **project01-03_txt.html** from the js01 ▶ project03 folder. Enter your name and the date in the comment section of the document and save it as **project01-03.html**.
2. Scroll down to the bottom of the file and locate the input element for the Submit button.
3. Add an onclick event handler to the <input> tag that changes the innerHTML value of the page element with the id "submitMsg" to the text message **Thank you for your order**. (Note: The entire JavaScript expression should be enclosed within a set of double quotation marks, but the id and the text message should be enclosed within single quotes.)
4. Save your changes to the file and then open **project01-03.html** in your web browser. Click the Submit button and verify that the text "Thank you for your order" appears on the bottom of the page.

Hands-On Project 1-4

In this chapter you learned how to dynamically change an image using the getElementById('id').src expression along with the onclick event handler. In this project you will use the onclick event handler to automatically fill delivery address input boxes with preassigned values using the expression:

```
document.getElementById('id').value = variable;
```

where *id* is the value of the id attribute of a web form element and *variable* is the variable value to write into the element. A preview of the completed project is shown in **Figure 1-26**.

Do the following:

1. Use your code editor to open **project01-04_txt.html** and **project01-04_txt.js** from the js01 ▶ project04 folder. Enter your name and the date in the comment section of each document and save them as **project01-04.html** and **project01-04.js,** respectively.
2. Go to the **project01-04.js** file in your code editor. Below the comment section declare the following variables and initial values: homeStreet = "1 Main St.", homeCity = "Sicilia", homeState = "MA", homeCode = "02103", workStreet = "15 Oak Ln.", workCity = "Central City", workState = "MA", workCode = "02104".

Hands-on Project 1-4

Shipping Address

Choose an address

Home — 1 Main St. Sicilia, MA 02103

Work — 15 Oak Ln. Central City, MA 02104

Street Address	15 Oak Ln.
City	Central City
State	MA
Zip	02104

Figure 1-26 Completed Project 1-4

3. Close the file, saving your changes.
4. Go to the **project01-04.html** file in your code editor. Directly below the closing `</head>` tag insert a `script` element accessing the project01-04.js file. Do not include the `defer` or `async` attributes so that the code in the external file loads as the HTML is loaded.
5. Directly below the closing `</div>` tag for the Home address, insert a `script` element. Within the script, insert commands to write the following two lines of HTML code:

```
homeStreet <br>
homeCity, homeState homeCode
```

   where *homeStreet*, *homeCity*, *homeState*, and *homeCode* are the variables you defined in Step 2. (Hint: You will have to use the add operator (+) to combine the variables with the literal text strings in these two lines of code.)
6. Directly below the closing `</div>` tag for the Work address, insert another `script` element. Within the script, insert commands the write the following two lines:

```
workStreet <br>
workCity, workState workCode
```

   where *workStreet*, *workCity*, *workState*, and *workCode* are once again the variables you defined in Step 2.
7. Go to the `input` element with the id "homeoption". Within the `<input>` tag insert an `onclick` event handler that contains the following four JavaScript commands: (a) Set the value of the of the element with the id "street" to the value of the `homeStreet` variable; (b) Set the value of the element with the id "city" to the `homeCity` variable; (c) Set the value of the element with the id "state" to the `homeState` variable; (d) Set the value of the element with the id "code" to the value of the `homeCode` variable.
8. Go to the `input` element with the id "workoption". Repeat the previous step except store the values of the `workStreet`, `workCity`, `workState`, and `workCode` variables.
9. Save your changes to the file and then load **project01-04.html** in your web browser. Verify that the contents of the page resemble that shown in Figure 1-26 and that you can switch the address information at the bottom of the page between home and work by clicking the corresponding option buttons.

Hands-On Project 1-5

Debugging Challenge

Learning to locate and fix errors is an important skill for anyone programming in JavaScript. You have been given a web page containing several errors that need to be fixed. When fixed, the page will display the content shown in **Figure 1-27**.

Figure 1-27 Completed Project 1-5

Do the following:

1. Use your code editor to open **project01-05_txt.html** from the js01 ▶ project05 folder. Enter your name and the date in the comment section of the document and save it as **project01-05.html**.
2. In the head section of the document there is a script that declares and initializes the `reopenDate` variable. There are two errors in this code. Fix both errors.
3. Scroll down to the script embedded within the `article` element. The code contains a total of four errors. Locate and fix the errors.
4. Save your changes to the file and then open the file in your web browser. Verify that the page resembles that shown in Figure 1-27.

Case Projects

Individual Case Project

The Individual Case Project for each chapter in this book will build on a website that you create on a subject of your choice. To begin, choose a topic for your website. This can be a topic related to your major, or a personal interest or activity. Plan a website containing at least four pages with a common layout and navigation system. Note that you'll add pages to your site in later chapters, so ensure that your navigation system can support additional content. Ensure that all of your web pages pass validation.

Team Case Project

Throughout the Team Case Projects in this book you will continue to work on a website on a subject chosen by your team. Working in a team of 4–8 people, discuss and agree on a topic for your website. This may be a topic related to your major, another area of study, your college or university, or a shared interest. Work together to plan a website containing, at a minimum, a number of pages equal to the number of group members, and to create a common layout and navigation system. Note that you'll add pages to your site in later chapters, so ensure that your navigation system can support additional content. Decide as a group who will create which page, and create the pages individually. When you've finished creating the individual pages, ensure they pass validation, and then work together to assemble the resulting website, identifying and fixing any issues as a group.

CHAPTER 2

Working with Functions, Data Types, and Operators

When you complete this chapter, you will be able to:

- Write and call functions to perform actions and calculate values
- Associate functions with events using event handlers and event listeners
- Use built-in JavaScript functions
- Understand the scope of variables and functions
- Understand the data types supported by JavaScript and write expressions with numeric values, text strings, and Boolean values
- Create expressions using arithmetic, assignment, comparison, logical, string, and special operators
- Understand order precedence and associativity of operations
- Work with events and values associated with form controls
- Access your browser's debugging console

So far, the code you have written has consisted of simple statements placed within script sections. However, like most programming languages, JavaScript allows you to group programming statements in logical units. In JavaScript, a group of statements that you can execute as a single unit is called a function. You'll learn how to create functions in this chapter, and you'll practice using them to organize your code.

In addition to functions, one of the most important aspects of programming is the ability to store values in computer memory and to manipulate those values. In the last chapter, you learned how to store values in computer memory using variables. The values, or data, contained in variables are classified into categories known as data types. In this chapter, you'll learn about JavaScript data types and the operations that can be performed on values of each type. You'll also explore the order in which different operations are performed by JavaScript processors, as well as how to change this order.

Working with Functions

A collection of statements that share a common purpose or calculate a value can be grouped into a programming structure known as a function. A function might be used to write messages to the user, calculate the total tax on an order, or estimate the shipping date for a product. The commands stored within a function can be called repeatedly throughout your program, simplifying your code and making it more efficient to run.

Defining a Function

Functions are classified as either named functions or anonymous functions. A named function is a function that is assigned a name and has the following syntax:

```
function functionName(parameters) {
   statements
}
```

where *functionName* is the name of the function, *parameters* is a comma-separated list of parameters, where each parameter is a variable used within the function, and *statements* are the commands contained with the function. For example, the following `writeMsg()` function encloses commands to display an alert box with part of the message determined by the `date` and `status` parameters:

```
function writeMsg(date, status) {
   window.alert("Today is " + date + ". Your order is " + status);
}
```

If `date` has a value of "October 3, 2024" and `status` is "pending", this function will display an alert box with the text: "Today is October 3, 2024. Your order is pending".

Function statements are always enclosed within opening and closing curly braces, a structure known as a command block that is used in many JavaScript statements to encapsulate multiple JavaScript statements. It is considered good practice to write the opening and closing curly braces on their own lines and indent the enclosed statements between those braces.

Functions do not have to contain parameters. No parameters are required in the following function that writes a canned message to an alert box:

```
function writeFinalMsg() {
   window.alert("Order completed. Thank you for your business");
}
```

Note The code in this book is indented using three space characters. The number of spaces used for indenting is not important, but you should use the same number consistently throughout your code. Some programmers prefer to use tab characters instead of spaces for indents; this choice is also a question of personal preference and has no effect on the quality of the code.

Functions are named so that they can be referenced and used elsewhere in the script in the same way that a variable is named so that it can referenced and used. If the function does not need to be referenced, it can be entered as an anonymous function without a name as in the following syntax:

```
function (parameters) {
   statements
}
```

As with named functions, you do not need to include a list of parameters unless the anonymous function requires it. Generally, named functions are used for functions that are accessed repeatedly in the program and anonymous functions are used for functions accessed only once. Anonymous functions are also important for use with event handlers as you will learn later in this chapter.

Writing a Function

In this chapter, you will create a program that calculates the total cost of photography services provided by Fan Trick Fine Art Photography. **Figure 2-1** shows a preview of the page with the selected service options and an estimate of the total overall cost.

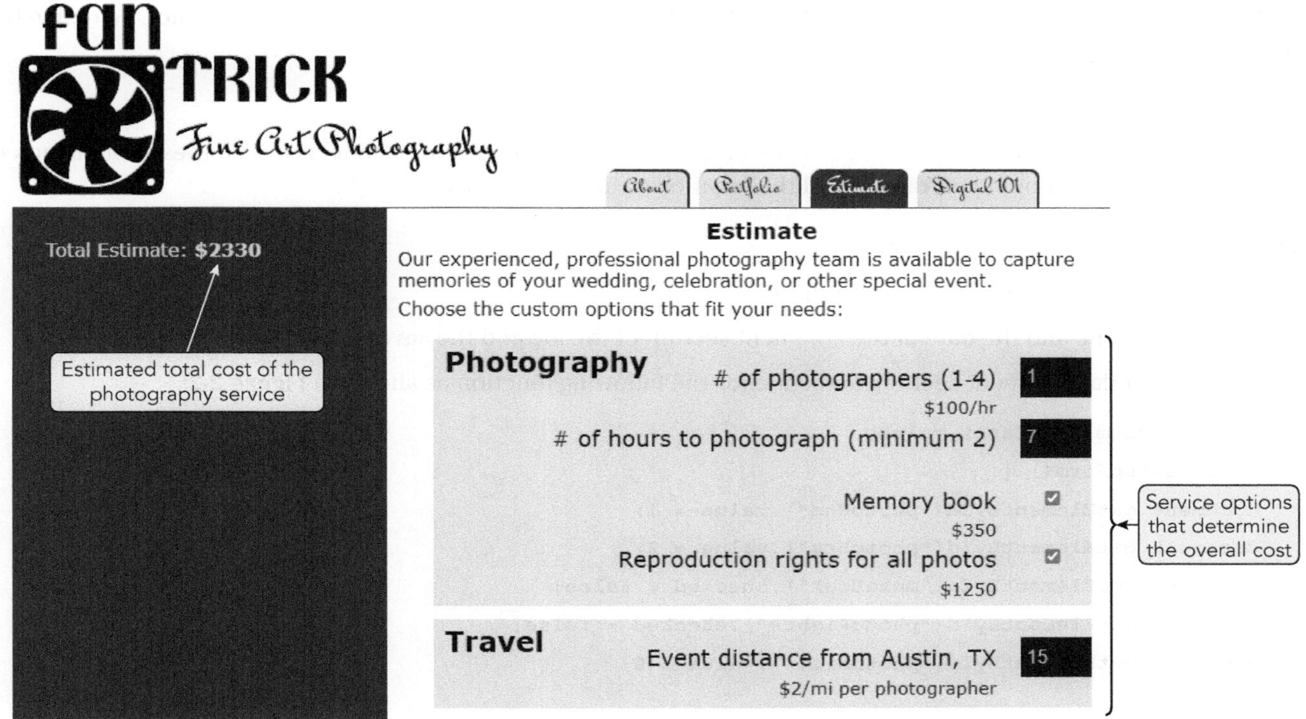

Figure 2-1 Estimating the total photography charge

The total charge is based on the number of photographers, the number of hours they worked, their travel distance, the publication of a memory book, and the granting of reproduction rights to digital copies. Your job will be to write the code that automatically calculates that total based on selections made by the customer in the web form. Open the data file for the web page now.

To open the fan trick photography page:

1. Use your code editor to go to the js02 ▶ chapter folder of your data files.
2. Open the **js02_txt.html** file in your code editor.
3. Enter your name and the date in the comment section of the file.
4. Scroll through the document to familiarize yourself with its contents.
5. Save the file as **js02.html** and load the file in your browser.
6. Add the following values to the web form using the controls on the form: # of photographers: **1**, # of hours **2**, click the **Memory book** checkbox to indicate that a memory book should be part of the purchase, and finally enter an travel distance in miles of **25**.
7. Refresh or reload the web page and notice that by refreshing or reloading the page, your values are erased.

You want to use JavaScript to open the web form with these default values already entered. One way of accomplishing that is with a function named `setupForm()` that defines those default values. To set the value of an input box, apply the JavaScript statement:

```
object.value = value;
```

where *object* is a reference to an input control on the web form and *value* is the value to insert into that control. If the control can be identified by the value of the *id* attribute, the statement has the syntax:

```
document.getElementById(id).value = value;
```

where *id* is the id of the input control.

Checkboxes have a property named `checked` that determines whether the checkbox is checked or not. To define the checked status, apply the JavaScript statement:

```
object.checked = status;
```

where *status* is `true` to check the checkbox or `false` to leave the checkbox unchecked. Use these commands in the `setupForm()` function now. You will add the function to an external JavaScript file.

To create the `setupform()` function:

1. Open the **js02_txt.js** file in your code editor.
2. Enter your name and the date in the comment section of the file and the save the file as **js02.js**.
3. Below the initial comment section, add code for the following function as shown in **Figure 2-2**:

```
// set the form's default values
function setupForm() {
   document.getElementById("photoNum").value = 1;
   document.getElementById("photoHrs").value = 2;
   document.getElementById("makeBook").checked = false;
   document.getElementById("photoRights").checked = false;
   document.getElementById("photoDist").value = 0;
}
```

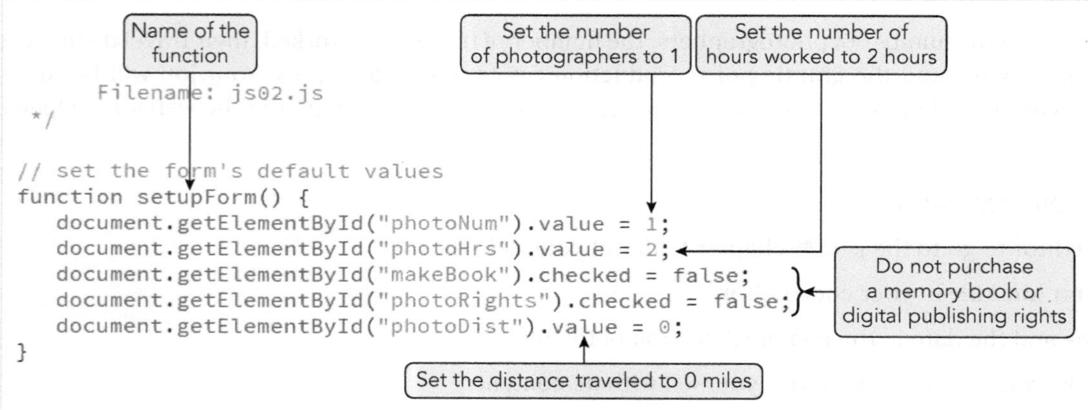

Figure 2-2 Creating the `setupForm()` function

Next, link the web page to this external script file.

4. Return to the **js02.html** file in your code editor.

5. Directly above the closing </head> tag insert the following element to load the js02.js script file, deferring the loading of the file until after the entire page has loaded.

```
<script src="js02.js" defer></script>
```

6. Save your changes to the file.

Functions like the `setupForm()` function cannot be run until they are called. You will explore how to call functions next.

Calling a Function

Any named function can be accessed or called by including the name of the function within the JavaScript expression:

```
functionName(paramValues);
```

where *functionName* is the name of the function and *paramValues* are the values assigned to the parameters (if any) of the function. The variables or values that you place in the parentheses of the function call statement are also called arguments or actual parameters. Sending arguments to the parameters of a called function is known as passing arguments. When you pass arguments to a function, the value of each argument is then assigned to the value of the corresponding parameter in the function definition. (Again, remember that parameters are simply variables that are declared within a function definition.)

For example, the following `showStatus()` function displays an alert box using values specified by the `name` and `status` parameters:

```
function showStatus(name, status) {
   window.alert("The " + name + " Contract is " + status);
}
```

and when called with the following parameter values

```
showStatus("Reynolds", "Pending");
showStatus("Dawson", "Approved");
```

the following text strings would be displayed within alert boxes:

```
The Reynolds Contract is Pending
The Dawson Contract is Approved
```

Functions are most effective when they can be reused with different parameter values to result in different outcomes, freeing the web developer from duplicating the same code within a program.

Returning a Value from a Function

So far you have only examined functions that perform an operation, but you may be more familiar with the concept of functions that perform calculations and return a value. JavaScript functions can also be used for that purpose. To create a function that returns a value, add the following `return` statement to the end of the function's command block:

```
function functionName(parameters) {
   statements
   return value;
}
```

where *value* is the calculated value returned by the function. The `return` statement marks the end of the function so that any code placed after it within the command block will never be executed. Note that only one value can be returned by a function, though some functions will have multiple `return` statements when one of several possible values could be returned at any given time.

The following `sum3()` function calculates the sum of three numeric values stored in `num1`, `num2`, and `num3` parameters. The `return` statement then returns the value of that sum.

```
function sum3(num1, num2, num3) {
   let sum = num1 + num2 + num3;
   return sum;
}
```

This `sum3()` function can then be used within any JavaScript statement just like one of JavaScript's built-in functions or methods. The following line of code calls the `sum3()` function with two sets of values, storing the result in the `finalTotal` variable:

```
let finalTotal = sum3(3, 4, 5) + sum3(1, 0, 5);
```

After running this command, the `finalTotal` variable would have a value of 18.

Managing Events with Functions

In your code you will often need to run functions in response to events occurring within the web page or browser, such as the user clicking a form button, or the browser having completed loading the web page. There are three ways of associating a function with an event: by adding an attribute to an HTML tag, by adding a property to a page object, or by attaching an event listener to a page object. Each approach has its advantages and disadvantages.

Using Event Handlers

The most direct way to associate a function with an event is to create an event handler as an attribute of the element within the HTML file. The general syntax is

```
<elem onevent = "function()">
```

where *`elem`* is the HTML element in which the event occurs, *`event`* is the name of a user- or browser-initiated event, and *`function()`* is the function that is called in response to the event. For example, the `calcTotal()` function would be run in response to the input button being clicked by the user:

```
<input type="button" id="total" value="Calculate"
 onclick="calcTotal()" />
```

In this example, the element is the input box, the name of the event is "click" and the function is `calcTotal()`. You can include multiple JavaScript statements with the event handler as in the following example in which both the `calcTotal()` and `writeMsg()` functions are called

```
<input type="button" id="total" value="Calculate"
 onclick="calcTotal(); writeMsg()" />
```

The statements specified with an event handler attribute do not need to be functions at all. Any set of JavaScript statements enclosed within the event handler attribute will be run in response to the event.

Note You can add parameter values to the function by including them within function parentheses. Parameter values that are text strings should be enclosed within single quotes.

One drawback of adding event handlers as HTML attributes is that they place JavaScript code within the HTML file. Just as developers want to keep HTML and CSS code separate, most developers prefer not to mix HTML and JavaScript code in the same document.

Events as Object Properties

To place an event handler within the JavaScript code, attach an event handler to a page object by specifying it as a property of that object. The general syntax is

```
object.onevent = function;
```

where *object* is the reference to an object within the document or browser, *event* is an event associated with the object, and *function* is the name of the function that will be run in response to the event. The following JavaScript command would run the `calcTotal()` function when the page object with the id *total* is clicked.

```
document.getElementById("total").onclick = calcTotal;
```

Note that you only specify the function name. You do not and cannot specify parameter values with this approach. Another limitation of setting an event handler as object property is that only one function can handle an event at a time. In the following code, the second event handler supersedes the first so that only the second function is run in response to the `load` event of the `window` object.

```
window.onload = function1;
window.onload = function2;
```

If your application requires multiple functions to be assigned to the same event, you can use an event listener.

Event Listeners

An event listener listens for an event as it propagates through a web page either through being captured or being bubbled. To understand the difference between the capturing and bubbling, imagine clicking an image on a page. In doing so, you have clicked more than the image; you have also clicked the browser window, the web page itself, and any page element containing the image. A single event interacts with a hierarchy of objects from the most general down through the most specific. JavaScript manages that event through an event model that describes how objects and events interact within the web page and web browser. Under JavaScript's event model, an event like `click` is first tracked in the capture phase, moving down the object hierarchy from the most general object (the browser window) down to the specific (the image itself). The capture phase is followed by the bubbling phase as the event moves back up the object hierarchy ending with the browser window. Thus, the event listener is always listening for the event as it goes down the object hierarchy (being captured) or goes up (being bubbled).

To attach an event listener to an object, apply the following method:

```
object.addEventListener("event", function, capture)
```

where *object* is the object in which to listen for the event, *function* is the name of the function that is run in response, and *capture* is an optional value equal to `true` (listen during the capture phase) or `false` (listen during the bubbling phase). The default value is `false` so that the event listener will only listen during the bubbling phase. The following statement listens for the `click` event occurring within the page object with the id `total` during the bubbling phase, running the `calcTotal()` function when that event occurs:

```
document.getElementById("total").addEventListener("click", calcTotal);
```

Unlike the event handler approach, event listeners can attach multiple functions to the same event. In the following code, both functions will be run in response to the `load` event of the `window` object:

```
window.addEventListener("load", function1);
window.addEventListener("load", function2);
```

Note

To remove an event listener from an object, apply the following command:

```
object.removeEventListener("event", function, capture)
```

Once the event listener has been removed, the event will no longer trigger a response from the script.

The distinction between the capture and bubbling phases is usually only important for more advanced applications, like online games. In this chapter and others, the *capture* argument will not be used so that events will only be listened to in the bubbling phase by default.

Events and Anonymous Functions

You can also use anonymous functions with event handlers and event listeners. One reason to do this is to allow parameter values to be used with the event. The following example shows how to nest a named function with parameter values within an anonymous function to respond to the `load` event of the `window` object:

```
window.onload = function() {
   showMsg("Dawson", "Approved");
}
```

Notice that in place of a function name, the entire structure of the anonymous function, including the command block, is added to the statement. To do the same with an event listener, enclose the entire structure of the anonymous function within the `addEventListener()` method in place of the function name. The following shows its application in response to the `load` event of the `window` object:

```
window.addEventListener("load", function() {
   showMsg("Dawson", "Approved");
   });
```

Whether you use named functions or anonymous functions depends on the needs of your application. Anonymous functions can provide more flexibility in your code, but they can also make your code more difficult to interpret and edit.

Applying a Function to an Event

Now that you have seen how to attach functions to events, you will run the `setupForm()` function when the browser window loads the web page. Add an event listener now to the js02.js file to accomplish this and then test your code.

To create an event listener for the `load` event:

1. Return to the **js02.js** file in your code editor.
2. Above the code for the `setupForm()` function insert the following event listener as shown in **Figure 2-3**:

```
// setup the form when the page loads
window.addEventListener("load", setupForm);
```

Attach an event listener to the browser window

Listen for the event of the window loading the web page

Run the `setupForm()` function in response to the event

```
// setup the form when the page loads
window.addEventListener("load", setupForm);

// set the form's default values
function setupForm() {
   document.getElementById("photoNum").value = 1;
   document.getElementById("photoHrs").value = 2;
   document.getElementById("makeBook").checked = false;
   document.getElementById("photoRights").checked = false;
   document.getElementById("photoDist").value = 0;
}
```

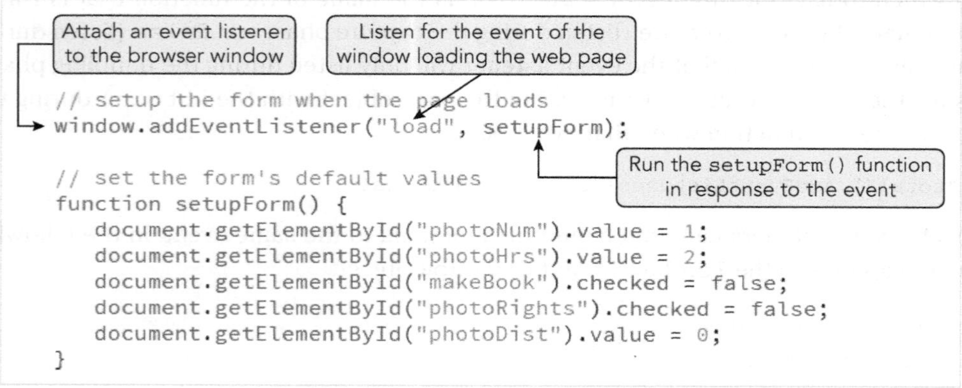

Figure 2-3 Creating an event listener

3. Save your changes to the file and then reload **js02.html** in your web browser.
4. Verify that the page opens with the number of photographs set to 1, the number of hours set to 2, the two checkboxes unselected, and the distance set to 0.

Having set the initial values in the web form you will next create a function to estimate the total cost of the photographic services. To do that however, you will first need to learn about variables, data types, and operators.

Using Built-in JavaScript Functions

In addition to custom functions that you create yourself, JavaScript allows you to use the built-in functions listed in **Figure 2-4**.

FUNCTION	DESCRIPTION
`decodeURI(`*string*`)`	Decodes text strings encoded with `encodeURI()`
`decodeURIComponent(`*string*`)`	Decodes text strings encoded with `encodeURIComponent()`
`encodeURI(`*string*`)`	Encodes a text string so it becomes a valid URI
`encodeURIComponent(`*string*`)`	Encodes a text string so it becomes a valid URI component
`eval(`*string*`)`	Evaluates expressions contained within strings
`isFinite(`*number*`)`	Determines whether a number is finite
`isNaN(`*number*`)`	Determines whether a value is the special value `NaN` (Not a Number)
`parseFloat(`*string*`)`	Converts string literals to floating-point numbers
`parseInt(`*string*`)`	Converts string literals to integers

Figure 2-4 Built-in JavaScript functions

In this book, you will examine several of the built-in JavaScript functions as you need them. For now, you just need to understand that you call built-in JavaScript functions in the same way you call custom functions. For example, the following code calls the `isNaN()` function to determine whether the `socialSecurityNumber` variable is not a number.

```
let socialSecurityNumber = "123-45-6789";
let checkVar = isNaN(socialSecurityNumber);
document.write(checkVar);
```

Because the Social Security number assigned to the `socialSecurityNumber` variable contains dashes, it is not a true number. Therefore, the `isNaN()` function returns a value of `true` to the `checkVar` variable.

Quick Check 1

1. What is the difference between a named function and an anonymous function?
2. What is a command block?
3. Provide an expression to call the `findSqr()` function using 10 as the parameter value.
4. What is the difference between the capture phase and the bubbling phase for an event occurring within a website?
5. An HTML file contains the following tag:

   ```
   <input type="button" value="Submit" id="SubmitButton" />
   ```

   Provide the code to run the `submitOrder()` function in response to the user clicking this input button using the following approaches: as a HTML attribute, as an object property entered as an event handler, and as an event listener (during the bubbling phase).

Understanding Variable Scope

Variables can be declared using either the `var` keyword or the `let` keyword. The difference between those approaches lies in the scope of the declared variable. Scope refers to where a variable or function can be called within the program.

let and var Declaration Scopes

Variables declared with `let` are block scoped, in that their scope is limited to the command block in which they are defined, or any code nested within that block. In the following code the `user` variable is recognized only within the command block, but outside of that command block it is not recognized and will produce an error if it is referenced in a statement:

```
{
   let user = "Dawson";
   document.write(user); // writes Dawson
}
   document.write(user); // produces an error
```

Constants declared with the `const` keyword are also block-scoped and, thus, can only be referenced within the command block in which they are declared.

Variables declared with the `var` keyword have function scope, in that their scope is limited to the function in which they are defined, or any code nested therein. In the following example, the `user` variable is only recognized within the `showUser()` function but not outside of it.

```
function showUser() {
   var user = "Reynolds";
   document.write(user); // writes Reynolds
}
document.write(user);    // produces an error
```

Because functions contain command blocks, any variable declared within a function using the `let` or `const` keywords is also not accessible outside of that function.

Local and Global Scope

Block scope and function scope are collectively referred to as local scope because they define variables and functions accessible locally within the command block or function in which they are defined. The other general type of scope is global scope, in which the variable or function is defined outside of any command block or function and, thus, is accessible throughout the entire program. Variables with local scope are called local variables, while variables with global scope are called global variables.

In the following code the `user` variable is a global variable and thus is accessible within any command block or function in the program:

```
let user = "Dawson";
function showUser() {
   document.write(user); //writes Dawson
}
```

If a global variable and a local variable share the same name, the local variable takes precedence. However, the value assigned to a local variable within a function or command block is not transferred outside of that context. In the following example the local value assigned to the `user` variable is limited to the scope of the function while the global value is unchanged outside of the function:

```
let user = "Dawson";
function showUser() {
   let user = "Reynolds";
   document.write(user);  // writes Reynolds
}
document.write(user);     // writes Dawson
```

Global variables are fine for smaller applications developed and maintained by a single programmer. They make it easier to share data between functions, freeing the programmer from having to declare variables within every function and command block. However, their use is strongly discouraged for larger applications, especially for applications that are managed by a team of programmers. The problem is that a global variable can be unexpectedly changed by one of the many functions scattered throughout a large and complex application. It is much easier for the team to confine their work to local variables whose scope is well-contained and easily tracked. If a value needs to be used within a function, it is much better to pass that value as a parameter of the function.

Note JavaScript is a forgiving language and will allow you to "bend the rules" on occasion. For example, you can create a variable without using the `let`, `const`, or `var` keywords. Variables created in this way are assigned global scope, even if they are created within a function or command block. The best practice, however, is to always declare a variable, so there is no ambiguity about its scope and role in the program.

You will create global variables for the photography web page containing the costs per hour for each photographer ($100), the cost of a memory book ($350), the reproduction rights for all photos ($1250), and the cost per mile for travel ($2). Because these variables will never change their value within the application, you will declare them using the `const` keyword.

To declare global constants:

1. Return to the **js02.js** file in your code editor.
2. Directly below the initial comment section, enter the following code declaring global constants (see **Figure 2-5**):

```
// declare global constants for the application
const EMP_COST = 100;     //cost of photographers per hour
const BOOK_COST = 350;    //cost of memory book
const REPRO_COST = 1250;  //cost of reproduction rights
const TRAVEL_COST = 2;    //cost of travel per mile
```

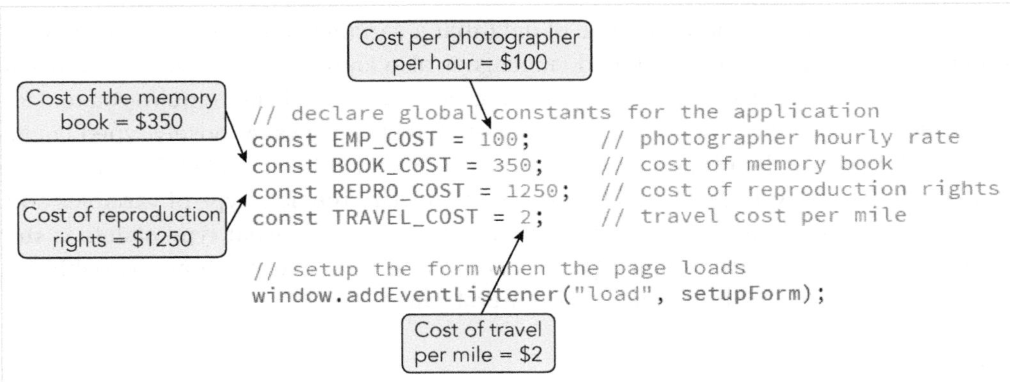

Figure 2-5 Declaring constant variables

3. Save your changes to the file.

Note It is common programming practice to distinguish constants from variables, by writing the names of constants in uppercase characters with words separated by underscores.

One of the advantages of declaring these global constants is that when the company changes its rates in the future, the programmer maintaining this application will only need to change these constant values once in the code and not every time they're used in a calculation or expression.

Working with Data Types

Variables can contain many different kinds of values such as the time of day, a dollar amount, or a person's name. A data type is the specific category of information that a variable contains. The data type determines how much memory is allocated for the data stored in the variable. The data type also governs the kinds of operations that can be performed on the variable.

Data types that can be assigned only a single value are called primitive types. JavaScript supports the five primitive data types described in **Figure 2-6**.

DATA TYPE	DESCRIPTION
number	A positive or negative number with or without decimal places, or a number written using exponential notation
Boolean	A logical value of `true` or `false`
string	Text such as "Hello World!"
undefined	An unassigned, undeclared, or nonexistent value
null	An empty value

Figure 2-6 Primitive JavaScript data types

> **Note** The JavaScript language also supports the object data type used for creating a collection of properties. You will learn about the object type in a later chapter.

You might be confused about the distinction between a null value and an undefined value. Null is both a data type and a value. You assign the `null` value to a variable to indicate that the variable does not contain any data. In contrast, an undefined variable is a variable that has never had a value assigned to it, has not been initialized or does not even exist. For example, a variable that has been declared but not given an initial value is undefined but not null.

Many programming languages require that you declare the type of data that a variable contains. Such languages are called strongly typed programming languages. A strongly typed language is also known as statically typed, because data types cannot be changed after they have been declared. Programming languages that do not require you to declare the data types of variables are called loosely typed or duck typed programming languages. A loosely typed language is also known as dynamically typed, because data types can change after they have been declared. JavaScript is a loosely typed programming language. In JavaScript, you are not required to declare the data type of variables and, in fact, are not allowed to do so. Instead, a JavaScript interpreter automatically determines what type of data is stored in a variable and assigns the variable's data type accordingly. The following code demonstrates how a variable's data type changes automatically each time the variable is assigned a new literal value:

```
diffTypes = "Hello World!"; // String
diffTypes = 8;              // Integer number
diffTypes = 5.367;          // Floating-point number
diffTypes = true;           // Boolean
diffTypes = null;           // Null
```

The next two sections focus on two especially important data types: number and Boolean data types.

Working with Numeric Values

JavaScript supports two types of numeric values: integers and floating point numbers. An integer is a positive or negative number with no decimal places like 13, 250, 0, 100, or 1000. Integer values in JavaScript range from 9007199254740990 (2^{-53}) to 9007199254740990 (2^{53}).

Numbers containing decimal places like −6.16, 0.314, or 10.5 or which are written in exponential notation are floating point numbers. Exponential notation, or scientific notation, is a shortened format for writing very large numbers or numbers with many decimal places. Exponential values in JavaScript are written with the letter e separating the decimal and exponent parts of the value, such as `2.0e6` for the value 2×10^6 or 2,000,000, or `3.1e-4` for 3.1×10^{-4} or 0.00031. Using exponential notation, JavaScript can represent floating point values as large as approximately $\pm 1.8 \times 10^{308}$ or as small as $\pm 5 \times 10^{-324}$. Floating point values beyond $\pm 1.8 \times 10^{308}$ are assigned the keywords `-Infinity` and `Infinity`.

Best Practices | Calculate with Whole Numbers, Not Decimals

JavaScript treats all numeric values as binary values, rather than as decimals—that is, the numbers are calculated using the two-digit binary system rather than the 10-digit decimal system. While the binary system can accurately represent any value that has a decimal equivalent, when it comes to floating point values, calculations performed on binary representations can result in slightly different results than the same calculations performed on decimal values. Because users enter decimal values in web interfaces and the interfaces display decimal results to users, this discrepancy can cause problems, especially when it comes to calculating exact monetary values such as dollars and cents. JavaScript programmers have developed a straightforward workaround, however: when manipulating a monetary value in a program, first multiply the value by 100, to eliminate the decimal portion of the number. In essence, this means calculating based on a value in cents (for instance, $10.51 * 100 = 1051¢). Because calculations on integer values are the same in binary and decimal, any calculations you perform will be accurate. When your calculations are finished, simply divide the result by 100 to arrive at the correct, final value in dollars and cents.

Working with Boolean Values

A Boolean value is a logical value of `true` or `false`. You can also think of a Boolean value as being yes or no, or on or off. Boolean values are most often used for deciding which code should execute and for comparing data. While a value of `true` or `false` looks like a text string, it is not. Boolean values should never be placed within quotes because they will be treated as text.

Working with Strings

As you learned in the previous chapter, a text string contains zero or more characters surrounded by double or single quotation marks. Examples of strings you may use in a script are company names, user names, and comments. You can use a text string as a literal value or assign it to a variable.

A literal string can also be assigned a zero-length string value called an empty string. For example, the following statement declares a variable named `customerName` and assigns it an empty string:

```
let customerName = "";
```

This practice specifies that the variable is a string variable with no content.

If quotation marks are themselves part of the text string, simply use double quotation marks to enclose single quotes and single quotation marks to enclose double quotes. The following statements demonstrate this technique by showing how to include first a single quote (') and then a double quote (") as part of a text string:

```
document.write("Welcome to 'Fan Trick Photography'");
document.write('Welcome to "Fan Trick Photography"');
```

JavaScript would then write the lines as

```
Welcome to 'Fan Trick Photography'
Welcome to "Fan Trick Photography"
```

Common Mistakes

A common mistake is to mix the two types of quotation marks or omit one of them as in the following statement in which a double quote begins the text string, but a single quote ends it:

```
document.write("Welcome to 'Fan Trick Photography');
```

You must always match a beginning quote with an ending quote of the same type or else an error will result in your code. Without matching quotes, the JavaScript interpreter cannot tell where the text string ends.

In writing your code you may have to deal with long text strings that will not fit on a single line. Although many JavaScript commands can be entered across several lines, a text string cannot split onto a new line without causing an error. If you have a long text string, there are several things you can do to make your code error-free:

- Fit as much of the text string as you can on one line and then close out the text with an ending quote followed by the addition operator (+) as in the following example:

```
let message = "This is a very long" +
" and complicated text string to enter.";
```

- End the line with the \ character indicating that the text string continues on the next line (this approach might not be supported by all browsers and browser versions).

```
let message = "This is a very long \
 and complicated text string to enter.";
```

Another approach is to enclose your text strings with the backtick character (`) rather than double or single quotes as in the following expression:

```
let message = `This is a very long
and complicated text string to enter`;
```

Using the backtick character (`) creates a structure known as a template literal introduced in ES6 to provide more tools for working with literal text strings. Note however that in the previous example, both the text and the line return are part of the text string and, thus, when printed the message text string will be rendered on two lines.

Note

Unlike other programming languages, JavaScript includes no special data type for a single character, such as the `char` data type in the C, C++, and Java programming languages.

Escape Characters and Sequences

Use extra care when using single quotation marks with possessives and contractions in strings, because JavaScript interpreters always look for the first closing single or double quotation mark to match an opening single or double quotation mark. For example, consider the following statement:

```
document.write('<p>My mom's favorite color is blue.</p>');
```

This statement causes an error. A JavaScript interpreter assumes that the literal string ends with the apostrophe following "mom" and looks for the closing parentheses for the `document.write()` statement immediately following "mom'". To get around this problem, you include an escape character before the apostrophe in "mom's". An escape character tells compilers and interpreters that the character that follows it has a special purpose. In JavaScript, the escape character is the backslash (\ ). Placing a backslash before an apostrophe tells JavaScript interpreters that the apostrophe is to be treated as a regular keyboard character, such as *a*, *b*, *1*, or *2*, and not as part of a single quotation mark pair that encloses a text string. The backslash in the following statement tells the JavaScript interpreter to print the apostrophe following the word "mom" as an apostrophe.

```
document.write('<p>My mom\'s favorite color is blue.</p>');
```

You can also use the escape character in combination with other characters to insert a special character into a string. When you combine the escape character with a specific other character, the combination is called an escape sequence. The backslash followed by an apostrophe (\') and the backslash followed by a double quotation mark (\") are both examples of escape sequences. Most escape sequences carry out special functions. For example, the escape sequence `\t` inserts a tab into a string. **Figure 2-7** describes the escape sequences that can be added to a string in JavaScript.

ESCAPE SEQUENCE	CHARACTER
`\\`	Backslash
`\b`	Backspace
`\r`	Carriage return
`\"`	Double quotation mark
`\f`	Form feed
`\t`	Horizontal tab
`\n`	Newline
`\0`	Null character
`\'`	Single quotation mark (apostrophe)
`\v`	Vertical tab
`\xXX`	Latin-1 character specified by the *XX* characters, which represent two hexadecimal digits
`\uXXXX`	Unicode character specified by the *XXXX* characters, which represent four hexadecimal digits

Figure 2-7 JavaScript escape sequences

Note If you place a backslash before any character other than those listed in Figure 2-7, the backslash is ignored.

Notice that one of the characters generated by an escape sequence is the backslash. Because the escape character itself is a backslash, you must use the escape sequence `\\` to include a backslash as a character in a string. For example, to include the path "C:\Users\me\Documents\Cengage\WebWarrior\JavaScript\" in a string, you must include two backslashes for every single backslash you want to appear in the string, as in the following statement:

```
document.write("<p>My JavaScript files are located in↵
   C:\\Users\\me\\Documents\\Cengage\\WebWarrior\\↵
   JavaScript\\</p>");
```

Quick Check 2

1. What is the difference between block scope and function scope?
2. What is the scope of variables declared with the `let` keyword?
3. What are the possible values for a Boolean variable?
4. What is the difference between a strongly typed and a loosely typed language? Which is JavaScript?
5. What is the escape sequence for the newline character?

Using Operators to Build Expressions

In the previous chapter, you learned the basics of how to create expressions using basic operators, such as the addition operator (+) and multiplication operator (*). In this section, you will learn about other types of operators you can use with JavaScript.

JavaScript operators are binary or unary. A binary operator requires an operand before and after the operator. The equal sign in the statement `myNumber = 100;` is an example of a binary operator. A unary operator requires just a single operand either before or after the operator. For example, the increment operator (++), an arithmetic operator, is used to increase an operand by a value of one. The statement `myNumber++;` changes the value of the `myNumber` variable to 101.

Note Another type of JavaScript operator, bitwise operators, operate on integer values; this is a fairly complex topic. Bitwise operators and other complex operators are beyond the scope of this book.

Arithmetic Operators

Arithmetic operators are used in JavaScript to perform mathematical calculations, such as addition, subtraction, multiplication, and division. You can also use an arithmetic operator to return the modulus of a calculation, which is the remainder left when you divide one number by another number.

Figure 2-8 describes the arithmetic operators supported by JavaScript.

OPERATOR	DESCRIPTION	EXPRESSION	RETURNS
+	Combines or adds two items	12 + 3	15
–	Subtracts one item from another	12 – 3	9
*	Multiplies two items	12*3	36
/	Divides one item by another	12/3	4
%	Returns the remainder after dividing one integer by another integer	18%5	3
**	Raising a value to a power	3**2	9

Figure 2-8 Arithmetic operators

Note The operand to the left of an operator is known as the left operand, and the operand to the right of an operator is known as the right operand.

You might be confused by the difference between the division (/) operator and the modulus (%) operator. The division operator performs a standard mathematical division operation so that the expression `15/6` returns a value of 2.5. The modulus operator returns the remainder after a division so that the expression `15%6` returns a value of 3 because that is the remainder when 15 is divided by 6.

Arithmetic operations can also be performed on a single variable using unary operators. **Figure 2-9** lists the arithmetic unary operators available in JavaScript.

OPERATOR	DESCRIPTION	EXPRESSION	RETURNS
++	Increases a value by 1	12++	13
--	Decreases a value by 1	12--	11
–	Changes the sign of a value	–12	–12

Figure 2-9 Unary operators

Unary operators provide a more simplified expression for increasing or decreasing a value by 1. The statement `count = count + 1` has the same result as the expression `count++`. Where things can be confusing is that the unary operator could also be placed before the variable as in the expression `++count`.

A prefix operator is a unary operator placed before the variable, while a postfix operator is placed after the variable. The distinction is important because placement indicates the order in which the operator is applied to the variable.

The following statement uses a prefix operator so that the value of x is first increased by 1, and then that value is assigned to the variable y, giving both variables a final value of 6:

```
let x = 5;
let y = ++x  // x = 6 and y = 6
```

But if the code is written using a postfix operator, a different result occurs:

```
let x = 5;
let y = x++  // x = 6 and y = 5
```

With a postfix operator, the value of x is first stored in y and only after that is x is increased by 1 so that the final value of x is 6 but the final value of y remains as 5. The same effect occurs if you use the decrement operator (--) to decrease the value of the variable by 1.

Skills at Work | Making Your Code Self-Documenting

While including comments in your code can make your code easier for you and other programmers to read and understand, using comments is not the only strategy for documenting code. Another strategy is to make your code self-documenting, meaning that the code is written as simply and directly as possible, so its statements and structures are easier to understand at a glance. For instance, it's a good idea to name variables with descriptive names so it's easier to remember what value is stored in each variable. Rather than naming variables `var1`, `var2`, and so on, you can use names like `firstName` or `lastName`. Creating statements that are easy to read is another instance of self-documenting code. For example, code that you create with the increment operator (++) is more concise than code that assigns a variable a value of itself plus 1. However, in this shortened form, the code can be more challenging to read and understand quickly. For this reason, some developers choose not to use the ++ operator at all, relying instead on the + and = operators to make their code easier for themselves and other developers to read. As you build your programming skills, you'll learn multiple ways to code many different tasks, but the best option is usually the one that results in code that is easy for you and other programmers to read and understand. This results in code that can be more easily maintained and modified by other developers when you move on to another job.

Assignment Operators

An assignment operator is used for assigning a value to a variable. The most common assignment operator is the equal sign (=), but JavaScript supports other operators known as compound assignment operators that both assign a value and perform a calculation. For example, the expression

```
x += y
```

both performs the addition operation and assigns a value so that this expression is equivalent to

```
x = x + y
```

Figure 2-10 lists other compound assignment operators supported by JavaScript.

OPERATOR	EXAMPLE	EQUIVALENT TO
=	x = y	x = y
+=	x += y	x = x + y
−=	x −= y	x = x − y
*=	x *= y	x = x * y
/=	x /= y	x = x/y
%=	x %=y	x = x % y
**=	x**=y	x = x**y

Figure 2-10 Assignment operators

You can use the += compound addition assignment operator to combine two strings as well as to add numbers. In the case of strings, the string on the left side of the operator is combined with the string on the right side of the operator, and the new value is assigned to the left operator. Before combining operands, a JavaScript interpreter attempts to convert a nonnumeric operand, such as a string, to a number. This means that unlike the + operator, which concatenates any string values, using the += operator with two string operands containing numbers results in a numeric value. For instance, the following code defines two variables with string values: `x` with a value of "5" and `y` with a value of "4". In processing the third line of code, a JavaScript interpreter first converts the strings to the values 5 and 4, respectively, then adds them, and then assigns the result, the value 9, to the `x` variable.

```
x = "5";
y = "4";
x += y; // a numeric value of 9 is returned for x
```

If a nonnumeric operand cannot be converted to a number, you receive a value of `NaN`. The value `NaN` stands for "Not a Number" and is returned when a mathematical operation does not result in a numerical value. The sole exception to this rule is +=, which simply concatenates operands if one or both can't be converted to numbers.

Comparison Operators

A comparison operator, or relational operator, is used to compare two operands and determine if one value is greater than another. A Boolean value of `true` or `false` is returned after two operands are compared. For example, the statement `5 < 3` would return a Boolean value of `false`, because 5 is not less than 3. **Figure 2-11** lists the JavaScript comparison operators.

OPERATOR	EXAMPLE	DECRIPTION
==	`x == y`	Tests whether x is equal in value to y
===	`x === y`	Tests whether x is equal in value to y and has the same data type
!=	`x != y`	Tests whether x is not equal to y or has a different data type
!==	`x !== y`	Tests whether x is not equal to y and/or doesn't have the same data type
>	`x > y`	Tests whether x is greater than y
>=	`x >= y`	Tests whether x is greater than or equal to y
<	`x < y`	Tests whether x is less than y
<=	`x <= y`	Tests whether x is less than or equal to y

Figure 2-11 Comparison operators

Note The comparison operators (`==` and `===`) consist of two and three equal signs, respectively, and perform a different function than the one performed by the assignment operator that consists of a single equal sign (=). The comparison operators compare values, whereas the assignment operator assigns values. Confusion between these two types of operators is a common mistake.

You can use number or string values as operands with comparison operators. When two numeric values are used as operands, JavaScript interpreters compare them numerically. For example, the statement `arithmeticValue = 5 > 4;` results in `true` because the number 5 is numerically greater than the number 4. When two nonnumeric values are used as operands, the JavaScript interpreter compares them in lexicographical order—that is, the order in which they would appear in a dictionary. The expression `"b" > "a";` returns `true` because the letter *b* comes after than the letter *a* in the dictionary. When one operand is a number and the other is a string, JavaScript interpreters attempt to convert the string value to a number. If the string value cannot be converted to a number, a value of `false` is returned. For example, the expression `10 === "ten";` returns a value of `false` because JavaScript interpreters cannot convert the string "ten" to a number.

Conditional Operators

Comparison operators are often used with conditional operators or ternary operators that return one of two possible values given the Boolean value of comparison. The general syntax of a comparison operator is

```
condition ? trueValue : falseValue;
```

where *`condition`* is an expression or value that is either `true` or `false`, *`trueValue`* is the returned value if the expression is `true`, while *`falseValue`* is the returned value if the expression is `false`. The `conditional` expression is often enclosed within parentheses to make the statement easier to read. For example, an online store might set a discount rate for prime members of 5%. The following statement sets the value of the `discount` variable based on whether the value of `member` variable is equal to "prime":

```
let discount = (member === "prime") ? 0.05 : 0.0;
```

If `member` equals "prime" then the value of the `discount` variable is set to 0.05 (5%); otherwise the `discount` variable is set to 0.0 (no discount). The condition can be any expression that equals `true` or `false`; it can even a Boolean variable as the following code demonstrates in which the `discount` variable equals 0.05 because the `primeMember` variable equals `true`:

```
let primeMember = true;
let discount = primeMember ? 0.05 : 0.0;
```

A conditional operator only returns *`trueValue`* if the *`condition`* is `true`. If *`condition`* is `false` or `undefined` or `null` or `NaN` (not a number), it will be treated as false by the conditional operator.

Note

You can nest one conditional operator within another to test two conditions. The general syntax is

```
condition1 ? trueValue : condition2 ? trueValue : falseValue;
```

where the expression returns *`trueValue`* if *`condition1`* is *`true`* or *`condition2`* is *`true`*; otherwise it returns *`falseValue`*.

Conditional operators can also be used with expressions in place of values. In the following statement, an alert box is displayed with the message "Enjoy your free shipping" if `primeMember` is `true` or the message "Go prime for free shipping" if it is `false`:

```
(primeMember) ? window.alert("Enjoy your free shipping") :
                window.alert("Go prime for free shipping");
```

Note that long expressions are often more easily written on several lines. As long as the text strings are all contained on a single line, you can break the statement at other points for better readability.

Understanding Falsy and Truthy Values

JavaScript includes six values that are treated in comparison operations as the Boolean value `false`. These six values, known as falsy values, are the following: `""`, `-0`, `0`, `NaN`, `null`, and `undefined`.

All values other than these six falsy values are the equivalent of Boolean `true`, and are known as truthy values.

Developers commonly take advantage of falsy and truthy values to make comparison operations more compact. In a conditional statement that tests whether a text field in a form contains a value, you could write the code for the conditional statement as

```
(document.getElementById("fname").value !== "") ?↵
   // code to run if condition is true :↵
   // code to run if condition is false;
```

However, it's simpler to test whether the value of the text field is falsy or truthy by omitting the comparison operator and writing the statement as follows:

```
(document.getElementById("fname").value) ?↵
   // code to run if condition is true :↵
   // code to run if condition is false;
```

Note that this code tests only the value of the text field. If it is an empty string (""), it is treated as `false`.

Logical Operators

Logical operators are used when combining expressions that will result in Boolean value of `true` or `false` or for negating a Boolean value, turning `true` to `false` or `false` to `true`. **Figure 2-12** lists the three logical operators supported by JavaScript.

OPERATOR	DEFINITION	EXAMPLE	DESCRIPTION
`&&`	and	`(x === 5) && (y === 8)`	Tests whether x is equal to 5 and y is equal to 8
`||`	or	`(x === 5) || (y === 8)`	Test whether x is equal to 5 or y is equal to 8
`!`	not	`! (x < 5)`	Test whether x is not less than 5

Figure 2-12 Logical operators

The following conditional operator uses the `And` operator (`&&`) to combine two conditions testing whether the value of the member variable is "prime" and the value of the plan variable is "gold". If both conditions are true, then discount rate is set to a value of 0.10; otherwise it is set to a value of 0.0.

```
let discount = (member === "prime" && plan === "gold") ? 0.10 : 0.0;
```

In the following expression, the `Or` operator (||) is used to return a discount rate of 0.05 if member is "prime" or sale is "yes":

```
let discount = (member === "prime" || sale === "yes") ? 0.05 : 0.0;
```

Using parentheses, you can create more complicated statements by grouping multiple conditions, as in the following statement that sets the discount rate at 0.10 if member equals "prime" and plan equals "gold" or sale equals "blowout":

```
let discount = ((member === "prime" && plan === "gold") || sale === "blowout") ? 0.10 : 0.0;
```

A common error when using multiple conditions is to omit an opening or closing parenthesis. You must have an equal number of opening and closing parentheses to avoid an error, so always count the number of opening and closing parentheses to verify that they match.

Note | Logical operators are often used within conditional and looping statements such as the `if`, `for`, and `while` statements. You will learn about conditional and looping statements in Chapter 3.

Special Operators

JavaScript also includes the special operators that are listed in **Figure 2-13**. These operators are used for various purposes and do not fit within any other category.

NAME	OPERATOR	DESCRIPTION
Property access	`.`	Appends an object, method, or property to another object
Array index	`[]`	Accesses an element of an array
Function call	`()`	Calls up functions or changes the order in which individual operations in an expression are evaluated
Comma	`,`	Separates multiple expressions in the same statement
Conditional expression	`?:`	Executes one of two expressions based on the results of a conditional expression
Delete	`delete`	Deletes array elements, variables created without the `var` keyword, and properties of custom objects
Property exists	`in`	Returns a value of `true` if a specified property is contained within an object
Object type	`instanceof`	Returns `true` if an object is of a specified object type
New object	`new`	Creates a new instance of a user-defined object type or a predefined JavaScript object type
Data type	`typeof`	Determines the data type of a variable
Void	`void`	Evaluates an expression without returning a result

Figure 2-13 Special operators

One of more useful special operators is the `typeof` operator, which returns the data type stored within a variable. The syntax of the `typeof` operator is

```
typeof(variable);
```

Values returned by the `typeof` operator are listed in **Figure 2-14**. Because JavaScript allows variables to change their data type, the `typeof` operator is often used to check that variables retain data type and that a number has not been changed to a text string or vice versa.

RETURN VALUE	RETURNED FOR
`number`	Integers and floating-point numbers
`string`	Text strings
`boolean`	True or false
`object`	Objects, arrays, and null variables
`function`	Functions
`undefined`	Undefined variables

Figure 2-14 Values of the `typeof` operator

Quick Check 3

1. What is the difference between a binary operator and a unary operator?
2. How does JavaScript deal with code that performs arithmetic operations on string values?
3. What is a comparison operator? What kind of value does it return?
4. What is a falsy value? What are the six falsy values in JavaScript?

Understanding Operator Precedence

When using operators you need to be aware of operator precedence, which determines the order in which operations in an expression are evaluated. **Figure 2-15** shows the order of precedence listed in descending order of precedence. Operators in the same grouping in Figure 2-15 have the same order of precedence. Operators listed in the same row of the table have their precedence determined by associativity, which is the order in which operators of equal precedence are executed. Associativity is evaluated from left-to-right or right-to-left, depending on the operators involved.

OPERATORS	DESCRIPTION	ASSOCIATIVITY
.	Objects—highest precedence	Left to right
[]	Array elements—highest precedence	Left to right
()	Functions/evaluation—highest precedence	Left to right
new	New object—highest precedence	Right to left
++	Increment	Right to left
--	Decrement	Right to left
-	Unary negation	Right to left
+	Unary positive	Right to left
!	Not	Right to left
typeof	Data type	Right to left
void	Void	Right to left
delete	Delete object	Right to left
**	Exponentiation	Left to right
* / %	Multiplication/division/modulus	Left to right
+ -	Addition/concatenation and subtraction	Left to right
< <= > >=	Comparison	Left to right
instanceof	Object type	Left to right
in	Object property	Left to right
== != === !==	Equality	Left to right
&&	Logical And	Left to right
||	Logical Or	Left to right
?:	Conditional	Right to left
=	Assignment	Right to left
+= -= *= /= %=	Compound assignment	Right to left
,	Comma—lowest precedence	Left to right

Figure 2-15 **Operator precedence**

Note The preceding list does not include bitwise operators. As explained earlier, bitwise operators are beyond the scope of this book.

In Figure 2-15, operators in a higher grouping have precedence over operators in a lower grouping. For example, the multiplication operator (*) has a higher precedence than the addition operator (+). Therefore, the expression `5 + 2 * 8` evaluates as follows: the numbers 2 and 8 are multiplied first for a total of 16, then the number 5 is added, resulting in a total of 21. If the addition operator had a higher precedence than the multiplication operator, then the statement would evaluate to 56, because 5 would be added to 2 for a total of 7, which would then be multiplied by 8.

However, multiplication and division have an equal order of precedence and, therefore, their precedence is determined by associativity, which for them is left-to-right. Thus the expression `30 / 5 * 2` results in a value of 12 because the division operator is applied first followed by the multiplication operator. See **Figure 2-16**.

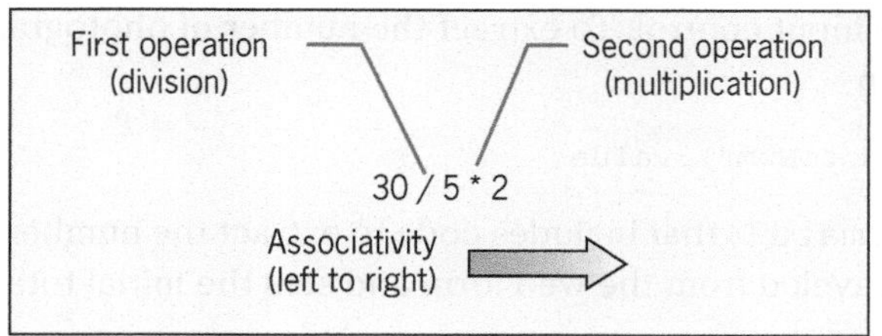

Figure 2-16 Left-to-right associativity

If the multiplication operator had higher precedence than the division operator, then the statement `30 / 5 * 2` would result in a value of 3 because the multiplication operation (`5 * 2`) would execute first. By contrast, the assignment operator and compound assignment operators, such as the compound multiplication assignment operator (`*=`), have an associativity of right to left as in the following example:

```
let x = 3;
let y = 2;
x = y *= ++x;
```

Moving right to left, the variable `x` is incremented by one *before* it is assigned to the `y` variable using the compound multiplication assignment operator (`*=`). Then, the value of variable `y` is assigned to the variable `x`, resulting a in final value of 8 for both variables. See **Figure 2-17**.

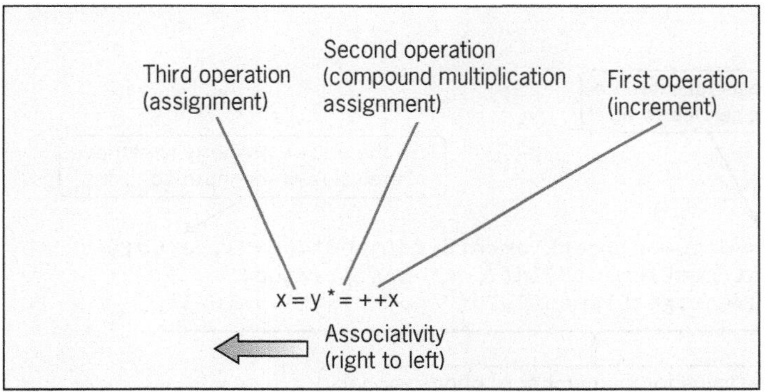

Figure 2-17 Right-to-left associativity

As shown in Figure 2-15, parentheses have among the highest precedence. For example, the expression `(5 + 2) * 8` is equal to `7 * 8` or `56`.

Using Expressions with Web Form Controls

Now that you have learned about expressions and operators, it is time to return to the Fan Trick Fine Art Photography page. The next task for the page is to provide an estimate for the total cost of the photography service. Recall that total cost is the sum of several factors:

- The number of photographers charged at a rate of $100 per hour per photographer
- The distance the photographers must travel to the photo shoot, charged at a rate of $2 per mile per photographer
- Whether a memory book is purchased at a cost of $350
- Whether full digital reproduction rights are granted to the customer at cost of $1250

To estimate the total cost, you will first have to extract information from the web form and then use JavaScript operators and expressions to calculate the total.

Working with Input Control Values

Recall from earlier in this chapter that the value inserted into an input control can be referenced using the following `value` property:

```
object.value
```

where *object* is a reference to the input control. To extract the number of photographers from the input box with the id "photoNum", use the expression

```
document.getElementById("photoNum").value
```

Create a function named `getEstimate()` that includes code to extract the number of photographers, the number of hours worked, and the distance traveled from the web form and sets the initial total cost of the service to $0.

To retrieve values from the web form:

1. Return to the **js02.js** file in your code editor.
2. At the bottom of the file insert the following `getEstimate()` function:

```
// estimate the total cost of the service
function getEstimate() {
   let totalCost = 0;
   let photographers = document.getElementById("photoNum").value;
   let hours = document.getElementById("photoHrs").value;
   let distance = document.getElementById("photoDist").value;
}
```

See **Figure 2-18**.

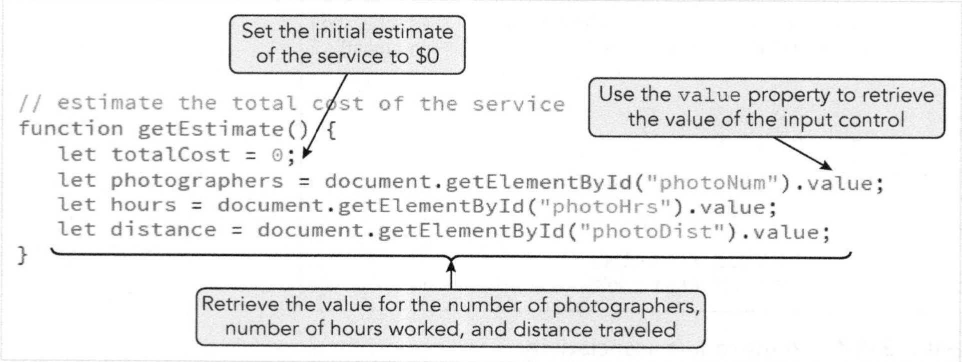

```
// estimate the total cost of the service
function getEstimate() {
   let totalCost = 0;
   let photographers = document.getElementById("photoNum").value;
   let hours = document.getElementById("photoHrs").value;
   let distance = document.getElementById("photoDist").value;
}
```

Figure 2-18 Retrieving input control values

Next, add the cost of the photographers per hour and the distance traveled per photographer and mile to the `totalCost` variable. To do these calculations you will use the += assignment operator to both perform the calculation and add it to the total cost estimate. To add the cost of photographers for the hours covered, use the statement

```
totalCost += photographers * hours * EMP_COST;
```

Notice that this expression uses the `photographers` and `hours` variables you declared in the last set of steps and `EMP_COST` is the global constant you declared in Figure 2-5. To add the cost of travel for the photographers, use the statement

```
totalCost += photographers * distance * TRAVEL_COST;
```

Add both of these statements to the `getEstimate()` function.

To add calculations to the `getEstimate()` function:

1. Add the following commands to the `getEstimate()` function as shown in **Figure 2-19**:

```
// Add the cost of photographers for the hours covered
totalCost += photographers * hours * EMP_COST;

// Add the cost of distance per photographer per mile
totalCost += photographers * distance * TRAVEL_COST;
```

```
// estimate the total cost of the service
function getEstimate() {
   let totalCost = 0;
   let photographers = document.getElementById("photoNum").value;
   let hours = document.getElementById("photoHrs").value;
   let distance = document.getElementById("photoDist").value;

   // Add the cost of photographers for the hours covered
   totalCost += photographers * hours * EMP_COST;

   // Add the cost of distance per photographer per mile
   totalCost += photographers * distance * TRAVEL_COST;
}
```

Add the photographer cost to the total estimate

Add the travel cost to the total estimate

Figure 2-19 Adding to the total cost estimate

2. Save your changes to the file.

Note Input control values are text strings even if they appear as numbers. If you use the + operator to add the values of two input controls, JavaScript will combine the two text strings and not add their numeric values. You can convert a text string by enclosing the text within the `Number()` function as in the expression `Number("12.3")`, which returns the numeric value 12.3.

Working with Checkboxes

As you learned earlier in this chapter, every checkbox control has a `checked` property, a Boolean value indicating whether the checkbox has been selected (`true`) or left unchecked (`false`). Thus, to retrieve the checked status of a checkbox, use the expression

```
object.checked
```

where *object* is a reference to checkbox control. The following expressions returns the checked status of the checkbox controls with the ids "makeBook" and "photoRights".

```
document.getElementById("makeBook").checked
document.getElementById("photoRights").checked
```

Add two variables named `buyBook` and `buyRights` to the `getEstimate()` to record the checked status of these two checkboxes.

To create variables for checkbox controls:

1. Below the statement declaring the distance variable in the `getEstimate()` function, add the following statement to determine whether the makeBook checkbox has been checked:

```
let buyBook = document.getElementById("makeBook").checked;
```

2. Next add the following statement to determine whether the photoRights checkbox has been checked. **Figure 2-20** shows the newly added code in the function.

```
let buyRights = document.getElementById("photoRights").checked;
```

```
// estimate the total cost of the service
function getEstimate() {
   let totalCost = 0;
   let photographers = document.getElementById("photoNum").value;
   let hours = document.getElementById("photoHrs").value;
   let distance = document.getElementById("photoDist").value;
   let buyBook = document.getElementById("makeBook").checked;
   let buyRights = document.getElementById("photoRights").checked;
```

buyBook will be true if the makeBook checkbox is checked

buyRights will be true if the photoRights checkbox is checked

Figure 2-20 Retrieving the checked status of web form checkboxes

The buyBook and buyRights variables will have a value of true if their respective checkboxes have been checked by the user and false if otherwise. You will use that fact as part of a conditional operator that adds the cost of the book and the reproduction rights if these variables values are true but adds $0 if they are false. The statements are

```
totalCost += buyBook ? BOOK_COST : 0;
totalCost += buyRights ? REPRO_COST: 0;
```

Note that the BOOK_COST and REPRO_COST variables represent the global constants you created in Figure 2-5. Add these statements to the getEstimate() function.

To add the cost of the memory book and digital rights:

1. At the bottom of the getEstimate() function, insert the following statements:

```
// Add the cost of the book if purchased
totalCost += buyBook ? BOOK_COST : 0;
// Add the cost of photo rights if purchased
totalCost += buyRights ? REPRO_COST: 0;
```

Figure 2-21 shows the revised code in the function.

```
// Add the cost of distance per photographer per mile
totalCost += photographers * distance * TRAVEL_COST;

// Add the cost of the book if purchased
totalCost += buyBook ? BOOK_COST : 0;

// Add the cost of photo rights if purchased
totalCost += buyRights ? REPRO_COST : 0;
}
```


Figure 2-21 Adding the cost of the memory book and the photo rights

2. Save your changes to the file.

The last statement in the getEstimate() function displays the value of the totalCost() variable. The js02.html file contains the following span element in which you will display the totalCost value:

```
<aside>
   <p>Total Estimate: <span id="estimate"></span></p>
</aside>
```

To display the totalCost value within the span element with the id "estimate", use the innerHTML property in the following statement:

```
document.getElementById("estimate").innerHTML = "$" + totalCost;
```

Note that this expression uses the + operator to add the $ character to the text string displayed in the element. Add this command to the getEstimate() function and then run the web page to verify the total cost is correctly calculated and shown in the page.

To calculate and display the total cost estimate:

1. At the bottom of the getEstimate() function, add the following code:

```
// Display the total cost estimate
document.getElementById("estimate").innerHTML = "$" + totalCost;
```

Figure 2-22 shows the final code in the getEstimate() function.

```
// estimate the total cost of the service
function getEstimate() {
   let totalCost = 0;
   let photographers = document.getElementById("photoNum").value;
   let hours = document.getElementById("photoHrs").value;
   let distance = document.getElementById("photoDist").value;
   let buyBook = document.getElementById("makeBook").checked;
   let buyRights = document.getElementById("photoRights").checked;

   // Add the cost of photographers for the hours covered
   totalCost += photographers * hours * EMP_COST;

   // Add the cost of distance per photographer per mile
   totalCost += photographers * distance * TRAVEL_COST;

   // Add the cost of the book if purchased
   totalCost += buyBook ? BOOK_COST : 0;

   // Add the cost of photo rights if purchased
   totalCost += buyRights ? REPRO_COST : 0;

   // Display the total cost estimate
   document.getElementById("estimate").innerHTML = "$" + totalCost;
}
```

Display `totalCost` prefaced by the $ character

Figure 2-22 Displaying the total cost estimate in the web page

2. Scroll up to the `setupForm()` function and at the end of the function insert the following command to call the `getEstimate()` function as shown in **Figure 2-23**.

```
getEstimate();
```

```
// set the form's default values
function setupForm() {
   document.getElementById("photoNum").value = 1;
   document.getElementById("photoHrs").value = 2;

   document.getElementById("makeBook").checked = false;
   document.getElementById("photoRights").checked = false;
   document.getElementById("photoDist").value = 0;

   getEstimate();
}
```

Run the `getEstimate()` function when the browser loads the page

Figure 2-23 Calling the `getEstimate()` function when the page loads

3. Save your changes to the file and then reload the **js02.html** file in your web browser. As shown in **Figure 2-24**, the initial page should show a total cost estimate of $200 for the default options entered the webform.

The total cost estimate needs to be automatically updated when the customer changes values and options in the form. You will add that feature next.

Note All modern browsers also support the `textContent` property for web page elements. This property is similar to the `innerHTML` property, except that a `textContent` value excludes any HTML markup, while `innerHTML` allows it.

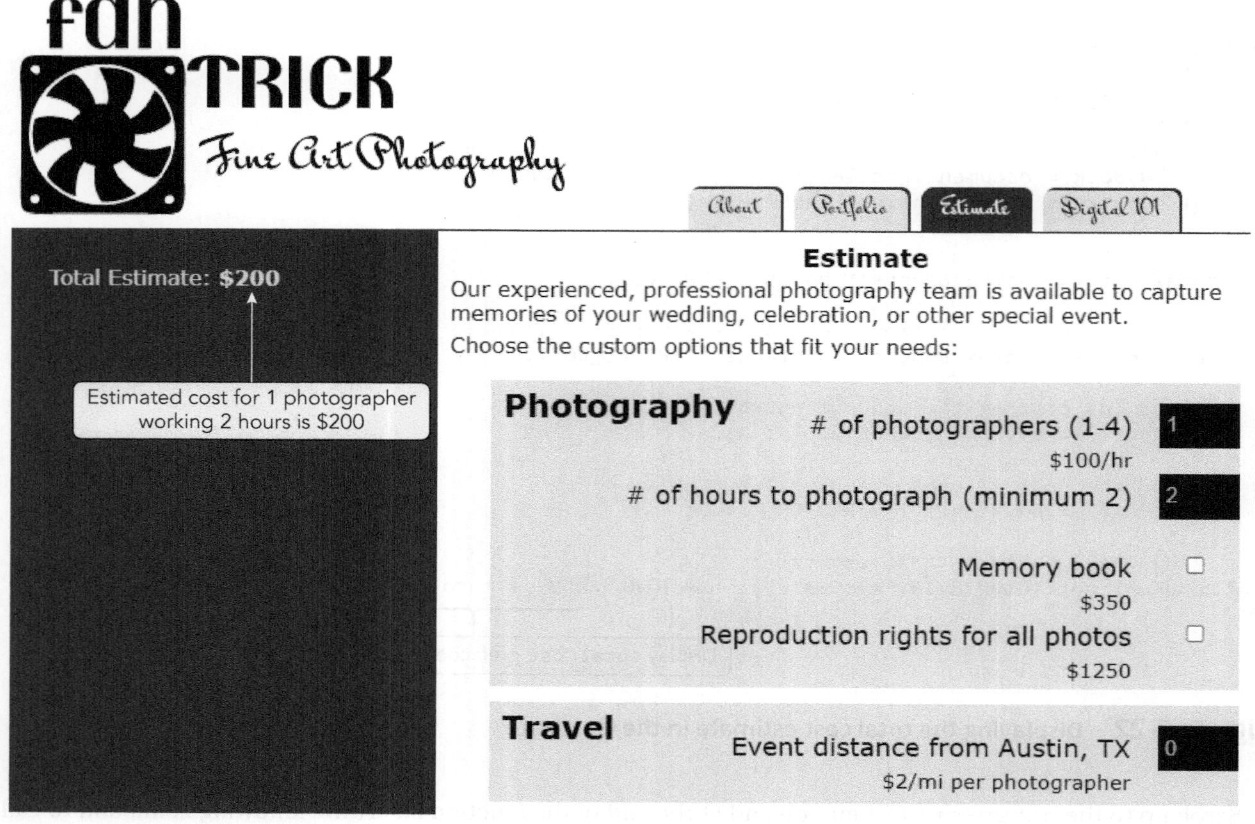

Figure 2-24 Initial Fan Trick Fine Art Photography page

Using the `change` Event with Web Form Controls

One of the events associated with web form controls is the `change` event, which is triggered when the value within the control is changed. The `change` event is triggered for an input box only when the control loses the focus by either tabbing out of the box or clicking outside of it. Checkboxes trigger the `change` event when they are clicked. To apply the `onchange` event handler to the form control, apply the statement

```
object.onchange = function;
```

With the event listeners, the statement appears as

```
object.addEventListener("change", function);
```

Attach the `getEstimate()` function to the `change` event associated with each of the five input controls on the Fan Trick web page. These commands are part of the `setupForm()` function that runs automatically when the browser loads the page.

To add onchange event handlers to the form controls:

1. Return to the **js02.js** file in your code editor.
2. At the bottom of the `setupForm()` function add the following statements:

```
// Add event handlers for each input control
document.getElementById("photoNum").onchange = getEstimate;
document.getElementById("photoHrs").onchange = getEstimate;
document.getElementById("photoDist").onchange = getEstimate;
document.getElementById("makeBook").onchange = getEstimate;
document.getElementById("photoRights").onchange = getEstimate;
```

Figure 2-25 shows the final code in the `setupForm()` function.

```
// set the form's default values
function setupForm() {
   document.getElementById("photoNum").value = 1;
   document.getElementById("photoHrs").value = 2;

   document.getElementById("makeBook").checked = false;
   document.getElementById("photoRights").checked = false;
   document.getElementById("photoDist").value = 0;

   getEstimate();

   // Add event handlers for each input control
   document.getElementById("photoNum").onchange = getEstimate;
   document.getElementById("photoHrs").onchange = getEstimate;
   document.getElementById("photoDist").onchange = getEstimate;
   document.getElementById("makeBook").onchange = getEstimate;
   document.getElementById("photoRights").onchange = getEstimate;
}
```

Run the `getEstimate()` function when the values of any of the 5 input controls are changed

Figure 2-25 Adding event handlers for each input control

3. Save your changes to the file and then reload the **js02.html** file in your browser.
4. Test the form, verifying that as you change the plan options the total cost estimate automatically updates. Note that you may have to tab out of a form control to trigger the change event. **Figure 2-26** shows the total estimate for a project that involves two photographers working for 3 hours traveling 30 miles to the event with both the memory book and photographic rights purchased by the customer. The total cost of the job would be $2320.

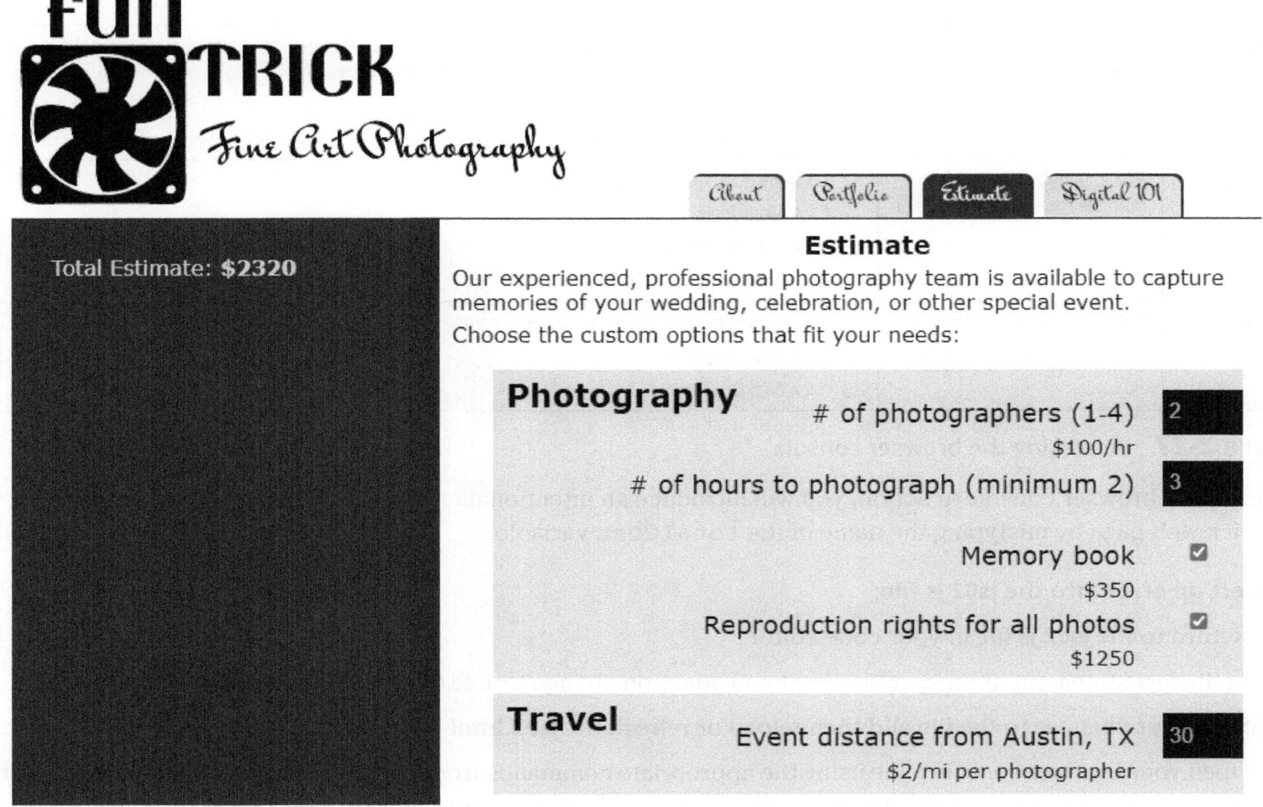

Figure 2-26 Estimating total cost for a photography job

If your page does not work, compare the code for your functions to that shown in Figures 2-22 and 2-25. Common mistakes include

- Misspelled JavaScript keywords
- Misspelled variable names or failing to match the use of uppercase and lowercase letters
- Misplaced or missing quotation marks, parentheses, or curly braces

If you still are having problems with your code, you can try to locate your coding error with your browser's console.

Locating Errors with the Browser Console

Even the most careful programmer makes mistakes. A small mistake, such as incorrect capitalization or the omission of a closing quote, parenthesis, or curly brace can prevent the browser from processing your code and result in an application filled with errors.

Accessing the Browser Console

When a browser encounters an error that prevents it from interpreting your code, it generates an error message displayed in a pane known as a browser console, or simply console, which is hidden from the user. However, developers can display the browser console pane to view errors in the application code. Almost every major browser supports a browser console, though there are slight differences in how to access and view the console details. **Figure 2-27** describes how to access the console in the major browsers at the time of this writing.

BROWSER	KEYBOARD SHORTCUT	MENU STEPS
Google Chrome	SHIFT + CTRL + J (Windows) Option + ⌘ + J (Macintosh)	1. Click the Chrome menu in the upper-right corner 2. Click More Tools 3. Click Developer Tools 4. Click Console from the Developer pane
Safari	Option + ⌘ + C	1. Enable the Developer tab by going into the Safari Menu > Preferences window, going to the Advanced tab and selecting Show Develop menu in menu bar checkbox 2. Click the Developer tab in the Safari menu 3. Click Show JavaScript Console
Microsoft Edge	F12 and then click Console from the Developer pane menu	1. Click the Edge menu in the upper-right corner 2. Click More Tools 3. Click Developer Tools 4. Click Console from the Developer pane
Firefox	SHIFT + CTRL + J (Windows) Option + ⌘ + J (Macintosh)	1. Click the Firefox menu in the upper-right corner 2. Click Web Developer 3. Click Web Console

Figure 2-27 Accessing the browser console

To view your browser console in action, you will introduce an intentional error in the application you created for the Fan Trick web page by mistyping the name of the `totalCost` variable.

To insert an error into the js02.js file:

1. Return to the **js02.js** file in your code editor.
2. In the last statement in the `getEstimate()` function change `totalCost` to **`totalcost`**.
3. Save your changes to the file and then reload or refresh the **js02.html** file.
4. Open your browser console pane using the appropriate commands from Figure 2-27. If your browser is not listed, use your browser's help system to determine how to open the console. **Figure 2-28** shows the console message from the Google Chrome browser (note that your browser's console might appear slightly different).

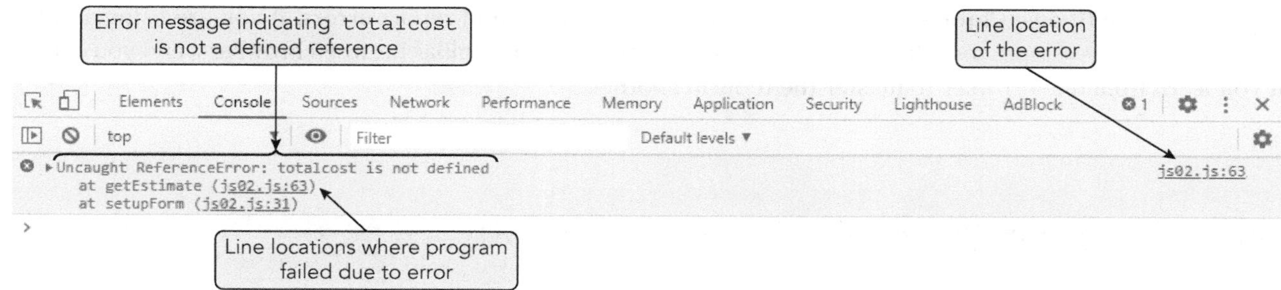

Figure 2-28 Browser console message in the Google Chrome browser

The console reports an unrecognized reference to `totalcost`. Because variable names are case sensitive and the variable should have been named `totalCost`, the JavaScript interpreter will not recognize the misspelled variable name.

Locating an Error in Your Program

In addition to error description, the console will indicate the location of the error that caused the program to fail. In this case, the location of the unrecognized reference is on line 63 of the js02.js file. Depending on how you wrote the code for your file, your line number might be different. The console also reports the lines in the code that the program failed to run: line 63 within the `getEstimate()` function and line 31 within the `setupForm()` function. This information helps the programmer locate the source of the error. With the browser console, you can click a link to jump to the location of the error. However, while you can make temporary changes to the program within the console, permanent changes should be made within your code editor.

To view the error location in the console:

1. Click the **js02.js:63** link in your console (if your line number is different, click the link to that line number).

   The console shows the file listing for the js02.js file, highlighting the line and the error within that line. See **Figure 2-29**.

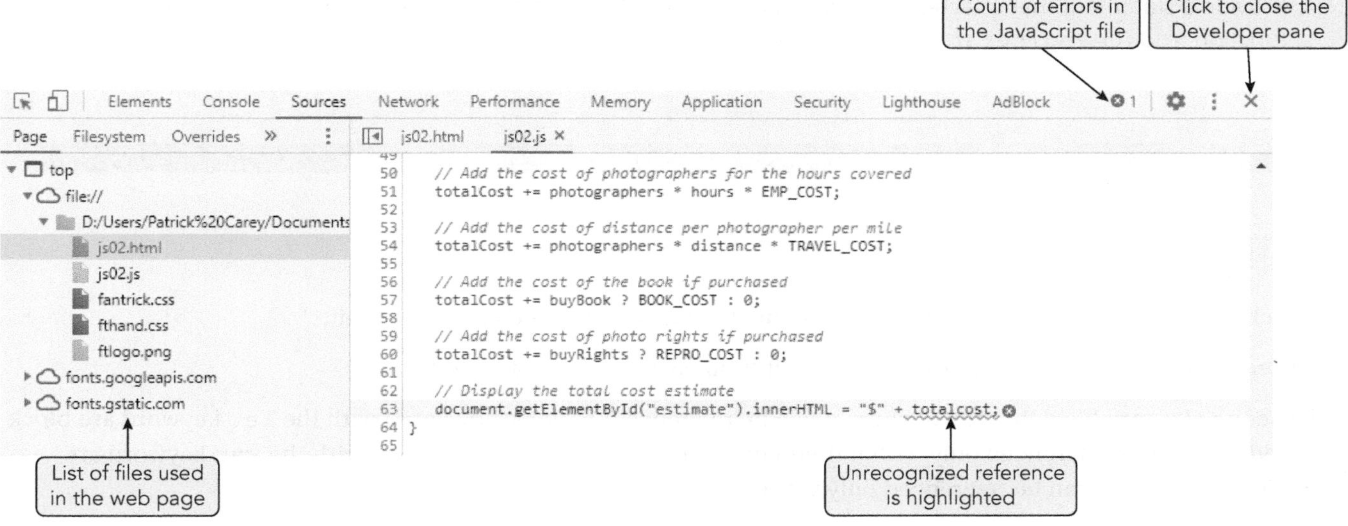

Figure 2-29 Console showing the location of the error

2. Now that you have viewed the source of the error, click the Close button in the upper right corner of the Developer pane.
3. Return to the **js02.js** file in your editor and fix the error from the last statement in the `getEstimate()` function, change `totalcost` back to **`totalCost`**.
4. Save your changes to the file and then reload the **js02.html** file in your browser and verify that the program is once again working correctly with no errors reported in the console.

This book uses the Google Chrome browser developer tools to check and report errors. If you are using a different browser, study the developer tools for your browser. Developer tools are similar between browsers, and you can apply what you learn from one browser to master the tools in another.

Programming Concepts | Creating Reusable Code

In a small JavaScript program, each function you create generally serves a specific purpose. However, when writing more complex code for larger sites, you should try to build functions that you can apply to multiple situations. For instance, instead of specifying an element name within a function, you could use a variable whose value is specified elsewhere in your program, depending on the context in which the function is called. Because such functions are reusable in multiple contexts within a website, they allow you to perform the same amount of work with less code than would be required to create functions for each specific situation. You'll learn additional strategies for creating reusable code in later chapters of this book.

Quick Check 4

1. When performing operations with operators in the same precedence group, how is the order of precedence determined?
2. Provide the expression to retrieve the value entered in the input control with the id "memberNumber".
3. Provide the expression to determine whether the checkbox control with the id "primeMember" has been checked.
4. Provide a statement that attaches an event listener to the input control with the id "memberNumber", running the function `updateRegistration()` when that control's value is changed.

Summary

- A function is a related group of JavaScript statements that are executed as a single unit.
- To execute a function, you must invoke, or call, it from elsewhere in your program.
- The scope of a variable determined where it can be referenced. Variables declared with the `let` keyword are block scoped and can be referenced only within their command block. Variables declared with the `var` keyword are function scoped and can be referenced only within their function.
- A global variable can be referenced anywhere within the program. A local variable can only be referenced within its command block or function.
- A data type (such as number, Boolean, or string) is the specific category of information that a variable contains.
- JavaScript is a loosely typed programming language, meaning it does not require you to declare the data types of variables.

- The numeric data type in JavaScript supports both integers (positive or negative numbers with no decimal places) and floating-point numbers (numbers that contains decimal places or that are written in exponential notation).
- A Boolean value is a logical value of `true` or `false`.
- The JavaScript escape character (\) tells compilers and interpreters that the character that follows it has a special purpose.
- Operators are symbols used in expressions to manipulate operands, such as the addition operator (+) and multiplication operator (*).
- A binary operator (such as +) requires operands before and after the operator, while a unary operator (such as ++) requires a single operand either before or after the operator.
- Arithmetic operators (such as +, -, *, and /) are used in JavaScript to perform mathematical calculations, such as addition, subtraction, multiplication, and division.
- An assignment operator (such as = or +=) is used for assigning a value to a variable.
- A comparison operator (such as === or >) is used to compare two operands and determine if one numeric value is greater than another.
- The conditional operator (? :) executes one of two expressions, based on the results of a conditional expression.
- Logical operators (&&, ||, and !) combine multiple Boolean expressions, resulting in a single Boolean value.
- Operator precedence is the order in which operations in an expression are evaluated.

Key Terms

anonymous function
actual parameters
arguments
arithmetic operators
assignment operator
associativity
binary operator
Boolean value
browser console
block scoped
bubbling phase
call
capture phase
command block
comparison operator
compound assignment operators
conditional operator
console
data type
duck typed
dynamically typed
empty string
escape character
escape sequence
event listener
event model
exponential notation
falsy values
floating point number
function
function scope
global scope
global variable
integer
local scope
local variable
logical operators
loosely typed
modulus
named function
operator precedence
parameter
passing arguments
postfix operator
prefix operator
primitive types
relational operator
scientific notation
scope
statically typed
strongly typed
template literal
ternary operator
truthy values
unary operator

Review Questions

1. Function statements are always enclosed within opening and closing curly braces in a structure known as a ____________.
   a. conditional operator
   b. command block
   c. parameter list
   d. return statement
2. Functions that are not named are called ____________.
   a. empty functions
   b. closed functions
   c. local functions
   d. anonymous functions
3. Variables declared with the `let` keyword ____________.
   a. have block scope
   b. have function scope
   c. have values that cannot be changed once declared
   d. act the same as variables declared with the `var` keyword
4. To return a value from a function, the last function statement must ____________.
   a. contain the `document.write()` method
   b. contain the `let` keyword
   c. contain the `return` keyword
   d. contain the `Return` keyword
5. Which of the following is a primitive data type in JavaScript?
   a. Boolean
   b. integer
   c. floating point
   d. logical
6. Which of the following describes JavaScript?
   a. strongly typed
   b. statically typed
   c. loosely typed
   d. untyped
7. Which of the following is an integer?
   a. −2.5
   b. 6.02e23
   c. −11
   d. 0.03
8. Which of the following is a Boolean value?
   a. 3.04
   b. `true`
   c. `"Greece"`
   d. 6.02e23
9. Which of the following creates an empty string?
   a. `null`
   b. `undefined`
   c. `""`
   d. 0
10. Which of the following is a valid JavaScript statement?
    a. `document.write('Boston, MA is called 'Beantown.'')`
    b. `document.write("Boston, MA is called "Beantown."")`
    c. `document.write("Boston, MA is called 'Beantown."')`
    d. `document.write("Boston, MA is called 'Beantown.'")`
11. To run the `showReport()` function when an input button is clicked, what attribute should be added to the HTML tag?
    a. `onclick = "showReport"`
    b. `click = "showReport()"`
    c. `onclick = "showReport()"`
    d. `addEvent = showReport`
12. One advantage of event listeners over event handlers is that____________.
    a. more than one function can be attached to the event
    b. event listeners work with local and global variables
    c. you can pass parameter values to event listeners
    d. event listeners work with mobile devices
13. If x = 10, the value of y in the following expression is____________.

    ```
    let y = x--;
    ```

    a. 9
    b. 10
    c. 11
    d. `undefined`
14. If `x = 10` and `y = 20`, the value of y in the following expression is____________.

    ```
    y /= x;
    ```

    a. 1/2
    b. 2
    c. 10
    d. 30

15. If `x = 5` the value of `y` in the following expression is ______________.

```
let y = (x === "5") ? 10 : 20;
```

   a. 5
   b. 10
   c. 20
   d. `undefined`

16. Write the code for a function named `mod10()` that has a single parameter named `x` and returns the remainder of `x` divided by 10.

17. Write the code for a function named `calcRatio()` that has three parameters named `x`, `y`, and `z` and returns the sum of `x` and `y` with that sum divided by `z`.

18. Explain the difference between a prefix and a postfix operator and provide an example of each.

19. Provide an expression that tests whether `x` is greater than or equal to `y` and returns the value of `x` if that condition is true and `y` if otherwise.

20. Write code that attaches an event listener for the `click` event for an element with the id "calc" that runs the function `calcRatio()` using 4, 8, and 3 as the parameter values. (Hint: You will have to use an anonymous function within the event listener.)

Hands-On Projects

Hands-On Project 2-1

In this project you will create an application to convert temperature readings between Fahrenheit and Celsius and between Celsius and Fahrenheit. The formula to convert a Fahrenheit temperature to the Celsius scale is

$Celsius = (Fahrenheit - 32)/1.8$

and the formula to convert a Celsius temperature to the Fahrenheit scale is

$Fahrenheit = Celsius \times 1.8 + 32$

Users will enter a value in a Celsius or Fahrenheit input box, press the Tab key and have the other input box automatically show the temperature reading in the other scale. A preview of the completed page is shown in **Figure 2-30**.

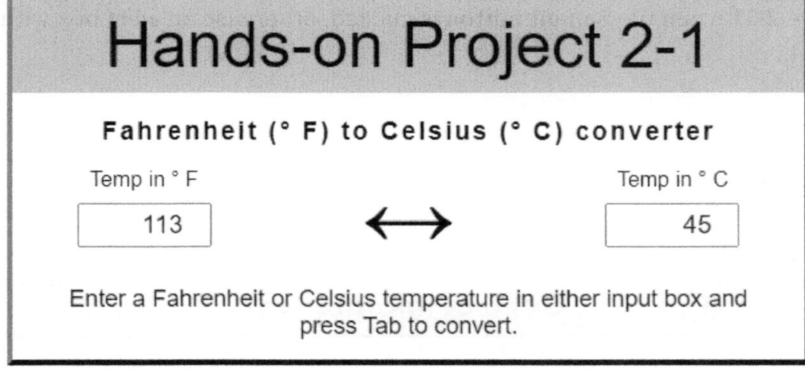

Figure 2-30 Completed Project 2-1

Do the following:

1. Use your code editor to open the **project02-01_txt.html** and **project02-01_txt.js** files from the js02 ► project01 folder. Enter your name and the date in the comment section of each file and save them as **project02-01.html** and **project02-01.js**, respectively.

2. Go to the **project02-01.html** file in your code editor and in the head section add a `script` element to load the project02-01.js file. Include the defer attribute to `defer` loading the external script file until the entire page is loaded. Study the contents of the HTML file and then save your changes.
3. Go to the **project02-01.js** file in your code editor. Create a function named `FahrenheitToCelsius()` containing a single parameter named `degree`. Insert a statement that returns the value of `degree` minus 32 and then divided by 1.8.
4. Create a function named `CelsiusToFahrenheit()` containing a single parameter named `degree`. Insert a statement that returns the value of `degree` multiplied by 1.8 plus 32.
5. Add an `onchange` event handler to the element with the id "cValue". Attach an anonymous function to the event handler and within the anonymous function do the following:
    a. Declare a variable named `cDegree` equal to the value of the element with the id "cValue".
    b. Set the value of the element with the id "fValue" to the value returned by the `CelsiusToFarenheit()` function using `cDegree` as the parameter value.
6. Add an `onchange` event handler to the element with the id "fValue". Attach an anonymous function to the event handler and within the anonymous function do the following:
    a. Declare a variable named `fDegree` equal to the value of the element with the id "fValue".
    b. Set the value of the element with the id "cValue" to the value returned by the `FarenheitToCelsius()` function using `fDegree` as the parameter value.
7. Save your changes to the file.
8. Open **project02-01.html** in your web browser. Verify that when you enter **45** in the Temp in °C box and press Tab a value of 113 appears in the Temp in °F box. Verify that when you enter **59** in the Temp in °F box and press Tab a value of 15 appears in the Temp in °C box.

Hands-On Project 2-2

In this project you will create an application that tests whether all fields within a web form have been completed. In creating this application, you will take advantage of the fact that empty text strings are falsy and in a conditional operator will be treated as having the Boolean value `false` and non-empty strings are treated as truthy with a Boolean value of `true`. If any of the form fields is left empty, the application will display the alert box shown in **Figure 2-31** when the Submit button is clicked, otherwise an alert box with the message "Thank you!" is displayed.

Figure 2-31 Completed Project 2-2

Do the following:

1. Use your code editor to open the project02-02_txt.html and project02-02_txt.js files from the js02 ▶ project02 folder. Enter your name and the date in the comment section of each file and save them as **project02-02.html** and **project02-02.js**, respectively.
2. Go to the **project02-02.html** file in your code editor and in the head section add a `script` element to load the project02-02.js file, deferring the loading the external script file until the entire page is loaded. Review the contents of the HTML file. Note that there are three input controls with the ids "name", "email", and "phone". Each of these controls must be filled out for the form to be submitted.
3. Go to the **project02-02.js** file in your code editor. Create a function named `verifyForm()` with no parameters. Within the function do the following:
   a. Declare the `name` variable equal to the value of the input control with the id "name".
   b. Declare the `email` variable equal to the value of the input control with the id "email".
   c. Declare the `phone` variable equal to the value of the input control with the id "phone".
   d. Insert a conditional operator that tests the truthy or falsy value of and `name` and `email` and `phone` using the && operator. If the result of this conditional expression is true, use the `window.alert()` method to display the message "Thank you!", otherwise display the message "Please fill in all fields".
4. Below the `verifyForm()` function insert a statement that attaches an event listener to the page element with the id "submit". When the click event occurs for this element, run the `verifyForm()` function.
5. Save your changes to the file and then open **project02-02.html** in your web browser.
6. Test the web form by clicking the Submit button with one or all the fields left blank, verifying that an alert box with the message "Please fill in all fields" is displayed. Enter text in all the fields and click the Submit button, verifying that an alert box with the message "Thank you!" is displayed.

Hands-On Project 2-3

In this project you will create an application that responds to the movements of the mouse over and out of a page object. The event that triggers the mouse over the object is called `mouseover` while moving the mouse out from an object triggers the `mouseout` event. In this application you will display a different message depending on the shape the mouse is hovering over or no message at all if the mouse is hovering over no shape. **Figure 2-32** shows a preview of the page with the message for the mouse hovering over the circle.

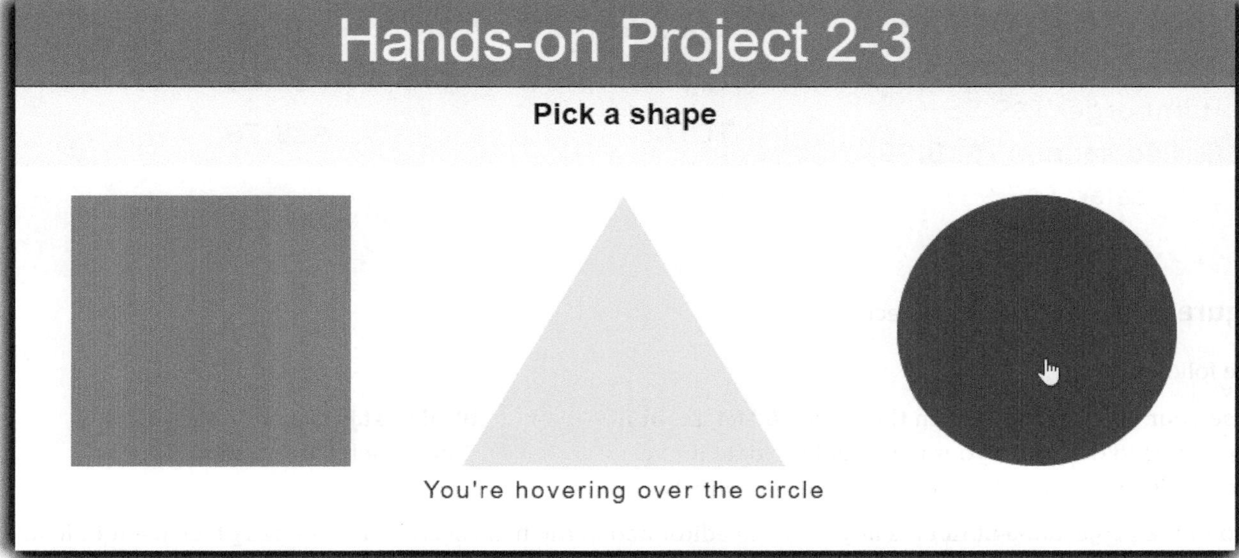

Figure 2-32 Completed Project 2-3

Do the following:

1. Use your code editor to open the **project02-03_txt.html** and **project02-03_txt.js** files from the js02 ▶ project03 folder. Enter your name and the date in the comment section of each file and save them as **project02-03.html** and **project02-03.js**, respectively.
2. Go to the **project02-03.html** file in your code editor and in the head section add a `script` element to load the project02-03.js file, deferring the loading the external script file until the entire page is loaded. Review the contents of the HTML file and note that the three shapes are placed within `div` elements with the ids "square", "triangle", and "shape". There is also an empty paragraph with the id "feedback". Save your changes to the file.
3. Go to the **project02-03.js** file in your code editor. Attach an `onmouseover` event handler to the element with the id "square". In response to the event run an anonymous function containing a statement that changes the `innerHTML` property of the element with the id "feedback" to the text string "You 're hovering over the square".
4. Attach an `onmouseout` event handler to the element with the id "square". In response to the event run an anonymous function containing a command that changes the `innerHTML` property of the element with the id "feedback" to an empty text string.
5. Repeat Steps 3 and 4 for the element with the id "triangle".
6. Repeat Steps 3 and 4 for the element with the id "circle".
7. Save your changes to the file and then open **project02-03.html** in your browser. Verify that as you hover your mouse pointer over each shape, a message indicating the shape in displayed on the page and when you move your mouse pointer away from the shape the message disappears.

Hands-On Project 2-4

In this project you will calculate the cost plus the tax of ordering items from a restaurant's online menu. So that the currency values are displayed with a leading `$` character, and to two decimal places you will call a function created for you named `formatCurrency()`, which takes a number and returns a text string in the format `$##.##`. The completed project appears as shown in **Figure 2-33**.

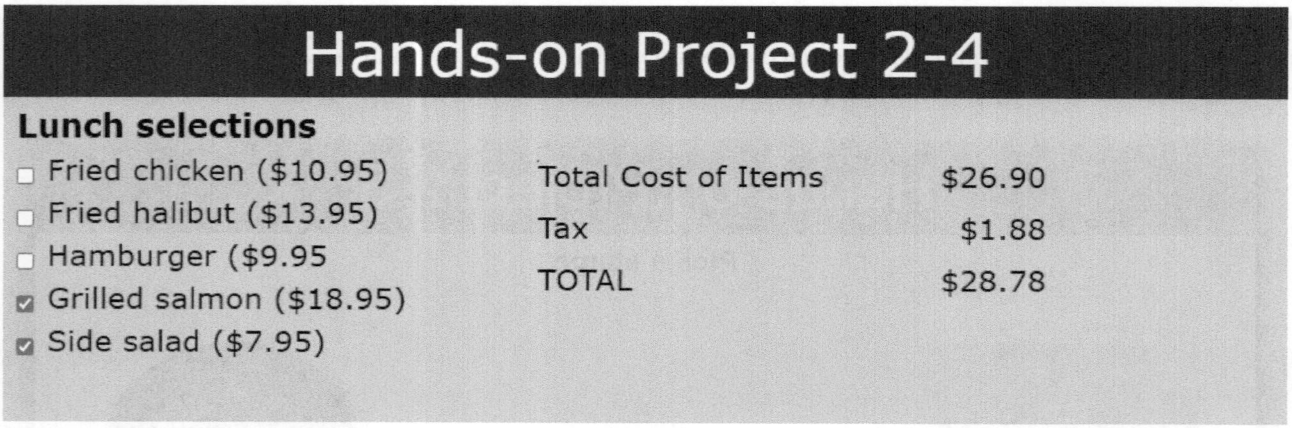

Hands-on Project 2-4

Lunch selections

- ☐ Fried chicken ($10.95)
- ☐ Fried halibut ($13.95)
- ☐ Hamburger ($9.95
- ☑ Grilled salmon ($18.95)
- ☑ Side salad ($7.95)

Total Cost of Items	$26.90
Tax	$1.88
TOTAL	$28.78

Figure 2-33 Completed Project 2-4

Do the following:

1. Use your code editor to open the **project02-04_txt.html** and **project02-04_txt.js** files from the js02 ▶ project04 folder. Enter your name and the date in the comment section of each file and save them as **project02-04.html** and **project02-04.js**, respectively.
2. Go to the **project02-04.html** file in your code editor and in the head section add a `script` element to load the project02-04.js file, deferring the loading the external script file until the entire page is loaded. Review the

contents of the HTML file, noting the ids of different page elements. You will display the calculated values in span elements with ids of "foodTotal", "foodTax", and "totalBill". Save your changes to the file.

3. Go to the **project02-04.js** file in your code editor. Below the comment section, declare the following constants with their initial values: CHICKEN_PRICE = 10.95, HALIBUT_PRICE = 13.95, BURGER_PRICE = 9.95, SALMON_PRICE = 18.95, SALAD_PRICE = 7.95, and SALES_TAX = 0.07.
4. Create the `calcTotal()` function containing the following:
   a. Declare the `cost` variable with an initial value of 0.
   b. Declare the `buyChicken` variable equal to the checked property of the element with the id "chicken". In the same way, declare the `buyHalibut`, `buyBurger`, `buySalmon`, and `buySalad` variables equal to the `checked` property of elements with ids of "halibut", "burger", "salmon", and "salad", respectively.
   c. Use a comparison operator to increase the value of the `cost` variable by the value of the CHICKEN_PRICE constant if `buyChicken` is `true` or by 0 if otherwise (see **Figure 2-21** as an example of your code). Do the same for the `buyHalibut`, `buyBurger`, `buySalmon`, and `buySalad` variables, increasing the value of total cost by the value of HALIBUT_PRICE, BURGER_PRICE, SALMON_PRICE, and SALAD_PRICE, respectively.
   d. Set the `innerHTML` property for the element with the id "foodTotal" to the value returned by the `formatCurrency()` function using `cost` as the parameter value.
   e. Declare the `tax` variable, setting its value equal to the `cost` variable multiplied by SALES_TAX.
   f. Set the `innerHTML` property for the element with the id "foodTax" to the value returned by the `formatCurrency()` function using `tax` as the parameter value.
   g. Declare the `totalCost` variable, setting its value equal to the `cost` variable plus the `tax` variable.
   h. Set the `innerHTML` property for the element with the id "totalBill" to the value returned by the `formatCurrency()` function using `totalCost` as the parameter value.
5. Directly above the `calcTotal()` function, insert an event handler that runs the `calcTotal()` function when the element with id "chicken" is clicked. Repeat this for the elements with the id "halibut", "burger", "salmon", and "salad".
6. Save your changes to the file and then open **project02-04.html** in your web browser. Verify that when you click each of the menu items the calculated cost and tax is automatically updated to reflect your choices.

Hands-On Project 2-5

Debugging Challenge

In this debugging challenge you will fix mistakes in code for an online calculator. The code has already been written for you but there are several syntax mistakes you will have to locate and correct. You can use your browser's debugging console to assist you in locating the errors. When the code has been fixed, you will be able to run the online calculator shown in **Figure 2-34** by clicking the calculator buttons and viewing the results in the calculator window. To erase the contents of the window, click the C button.

Do the following:

1. Use your code editor to open the **project02-05_txt.html** and **project02-05_txt.js** files from the js02 ► project05 folder. Enter your name and the date in the comment section of each file and save them as **project02-05.html** and **project02-05.js**, respectively.
2. Go to the **project02-05.html** file in your code editor and in the head section add a `script` element to load the project02-04.js file, deferring the loading the external script file until the entire page is loaded. Review the contents of the HTML file. Notice that the calculator buttons are arranged in a web table with each calculator button having a separate id related to the button's value. Save your changes to the file.

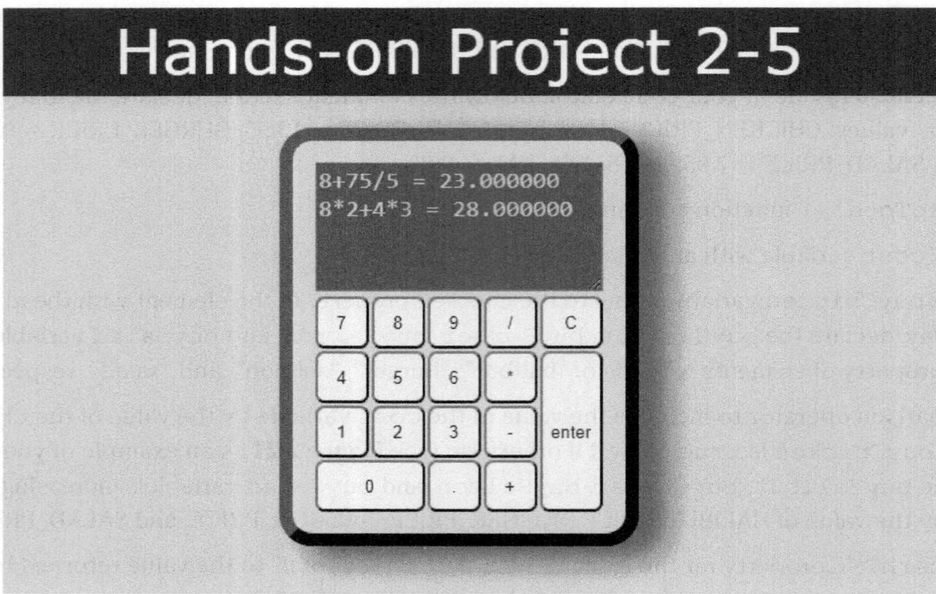

Figure 2-34 Completed Project 2-5

3. Go to the **project02-05.js** file in your code editor. The first part of the code contains several event handlers for running functions in response to the `click` event (in future chapters you will learn a more efficient way of specifying these event handlers). Within this section there are four syntax errors. Locate and fix those errors.
4. The next section in the file contains the `runCalculator()` function used to edit the contents of the calculator window in response to the clicking of calculator buttons. The `calcValue` variable will be used to store the text string of the expression in the calculator window. There are two syntax errors in this function. Fix them both.
5. The next section contains the `clearCalculator()` function to clear contents of the calculator window. There is one syntax error in this function. Locate and fix the error.
6. Save your changes to the file and then open **project02-05.html** in your browser. Test your calculator by clicking the calculator buttons, verifying that you can enter expressions into the calculator window and evaluate those expressions by clicking the Enter button. Also verify that you can clear the calculator window by clicking the C button. If the online calculator does not work correctly, use the browser console to locate and fix any undiscovered errors.

Case Projects

Individual Case Project

Plan and add a feature to one of the web pages in your personal site that uses at least one function to perform a mathematical calculation based on user input. Test the page to ensure it works as planned.

Team Case Project

Choose one of the web pages from your team website to enhance with at least two functions. Common uses of functions include performing actions based on user input (validation, personalization of the web page) and performing calculations. Divide your team into subgroups equal to the number of functions your page will include. After each subgroup has created its function, come back together as a full group and incorporate the functions in the web page. Test the functions to verify the page works as planned, doing any troubleshooting and making any edits to the functions as a full team.

CHAPTER 3

Building Arrays and Controlling Flow

When you complete this chapter, you will be able to:

- Create an array containing a list of data values
- Access a collection of HTML elements by type
- View arrays and HTML collections using the browser console
- Create program loops using `while`, `do while`, and `for` loops
- Explore array methods to replace program loops
- Make decisions with `if` statements and `switch` statements
- Manage program loops and conditional statements with the `break`, `continue`, and `label` commands

---

The code you have written so far has been linear in nature. In other words, your programs start at the beginning and end when the last statement in the program executes. However, sometimes it can be useful to change this default order of execution. Changing the order in which JavaScript code is executed is known as controlling flow. Controlling the flow of code is one of the most fundamental skills required in programming. Before learning how to control program flow, you will first learn about the array data type, which is often used with that task.

Storing Data in Arrays

An array is a set of data represented by a single variable name. You use an array when you want to store a group or a list of related information in a single, easily managed location. Lists of names, courses, test scores, and prices are typically stored in arrays.

Note The identifier you use for an array name must follow the same rules as identifiers for variables. It must begin with an uppercase or lowercase ASCII letter, dollar sign ($), or underscore (_), can include numbers (but not as the first character), cannot include spaces, and cannot be reserved words.

Declaring and Initializing Arrays

The most common way to create an array is with an array literal, a single statement that declares a variable and specifies array values as its content. The syntax of the array literal is:

```
let array = [values];
```

where *array* is the variable name assigned to the array, and *values* is a comma-separated list of values stored within the array.

For example, the following statement creates an array, storing within it the three-letter abbreviations of the months of the year:

```
let months = ["Jan", "Feb", "Mar", "Apr", "May", "Jun",
"Jul", "Aug", "Sep", "Oct", "Nov", "Dec"];
```

Notice that the contents of the array do not have to be confined within a single line of code if you do not start a new line within a text string. Values stored within an array can involve several different data types. The following `dataValues` array stores a text string, a numeric value, a Boolean value, and the `null` value:

```
let dataValues = ["April", 3, true, null];
```

The ability to store data of different types within an array is not true of other programming languages in which all values within an array must be of the same type. Nor do you have to specify array values. You can initialize an array with no data values by leaving the contents within the brackets empty as the following statement demonstrates:

```
let dataValues = [];
```

Arrays are objects, so another way to declare and initialize an array is with the following `new Array()` object constructor:

```
let array = new Array(values)
```

where *values* is a comma-separated list of values stored in the array. You could declare and initialize the `months` array as an `Array` object using the following object constructor:

```
let months = new Array("Jan", "Feb", "Mar", "Apr",
"May", "Jun", "Jul", "Aug","Sep", "Oct", "Nov", "Dec");
```

The `new Object()` constructor also defines arrays based on the number items within the array. The general syntax of the statement is:

```
let array = new Array(length)
```

where *length* is the number of values within the array. The *length* argument must be entered as an integer between 0 and $2^{32} - 1$. The following statement creates the `monthName` array with 12 elements:

```
let monthName = new Array(12);
```

While the `monthName` array has been declared, it has not been initialized. The only thing that has happened is that memory for an array of length 12 has been allotted to the `monthName` variable. You can do the same thing with an array literal if you do not specify any values in the comma-separated list as in the following statement, which creates the `dataValues` array with four undefined values:

```
let dataValues = [,,,];
```

Notice that three commas separate the four undefined values within the array.

Elements and Indexes

Each value stored in an array is called an element, and each element is identified by its position or index within the array. Indexes always start with the number 0, so the first element in any array has an index of 0, the second has an index of 1, and so forth. You can set a specific array value by its index using the expression

```
array[index] = value;
```

where *index* is the index number of the array element and *value* is the value stored at that location within the array. The values of the first several elements in the `monthName` array could be defined using the following statements:

```
monthName[0] = "January";
monthName[1] = "February";
monthName[2] = "March";
...
```

and so forth.

Unlike with many other programming languages, arrays in JavaScript are dynamic in that they will automatically expand to allow for new elements. In the following code the `dataValues` array is declared with four elements. The next statement setting the value of an element with an index of four increases the length the `dataValues` array to five:

```
let dataValues = [10, 20, 30, 40];
dataValues[4] = 50;    // 10, 20, 30, 40, and 50 stored in the array
```

JavaScript also allows for the creation of sparse arrays in which some array values are left undefined so that the length of the array is greater than the number of defined values. The following commands create a sparse array with only two defined values out of 100 elements:

```
let x = new Array();
x[0] = "Aaron";
x[99] = "Zukov";
```

Sparse arrays occur frequently in applications involving customer data where items such as mobile phone numbers or postal codes have not been stored for every individual.

Note

JavaScript can treat the entire content of your array as text entries in a comma-separated list. For example, the following statements

```
let x = ["Iowa", "Kansas", "Illinois"];
document.write(x);
```

will write the text string "Iowa,Kansas,Illinois" into the web page.

To determine an array's current size, use the property:

```
array.length
```

were *array* is a reference to the variable storing the array. The value returned by the `length` property is equal to one more than the highest index number in the array (because array indexes start at 0 rather than 1.) So, if the highest index number is 11, then the value returned by the `length` property would be 12.

Creating an Array

In this chapter, you will work on a web page displaying game results for the Tipton Turbines, a minor league baseball team in Tipton, Iowa. The page will retrieve game information from several arrays and display that content in an easy-to-read table. **Figure 3-1** shows a preview of the page you will create.

TIPTON TURBINES

Tickets Calendar Players News Community

Calendar

August 2024

Sunday	Monday	Tuesday	Wednesday	Thursday	Friday	Saturday
28 vs. Bettendorf W: (2 - 1)	29	30	31	1 @ Marion W: (4 - 2)	2 vs. Clinton W: (2 - 0)	3 vs. Clinton L: (1 - 5) [6]*
4 vs. Clinton L: (0 - 3)	5	6 vs. Urbandale L: (2 - 3)	7	8 @ Cedar Falls W: (2 - 1) [12]	9 @ Cedar Falls L: (1 - 5) [7]*	10 @ Cedar Falls W: (8 - 3)
11 @ Bettendorf W: (3 - 1)	12 @ Bettendorf W: (4 - 3)	13	14 vs. Ames W: (7 - 6) [11]	15	16 vs. Ames L: (4 - 7)	17 vs. Ames S: (1 - 4) [4.5]***
18 @ Waukee L: (2 - 6)	19	20 @ Waukee L: (0 - 3)	21	22 @ Mason City W: (8 - 2)	23 @ Mason City W: (6 - 4)	24 @ Mason City W: (3 - 1)
25 @ Clinton P: (0 - 0) [0]***	26	27	28 vs. Marion S: (5 - 3) [2]***	29	30 vs. Cedar Falls W: (7 - 2)	31 vs. Cedar Falls L: (3 - 4) [10]

Win Loss Suspended Postponed

Tipton Turbines Baseball • Tipton, Iowa

Figure 3-1 Tipton Turbines game calendar

Open the HTML file and web page now.

To open the Tipton Turbines web page:

1. Use your code editor to go to the js03 ▶ chapter folder of your data files.
2. Open the **js03_txt.html** file in your code editor and enter your name and the date in the comment section of the file.
3. Scroll through the document to familiarize yourself with its contents. Notice that the page contains a web table in which the table body consists of five rows of seven table cells with the table cell ids containing calendar dates ranging from "2024-7-28" up to "2024-8-31".
4. Save the file as **js03.html** and load the file in your browser.

Currently, the web table contains no data other than the calendar days. The table head section should display the names of the days of the week. Although you can enter this content directly into the HTML file, you can also generate that content using an array. You will create an array of weekday names for that purpose.

To create an array of weekday names:

1. Open the **js03_txt.js** file in your code editor and enter your name and the date in the comment section of the file.
2. Directly below the comment section, enter the following code for the `weekDays` array as shown in **Figure 3-2**.

```
// Days of the week
let weekDays = ["Sunday", "Monday", "Tuesday", "Wednesday",
"Thursday", "Friday", "Saturday"];
```

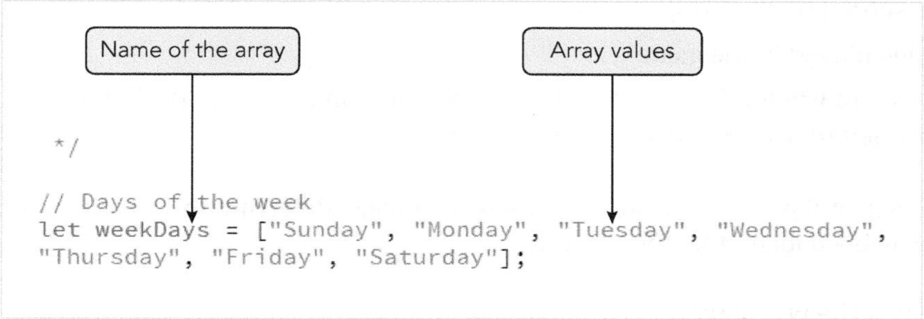

Figure 3-2 Creating the `weekDays` array

3. Save the file as **js03.js**.

You have also been given a JavaScript file named schedule.js, containing arrays with information on the 23 games that Tipton played from July 31 to August 31. **Figure 3-3** shows the content of the arrays in that file.

```
// date of games played
let gameDates = ["2024-7-28", "2024-8-1", "2024-8-2", "2024-8-3",
                 "2024-8-4", "2024-8-6", "2024-8-8", "2024-8-9", "2024-8-10",
                 "2024-8-11", "2024-8-12", "2024-8-14", "2024-8-16", "2024-8-17",
                 "2024-8-18", "2024-8-20", "2024-8-22", "2024-8-23", "2024-8-24",
                 "2024-8-25", "2024-8-28", "2024-8-30", "2024-8-31"];

// game opponents
let gameOpponents = ["Bettendorf", "Marion", "Clinton", "Clinton",
                     "Clinton", "Urbandale", "Cedar Falls", "Cedar Falls", "Cedar Falls",
                     "Bettendorf", "Bettendorf", "Ames", "Ames", "Ames",
                     "Waukee", "Waukee", "Mason City", "Mason City", "Mason City",
                     "Clinton", "Marion", "Cedar Falls", "Cedar Falls"];

// game locations: h (home) or a (away)
let gameLocations = ["h", "a", "h", "h", "h", "h", "a", "a", "a", "a", "a", "h", "h", "h",
                     "a", "a", "a", "a", "a", "a", "h", "h", "h"];

// runs scored in each game
let runsScored =    [2, 4, 2, 1, 0, 2, 2, 1, 8, 3, 4, 7, 4, 1, 2, 0, 8, 6, 3, 0, 5, 7, 3];

// runs allowed in each game
let runsAllowed =   [1, 2, 0, 5, 3, 3, 1, 5, 3, 1, 3, 6, 7, 4, 6, 3, 2, 4, 1, 0, 3, 2, 4];

// innings played in each game
let gameInnings =   [9, 9, 9, 6, 9, 9, 12, 7, 9, 9, 9, 11, 9, 4.5, 9, 9, 9, 9, 9, 0, 2, 9, 10];

// game outcome: W (win), L (lose), S (suspended prior to completion), P (postponed to later date)
let gameResults =    ["W", "W", "W", "L", "L", "L", "W", "L", "W", "W", "W", "W", "L", "S",
                      "L", "L", "W", "W", "W", "P", "S", "W", "L"];
```

Figure 3-3 Arrays describing the results of 23 games

The schedule.js file contains the following arrays and data:

- `gameDates`—the dates of the 23 games played by the team
- `gameOpponents`—the opponent on each of those 23 game days
- `gameLocations`—whether the game was at home ("h") or away ("a")
- `runsScored`—the number of runs the Tipton Turbines scored in the game

- `runsAllowed`—the number of runs scored by their opponents
- `gameInnings`—the number of innings played in the game
- `gameResults`—the result of game: "W" (a win for Tipton), "L" (a loss), "S" (the game was suspended due to weather), or "P" (the game was postponed to a later date due to weather.)

Add both the js03.js and schedule.js JavaScript files to the Tipton Turbines web page, deferring the loading of both script files until the complete HTML file has been loaded by the browser.

To load the js03.js and schedule.js files into the web page:

1. Return to the **js03.html** file in your code editor.
2. Directly above the closing </head> tag, insert the following `script` elements:

```
<script src="schedule.js" defer></script>
<script src="js03.js" defer></script>
```

3. Save your changes to the file.

Note that all the arrays in two JavaScript files are defined as global variables (because they are not placed within a function or command block) and will be accessible to any function you create in developing this project.

Multidimensional Arrays

Many applications store data in a rectangular format known as a matrix, in which the values are arranged in a rectangular grid. The following is an example of a matrix laid out in a grid of three rows and four columns:

$$\begin{pmatrix} 4 & 2 & 1 & 2 \\ 1 & 3 & 18 & 6 \\ 3 & 7 & 3 & 4 \end{pmatrix}$$

Entries in a matrix are identified by the indexes for the rows and columns. The value 18 from this matrix is referenced using the index pair (2, 3) because that value is placed at the intersection of the second row and third column.

JavaScript does not support matrices. However, you can mimic the behavior of matrices by nesting one array within another in a structure called a multidimensional array. The following code recreates that matrix with an array containing three elements, each of which is an array containing four elements:

```
var mArray = [
    [4, 2, 1, 2],
    [1, 3, 18, 6],
    [3, 7, 3, 4]
];
```

Values within a multidimensional array are referenced using the expression:

```
array[x][y] ,
```

where *x* is the index of the outer array (the row) and *y* is the index of the inner array (the column.) Thus the expression `mArray[1][2]` would return the value 18 from the matrix's second row and third column (remember that indexes start with 0 and not 1.) The expression `mArray[2][1]` would return the value from the third row and second column, which in this example is the number 7.

The number of rows in a multidimensional array is given by the `length` property. The number of columns can be determined by applying the `length` property to the first table row. For example, the expressions

```
mArray.length;
mArray[0].length
```

would return values of 3 (the number of rows) and 4 (the number of columns). This assumes that every row has the same number of elements as the first row. You can continue to nest arrays in this fashion to create matrices of even higher dimensions.

One reason to use multidimensional arrays is to match values from different arrays within a single variable. For example, the game data shown in Figure 3-3 could be placed within a single multidimensional array as follows:

```
let games = [
   ["2024-7-28","Bettendorf","h",2,1,9,"W"] ,
   ["2024-8-1","Marion","a",4,2,9,"W"] ,
   ["2024-8-2","Clinton","h",2,0,9,"W"] ,
   ["2024-8-3","Clinton","h",1,5,6,"L"] ,
...
```

Information on Tipton's second game would come from the entries in the second element of the `games` array with the date given by the expression `games[1][0]`, the opponent given by `games[1][1]`, the location by `games [1][2]`, and so forth. As you become more comfortable with arrays, you might find it easier to place your data within a single multidimensional array rather than spread across several arrays.

Exploring HTML Collections

The Document Object Model organizes HTML elements into collections where each element is an HTML Collection Object. For example, all hyperlinks are part of a collection of links, all input controls are part of a collection of form elements, and so forth. Though these collections are not arrays, they share many of the features of arrays. **Figure 3-4** lists the JavaScript properties and methods used to access HTML collections within the DOM.

HTML COLLECTION	COLLECTION OF
`embeds`	`<embed>` elements in the document
`forms`	`<form>` elements in the document
`form.elements`	Elements within a web form
`getElementsByClassName(`*`class`*`)`	Elements in the document with belonging to the class *`class`*
`getElementsByName(`*`name`*`)`	Elements in the document with a *`name`* attribute equal to *`name`*
`getElementsByTagName(`*`tag`*`)`	Elements in the document with a tag name equal to *`tag`*
`images`	`<img>` elements in the document
`links`	`<a>` elements and `<area>` elements with a `href` attribute
`scripts`	`<script>` elements in the document
`styleSheets`	Stylesheet objects associated with the document

Figure 3-4 HTML Collection objects

Referencing an Element within a Collection

To reference a specific element within an HTML collection, use either of the following expressions:

```
objects[idref]
```

or

```
objects.idref ,
```

where *`objects`* is a reference to an HTML collection of elements and *`idref`* is either an index number representing the position of the element within the collection or the value of the `id` attribute assigned to the element. As with arrays, the first element in a collection has an index value of 0, the second element has an index value of 1, and so forth. Thus, if the first inline image within a document has the tag

```
<img src="logo.png" id="TiptonLogo" alt="Tipton Turbines">
```

it can be referenced with any of the following expressions:

```
document.images[0]
document.images["TiptonLogo"]
document.images.TiptonLogo
```

Other element collections are referenced in a similar way. As with JavaScript arrays, you can determine the number of elements within a collection with the `length` property. The following expression will return the number of images within the entire document:

```
document.images.length
```

Note | The ordering of the elements within an HTML collection reflects the order of the element tags within the HTML file.

Searching through the DOM

HTML collections can also be formed by searching through elements within the Document Object Model based on their `class` attribute, tag name, or `name` attribute using the following methods:

```
document.getElementsByClassName(class)
document.getElementsByTagName(tag)
document.getElementsByName(name)
```

where *`class`* is the value of the `class` attribute, tag is the name of the HTML tag and *`name`* is the value of the `name` attribute. For example, to reference the first `h1` element within the document, apply the following expression:

```
document.getElementsByTagName("h1")[0]
```

To reference the second element in the document belonging to the "sideBar" class, use the expression

```
document.getElementsByClassName("sideBar")[1]
```

And to reference the third element in the document whose `name` attribute equals "menuChoice", use

```
document.getElementsByName("menuChoice")[2]
```

Notice that three methods all use the phrase "`document.getElements`" (plural) as opposed to the `document.getElementById()` method, which uses the singular form because it returns only one object instead of a collection. A common mistake is to use the singular form, as in `document.getElementByName()`, which will result in an error.

Each of these three expressions returns all matching elements within the entire document. You can also return HTML collections within a specified part of the document by nesting the object references in the following format:

```
object.objects
```

where *`object`* is an element that contains other elements and *`objects`* is a collection within that container. Thus, the following expression returns the collection of paragraphs nested within the first table cell element of the web page:

```
document.getElementsByTagName("td")[0].getElementsByTagName("p")
```

Continuing in this fashion, you can nest one object collection within another and then another to create an element collection specific to one branch of the document hierarchy.

Common Mistakes

Working with Arrays and Indices

Assuming that the first element in an array or an HTML collection has an index number of 1 rather than 0 is a common programming error for beginners. If you are working with an array collection and are seeing results offset by 1 from what you expect, check that your code accounts for 0 as the first index number.

Another common mistake is to omit the index number when using properties that should be applied to a specific element within a collection. For example, the expression

```
document.getElementsByTagName("input").checked
```

will result in an error because it attempts to apply the `checked` status to a collection of `input` elements. Instead, you must specify only a single element from the collection, as in the following expression that applies the `checked` status to the first `input` element:

```
document.getElementsTagName("input")[0].checked
```

Viewing Arrays and HTML Collections with the Console

Your browser's console supports commands to view the contents of arrays and HTML collections, a useful feature for confirming that your arrays and collection are storing the correct data. You will use the console now to confirm that your web page has loaded the arrays containing the results of the Tipton games correctly.

To view arrays in your browser console:

1. Return to the **js03.html** file in your web browser.
2. Open the console using commands appropriate for your web browser. (Hint: You can view your browser's online help if you are unsure how to access the Developer Console.)
3. Within the console type **gameDates.length** and press **Enter**. The console returns a value of 23, indicating that there 23 elements in the `gameDates` array for the 23 games played by the team.

   Note that the console may try to automatically complete your entry or show a list of names matching the first few characters of your entry. You can speed up the process and save yourself some typing by pressing Tab or double-clicking the name from the list provided by the console.
4. Type **gameOpponents[4]** and press **Enter**. The console returns the text string "Clinton" which is the fifth opponent listed in the calendar shown earlier Figure 3-1.
5. Type **gameResults[4]** and press **Enter**. The console returns the text string "L" indicating that the fifth game was a loss.

   You can also use the console to view information about the elements in your document. Use this feature now to determine the number of hypertext links in the document.
6. Type **document.links.length** and press **Enter**. The console reports 5 links in the document.
7. Type **document.links[1].innerHTML** and press **Enter**. The console returns the text string "Calendar", indicating that the HTML code stored in the second text string is the word "Calendar".

   Finally, if you attempt to retrieve a value that is undefined, the console will report that error.
8. Type **gameOpponents[23]** to retrieve the opponent for a non-existent 24th game. The console returns the value undefined, indicating that there is no value matching this reference.

   Figure 3-5 shows the results of Google Chrome's console for retrieving information on arrays and HTML collections.

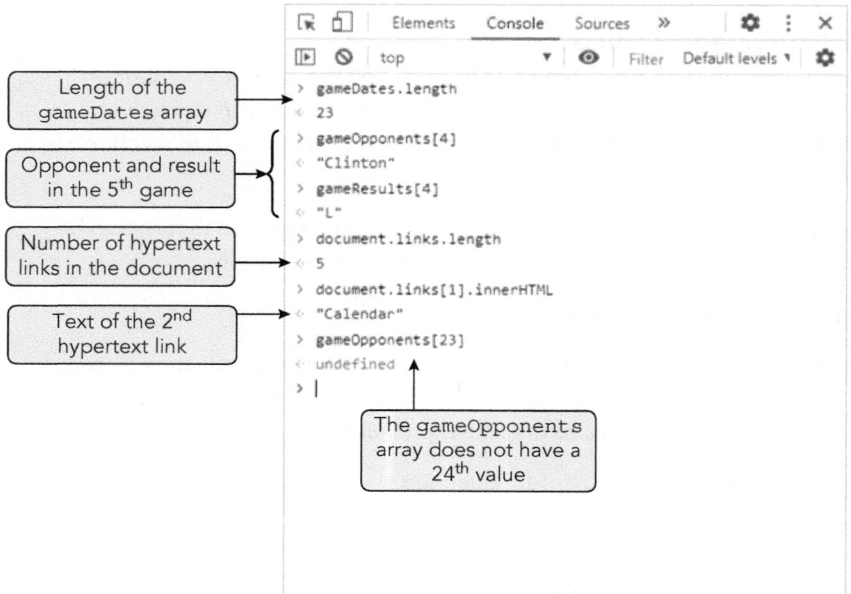
Elements Console Sources
top
Filter Default levels
Length of the gameDates array
> gameDates.length
23
Opponent and result in the 5th game
> gameOpponents[4]
"Clinton"
> gameResults[4]
"L"
Number of hypertext links in the document
> document.links.length
5
> document.links[1].innerHTML
Text of the 2nd hypertext link
"Calendar"
> gameOpponents[23]
undefined
The gameOpponents array does not have a 24th value

Figure 3-5 Information on arrays and collections viewed in the Console

9. Continue exploring arrays and collections using the console. It is a great tool for becoming more familiar with these concepts and techniques. Close the console when finished.

Next you will learn how to use arrays to generate content for a web page.

Quick Check 1

1. Show how to create an array named `foodMenu` containing the text strings "Breakfast", "Lunch", and "Dinner" as an array literal and using the `new Array()` object constructor.
2. Provide a command to return the size of the array `customerOrders`.
3. Provide a command to return the tenth entry in the `customerOrders` array.
4. Provide the expression to reference to fifth inline image in the document.
5. Provide the expression to reference the third element belonging to the `blogpost` class.

Working with Program Loops

In your applications you will often need to repeat the same group of statements several times. Imagine if you had to repeat essentially the same command block dozens, hundreds, or even thousands of times—the code would become unmanageably long. Programmers deal with this kind of situation by creating program loops. A program loop is a command block that executes repeatedly until a stopping condition is met. For example, a program that writes content from an array could be written as a program loop that goes through each array item, writing content as it goes, and stopping only when it has reached the end of the array. There are several different types of program loops. The first to consider is the `while` loop.

The `while` Loop

In a `while` loop, a command block is executed while a given condition is true but stops once that condition is no longer true. The syntax of a `while` loop is:

```
while (condition) {
   statements;
}
```

where *`condition`* is a conditional expression that is either `true` or `false` and *`statements`* are the statements within the command block that are repeatedly executed as long as that conditional expression is `true`. Each repetition of the command block is called an iteration.

To avoid loops that never end, also known as infinite loops, the command block needs to include at least one statement that eventually results in a falsy value for the condition. Command blocks often use a counter, which is a variable whose value changes with each iteration. Once that counter fails to match the condition, the loop ends. For example, the following code includes a counter variable named `i` with an initial value of 1. With each iteration, the value of `i` increases by 1. The loop continues while `i` is less than or equal to 5.

```
let i = 1;
while (i <= 5) {
   document.write(i + "<br>");
   i++; // increase the value of i by 1
}
// after the loop ends
document.write("<p>The value of i is equal to " + i +
"</p>");
```

Through the iterations, the value of `i` steadily increases. When the counter exceeds a value of 5 the `while` condition is no longer met and the loop ends, continuing onto the next statement in the program. The following content is written to the web page:

```
1<br>2<br>3<br>4<br>5<br>
<p>The value of i is equal to 6</p>
```

It is common for programmers to use variables named `i`, `j`, or `k` as counters for program loops. This standard practice makes it easy for other programmers to recognize the loop counter without having to read detailed commentary about the code.

Note If you forget a stopping condition and inadvertently create an infinite loop, you must close the browser tab or browser window to cancel the loop. The method for forcing an app to close varies between operating systems. In Windows, press Ctrl+Alt+Del to open the Task Manager, click the Application tab, right-click the browser name and click End Task. On the Macintosh, press Command+Option+Esc, select the browser name from the application list, and click Force Quit. Once you have closed the browser, return to the code, and correct your mistake.

You can use a wide variety of counters with `while` loops by varying the initial value, the iteration of the counter, and the conditional expression. **Figure 3-6** shows a few examples.

INITIAL VALUE	ITERATION	WHILE CONDITION	ITERATED VALUES
`let i = 5`	`i++`	`i <= 10`	`i` = 5, 6, 7, 8, 9, 10
`let i = 5`	`i--`	`i > 0`	`i` = 5, 4, 3, 2, 1
`let i = 0`	`i += 60`	`i <= 180`	`i` = 0, 60, 120, 180
`let i = 1`	`i *= 2`	`i <= 50`	`i` = 1, 2, 4, 8, 16, 32
`let i = 90`	`i /= 3`	`i > 5`	`i` = 90, 30, 10

Figure 3-6 HTML Collection objects

The Tipton Turbines calendar contains a header row with seven empty table heading (`th`) cells. Apply a `while` loop to write the contents of the `weekDays` array you created earlier into those seven cells. The loop will iterate through the collection of cells and for each cell it will write the value from an element in the `weekDays()` array. To reference the seven cells, use the HTML collection:

```
document.getElementsByTagName("th")
```

Add the `while` loop within a function that will run after the browser window loads the web page.

To create the `while` loop:

1. Return to the **js03.js** file in your code editor.
2. At the bottom of the file insert the following event listener to run the `addWeekDays()` function when the page is loaded:

```
window.addEventListener("load", addWeekdays);
```

3. Below this statement, add the following `addWeekDays()` function as described in **Figure 3-7**:

```
// Function to write weekday names into the calendar
function addWeekDays() {
   let i = 0; // initial counter value

   // reference the collection of heading cells
   let headingCells = document.getElementsByTagName("th");

   // write each of the seven days into a heading cell
   while (i < 7) {
      headingCells[i].innerHTML = weekDays[i];

      // increase the counter by 1
      i++;
   }
}
```

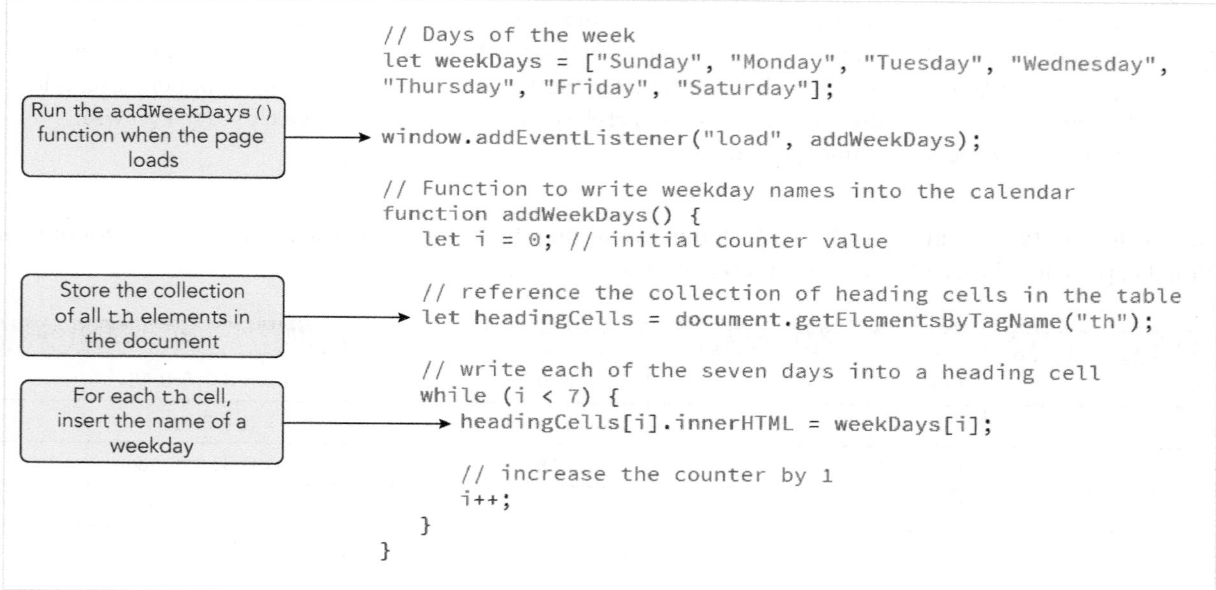


```
// Days of the week
let weekDays = ["Sunday", "Monday", "Tuesday", "Wednesday",
"Thursday", "Friday", "Saturday"];

window.addEventListener("load", addWeekDays);

// Function to write weekday names into the calendar
function addWeekDays() {
   let i = 0; // initial counter value

   // reference the collection of heading cells in the table
   let headingCells = document.getElementsByTagName("th");

   // write each of the seven days into a heading cell
   while (i < 7) {
      headingCells[i].innerHTML = weekDays[i];

      // increase the counter by 1
      i++;
   }
}
```

Figure 3-7 Creating a `while` loop

4. Save your changes to the file and then reload the **js03.html** file in your web browser. As shown in **Figure 3-8**, the calendar now includes a table row displaying the days of the week.

Note that the scope of the `i` counter variable is limited to the `addWeekDays()` function so that you can use `i` as a counter in other functions without affecting its value within this function.

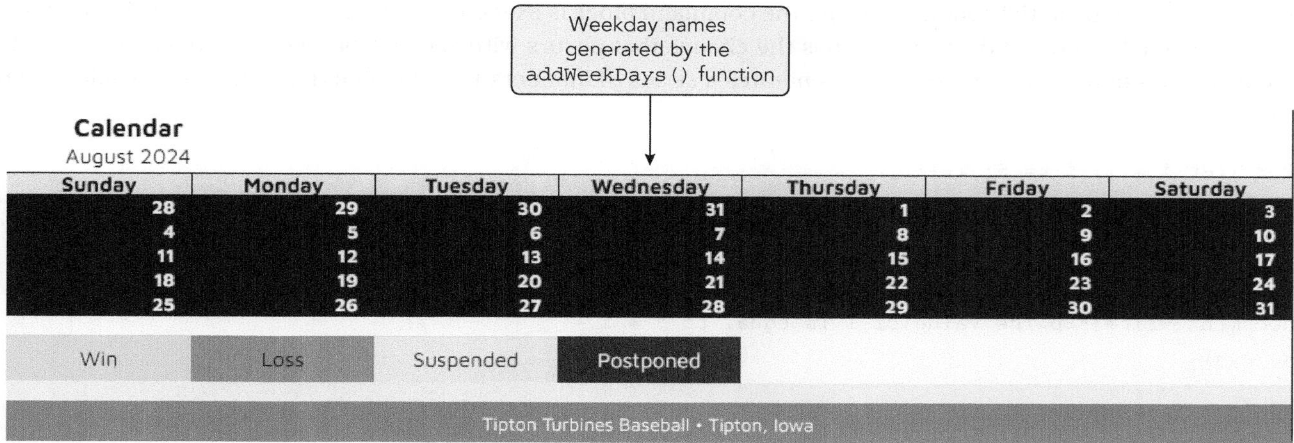

Figure 3-8 Adding the weekday names to the table

The `do while` Loop

The `while` loop is an example of a pretest loop in that the condition is evaluated before each iteration of the command block. Because of this, it is possible that command block will be halted before the first iteration. Another type of program loop, called the `do while` loop, is a posttest loop in which the condition is evaluated after the command block has been executed at least once. The syntax of the `do while` loop is:

```
do {
   statements;
} while (condition);
```

Notice that the condition is placed at the end of the loop so that the command block is not tested prior to the first iteration. The following code uses a `do while` loop to generate a series of numbers and a concluding statement:

```
let i = 1;
do {
   document.write(i + "<br>");
   i++; // increase the value of i by 1
} while (i <= 5);
// after the loop ends
document.write("<p>The value of i is equal to " + i +
"</p>");
```

resulting in the following content being written to the web page:

```
1<br>2<br>3<br>4<br>5<br>
<p>The value of i is equal to 6</p>
```

Aside from the location of the stopping condition, there is no difference between the `while` and `do while` loops. Use the `do while` loop when you want to ensure that the command block will be executed at least once; use the `while` loop when your program does not require such a guarantee.

The `for` Loop

Another pretest loop is the `for` loop, in which the initial condition, stopping condition, and iterative expression are placed within a single line of code. The syntax of the `for` loop is:

```
for (initial; condition; iteration) {
   statements;
}
```

where *initial* is the initial condition before the command block is executed, *condition* is the condition that must be true for each iteration, and *iteration* is the change that occurs with each iteration of the command block. For example, the version of the `for` loop that generates a series of numbers with a concluding statement would be written as:

```
for (let i = 1; i <= 5; i++) {
   document.write(i + "<br>");
}
// after the loop ends
document.write("<p>The value of i is equal to " + i +
"</p>");
```

resulting in the following output:

```
1<br>2<br>3<br>4<br>5<br>
ReferenceError: i is not defined
```

The `for` loop is simpler and more compact than either the `while` or `do while` loops and thus `for` loops are the preferred method for writing loops. Note that the scope of the `i` counter is limited to the `for` loop. Attempting to reference the counter outside of the `for` loop will produce an error. If you need to reference the final value of the counter variable outside of the loop, you should use either the `while` or `do while` loops, but otherwise to avoid confusion use a `for` loop to limit the scope of your counters.

`For` loops can also be nested within one another to create code that iterates through two sets of counters. The following code demonstrates how to generate a web table by creating an outer loop that iterates through a set of table rows and an inner loop that iterates through a set of table cells within each row:

```
document.write("<table>");
for (let i = 1; i <= 2; i++) {
   document.write("<tr>");
   for (let j = 1; j <= 3; j++) {
      document.write("<td>" + i + "," + j + "</td>");
   }
   document.write("</tr>");
}
document.write("</table>");
```

The resulting web table has two table rows and three table data cells within each of those rows:

```
<table>
   <tr>
      <td>1,1</td><td>1,2</td><td>1,3</td>
   </tr>
   <tr>
      <td>2,1</td><td>2,2</td><td>2,3</td>
   </tr>
</table>
```

There is no practical limit to the number of nested `for` loops you can employ in your program. Nested `for` loops are often used with multidimensional arrays to loop through each level of the nested arrays.

Writing a `for` Loop

To create a `for` loop that iterates through the contents of an array or HTML collection, apply the following general structure:

```
for (let i = 0; i < objects.length; i++) {
   statements;
}
```

where *objects* is a reference to either an array or HTML collection. The counter starts with a value of 0 (because 0 is the index of the first element in the list) with the loop continuing if the counter is less than the value of the `length` property. Recall that the index of the last item in an array or collection will always be one less than the `length` value. For example, an array with 100 items will have indexes that range from 0 up to 99.

> **Note** A common mistake is to make the stopping condition `i <= objects.length`, resulting in an error because the last iteration will go beyond the last item in the array.

Once you have defined a collection, you can work with individual collection objects as you would individual array elements. The following code demonstrates how to apply an event handler to every `input` element within a document:

```
let allInputs = document.getElementsByTagName("input");
for (let i = 0; i < allInputs.length; i++) {
   allInputs[i].addEventListener("click", checkOrder);
}
```

By applying this code, whenever an `input` element in the document is clicked, the `checkOrder()` will run in response.

Use a `for` loop to write the game results into cells of the calendar table. The `for` loop will have the following general structure:

```
for (let i = 0; i < gameDates.length; i++) {
   write a game result into a table cell
}
```

with the number of games determined by the `gameDates` array shown earlier in Figure 3-1. With each iteration of the loop, the following contents will be written into the table cell matching the date on which the game was played:

```
<p>gameOpponents[i]<br>
gameResults[i]: (runsScored[i] - runsAllowed[i])
</p>
```

where the `gameOpponents` array provides the opponent for a particular day, the `gameResults` array provides the result of the game, the `runsScored` array retrieves the number of runs scored by Tipton, and the `runsAllowed` array retrieves the number of runs scored by Tipton's opponent. For example, the information on Tipton's first game will be written as:

```
<p>Bettendorf<br>
W: (2 - 1)
</p>
```

To match a game to a table cell, use the date stored in the `gamesDate` array and match it to the `id` value of a table cell (recall that each table cell has an `id` for a specific calendar date.) Thus, the table cell matching a game played on a specific date would be referenced using the expression

```
let tableCell = document.getElementById(gameDates[i])
```

Finally, the table cells are not empty, so any content will have to be added to the HTML content already present in the cell instead of overwriting it. JavaScript provides the following `insertAdjacentHTML()` method to insert additional content into an element:

```
element.insertAdjacentHTML(position, text)
```

where *`element`* is the element into which the new content is inserted, *`position`* is the location of the new content, and *`text`* is the text of the content. The *`position`* argument has the following values:

- `"beforeBegin"`—to insert new content directly before the element's opening tag
- `"afterBegin"`—to insert new content directly after the element's opening tag
- `"beforeEnd"`—to insert new content directly before the element's closing tag
- `"afterEnd"`—to insert new content directly after the element's closing tag

For this application, you will insert the new content directly before each table cell's closing tag, using a position value of `"beforeEnd"`.

Put all of these pieces together in a new function named `showGames()` that will run when the page is loaded by the browser.

To create the `showGames()` function:

1. Return to the **js03.js** file in your code editor.
2. At the bottom of the file insert an event listener to run the `showGames()` function when the page is loaded:

```
window.addEventListener("load", showGames);
```

   Remember that because multiple functions can be attached to an event listener, this event listener will supplement the event listener created earlier for the `addWeekDays()` function.

3. Below the event listener, add the following `showGames()` function as described in **Figure 3-9**:

```
// Function to write game information into the calendar
function showGames() {
   for (let i = 0; i < gameDates.length; i++) {
      let gameInfo = "";

      // Open the paragraph
      gameInfo += "<p>";

      // Include the opponent
      gameInfo += gameOpponents[i] + "<br>";

      // Include the result and score
      gameInfo += gameResults[i] + ": (" + runsScored[i] +
" - " + runsAllowed[i] + ")";

      // Close the paragraph
      gameInfo += "</p>";

      // Write the information into a table cell
      let tableCell = document.getElementById(gameDates[i]);
      tableCell.insertAdjacentHTML("beforeEnd", gameInfo)
   }
}
```

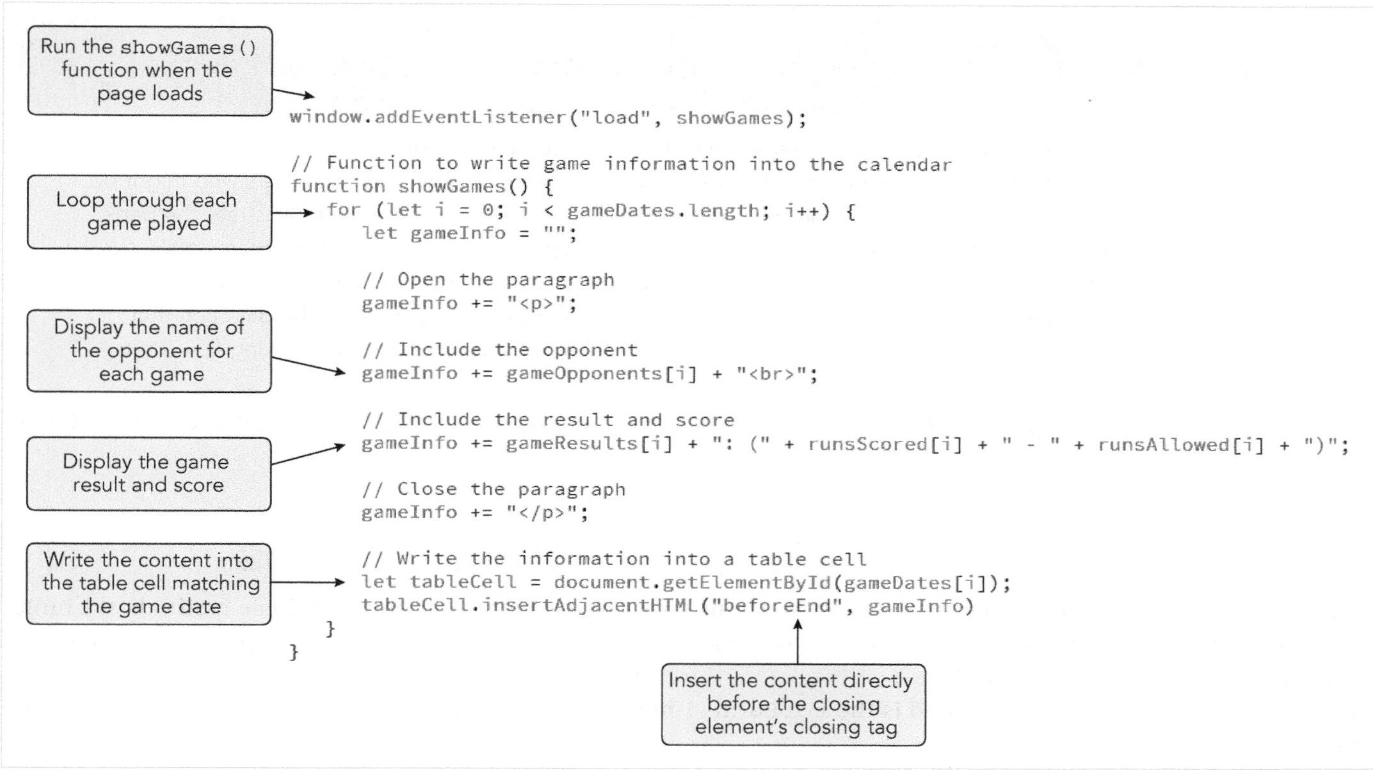
Run the showGames() function when the page loads
window.addEventListener("load", showGames);
// Function to write game information into the calendar
function showGames() {
Loop through each game played
for (let i = 0; i < gameDates.length; i++) {
let gameInfo = "";
// Open the paragraph
gameInfo += " ";
Display the name of the opponent for each game
// Include the opponent
gameInfo += gameOpponents[i] + "<br>";
// Include the result and score
Display the game result and score
gameInfo += gameResults[i] + ": (" + runsScored[i] + " - " + runsAllowed[i] + ")";
// Close the paragraph
gameInfo += " ";
Write the content into the table cell matching the game date
// Write the information into a table cell
let tableCell = document.getElementById(gameDates[i]);
tableCell.insertAdjacentHTML("beforeEnd", gameInfo)
}
}
Insert the content directly before the closing element's closing tag

Figure 3-9 Add information on each game to the calendar

4. Save your changes to the file and then reload the **js03.html** file in your web browser. Information on each game is added to a table cell matching the game date. See **Figure 3-10**.

Sunday	Monday	Tuesday	Wednesday	Thursday	Friday	Saturday
28	29	30	31	1	2	3
Bettendorf W: (2 - 1)				Marion W: (4 - 2)	Clinton W: (2 - 0)	Clinton L: (1 - 5)
4	5	6	7	8	9	10
Clinton L: (0 - 3)		Urbandale L: (2 - 3)		Cedar Falls W: (2 - 1)	Cedar Falls L: (1 - 5)	Cedar Falls W: (8 - 3)
11	12	13	14	15	16	17
Bettendorf W: (3 - 1)	Bettendorf W: (4 - 3)		Ames W: (7 - 6)		Ames L: (4 - 7)	Ames S: (1 - 4)
18	19	20	21	22	23	24
Waukee L: (2 - 6)		Waukee L: (0 - 3)		Mason City W: (8 - 2)	Mason City W: (6 - 4)	Mason City W: (3 - 1)
25	26	27	28	29	30	31
Clinton P: (0 - 0)			Marion S: (5 - 3)		Cedar Falls W: (7 - 2)	Cedar Falls L: (3 - 4)

Figure 3-10 Game data for July and August

Because arrays, collections, and program loops are so often used together, JavaScript supports several methods to work with array items directly without creating a loop.

Skills at Work | Communicating the Structure of a Program with a *Flowchart*

When designing a program that involves loops, especially a large and complex program, it can be challenging to explain the structure of the program and the relationships between its parts to other team members who might be working with you to create it. It's common for programmers to create a visual representation to illustrate the parts of a program and how they fit together both before and during development. For loops, such diagrams often take the form of a flowchart, which shows program components as boxes of different shapes, with lines connecting those components that communicate with each other. A flowchart often includes arrows to indicate the direction that information flows between components. Although software is available to create professional-looking flowcharts, most programmers create flowcharts on white boards.

Exploring Array Methods for Generating Loops

Array methods that replace program loops are a useful JavaScript feature, and because these methods are built into the language, they are usually faster than program loops and will make your code simpler and more compact. Each of these methods employs a callback function, which is a function passed as a parameter to another function or method. One such method is the `forEach()` method, which calls a function for each element within an array:

```
array.forEach(callback, thisArg)
```

where *`array`* is a reference to an array, *`callback`* is the function called for each array element, and *`thisArg`* is an optional parameter containing a value that can be passed to the callback function. The callback function has the syntax:

```
function callback(arrValue, index, array) {
   statements;
}
```

where *`arrValue`* is the value of the current array element during each iteration within the array, *`index`* is the index of the current array element, and *`array`* is the name of the array. Only the *`arrValue`* parameter is required; the other two are optional.

The following code uses the `forEach()` method to apply the `writeValue()` function to each element within the x array:

```
let x = [1, 3, 5, 10];
x.forEach(writeValue);

function writeValue(arrValue) {
   document.write("<td>" + arrValue + "</td> ");
}
```

resulting in the following content written to the web page:

```
<td>1</td> <td>3</td> <td>5</td> <td>10</td>
```

With the `forEach()` method, you don't have to explicitly write the code for the program loop, calculate the size of the array, or worry about iterating past the last array element. The method automatically applies the callback function to each array element for you.

Note You can replace the name of the callback function with the code of an anonymous function, written directly within the `forEach()` method.

The `forEach()` method can also be used to change array values. The following code calls the `stepUp5()` function to increase the value of each item in the `x` array by 5:

```
let x = [1, 3, 5, 10];
x.forEach(stepUp5);
function stepUp5(arrValue, i, arr) {
   arr[i] = arrValue + 5;
}
```

In this example, the `stepUp5()` function has three parameters: the `arrValue` parameter representing the value of the array element at each iteration, `i` representing the index number at each iteration, and `arr` representing the name of the array. The result is that value of the `x` array will be changed from [1, 3, 5, 10] to [6, 8, 10, 15].

Figure 3-11 describes some of the other array methods that can be used in place of a program loop. However, note that none of these methods can be applied to HTML collections, which, though they often act like arrays, are not arrays.

ARRAY METHOD	DESCRIPTION
`every(`*`callback, thisArg`*`)`	Tests whether the value of the *`callback`* function is `true` for all array elements
`filter(`*`callback, thisArg`*`)`	Creates a new array populated with the elements of the array that return a value of `true` from the *`callback`* function
`forEach(`*`callback, thisArg`*`)`	Applies the *`callback`* function to each array element
`map(`*`callback, thisArg`*`)`	Creates a new array by passing the original array elements to the *`callback`* function, which returns the mapped value of those elements
`reduce(`*`callback, thisArg`*`)`	Reduces the array by keeping only those elements returning a `true` value from the *`callback`* function
`reduceRight(`*`callback, thisArg`*`)`	Reduces the array starting from the last element by keeping only those elements returning a `true` value from the *`callback`* function
`some(`*`callback, thisArg`*`)`	Tests whether the value of *`callback`* function is `true` for at least one array element
`find(`*`callback, thisArg`*`)`	Returns the value of the first array element returning a `true` value from the *`callback`* function
`findIndex(`*`callback, thisArg`*`)`	Returns the index of the first array element returning a `true` value from the *`callback`* function

Figure 3-11 Looping methods for JavaScript arrays

As you expand your mastery of JavaScript you will find that you can save yourself a lot of time and trouble by using array methods in place of program loops whenever possible.

Quick Check 2

1. Show how to use a `while` loop to write the HTML code `<td>`*`counter`*`</td>` for integer values of *`counter`* ranging from 1 to 100 by 1.
2. What is the most important difference between a `while` loop and a `do while` loop?
3. Provide code for a `for` loop that writes the following HTML code:

```
<td>3</td> <td>6</td> <td>12</td> <td>24</td> <td>48</td>
<td>96</td>
```

4. What JavaScript method can be used to insert HTML code just after an element's opening tag?
5. What JavaScript method can be used to apply a function to each element of an array without writing a program loop?

Programming Concepts | Creating an Efficient Loop

As your programs increase in size and complexity, the ability to write efficient code becomes essential. Bloated, inefficient code is particularly noticeable with program loops that might repeat the same set of commands hundreds or thousands of times. A millisecond wasted due to one poorly written command can mean an overall loss of several seconds when repeated a thousand times.

There are several ways of adding efficiency to your program loops. One is to place all calculations that will not change during the loop, outside of the loop. For example, the expression

```
document.getElementsByTagName("p").length
```

searches through the entire document tree to count the number of paragraphs. The following `for` statement

```
for (let i = 0; i < document.getElementsByTagName("p").length;
i++)
```

will perform that search with each iteration. In a long document, this can result is a serious performance hit. Instead, place the `length` calculation outside the loop as follows:

```
let pCount = document.getElementsByTagName("p").length;
for (let i = 0; i < pCount; i++)
```

The paragraph count will only be performed once and not hundreds or thousands of times.

Adding Decision Making to Your Code

Often an application will need to execute a different set of statements depending on varying conditions. A shopping cart application might need to run different code depending on the customer's choice of shipping or payment. The shopping cart might need to run one set of operations for overnight shipping and different set of operations for standard shipping. A payment using a credit card might require a different set of functions from functions applied to payment using a gift card.

The process of choosing which code to execute in response to circumstance is known as decision making. The special types of JavaScript statements used for making decisions are called decision-making statements, decision-making structures, or conditional statements. The most common type of decision-making statement is the `if` statement.

The `if` Statement

The syntax of the `if` statement is:

```
if (condition) {
   statements
}
```

where *`condition`* is a Boolean expression that is either `true` or `false` and *`statements`* are part of the command block that runs when that condition is true. If the command block contains only a single statement you can dispense with the command block and write the `if` statement as:

```
if (condition) statement;
```

but it is considered good programming practice to always enclose even a single statement within a command block. The following `if` statement tests whether the `day` variable is equal to "Friday" and if that condition is true, displays a special greeting message:

```
if (day === "Friday") {
   window.alert("Get ready for the Weekend!");
}
```

Note A very common error is to use the = symbol in place of the === conditional operator to test for the truth of a condition. The = symbol is an assignment operator and assigns one value to another; it does not test their equality.

The `if else` Statement

The `if` statement will only take an action if the condition is true; otherwise it will take no action. To run one command block if the condition is true and a different command block if the condition is not true, use the `if else` statement:

```
if (condition) {
   statements if condition is true
} else {
   statements if condition is not true
}
```

The following `if else` statement displays one greeting if the day variable equals "Friday" and a different greeting if otherwise:

```
if (day === "Friday") {
   window.alert("Get ready for the Weekend!");
} else {
   window.alert("Have a great day!");
}
```

The `else` command block runs if the condition has any falsy value. Thus, a condition that evaluates to `false` or `null` or `undefined` will trigger the `else` command block.

The `else if` Statements

In some applications, there might be several possible conditions to consider. For example, a shopping cart payment might be made with a credit card, a gift card, or an online banking account. For those situations, you can apply multiple `if` statements in the following structure:

```
if (condition1) {
   statements if condition1 is true
} else if (condition2) {
   statements if condition2 is true
} else {
   statements if neither condition1 nor condition2 are true
}
```

In the `else if` structure, *`condition1`* is tested first. If that condition is `true`, the corresponding command block executes. Only if it is not true is *`condition2`* tested. If that condition is `true`, its command block runs. If neither *condition1* nor *condition2* are `true`, only then does the final command block run. In the following example, one of three possible greetings is displayed based on the value of the `day` variable.

```
if (day === "Friday") {
   window.alert("Get ready for the Weekend!");
} else if (day === "Monday") {
   window.alert("Start of another work week.");
} else {
   window.alert("Have a great day!");
}
```

Note | The `else` condition is considered the "default" option, applied only when all other possibilities have been tested and rejected.

Proceeding in this fashion, you can add as many `else if` statements as your application requires until you have covered all possible contingencies.

There are only two possible locations for Tipton's game: home (indicated by "h" in the `gameLocations` array) and away (indicated by "a"). The calendar should display the location using "vs." for home games and "@" for away games as in "vs. Bettendorf" or "@ Marion". Use an `else if` statement now to write the home/away information on the game calendar.

To create an `else if` statement:

1. Return to the **js03.js** file in your code editor and scroll down to the `showGames()` function.
2. Directly after the statement that writes the opening `<p>` tag, insert the following `else if` statement as shown in **Figure 3-12**.

```
// Display the game location
   if (gameLocations[i] === "h") {
      gameInfo += "vs. ";
   } else if (gameLocations[i] === "a") {
      gameInfo += "@ ";
}
```

```
// Function to write game information into the calendar
function showGames() {
   for (let i = 0; i < gameDates.length; i++) {
      let gameInfo = "";

      // Open the paragraph
      gameInfo += "<p>";

      // Display the game location
      if (gameLocations[i] === "h") {
         gameInfo += "vs. ";
      } else if (gameLocations[i] === "a") {
         gameInfo += "@ ";
      }
```

If the game is at home, display the text string "vs."
If the game is away, display the @ character

Figure 3-12 Inserting an `else if` statement

Note that there is no `else` condition in this statement because all games should be either home ("h") or away ("a") and if a different value was entered in the `gameLocations` array or no value at all, that situation should be flagged by not displaying the "vs." or @ characters. You should always write your code to help catch potential errors in your data.

3. Save your changes to the file and then reload the **js03.html** file in your web browser. Verify that all games are listed as either home or away on the calendar (see **Figure 3-13**.)

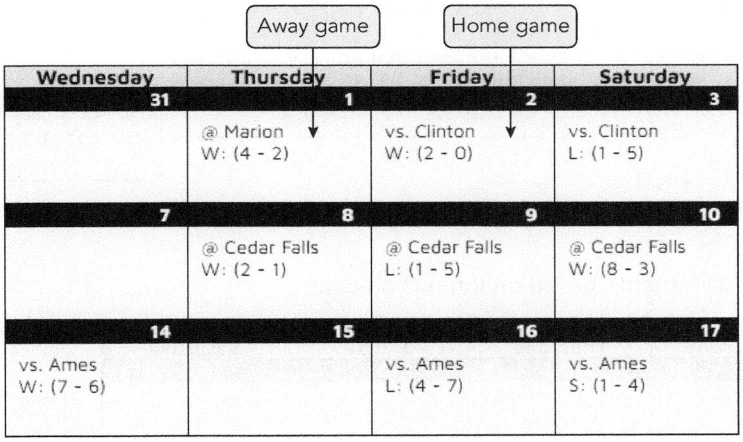

Away game
Home game

Wednesday	Thursday	Friday	Saturday
31	1	2	3
	@ Marion W: (4 - 2)	vs. Clinton W: (2 - 0)	vs. Clinton L: (1 - 5)
7	8	9	10
	@ Cedar Falls W: (2 - 1)	@ Cedar Falls L: (1 - 5)	@ Cedar Falls W: (8 - 3)
14	15	16	17
vs. Ames W: (7 - 6)		vs. Ames L: (4 - 7)	vs. Ames S: (1 - 4)

Figure 3-13 Home and away games

The only other piece of information not displayed in the calendar is the number of innings played. By default baseball games last nine innings, but in case of a tie, a game may go into extra innings, or a game might be shortened due to weather, or suspended prior to the fifth inning to be completed at a later date. For these different situations, have the calendar display the following:

- For nine-inning games, do not display the innings played
- For extra-inning games, display the innings enclosed in brackets, such as `[11]`
- For shortened games in which the result is still final, display the inning enclosed in brackets followed by an asterisk, such as `[7]*`
- For games suspended prior to the fifth inning, display the inning enclosed in brackets followed by three asterisks, such as `[4]***`

Add these conditions to the `showGames()` function using an `if` statement with multiple `else if` conditions to cover all possibilities.

To display the innings played:

1. Return to the **js03.js** file in your code editor and go to the `showGames()` function.
2. Directly above the comment for closing the paragraph insert the following `else if` statement (see **Figure 3-14**).

```
// Display innings played for suspended, shortened, or extrainning games
if (gameInnings[i] < 5) {
   gameInfo += " [" + gameInnings[i]+"]***";
} else if (gameInnings[i] < 9) {
   gameInfo += " [" + gameInnings[i]+"]*";
} else if (gameInnings[i] > 9) {
   gameInfo += " [" + gameInnings[i] + "]";
}
```

3. Save your changes to the file and then reload the **js03.html** file in your web browser. As shown in **Figure 3-15**, innings are added to those games that are suspended, shortened, or go into extra innings, but games that went for nine innings are not changed.

```
// Include the result and score
gameInfo += gameResults[i] + ": (" + runsScored[i] + " - " + runsAllowed[i] + ")";

// Display innings played for suspended, shortened, or extra-inning games
if (gameInnings[i] < 5) {
   gameInfo += " [" + gameInnings[i]+"]***";
} else if (gameInnings[i] < 9) {
   gameInfo += " [" + gameInnings[i]+"]*";
} else if (gameInnings[i] > 9) {
   gameInfo += " [" + gameInnings[i] + "]";
}

// Close the paragraph
gameInfo += "</p>";
```

Display suspended games as *[innings]****

Display shortened games as *[innings]**

Display extra-inning games as *[innings]*

Do not do anything for games that go exactly 9 innings

Figure 3-14 Conditional statements based on innings played

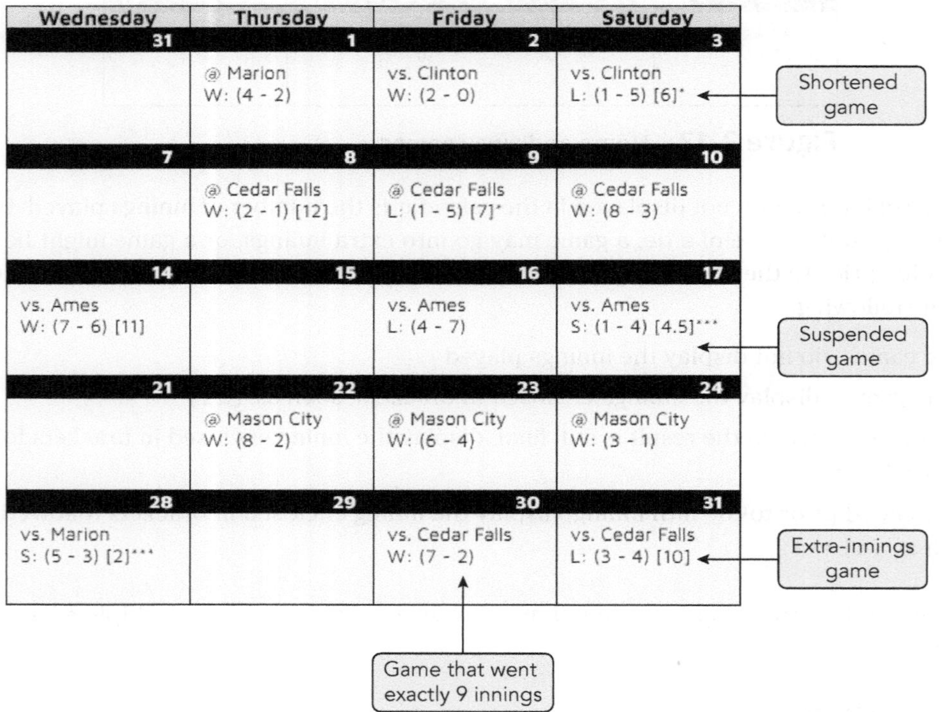

Wednesday	Thursday	Friday	Saturday
31	1	2	3
	@ Marion W: (4 - 2)	vs. Clinton W: (2 - 0)	vs. Clinton L: (1 - 5) [6]*
7	8	9	10
	@ Cedar Falls W: (2 - 1) [12]	@ Cedar Falls L: (1 - 5) [7]*	@ Cedar Falls W: (8 - 3)
14	15	16	17
vs. Ames W: (7 - 6) [11]		vs. Ames L: (4 - 7)	vs. Ames S: (1 - 4) [4.5]***
21	22	23	24
	@ Mason City W: (8 - 2)	@ Mason City W: (6 - 4)	@ Mason City W: (3 - 1)
28	29	30	31
vs. Marion S: (5 - 3) [2]***		vs. Cedar Falls W: (7 - 2)	vs. Cedar Falls L: (3 - 4) [10]

Figure 3-15 Displaying innings played

Note that because decision-making statements end with the first `true` condition, you need to order your statements to remove overlapping conditions. In this case, you first test for games that end in less than five innings *and then* test for games that end in less than nine innings. Switching the order would have treated all games with less than nine innings as shortened but finalized games, even those that lasted a single inning.

Nested `if` and `if else` Statements

As with program loops, you can nest decision-making statements within one another, creating a series of conditions that all must be true before an action is taken. This type of structure is called a nested decision-making structure. The following code shows an example of nested `if` statements:

```
if (day === "Friday") {
   if (time === "8am") {
      window.alert("Start of the last day of the week.");
```

```
    } else if (time === "5pm") {
        window.alert("Time to start the weekend!");
    } else {
        window.alert("A few more hours until the weekend.");
    }
} else if (day === "Monday") {
    window.alert("Start of another work week.");
} else {
    window.alert("Have a great day!");
}
```

In this example, if the day is "Friday", one of 3 possible messages will be displayed based on the value of the time variable; otherwise two possible messages will be displayed depending on whether the day is "Monday" or another day.

> **Note** With nested statements, it is very easy to lose track of the opening and closing braces. Mismatching the braces will most likely result in an error. To assist you, most code editors will include visual clues matching opening and closing braces.

Conditional Statements and Browser Testing

A great challenge for any web developer is ensuring that program code is supported by the browser. Older browser versions may not recognize the latest enhancements made to ECMAScript, and customers running those browsers will be faced with an application that fails due to its lack of support. If you feel that a feature of your code might not be universally supported, you can add a browser test confirming that the feature is recognized by the JavaScript interpreter and providing alternate statements if it is not. The general syntax is:

```
if (feature) {
    statements that use the feature
} else {
    statements that use replacement code
}
```

where *`feature`* is a JavaScript object, property, or method that should be tested for browser support. If the feature returns `true`, you can apply statements that use the feature; but if the condition returns a falsy value (such as `undefined`), you can supply an alternate set of commands that use a different feature that is supported.

For example, the method `find()` (listed in Figure 3-11) is an array method that locates the first element in array returning a `true` value from a callback function. However, the method was introduced in 2015 with ES6 and thus might not be supported by some older browsers. The following code shows how to conduct a browser test for the `find()` method in a program that analyzes customer orders:

```
// array of order ids
let orders = ["33-104", "21-098", "88-001", "14-791"];

// find the first order that has not shipped
if (orders.find) {
    // the find method is supported by the browser
    let firstUnshipped = orders.find(unshipped);
} else {
```

```
   // alternate code in place of the find method
}

function unshipped(arrValue) {
   // callback function to determine whether an order has shipped
}
```

If the expression `orders.find` is not recognized, the JavaScript interpreter will return the falsy value `undefined` and the test condition fails so that the `else` command block is executed with an alternate set of commands; but if the test condition is `true`, the `find()` method is applied to accomplish the task.

Browser testing is often used to ease the transition into new ECMAScript features, so that the most current features are applied where supported and older features are used where needed. As newer features become more widely supported, developers can simplify their code by removing the browser test and the alternate set of instructions. Throughout the years, many statements using outdated methods have been winnowed away in this fashion, resulting in faster, more efficient code.

The `switch` Statement

As the number of possible conditions increases, the entire `if else if` structure can become large and unwieldy. An alternative to a long list of `else if` conditions is the following `switch` statement:

```
switch (expression) {
   case label1 : statements; break;
   case label2 : statements; break;
   case label3 : statements; break;
...
   default: statements; break;
}
```

where *`expression`* is a statement that returns a value, *`label1`*, *`label2`*, *`label3`*, and so on are possible values of that expression, *`statements`* are the commands run with each possible value, and the final default option is run if none of the listed labels match the expression's value.

The following `switch` statement demonstrates how to run a different set of statements based on the value of the `day` variable:

```
switch (day) {
   case "Friday": alert("Thank goodness it's Friday!"); break;
   case "Monday": alert("Blue Monday"); break;
   case "Saturday": alert("Sleep in today."); break;
   default: alert("Today is " + day);
}
```

This `switch` statement tests for three possible `day` values, "Friday", "Monday", and "Saturday", with different messages displayed for each day. If `day` equals none of those values, the default message is displayed.

> **Note** Case labels must be discrete values and cannot use operators. Thus, you cannot define a case label based on numeric ranges like `< 20` or `>= 10`. If you need a numeric range, use an `else if` construction instead of a `switch` statement.

The `break` statement, marking the end of each case, is an optional keyword that halts the execution of the `switch` statement once a matching case has been found. For programs in which more than one label might match the expression, omit the `break` statements and the JavaScript interpreter will continue moving through the `case` labels, running all statements in which a match has been found. This situation is known as fallthrough.

Use a `switch` statement to add one last feature to the game calendar. The calendar needs to show wins, losses, suspended games, and postponed games with differing font and background colors. Styles for each result have been saved in the CSS stylesheet under different class names. To use the style sheet, your program must change the paragraph tag containing the game result to one of following depending on the game outcome:

- `<p class = "win"> … </p>`
- `<p class = "lose"> … </p>`
- `<p class = "suspended"> … </p>`
- `<p class = "postponed"> … </p>`

Create a `switch` statement now to write a different opening tag for the paragraph based on the value in the `gameResults` array.

To apply a `switch` statement:

1. Return to the **js03.js** file in your code editor and go to the `showGames()` function.
2. Replace the statement `let gameInfo = "<p>"` that writes the paragraph's opening tag with the following `switch` statement that chooses one of four possible opening paragraph tags:

```
switch (gameResults[i]) {
   case "W":
      gameInfo += "<p class='win'>";
      break;
   case "L":
      gameInfo += "<p class='lose'>";
      break;
   case "S":
      gameInfo += "<p class='suspended'>";
      break;
   case "P":
      gameInfo += "<p class='postponed'>";
      break;
}
```

Figure 3-16 shows the newly added code in the function.

```
// Function to write game information into the calendar
function showGames() {
   for (let i = 0; i < gameDates.length; i++) {
      let gameInfo = "";

      // Open the paragraph
      switch (gameResults[i]) {
         case "W":
            gameInfo += "<p class='win'>";
            break;
         case "L":
            gameInfo += "<p class='lose'>";
            break;
         case "S":
            gameInfo += "<p class='suspended'>";
            break;
         case "P":
            gameInfo += "<p class='postponed'>";
            break;
      }

      // Display the game location
```


Figure 3-16 Creating a `switch` statement

3. Save your changes to the file and then reload the **js03.html** file in your web browser. **Figure 3-17** shows the final version of the calendar.

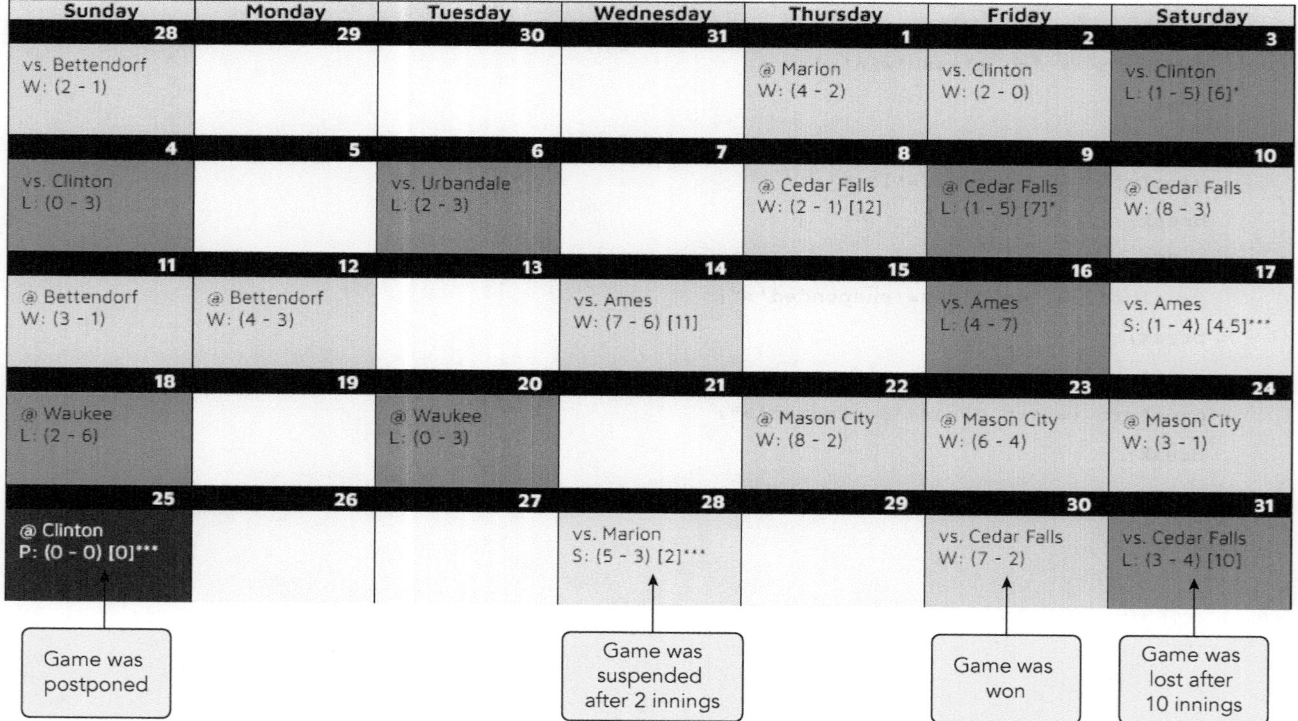

Figure 3-17 Final monthly calendar for the Tipton Turbines

Managing Program Loops and Conditional Statements

Although you are finished with the calendar, you still should become familiar with some features of program loops and conditional statements for future work with these JavaScript structures. You will examine three features in more detail—the `break`, `continue`, and `label` statements.

The `break` Statement

The `break` statement can be used anywhere within any program loop or conditional statement. When a `break` statement is encountered, the execution of the code passes to the next set of statements. Breaks are most often used to exit a program loop before the stopping condition is met, as in the following program loop that examines the `customerID` array for a specific customer ID number:

```
for (let i = 0; i< customerID.length; i++) {
   if (customerID[i] === "C-14281") {
      window.alert("C-14281 is found");
      break; // stop processing the for loop
   }
}
```

Once the specific customer ID has been located, there is little point in continuing the `for` loop. The `break` command saves the JavaScript interpreter from having to fruitlessly examine the rest of an array that might contain tens of thousands of elements.

The `continue` Statement

The `continue` statement is like the `break` statement except that instead of stopping a program loop altogether, the `continue` statement stops only the current iteration and continues on to the next iteration. A `continue` statement is useful in programs that need to avoid undefined values that can cause the program to fail. In the following code, a `for` loop is used to examine the contents of an array of customer email addresses. However, the `customerEmail` array may be sparse with several undefined values that would result in errors if processed. This problem is avoided with an `if` statement that continues the loop to the next iteration when an undefined value is detected:

```
for (let i = 0; i< customerEmail.length; i++) {
   if (customerEmail[i] === undefined) {
      continue;
   } else {
      // statements to process the e-mail address
   }
}
```

Statement Labels

Statement labels identify statements in the code so that they can be referenced elsewhere in the program. The syntax of the statement label is:

```
label: statements
```

where *`label`* is the text of the label and *`statements`* are the statements identified by the label. You have already seen labels with the `switch` statement, but labels can also be used with other program loops and conditional statements to provide more control over how statements are processed. Labels often are used with `break` and `continue` statements to direct the program flow to a specific set of statements. The syntax to reference a label in such cases is simply

```
break: label;
```

or

```
continue: label;
```

For example, the following `for` loop uses a statement label not only to jump out of the programming loop when the text string “C-14281” is found but also to jump to a location in the script identified by the `nextReport` label and to continue to process the statements found there:

```
for (let i = 0; i< customerID.length; i++) {
   if (customerID[i] === "C-14281") {
      window.alert("C-14281 is found");
      break: nextReport; // stop processing the for loop
   }
}

nextReport: statements
```

Labels are most often used with nested loops when you need to break out of a loop completely, no matter how deeply nested you might be.

Best Practices | *Avoiding Spaghetti Code*

Spaghetti code is a pejorative programming term that refers to convoluted or poorly written code. One hallmark of spaghetti code is the frequent branching from one section of code to another, making it difficult to track the program line-by-line as it is executed. A change in one part of the program could lead to unpredictable changes in a completely different section of the code.

Many developers discourage the use of label statements unless absolutely necessary. They can confuse a programmer trying to fix code in which a program loop can end before its stopping condition, or code in which statements are not processed in the order that they are written in a document. Almost all of the tasks in a program can also be performed by carefully setting up the conditions for program loops without forcing jumps to labeled sections.

Even with the best of intentions, spaghetti code can easily occur in environments in which the same code is maintained by several people or passed from one employee to another. A programmer might add a new feature that is needed right away without adequately documenting the changes made to the code or without considering the impact of those changes on other programs. To avoid or at least reduce the occurrence of spaghetti code, always document your code, and develop a structure that is easy for others to follow.

Quick Check 3

1. Provide the code for an `if` statement that displays an alert window with the message "You passed with an A" if the value of the `exam` variable is greater than 90.
2. Provide the code for an `if else` statement that displays an alert window with the message "You passed with an A" if the value of the `exam` variable is greater than 90 and the message "Not an A" if otherwise.
3. Provide the code for an `else if` statement that displays the message "You passed with an A" if `exam` is greater than 90, else if `exam` is greater than 80 the browser displays the message "You passed with a B". else if `exam` is greater than 70, the message "You passed with an C" is displayed, else the message "You did not pass" is displayed.
4. Provide the general code for a browser test that tests whether or not the browser supports the `findIndex()` method when applied to an array named `xValues`.
5. How should you write the code for a `switch` statement to allow more than one condition to be run by the JavaScript interpreter?

Summary

- An array contains a set of data represented by a single variable name. You can think of an array as a collection of variables contained within a single variable. Each piece of data contained in an array is called an element. An index is an element's numeric position within the array.
- A loop statement is a control flow statement that repeatedly executes a statement or a series of statements while a specific condition is true or until a specific condition becomes true. Loop statements in JavaScript include the `while`, `do while`, and `for` statements.
- The `while` statement is used for repeating a statement or series of statements as long as a given conditional expression evaluates to `true`.
- Each repetition of a looping statement is called an iteration.
- An infinite loop is a situation in which a loop statement never ends because its conditional expression is never false.
- The `do while` statement executes a statement or statements once, and then it repeats the execution as long as a given conditional expression evaluates to `true`.
- The `for` statement is used to repeat a statement or series of statements as long as a given conditional expression evaluates to `true`.
- The `continue` statement halts a looping statement and restarts the loop with a new iteration.
- The process of choosing which code to execute at a given point in an application is known as decision making. In JavaScript, you use the `if`, `if else`, `else if`, and `switch` statements to create decision-making structures.
- The `if` statement is used to execute specific programming code if the evaluation of a conditional expression returns a value of `true`.
- An `if` statement that includes an `else` clause is called an `if else` statement.
- When one decision-making statement is contained within another decision-making statement, they are referred to as nested decision-making structures.
- The `switch` statement controls program flow by executing a specific set of statements, depending on the value of an expression.
- A `break` statement is used to exit control statements, such as the `switch` statement or the `while`, `do while`, and `for` looping statements.

Key Terms

array
array literal
browser test
callback function
conditional statement
controlling flow
counter
decision making
decision-making statement
decision-making structure
element
fallthrough
HTML Collection Object
index
infinite loop
iteration
matrix
multidimensional array
nested decision-making structure
posttest loop
pretest loop
program loop
spaghetti code
sparse array

Review Questions

1. What is the correct syntax for creating an empty array named `taxRules`?
   a. `var taxRules = {};`
   b. `var taxRules;`
   c. `var taxRules = [];`
   d. `var taxRules[5];`

2. Which of the following statements adds the value "oak" as the third element of the `trees` array?
   a. `trees += "oak";`
   b. `trees += "","","oak";`
   c. `trees[2] = "oak";`
   d. `trees[3] = "oak";`

3. Which of the following properties returns the number of elements in an array?
   a. `length`
   b. `size`
   c. `elements`
   d. `indexes`

4. To create a multidimensional array in JavaScript, you must ______________.
   a. use the `new Matrix()` object constructor
   b. nest one array within another
   c. load a JavaScript library with special array tools
   d. apply the `forEach()` array method

5. To reference the element in the third row and fourth column of the multidimensional array `xValues`, use:
   a. `xValues(3, 4)`
   b. `xValues[3, 4]`
   c. `xValues[2][3]`
   d. `xValues[2, 3]`

6. To reference the third inline image found within the web page document, use:
   a. `document.images.3`
   b. `document.images[3]`
   c. `image.2`
   d. `document.images[2]`

7. If you do not include code that changes the counter value in a loop statement, your program will be caught in a(n) ______________.
   a. iteration
   b. condition
   c. fallthrough
   d. infinite loop

8. To access HTML elements by the value of their `class` attribute, which of the following would you use?
   a. `document.getElementsByClassName()`
   b. `document.getElementByClassName()`
   c. `document.getElementsByClass()`
   d. `document.getClasses()`

9. Each repetition of a program loop is called a(n) ______________.
   a. command block
   b. counter
   c. iteration
   d. `while` loop

10. Posttest loops are ______________.
    a. program loops in which the stopping condition is evaluated before each iteration of the command block
    b. program loops in which the stopping condition is evaluated after the command block has been executed at least once
    c. used in `while` loops and `for` loops
    d. loops that have no stopping condition

11. Which of the following can be used as part of a `for` loop to go through all the elements in the `xValues` array?
    a. `for (let i = 1; i < xValues.length; i++)`
    b. `for (let i = 0; i <= xValues.length; i++)`
    c. `for (let i = 0; i < xValues.length; i++)`
    d. `for (let i = 1; i = xValues.lenght; i++)`

12. A simple `if else` statement enables you to specify code for ______________ alternatives.
    a. 2
    b. 3
    c. 4
    d. unlimited

13. To insert HTML code within an element without overwriting code already in that element, use the ______________ method.
    a. `innerHTML()`
    b. `insertAdjacentHTML()`
    c. `document.write()`
    d. `insertHTML()`

14. The forEach() method _______________.
 a. requires a JavaScript extension
 b. is an example of a pretest loop
 c. is an example of a posttest loop
 d. is used to apply a function to every element within an array without using a program loop

15. In an if else statement, the else command block will run when _______________.
 a. the conditional expression is true
 b. the conditional expression is false
 c. the conditional expression is undefined
 d. the conditional expression is falsy

16. Describe two ways of declaring a JavaScript array.

17. Provide the code to reference the fourth element in the projectTeam array.

18. Provide the code to reference the third div element within a web document.

19. Provide the general code of a for loop that loops through all the div elements within a web document.

20. Provide code to insert the HTML text string <h1>Main Heading</h1> directly after the opening tag of the div element with the id "Main".

Hands-On Projects

Hands-On Project 3-1

In this project you create an application that calculates the total cost of items selected from a lunch menu using a for loop and an if statement as part of the program code. The cost of each menu item is stored in the value attribute of an input control on a web form. Because attribute values are treated as text strings, you will have to convert the attribute value to a number using the following JavaScript function:

```
Number(object.value)
```

where *object* is a reference to an input box within the web page. Your application will automatically update the total order cost whenever the user clicks a menu item checkbox. **Figure 3-18** shows a preview of the completed project.

Hands-on Project 3-1

Lunch selections

Total Order Cost: $22.90

☐ Fried chicken ($11.95)
☑ Fried halibut ($13.95)
☐ Hamburger ($10.95)
☐ Grilled salmon ($17.95)
☑ Side salad ($8.95)

Figure 3-18 Completed Project 3-1

Do the following:

1. Use your code editor to open the **project03-01_txt.html** and **project03-01_txt.js** files from the js03 ▶ project01 folder. Enter your name and the date in the comment section of each file and save them as **project03-01.html** and **project03-01.js**, respectively.

2. Go to the **project03-01.html** file in your code editor and in the head section add a `script` element to load the project03-01.js file. Include the `defer` attribute to defer loading the file until the entire page is loaded. Study the contents of the HTML file, noting that all checkboxes for the menu items belong to the `menuItems` class. Save your changes to the file.
3. Go to the **project03-01.js** file in your code editor. Below the initial comment section, declare a variable named **menuItems** containing the collection of HTML elements belonging to the `menuItem` class using the `getElementsByClassName()` method.
4. Create a `for` loop that loops through the contents of the `menuItems` collection with a counter variable that starts with an initial value of 0 up to a value less than the length of the `menuItems` collection. Increase the counter by 1 with each iteration. Within the `for` loop, add an event listener to the `menuItems[i]` element in the collection (where *i* is the value of the counter), running the `calcTotal()` function when that item is clicked.
5. Create the **calcTotal()** function to calculate the total cost of the customer order given the selected menu items. Add the following commands to the function:
   a. Declare the **orderTotal** variable, setting its initial value to 0.
   b. Create a `for` loop that loops through the contents of the `menuItems` collection. For `menuItems[i]` (where *i* is the counter), apply an `if` statement that tests whether the item has been checked. If true, increase the value of the `orderTotal` variable by the value of `menuItems[i]`. (Hint: Use the `Number()` function to convert the value of `menuItems[i]` to a number.)
   c. After the `for` loop, insert a command to change the `innerHTML` property of the element with the id "billTotal" to the value returned by the `formatCurrency()` function using `orderTotal` as the parameter value.
6. Save your changes to the file and then open **project03-01.html** in your browser. Verify that the total cost of the order is automatically updated as you select and deselect menu items in the web form.

Hands-On Project 3-2

In this project you will generate an image gallery using images of the International Space Station. Each image will be placed within a figure box accompanied by a caption taken from an array of caption text. A preview of the completed project is shown in **Figure 3-19**.

Do the following:

1. Use your code editor to open the **project03-02_txt.html** and **project03-02_txt.js** files from the js03 ▶ project02 folder. Enter your name and the date in the comment section of each file and save them as **project03-02.html** and **project03-02.js**, respectively.
2. Go to the **project03-02.html** file in your code editor and in the head section add a `script` element to load the project03-02.js file, deferring the loading of the JavaScript source file until the entire HTML file is loaded. Study the contents of the HTML file and save your changes.
3. Go to the **project03-02.js** file in your code editor. Below the code that creates and populates the `captions` array, declare the **htmlCode** variable, setting its initial value to an empty text string.
4. Create a `for` loop with a counter that goes from 0 to less the length of the `captions` array in increments of 1. With each iteration, add the following text to the value of the `htmlCode` variable:

   ```
   <figure>
   <img alt='' src='slidei.jpg' />
   <figcaption>caption[i]</figcaption>
   </figure>
   ```

   where *i* is the value of the counter for that iteration and `captions[i]` is the corresponding element from the `captions` array.

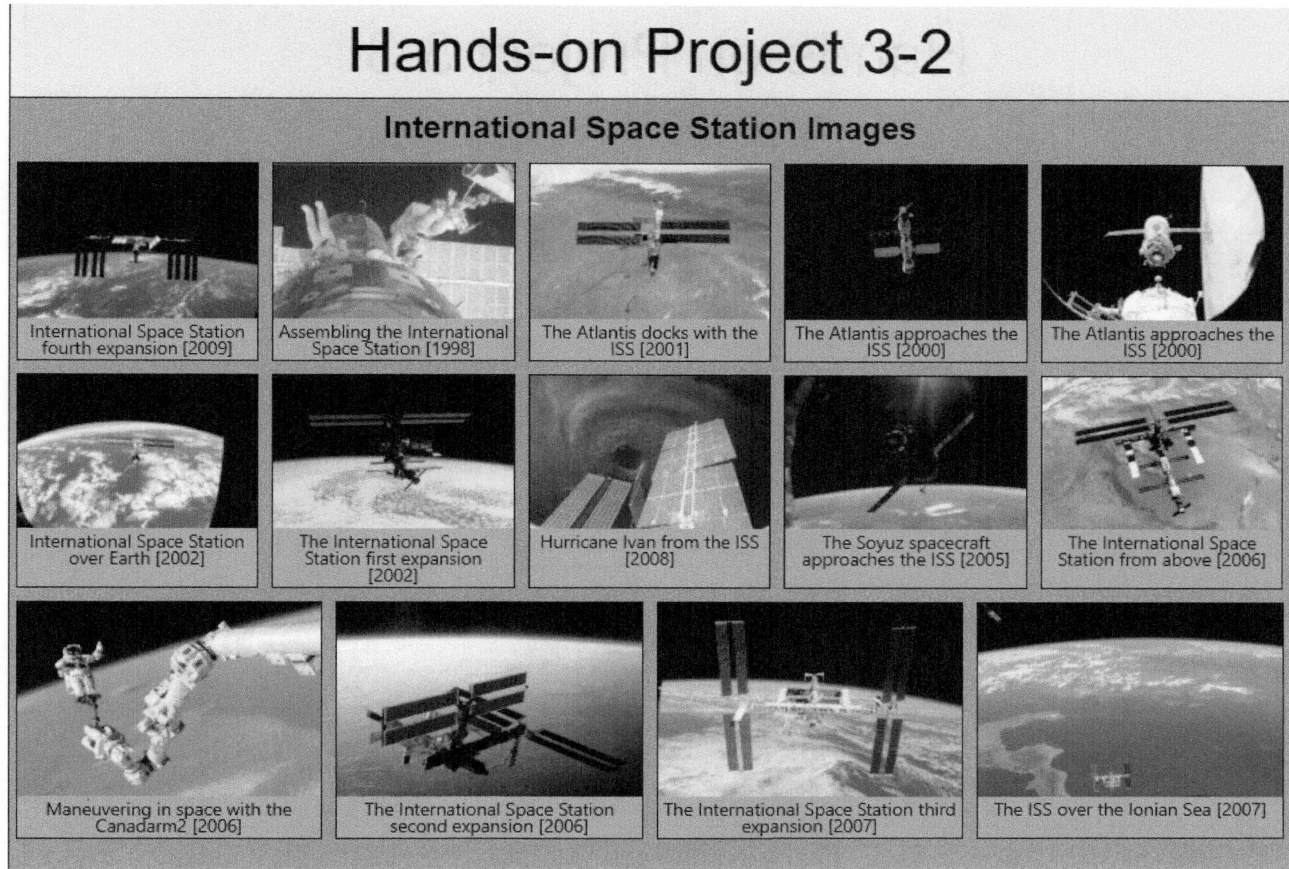

Figure 3-19 Completed Project 3-2 *NASA*

5. After the `for` loop, change the inner HTML of the document element by the id "gallery" to the value of the `htmlCode` variable.
6. Save your changes to the file and then load **project03-02.html** in your browser. Verify that the page displays the 14 images in the slide gallery along with their captions.

Hands-On Project 3-3

In this project you will generate the HTML code for a web table displaying the top 10 movies from the IMDB website. Information on each movie is stored in arrays that have been created for you. Your job will be to create a program loop that loops through the content of the arrays and writes the information as new table rows in the web table. A preview of the completed project is shown in **Figure 3-20**.

Do the following:

1. Use your code editor to open the **project03-03_txt.html** and **project03-03_txt.js** files from the js03 ▶ project03 folder. Enter your name and the date in the comment section of each file and save them as **project03-03.html** and **project03-03.js**, respectively.
2. Go to the **project03-03.html** file in your code editor and in the head section add a `script` element to load the project03-03.js file, deferring the loading of the JavaScript source file until the entire HTML file is loaded. Study the contents of the HTML file and save your changes.
3. Go to the **project03-03.js** file in your code editor. Below the code that creates and populates the `links` array, declare the **htmlCode** variable, setting its initial value to an empty text string.

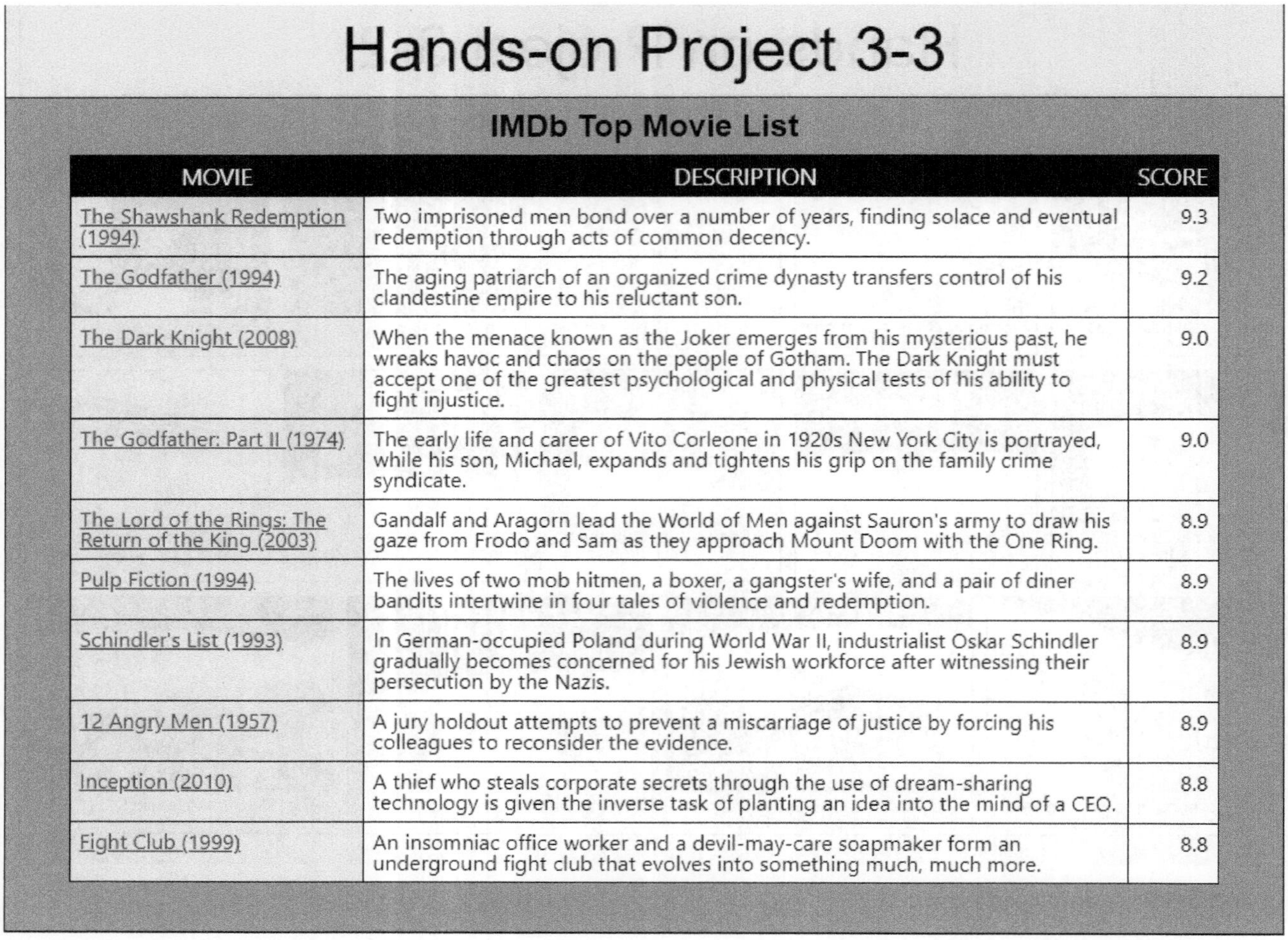

Hands-on Project 3-3

IMDb Top Movie List

MOVIE	DESCRIPTION	SCORE
The Shawshank Redemption (1994)	Two imprisoned men bond over a number of years, finding solace and eventual redemption through acts of common decency.	9.3
The Godfather (1994)	The aging patriarch of an organized crime dynasty transfers control of his clandestine empire to his reluctant son.	9.2
The Dark Knight (2008)	When the menace known as the Joker emerges from his mysterious past, he wreaks havoc and chaos on the people of Gotham. The Dark Knight must accept one of the greatest psychological and physical tests of his ability to fight injustice.	9.0
The Godfather: Part II (1974)	The early life and career of Vito Corleone in 1920s New York City is portrayed, while his son, Michael, expands and tightens his grip on the family crime syndicate.	9.0
The Lord of the Rings: The Return of the King (2003)	Gandalf and Aragorn lead the World of Men against Sauron's army to draw his gaze from Frodo and Sam as they approach Mount Doom with the One Ring.	8.9
Pulp Fiction (1994)	The lives of two mob hitmen, a boxer, a gangster's wife, and a pair of diner bandits intertwine in four tales of violence and redemption.	8.9
Schindler's List (1993)	In German-occupied Poland during World War II, industrialist Oskar Schindler gradually becomes concerned for his Jewish workforce after witnessing their persecution by the Nazis.	8.9
12 Angry Men (1957)	A jury holdout attempts to prevent a miscarriage of justice by forcing his colleagues to reconsider the evidence.	8.9
Inception (2010)	A thief who steals corporate secrets through the use of dream-sharing technology is given the inverse task of planting an idea into the mind of a CEO.	8.8
Fight Club (1999)	An insomniac office worker and a devil-may-care soapmaker form an underground fight club that evolves into something much, much more.	8.8

Figure 3-20 Completed Project 3-3

4. Create a `for` loop with a counter that goes from 0 to less the length of the `titles` array in increments of 1. With each iteration, add the following text to the value of the `htmlCode` variable:

```
<tr>
<td><a href='links[i]'>titles[i]</a><td>
<td>summaries[i]</td>
<td>ratings[i]</td>
</tr>
```

   where *i* is the value of the counter for that iteration, and `links[i]`, `titles[i]`, `summaries[i]`, and `ratings[i]` are the values from the corresponding elements in the `links`, `titles`, `summaries`, and `ratings` arrays.

5. After the `for` loop, declare a variable named **tableBody** referencing the first (and only) element in the web document with the tag name "tbody". (Hint: Use the `getElementsByTagName()` method to access the HTML collection and don't forget to reference the first element in that collection and not the whole collection.)
6. Change the `innerHTML` property of `tableBody` to the value of the `htmlCode` variable.
7. Save your changes to the file and then load **project03-03.html** in your browser. Verify that the page displays the top 10 movies in the IMDB ratings.

Hands-On Project 3-4

In this project you will display customer reviews for a new digital game. Information on each customer and review is contained within several arrays. Customers give the game a rating from one to five stars, which you will display as star images in the web page. A preview of the completed project is shown in **Figure 3-21**.

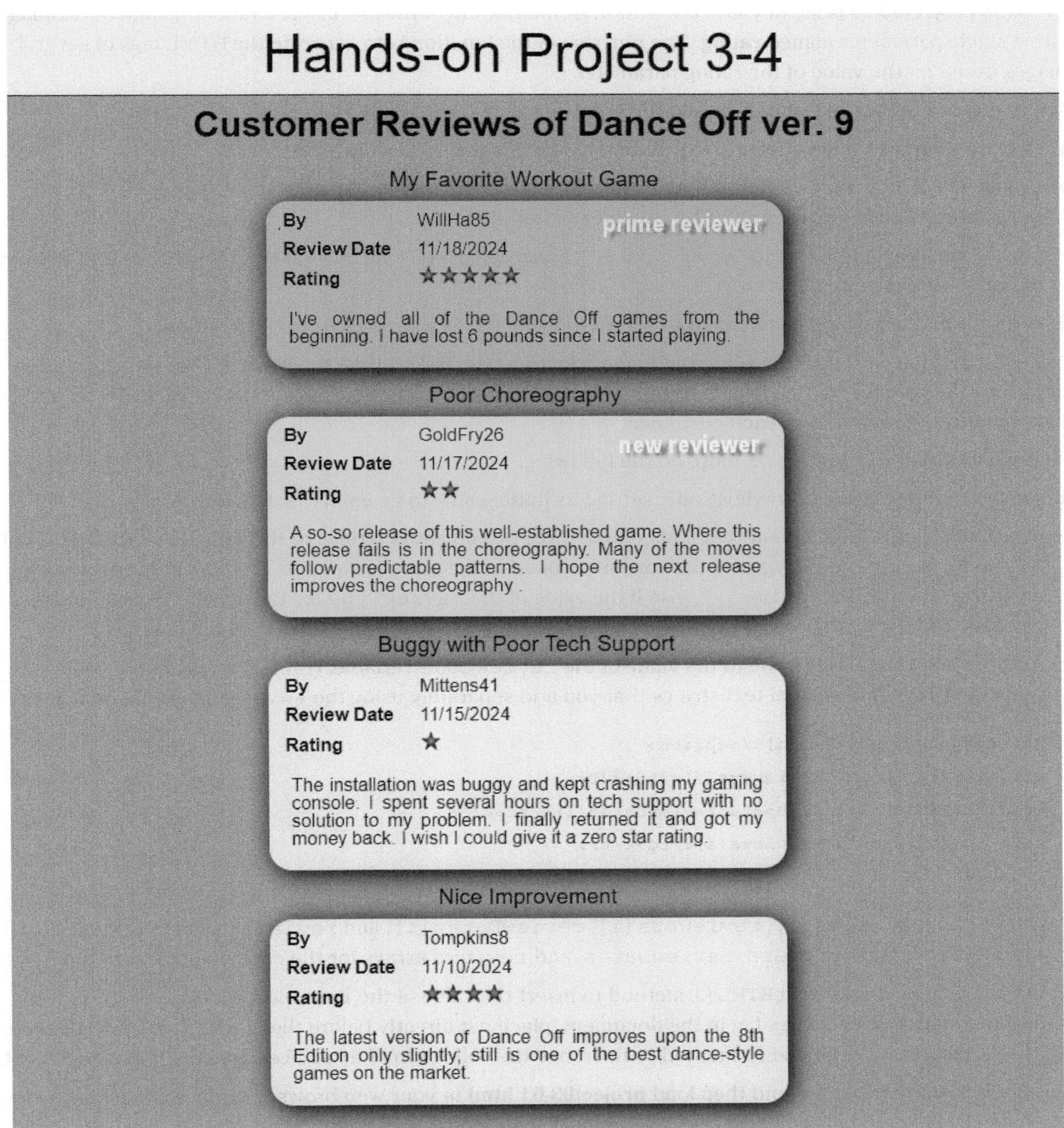

Figure 3-21 Completed Project 3-4

Do the following:

1. Use your code editor to open the **project03-04_txt.html** and **project03-04_txt.js** files from the js03 ▶ project04 folder. Enter your name and the date in the comment section of each file and save them as **project03-04.html** and **project03-04.js**, respectively.
2. Go to the **project03-04.html** file in your code editor and in the head section add a `script` element to load the project03-04.js file, deferring the loading of the JavaScript source file until the entire HTML file is loaded. Study the contents of the HTML file and save your changes.
3. Go to the **project03-04.js** file in your code editor. At the bottom of the file, insert a function named **starImages()** with a single parameter named **rating**. The purpose of the function is to generate the HTML tags of several star images based on the value of the rating parameter.
4. Within the `starImages()` function add the following:
   a. Declare a variable named **imageText**, setting its initial value to an empty text string.
   b. Create a `for` loop with a counter that goes from 1 up to less than or equal to the value of the `rating` parameter, increasing the counter by 1 with each iteration.
   c. In the `for` loop, add the text `"<img src = 'star.png' alt = ">"` to the value of the `imageText` variable with each iteration.
   d. After the `for` loop, add a statement to return the value of `imageText` from the function.
5. Create a `for` loop with the counter variable ranging from 0 up to less than the length of the `reviewers` array, increasing the counter by 1 with each iteration. In this `for` loop you will generate the HTML code for a table that contains the review from each customer.
6. For each iteration within the `for` loop, do the following:
   a. Declare a variable named **reviewCode**, setting its initial value to an empty text string.
   b. Insert an `else if` statement that adds one of three possible text strings to the value of `reviewCode`: if the value of the `reviewType` for the current element in the array is equal to "P" then add the text string `"<table class = 'prime'>"`, else if the value of the `reviewType` for the current element is equal to "N" then add the text string, `"<table class = 'new'>"` else add the text string, `"<table>"`.
   c. Add the following HTML code to the value of the `reviewCode` variable. (Hint: You may find it easier to break this code into several text strings that you add separately using the += assignment operator.)

   ```
   <caption>reviewTitles[i]</caption>
   <tr><th>By</th><td>reviewers[i]</td></tr>
   <tr><th>Review Date</th><td>reviewDates[i]</td></tr>
   <tr><td colspan='2'>reviews[i]</td></tr>
   </table>
   ```

   where `reviewTitles[i]`, `reviewers[i]`, `reviewDates[i]`, and `reviews[i]` are the values from the `reviewTitles`, `reviewers`, `reviewDates`, and `reviews` arrays for the current element in the iteration.
   d. Use the `insertAdjacentHTML()` method to insert the value of the `reviewCode` variable into the first (and only) `<article>` tag in the document, placing it directly before the closing tag. (Hint: Use the `getElementsByTagName()` method to reference the collection of `article` elements in the document.)
7. Save your changes to the file and then load **project03-04.html** in your web browser, verify that all four reviews are shown as indicated in Figure 3-21.

Hands-On Project 3-5

Debugging Challenge

In this debugging challenge you will fix the mistakes in a program that generates a horizontal bar chart describing the relative sales of five brands of cell phones sold by a company. You can use the browser console to evaluate the code and the arrays the program uses to locate any errors. When the code has been fixed, it will display the bar chart shown in **Figure 3-22**.

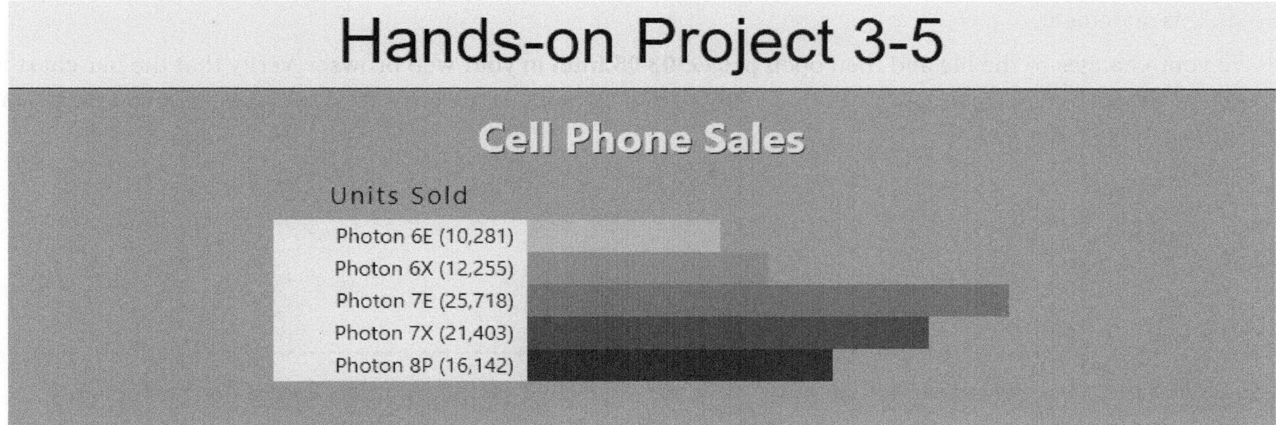

Figure 3-22 Completed Project 3-5

The horizontal bar chart is created by generating a web table with each phone model displayed on a separate table row. The bars themselves are generated using `<td></td>` tags with the number of `td` elements in each row equal to the percentage of the total sales (to nearest 1%). For example, a phone that accounts for 40% of sales will have 40 `td` elements in its table row. The width and color of each `td` element is set in a style sheet so that different background colors are applied to the different phone models.

Do the following:

1. Use your code editor to open the **project03-05_txt.html** and **project03-05_txt.js** files from the js03 ► project05 folder. Enter your name and the date in the comment section of each file and save them as **project03-05.html** and **project03-05.js**, respectively.
2. Go to the **project03-05.html** file in your code editor and in the head section add a `script` element to load the project03-05.js file, deferring the loading of the JavaScript source file until the entire HTML file is loaded. Study the contents of the HTML file and save your changes.
3. Go to the **project03-05.js** file in your code editor. Comments have been added to help you understand the code used in this application.
4. Locate and fix the following errors in the code:
   a. The program declares two arrays named `phones` and `sales` that contain the names of the five phone models and their units sold. There is an error in declaring each of these arrays. Locate and fix those errors.
   b. The program uses the `forEach()` method with the `addToTotal()` function as the callback function to calculate the total sales across all phone models. Fix the error in the statement that runs the `forEach()` method.

c. In the `for` loop that writes the `td` elements for the bar chart, there are errors defining the counter values. Locate and fix the errors involved.

d. Fix the error in the statement that declares and initializes the `barPercent` variable (which calculates the sales percentage for a specific phone model.)

e. Fix the syntax errors in the `switch` statement that sets the value of the `cellTag` variable based on name of the phone model.

f. At the end of the `for` loop, the program inserts the value of the `barChart` variable into HTML code of the first `<tbody>` element in the document, directly before the closing `</tbody>` tag. Locate and fix the error in this statement.

5. Save your changes to the file and then open **project03-05.html** in your web browser. Verify that the bar chart is generated as shown in Figure 3-22. If you are still getting errors, use the browser console to help you locate and fix errors in the code.

Case Projects

Individual Case Project

Plan and add a feature to one of the web pages in your personal site that incorporates content or functionality created by a series of `if`, `if else`, and/or `else if` statements, or by a `switch` statement. View and test your page in one or more browsers as appropriate to ensure it works as you expect.

Team Case Project

Choose one of the web pages from your team web site to enhance with code that uses an array and a loop. Arrays are often used to store a set of related data, either provided by the developer or added by a user. Loops are often used in combination with arrays to perform a common action on each element in an array. Plan the structure of the code as a team, then divide into two groups. One group should create the code for the array, and the other the code for the loop. After each group has completed its work, come back together as a full group and incorporate the code in the group web page. Test the code to verify the page works as planned, doing any troubleshooting and making any edits to the functions as a full team.

CHAPTER 4

Debugging and Error Handling

When you complete this chapter, you will be able to:

- Understand four different types of errors that programmers must deal with
- Use the debugger console to locate errors in a program
- Use JavaScript in strict mode
- Trace an error to its source
- Track the flow of your program using debugger tools
- Manage errors in your code using a `try catch` statement
- Control how a browser handles errors

The more JavaScript programs you write, the more likely you are to write programs that generate error messages. At times it may seem like your programs never function quite the way you want. Regardless of experience, knowledge, and ability, all programmers introduce errors in their programs at one time or another. Thus, all programmers must devote part of their programming education to mastering the art of debugging, which is the process of tracing and resolving errors in a program. Debugging is an essential skill for any programmer, regardless of the programming language.

In this chapter, you will learn techniques and tools that you can use to trace and resolve errors in JavaScript programs. However, you will not create any new programs. Instead, you will learn how to locate errors in an existing program.

Introduction to Debugging

All programming languages, including JavaScript, have their own syntax, or rules. To write a program, you must understand the syntax of the programming language you are using. You must also understand computer-programming logic. The term logic refers to the arrangement of operations within the program to achieve its intended goal. You may know how to operate a car correctly (i.e., with correct syntax) but unless you follow the correct route (with correct logic) you are unlikely to arrive at your destination. One of the goals of programming is to arrive in the most efficient way possible and in programming, this is as much an art as a science.

Any error in a program that causes it to function incorrectly, whether because of incorrect syntax or flaws in logic, is called a bug. The term debugging refers to the act of tracing and resolving errors in a program. Grace Murray Hopper, a mathematician who was instrumental in developing the Common Business-Oriented Language (COBOL) programming language, is said to have first coined the term. A moth short-circuited a primitive computer that Hopper was using. Removing the moth "debugged" the system and resolved the problem. Today, the term "bug" refers to any sort of problem in the design and operation of a program. There are three general types of errors within a program: load-time errors, runtime errors, and logic errors.

Note Do not confuse bugs with computer viruses or worms. Bugs are problems within a program that occur because of syntax errors, design flaws, or runtime errors. Viruses and worms are self-contained programs designed to infect a computer system and cause damage, compromise security, and/or steal information.

Load-Time Errors

A load-time error, also known as a syntax error, occurs when the program is initially loaded by the browser. One of the tasks of a JavaScript interpreter is to confirm that there are no errors in the syntax. A common syntax error is the misspelling of a JavaScript keyword such as using `document.writ()` in place of `document.write()`. Other syntax errors would be forgetting to end a command block with a closing curly brace or forgetting to enclose a text string within a set of quotation marks. A good code editor will highlight syntax errors for you, saving you the trouble of running the code in your browser and discovering the mistake there.

The following code contains two syntax errors. The first is that the keyword `function` is written as `Function` and the second is the lack of a closing brace for the command block:

```
Function sayHello() {
   let message = "Hello World";
   window.alert(message);
```

When this code is loaded by the browser, an error message like the one shown in **Figure 4-1** is generated by the browser debugging console. In this figure, the browser is the Google Chrome browser.

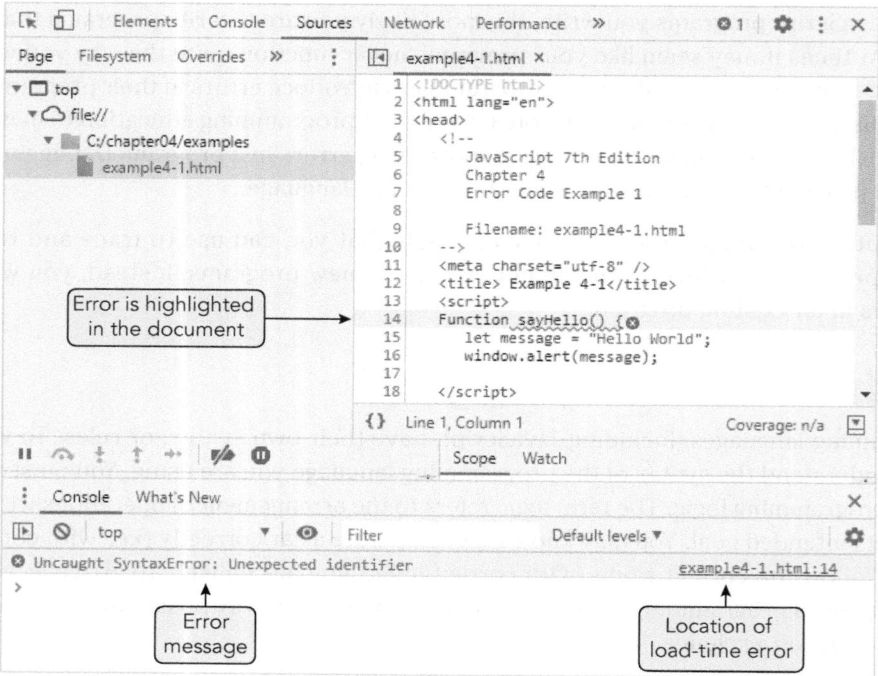

Figure 4-1 Load-time error viewed in the Chrome browser console

The console highlights the error within the code, provides the line number, and offers a brief description of what might have caused the error. The message `Uncaught SyntaxError: Unexpected identifier` tells the programmer that there is a syntax error within the statement `Function sayHello()`. Notice, however, that the console says nothing about the syntax error in omitting the closing brace. When the debugger encounters a syntax error, it stops processing the code so that any subsequent errors are not reported. In fixing a syntax error, you might find that fixing one error leads you further down the code to the next error.

Runtime Errors

When the interpreter loads the script without finding any syntax errors, it will next attempt to run the code. At this point, a runtime error may appear, which is an error that occurs when the interpreter is unable to run the code. Runtime errors may manifest themselves for several reasons such as attempting to reference a function or variable that has not been declared, using an undefined value in an expression, or performing an illegal mathematical operation such as calculating the square root of a negative number.

The following code contains two runtime errors that will prevent the code from running successfully:

```
function defineVariables() {
   let pct = 25;    // percent value
   let amt = 1600; // amount value
}

function calculatePercent() {
   let result = amt * pct/100;
   document.write("<p>" + pct + "% of " + amt + " is: ");
   document.write(result + "</p>");
}

defineVariables();
calculatePercent();
```

The interpreter does not report an error when it loads the program because there are no problems with the syntax, but it will report a runtime error when it calls the `calculatePercent()` function as shown in **Figure 4-2**.

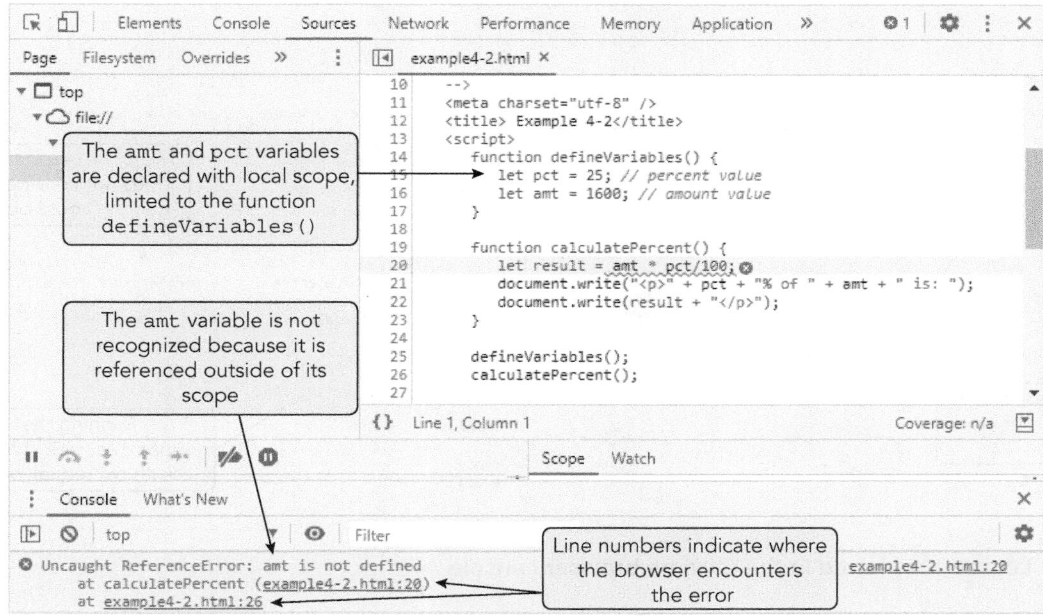

Figure 4-2 Runtime error viewed in the Chrome browser console

The runtime error is due to the `pct` and `amt` variables being declared within the `defineVariables()` function and thus with scope limited to that function. Attempts to reference those variables outside of that scope caused the error. The console only reports the error with the `amt` variable, because the browser stops running the program at the first runtime error. This particular runtime error manifests in two locations. The error on line 20 occurs when the interpreter tries to calculate the value of the `result` variable using the unrecognized `amt` variable. The error on line 26 occurs when the `calcPercent()` function is called and fails. From the line numbers you can trace an error as it propagates during the running of the program. It is not unusual for a single error to result in multiple error locations.

Logic Errors

The third type of error, a logic error, is a flaw in a program's design that prevents the program from reaching its intended goal. There is nothing wrong with the syntax or with the statements themselves; the result is simply wrong.

Logic errors can result from performing essential steps in the wrong order. When you do the laundry, you sort, then wash, then dry, and finally fold your clothes. A logic error in which you fold, sort, dry, and then wash the clothes would leave you with a pile of wet, unsorted, and unfolded laundry! Or the problem might come from missing an important step, such as forgetting the laundry detergent, leaving you with dirty clothes. Or the problem might lie in misinterpreting the data involved. If you accidently mix reds and whites in the sorting step, you could end with a pink mess.

The following function is correct in its syntax and structure, but will nevertheless not work correctly due to an error in logic. Can you spot the mistake?

```
function compareValues(a, b) {
   if (a > b) {
      window.alert(a + " is greater than " + b);
   } else {
      window.alert(a + " is less than " + b);
   }
}
```

The mistake is that there are three possible outcomes: `a` could be greater than `b`, `a` could be less than `b`, or `a` could be equal to `b`. That third possibility, never tested by the code, results in the nonsensical statement shown in **Figure 4-3**.

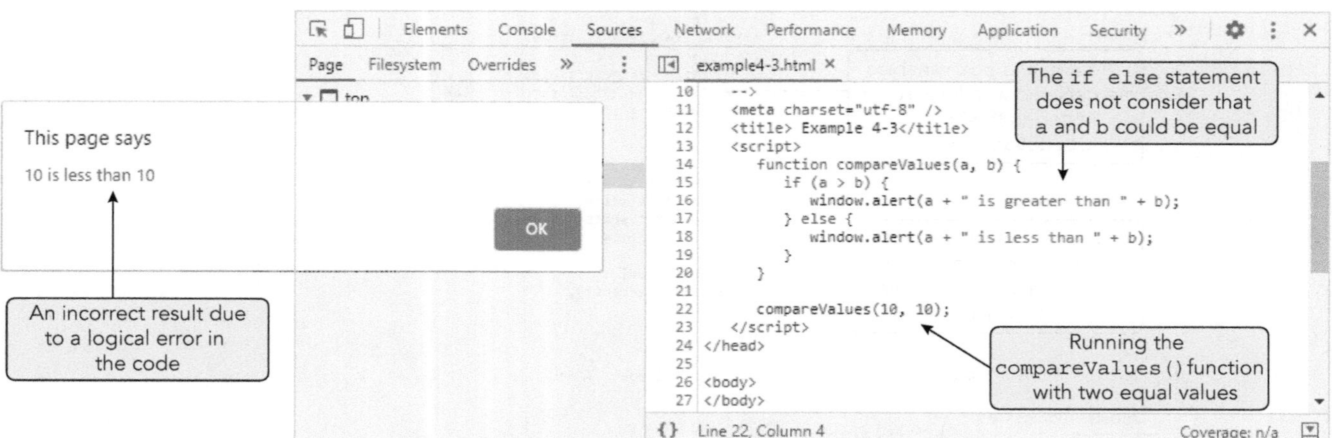

Figure 4-3 Logic error viewed in the Chrome browser console

Finding and fixing logic errors is the most difficult part of programming. You must analyze the logic at each step of your code, comparing the results you expected with the results you got. A debugger can provide tools to make that comparison easier, but the analysis must be done by the programmer.

> **Note** You can locate errors in your code using linting, a process that involves sending your code through a third-party program that analyzes and produces a detailed error report. Some of the most popular linting programs for JavaScript are jslint, ESLint, and JSHint. Also, many code editors offer their own set of linting tools.

Starting Debugging with the Browser Console

You have been hired by Tuba Farm Equipment, located in Fargo, North Dakota, to finalize a web application that selects tractor models based on the acreage to be cultivated, the crop to be planted, the months of work, and the preferred fuel source. The web application has been coded but does not work. You will use debugging techniques to identify and fix the bugs in the program, so it functions as designed. **Figure 4-4** shows how the completed page should perform.

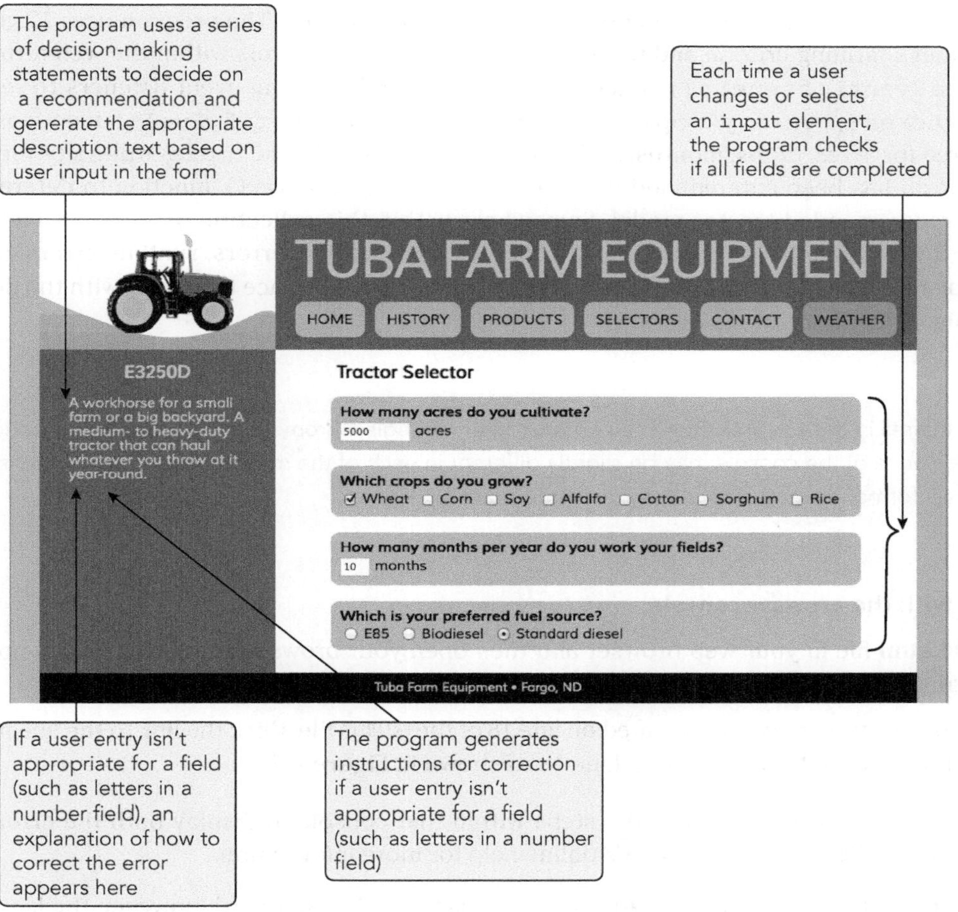

Figure 4-4 Tuba Farm Equipment page

Start your work on fixing this program by opening the page in its current state and viewing the errors.

To open the Tuba Farm Equipment page:

1. Go to the js04 ▶ chapter folder of your data files.
2. Use your code editor to open the **js04_txt.html** and **js04_txt.js** files and enter your name and the date in the comment section of each file.
3. Return to the **js04.html** file in your code editor. Scroll through the document to familiarize yourself with its content. The `article` element contains the form, and the `aside` element contains empty `h2` and `p` elements where the program will display its tractor recommendation.
4. Open the **js04.html** file in your browser, and then in the first text box (with the label "acres"), type your first name. Because the program expects a number in this box, your entry of text should generate an error. However, nothing happens when you type text in the box.
5. Complete the form as follows: Enter **5000** in the acres input box, click the **Wheat** checkbox to select it as a crop to grow, enter **10** in the months input box, and click the **Standard diesel** option button as the preferred fuel source.

   Notice that even though you have completed the form correctly, no recommendation for a tractor model appears in the left sidebar. The program is not working as intended because of one or more errors within the code.
6. Return to the **js04.js** file in your code editor and take some time to examine the contents of the file.

The program code in the js04.js file involves multiple variables and functions. The program uses 12 global variables to record the customer's farming criteria and to reference elements and controls within the web form. The file also contains the `createEventListeners()` function for defining and applying event listeners to respond to user actions, the `verifyAcres()`, `verifyCrops()`, `verifyMonths()`, and `verifyFuel()` functions to verify that correct data is entered for acres, crops, months, and fuel values, the `testFormCompleteness()` function to verify that all data in the form has been entered, and the `createRecommendation()` function to determine and write information on the recommended tractor model. Somewhere within this collection of variables and functions are errors that prevent the program from running. Whether those are load-time errors, runtime errors, logic errors, or some combination of all three is for the programmer to determine. The best place to start is with the debugging tools in the browser's console.

Note | The figures in this chapter show the contents of the Google Chrome browser console. Although the appearance of the console may be slightly different in each of the major browsers, they all display the same information in roughly the same layout.

To start debugging with the browser console:

1. Reload the **js04.html** file in your web browser and then open your browser's console. You do not, at this time, have to enter any data in the web form.
2. The console reports one syntax error located on line 18 of the js04.js file. Click the link to the line number to view the contents of that file and scroll down to Line 18 as shown in **Figure 4-5**.

   If you are using a different browser, use the steps within that console to display both the error message and content of the js04.js file. See your browser's online help for more information.

Line 17 is supposed to declare the `fuelComplete` variable using the `let` keyword; however, the keyword has been mistyped as `et`. Correct this syntax error now and continue the debugging process.

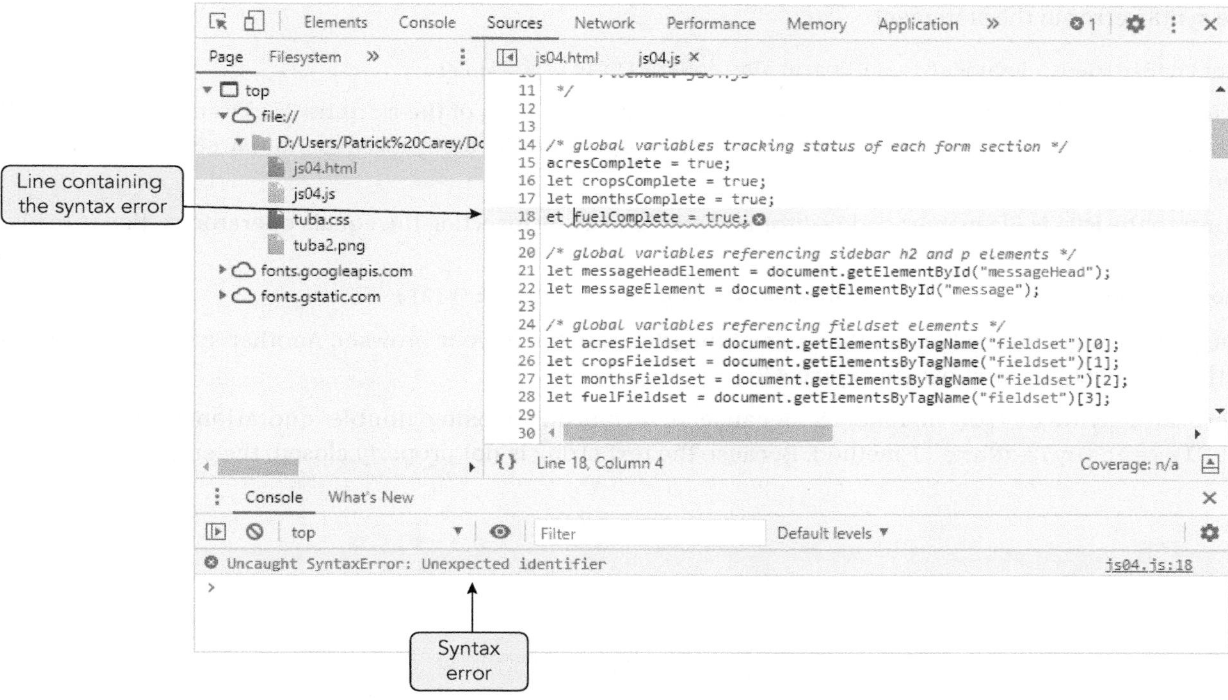

Figure 4-5 Syntax error in the js04.js file

To correct the syntax error:

1. Go to the **js04.js** file in your code editor and scroll down Line 17 declaring the `fuelComplete` variable.
2. Edit the line so that it reads as follows:

```
let fuelComplete = true;
```

3. Save your changes to the file and then reload the **js04.html** file in your browser (you do not have to close the console.) As shown in **Figure 4-6**, another syntax error is discovered in Line 27.

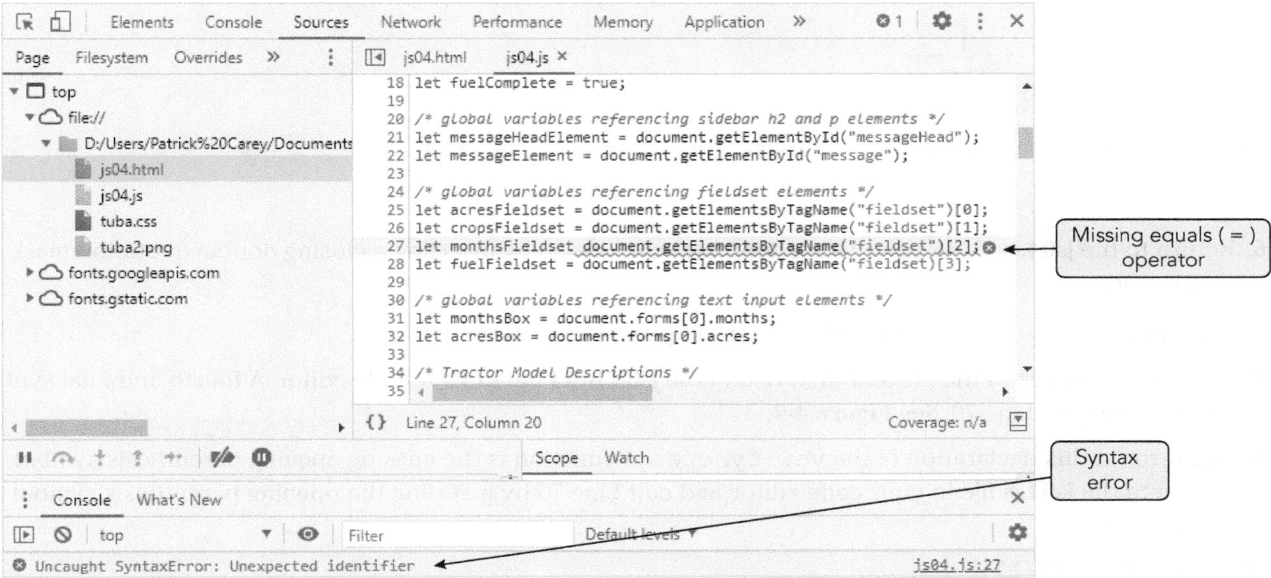

Figure 4-6 Syntax error declaring a variable

The syntax error in the statement

```
let monthsFieldset document.getElementsByTagName("fieldset")[2];
```

occurs because there is no equals symbol between the declaration of the `monthsFieldset` variable and the reference to the HTML collection object. Without that operator, the interpreter cannot parse the statement and reports an error.

4. Return to the **js04.js** file in your code editor and edit Line 27 by inserting the equals operator, so that it reads as follows:

```
let monthsFieldset = document.getElementsByTagName("fieldset")[2];
```

5. Save your changes to the file and then reload the **js04.html** file in your browser. Another syntax error appears on the very next line as shown in **Figure 4-7**.

   There is a syntax error in Line 28 because of a missing closing double quotation mark within the `getElementsByTagName()` method. Because the text string is not properly closed, the entire line is invalid.

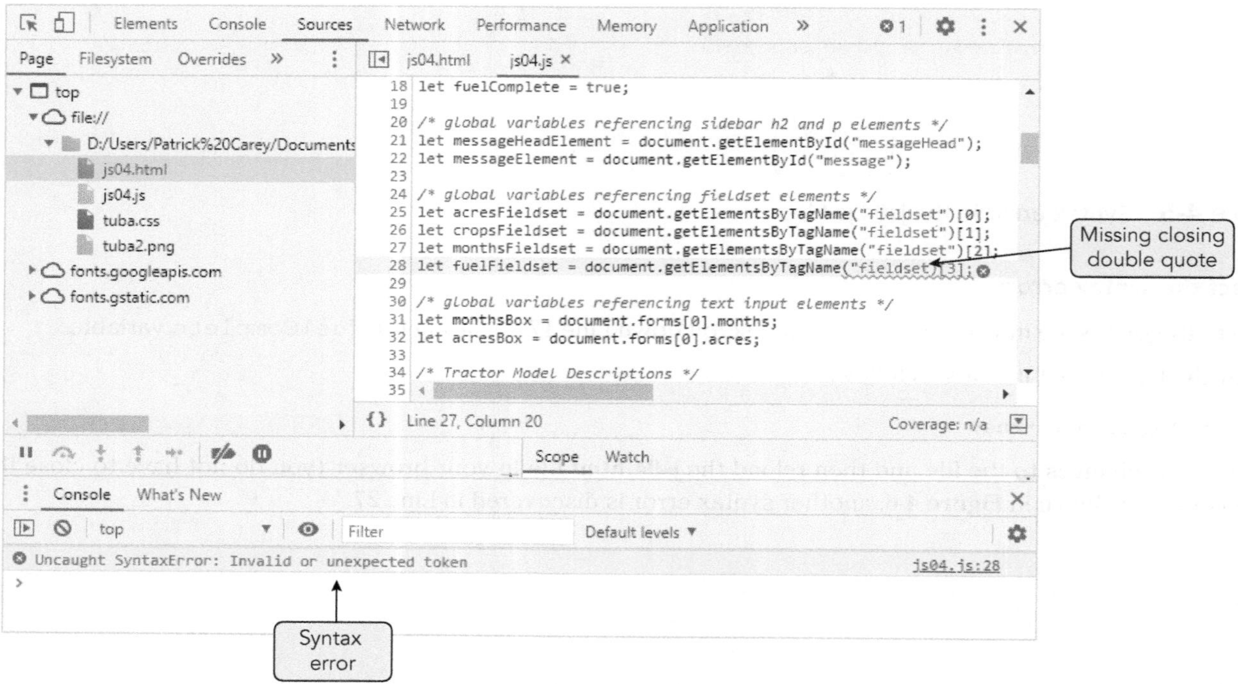

Figure 4-7 Syntax error with the `getElementsByTagName()` method

6. Return to the **js04.js** file in your code editor and edit Line 28 by inserting a closing double quotation mark so that it reads:

```
let fuelFieldset = document.getElementsByTagName("fieldset")[3];
```

7. Save your changes to the file and then reload the **js04.html** file in your code editor. A fourth and final syntax error appears on Line 70. See **Figure 4-8**.

8. The error in this declaration of the `verifyAcres()` function is the missing opening parenthesis symbol, `(`. Return to the **js04.js** file in your code editor and edit Line 70 by inserting the opening parenthesis symbol so that it reads:

```
function verifyAcres() {
```

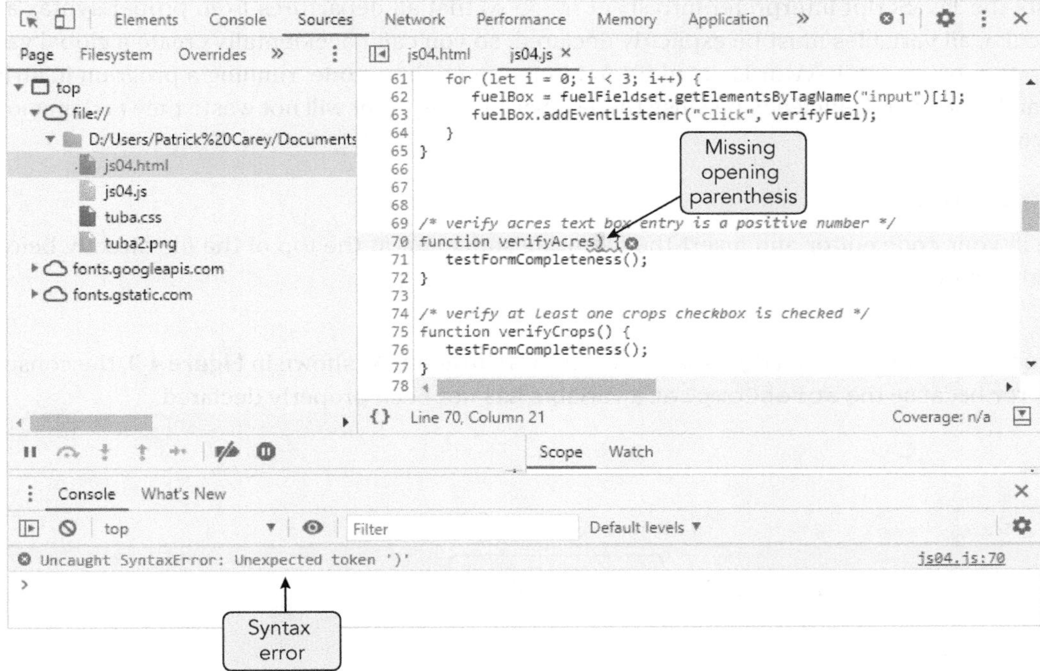

Figure 4-8 Syntax error declaring a function

9. Save your changes to the file and then reload the **js04.html** file in your browser. You should see no more syntax errors in the browser console.

You have located all the syntax errors in the program, but is the code properly written? To answer that question, you will set up the browser to strictly interpret the code.

> **Note** You can use the console to write commands that will be executed as the program is paused. The commands will exist in memory only during the current session. Any permanent commands should be added directly to the JavaScript file and saved in your code editor.

Running Javascript in Strict Mode

JavaScript interpreters are very forgiving of lapses in syntax and structure. You can create a variable without using the `let`, `var`, or `const` keywords. If you forget to end a statement with the semicolon, your program will most likely still run without fail. Though this may sound like an advantage for beginning programmers, many developers disapprove of the feature because it can lead to a casualness in coding that makes such errors more likely to occur with future programs.

Most languages, like C++ and Java, require strict adherence to syntax and will reject programs that depart from syntax rules in even the smallest way. To enforce that level of scrutiny in JavaScript, add the following text string to the beginning of the code:

```
"use strict";
```

Adding this statement puts the JavaScript interpreter into strict mode so that all departures from proper syntax are flagged as errors. In particular, all variables must be explicitly declared, so you can't accidentally create a global variable by omitting the `let`, `var`, or `const` keywords. In addition to creating tighter code, running a program in strict mode increases the program's speed and efficiency because the JavaScript interpreter will not waste time and memory resolving poorly written code.

To test the page under strict mode:

1. Go to the **js04.js** file in your code editor and insert the following statement at the top of the file directly before the commented head section.

```
"use strict";
```

2. Save your changes to the file and then reload **js04.html** in your web browser. As shown in **Figure 4-9**, the console flags Line 16 as an error because the `acresComplete` variable has not been properly declared.

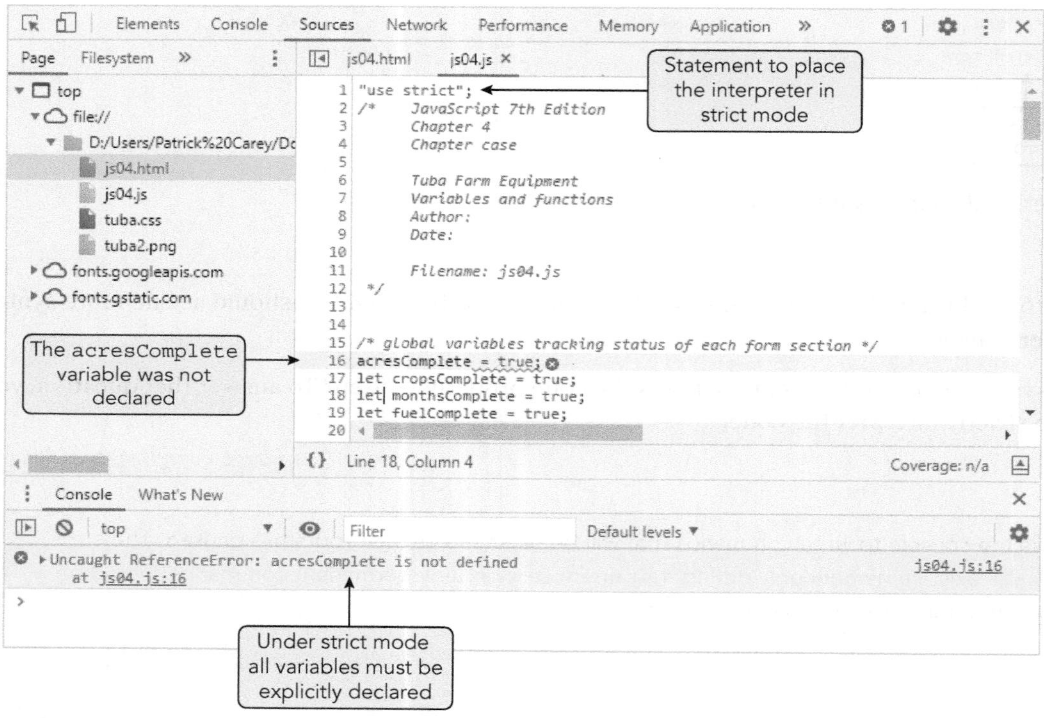

Figure 4-9 Syntax error under strict mode

3. Return to the **js04.js** file in your code editor. Scroll down and change the statement `acresComplete = true;` to

```
let acresComplete = true;
```

4. Save your changes to the file and then reload the **js04.html** file in your browser. Verify that no errors are reported in the code.
5. Close the browser console.

The `"use strict";` statement can be placed anywhere within your code. If you want to apply strict mode only to code within a function, add the statement as the first line in that function's command block. The JavaScript interpreter will interpret the function's code strictly and code elsewhere in your program less strictly.

Common Mistakes

Interpreting Error Messages

As you debug your programs, you might find the debugger's error messages difficult to interpret. Here are some error messages and their common sources:

- **Uncaught TypeError: Cannot Read Property**—The object, such as a variable or function, has not yet been defined and thus has no properties associated with it.
- **TypeError: 'undefined' Is Not an Object**—The object has not yet been defined or initialized.
- **TypeError: null is Not an Object**—A property or method is being applied to a null object that has not been created or initialized.
- **TypeError: Object doesn't support property**—A property or method either doesn't exist (perhaps because of a typing error) or is not associated with the object.
- **Uncaught TypeError: Cannot set property**—A variable has an undefined value and thus cannot be used to set or return a property value.
- **ReferenceError: Object is Not Defined**—A variable is being referenced outside of its scope.

Quick Check 1

1. Describe the three types of program errors.
2. What is the error in the following code and what type of error is it?

```
document.writ("Hello World");
```

3. What is the error in the following code and what type of error is it?

```
let firstValue = 10;
let secondValue = 20;
let result = firstvalue + secondValue;
```

4. If the browser console reports a single syntax error, does that mean there is only one syntax error in the code?

Tracing Errors to Their Source

Although error and warning messages will help you catch basic syntax errors, some syntax errors are difficult to pinpoint. For example, if you have a deeply nested set of control structures and one of the control structures is missing a closing brace, the syntax error may not be able to tell you exactly which control structure is malformed. This section covers a few basic techniques for debugging JavaScript.

Tracing Errors with the `window.alert()` Method

If you are unable to locate a bug in your program by using error messages, or if you suspect a logic error (which does not generate error messages), then you must trace your code. Tracing is the examination of individual statements in an executing program. For example, the following function calculates weekly net pay by adjusting the gross pay for taxes and withholdings. There are no syntax errors, but the function returns a value of $171,072 instead of the correct value, $485.

```
function calculatePay() {
   let payRate = 15; numHours = 40;
   let grossPay = payRate * numHours;
   let federalTaxes = grossPay * 0.07;
   let stateTaxes = grossPay * 0.05;
```

```
        let socialSecurity = grossPay * 0.06;
        let medicare = grossPay * 0.015;
        let netPay = grossPay - federalTaxes;
        netPay -= stateTaxes;
        netPay *= socialSecurity;
        netPay *= medicare;
        return netPay;
    }
```

The function obviously contains one or more logic errors. One method of tracing the errors is to display alert boxes, using the `window.alert()` method at different points in the code, showing partial results of the function. Each time the JavaScript interpreter encounters the `window.alert()` method, it pauses the program to display contents of the alert box to the user. The important goal of this technique is to take a long and complex program and break it into discrete sections of a few lines, which you can then examine in detail to discover the error. Once you have confirmed that one section of the code is working correctly, you can remove the alert boxes in that section and focus on other sections.

Figure 4-10 shows the revised code along with three alert boxes that display partial calculations during the running of the program.

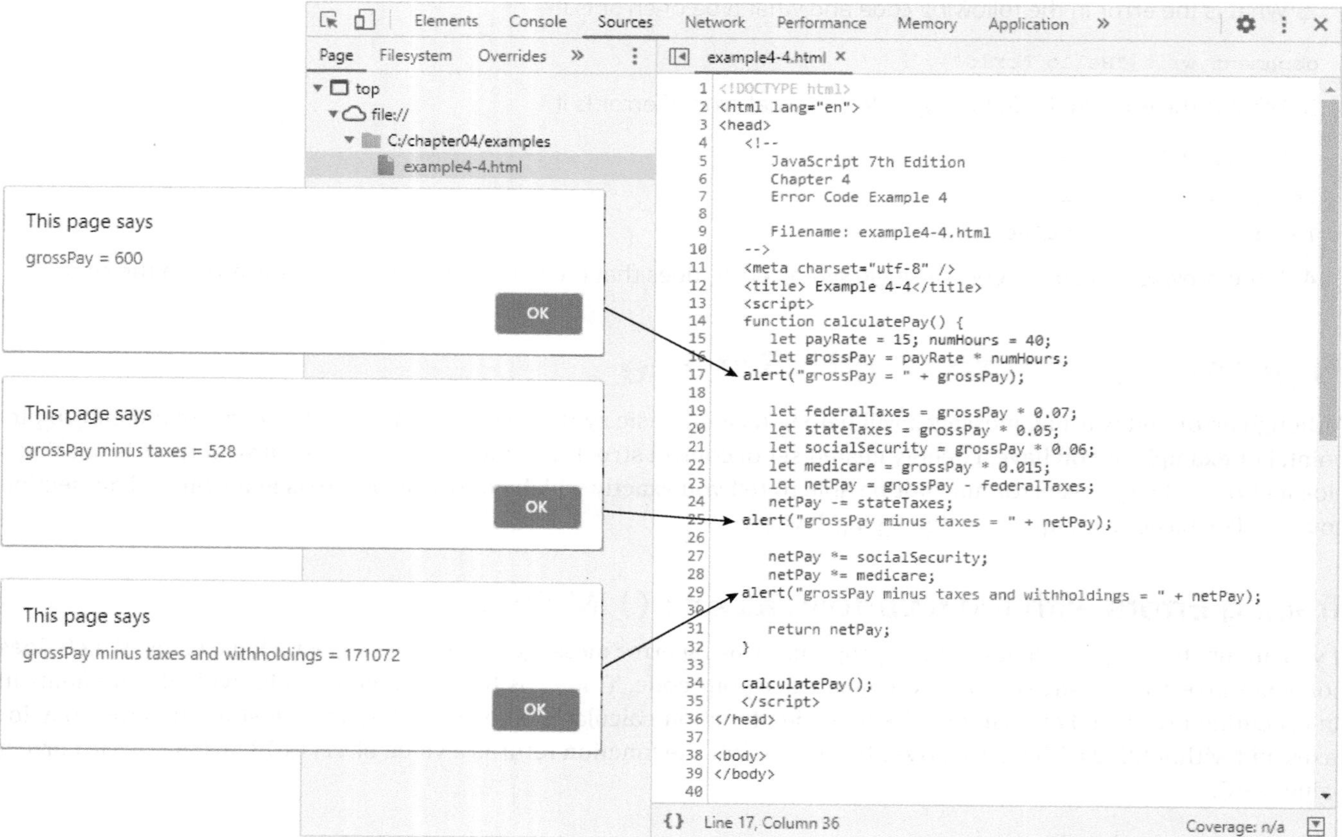

Figure 4-10 Using alert boxes to trace program values

> **Note** When you use the alert box approach, include the variable name alongside the variable values, so you will be able to interpret the results of your code.

Based on the alert boxes, you determine that the payment values are reasonable through the calculation of gross pay and gross pay after subtracting taxes. It is only in the third alert box, after subtracting withholding for Social Security and Medicare, that payment values are unreasonable. Therefore, the error must lie with the following lines of code:

```
netPay *= socialSecurity;
netPay *= medicare;
```

The logic error is that the multiplication assignment operator (`*=`) was mistakenly used to calculate the net pay after withholding rather than the subtraction operator (`-=`). Once that mistake is corrected, the function will return the correct result. Note that when adding statements such as `window.alert()` to trace your code, it is helpful to place them at a different level of indentation to clearly distinguish them from the actual program and make it easier to remove them after debugging.

You have already removed the syntax errors from the Tuba Farm Equipment page. Now you will explore whether there are logic errors in the code.

To start debugging with the browser console:

1. If necessary, load the **js04.html** file in your web browser.
2. Enter **5** in the acres input box. Check the **Wheat** check box, enter **8** in the months input box, and then click the **E85** option button for the preferred fuel choice. See **Figure 4-11**.

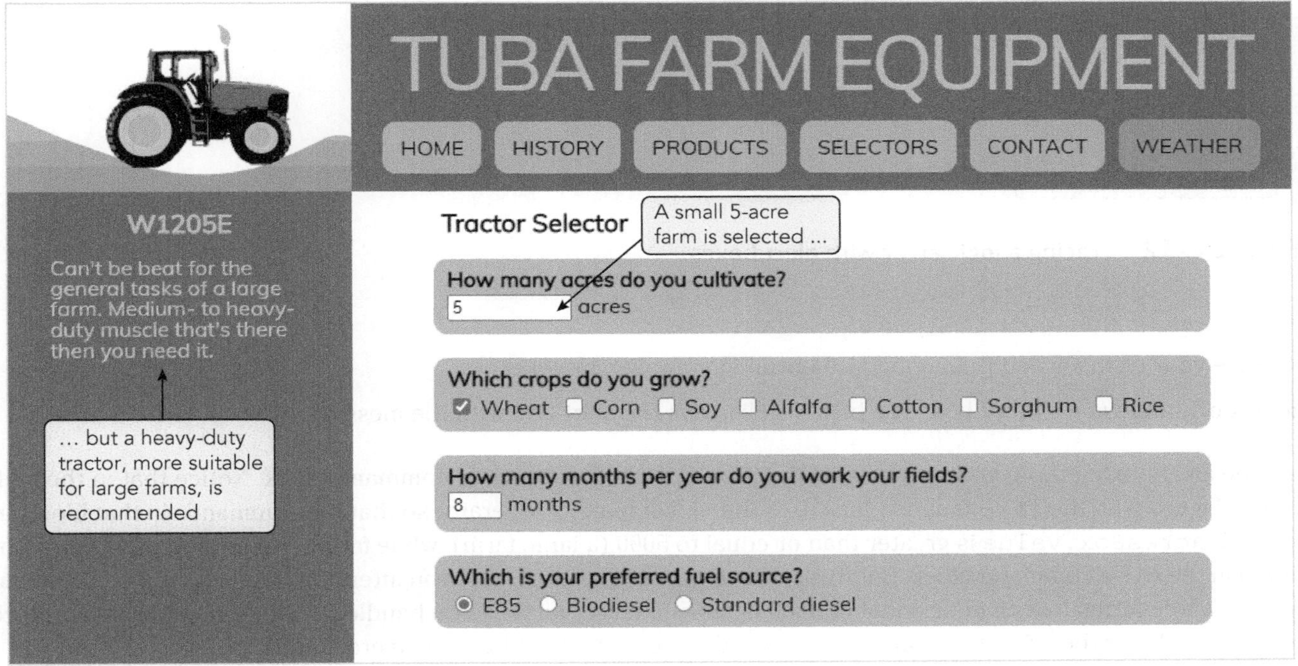

Figure 4-11 Logic error in selecting a tractor model

The web page recommends the W1205E tractor, but that model is best suited for larger farms. A 5-acre farm is not considered large, so that must be due to a logic error in the conditional statements that select one model over another. Use the alert box method to trace the actions of the conditional statement used for your selections.

To trace conditional statements with alert boxes:

1. Return to the **js04.js** file in your code editor and scroll down to the `createRecommendation()` function.
2. Directly after the `if (acresBox.value >= 5000)` statement, insert the following command to display an alert box if the program reaches this first condition in the `if` statement:

```
window.alert("First if block for " + acresBox.value + " acres");
```

3. Scroll down to the `} else { // more than 5000 acres` statement and directly below that `else` clause, insert the following command:

```
window.alert("Else block for " + acresBox.value + " acres");
```

Figure 4-12 shows the newly added code in the file.

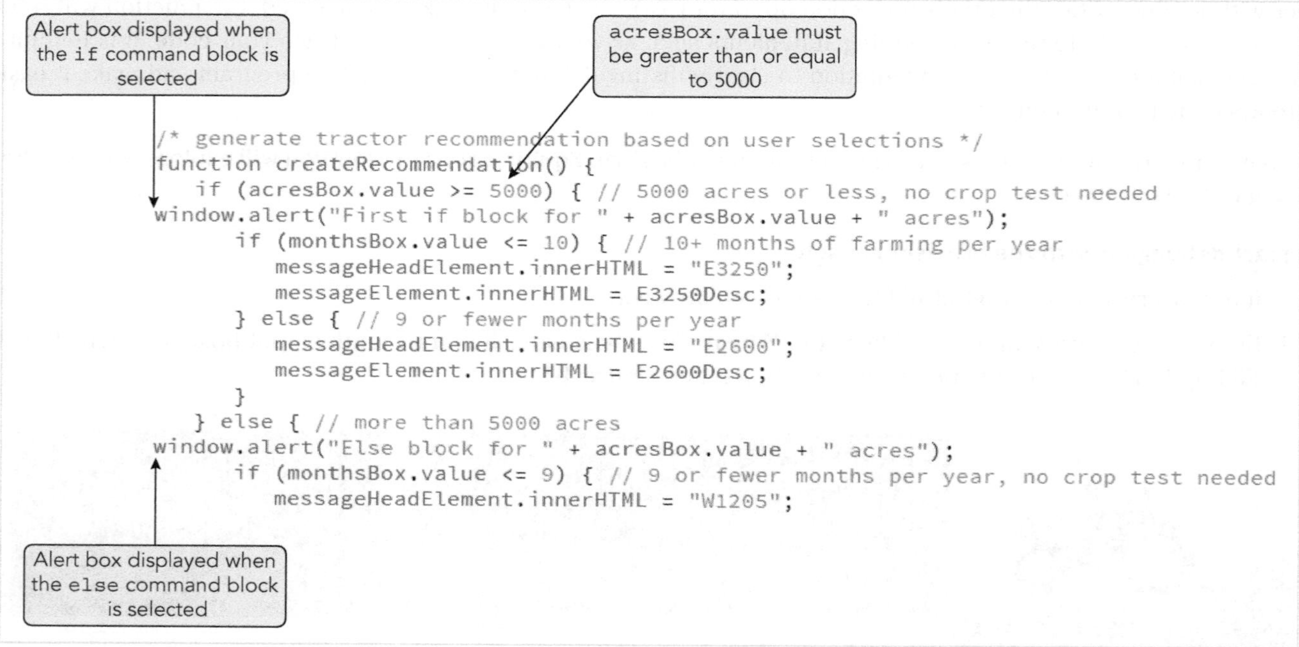

Alert box displayed when the `if` command block is selected

`acresBox.value` must be greater than or equal to 5000

```
/* generate tractor recommendation based on user selections */
function createRecommendation() {
   if (acresBox.value >= 5000) { // 5000 acres or less, no crop test needed
window.alert("First if block for " + acresBox.value + " acres");
      if (monthsBox.value <= 10) { // 10+ months of farming per year
         messageHeadElement.innerHTML = "E3250";
         messageElement.innerHTML = E3250Desc;
      } else { // 9 or fewer months per year
         messageHeadElement.innerHTML = "E2600";
         messageElement.innerHTML = E2600Desc;
      }
   } else { // more than 5000 acres
window.alert("Else block for " + acresBox.value + " acres");
      if (monthsBox.value <= 9) { // 9 or fewer months per year, no crop test needed
         messageHeadElement.innerHTML = "W1205";
```

Alert box displayed when the `else` command block is selected

Figure 4-12 Tracing a logic error with alert boxes

4. Save your changes and then reload **js04.html** in your web browser.
5. Type **5** in the acres input box. The browser displays the alert box with the message “Else block for 5 acres”.

Using the alert box method, you have traced the program flow to the `else` command block. Notice that in the code shown in Figure 4-12, the `if` command block uses the >= comparison operator so that the commands in that block are only run if `acresBox.value` is greater than or equal to 5000 (a large farm), while farms smaller than 5000 acres are handled in the `else` command block. But this is exactly the opposite of what you intended. You want the `if` command block to handle farms less than or equal to 5000 acres and larger farms to be handled in the `else` command block. Modify the code for the `if else` statement now and remove the alert boxes you created.

To fix the logic error in the `if else` statement:

1. Return to the **js04.js** file in your code editor and go to the `createRecommendation()` function.
2. Change the condition in the `if` statement from `acresBox.value >= 5000` to the following:

```
acresBox.value <= 5000
```

3. Remove the statements displaying the alert boxes within the `if` condition and the `else` clause.
4. Save your changes to the file.
5. Reload **js04.html** in your web browser.
6. Type **5** in the acres box and verify that the page now recommends the E3250D tractor, a model more suitable for small farms or big backyards (see **Figure 4-13**).

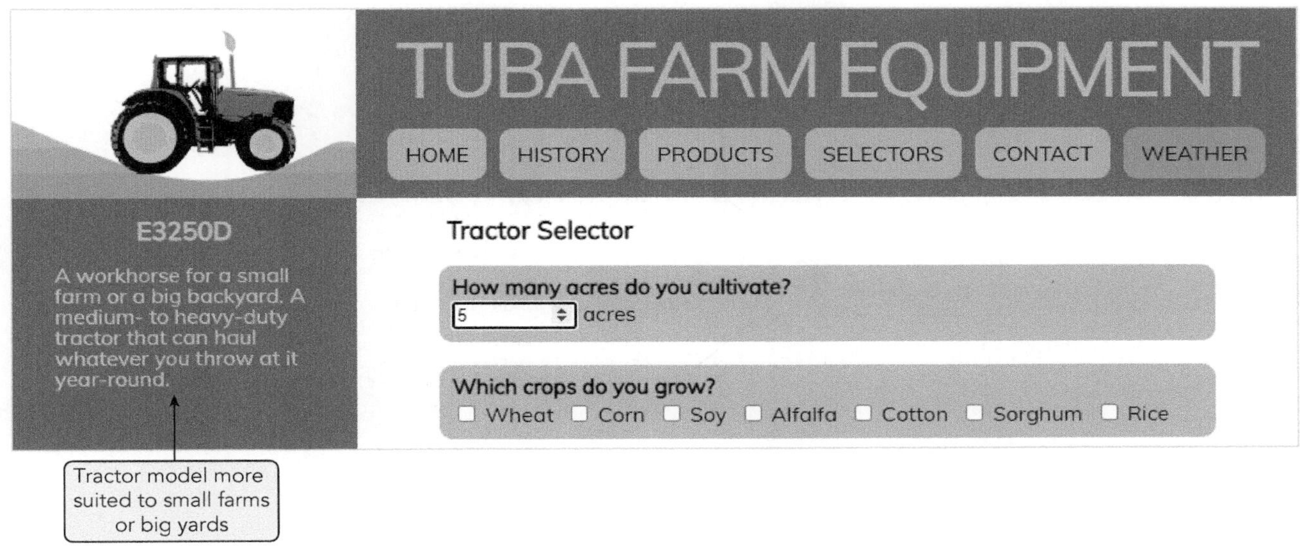

Figure 4-13 Selecting a tractor model for a small farm

Using alert boxes to trace the progress of your program is a fast and easy approach to debugging, but there are several limitations with this method:

- Alert boxes interfere with the normal operation of the code and must be deleted after their use.
- Alert boxes do not perform well in tracing a long sequence of operations. Imagine displaying an alert box for each iteration in a `for` loop that goes through hundreds of iterations.
- You cannot compare the contents of one alert box with subsequent boxes, because closing the alert box removes it from the browser window.

A better alternative to alert boxes is the console log.

Tracing Errors with the Console Log

As your program runs, you can trace the changing values in the program by writing or logging those values in the console log with the following method:

```
console.log(text)
```

where *text* is a text string that will be written into the console, which can then be viewed within the debugger. **Figure 4-14** shows how to use the console log to locate the error in the program that incorrectly calculates take-home pay after adjusting the gross pay for taxes and other withholdings.

Compared to the tracing method using alert boxes shown earlier in Figure 4-12, the console log approach is much cleaner. It does not impede the operation of the program with a series of distracting alert boxes and you can easily view the progression of values displayed in the log, comparing the payment total at different stages in the calculation. The console includes a link to each location of a `console.log` method, so you can easily jump to that location in the code, viewing the program in more detail. As before, it is obvious that the logic error had to occur in the commands that adjusted pay for Social Security and Medicare withholdings.

Note Because the console log is hidden in the debugger user, you can leave the `console.log` commands in your program; however you might want to remove them to speed up the operation of your code, especially if your app involves processing hundreds or thousands of statements.

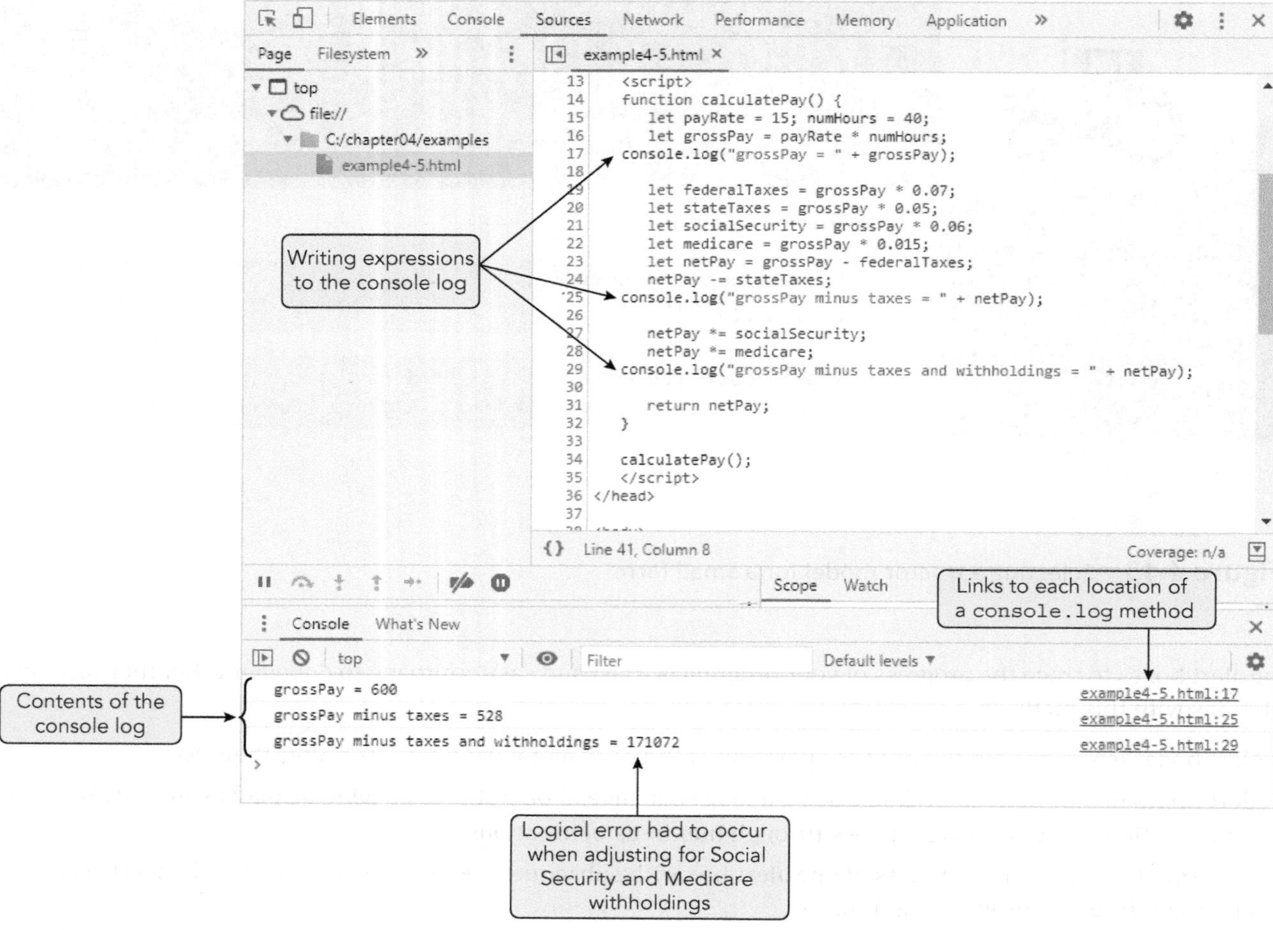

Figure 4-14 Using the console log to trace program values

You continue to explore the operations of the tractor recommendations page. Determine the type of tractor that would be recommended for 8 months of work in a 5-acre wheat field.

To view the recommended tractor for 8 months of work:

1. Reload the **js04.html** file in your web browser.
2. Enter **5** in the acres box, check the **Wheat** checkbox, and enter **8** in the months box to indicate the field will be worked on for eight months. As shown in **Figure 4-15**, the page recommends the E3250E tractor.

The E3250E tractor does not match the customer's specifications, recommending a year-round tractor for heavy-duty use when a medium-duty tractor might be a better match. Once again, there appears to be a logic error in the program code. Use the console log to trace the error to its source.

To trace the error with the console log:

1. Return to the **js04.js** file in your code editor and scroll down to the `createRecommendation()` function.
2. Within the nested `if` statement, directly below the statement `messageElement.innerHTML = E3250Desc;` add the following statement to write the month value to the console log:

```
console.log("Nested if: " + monthsBox.value + " months");
```

3. Directly below the statement `messageElement.innerHTML = E2600Desc;` within the nested `else` statement, insert the following command:

```
console.log("Nested else: " + monthsBox.value + " months");
```

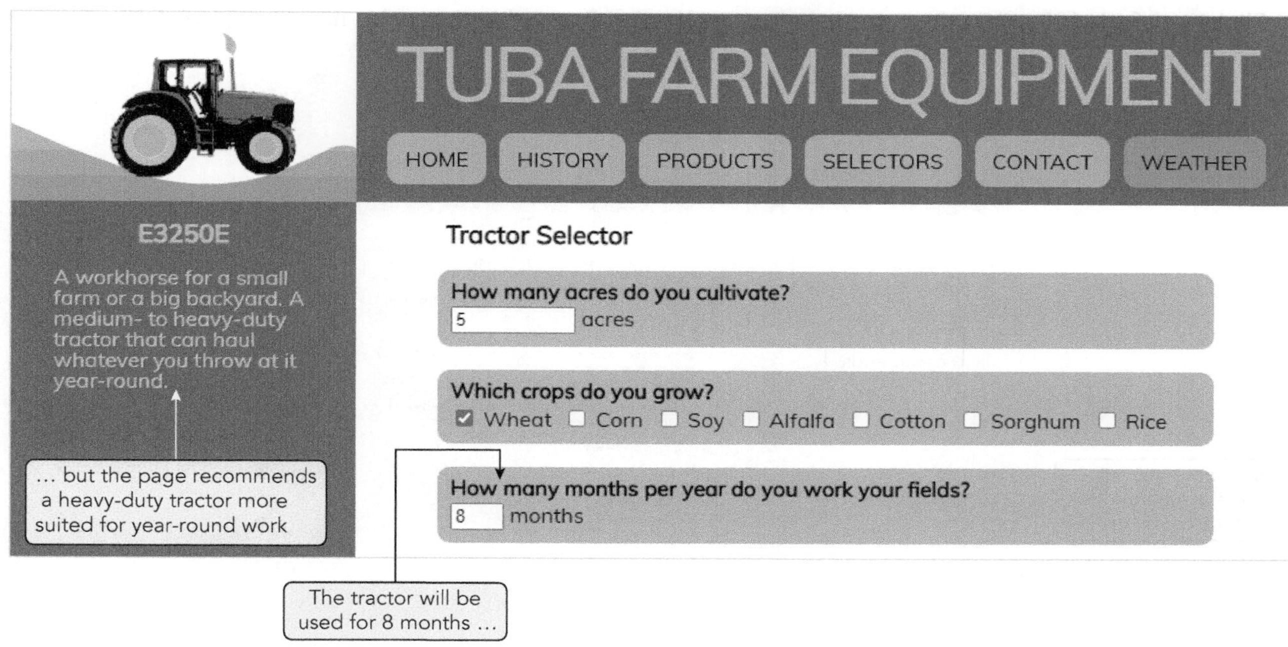

Figure 4-15 Logic error in selecting a tractor model for the number of months

Figure 4-16 highlights the revised code in the file.

`monthsBox.value` must be less than or equal to 10

```
/* generate tractor recommendation based on user selections */
function createRecommendation() {
   if (acresBox.value <= 5000) { // 5000 acres or less, no crop test needed
      if (monthsBox.value <= 10) { // 10+ months of farming per year
         messageHeadElement.innerHTML = "E3250";
         messageElement.innerHTML = E3250Desc;
console.log("Nested if: " + monthsBox.value + " months");
      } else { // 9 or fewer months per year
         messageHeadElement.innerHTML = "E2600";
         messageElement.innerHTML = E2600Desc;
console.log("Nested else: " + monthsBox.value + " months");
      }
   } else { // more than 5000 acres
```

Write to the console when the `if` command block is selected

Write to the console when the `else` command block is selected

Figure 4-16 Tracing a logic error with the console log

4. Save your changes to the file and then reload **js04.html** in your web browser.
5. Open your browser's debugging console and then click **Sources** from the Debugger menu at the top of the pane to view the source and console. If you do not see the console, press the **Esc** key to display it or click the ⋮ character in the upper-right of the Developer pane and click **Show console drawer**.
6. Type **5** in the acres box of the web page. The program is set up to run the `createRecommendation()` function whenever data is input into the form. In this case, the console log displays a message with a null value for months, because you have not entered that information yet.
7. Click the **Wheat** checkbox and note that another message is sent to the console as the `createRecommendation()` function is once again run in response to the click event.
8. Type **12** in the months box. Notice that with the input of each keystroke, another message is logged to the console.

9. Click the **js04.js:107** link in the console log to display that line within the js04.js file. See **Figure 4-17**.

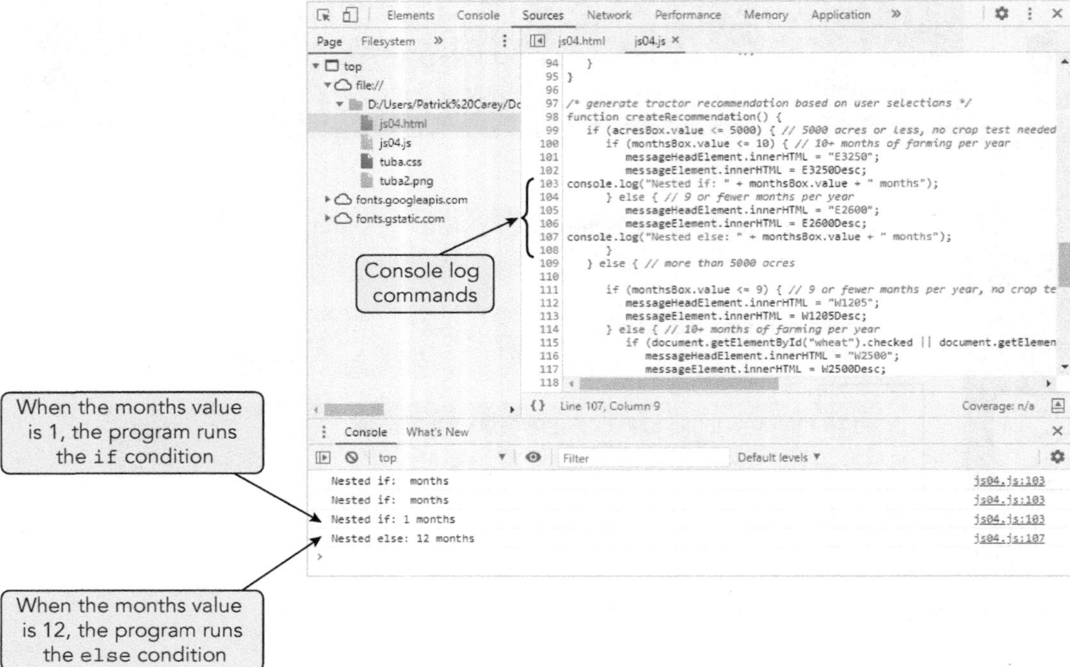
Console log commands
When the months value is 1, the program runs the if condition
When the months value is 12, the program runs the else condition
Nested if: months
Nested if: months
Nested if: 1 months
Nested else: 12 months
js04.js:103
js04.js:107
Line 107, Column 9

Figure 4-17 Console log entries

Depending on your browser and its configuration, your browser window might not exactly match that shown in Figure 4-17.

10. Close the console pane in your browser.

From the console log you know that the `if` condition is run when the months value is 1 and the `else` condition is selected when the months value is 12. However, this is just the opposite of what the Tuba Farm Equipment page wants. The `if` statement should be run when the months value is 10 or greater and the `else` statement should be run for month values less than 10. Modify the program code to fix this error and remove the `console.log` commands.

To fix the logic error in the `if else` statement:

1. Return to the **js04.js** file in your code editor and go to the `createRecommendation()` function.
2. Change the nested if statement that reads `if (monthsBox.value <= 10) {` to:

```
if (monthsBox.value >= 10) {
```

3. Remove the two `console.log` commands from the program and then save your changes.
4. Reload the **js04.html** file in your browser and enter **5** in the acres box, click the **Wheat** checkbox, and enter **8** in the months box. The page recommends the E2600D tractor, a medium-duty model geared towards small farms that do not need a year-round tractor.

You have corrected another logic error found in the code.

> **Note**
>
> When using the `console.log()` method to trace bugs, it can be helpful to use a driver program, which is a simplified, temporary program that is used for testing functions and other code. A driver program is simply a JavaScript program that contains only the code you are testing. Driver programs do not have to be elaborate; they can be as simple as a single function you are testing. This technique allows you to isolate and test an individual function without having to worry about web page elements, event handlers, global variables, and other code that complete your program's purpose.

Using Comments to Locate Bugs

Another method of locating bugs in a JavaScript program is identifying lines that may be causing problems and transforming them into comments by adding // to the start of each line or enclosing a block of statements within the /* and */ characters. This process, known as commenting out code, allows you to isolate a particular statement or set of statements that may be causing an error. If there are no errors after you have commented out a section, you will know that the error in your code lies within that section. Proceeding with this technique, you can take a long and complicated program and break it down into smaller sections that merit more focused attention.

In the following code, several lines have been commented out that adjust the net pay value for state taxes, Social Security, and Medicare:

```
function calculatePay() {
   let payRate = 15; numHours = 40;
   let grossPay = payRate * numHours;
   let federalTaxes = grossPay * 0.07;
   let stateTaxes = grossPay * 0.05;
   let socialSecurity = grossPay * 0.06;
   let medicare = grossPay * 0.015;
   let netPay = grossPay - federalTaxes;
/*
   netPay -= stateTaxes;
   netPay *= socialSecurity;
   netPay *= medicare;
*/
   return netPay;
}
```

If the function returns an error-free value without those lines, you can narrow the comment section until you uncomment the line or lines that are causing the error. At that point you can focus your attention on those few lines to find the error preventing your code from running correctly.

Programming Concepts | Dependencies

Any program longer than a handful of lines includes statements that depend on the successful execution of other statements or functions. These relationships, known as dependencies, add an extra layer of complexity to debugging. An error reported in one function can be the result of an error from a different part of the program. In addition, an error in one part of the code can stop dependent code from executing, preventing you from receiving error messages for the dependent code. After finding and fixing a bug, it is important to test related functionality that worked correctly before the bug fix. In some cases, fixing one bug exposes another, or itself creates another problem, so it is important not to assume that everything that worked before fixing a bug will continue to work after fixing it.

Quick Check 2

1. The `orderCost` variable in a long and elaborate program might be incorrectly calculated. Provide code to display the value of the variable within an alert box.
2. Provide code to write the value of `orderCost` to the console log.
3. What are three reasons to use the console log approach over the alert box approach?
4. Why would you comment out sections of a program that is producing errors?

Tracking Program Flow with Debugging Tools

Examining your code manually with alert boxes or the console log is the first step in debugging. These techniques work fine with smaller programs. However, as a program expands in size and complexity, such errors become more difficult to spot. For instance, you may have several functions that perform calculations and pass the results to other functions for further processing. Attempting to track the logic and flow of the code can be extremely difficult. Browser debuggers provide several tools to trace each line of code, creating a much more efficient method of finding and resolving logic errors.

Accessing your Browser's Debugging Tools

In all the major browsers, these debugging tools are accessible through the same pane that opens with the console. The tools can track and find errors in HTML, CSS, and JavaScript code, gauge a page's performance and response over different connections, and preview the page's appearance for various devices and screen resolutions.

Each browser is slightly different in how it organizes and presents these debugging tools, so you have to spend some time evaluating your browser's debugging environment to fully utilize its features. **Figure 4-18** describes how to access the debugging tools in four major browsers.

BROWSER	KEYBOARD SHORTCUT	MENU STEPS
Google Chrome	SHIFT + CTRL + J (Windows) Option + ⌘ + J (Macintosh)	1. Click the Chrome menu in the upper-right corner 2. Click More tools 3. Click Developer tools 4. Click Sources from the Developer pane
Safari	Option + ⌘ + C	1. Enable the Developer tab by going into the Safari Menu > Preferences window, going to the Advanced tab and selecting Show Develop menu in menu bar checkbox 2. Click the Develop tab in the Safari menu 3. Click Show JavaScript Console 4. Click the Debugger tab
Microsoft Edge	F12 and then click Console from the Developer pane menu	1. Click the Edge menu in the upper-right corner 2. Click More tools 3. Click Developer tools 4. Click Sources from the Developer pane
Firefox	SHIFT + CTRL + J (Windows) Option + ⌘ + J (Macintosh)	1. Click the Firefox menu in the upper-right corner 2. Click Web Developer 3. Click Debugger

Figure 4-18 Accessing browser debuggers

This chapter demonstrates debugging tools within the Chrome browser running on Windows, but the techniques discussed can be applied equally well to Safari, Edge, and Firefox.

To open the Chrome browser debugger:

1. If necessary, reopen the **js04.html** file in your browser.
2. Click the Chrome menu ⋮ in the upper-right corner of the page, click **More tools** and then **Developer tools**.
3. Click **Sources** in the Developer pane.

   The pane itself can be docked with the left, right, or bottom side of the browser window. It can also be floated as its own window. For this demonstration, the pane will be docked on the right side of the window.

4. Click the ⋮ icon on the top-right corner of the pane and click the **Dock to right** icon (the last entry in the Dock side list.)

The Developer pane has several different sections arranged within different windows. There is the Navigator section that shows the files in use with the web page, a section showing the content of those sections, the Debugger section that shows the debugging tools, and the Console. Those sections can be arranged vertically or horizontally within the pane.

5. Click the **gear** icon ⚙ located in the top-right corner of the Developer pane to display the Settings options for the pane.
6. Go to the **Preferences** section, click the **Panel layout** list box and click **horizontal** to arrange the sections horizontally.
7. Click the **close** button **(×)** located in the top-right corner of the Settings window to return to the Developer pane.

Figure 4-19 shows the contents and layout of the Developer pane in the Chrome browser.

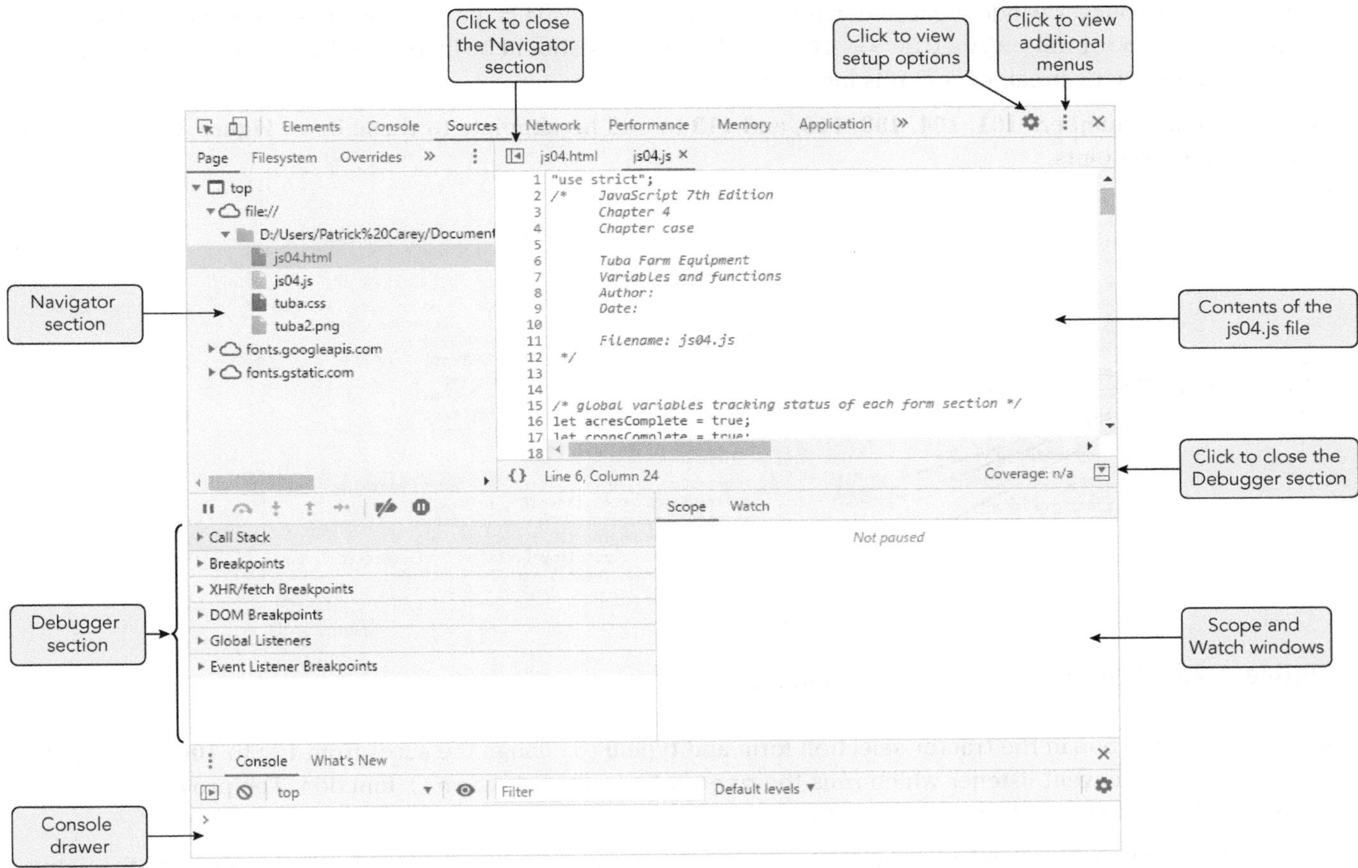

Figure 4-19 Developer pane in Google Chrome

Depending on your browser and its configuration, your window might not match that shown in the figure. Layout and configuration options can be accessed by clicking the ⋮ menu button and the gear icon ⚙ if you wish to edit or modify your Developer pane layout.

Adding and Removing Break Points

The browser debugging tools include the ability to run programs in break mode in which the program execution is suspended to allow the programmer to review the current state of variables and functions. Entering break mode requires inserting breakpoints into the debugger, where each breakpoint marks the location where execution is suspended.

Once the execution is paused, you use the debugger to view the status of the program at the point at which it was paused.

> **Note** | Adding a breakpoint does not the alter the code; only how the JavaScript interpreter interacts with the running program.

You will use the debugger now to add breakpoints to the program that determines the recommended tractor model for specified conditions.

To set breakpoints in the `createRecommendation()` function:

1. Enter **100** in the acres box, click the **Wheat** checkbox, enter **12** in the months box, and then click the **E85** options button. The recommended tractor for these options should be E3250E.
2. Within the debugger window, scroll down the contents of the js04.js file and click the line number **100** next to the line `if (monthsBox.value >= 10)`. The line number should be highlighted after you click it to indicate that you have set a breakpoint at this location.
3. Click the line numbers **101**, **104**, **109**, **110**, and **113** to add breakpoints to those lines. **Figure 4-20** shows the selected breakpoints.

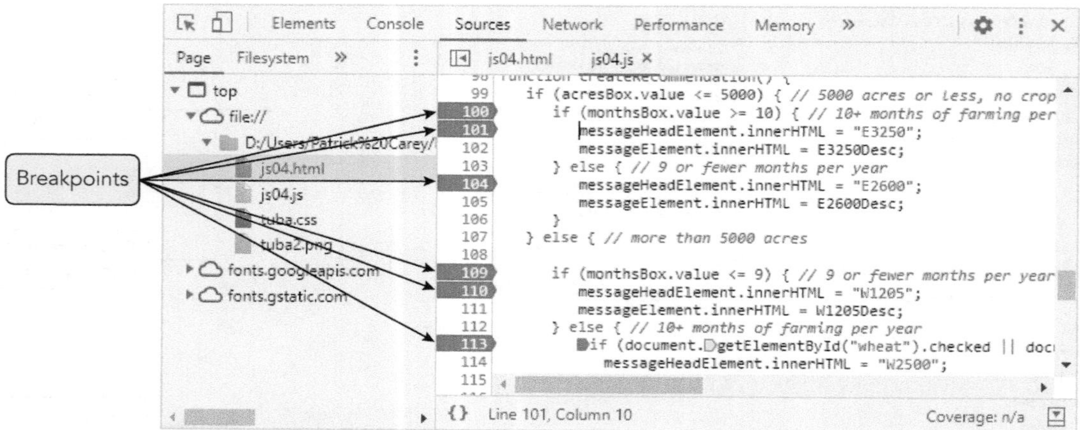

Figure 4-20 Adding breakpoints to the debugger

4. Click the **acres** box in the tractor selection form and type **0** to change the acres from 100 to **1000**. Typing that digit triggers an event listener which runs the `createRecommendation()` function. The program pauses at the breakpoint in Line 100. See **Figure 4-21**.

   When the program is paused, you can hover your mouse pointer over any expression in the code and the debugger will display a popup with the expression's value or a scroll box listing properties and values associated with that expression.

5. Hover your mouse pointer over `monthsBox.value` expression in Line 100. The debugger displays the popup value 12, which is the value entered in the months box. See Figure 4-21.

You can resume the program from its breakpoint using the Resume script execution button. The program will then continue to run until it hits the next breakpoint. The program will only pause at those breakpoints within its flow. A breakpoint within a branch that is not reached will have no effect on the execution of the script.

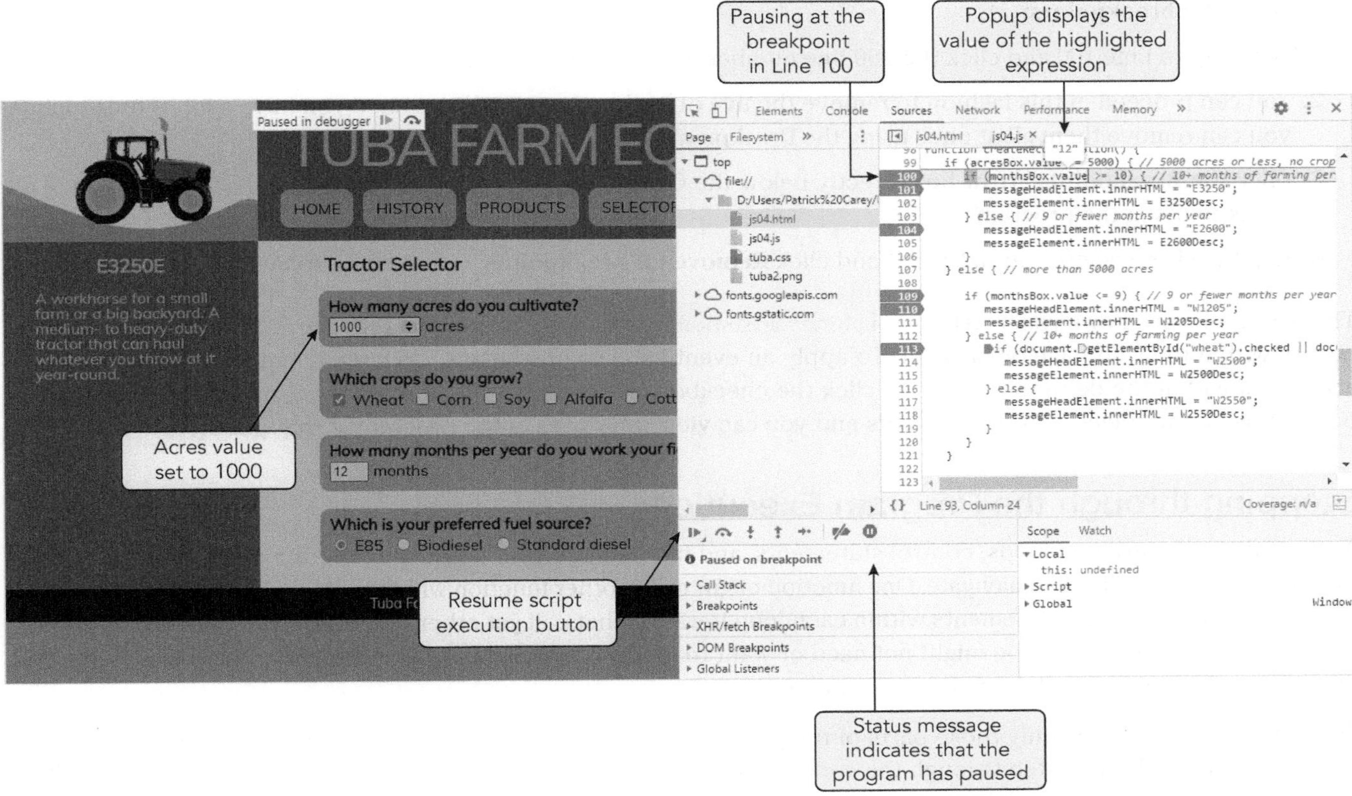

Figure 4-21 Pausing at a breakpoint

To continue the program execution:

1. Click the **Resume script execution** button located either in the debugger or in the popup displayed above the browser or press the keyboard shortcut **F8**.

   The script pauses at the next breakpoint in Line 101.

2. Resume the program again using the **Resume script execution** button or the **F8** shortcut key.

   The interpreter continues to the end of the program without pause. The other breakpoints are never executed because the flow of the program never reaches them.

3. Type **0** in the acres box, increasing the number of acres from 1000 to **10000**.

   The program pauses at the breakpoint in Line 109, a line of code that is reached only when acres value exceeds 5000.

4. Continue the program execution using either the **Resume script execution** button or the **F8** shortcut key.

   The program pauses at Line 113—the next line of code used when the number of months exceeds 10.

5. Continue the program execution once more. The program continues running to its end, without hitting any other breakpoints.

Breakpoints are extremely useful in tracing the execution of the program as it moves through several logical conditions. By viewing the breakpoints, you can determine which branch the program chose and why. Once you have confirmed that the flow of the program is working correctly, you can remove the breakpoints.

To remove the breakpoints:

1. Scroll up to Line 100 and click the **100** line number to remove the breakpoint.
2. You can proceed in this fashion to remove the five other breakpoints. However, if you have a lot of breakpoints you can remove them all at once using the Breakpoints list in the debugger.
3. Click the **Breakpoints** arrow box directly below the Call Stack arrow box in the debugger to display a list of all breakpoints in the program.
4. Right-click anywhere within the list and click **Remove all breakpoints** from the popup menu.

The debugger also allows you to set event listener breakpoints, which are breakpoints that are activated when an event occurs within the web page or browser. To apply an event listener breakpoint, click the Event Listener Breakpoints arrow box within the debugger and then click the checkbox for the event. The program execution will pause at the occurrence of the selected event or events and you can view the status of the program at that point.

Stepping through the Program Execution

As you add more program loops, control statements, and functions to your code, the program flow becomes increasingly complex and difficult to navigate. One function might call another function which itself contains a series of nested `for` loops with `if else` statements within each loop iteration that call yet other functions. If you are trying to trace the execution of your code, you might not need or want to follow every possible branch of the code's execution. You might want to skip past certain functions or loops.

To make it easier to trace only those parts of the program that interest you, the debugger provides a set of stepping options to choose how to step through the code. You can step in or step into the code so that any function called by the program is traced by the debugger one step at a time. However, if you do not need to evaluate those functions in detail, you can step over them so that the function is still run but the debugger does not show each step of the process. You would use the step over option when you are convinced that a function is working correctly and thus does not need your attention as you debug other sections of the program. Finally, you can step out of the code, so the debugger executes all the remaining code within the function without pause. The step out option is used to jump out of a function that no longer requires your direct attention.

To apply stepping options when tracing code:

1. Scroll to Line 87 and click **87** to establish a breakpoint at that line.
2. On the web form, click the **E85** option button, which triggers the event listener for that button.
3. The program pauses at the statement that calls the `testFormCompleteness()` function.
4. Click the **Step Into** button in the debugger or press the **F11** shortcut key (see **Figure 4-22**).

   The debugger moves to Line 92, which is the first line within the `testFormCompleteness()` function.
5. Click the **Step Into** button to move to the next statement, Line 93 which calls the `createRecommendation()` function.
6. Because you have already explored the code in the `createRecommendation()` function, click the **Step Over** button to execute the code within the function but not proceed through it step-by-step.

   The debugger moves to Line 95, which marks the end of the `testFormCompleteness()` function.
7. Click the **Step Into** button. The debugger goes to Line 88, which marks the end of the `verifyFuel()` function.
8. Click the **Step Out** button to step out of the `verifyFuel()` function and complete the execution of the program.
9. Click the Line **87** breakpoint to remove it.

If you are not sure which button to click as you trace the program's execution, hover your mouse pointer over the buttons to view the popup information associated with each button.

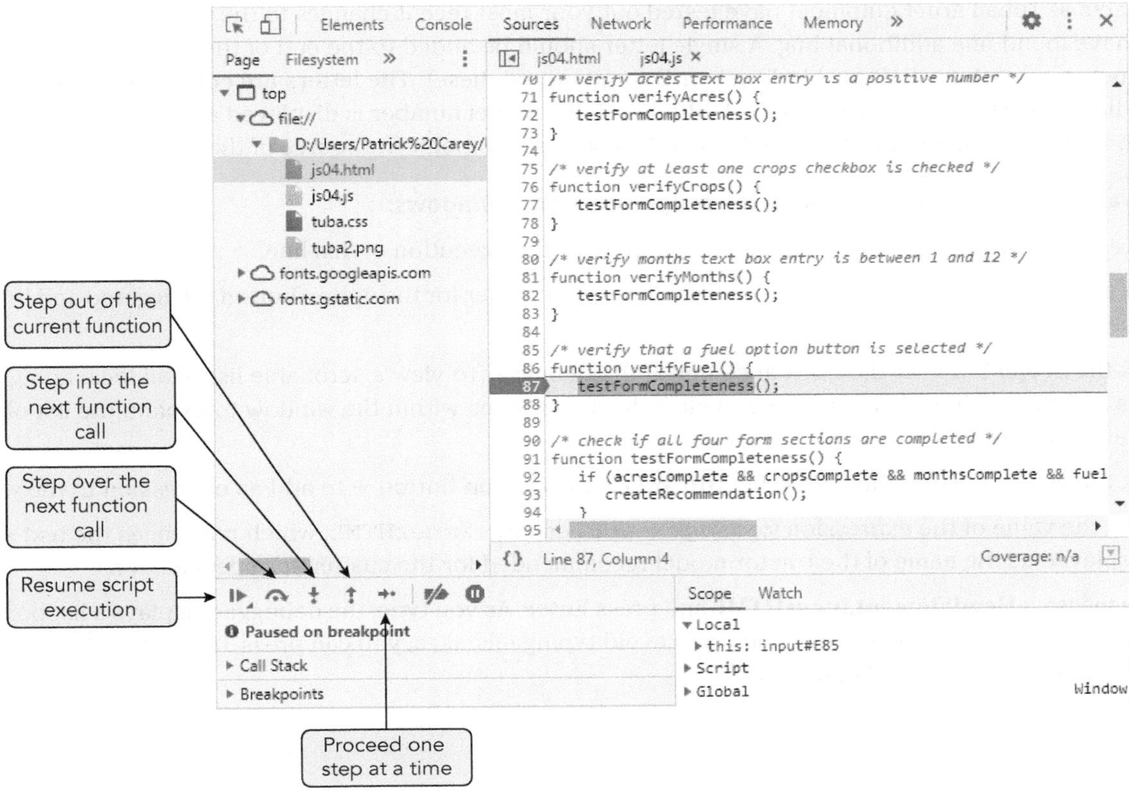

Figure 4-22 Stepping into a function

> **Note**
>
> You can insert a breakpoint directly into your program by adding the statement `debugger;` to the code. When the browser encounters this statement, it will pause the program execution until you manually restart it using the step buttons in the debugger.

Tracking Variables and Expressions

As you trace program execution with step commands and breakpoints, you may also need to track how variables and expressions change during that execution. For example, suppose you have following statement in your code:

```
let squareRoot = number**(1/2);
```

Unfortunately, somewhere in the program, `number` was given a negative value, and because you cannot calculate the square root of a negative, this expression returns the value `NaN` (Not a Number). But it is a long and complicated program, so you do not know when and how `number` became negative.

To assist you, the debugger displays a Scope window listing all the local and global variables and objects available to the program and their current values. As the program executes, the Scope window will update the list to reflect the operations of the code. If you do not need to track all variables, the debugger also provides a Watch window to specify the variable or expression whose value you wish to track during the program's execution. To add a variable or an expression to the Watch window, locate an instance of the variable or expression in the program, select it, and copy it to the Clipboard. You can then paste the copied text into the Watch window. You can also type the variable or expression directly into the Watch window.

Your contacts at Tuba Farm Equipment have tested out your most recent changes to the tractor selector application, and they have found one additional bug. A single letter should be added to the end of the model name to denote the selected fuel source—E for E, B for biodiesel, or D for standard diesel. The letters are correctly appended for E and standard diesel. However, when a user selects Biodiesel, the model number is displayed as simply "B". Use the Scope and Watch windows now to track the variables in the code and pinpoint the source of the error.

To track variables and expressions with the Scope and Watch windows:

1. Add a breakpoint at Line **123** to pause the program at the execution of this line.
2. Click the **E85** option button in the web form. The event handler for the option button is triggered and the program pauses at Line 123.
3. Click the **Scope** tab near the bottom center of the debugger to view a scrollable list of all local and global variables and their values. You may have to click the arrow icons within the window to expand the list of variables and expressions.
4. Click the **Watch** tab and then click the **Add Watch Expression** button + to add an expression to the window.

   Watch the value of the expression `messageHeadElement.innerHTML`, which references the text string that is displayed as the name of the tractor model recommended for the customer's specifications.
5. Type **messageHeadElement.innerHTML** and press **Enter**. As you type, the debugger displays a list box of names and expressions. To reduce your typing and avoid typing mistakes, you can press **Tab** to select the option highlighted in the list box. See **Figure 4-23**.

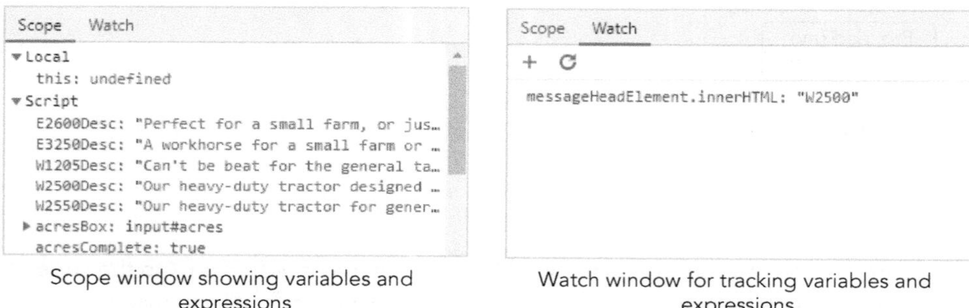

Figure 4-23 The Scope and Watch windows

6. Click the **Step In** button twice. The debugger moves to Line 124 and then to the end of the `if else` statement. Again click the **Resume script execution** button to continue running the program to the end.
7. Next, click the **Biodiesel** option button on the web form. The script pauses once again at Line 123.
8. Click the **Step In** button to first move to Line 125 and then to Line 126. The value of the `messageHeadElement.innerHTML` expression shown in the Watch window changes to "B". A value which is incorrect and thus must be the source of the error in the program.
9. Click the **Resume script execution** button to run the program to its end.
10. Remove the breakpoint in Line 123.

From tracking the value of the `messageHeadElement.innerHTML`, you have determined that the value is incorrectly set in Line 126:

```
messageHeadElement.innerHTML = "B";
```

But that code is incorrect because the program should append the letter "B" to the tractor name and not replace the name altogether. The expression should use the following assignment operator:

```
messageHeadElement.innerHTML += "B";
```

Make this change to the program and rerun it.

To fix the logic error in the program:

1. Go to the **js04.js** file in your code editor.
2. Scroll down to the bottom of the file and change the statement `messageHeadElement.innerHTML = "B";` to:

```
messageHeadElement.innerHTML += "B";
```

See **Figure 4-24**.

```
if (document.getElementById("E85").checked) { // add suffix to model name based on fuel choice
   messageHeadElement.innerHTML += "E";
} else if (document.getElementById("biodiesel").checked) {
   messageHeadElement.innerHTML += "B";
} else {
   messageHeadElement.innerHTML += "D";
}
```

Revised statement to append "B" to the tractor model name

Figure 4-24 Fixing a logical error

3. Save your changes to the file and then reload **js04.html** in your browser.
4. Enter **10000** in the acres box, click the **Wheat** checkbox, enter **12** in the months box, and click the **Biodiesel** option button. The web page returns a recommendation for the W2500B tractor, a heavy-duty tractor designed for the needs of wheat, corn, and soy farmers.

Examining the Call Stack

As programs become more complex, they will often involve functions that call other functions that call even more functions. For example, an accounting program might have an `accountsPayable()` function that calls the `accountsReceivable()` function that might call the `depositFunds()` function, all nested within the `balanceBooks()` function that is called by the `reportBudget()` function. With such a complex set of nested functions, you might get lost as you trace the execution of the program code. To aid in knowing where you are in the code, the debugger provides a call stack that lists the functions currently running, displayed in a hierarchical list of function names and properties. Each time the program calls a function or procedure, it is added to the top of the call stack. After the function or procedure finishes executing, it is removed from the stack.

The call stack is useful to trace the changing values of a variable that is passed as an argument among several functions. If variable is assigned a wrong value, the call stack makes it easier to locate the specific function causing the problem. Use the call stack to view the order of execution among the many functions used the Tuba Farm Equipment web page.

To view the call stack during program execution:

1. Add a breakpoint to Line **87** containing the statement that calls the `testFormCompleteness()` function.
2. Click the **E85** option button the web form to initiate the event handler and run the program.
3. Within the debugger tools click the **Call Stack** arrow if necessary, to view its contents. The `verifyFuel()` function is listed within the stack along with the location indicating both the file name and the line number (js04.js:87).
4. Click the **Step Into** button to step into the `verifyFuel()` function on Line 92 as the program continues.
5. The `testFormCompleteness` function is added to the top of the call stack, indicating that the `testFormCompleteness()` function is the currently active function and when it is completed, the program will return to the `verifyFuel()` function.
6. Click the **Step Into** button twice to trace the program into the `createRecommendation()` function located on Line 99. **Figure 4-25** shows the current contents of the call stack.
7. Continue clicking the **Step Into** button to complete the `createRecommendation()` function and return to the `testFormCompleteness()` function. The call stack is revised to show the current hierarchy of the active functions in the code.

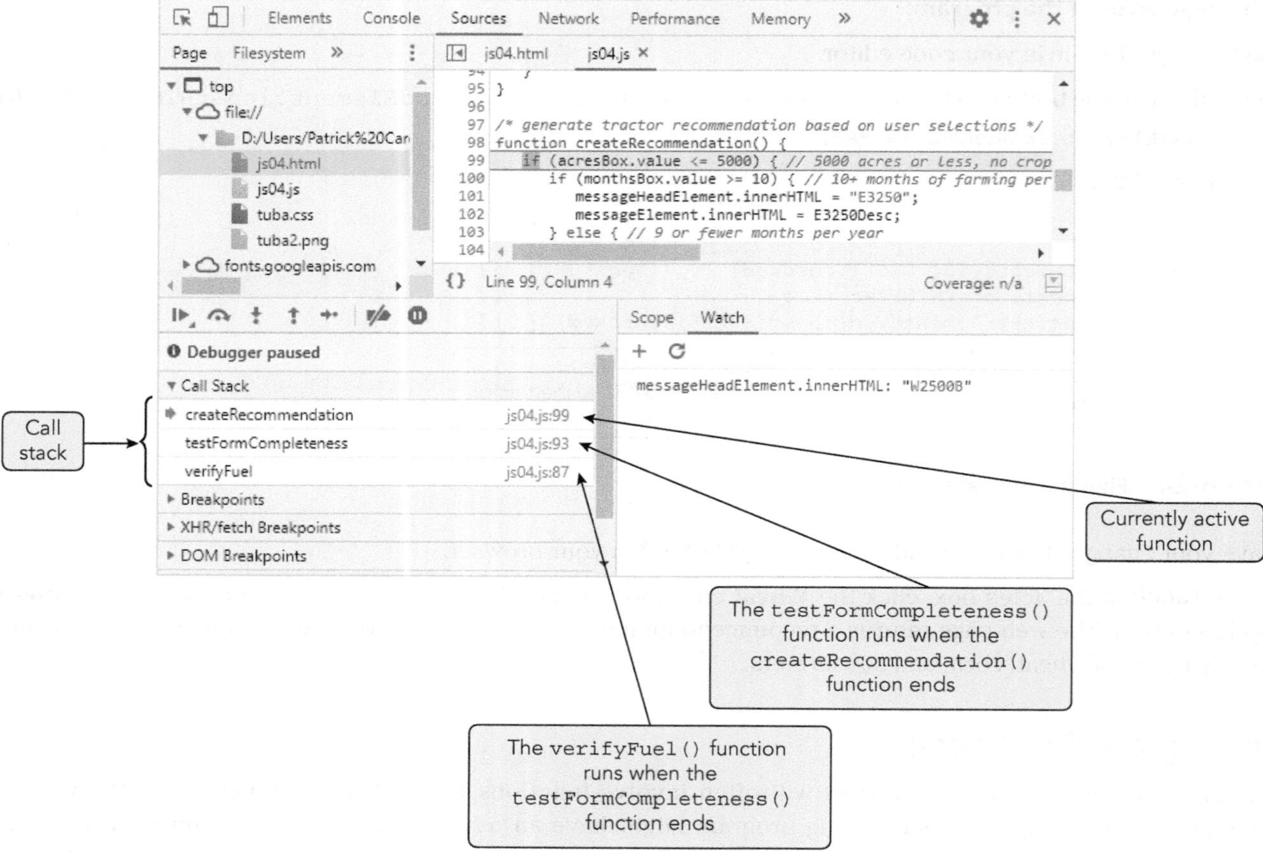

Figure 4-25 Viewing the call stack

8. Click the **Step Into** function again to move back to the `verifyFuel()` function on Line 87.
9. Click the **Resume script execution** button to complete the running of the program.
10. Remove the breakpoint on Line 87 and close the debugger.

With the call stack and the code window, you will always know where you are within the program, making it easier to determine which line or lines are causing the errors.

Skills at Work | Reporting Bugs

Working as a member of a development team or providing technical support, you need to describe clearly and concisely any bugs encountered in an application. The following are some tips to ensure your reporting will be useful to the programmers tasked with fixing the error:

- Provide the exact text of the error message, do not simply summarize it.
- Describe in detail the steps required to reproduce the error, what you expected would result from these steps, and what you observed instead.
- Do not jump to conclusions about what may be causing the error.
- Make yourself available for further tests and demonstrations.

The more complex the program, the more difficult it will often be to fix the bug, so you should not expect a quick turnaround on every bug report.

Quick Check 3

1. What is a breakpoint?
2. Explain the difference between stepping into, stepping over, and stepping out of the program execution.
3. What is the call stack? How do you use it to aid in debugging a program?

Managing Errors

A fourth type of error is one that is often not under a programmer's direct control: user error. A user error occurs when the user mistakenly runs the program in a way not intended by the developer, such as an entering a text string when a numeric value is called for or neglecting to enter all required data. Programmers employ bulletproofing to anticipate and handle potential user error before it causes major problems in the code. For example, form data should be validated before it is acted upon by the program and input controls should be designed to restrict the user's ability to enter data in the wrong format.

Anticipating and preventing user error is one of the developer's greatest challenges because, quite frankly, users are very resourceful. Therefore, programs need to be written in such a way that user error, when it does occur, is least disruptive to the program and the user experience. One oft-employed technique is exception handling in which the program handles errors rather than leaving that task to the JavaScript interpreter.

Handling Exceptions with the `try catch` Statement

Statements that may result in an error can be enclosed within the following `try catch` statement:

```
try {
   statements that might contain an error;
} catch (error) {
   statements that respond to the error
}
```

In this structure, the statements that might contain an error are tested within the `try` command block. If an error is present the statements within the `catch` command block are run. The *`error`* parameter in the `catch` command block is an error object that contains information about the error. The *`error`* parameter can be given any name that does not conflict with a JavaScript keyword.

The statements in the `catch` command block override the browser's default error handling. For example, you can create a customized error message that appears within the browser window rather than relying on the default error message written to the debugger console. The following code contains a mistake in which a variable named `username` is referenced, but because the variable's correct name is `userName`, a runtime error is generated. By enclosing the code within a `try catch` statement, the JavaScript interpreter "tries out" the code first, catches the error, and handles it using the commands in the `catch` command block.

```
let userName = "Jenkins";
try {
   window.alert("The user is " + username);
} catch(err) {
   window.alert("Invalid code");
}
```

The result is an alert box containing the message "Invalid code" displayed within the web browser. Note that the browser will run all the code within the `try` command block until the first error is caught after which the commands in the `catch` command block are run. The runtime error will not cause the program to halt because the `catch` statements provide an alternate way of managing the error.

Throwing an Exception

The `try catch` statement is not much help in managing user error because those would not be recognized as errors by the JavaScript interpreter. However, you can define your own errors called exceptions using the following `throw` operator:

```
throw id
```

where *id* is a value or text string that that identifies the error. The id will appear in the debugger console as the explanation for the error.

The following code uses the `**` operator to calculate the square root of a given number. While this is an illegal math operation for negative values, it is not a fatal error because the program will simply generate a `NaN` value and continue on. To create an exception for this event, the code first tests whether `number` is less than zero. If it is, the code will throw an exception, and the program halts; otherwise, the program continues as normal.

```
let number = -9;
if (number < 0) throw "Attempt to calculate the square root of a negative value.";
let sqrt = number**0.5;
window.alert("The square root of " + number is + " is " + sqrt);
```

Because `number` is negative in this example, the debugger would stop at the `throw` statement, writing the message "Attempt to calculate the square root of a negative value." to the debugger console.

Thrown exceptions can be combined with the `try catch` statement to create a customized error response. The following code employs a `try catch` statement with the `throw` operator to catch a user error in which the value of the `IDBox` input box has been left blank.

```
try {
   userID = document.getElementById("IDBox").value;
   if (userID === "") throw "Missing user ID";
   window.alert("Your user ID is " + userID);
} catch(err) {
   window.alert("You must enter a user ID");
}
```

If the `IDBox` control has been left blank, an exception is thrown, generating an alert box with the message "You must enter a user ID". If `IDBox` is not blank, there is no error, and the program displays an alert box showing the user ID.

The `try catch finally` Statement

JavaScript supports the following optional `finally` clause to supplement exception handling:

```
try {
   statements that might contain an error;
} catch (error) {
   statements to respond to the error
} finally {
   statements to run with or without an error
}
```

Statements in the `finally` command block are always run, whether or not an error is found. The `finally` command block is often used to perform those tasks that are necessary even in the presence of an error. In the following code, an alert box with the Thank You message is always displayed after the error checking is performed.

```
try {
   userID = document.getElementById("IDBox").value;
   if (userID === "") throw "Missing user ID";
   window.alert("Your user ID is " + userID);
} catch(err) {
   window.alert("You must enter a user ID");
} finally {
   window.alert("Thank You");
}
```

You can have multiple `catch` statements within a program to deal with multiple types of thrown exceptions. Whenever a `try` statement throws an exception, the JavaScript interpreter executes the nearest `catch` statement. If a `catch` statement is not located within the construct that throws the exception, the JavaScript interpreter looks at the next higher levels of code for a `catch` statement until it locates one.

> **Note** Every `try` statement must be followed by a `catch` or a `finally` statement or both. If the `catch` statement is omitted, the program terminates in the presence of the error or exception after it has run the commands in the `finally` statement. If both are included, an error will cause the commands in the `catch` statement to be run followed by the commands in the `finally` statement.

The *`error`* Parameter in the `catch` Statement

The `catch` statement includes an *error* parameter that contains information about the error that was caught. For built-in errors, the object has two properties: the `name` property storing the name of the error and the `message` property storing text describing the error. Thus, in the following code, the alert box will display the error name followed by its description:

```
catch(err) {
   window.alert(err.name + ": " + err.message);
}
```

There are six `name` property values for built-in errors: `EvalError`, `RangeError`, `ReferenceError`, `SyntaxError`, `TypeError`, and `URIError` with each indicating the general type of error that occurred. The values of the `message` property are based on information that provides details on the source of the error. Custom errors created by throwing an exception do not have the `name` or `message` properties. Instead, the *id* specified in the `throw` operator is stored as the text of the error message and provides all the information the developer requires.

In ES10 released in 2019, the *`error`* parameter is optional. If you are not using the *`error`* parameter in your code, apply the simpler form:

```
catch {
   statements
}
```

to catch a thrown exception.

Applying Exception Handling to a Program

One possible source of user error in the Tuba Farm Equipment page is a customer specifying zero or a negative acreage for the area to be cultivated. You will anticipate this error by adding a `try catch` statement to the code to throw an exception if that error occurs. To test for an invalid acreage, apply the following statement:

```
if (!(acresBox.value > 0)) throw "Enter a positive acreage";
```

The statement uses the negation operator `!` that returns a `true` value if `acresBox.value` has any other value but a positive number. Use this expression now in a `try catch` statement that throws an exception when the expression is `true`.

To test for a valid acreage:

1. Return to the **js04.js** file in your code editor and scroll down to the `verifyAcres()` function.
2. Replace the statement that calls the `testFormCompleteness()` function with the following `try catch` statement:

```
try {
   if (!(acresBox.value > 0)) throw "Enter a positive acreage";
   testFormCompleteness();
} catch(error) {
   messageElement.innerHTML = error;
   messageHeadElement.innerHTML = "";
}
```

   If an error is detected, the browser will throw an exception and run the catch commands. If no error is detected, the browser will call the `testFormCompleteness()` function as before. See **Figure 4-26**.

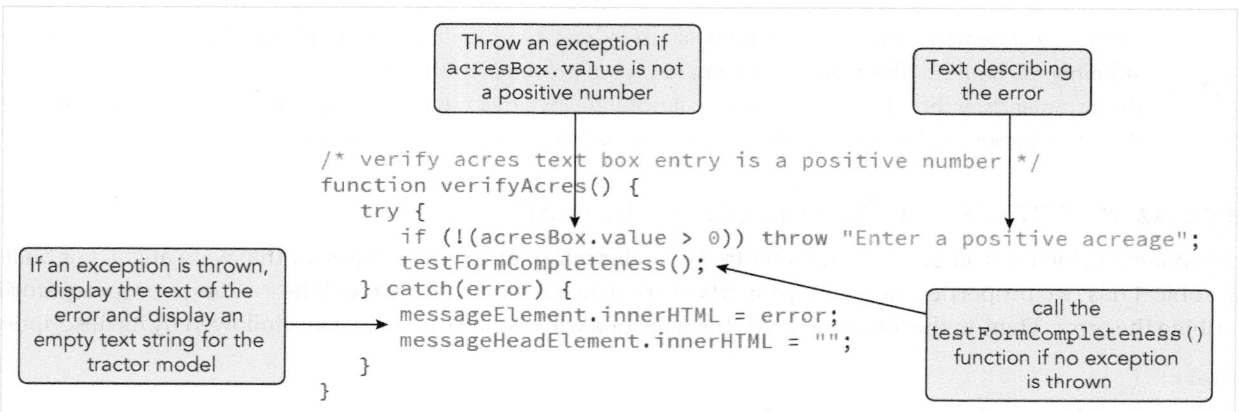

Figure 4-26 Creating a `try catch` statement

3. Save your changes to the file and then reload **js04.html** in your web browser.
4. Enter **0** in the acres box. The event handler immediately responds to the action, running the `verifyAcres()` function. Because this is not a positive value, an exception is thrown, and the error text is displayed in the left sidebar shown in **Figure 4-27**.

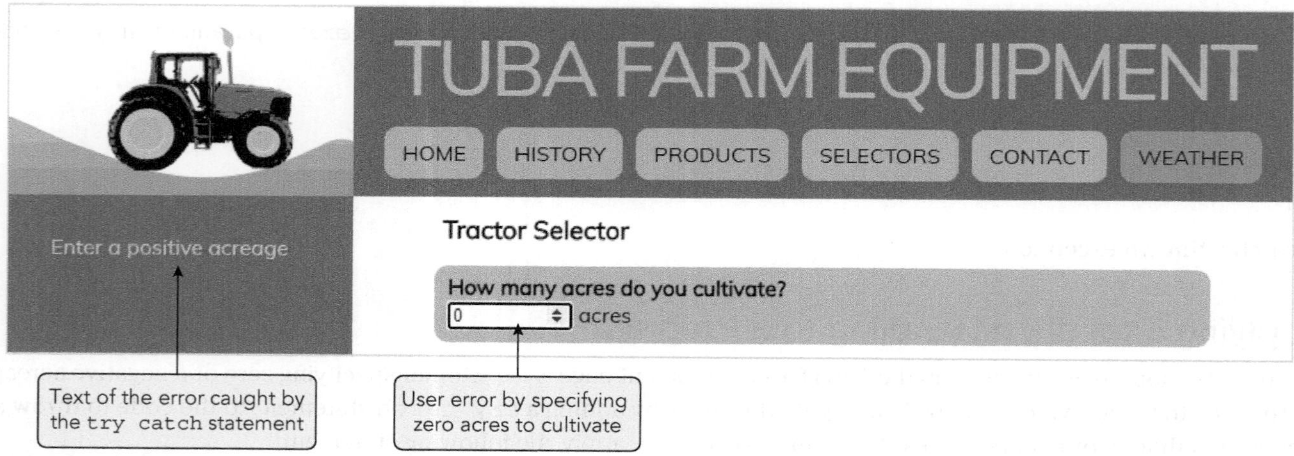

Figure 4-27 Catching an invalid acreage

5. Change the value in the acres box to **1000** and verify that no exception is thrown, and the sidebar displays the details of the E2600D tractor.

Users should specify that the tractor should be in operation from 1 to 12 months. To catch user errors in which a customer specifies a duration outside of this range you will add another `try catch` statement to the program. The statement to throw the exception is:

```
if (!(monthsBox.value >= 1 && monthsBox.value <= 12))
   throw "Enter months between 1 and 12";
```

This statement also uses the negation operator `!` to throw an exception for any condition other than `monthsBox.value` having a duration between 1 and 12 months, inclusive. Create and test the `try catch` statement now.

To test for a valid duration of operation:

1. Return to the **js04.js** file in your code editor and scroll down to the `verifyMonths()` function.
2. Replace the statement calling the `testFormCompleteness()` function with the following:

```
try {
   if (!(monthsBox.value >= 1 && monthsBox.value <= 12))
      throw "Enter months between 1 and 12";
   testFormCompleteness();
} catch(error) {
   messageElement.innerHTML = error;
   messageHeadElement.innerHTML = "";
}
```

See **Figure 4-28**.

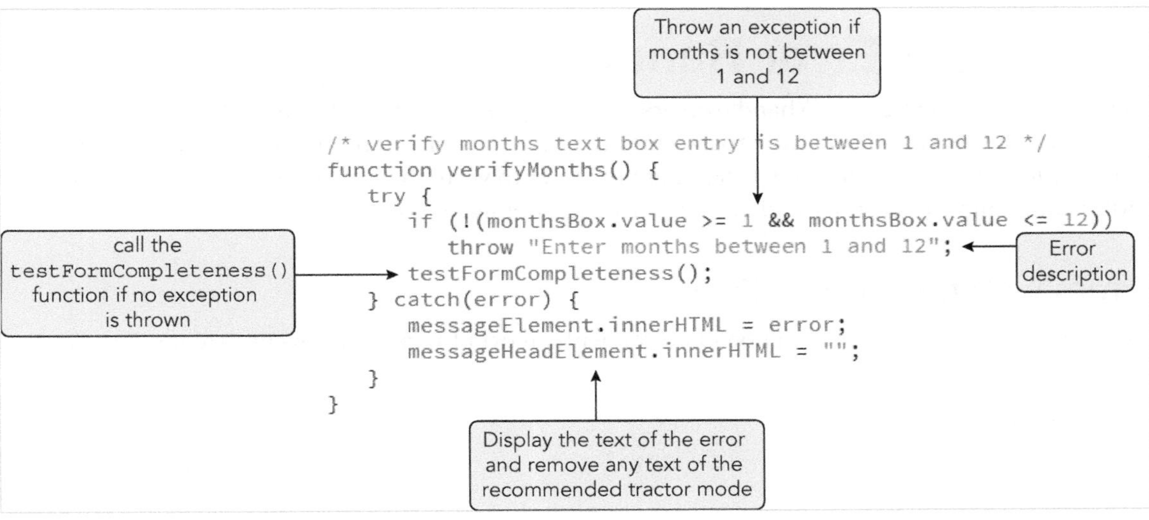

Figure 4-28 Testing for invalid months of operation

3. Save your changes to the file and then reload **js04.html** in your web browser.
4. Enter **14** in the months box. The event handler runs the `verifyMonths()` function, catching the user error and displaying the message shown in **Figure 4-29** in the left sidebar.
5. Change the value in the acres box to **6** and verify that the sidebar displays information on the E2600D tractor.

You have completed your work on the Tuba Farm Equipment page by locating and fixing all the errors in the code and adding code to catch possible user errors.

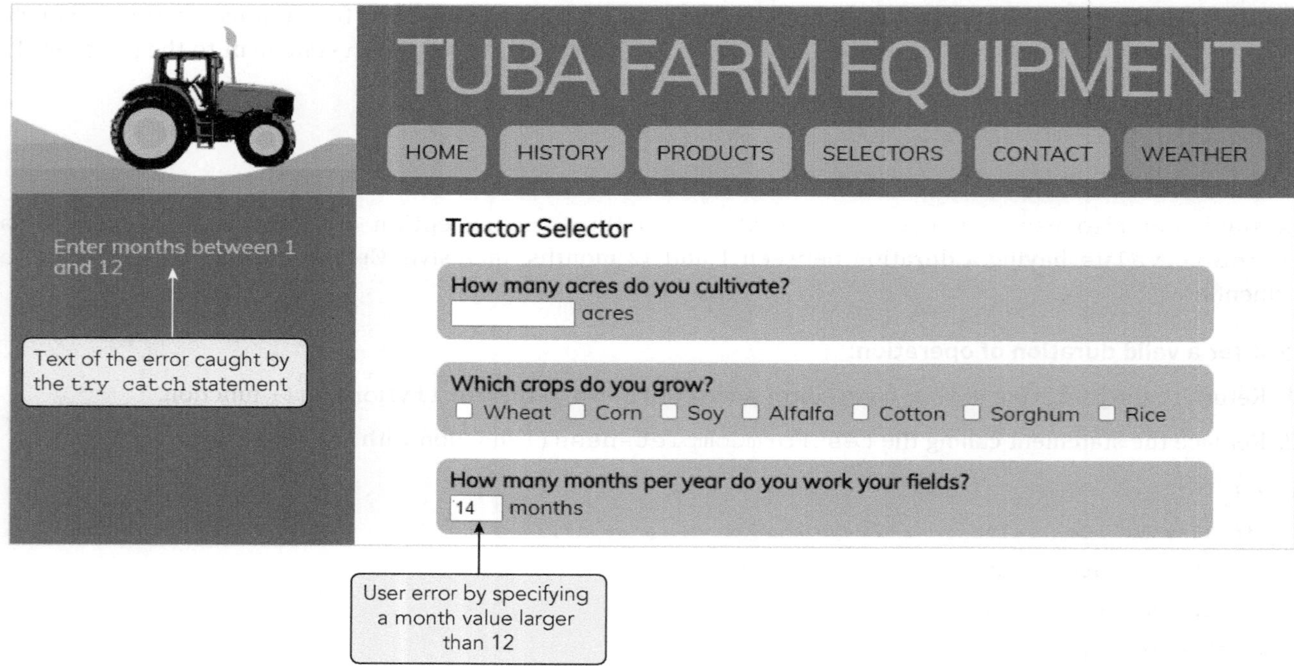

Figure 4-29 Catching an invalid duration of operation

> **Note** To have a customized error message appear in the console log in error message format, apply the `console.error()` method in place of `console.log()`.

Customizing Your Error Handling

Exception handling provides a graceful way to handle errors, especially user error. In addition to handling errors within a specific section of code, JavaScript allows the programmer to create custom methods for handling any errors that may appear anywhere within the program. Many programmers prefer to write their own error handlers in place of the default error handlers built into the browser and viewed within the debugger console.

Catching Errors with the `error` Event

The occurrence of an error is an event, so it can be managed with an event handler or event listener. The syntax for managing an error event is

```
window.onerror = function;
```

or

```
window.addEventListener("error", function)
```

where *`function`* is the function that will be run whenever an error occurs anywhere within the program, including custom errors generated by throwing an exception. For example, the following statement runs the `processErrors()` function in response to errors occurring with the program or browser:

```
window.addEventListener("error", processErrors)
```

Note that running a function in response to an error will not fix the error. The function's only purpose it to create a customized method of handling errors.

Error Handling Functions

Error handling functions have the following general syntax:

```
function errorFn(message, url, line) {
    statements;
    return value;
}
```

where *message*, *url*, and *line* are optional parameters that provide the message, file URL, and line location associated with the error. The `return` statement's value is either `true` or `false`. If `return` is `true`, the error handling function replaces the browser's default error handling; if `return` is `false` or omitted, the error handling function supplements the actions of the browser but does not replace them.

The following `processErrors()` function writes a specialized message to the console log, specifying the name of the file, the type of error that occurred, and its line location.

```
function processErrors(msg, url, line) {
    console.log("The file " + url
    + " generated the following error: "
    + msg + " on line: " + line);
    return true;
}
```

Note that because the `return` value is `true`, this error handling function will override the default way the browser manages errors.

Best Practices | Minimizing Bugs in your Code

What can you do to mitigate bugs in your JavaScript programs? First, always use good syntax, such as ending statements with semicolons and declaring variables with the `let` or `var` keywords. The more disciplined you are in your programming techniques, the fewer bugs you will introduce in your code.

Second, be sure to thoroughly test your JavaScript programs with every browser type and version on which you anticipate your program will run. Most desktop users run Chrome, Safari, Firefox, or Edge, and mobile web use is dominated by Safari for iOS and Chrome for Android. Write your code so that it is compatible with current versions of all major web browsers, as well as any older versions that may continue to have significant market share among your users.

One rule of thumb is that if a browser is used by more than 1 percent of the market, then you need to write and debug your JavaScript programs for that browser. After all, if you were running a business, would you want to write off 1 percent of your customers if you did not have to?

Finally bugs in your web page are not limited to JavaScript. Always run your HTML file and your CSS stylesheet through a validator such as the one at *http://validator.w3.org* to ensure that you have made no mistakes in those files.

Quick Check 4

1. Under what circumstances will the `catch` command block be run by the browser?
2. Under what circumstances will the `finally` command block be run by the browser?
3. Provide code to generate an exception with the message, "Supply a positive value", if the value of the `age` variable is less than zero.
4. What must be included within an error handling function to replace the browser's default error reporting methods?

Summary

- Three types of errors can occur in a program: syntax errors, runtime errors, and logic errors. Syntax errors occur when the interpreter fails to recognize code. Runtime errors occur when the JavaScript interpreter encounters a problem while a program is executing. Logic errors are flaws in a program's design that prevent the program from running as you anticipate.
- The first line of defense in locating bugs in JavaScript programs consists of the error messages you receive when the JavaScript interpreter encounters a syntax or runtime error.
- Tracing is the examination of individual statements in an executing program. You can use the `window.alert()` and `console.log()` methods to trace JavaScript code.
- When using the `console.log()` method to trace bugs, it is helpful to use a driver program, which is a simplified, temporary program that is used for testing functions and other code.
- Another method of locating bugs in a JavaScript program is to identify lines that you think may be causing problems and transform them into comments.
- The current versions of all major browsers contain built-in debugging tools.
- The term "break mode" refers to the temporary suspension of program execution so that you can monitor values and trace program execution.
- A breakpoint is a statement in the code at which program execution enters break mode.
- The step in (or into), step over, and step out options in browser debugging tools allow you to continue program execution after you enter break mode.
- You can add an expression to the watch list in browser debugging tools to monitor its value as you step through the program.
- The term "call stack" refers to the order in which procedures, such as functions, methods, or event handlers, execute in a program.
- Writing code that anticipates and handles potential problems is often called bulletproofing.
- Exception handling allows programs to handle errors as they occur in the execution of a program. The term "exception" refers to some type of error that occurs in a program.
- You execute code that may contain an exception in a `try` statement. You use a `throw` statement to indicate that an error occurred within a `try` block. After a program throws an error, you can use a `catch()` statement to handle, or "catch" the error. A `finally` statement that is included with a `try` statement executes regardless of whether its associated `try` block throws an exception.
- You can assign a custom function to JavaScript's `error` event for handling any types of errors that occur on a web page.

- Additional methods and techniques for locating and correcting errors in your JavaScript programs include checking your HTML elements, analyzing your logic, testing statements with the console command line, using the `debugger` statement, executing code in strict mode, linting, and reloading a web page.

Key Terms

break mode
breakpoint
bug
bulletproofing
call stack
commenting out
debugging
dependencies
driver program
event listener breakpoint
exception
exception handling
linting
load-time error
logging
logic
logic error
runtime error
Scope window
step in
step into
step out
step over
stepping options
strict mode
syntax
syntax error
throw
tracing
user error
Watch window

Review Questions

1. What type of error occurs when the interpreter fails to recognize code?
   a. debugging
   b. syntax
   c. runtime
   d. logic
2. ______________ errors are problems in the design of a program that prevent it from running as you anticipate.
   a. Application
   b. Syntax
   c. Logic
   d. Runtime
3. When a JavaScript interpreter encounters a problem while a program is executing, that problem is called a(n) ______________ error.
   a. application
   b. syntax
   c. logic
   d. runtime
4. Which of the following statements causes a syntax error?
   a. `let firstName = "";`
   b. `document.write(Available points: " + availPoints);`
   c. `readyState = true;`
   d. `"use strict";`
5. Which of the following statements writes the value of the `selection` variable to the console?
   a. `console.log("selection");`
   b. `document.console("selection");`
   c. `console.alert(selection);`
   d. `console.log(selection);`
6. Which of the following `for` statements is logically incorrect?
   a.
   ```
   for (var count = 10; count <= 0;
       count++) {
           document.write(count);}
   ```
   b.
   ```
   for (var count = 0; count <= 10;
       count++) {
           document.write (count);}
   ```
   c.
   ```
   for (var count = 10; count >= 0;
       count--) {
           document.write (count);}
   ```
   d.
   ```
   for (var count = 5; count >= 0;
       count--) {
           document.write (count);}
   ```
7. Which of the following modes temporarily suspends, or pauses, program execution so that you can monitor values and trace program execution?
   a. Suspend
   b. Step
   c. Break
   d. Continue

8. Which command executes all the statements in the next function in browser debugging tools?
   a. Step out
   b. Step over
   c. Step
   d. Step in/into

9. After you throw an exception, you use a ______________ statement to handle the error.
   a. `try`
   b. `throw`
   c. `catch`
   d. `finally`

10. In ______________, some features are removed from the JavaScript language, while other features require more stringent syntax.
    a. exception handling
    b. strict mode
    c. debugging tools
    d. debugger mode

11. Which of the following pieces of information is passed as an argument from a `throw` statement to a `catch` statement?
    a. error number
    b. error message
    c. line number
    d. URL

12. What statement can you add to your code to effectively serve the same role as a breakpoint?
    a. `break;`
    b. `breakpoint;`
    c. `debug;`
    d. `debugger;`

13. The Watch window in the debugger lets you monitor the value of a(n) ______________ during program execution.
    a. function
    b. exception handler
    c. expression
    d. statement

14. The ______________ is the ordered list maintained by a JavaScript processor containing all the procedures, such as functions, methods, or event handlers, that have been called but have not yet finished processing.
    a. Scope window
    b. Watch window
    c. strict mode
    d. call stack

15. Which of the following exception handling code executes regardless of whether its associated `try` block throws an exception?
    a. `throw "Please enter your last name.";`
    b.
    ```
    catch(lNameError) {
        return false;
    }
    ```
    c.
    ```
    catch(lNameError) {
        window.alert(lNameError)
        return false;
    }
    ```
    d.
    ```
    finally {
        lNameValid = true;
    }
    ```

16. What is the advantage of tracing errors using the `window.alert()` method? What is the advantage of using the `console.log()` method instead?

17. Explain how to debug code by commenting it out.

18. Explain two different ways that a text editor specialized for web development can help you in preventing errors and debugging code.

19. When and why should you use exception handling with your JavaScript programs?

20. Explain what strict mode is, how to implement it, and how it's useful in reducing coding errors.

Hands-On Projects

Hands-On Project 4-1

Debugging Challenge

In this project you will finish an application that provides a general estimate of costs from a moving company. The company charges 50 cents per pound of items moved and 75 cents per mile plus an optional $500 fee for setting and installing furniture and appliances. The program code needs some debugging work and extra code to account for user error. A preview the completed page is shown in **Figure 4-30**.

Figure 4-30 Completed Project 4-1

Do the following:

1. Use your code editor to open the **project04-01_txt.html** and **project04-01_txt.js** files from the js04 ▶ project01 folder. Enter your name and the date in the comment section of each file and save them as **project04-01.html** and **project04-01.js**, respectively.
2. Go to the **project04-01.html** file in your code editor and in the head section add a `script` element to load the project04-01.js file, deferring the loading of the program until the web page finishes loading. Study the contents of the HTML to become family with the elements and the ids associated with each element. Save your changes to the file.
3. Go to the **project04-01.js** file in your code editor. At the top of the file above the comment section, insert a statement that indicates this program adheres to a strict interpretation of JavaScript syntax.
4. There are two logic errors in setting up the global constants. Locate and fix those errors.
5. Go to the `calcTotal()` function. To guard against users entering a zero or negative value for the estimated weight, replace the statement `totalCost += wgtBox.value * COST_PER_LB;` with a `try catch` statement that does the following:
   a. Tests whether `wgtBox.value` is not greater than 0 by using the expression `!(wgtBox.value > 0)`. If that expression is true, throw an exception with the error message **"!! Enter a positive weight"**
   b. If no exception is thrown then run the command `totalCost += wgtBox.value * COST_PER_LB;`.
   c. If an exception is caught, set the value of `msgBox.innerHTML` to the error message you defined for the thrown exception.
6. Repeat Step 5, for the estimated distance cost using `distBox.value`. Throw the error message **"!! Enter a positive mileage"** for a caught exception.
7. Save your changes to the file.
8. Open the **project04-01.html** file in your web browser. Open the debugger and confirm that there are no syntax errors. If there are, fix your code in your code editor.
9. Test your code by entering **0** for the estimated weight and **1200** for the mileage. Confirm that the error message "!! Enter a positive weight" appears next to the total box.
10. Change the weight to **2500** and enter a **0** for the estimated mileage. Confirm that the error message "!! Enter a positive mileage" appears next to the total box.
11. Enter a mileage of **1200** miles and click the Setup and Installation box. Confirm that the estimated moving cost is calculated to be $2650.

Hands-On Project 4-2

Debugging Challenge

In this project you have been given a program that generates a random Jane Austen quote each time a page reloads. The application calls the following function to generate a random integer used in picking the quote from an array of quotes:

```
randomInt(lowest, highest)
```

where *`lowest`* is the lowest integer in the range and *`highest`* is the highest integer. Thus, the statement

```
randomInt(0, 5)
```

will generate a randomly selected integer from 0 up to 5 (including both 0 and 5). However, there are several bugs in the application that need to be fixed before the page will work properly. **Figure 4-31** shows a preview of the page with a randomly selected quote.

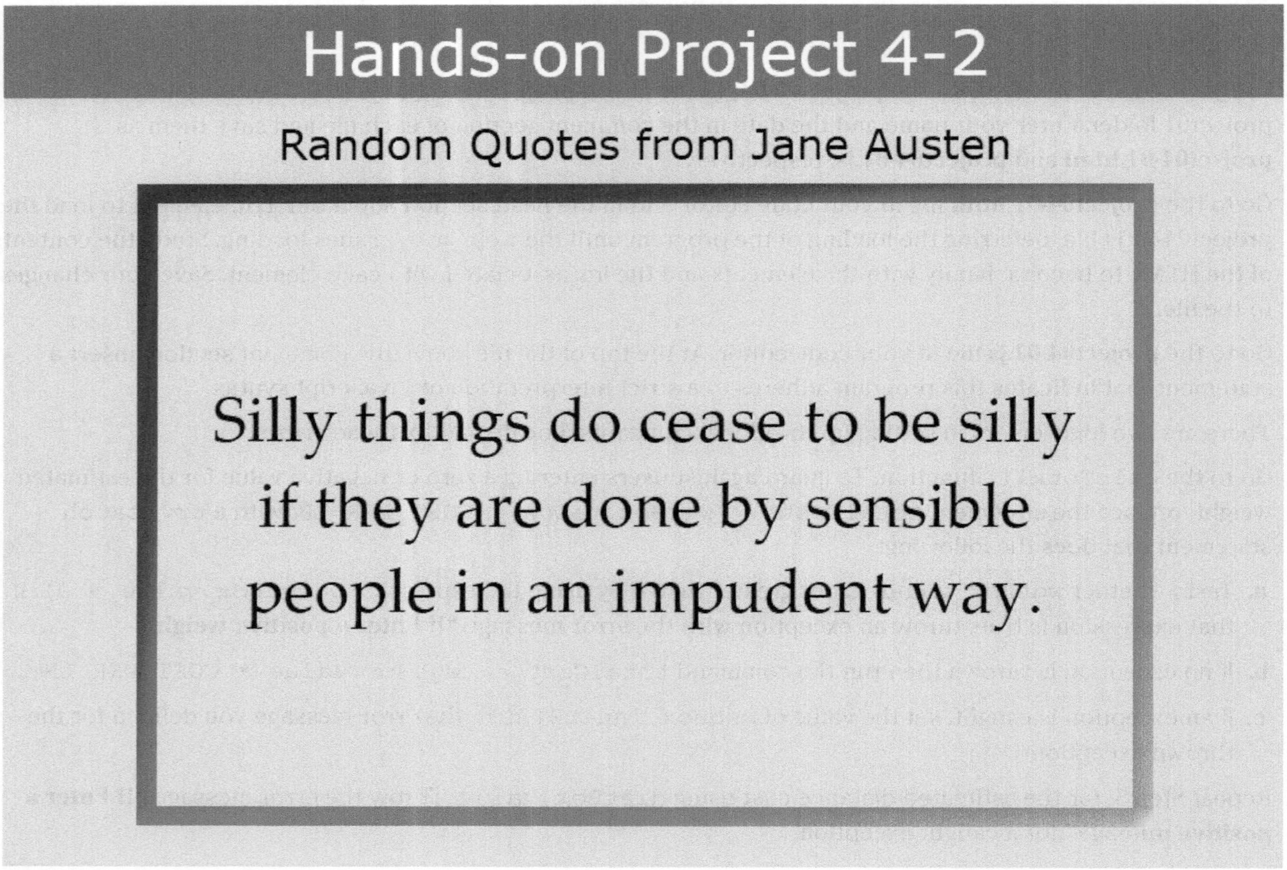

Figure 4-31 Completed Project 4-2

Do the following:

1. Use your code editor to open the **project04-02_txt.html** and **project04-02_txt.js** files from the js04 ▶ project02 folder. Enter your name and the date in the comment section of each file and save them as **project04-02.html** and **project04-02.js**, respectively.
2. Go to the **project04-02.html** file in your code editor and in the head section add a `script` element to load the project04-02.js file, deferring the loading of the JavaScript source file until the entire HTML file is loaded. Study the contents of the HTML file and save your changes.

3. Go to the **project04-02.js** file in your code editor. At the top of the file insert a command to have the JavaScript interpreter parse the code using strict standards.
4. Save your changes to the file and then load **project04-02.html** in your browser.
5. Use the debugger to locate the syntax and runtime errors within the document. Fix the errors using your code editor.
6. Once you have fixed the syntax and runtime errors, continually reload the web page. Each time the page is loaded, a Jane Austen quote is randomly selected from the array. Occasionally, an `undefined` value appears where the quote should be. Find the source of this logic error by setting a breakpoint at Line 48 and watch the values of the `randomQuote` and `quotes[randomQuote]` expression. What are their values that result in an undefined quote?
7. Return to the code editor and fix the program to remove the logic error. (Hint: What is the largest index in the quotes array and what would happen if you tried to retrieve an entry larger that index?)
8. Return to the **project04-02.html** file in your browser and continually reload it to verify that the undefined quote no longer appears.

Hands-On Project 4-3

Debugging Challenge

In a comment text box, reviewers are often given a character limit that they cannot exceed. In this project, you will debug the code for an application that counts the number of characters in a posted comment to ensure the comment does not exceed a predetermined limit. The app makes use of the `keyup` event which is triggered when a key is pressed and then released up from the keyboard as part of typing a character. A function named `countCharacters()` has been provided that counts the characters in the review. Your job will be to locate and fix the errors in the code and to catch user error when the review exceeds the character count limit. A preview of the page for a character count limit of 100 is shown in **Figure 4-32**.

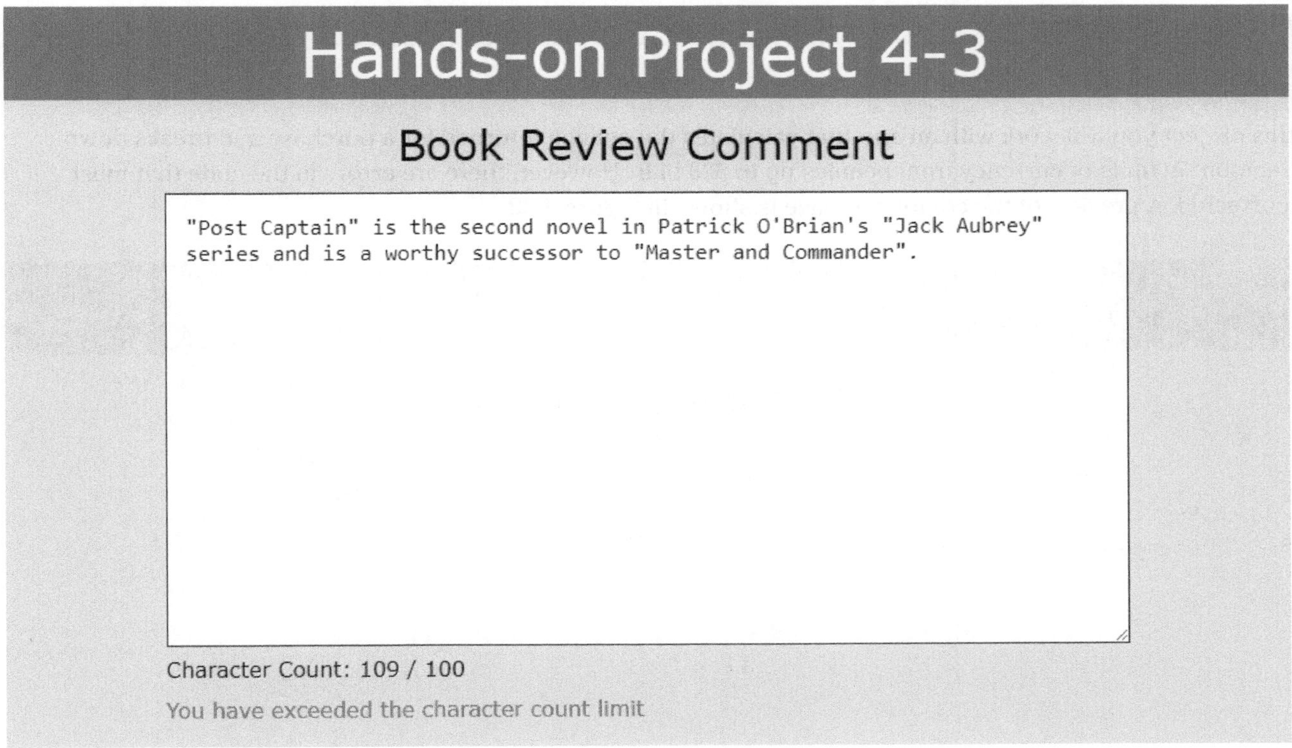

Figure 4-32 Completed Project 4-3

Do the following:

1. Use your code editor to open the **project04-03_txt.html** and **project04-03_txt.js** files from the js04 ▶ project04 folder. Enter your name and the date in the comment section of each file and save them as **project04-03.html** and **project04-03.js**, respectively.
2. Go to the **project04-03.html** file in your code editor and in the head section add a `script` element to load the project04-03.js file, deferring the loading of the JavaScript source file until the entire HTML file is loaded. Study the contents of the HTML file and save your changes.
3. Go to the **project04-03.js** file in your code editor. At the top of the file, insert a statement directing that the code be interpreted under strict standards.
4. Go to the `updateCount()` function. Insert at the bottom of the function a `try catch finally` statement that does the following:
   a. Within the `try` statement, test if the `charCount` variable is greater than the value of the `MAX_REVIEW` constant. If it is, throw an exception with the error message "**You have exceeded the character count limit**".
   b. For caught exceptions, display the error message within the `innerHTML` of the `warningBox` object.
   c. Whether the exception is thrown or not, change the `innerHTML` of the `wordCountBox` object to the value of the `charCount` variable.
5. Save your changes to the file and then load **project04-03.html** in your web browser. Start typing text into the comment box.
6. There are several errors within the code. Use the debugger to find any syntax or runtime errors you encounter. Fix the errors in your code editor.
7. When the app is free of errors, attempt to type more than 100 characters into the comment box. Verify that when you exceed the character limit, a warning message appears on the page.
8. Return to your code editor and increase the value of `MAX_COUNT` from 100 to **1000**.

Hands-On Project 4-4

Debugging Challenge

In this project you will work with an app that calculates the change returned for a purchase and breaks down the amount in units of currency from pennies up to $20 bills. However, there are errors in the code that must be corrected. A preview of the completed page is shown in **Figure 4-33**.

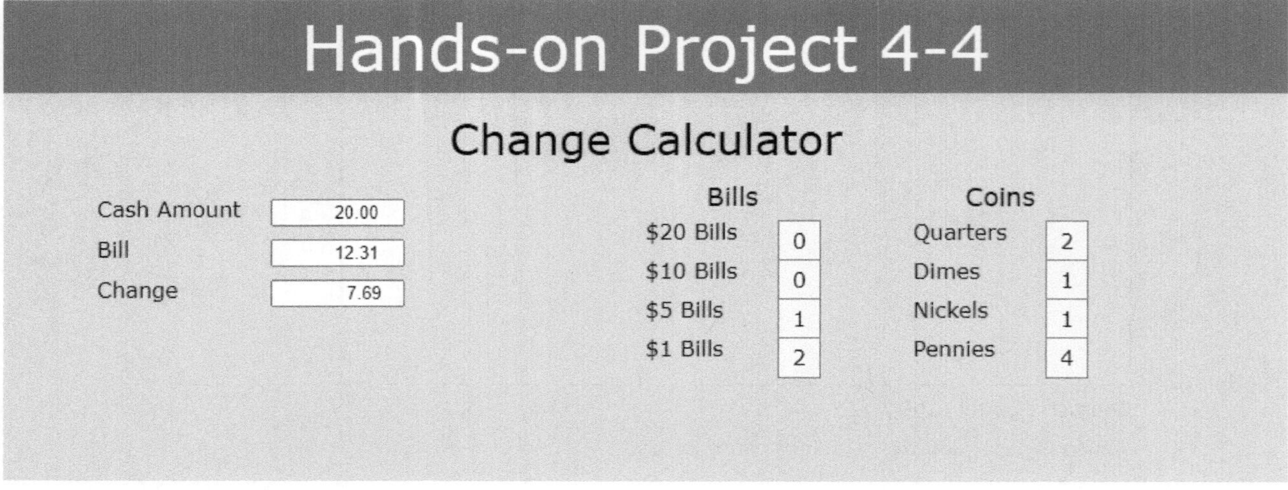

Figure 4-33 Completed Project 4-4

Do the following:

1. Use your code editor to open the **project04-04_txt.html** and **project04-04_txt.js** files from the js04 ▶ project04 folder. Enter your name and the date in the comment section of each file and save them as **project04-04.html** and **project04-04.js**, respectively.
2. Go to the **project04-04.html** file in your code editor and in the head section add a `script` element to load the project04-04.js file, deferring the loading of the JavaScript source file until the entire HTML file is loaded. Take some to study the contents of the file, paying special attention to the ids of the different elements in the page. Save your changes to the file.
3. Go to the **project04-04.js** file in your code editor. At the top of the file insert a command so that the code in the file is interpreted with strict adherence to the JavaScript standards for syntax.
4. Study the contents of the file, noting the different functions that are used to create the change calculator. Save your changes to the file.
5. Open the **project04-04.html** file in your web browser. To run the program, enter a cash value in the Cash Amount box and the bill in the Bill box. An event handler should calculate the change in response to those events. There are several syntax and runtime errors in the program. Use the debugger to assist you in locating the errors. Use your code editor to fix the errors you find.
6. Once the program operates without syntax or runtime errors, use it to calculate the change from \$20 for a bill of \$12.31. While the change is correctly calculated, the breakdown in units of currency is not. Use the tracing features of the debugger to trace the error to its source. Use your code editor to fix the problem. When the program works as intended, the change and currency amounts should match that shown in Figure 4-33.
7. Return to the **project04-04.js** in your code editor. If the bill is greater than the cash amount, no change can be given. Handle this user error by adding a `try catch` statement to the `runTheRegister()` function. Within the `try catch` statement do the following:
   a. Within the `try` statement test if `changeValue` is not greater than or equal to zero. If that condition is `true`, throw an exception with the error message "**Cash amount doesn't cover the bill**".
   b. Run the following commands
   ```
   changeBox.value = formatCurrency(changeValue);
   calcChange(changeValue);
   ```
   c. Within the `catch` statement set the `innerHTML` of the element with the id "warning" to the value of thrown exception.
8. Save your changes to the file. Reload **project04-04.html** in your browser. Verify that if the Bill value is greater than the Cash Amount value, no calculation is done on the change and a warning message appears on the page.

Hands-On Project 4-5

Debugging Challenge

In this debugging challenge you will debug a program that converts angular measurements between degrees and radians. The formula to convert an angle measured in degrees to radians is as follows:

$$radians = degrees \times \frac{\pi}{180}$$

and the formula to convert radians to degrees is:

$$degrees = radians \times \frac{180}{\pi}$$

The value of π can be entered with the built-in JavaScript constant `Math.PI`. The code to do the calculations has been entered for you, but you will have to fix the bugs in the program. A preview of the completed page is shown in **Figure 4-34**.

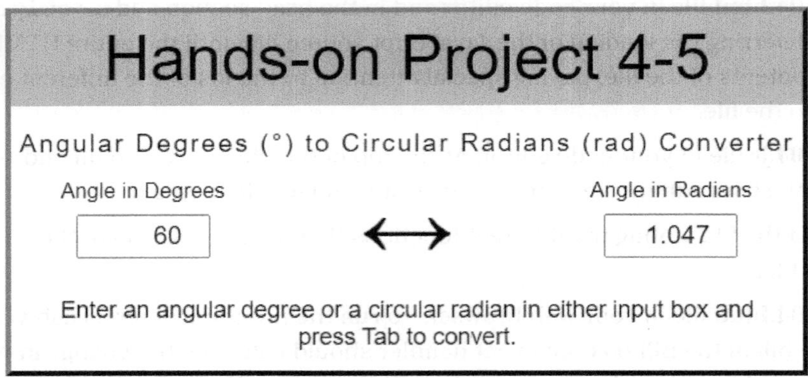

Figure 4-34 Completed Project 4-5

Do the following:

1. Use your code editor to open the **project04-05_txt.html** and **project04-05_txt.js** files from the js04 ► project05 folder. Enter your name and the date in the comment section of each file and save them as **project04-05.html** and **project04-05.js**, respectively.
2. Go to the **project04-05.html** file in your code editor and in the head section add a `script` element to load the project04-05.js file, deferring the loading of the JavaScript source file until the entire HTML file is loaded. Study the contents of the HTML file and save your changes.
3. Go to the **project04-05.js** file in your code editor. At the top of the file, insert a command so that the code is strictly interpreted.
4. Directly below the command that declares the radians variable, insert a command that writes the radians value to the debugger console in the form: "Radians = *radians*".
5. Directly below the command that declares the degrees variable, insert a command that writes the degrees value to the debugger console in the form: "Degrees = *degrees*".
6. Save your changes to the file and then load **project04-05.html** in your web browser.
7. Use the debugger to locate syntax and runtime errors in the code. Fix those errors in your code editor.
8. Enter **60** in the Angle in Degrees box. The value for Angle in Radians should be 1.047, but it is not. Locate and fix the logic error that resulted in the incorrect value being calculated.

Case Projects

Individual Case Project

Add exception handling to the code for one of the forms on your personal website. If your site does not include a form, add one first. Your code should display one or more relevant error messages in an appropriate location. After you finalize your code, write a summary of the debugging methods from this chapter that you used in this project, describing how you used each one in your code.

Team Case Project

Divide your team into two subgroups and assign each group a page from your team project website that includes JavaScript code. Within each subgroup, introduce at least three bugs into the code for the page you've been assigned. Exchange documents with the other subgroup, and then work as a team to debug the code provided by the other team. As you debug, record which debugging methods you use, including whether each was helpful in resolving a given issue. When the document works as expected, create a report. For each bug, describe the behavior you expected as well as the erroneous behavior that the bug caused and describe the methods you used to debug it, including whether each method was helpful or not. Also specify the line number or numbers of the code that contained the error, and show the incorrect as well as the corrected code in your report.

CHAPTER 5

Creating a Web App Using the Document Object Model

When you complete this chapter, you will be able to:

- Understand the principles of building a web app
- Create nodes and append them to a web document
- Restructure a web document by adding, deleting, copying, and moving element nodes
- Define a timed command that repeats a function or command block at set intervals
- Create system dialog boxes that receive user input
- Open and configure a browser popup window
- Create an overlay that lies on top of a web document
- Work with the objects within the Browser Object Model

Designing a Web App

In this chapter you will create a web app that displays a slideshow or lightbox in which multiple images are displayed in a scrolling gallery with individual images expanded to fill the entire screen, dimming the rest of the page. **Figure 5-1** shows a preview of the lightbox you will create and the features it will support.

A web app like the lightbox is built on four foundations:

- The HTML code that provides a container for the web app
- The CSS code that defines the look of the app
- The JavaScript code that manages the operation and output from the app
- The data used by the app, often stored in an external file, or retrieved from a database server

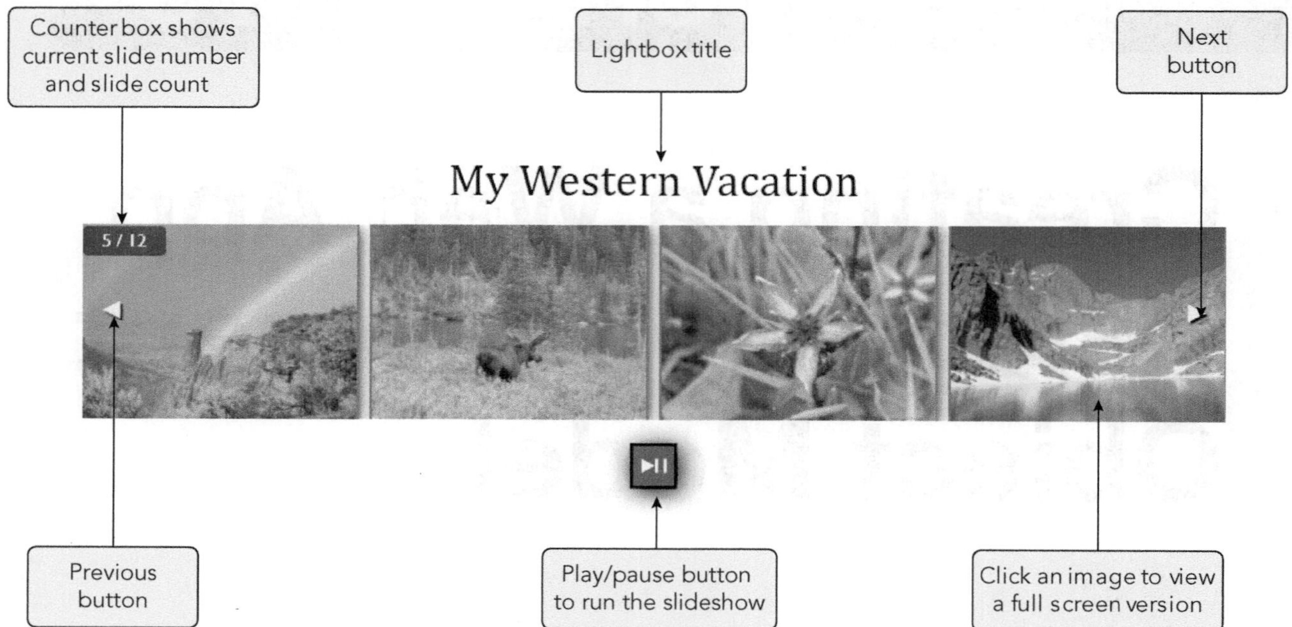

Figure 5-1 Preview of the lightbox app *Joan Carey*

In some environments these features might not even by handled by the same person. A team of designers might work with the HTML and CSS code while a team of programmers manages the JavaScript code, and a third team is responsible for data. For the lightbox app, you are responsible for the JavaScript code; the images and the code for the HTML and CSS files are already created for you.

To open the files for the lightbox app:

1. Go to the js05 ▶ chapter folder of your data files.
2. Use your code editor to open the **js05_txt.html** and **js05_txt.js** files and enter your name and the date in the comment section of each file.
3. Return to the **js05.html** file in your code editor. With the head section, add the following code to link the page to a stylesheet with the styles used by the lightbox, a script file containing data on the lightbox images, and the script you will write that creates the lightbox.

```
<link rel="stylesheet" href="lightbox.css" />
<script src="lightbox_data.js" defer></script>
<script src="js05.js" defer></script>
```

4. Scroll to the bottom of the file and directly above the closing `</article>` tag insert the following `div` element that will contain the lightbox app.

```
<div id="lightbox"></div>
```

   Figure 5-2 shows the revised code in the HTML file.

5. Close the file, saving your changes.

Figure 5-3 shows the contents of the lightbox_data.js file. In this app, the title of the lightbox is stored in the `lightboxTitle` variable, the image file names are stored in the `imgFiles` array, the captions associated with each image are stored in the `imgCaptions` array, and the total number of images is calculated and stored in the `imgCount` variable.

There are 12 images in this example, but you will write your code so that the lightbox app can manage any number of images.

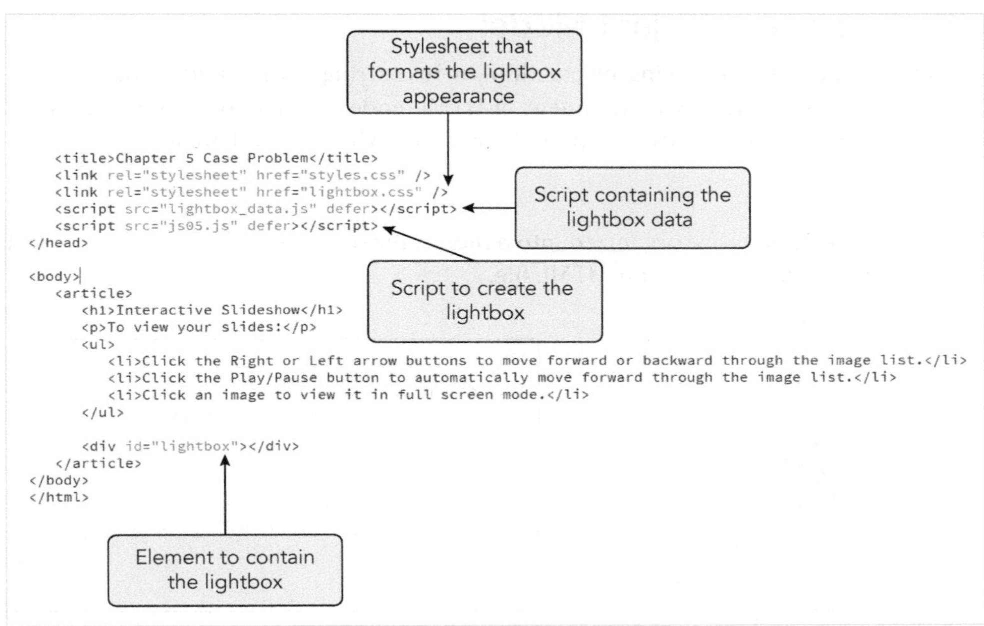

Figure 5-2 Parts of the lightbox app

```
// Title of the slideshow
let lightboxTitle = "My Western Vacation";

// Names of the image files shown in the slideshow
let imgFiles = ["photo01.jpg", "photo02.jpg", "photo03.jpg", "photo04.jpg",
                "photo05.jpg", "photo06.jpg", "photo07.jpg", "photo08.jpg",
                "photo09.jpg", "photo10.jpg", "photo11.jpg", "photo12.jpg"]

// Captions associated with each image
let imgCaptions = new Array(12);
imgCaptions[0]="Sky Pond (Rocky Mountain National Park)";
imgCaptions[1]="Buffalo on the Plains (South Dakota)";
imgCaptions[2]="Garden of the Gods (Colorado Springs)";
imgCaptions[3]="Elephant Head Wild Flower (Rocky Mountain National Park)";
imgCaptions[4]="Double Rainbow (Colorado National Monument)";
imgCaptions[5]="Moose in the Wild (Grand Lake, Colorado)";
imgCaptions[6]="Camas Wild Flower (Rocky Mountain National Park)";
imgCaptions[7]="Chasm Lake (Rocky Mountain National Park)";
imgCaptions[8]="Teton Crest Trail (Grand Teton National Park)";
imgCaptions[9]="The Notch Trail (Badlands National Park)";
imgCaptions[10]="Sprague Lake (Rocky Mountain National Park)";
imgCaptions[11]="Longs Peak Trail (Rocky Mountain National Park)";

// Count of images in the slideshow
let imgCount = imgFiles.length;
```

Figure 5-3 Content of the lightbox_data.js file

Introducing Nodes

To generate web page content you've been limited to the `document.write()` method, the `innerHTML` property, and the `textContent` property. In each of these approaches the HTML code is submitted as a text string that the browser parses and adds to the web document. While effective for small and simple scripts, these approaches quickly become unwieldy when the app needs to write longer sections of HTML code or must constantly revise the structure of that code. A better approach to deal with those challenges is to work with nodes.

Nodes and the Document Object Model

Each element, attribute, comment, processing instruction, or text string within a web document is a distinct entity known as a node. For example, the following fragment of HTML code consists of two nodes—one node for the `h1` element and one node for the text string "My Slideshow" contained within that element.

```
<h1>My Slideshow</h1>
```

In the Document Object Model, nodes are organized into a hierarchical structure called a node tree. **Figure 5-4** shows the representation of the node tree for a sample HTML file.

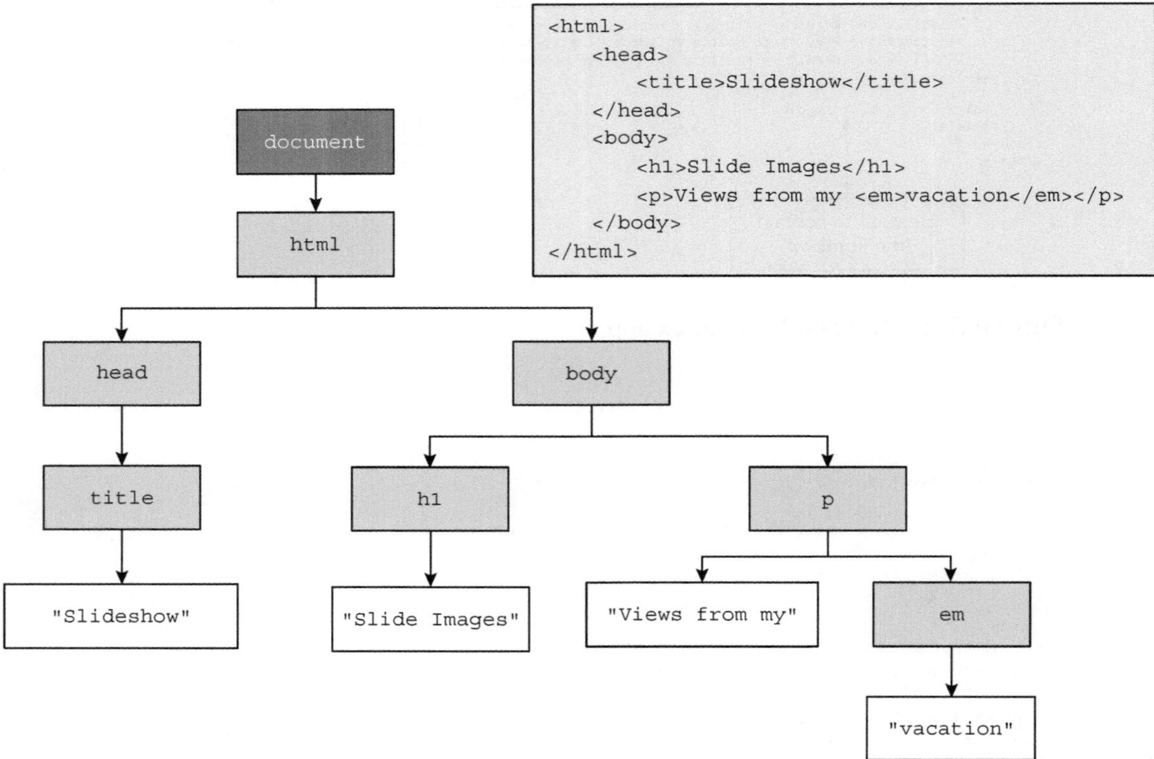

Figure 5-4 A node tree

Nodes in the node tree have a familial relationship—each node can be a parent, child, and/or sibling of other nodes. In the node tree shown in Figure 5-4, the parent of the `body` node is the `html` node, and the parent node at the top of the node tree is known as the root node. The `body` element has two child nodes: an `h1` element and a paragraph (`p`) element. The `h1` element and the paragraph element are siblings of each other because they share a common parent.

Note The root node can be referenced using the `documentElement` object. The page body itself can be referenced using the `document.body` object.

Each of these familial relationships can be referenced using the JavaScript properties shown in **Figure 5-5**.

For example, the following expression references the parent of a node within the node tree.

```
node.parentNode
```

EXPRESSION	DESCRIPTION
node.firstChild	The first child of *node*
node.lastChild	The last child of *node*
node.childNodes	A node list of all nodes which are direct children of *node*
node.previousSibling	The sibling listed before *node* on the same level in the node tree
node.nextSibling	The sibling listed after *node* on the same level in the node tree
node.ownerDocument	The root node of the document
node.parentNode	The parent of *node*

Figure 5-5 Node relationships

To go two levels up (to the "grandparent") add another `parentNode` property to the expression:

```
node.parentNode.parentNode
```

and to go to an "aunt or uncle" node, go up to the parent node and move to either sibling:

```
node.parentNode.previousSibing
node.parentNode.nextSibling
```

By combining the properties listed in Figure 5-5, you can start from any node in the node tree and navigate to any other node. Nodes can also be referenced as part of collection within a node list. The following `childNodes` property references a collection of all nodes that are children of the *node* object:

```
node.childNodes
```

As with arrays and HTML collections, a node list is indexed starting with an index of 0 and the total number of nodes within the list indicated by the `length` property. Both of the following expressions reference the first child node of its parent:

```
node.firstChild
node.childNodes[0]
```

The properties in Figure 5-5 make no distinction between nodes that represent elements and nodes that represent text strings, comments, and other types of nodes in the node tree. Most applications are concerned only with element nodes. To work directly with those, JavaScript provides the properties listed in **Figure 5-6**.

EXPRESSION	DESCRIPTION
node.children	A node list of all elements which are direct children of *node*
node.firstElementChild	The first element within *node*
node.lastElementChild	The last element within *node*
node.previousElementSibling	The sibling element immediately prior to *node* in the node tree
node.nextElementSibling	The sibling element immediately following *node* in the node tree
node.parentElement	The parent element of *node*

Figure 5-6 Element node relationships

One of the reasons to use nodes to create page content instead of using a property like `innerHTML` is that nodes provide the ability to create, add, remove, and rearrange elements within the node tree, giving the programmer control over not just the content of the web document but also its structure.

Common Mistakes

Referencing Child Elements

In some scripts you might need to reference the children of a parent node. Make sure you reference the right node list. To reference only element nodes, use the `children` property. To reference nodes of any kind, use the `childNodes` property.

Selecting Nodes with the `querySelectorAll()` Method

You can define a node list based on a CSS query using the following `querySelectorAll()` method:

```
document.querySelectorAll(css)
```

where *css* is the text of CSS selector. For example, the following expression creates a node list by selecting all paragraph element nodes belonging to the review class:

```
document.querySelectorAll("p.review");
```

The `querySelectorAll()` method gives the programmer more options selecting elements than could be achieved by the `getElementsByClassName()` or `getElementsByTagName()` methods. However, the `querySelectorAll()` method creates a node list, not an HTML collection, and there are some important differences. JavaScript also provides the `querySelector()` method, which returns the first element node that matches the CSS selector rather than the complete node list.

Programming Concepts | Node Lists vs. HTML Collections

Node lists and HTML collections are similar, but there are some important differences. Items within an HTML collection can be referenced by index number, element id, or element name. Items within a node list can only be referenced by their index number. HTML collections can only contain elements. A node list can contain a variety of node types including elements, text strings, and attributes.

Finally, HTML collections are dynamic so that changes in the structure of the web page will be automatically reflected in the HTML collection. A node list is static. Once it has been created it will not automatically update itself even as the document changes.

Creating and Connecting Nodes

Like objects and variables, nodes can be created using JavaScript and stored as variables. The methods employed by JavaScript to create or copy nodes are described in **Figure 5-7**.

EXPRESSION	DESCRIPTION
`document.createAttribute(`*`att`*`)`	Create an attribute node with the name *`att`*
`document.createComment(`*`text`*`)`	Creates a comment node containing the comment *`text`*
`document.createElement(`*`elem`*`)`	Creates an element node with the name *`elem`*
`document.createTextNode(`*`text`*`)`	Creates a text node containing the text string *`text`*
`node``.cloneNode(`*`deep`*`)`	Creates a copy of *`node`*, where *`deep`* is `true` to copy all the node's descendants or `false` to copy only *`node`* itself

Figure 5-7 Methods to create or copy a node

For example, the following code creates an element node for an `h1` heading and a text node containing the text string "My Slideshow":

```
let mainHeading = document.createElement("h1");
let headingTxt = document.createTextNode("My Slideshow");
```

Nodes can be combined to create a document fragment. The document fragment resides only within computer memory and is not yet part of the web page. **Figure 5-8** describes the JavaScript methods used to combine, replace, or remove nodes.

EXPRESSION	DESCRIPTION
node.appendChild(*new*)	Appends *new* node as the last child of *node*
node.insertBefore(*new*, *child*)	Insert *new* node as a sibling directly before *child* node (if no *child* node is specified then *new* node is added as a sibling after the last child node)
node.removeChild(*old*)	Remove *old* node from *node*
node.replaceChild(*new*, *old*)	Replaces *old* node with new *node*

Figure 5-8 Methods to add or remove nodes

The following code appends the headingTxt node as a child of the mainHeading node:

```
mainHeading.appendChild(headingTxt);
```

resulting in the following document fragment:

```
<h1>My Slideshow</h1>
```

To place mainHeading into the web document it must be attached to a node already present in that document's node tree. If the document had a div element with the id "intro", the mainHeading node could be attached to that element using the following code:

```
let introDIV = document.getElementById("intro");
introDiv.appendChild(mainHeading);
```

and the web page would then include the following content:

```
<div id="intro">
   <h1>My Slideshow</h1>
</div>
```

Proceeding in this fashion, you can continue to append nodes to each other and to elements within the web page, creating an elaborate hierarchy of parent and child elements.

Note | Nodes support the innerHTML and textContent properties so you can always add HTML code and text to a node as a quick way of creating a document fragment.

Elements Nodes and HTML Attributes

Attributes are considered nodes and JavaScript supports a wealth of tools for working with attribute nodes, but it is often easier to enter the attribute and its value directly as a property of a node. Every HTML attribute has a corresponding node property. For example, the following code attaches the id property with the value "main" to the mainHeading node created previously:

```
mainHeading.id = "main";
```

resulting in the following HTML content:

```
<div id="intro">
   <h1 id="main">My Slideshow</h1>
</div>
```

In the same way, you can use the src property to add a src attribute to the element node for an inline image or the href property to define the href attribute for the <a> tag. One exception to this approach is HTML's class attribute. Because class is a reserved JavaScript keyword, it cannot be used as a property of an element node. Instead,

JavaScript uses the `className` property as in the following example that sets a value for the `class` attribute of the `mainHeading` element node:

```
mainHeading.className = "lightbox";
```

resulting in the following modification to the `<h1>` tag:

```
<div id="intro">
   <h1 id="main" class="lightbox">My Slideshow</h1>
</div>
```

A similar property to the `className` property is the `classList` property, which is used with HTML elements associated with more than one class. With the `classList` property you can add, remove, or replace class values from an element with multiple classes.

Nodes and Inline Styles

Inline styles are added to HTML elements using the `style` attribute. Thus, the following HTML code

```
<h1 id="main" style="font-size: 1.5em; color: blue">
   My Slideshow
</h1>
```

can be replaced with the JavaScript statements:

```
let mainH1 = document.getElementById("main");
mainH1.style = "font-size: 1.5em; color: blue;";
```

However, you can also define individual styles by appending the `style` property and a style value to the object. For example, you can set values of the `font-size` and `color` properties using the following:

```
mainH1.style.fontSize = "1.5em";
mainH1.style.color = "blue";
```

Notice that because JavaScript does not support hyphens in property names, the CSS `font-size` style is written in camel case as `fontSize`. Similarly, the `background-color` style would be written as `backgroundColor`, the `font-family` style would be entered as `fontFamily`, and so forth. Any styles defined using the `style` property are treated as inline styles and thus will have precedence over styles defined in an embedded or external style sheet.

Creating a Document Fragment in an App

You will use nodes to develop the content of the lightbox app. The general structure of the lightbox is as follows:

```
<div id="lightbox">
   <h1>Lightbox Title</h1>
   <div id="lbCounter"></div>
   <div id="lbPrev"></div>
   <div id="lbNext"></div>
   <div id="lbPlay"></div>
   <div id="lbImages">
      images
   </div>
</div>
```

Compare this HTML code to the preview of the completed lightbox shown earlier in Figure 5-1. You have already added the lightbox container element to the web page, so any nodes appended to it will automatically be added to the page. While you could add this general structure using the `innerHTML` property, such a text string would be long and cumbersome to create and manipulate. The content and the structure will be more easily managed with nodes. Commands to create this lightbox structure will be placed within a `createLightbox()` function that runs when the browser initially loads the page.

To create nodes for the lightbox app:

1. Go to the **js05.js** file in your code editor.
2. Below the initial comment section insert the event listener:

```
window.addEventListener("load", createLightbox);
```

3. Add the following initial code for the `createLightbox()` function as shown in **Figure 5-9**:

```
function createLightbox() {
   // Lightbox Container
   let lightBox = document.getElementById("lightbox");

   // Parts of the lightbox
   let lbTitle = document.createElement("h1");
   let lbCounter = document.createElement("div");
   let lbPrev = document.createElement("div");
   let lbNext = document.createElement("div");
   let lbPlay = document.createElement("div");
   let lbImages = document.createElement("div");
}
```

```
window.addEventListener("load", createLightbox);

function createLightbox() {
   // Lightbox Container
   let lightBox = document.getElementById("lightbox");

   // Parts of the lightbox
   let lbTitle = document.createElement("h1");
   let lbCounter = document.createElement("div");
   let lbPrev = document.createElement("div");
   let lbNext = document.createElement("div");
   let lbPlay = document.createElement("div");
   let lbImages = document.createElement("div");
}
```

Create h1 and div element nodes

Figure 5-9 Creating element nodes

Next, append each part of the lightbox to the lightbox container using the `appendChild()` method, adding an `id` attribute to each element to identify it for the styles defined in the lightbox.css stylesheet.

To append the element nodes:

1. Within the `createLightbox()` function add the following code to append the element nodes to the lightbox container and to assign each of them a unique id.

```
// Design the lightbox title
lightBox.appendChild(lbTitle);
lbTitle.id = "lbTitle";
```

```
// Design the lightbox slide counter
lightBox.appendChild(lbCounter);
lbCounter.id = "lbCounter";

// Design the lightbox previous slide button
lightBox.appendChild(lbPrev);
lbPrev.id = "lbPrev";

// Design the lightbox next slide button
lightBox.appendChild(lbNext);
lbNext.id = "lbNext";

// Design the lightbox Play-Pause button
lightBox.appendChild(lbPlay);
lbPlay.id = "lbPlay";

// Design the lightbox images container
lightBox.appendChild(lbImages);
lbImages.id = "lbImages";
```

Figure 5-10 shows the revised code in the function.

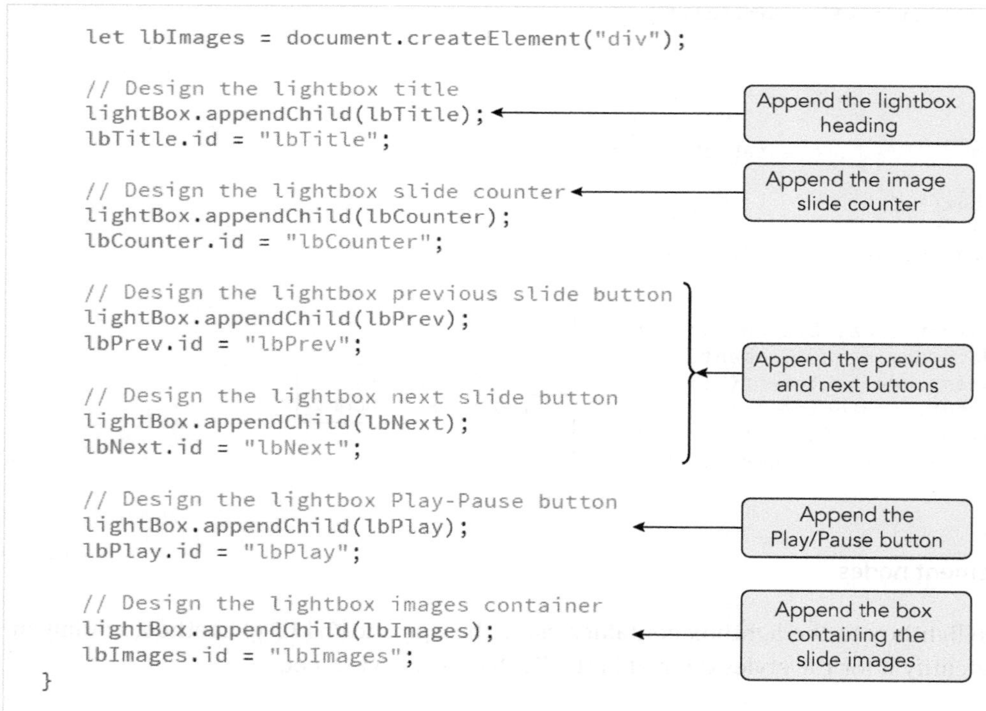

Figure 5-10 Attaching element nodes to the lightbox container

2. Save your changes to the file.

Note The `appendChild()` method always places the node at the end of the parent node's children. To insert a node at a different position—such as at the beginning of the child list—use the `insertBefore()` method.

Viewing Elements within the Browser Debugger

Currently, the lightbox has no images, so there is nothing that would appear on the web page, but in developing this app you want to ensure that your code has generated the correct node structure. Before going further in developing this app, examine the contents and structure of the web page using tools in your browser's debugger.

To view the elements within a web page:

1. Reload the **js05.html** file in your browser.
2. To view the node tree in Google Chrome and Microsoft Edge, open the Developer tools pane and click the Elements tab. For the Firebox browser, open the Debugger and click the Inspector tab. For the Safari browser, open the Web Inspector from the Develop menu.
3. The elements are displayed in a hierarchy. Click the ▶ icon next to an element to expand a lower branch of the hierarchy and view its contents.
4. Navigate through the representation of the node tree, expanding the branches down through the `body` element, the `article` element, and finally the contents of the `div` element with the lightbox id.
5. Hover over and click the lightbox `div` element in the node tree. The web browser highlights the location of the element within the web page and a styles box provides information on the styles applied to the element. See **Figure 5-11**.

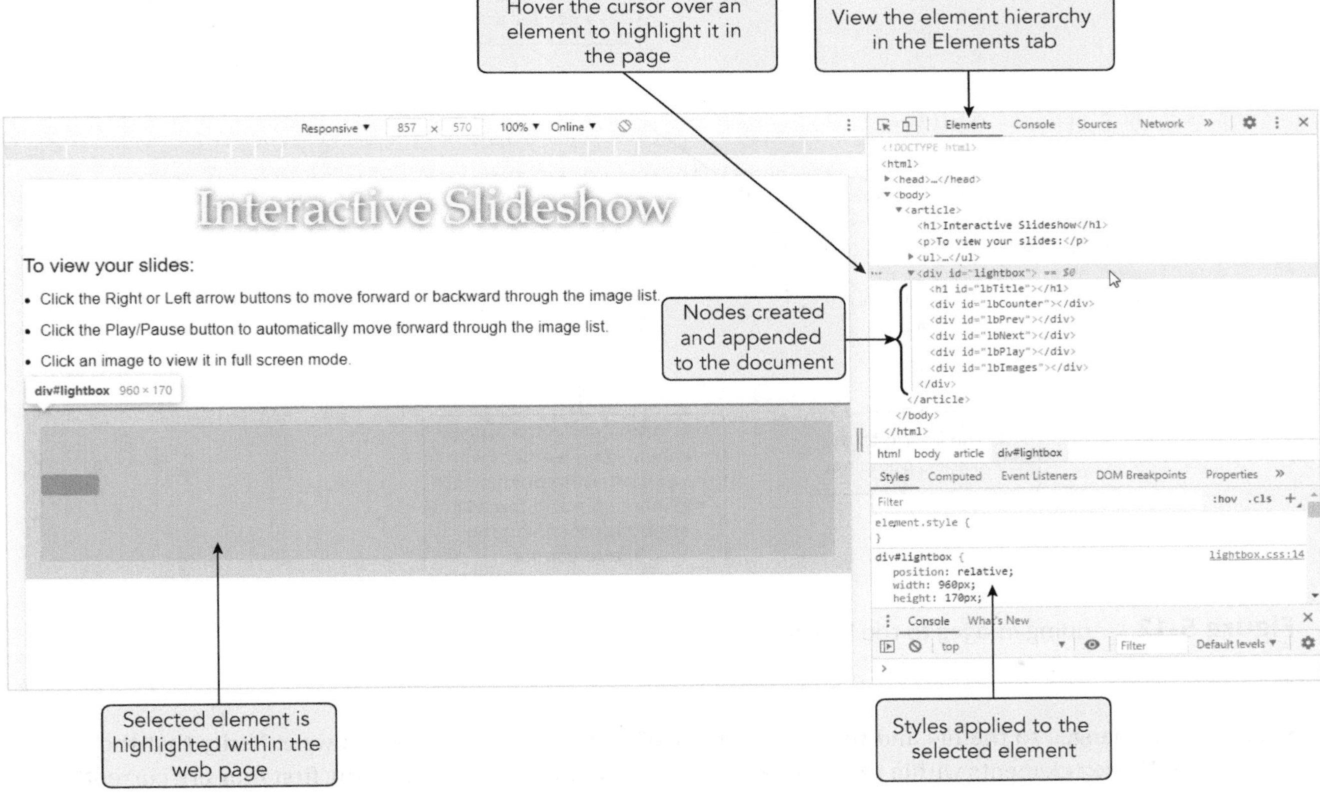

Figure 5-11 Viewing the element hierarchy in the Elements tab

If your page does not contain the elements shown in Figure 5-11, return to the js05.js file in your code editor. Check your code against the code shown in Figures 5-9 and 5-10. Common errors might involve the misspelling of id names, node variables, or node properties.

To add images to the lightbox, use a `for` loop to iterate through the `imgFiles` array, creating an `img` element node for each item in the array and appending it as a child of the `lbImages` element node. Notice that the code uses the imgCount variable whose value was already calculated in the lightbox_data.js file and stores the number of images in the lightbox.

To add the light box images:

1. Return to the **js05.js** file in your code editor.
2. At the bottom of the `createLightbox()` function, insert the following `for` loop to populate the `lbImages` element node with inline images (see **Figure 5-12**):

```
// Add images from the imgFiles array to the container
for (let i = 0; i < imgCount; i++) {
   let image = document.createElement("img");
   image.src = imgFiles[i];
   image.alt = imgCaptions[i];
   lbImages.appendChild(image);
}
```

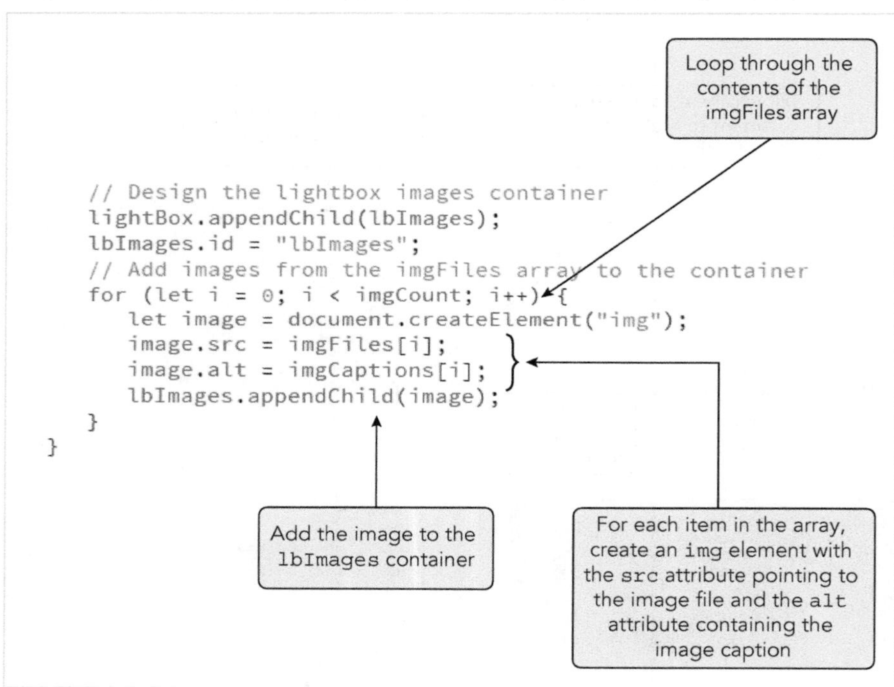

Figure 5-12 Adding images to the lightbox

3. Save your changes to the file and then reload the **js05.html** file in your web browser. Verify that the page now contains 12 `img` elements within the `lbImages div` container of which only the first four are currently visible in the web page.

Next you will use the `textContent` property to insert the title of the lightbox slideshow and the text of the slide counter. The counter text will have the format:

currentImg / imgCount

where *currentImg* is the number of the image currently shown in the lightbox and *imgCount* is the total number of images.

To add the lightbox title and image counter:

1. Directly below the statement that defines the id for the `lbTitle` node, add:

```
lbTitle.textContent = lightboxTitle;
```

2. Below the statement defining the id for the `lbCounter` node, add:

```
let currentImg = 1;
lbCounter.textContent = currentImg + " / " + imgCount;
```

See **Figure 5-13**.

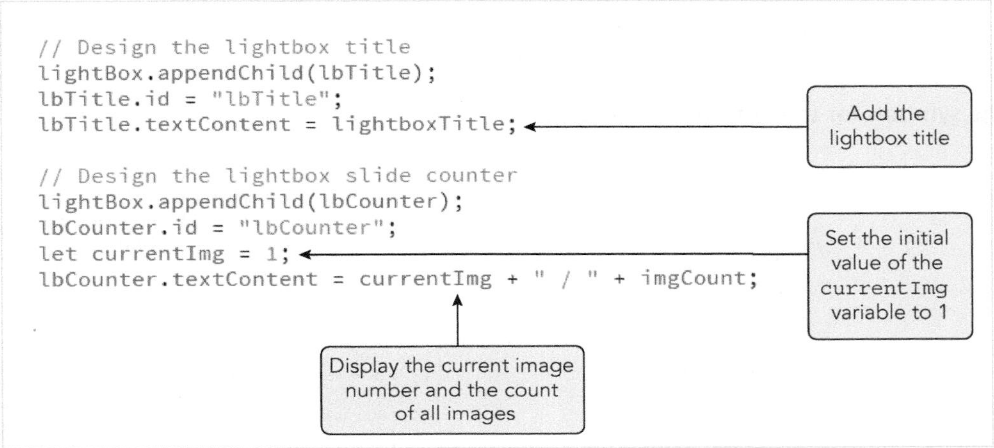

```
// Design the lightbox title
lightBox.appendChild(lbTitle);
lbTitle.id = "lbTitle";
lbTitle.textContent = lightboxTitle;

// Design the lightbox slide counter
lightBox.appendChild(lbCounter);
lbCounter.id = "lbCounter";
let currentImg = 1;
lbCounter.textContent = currentImg + " / " + imgCount;
```

Add the lightbox title
Set the initial value of the currentImg variable to 1
Display the current image number and the count of all images

Figure 5-13 Adding the lightbox title and counter

3. Save your changes and reload **js05.html** in your web browser. Verify that the title "My Western Vacation" appears above the lightbox images and that the counter text "1 / 12" appears superimposed on the first image.

To complete the lightbox content, add symbols for the previous (◀), next (▶), and play/pause (⏯) buttons, using the HTML entity references ◀, ▶, and ⏯, respectively. Because these symbols are entered as HTML code, they must be added using the `innerHTML` property.

To add symbols to the lightbox buttons:

1. Return to the **js05.js** file in your code editor.
2. Directly below the statement defining the id for the `lbPrev` node, add:

```
lbPrev.innerHTML = "&#9664;";
```

3. Below the statement defining the id for the `lbNext` node, add:

```
lbNext.innerHTML = "&#9654;";
```

4. Finally, directly below the statement defining the id for the `lbPlay` node, add:

```
lbPlay.innerHTML = "&#9199;";
```

Figure 5-14 shows the revised code in the `createLightbox()` function.

5. Save your changes and reload **js05.html** in your web browser. **Figure 5-15** shows the complete content of the lightbox including the structure of the `div` and `img` elements.
6. Close the browser debugger.

The lightbox displays only the first four of the 12 images. The other image files are part of the page but hidden using a style rule defined in the lightbox.css style sheet that hides any overflowing content in the lightbox container.

```
// Design the lightbox previous slide button
lightBox.appendChild(lbPrev);
lbPrev.id = "lbPrev";
lbPrev.innerHTML = "&#9664;";

// Design the lightbox next slide button
lightBox.appendChild(lbNext);
lbNext.id = "lbNext";
lbNext.innerHTML = "&#9654;";

// Design the lightbox Play-Pause button
lightBox.appendChild(lbPlay);
lbPlay.id = "lbPlay";
lbPlay.innerHTML = "&#9199;";
```

Display the ◀ symbol

Display the ▶ symbol

Display the ⏯ symbol

Figure 5-14 **Adding the symbols for the buttons in the lightbox**

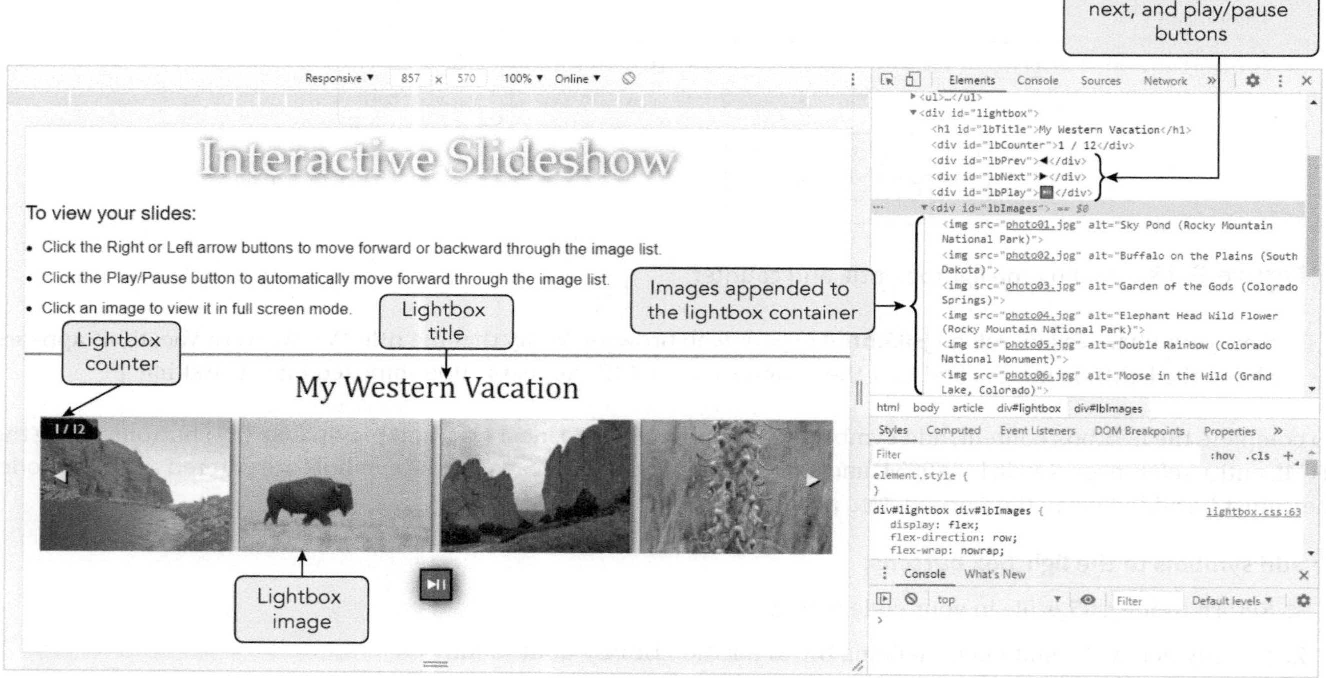

Figure 5-15 **Lightbox images and text** *Joan Carey*

In the next session you will work with commands to allow the user to scroll through image list manually or automatically to view all the images one-by-one.

Quick Check 1

1. Provide the code to reference the last child element of the element with the id "main".
2. What properties would you combine to reference the "cousin" of a node (where cousin refers to the first child of the previous sibling of the parent of node)?
3. Provide code to create a `span` element node named `rating` belonging to the "review" class.
4. Provide code to append the `rating` element node to a `div` element with the id "reviews".
5. Provide code to change the font size of the rating element to 1.2em.

Restructuring a Node Tree

In the next part of the lightbox app you provide the ability to move forward and backward through the image list. Because only four images are displayed at any one time, to move forward the lightbox app must send the first image to the back of the image list, shifting the remaining images forward one place in line. See **Figure 5-16**.

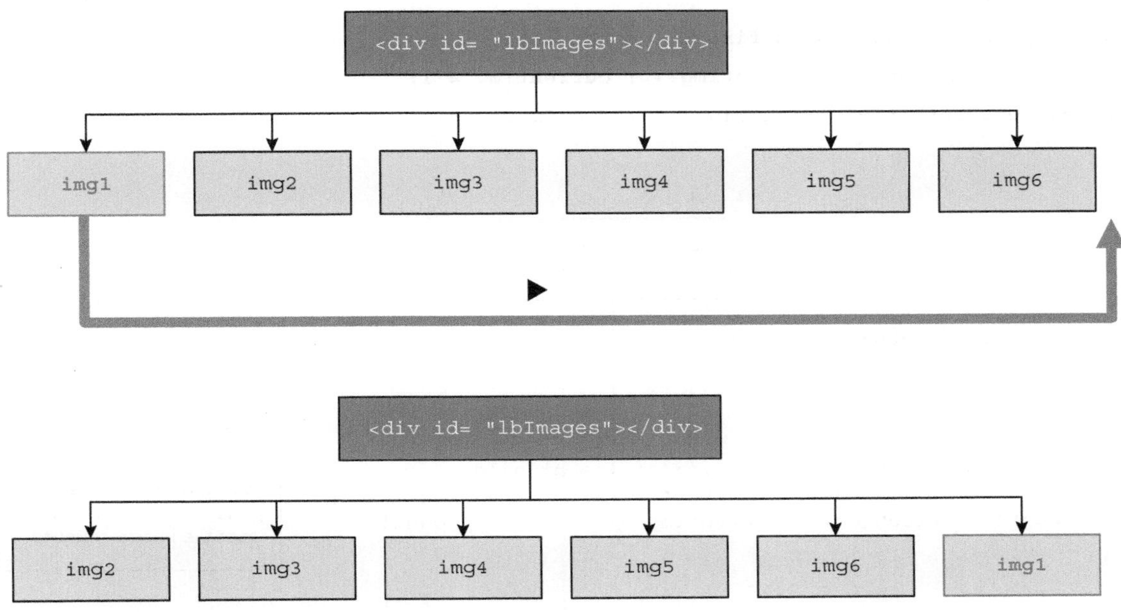

Figure 5-16 Moving forward through the list of images

The app does not need to create or copy any elements, it only needs to move a node that already exists.

Moving Nodes with the `appendChild()` Method

You have already used the `appendChild()` method to add a new child to a parent node. As the name implies, the method appends the node, placing it at the end of the child list. If the node is already part of a document tree, the `appendChild()` method moves the node from its current location to that new position. Thus, the following statement:

```
lbImages.appendChild(lbImages.firstElementChild);
```

moves the first image, referenced with the expression `lbImages.firstElementChild` to the *end* of the list of images. All the other images will move up in position so that the second image is now the first, the third image is now the second, and so forth.

As the user moves through the image list the value of the `currentImg` variable should increase by 1 with each image moved. When the user goes beyond the last image the `currentImg` variable should reset to 1 as the lightbox "loops" back to the beginning of the list. You can determine the value of `currentImg` with the following conditional operator that tests whether the `currentImg` value is less than the total number of images. If it is, the counter is increased by 1; otherwise it is reset to 1.

```
(currentImg < imgCount) ? currentImg++ : currentImg = 1;
lbCounter.textContent = currentImg + " / " + imgCount;
```

Add these statements as part of a `showNext()` function that runs whenever the Next button is clicked within the lightbox.

To create the `showNext()` function:

1. Return to the **js05.js** file in your code editor.
2. Directly before the closing brace of the `createLightbox()` function command block insert the following code as described in **Figure 5-17**:

```
// Function to move forward through the image list
function showNext() {
   lbImages.appendChild(lbImages.firstElementChild);
   (currentImg < imgCount) ? currentImg++ : currentImg = 1;
   lbCounter.textContent = currentImg + " / " + imgCount;
}
```

```
      lbImages.appendChild(image);
   }

   // Function to move forward through the image list
   function showNext() {
      lbImages.appendChild(lbImages.firstElementChild);
      (currentImg < imgCount) ? currentImg++ : currentImg = 1;
      lbCounter.textContent = currentImg + " / " + imgCount;
   }
}
```

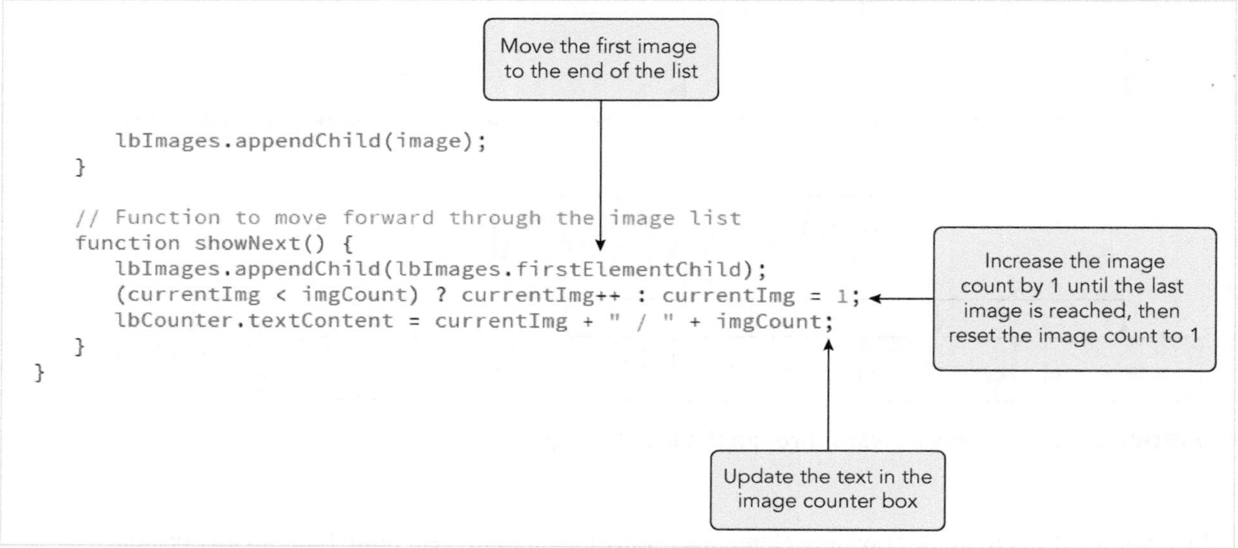

Figure 5-17 The `showNext()` function

3. Scroll up to the line that sets the `innerHTML` value of the `lbNext` element node and add the following event hander (see **Figure 5-18**):

```
lbNext.onclick = showNext;
```

```
// Design the lightbox next slide button
lightBox.appendChild(lbNext);
lbNext.id = "lbNext";
lbNext.innerHTML = "&#9654;";
lbNext.onclick = showNext;
```

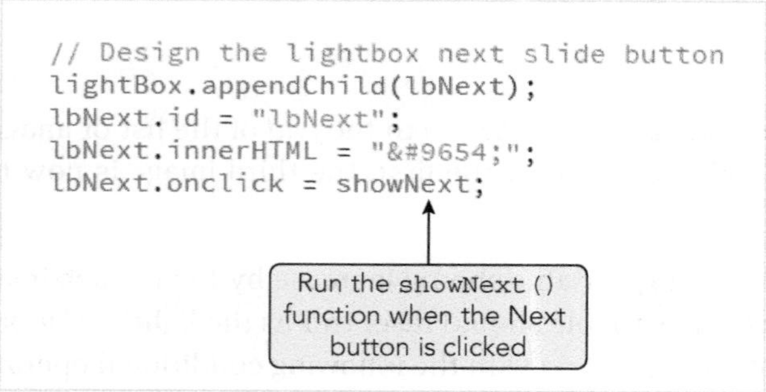

Figure 5-18 Event handler for the `showNext()` function

4. Save your changes to the file and then reload **js05.html** in your web browser.
5. Click the ► button repeatedly in the lightbox to verify that the app advances forward through the image list and the image counter increases by 1.
6. Continue clicking the ► button to verify that the images loop around to the beginning after moving through the first 12 images and that the image counter returns to a value of 1.

Notice that by placing the `showNext()` function within the command block, you have given the function local scope, confined to the `createLightbox()` function. When creating apps that may be used by third parties, you want to give your variables and functions local scope so they do not interfere with any other code your users might be running. It is not uncommon for an app to have a single function with several nested functions doing the work.

Moving Nodes with the `insertBefore()` Method

To move backwards through the list of images, the lightbox app must move the last image to the beginning of the line, shifting the subsequent images back one position. See **Figure 5-19**.

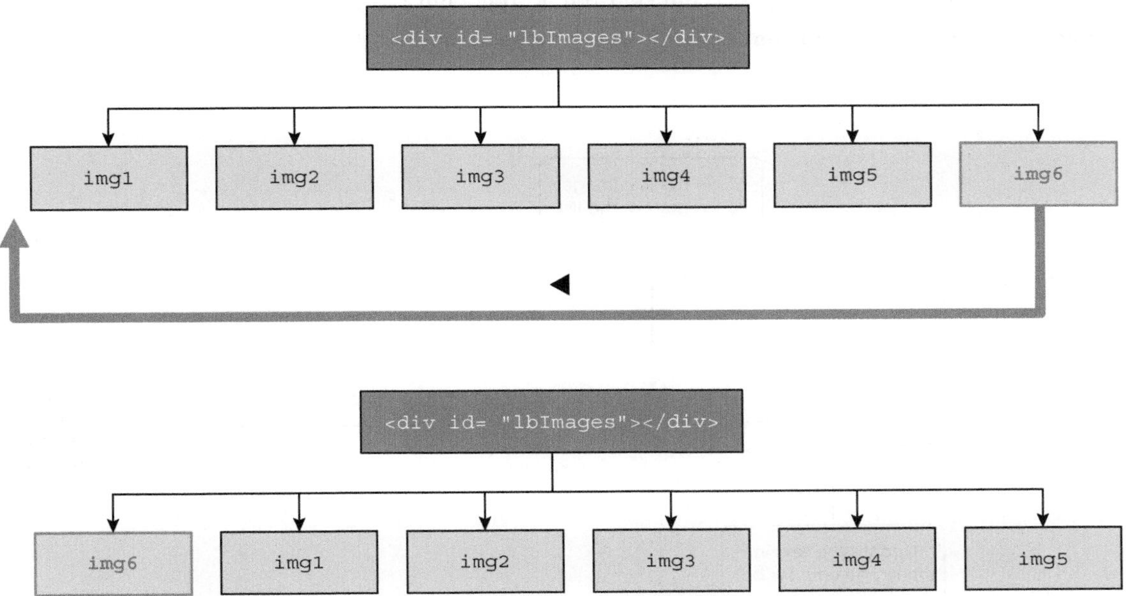

Figure 5-19 Moving backward through the list of images

To insert a node at any position other than the end of the list of child nodes, apply the following `insertBefore()` method:

```
node.insertBefore(new, child)
```

where *`node`* is the parent node, *`new`* is the node that will be inserted as a new child of the parent, and *`child`* is a child node before which the new node is to be placed. As with the `appendChild()` method, if the *`new`* node is already part of the node tree it will be moved from its current location to its new location.

For the lightbox, the *`new`* node would be the last image referenced with the expression `lbImages.lastElementChild` and the *`child`* node would be first image referenced with the expression `lbImages.firstElementChild`. The following command would then move the last image to the front of image list:

```
lbImages.insertBefore(lbImages.lastElementChild,lbImages.firstElementChild);
```

As the user moves backward through the image list, the image counter should decrease by 1 with each image displayed until the first image is reached. At that point, the counter will have “looped” to the end of the list and the next image should have a counter value equal to number of the last image. The code to update the counter value would use the following conditional operator:

```
(currentImg > 1) ? currentImg-- : currentImg = imgCount;
lbCounter.textContent = currentImg + " / " + imgCount;
```

As long as `currentImg` is greater than 1, its value will decrease by 1, otherwise its value will be set to the number of the last slide image as the slideshow loops back to the end of the image list. Add these statements to the `showPrev()` function that will be called when the Previous button is clicked.

To create the `showPrev()` function:

1. Return to the **js05.js** file in your code editor.
2. Directly below the `showNext()` function add the following code as described in **Figure 5-20**:

```
// Function to move backward through the image list
function showPrev() {
   lbImages.insertBefore(lbImages.lastElementChild,
lbImages.firstElementChild);
   (currentImg > 1) ? currentImg-- : currentImg = imgCount;
   lbCounter.textContent = currentImg + " / " + imgCount;
}
```

```
      lbCounter.textContent = currentImg + " / " + imgCount;
   }

   // Function to move backward through the image list
   function showPrev() {
      lbImages.insertBefore(lbImages.lastElementChild, lbImages.firstElementChild);
      (currentImg > 1) ? currentImg-- : currentImg = imgCount;
      lbCounter.textContent = currentImg + " / " + imgCount;
   }
}
```

Move the last image to the start of the list
Decrease the image count by 1 until the first image is reached, then reset the image count to the total number of images
Update the text in the image counter box

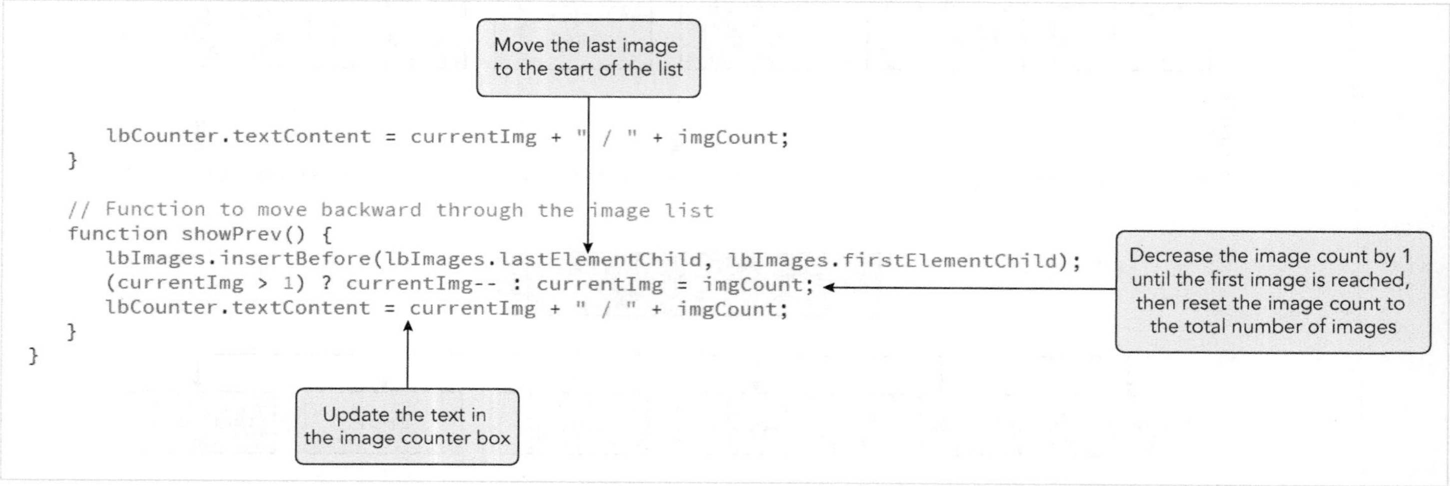

Figure 5-20 The `showPrev()` function

3. Scroll up to the line that sets the `innerHTML` value of the `lbPrev` element node and add the following event hander (see **Figure 5-21**):

```
lbPrev.onclick = showPrev;
```

```
// Design the lightbox previous slide button
lightBox.appendChild(lbPrev);
lbPrev.id = "lbPrev";
lbPrev.innerHTML = "&#9664;";
lbPrev.onclick = showPrev;
```

Run the showPrev() function when the Previous button is clicked

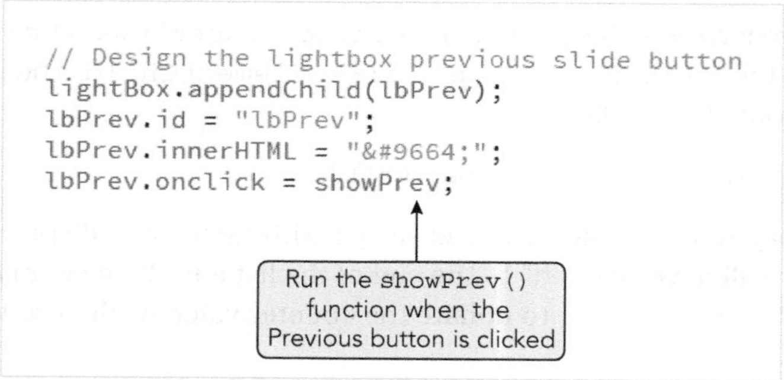

Figure 5-21 Calling the `showPrev()` function

4. Save your changes to the file and reload **js05.html** in your web browser.
5. Click the ◀ button to verify that the lightbox moves backward through the image list and that the image counter displays a decreasing image count.

If the slideshow is not moving through image list as expected, use your browser's debugger, and view the list of `img` elements with the document. Verify that the sequence of `img` elements changes as you move forward and backward in the list. If you have an error in your code, check that your program matches the code shown in Figures 5-17, 5-18, 5-20, and 5-21.

Cloning a Node

In some of your applications you may need to create and move a copy of a node rather than the node itself. To create a node copy, apply the command:

```
node.cloneNode(deep)
```

where *`node`* is the node to be copied and *`deep`* is a Boolean value that is *`true`* to create a deep copy that copies the node and all of its descendants or `false` to copy only the node and not any descendants. In the following code, the `mainCopy` node is a copy of all the content of the `mainElem` node, including any nested headings, paragraphs, text, inline image tags, etc.

```
let mainElem = document.getElementById("main");
let mainCopy = mainElem.cloneNode(true);
```

The `cloneNode()` method will copy all of the node's DOM content, but it will not copy any JavaScript properties attached to the node. For example, it will not copy event handlers, so those will have to added individually to any node copies.

Running Timed Commands

Many slideshows give users the option of automatically running the show rather than clicking a button to go to the next image. You will add that capability to the lightbox app.

Repeating Commands at Specified Intervals

A timed command is a command or function that is run at a specified time or repeated at set intervals. To repeat a command at set intervals, apply the following `setInterval()` method:

```
timeVar = window.setInterval(command, interval)
```

where *`timeVar`* is a variable that stores an id identifying the timed command, *`command`* is a statement or command that will be repeatedly run, and *`interval`* is the interval in milliseconds between runs. For example, the following statement runs the `moveNext()` function every 2000 milliseconds (2 seconds) after an initial 2-second delay. The `id` of the timed command is stored in the `timeID` variable.

```
let timeID = window.setInterval(moveNext, 2000);
```

Note | To run a timed command with no initial delay, include two statements: the first statement running the command immediately and a second statement using the `setInterval()` method to run the command after a specified time interval.

Use the `setInterval()` method to run the `moveNext()` command every 1.5 seconds or 1500 milliseconds, storing the id of the timer in the `timeID` variable. Initiate this process by adding an event handler to the `lbPlay` element node that runs the time command when the Play-Pause button is clicked.

To create a timed command:

1. Return to the **js05.js** file in your code editor.
2. Directly below the command that sets the `innerHTML` property of the `lbPlay` element node, add the following command to declare the `timeID` variable, but leaving its value undefined (because no timed command has been initialized yet).

```
let timeID;
```

3. Next, apply an event handler to the `lbPlay` element node that runs the following anonymous function when that button is clicked:

```
lbPlay.onclick = function() {
   showNext();
   timeID = window.setInterval(showNext, 1500);
}
```

See **Figure 5-22**.

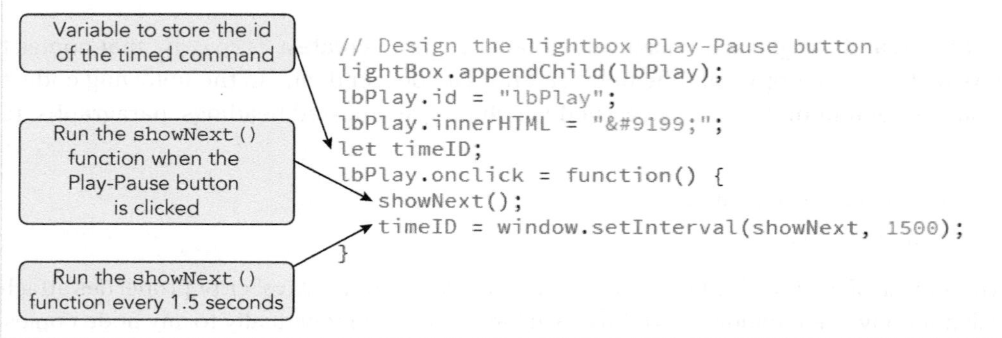

Figure 5-22 Running a timed command

4. Save your changes to the file and then reload **js05.html** in your web browser.
5. Click the ⏯ button to verify that the lightbox starts moving through the images every 1.5 seconds without stopping.

Once the slideshow is started, there is no way to stop it save reloading the web page. You need to modify the ⏯ button so that it pauses the slideshow if it is already running and restarts the slideshow if it is currently paused.

Stopping a Timed Command

Once a timed command is initiated, it can be stopped using the following `clearInterval()` method:

```
window.clearInterval(timeVar)
```

where *`timeVar`* is the variable storing the id of the timed command. An application might have several timed commands running simultaneously, so the id is necessary to distinguish one timed command from another.

The lightbox's play/pause button needs to toggle between two states: (1) If the slideshow is not running, clicking the ⏯ button starts the show; and (2) if the slideshow is running, clicking the ⏯ button stops the show by clearing the timed command. The following `if else` statement covers both conditions:

```
if (timeID) {
   window.clearInterval(timeID);
   timeID = undefined;
} else {
   showNext();
   timeID = window.setInterval(showNext, 1500);
}
```

The `if` condition is `true` only if `timeID` has a truthy (defined) value and the slideshow is running. The `if` statement clears the timed command and sets `timeID` back to `undefined`; otherwise the slideshow is not running and the `else` condition starts the slideshow by running the `showNext()` function and storing the id of the timed command.

Add this `if else` statement to the code for the lightbox app.

To clear a timed command:

1. Return to the **js05.js** file in your code editor.
2. Replace the two commands in the anonymous function you created in the last set of steps with the following `if else` structure:

```
if (timeID) {
   // Stop the slideshow
   window.clearInterval(timeID);
   timeID = undefined;
} else {
   // Start the slideshow
   showNext();
   timeID = window.setInterval(showNext, 1500);
}
```

See **Figure 5-23**.

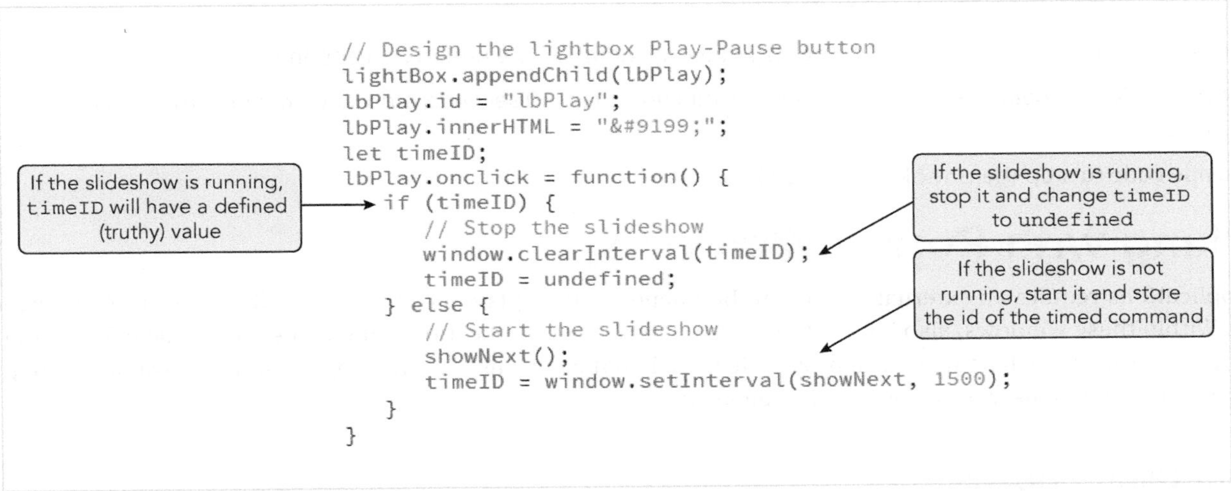

```
// Design the lightbox Play-Pause button
lightBox.appendChild(lbPlay);
lbPlay.id = "lbPlay";
lbPlay.innerHTML = "&#9199;";
let timeID;
lbPlay.onclick = function() {
   if (timeID) {
      // Stop the slideshow
      window.clearInterval(timeID);
      timeID = undefined;
   } else {
      // Start the slideshow
      showNext();
      timeID = window.setInterval(showNext, 1500);
   }
}
```

If the slideshow is running, `timeID` will have a defined (truthy) value

If the slideshow is running, stop it and change `timeID` to `undefined`

If the slideshow is not running, start it and store the id of the timed command

Figure 5-23 Toggling between starting and stopping the slideshow

3. Save your changes to the file and then reload **js05.html** in your web browser.
4. Click the ⏯ button to start the slideshow. Click the ⏯ button again the stop the show. Continue clicking the ⏯ button to verify that the state of lightbox toggles between running and pausing the slideshow.

Note that the browser is not guaranteed to run a timed command at exactly the specified time. While the command is scheduled to be run at that time, it is also placed within a queue along with other commands. Commands are only run when they reach the top of the queue and thus a timed command might not always start exactly at the specified time.

Using Time-Delayed Commands

Another type of timed command is one in which the command is run once after a specified delay. To run a delayed command use the following `setTimeout()` method:

```
let timeVar = window.setTimeout(command, delay);
```

where *`delay`* is the delay time in milliseconds. The following command runs the `showNext()` function but only after a 2-second delay.

```
let timeID = window.setTimeout(showNext, 2000);
```

As with the `setInterval()` method, time-delayed commands can be assigned an id that distinguishes the command from other timed commands. To prevent a delayed command from running, apply the following `clearTimeout()` method:

```
window.clearTimeout(timeVar)
```

Once a time-delayed command runs or is cleared, it is removed from the queue and will not run unless another `setTimeout()` method is applied to place it back in the queue.

Note With all properties and methods of the `window` object, you can omit the `window` part of the reference name, for example, using `setInterval()` in place of `window.setInterval()`. You can use the `window` part of the reference to apply the property or method to a specific browser window in the case of a script that involves working with multiple open windows.

You have completed your work on the lightbox tools that enable the user to move through the slideshow images. Your final task will be to add a feature that displays full-screen versions of individual images from the lightbox.

Quick Check 2

1. Where does the `appendChild()` method place nodes?
2. Provide code to create a copy of the `rating` node, including all the node's descendants.
3. Provide code to repeat the `checkAnswers()` function every 10 seconds; store the time id in the variable `timeID`.
4. Provide code to stop the `checkAnswers()` function from repeating.

Working with Popup Windows

Many applications require an external window to be opened and displayed on top of or adjacent to the application content. Within these windows, also known as popup windows, the application can include additional information to users or provide an area where users can provide feedback that can be used by the application. For example, a popup window might prompt a user for a password or email address.

System Dialog Boxes

One popup window that you've already seen is the alert window created with the `window.alert()` method. The alert window simply displays a message along with an OK button to close the window, but the method does not ask for any response from the user.

A window that does provide the ability for the user to respond is a confirmation window that displays a message along with an OK and Cancel button. The window returns a value of `true` or `false` depending on whether the user closed the window by clicking the OK button or the Cancel button. To create a confirmation window, apply the following `window.confirm()` method:

```
response = window.confirm(message)
```

where *`response`* is a Boolean value that is `true` if the user clicks the OK button and `false` if the user clicks the Cancel button, and *`message`* is the text that appears in the window.

For a more general response, JavaScript provides the prompt window that displays a message along with an input box into which the user can enter a text string. To create a prompt window, apply the following `window.prompt()` method:

```
response = window.prompt(message, default)
```

where *response* is the text of the user's response, *message* is the prompt message, and *default* is the input box's default value. **Figure 5-24** shows examples of each window along with the code that generated it.

```
window.alert("Welcome to the game!")
```

This page says

Welcome to the game!

OK

```
window.confirm("Quit the game?")
```

This page says

Quit the game?

OK Cancel

```
window.prompt("Which game to play?", "Poker")
```

This page says

Which game to play?

Poker

OK Cancel

Figure 5-24 JavaScript popup windows

The exact appearance of the window is determined by the operating system and the browser. There are no JavaScript properties or CSS styles to modify these windows.

Working with Browser Windows

Another approach to creating a popup window is to open a new browser window. The browser window then becomes its own `window` object with its own collection of properties and methods. You can use JavaScript to create a new `window` object and define the window's appearance and content. **Figure 5-25** describes some of the JavaScript properties associated with the `window` object.

PROPERTY	DESCRIPTION
`window.closed`	Returns true if the browser window or tab has been closed
`window.document`	References the document stored in the window
`window.history`	References the browsing history stored with the window
`window.innerHeight`	Returns the height of the window's content area, including the scrollbar
`window.innerWidth`	Returns the width of the window's content area, including the scrollbar
`window.location`	Returns information about the current URL displayed in the window
`window.name`	Sets or returns the name of the window
`window.navigator`	References an object containing information about the browser displaying the window
`window.outerHeight`	Returns the height of the browser window, including the scrollbar
`window.outerWidth`	Returns the width of the browser window, including the scrollbar
`window.screen`	References an object containing information about the user's viewscreen
`window.status`	Sets or returns the text displayed in the browser window status bar

Figure 5-25 Properties of the `window` object

Figure 5-26 describes some of the methods that can be applied to the `window` object.

METHOD	DESCRIPTION
`window.blur()`	Removes the focus from the browser window or tab
`window.close()`	Closes the browser window or tab
`window.focus()`	Makes the `window` object the active window or tab
`window.moveBy(x, y)`	Moves the browser window *x* pixels horizontally and *y* pixels vertically
`window.moveTo(x, y)`	Moves the browser window to the screen coordinates (*x*, *y*)
`window.open(url, name, option, replace)`	Opens a new browser window or tab where *`url`* is the location of a file loaded into the window, *`name`* is the window's name, *`options`* defines the window's appearance, and *`replace`* is Boolean value that specifies whether *`url`* should create a new entry in the window's history list (`true`) or replace the existing entry (`false`)
`window.print()`	Opens the print dialog box displaying the content of the browser window
`window.resizeBy(width, height)`	Resizes the window by specified *`width`* and *`height`* relative to its current size
`window.resizeTo(width, height)`	Resizes the window to a specified *`width`* and *`height`*
`window.scrollBy(xnum, ynum)`	Scrolls the browser window or tab by a specified amount in the horizontal (*xnum*) and vertical direction (*ynum*)
`window.scrollTo(xpos, ypos)`	Scrolls the browser window or tab to a specified (*xpos*, *ypos*) coordinate in the document

Figure 5-26 Methods of the `window` object

To create a new browser window, apply the following `window.open()` method:

```
window.open(url, title, options, replace)
```

where *`url`* is the location of the file displayed in the window, *`title`* is the window's title, *`options`* is a comma-separated list of features defining the window's appearance, and *`replace`* is an optional Boolean value that specifies whether *`url`* should create a new entry in the window's history list (`true`) or replace the existing entry (`false`). You can include all or none of the arguments for the `window.open()` method.

Depending on the arguments used with the `window.open()` method, the new content might open as a popup window or it might appear as a new tab within the browser. For example, the statement `window.open("http://www.example.com");` opens the page at *www.example.com* in a new browser window or tab. If you exclude a *`url`* value or specify and empty text string, a blank browser window or tab opens.

You can customize the appearance of a new browser window or tab using the *`options`* argument in the `window.open()` method. **Figure 5-27** lists options common to all major browsers. Because the `window` object is part of the Browser Object Model, the exact list of features is determined by the browser. Some browsers also include the ability to turn off the address bar or allow the window to be resized; others do not.

NAME	DESCRIPTION
`height=value`	Sets the window's height in pixels
`left=value`	Sets the horizontal position of the window in pixels
`menubar=yes|no|1|0`	Displays the menu bar (`yes` or `1`) or hides it (`no` or `0`)
`scrollbars=yes|no|1|0`	Displays scrollbars (`yes` or `1`) or hides them (`no` or `0`)
`status=yes|no|1|0`	Displays the status bar (`yes` or `1`) or hides it (`no` or `0`)
`toolbar=yes|no|1|0`	Displays the browser toolbar (`yes` or `1`) or hides it (`no` or `0`)
`top=value`	Sets the vertical position of the window in pixels
`width=value`	Sets the window's width in pixels

Figure 5-27 Options of the `window.open()` method

If you omit an option list in the `window.open()` method, then all standard options are included in the new browser window. However, if the `window.open()` method does include an option list, only those features specified in that list will be applied to the new window or tab. To force the browser to display a new browser window rather than a new tab, always include a width and height value in the option list of the `window.open()` method.

The following statement creates a browser window that is 400 pixels wide by 600 pixels tall displaying the contents of the page at *www.example.com* without a toolbar, menu bar, location box, or status bar.

```
let newWin = window.open("http://www.example.com", "win", "width=400, height=600, toolbar=0,
menubar=0, scrollbars=0, status=0");
```

The window is stored in an object variable named `newWin`. When a window has been saved under a variable name, you can apply the properties and methods described in Figures 5-25 and 5-26 to it. For example, the following statement moves the `newWin` browser window to a position 300 pixels to left and 400 pixels down from the top-left corner of the screen and then increases its width and height by 50 pixels.

```
newWin.moveTo(300,400);
newWin.resizeBy(50, 50);
```

Values for moving, sizing, or scrolling browser windows are always measured in pixels. You do not have to include the `px` unit, only the value itself.

> **Note** You can reference the window from which the popup window was opened using the `opener` property. The expression `newWin.opener` would refer to the original window that opened the `newWin` popup. In this way, the two windows can exchange information and content.

Writing Content to a Browser Window

The new window contains a web document and thus all document properties and methods can be applied to that document. The document body contained within the window is referenced using the *`window`*`.document.body` object where *`window`* is the name assigned to the window object. Thus, the following code creates a blank window named `newWin` and adds the `h1` heading `<h1>My slideshow</h1>` to the document body.

```
let newWin = window.open("", "slideshow", "width=500, height=300");
let mainHeading = document.createElement("h1");
mainHeading.textContent = "My Slideshow";
newWin.document.body.appendChild(mainHeading);
```

You can also use the `document.write()` method to write the content into the document as a single text string:

```
let newWin = window.open("", "slideshow", "width=500, height=300");
newWin.document.write("<h1>My Slideshow</h1>");
```

Unlike windows created with the `confirm()` or `prompt()` methods, a browser popup window can be designed in whatever fashion the application requires. You can include form elements, tables, and embedded images to design a customized dialog box suitable for your app.

Limitations of Browser Windows

While you can do a lot with browser windows, they do suffer from some very important limitations:

- Popup browser windows can be blocked by popup blockers installed by the user or built into the browser itself.
- Browser windows do not scale well to small mobile devices such as cell phones, which put a premium on screen space.
- For security reasons, browser windows cannot display files that are loaded locally on the user's computer.
- Browsers are not consistent in how they handle browsers windows. A feature that is supported in one browser might not be supported in a different browser.

All of this is not to say you should never use a browser window as a popup. They are flexible and easy to apply and make sense for some applications. However, their use has declined in recent years due to their limitations.

> **Note** Popup blockers generally will not block popup windows that are opened in response to user-initiated events, such as clicking a form button.

Creating an Overlay

An alternative to a popup window is an overlay, which is an element that lays on top of the rest of the page content, partially obscuring that content. An overlay is sometimes referred to as a modal or modal window, a window that takes control of an application and must be closed before the user can continue using the app. Examples of modal windows include popup dialog boxes that must be completed before returning a user to the web form or, annoyingly, a popup ad that must be clicked before a user can return to a web page.

The final piece of the lightbox app will be an overlay that is generated whenever the user clicks an image from the lightbox slideshow. The overlay will display a full-sized version of the clicked image alongside the image caption. Included with the overlay will be a Close button that closes the overlay when clicked. See **Figure 5-28**.

Figure 5-28 Image overlay for the lightbox app *Joan Carey*

The image overlay will contain the following HTML code:

```
<div id="lbOverlay">
   <figure>
      <img src="url" alt="text" />
      <figcaption>text</figcaption>
   </figure>
   <div id="lbOverlayClose">&times;</div>
</div>
```

where `url` is the URL of the clicked image and `text` is the caption text associated with that image. The styles for the overlay have already been entered into the lightbox.css stylesheet, using the following style rules:

```
div#lbOverlay {
   position: fixed;
   top: 0;
```

```
    left: 0;
    z-index: 1;
    width: 100%;
    height: 100%;
    background-color: rgba(104, 49, 0, 0.85);
}
```

The style rule fixes the `div` element within the browser window and sizes it to cover the complete window. A semi-transparent browser background is used so that the contents of the page are still partially visible beneath the overlay.

Add the `createOverlay()` function to begin creating the structure and content of the overlay.

To begin creating the image overlay:

1. Return to the **js05.js** file in your code editor.
2. Directly before the closing curly brace of the `createLightbox()` function, insert the following initial code for the `createOverlay()` function as described in **Figure 5-29**:

```
function createOverlay() {
    let overlay = document.createElement("div");
    overlay.id = "lbOverlay";

    // Add the figure box to the overlay
    let figureBox = document.createElement("figure");
    overlay.appendChild(figureBox);

    document.body.appendChild(overlay);
}
```



```
function createOverlay() {
    let overlay = document.createElement("div");
    overlay.id = "lbOverlay";

    // Add the figure box to the overlay
    let figureBox = document.createElement("figure");
    overlay.appendChild(figureBox);

    document.body.appendChild(overlay);
  }
}
```

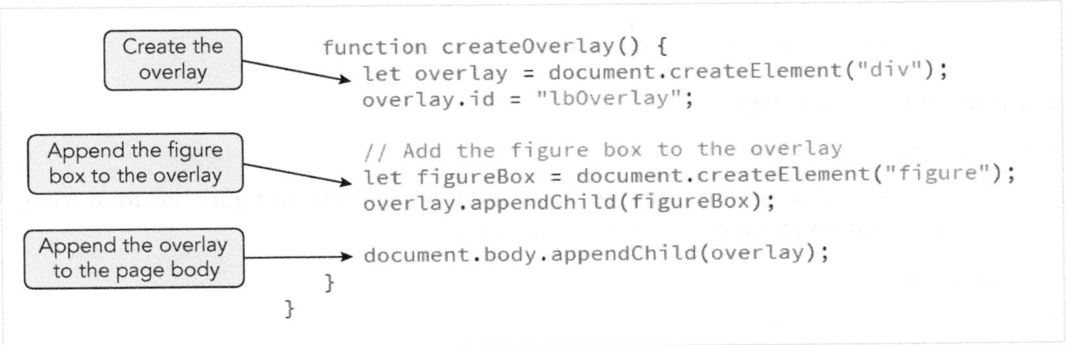

Figure 5-29 Initial `createOverlay()` function

3. Scroll up to the `for` loop that adds images to the container and directly below the statement that sets the value of the `alt` property, and insert the following statement to run the `createOverlay()` function whenever an lightbox image is clicked (see **Figure 5-30**):

```
image.onclick = createOverlay;
```

4. Save your changes and then reload **js05.html** in your web browser.
5. Click any image within the lightbox and verify that a semi-transparent brown overlay covers the entire page. If the overlay is not generated, use your browser's debugger to examine the elements within the web page to verify that overlay box was created. Check the code in your file against the code shown in Figures 5-29 and 5-30.

Next you will add the image and caption to the overlay. To do that the app needs to know which image was clicked by the user. That can be accomplished using the `this` object.

```
// Add images from the imgFiles array to the container
for (let i = 0; i < imgCount; i++) {
   let image = document.createElement("img");
   image.src = imgFiles[i];
   image.alt = imgCaptions[i];
   image.onclick = createOverlay;
   lbImages.appendChild(image);
}
```

Call the createOverlay() function when any image is clicked

Figure 5-30 Adding an event handler for the `createOverlay()` function

Introducing the `this` Object

The this object references the owner of a currently running segment of JavaScript code. That general definition can be confusing because its meaning depends on context. How do you determine who "owns" the code? For an anonymous function called by an event handler or event listener, the owner of the function is the object that initiated the event. If clicking an image initiated an event that called an anonymous function, that image is the called function's owner.

From within the `createOverlay()` function, you can reference the image that called the function using the `this` object. The following code uses the `this` object to append a copy of the image node to the overlay's figure box:

```
let overlayImage = this.cloneNode("true");
figureBox.appendChild(overlayImage);
```

In the same way, the following code creates the figure caption based on the `alt` attribute of the image node and appends it to the figure box:

```
let overlayCaption = document.createElement("figcaption");
overlayCaption.textContent = this.alt;
figureBox.appendChild(overlayCaption);
```

Add both sections of code to the `createOverlay()` function and retest your app.

To append the image and caption to the overlay:

1. Return to the **js05.js** file in your code editor.
2. Within the `createOverlay()` function directly after the statement that appends the figure box to overlay, add the following code to copy the image and append it to the figure box:

```
// Add the image to the figure box
let overlayImage = this.cloneNode("true");
figureBox.appendChild(overlayImage);
```

3. Next, add the following code as described in **Figure 5-31** to add the figure caption, set the caption text, and append the caption to the figure box:

```
// Add the caption to the figure box
let overlayCaption = document.createElement("figcaption");
overlayCaption.textContent = this.alt;
figureBox.appendChild(overlayCaption);
```

4. Save your changes to the file and then reload **js05.html** in your web browser.
5. Click any image within the lightbox app and verify that a larger version of the image along with the image caption is overlaid on the page. Note that this overlaying is done with an animated zoom effect that was created within the lightbox.css stylesheet.

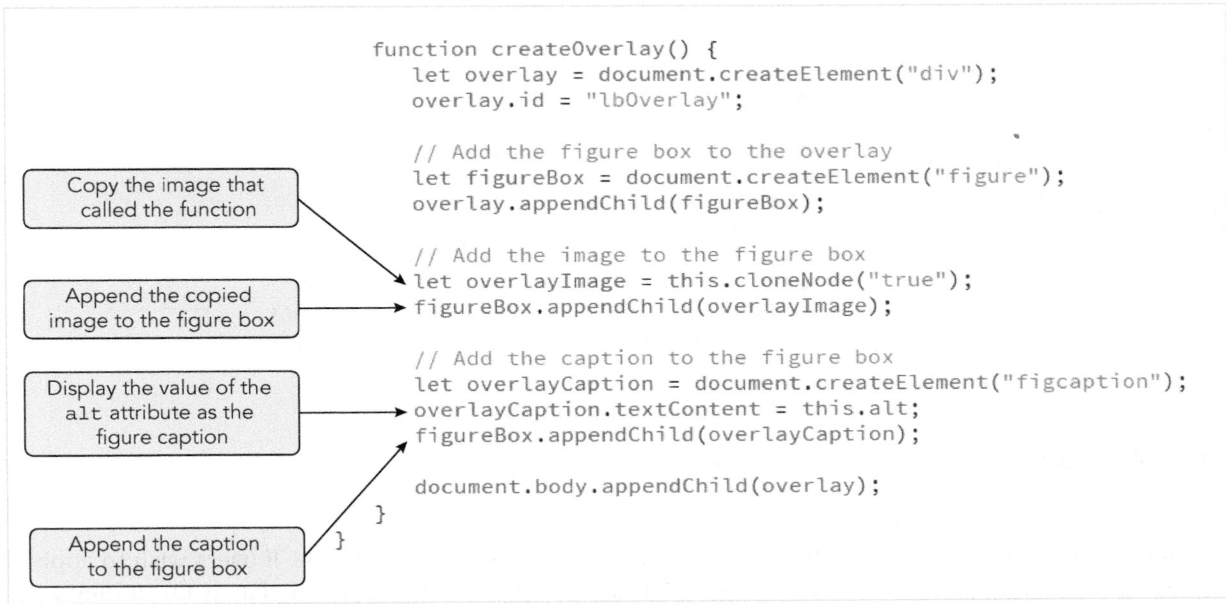

Figure 5-31 Adding an image and caption to the overlay

Removing a Node

To complete the lightbox app, you will add a close button that removes the overlay from the web page, returning the user to the lightbox slideshow. To remove a node, apply the method:

```
node.removeChild(old)
```

where *node* is the parent node and *old* is the child node that will be removed from the parent. Add a close button to the overlay and create an event handler that removes the overlay when that button is clicked.

To create the overlay close button:

1. Return to the **js05.js** file in your code editor.
2. Within the `createOverlay()` function directly after the statement that appends the caption to the figure box add the following code to create the close button:

```
// Add a close button to the overlay
let closeBox = document.createElement("div");
closeBox.id = "lbOverlayClose";
closeBox.innerHTML = "&times;";
```

3. Next, add an event handler that calls an anonymous function to remove the overlay from the document body when the close button is clicked:

```
closeBox.onclick = function() {
   document.body.removeChild(overlay);
}
```

4. Finally, append the close button to the overlay:

```
overlay.appendChild(closeBox);
```

   Figure 5-32 describes the code added to the `createOverlay()` function.

5. Close the file, saving your changes.
6. Reload the **js05.html** file in your browser. Verify that you can open the overlay when any image in the lightbox is clicked and that you can close the overlay by clicking the close button in the upper-right corner of the browser window.

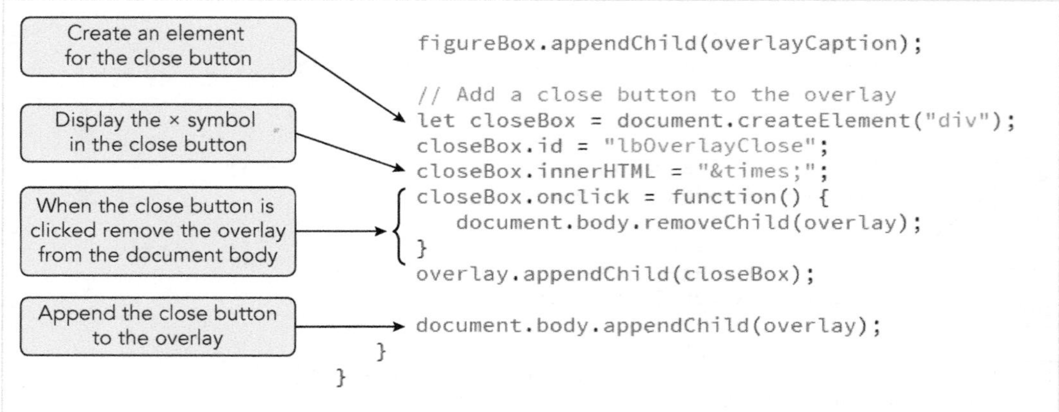

Figure 5-32 Adding the close box to the overlay

You have completed your work on the lightbox app. The app is reasonably customizable. If users wish to apply this app to their own projects, they can change the images and captions listed in the lightbox_data.js file. If they wish to change the look and feel of the lightbox or the overlay, they can make changes to the lightbox.css stylesheet without having to touch the JavaScript code.

Best Practices | Designing the Look of an App

When you plan the visual design for your app, you want to create a design that can be easily modified in the future. For that reason, put as much of your design choices within a CSS stylesheet and not within your JavaScript code. One way of accomplishing this is with classes. For example, you could include the following statement in your app to increase the font size of text in a "major" element:

```
document.getElementById("major").style.fontSize = "1.8em";
```

But a better approach is the following statement that changes that element's class name:

```
document.getElementById("major").className = "majorText";
```

and leaves the style definition in the CSS style sheet. If at a later date you and your team decide that your app needs a facelift, you can make all the modifications to the style definitions for that class in the stylesheet, saving you the trouble of wading through what might be long and complicated script looking for all the style settings.

Quick Check 3

1. Provide code to create a confirmation window with the message "Do you wish to continue?", storing the response in the `continuePlay` variable.
2. Provide code to create a prompt window with the message "Enter your state" with the default value, "Texas". Store the response in the `state` variable.
3. Provide code for the URL "http://www.microsoft.com" in a new browser window named `newWin` that is 600 pixels wide and 400 pixels tall. Store the window object in variable named `myWindow`.
4. Provide code to increase the width of `myWindow` by 100 pixels and the height by 50 pixels.
5. What do you use the `this` object for?

Exploring the Browser Object Model

In some situations, an app may need to work with the user's browser or device. In this section you will review some of the objects, properties, and methods associated with the Browser Object Model (BOM). Like objects in the Document Object Model, objects in the BOM are also arranged in a hierarchy with the browser window at the top of the tree. See **Figure 5-33**.

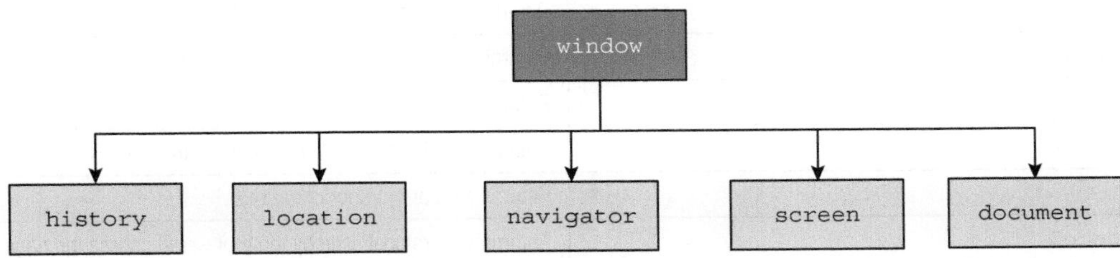

Figure 5-33 Browser Object Model

The browser automatically creates the `window` object and the other objects in tree. The `window` object is also referred to as a global object because all other objects in the BOM are contained within it.

The `History` Object

Each browser window maintains a history of all the pages that have been opened during the current session within a history list. Under the BOM, this information is stored in the `history` object. For security and privacy reasons, the `history` object does not store the actual contents or addresses of those pages, but you can go back and forth through the history list using the `back()`, `forward()`, and `go()` methods described in **Figure 5-34**.

HISTORY METHOD	DESCRIPTION
`history.back()`	Go back one page in the history list
`history.forward()`	Go forward one page in the history list
`history.go(`*`integer`*`)`	Go to a page whose index is indicated by *`integer`*. Negative integers cause the browser to go back in the history list; positive integers cause the browser to go forward. An integer value of 0 reloads the page.

Figure 5-34 Methods of the `History` object

For example, to go back one page in the history list, apply either of the following statements:

```
window.history.back();
window.history.go(-1);
```

To go forward one page, apply either command:

```
window.history.forward();
window.history.go(1);
```

These navigation methods are often used for applications that involve data entry in web forms spread across multiple pages. By applying these methods, users can go back or forward through the pages to review or revise their answers. To navigate through the history list of a popup window, use the name assigned to the window object as part of the history statement.

Note The total number of pages stored in the history list is provided by the `window.history.length` property.

The location Object

Information about the current page opened in the browser is stored in the location object. Properties and methods of the location object are described in **Figure 5-35**.

PROPERTY	DESCRIPTION
location.hash	Returns the anchor part (#) of the location URL
location.host	Returns the name of the server and the port number, if present
location.hostname	Returns the name of the server hosting the URL
location.href	Returns the full text of the URL address
location.pathname	Returns the directory and/or filename within the URL
location.port	Returns the port number of the URL
location.protocol	Returns the protocol used by the browser to access the page
location.search	Returns the query string portion of the URL
location.assign(*url*)	Loads the page at the *url* address
location.reload()	Reloads the current page
location.replace(*url*)	Replaces the current document with the page at the *url* address

Figure 5-35 Properties and methods of the location object

The location object is a property of both the document and window objects, so you can write the entire reference as either document.location or window.location. If you omit the document or window object, the location is assumed to refer to the current document being viewed in the currently active window.

The location object is useful for apps that must load certain web pages or extract important information from page addresses. A navigation app might need to load specific web page maps or geolocation websites to function properly. Web forms often include field names and values as part of the web address so that by accessing the location object, the app can extract those field names and values from the address. For example, following statement uses the location object to load the Google home page into a popup browser window named newWin.

```
let newWin = window.open("", "searchbox", "width=700, height=700");
newWin.location.href = "http://www.google.com";
```

You can also load the Google home page using either of the following statements:

```
location.assign("http://www.google.com");
location.replace("http://www.google.com");
```

The difference is that replace() method removes the URL of the current page, so that the user won't be able to use the back button to navigate back to the original document.

The navigator Object

Originally introduced with the Netscape Navigator browser in 1995, the navigator object is used to obtain information about the user's browser. Different browsers support different properties, but the properties described in **Figure 5-36** are supported by all current versions of the major browsers.

The navigator object is primarily used for debugging or for verifying that the user is running a compatible browser or operating system. For example, the following code tests whether the language of the browser is based on United States English, running a different command block if it is not:

```
if (navigator.language !== "en-US") then {
   statements to work with browsers of other languages
}
```

PROPERTY	DESCRIPTION
navigator.appName	Returns the name of the browser
navigator.appVersion	Returns version information about the browser
navigator.geolocation	Returns a geolocation object that can be used to extract information about the user's current position
navigator.language	Returns information on the browser's primary language
navigator.onLine	Determines whether the browser is currently online
navigator.platform	Returns information about the platform on which the browser is running
navigator.userAgent	Returns information about the browser, platform name, and compatibility

Figure 5-36 Properties of the `navigator` object

In the past, the `navigator` object was sometimes used for to choose which code to run based on the user's browser. For example, an application would run one set of code for Netscape and another for Internet Explorer. However, it is usually better and more effective to use object detection to determine whether the browser (regardless of its vendor) supports a section of code and using a `try catch` statement to handle exceptions.

The `screen` Object

Computer displays vary widely depending on the type of device, the size and resolution of the monitor, the features of the graphics card and screen settings chosen by the user. Information about the screen is stored in the `screen` object. **Figure 5-37** describes the properties associated with the object.

PROPERTY	DESCRIPTION
screen.availHeight	Returns the height of the screen in pixels, excluding parts of the browser such as the taskbar, menu, or scrollbars
screen.availWidth	Returns the width of the screen in pixels, excluding parts of the browser such as the taskbar, menu, or scrollbars
screen.colorDepth	Returns the bit depth of the screen's color palette
screen.height	Return the total height of the screen in pixels
screen.pixelDepth	Returns the color resolution in bits per pixel of the screen
screen.width	Returns the total width of the screen in pixels

Figure 5-37 Properties of the `screen` object

If your app employs popup windows, you can use the `width` and `height` properties of the `screen` object to center the popup within the screen. To center a popup window, subtract the width and height of the popup from the screen's width and height and divide those differences by two. Assign the two calculated values to the popup window's left and top position. The following code show a function that opens a popup window centered on the screen for a given width and height value:

```
function centerPopup(url, popName, popWidth, popHeight) {
   let leftPos = (screen.width - popWidth)/2;
   let topPos = (screen.height - popHeight)/2;
   let popOptions = "width="+popWidth + ", height=" + popHeight +
            ", left=" + leftPos + ", top=" + topPos;
   let popWin = window.open(url, popName, popOptions);
}
```

Note that this method will not work for users running multiple monitors; however, there are workarounds involving using the available height and width within the current browser window.

Skills at Work | Designing your Web App

A successful web app is one that is easy to use with clear and consistent feedback to the user. As you think about your own apps, keep in mind the following tips:

- **Know your users.** Learn their strengths and weakness. An app created for the elderly might have very different design features than an app produced for a much younger generation.
- **Determine how your app will be used.** Are your users going to be on mobile devices or at a kiosk? Plan your design with the most likely devices in mind.
- **Provide constant feedback.** Whenever a user interacts with your app there should always be feedback indicated that the app has recognized the user activity and is responding. Don't leave the user with "dead air," unsure whether the app is really working as intended.
- **Anticipate user error.** User error is perhaps the most common kind of error. Make sure you build in safeguards that can prevent user error as much as possible so that user experience is enjoyable and free of frustration.
- **Keep it simple.** An app with a lot of busy and distracting design features is not as effective as a clean and direct interface. Focus on only a few things at any one time and have your app direct the users to those tasks.

The best web apps are the ones that meet the needs of the customers and help them to be effective in their tasks.

Quick Check 4

1. Provide two statements that display the previous page in the browser history.
2. What is the difference between the `assign()` method and the `replace()` method?
3. Provide an expression to return the width of screen after adjusting for browser features such as toolbars, menus, and scrollbars.

Summary

- A document is made up of objects called nodes organized into a hierarchical structure called a node tree. Nodes can represent elements, text strings, attributes, and other document objects.
- Nodes have a familial relationship and can be parents, children, siblings, or descendants of other nodes.
- A node can be connected to other nodes to create document fragments, which can then be connected to the document's node tree.
- HTML attributes are matched in JavaScript by properties attached to element nodes.
- A node tree can be restructured using the `appendChild()` and `insertBefore()` methods, which move nodes from one location to another.
- A node can be copied using the `cloneNode()` method.
- The `setInterval()` method repeats a function or command block at set intervals. To stop a function or command block from repeating, apply the `clearInterval()` method.
- The `setTimeout()` method runs a function or command block after a specified time has elapsed. To cancel the function or command, apply the `clearTimeout()` method.

- System dialog boxes that receive user input can be created with the `window.confirm()` and `window.prompt()` methods.
- Properties of the browser window itself can be set using the `window` object.
- A new browser window can be created and configured using the `window.open()` method.
- The Browser Object Model contains a hierarchy of objects relating to the operation of the browser.
- The `history` object contains information on the history of pages viewed by the user. The `location` object contains information on the current page. The `navigator` object contains information about the browser itself. The `screen` object contains information on the screen in which the page is rendered.

Key Terms

confirmation window
deep copy
document fragment
global object
history list
`history` object
lightbox
`location` object
modal
modal window
`navigator` object
node
node list
node tree
overlay
popup window
prompt window
root node
`screen` object
`this` object
timed command

Review Questions

1. The node at the top of the document node tree containing all other nodes is the ______________ node.
   a. parent
   b. root
   c. head
   d. body
2. To reference the third child node of a parent node, use ______________.
   a. `childNodes[3]`
   b. `childNodes[4]`
   c. `childNodes.2`
   d. `childNodes[2]`
3. To create a node list of all `img` element belonging to the slideshow class, use ______________.
   a. `document.querySelectorAll("img.slideshow")`
   b. `document img.slideshow`
   c. `document.selector("img.slideshow")`
   d. `document.querySelector("img.slideshow")`
4. Which of the following is an important difference between node lists and HTML collections?
   a. HTML collections are created using HTML elements.
   b. Node lists are dynamic, HTML collections are static.
   c. Node lists are static, HTML collections are dynamic.
   d. HTML collections include attributes and text strings.
5. Which of the following is an action performed by the `appendChild()` method?
   a. It adds the node to the end of the parent node's child list.
   b. It adds the node to the beginning of the parent node's child list.
   c. It replaces any child nodes of the parent node.
   d. It copies the parent node and adds it as a child of the parent.
6. Provide the JavaScript equivalent of the HTML tag: <img id="logo" src="photo1.jpg" />.
   a. `document.logo[src] = "photo1.jpg"`
   b. `document.getElementById("logo").src = "photo1.jpg"`
   c. `document[logo].src = "photo1.jpg"`
   d. `document.image[0].src = "photo1.jpg";`

7. What is the JavaScript equivalent of the HTML class attribute?
   a. `class`
   b. `classVar`
   c. `classValue`
   d. `className`
8. Provide the JavaScript equivalent of the HTML tag: `<p id="main" style="color: red">`
   a. `document.getElementById("main").color = "red";`
   b. `document.getElementById("main").style = "red";`
   c. `document.getElementById("main").style.color = "red";`
   d. `document.getElementById("main").red = true;`
9. In JavaScript, the CSS `border-color` property is entered as ________________.
   a. `bordercolor`
   b. `border-color`
   c. `border.color`
   d. `borderColor`
10. Which of the following moves the third child of a parent *node* to the end of the child node list?
    a. `node.appendChild(node.children[3]);`
    b. `node.lastChild(node.children[2]);`
    c. `node.appendChild(node.children[2]);`
    d. `node.moveTo(node.children[2], node.lastChild);`
11. Which of the following creates of copy of a node including all the node's descendants?
    a. `node.cloneNode(true);`
    b. `node.cloneNode(false);`
    c. `node.copy(deep);`
    d. `node.copy(true);`
12. Which method do you use to repeat a function or command block at a set interval?
    a. `setRepeat()`
    b. `repeatCommand()`
    c. `setInterval()`
    d. `repeatFunction()`
13. What method do you use to create a system dialog box with a message, an OK button, and a Cancel button?
    a. `window.alert()`
    b. `window.prompt()`
    c. `window.confirm()`
    d. `window.open()`
14. Which of the following provides code to create a browser window that displays the website http://www.example.com with the title "new" sized to 800 pixels wide by 600 pixels tall?
    a. `window.open("new", "http://www.example.com", "width=800, height=600")`
    b. `window.open("http://www.example.com", "new", "width=800, height=600")`
    c. `window.open("http://www.example.com", "new", "width=800px, height=600px")`
    d. `window.create("http://www.example.com", "new", "width=800, height=600")`
15. Which object provides information about the URL of a currently displayed website?
    a. `navigator`
    b. `document`
    c. `location`
    d. `screen`
16. What is the advantage of using nodes over writing HTML content using the `innerHTML` property?
17. What is an advantage and disadvantage of the using the `document.querySelectorAll()` method for selecting elements from an HTML document?
18. What are some disadvantages in using popup windows to convey information or content in a web app?
19. What is the `this` object and why would you reference it with an event handler or event listener?
20. Why should you use JavaScript to change an element class instead of directly changing the element's style to change the element's appearance?

Hands-On Projects

Hands-On Project 5-1

In this project you will create an online practice quiz for an Algebra I class. All questions must be answered within a specified time limit. A countdown clock will show the number of seconds remaining to complete the quiz. At the end of the quiz the number of correct answers will be totaled, and incorrect answers will be marked in red so that students can retake the quiz to correct their mistakes. When the clock is not running, the quiz should be hidden from the student. A preview of the completed page during the quiz is shown in **Figure 5-38**.

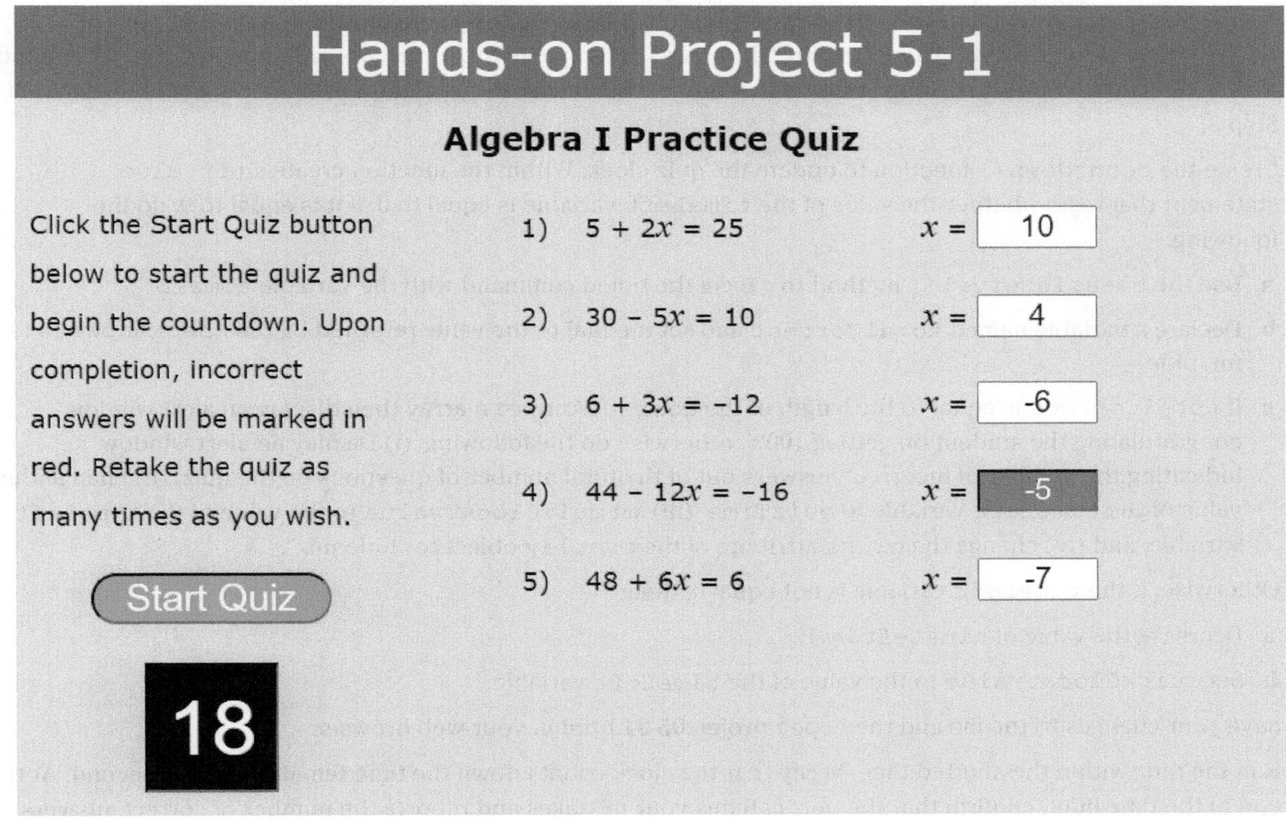

Figure 5-38 Completed Project 5-1

The project uses an overlay to hide the quiz when the clock is not running. The styles for the overlay and other page elements are saved in the style.css file. To change the overlay from visible to invisible, your project will change the value of the overlay's `class` attribute so that a different visual style is applied to the overlay.

Do the following:

1. Use your code editor to open the **project05-01_txt.html** and **project05-01_txt.js** files from the js05 ▶ project01 folder. Enter your name and the date in the comment section of each file and save them as **project05-01.html** and **project05-01.js**, respectively.
2. Go to the **project05-01.html** file in your code editor and in the head section add a `script` element to load the project05-01.js file, deferring the app until the page is loaded. Review the contents and structure of the web document and then close the file, saving your changes.
3. Go to the **project05-01.js** file in your code editor. Below the initial code at the top of the file declare the **`timeID`** variable but do not set an initial value.
4. Declare the **`questionList`** variable, storing in it the node list created by the `querySelectorAll()` method using "`div#quiz input`" as the CSS selector.
5. Add an `onclick` event handler to the `startQuiz` object, running an anonymous function that sets the `class` attribute of the `overlay` object to "showquiz" and repeats the `countdown()` function every 1 second (every 1000 milliseconds), storing the id of the timed command in the global `timeID` variable you declared in Step 3.
6. Create the `countdown()` function to update the quiz clock. Within the function create an `if else` statement that tests whether the value of the `timeLeft` variable is equal to 0. If it is equal to 0, do the following:
   a. Use the `clearInterval()` method to cancel the timed command with the variable `timeID`.
   b. Declare a variable named **`totalCorrect`** and set it equal to the value returned by the `checkAnswers()` function.
   c. If `totalCorrect` is equal to the length of the `correctAnswers` array then display an alert window congratulating the student on getting 100%, otherwise do the following: (i) Display an alert window indicating the number of incorrect answers out of the total number of questions on the quiz, (ii) change the value of the `timeLeft` variable to `quizTime`, (iii) set `quizClock.value` to the value of the `timeLeft` variable, and (iv) change the `class` attribute of the `overlay` object to "hidequiz".
7. Otherwise, if the `timeLeft` variable is not equal 0, then:
   a. Decrease the value of `timeLeft` by 1.
   b. Set `quickClock.value` to the value of the `timeLeft` variable.
8. Save your changes to the file and then open **project05-01.html** in your web browser.
9. Run the quiz within the allotted time. Verify that the clock counts down the time remaining every second. At the end of the time limit, confirm that the quiz catches your mistakes and reports the number of correct answers out of the total number of questions. Verify that when you get all the answers correct, a congratulatory message is given.
10. Return to the **project05-01.js** file in your code editor. Increase the value of the `timeLimit` variable to **90** and the close the file, saving your changes.

Hands-On Project 5-2

In this project you will create an app that allows users to rank photos by clicking the images in a "photo bucket" to move them from the bucket to an ordered list of images. Clicking an image in the list returns the photo to the bucket while automatically renumbering the list. A preview of the completed project is shown in **Figure 5-39**.

Hands-on Project 5-2

Rank the Photos

The following are the photo entries for this month's contest. Click the images in the photo bucket below to add them to the list at the right. Click an image from the list to return it to the photo bucket.

1. 5. 2. 6. 3. 7. 4.

Figure 5-39 Completed Project 5-2 *Joan Carey*

Do the following:

1. Use your code editor to open the **project05-02_txt.html** and **project05-02_txt.js** files from the js05 ► project02 folder. Enter your name and the date in the comment section of each file and save them as **project05-02.html** and **project05-02.js**, respectively.
2. Go to the **project05-02.html** file in your code editor and in the head section add a `script` element to load the project05-02.js file, deferring the app until the page is loaded. Review the contents and structure of the web document and then close the file, saving your changes.
3. Return to the **project05-02.js** file in your code editor. Below the initial comment section declare the following variables:
   a. The **`images`** variable containing an HTML collection of all elements with the tag name "img".
   b. The **`photoBucket`** variable referencing the element with the id "photo_bucket".
   c. The **`photoList`** variable referencing the element with the id "photo_list".
4. Create a `for` loop that iterates through all of the items in the images collection.
5. Within the `for` loop insert an `onclick` event handler that runs an anonymous function when an image is clicked.

6. When an image is clicked it is either moved from the photo bucket to the photo list or from the photo list back to the photo bucket. To determine which action to perform, add the following if else statement to the anonymous function:
   a. If the parent element of the clicked image has an id equal to "photo_bucket" then do the following: (i) Create an element node named **newItem** for the `li` element, (ii) append `newItem` to the `photoList` object, and (iii) append the image to the `newItem` object using the `appendChild()` method. Note: Use the `this` object to reference the image that was clicked by the user.
   b. Otherwise, do the following: (i) Declare a variable named **oldItem** equal to the parent element of the clicked image, (ii) append the clicked image to `photoBucket` object, and (iii) remove `oldItem` from the parent element of `oldItem` using the `removeChild()` method.
7. Save your changes to the file and then load **project05-02.html** in your web browser.
8. Verify that you can move items between the photo bucket and the photo list by clicking the image within either location.

Hands-On Project 5-3

In this project you will explore more about the properties and uses of nodes. The first feature you will use is the `nodeName` property which, for element nodes, returns the tag name in uppercase letters. Thus, the expression `n.nodeName` would return a value of "P" if the node `n` represents a paragraph element. The second feature is a `for` loop that doesn't use a counter variable, but instead iterates through each child element of a parent node. The general structure is the following:

```
for (let n = node.firstElementChild; n != null; n = n.nextElementSibling) {
   commands applied to each child node
}
```

The `for` loop starts with the first child of *node*, storing that child node in the node variable `n`. With each new iteration, `n` proceeds to next sibling until it tries to go past the last child node. At that iteration, the next sibling would be `null` (because there is no next sibling) and the loop ends.

You will use these node techniques in a project that automatically generates a table of contents for a document of any length. In this project the document is the text of the amendments to the U.S. Constitution and the name of each amendment is marked with an `h2` heading. The completed project shown in **Figure 5-40** extracts the text of each `h2` heading, creating a list of internal hypertext links that will jump to each amendment listed in the document.

Do the following:

1. Use your code editor to open the **project05-03_txt.html** and **project05-03_txt.js** files from the js05 ▶ project03 folder. Enter your name and the date in the comment section of each file and save them as **project05-03.html** and **project05-03.js**, respectively.
2. Go to the **project05-03.html** file in your code editor and add a `script` element loading the project05-03.js file, deferring the app until the entire page is loaded. Take some time to study the contents and structure of the document. Note that the table of contents will be written to an ordered list with the id "toc" and the source of the table of contents is stored in element with the id "source_doc". Close the file, saving your changes.
3. Go to the **project05-03.js** file in your code editor. Below the initial comment section declare the following variables:
   a. The `sourceDoc` variable referencing the element with the id "source_doc".
   b. The `toc` variable referencing the element with the id "toc".
   c. The `headingCount` variable with an initial value of 1.
   d. A constant named `heading` with a value of "H2".

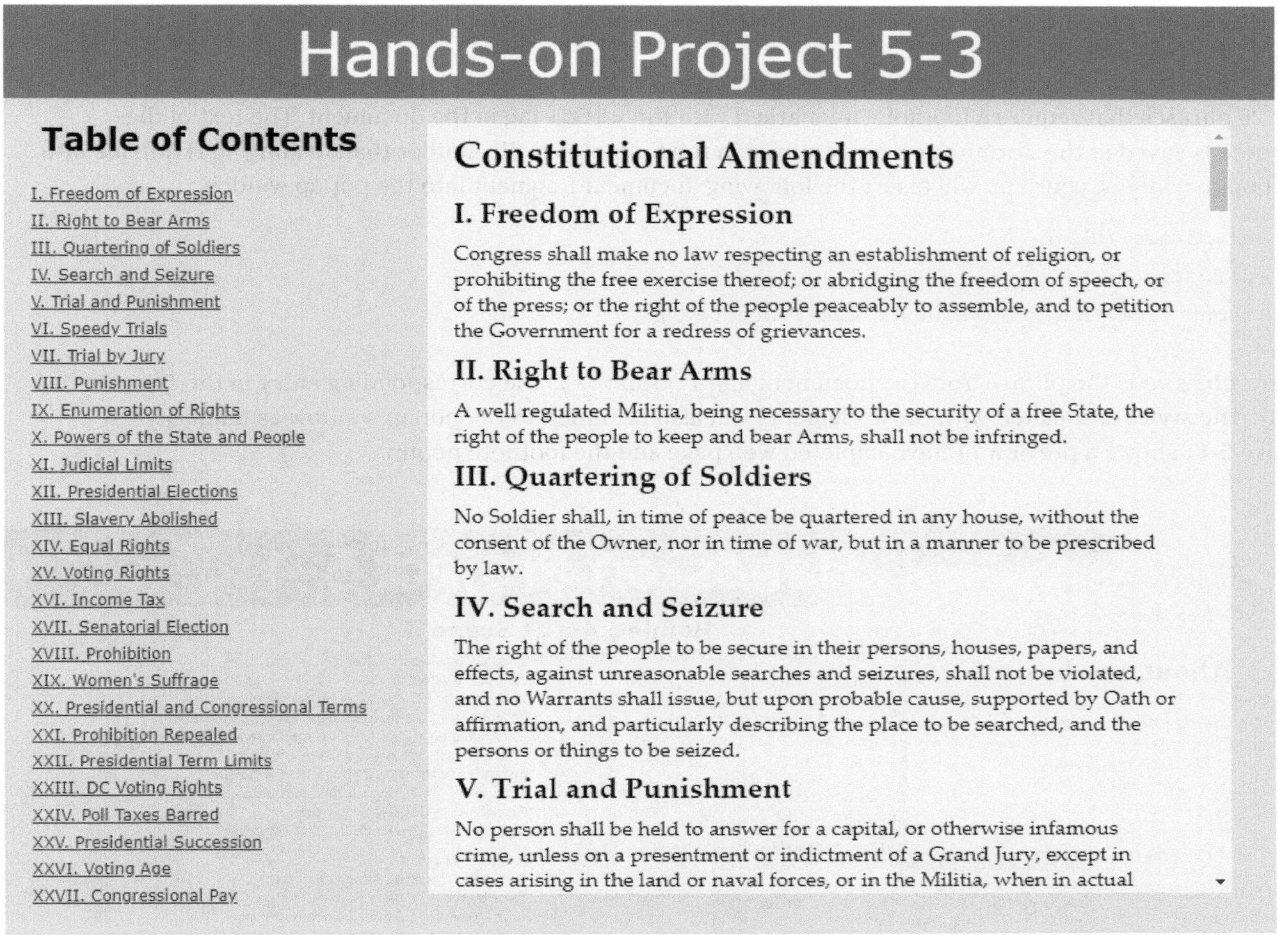

Hands-on Project 5-3

Table of Contents

I. Freedom of Expression
II. Right to Bear Arms
III. Quartering of Soldiers
IV. Search and Seizure
V. Trial and Punishment
VI. Speedy Trials
VII. Trial by Jury
VIII. Punishment
IX. Enumeration of Rights
X. Powers of the State and People
XI. Judicial Limits
XII. Presidential Elections
XIII. Slavery Abolished
XIV. Equal Rights
XV. Voting Rights
XVI. Income Tax
XVII. Senatorial Election
XVIII. Prohibition
XIX. Women's Suffrage
XX. Presidential and Congressional Terms
XXI. Prohibition Repealed
XXII. Presidential Term Limits
XXIII. DC Voting Rights
XXIV. Poll Taxes Barred
XXV. Presidential Succession
XXVI. Voting Age
XXVII. Congressional Pay

Constitutional Amendments

I. Freedom of Expression

Congress shall make no law respecting an establishment of religion, or prohibiting the free exercise thereof; or abridging the freedom of speech, or of the press; or the right of the people peaceably to assemble, and to petition the Government for a redress of grievances.

II. Right to Bear Arms

A well regulated Militia, being necessary to the security of a free State, the right of the people to keep and bear Arms, shall not be infringed.

III. Quartering of Soldiers

No Soldier shall, in time of peace be quartered in any house, without the consent of the Owner, nor in time of war, but in a manner to be prescribed by law.

IV. Search and Seizure

The right of the people to be secure in their persons, houses, papers, and effects, against unreasonable searches and seizures, shall not be violated, and no Warrants shall issue, but upon probable cause, supported by Oath or affirmation, and particularly describing the place to be searched, and the persons or things to be seized.

V. Trial and Punishment

No person shall be held to answer for a capital, or otherwise infamous crime, unless on a presentment or indictment of a Grand Jury, except in cases arising in the land or naval forces, or in the Militia, when in actual

Figure 5-40 Completed Project 5-3

4. Create a `for` loop using the code structure described above going from the first child element of the `sourceDoc` variable through the last child where the next sibling element would be `null`.
5. Within the `for` loop insert an `if` statement that tests whether the value of `n.nodeName` is equal to the value of the `heading` constant.
6. Within the `if` statement insert the following commands to be run if the condition is true:
   a. Create an element node named `anchor` for the a element.
   b. Set the value of the `name` attribute of anchor to the text string: `"doclink" + headingCount`.
   c. Use the `insertBefore()` method to insert `anchor` before first child of the `n` node.
   d. Create an element node named `listItem` for the `li` element and an element node named `link` for the a element. Use the `appendChild()` method to append `link` to `listItem`.
   e. Set the value of the `textContent` property of `link` to `n.textContent`.
   f. Set the value of the `href` property of `listItem` to the text string: `"#doclink" + headingCount;`
   g. Use the `appenChild()` method to append `listItem` to the `toc` object.
   h. Increase the value of the `headingCount` variable by 1.
7. Save your changes to the document and then load **project05-03.html** in your web browser.
8. Verify that the app populates the table of contents with the names of each of the 27 amendments and that when an amendment is clicked the browser jumps to that amendment's location in the source document.

Hands-On Project 5-4

In this project you will create a browser popup window that displays footnotes for a soliloquy from *Hamlet*. The 26 phrases that require a footnote are marked with the `<dfn>` tag in the document. The text of the footnote is saved in the `footnotes` array stored in the footnotes.js file. Rather than loading an HTML file into the popup window, your app will insert the following document fragment into the popup window:

```
<h1>phrase</h1>
<p>footnote</p>
<input type="button" value="Close Footnote" />
```

where *`phrase`* is the phrase from the document and *`footnote`* is the corresponding entry in the `footnotes` array. The styles associated with these elements will also be added to the popup window as inline styles. **Figure 5-41** shows a preview of the completed web page and the footnote popup.

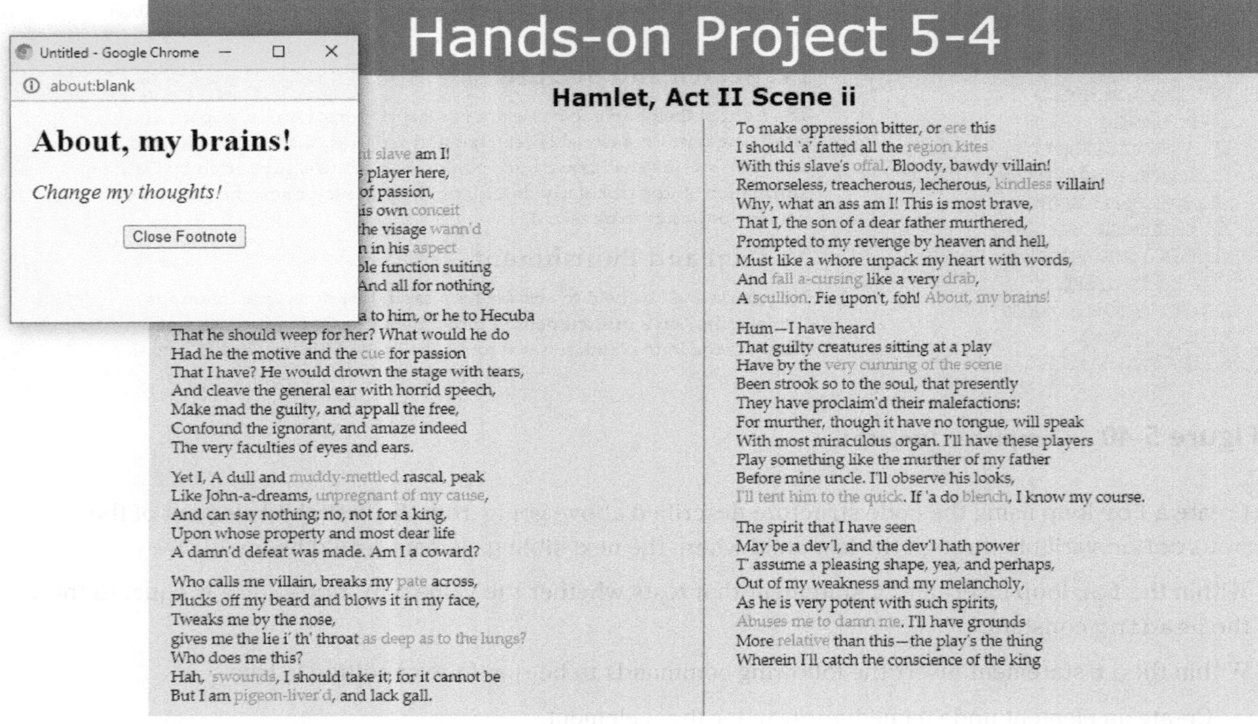

Figure 5-41 Completed Project 5-4

Do the following:

1. Use your code editor to open the **project05-04_txt.html** and **project05-04_txt.js** files from the js05 ► project02 folder. Enter your name and the date in the comment section of each file and save them as **project05-04.html** and **project05-04.js**, respectively.
2. Go to the **project05-04.html** file in your code editor and in the head section add a `script` element to load the footnotes.js and project05-04.js files, deferring both files until the page is loaded. Review the text of the document, noting the phrases that are marked with the `<dfn>` tag. Close the file, saving your changes.
3. Return to the **project05-04.js** file in your code editor. Create a `for` loop that uses a counter variable, `i`, to loop through all the items in `phrases` node list. For each `phrases[i]` item in that list, apply an `onclick` event handler that runs an anonymous function. Add the statements described in Steps 4 through 10 to that anonymous function.

4. Create the **phrase** variable containing an h1 element. Set the value of the textContent property to the value of the textContent property of the this object. (Note that in this context, the this object references the dfn element clicked by the user.)
5. Create the **footnote** variable containing a p element. Set the value of the textContent property of that element to the value of footnotes[i], where i is the counter from the for loop. Apply the style rule "font-style: italic; font-size: 1.2em;" to the footnote.style object property.
6. Create the **closeButton** variable containing an input element. Set the value of the button's type attribute to "button" and the value attribute to "Close Footnote". Apply the style rule "display: block; margin: 10px auto" to the closeButton.style object property.
7. Use the window.open() method to create a popup window, storing the window in a variable named popup. The *url* parameter should be an empty text string, the *title* parameter be "footnote" and the *options* parameter should set the width of the popup to 300, the height to 200, and the top and left values to 100.
8. Apply the style rule "background-color: ivory; font-size: 16px; padding: 10px;" to the popup.document.body.style object property.
9. Use the appendChild() method to append the phrase, footnote, and closeButton objects to popup.document.body.
10. Add an onclick event handler to the closeButton element node, running an anonymous function containing the single statement popup.close() to close the popup window when the button is clicked.
11. Save your changes to the file and then load **project05-04.html** in your web browser. Verify that clicking a marked phrase in the document opens a popup window with the text of the phrase and footnote as well as the Close Footnote button. Confirm that clicking the Close Footnote button closing the popup window.

Hands-On Project 5-5

Debugging Challenge

In this debugging challenge you will work on an online version of the Concentration game. In the game pairs of image tiles are randomly placed on a board face down. To view an image, click the tile followed by another tile that you believe contains the matching image. If the images match, the tiles remain face up; otherwise they are automatically flipped face down after 1 second.

In this online version, the tile image and back of the tile image are placed within div elements belonging to the tile class. The second of the two images is always the one displayed on the page. When a tile is flipped, the order of the two images is switched and then switched again to flip the tile back. Tiles can only be clicked if they are face down and only two tiles can be clicked at any time. The code for the game has several errors that prevent it from working correctly. A preview of the completed page is shown in **Figure 5-42**.

Do the following:

1. Use your code editor to open the **project05-05_txt.html** and **project05-05_txt.js** files from the js05 ▶ project02 folder. Enter your name and the date in the comment section of each file and save them as **project05-05.html** and **project05-05.js**, respectively.
2. Go to the **project05-05.html** file in your code editor and in the head section add a script element to load the project05-05.js file, deferring it until the entire page is loaded. Take some time to review the contents and structure of the game board. Close the file, saving your changes.
3. Return to the **project05-05.js** file in your code editor. Comments have been added to help you interpret the code in the file.
4. The page initially loads the scrambleTiles() function to randomize the order of the tiles on the game board. There are two errors within the function. Locate and correct the errors. Note: There is no error in the statement that declares the randomIndex variable.

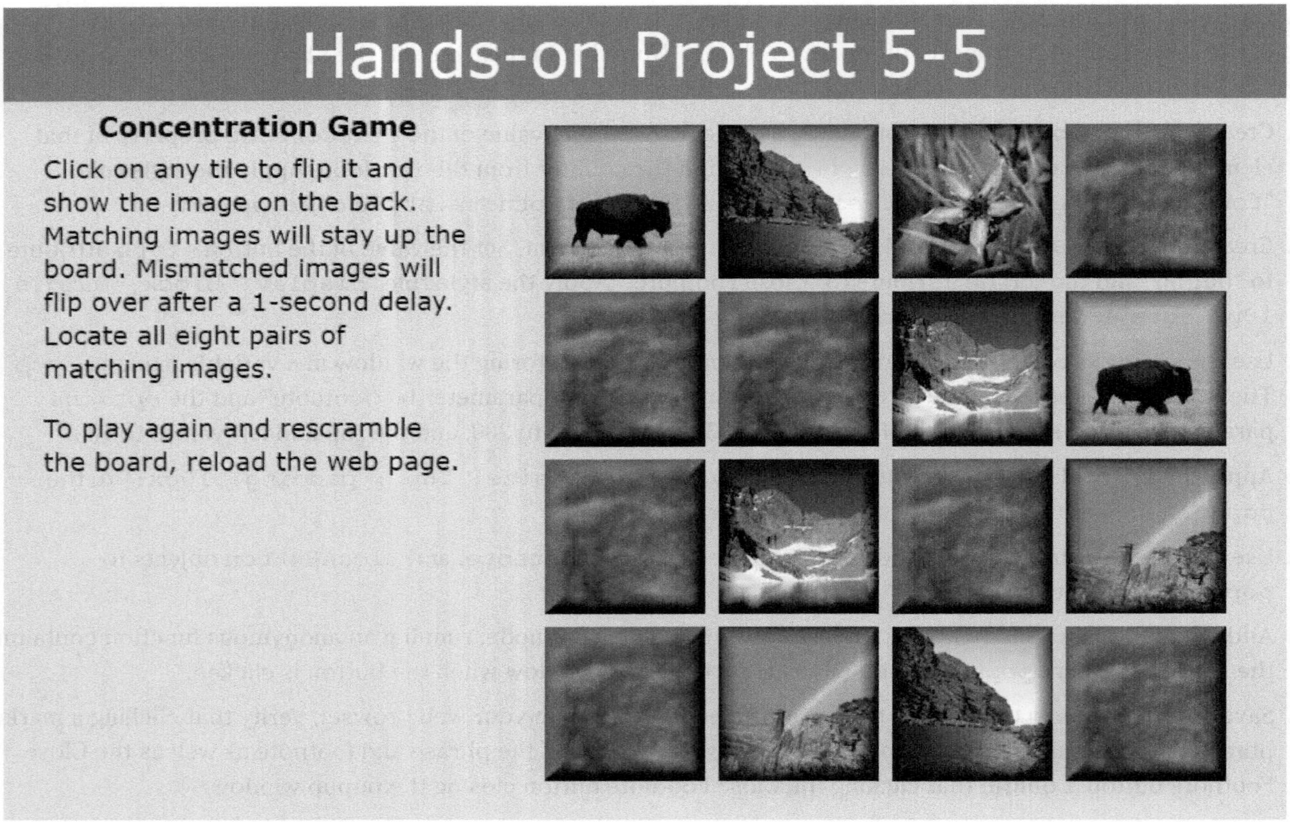

Hands-on Project 5-5

Concentration Game

Click on any tile to flip it and show the image on the back. Matching images will stay up the board. Mismatched images will flip over after a 1-second delay. Locate all eight pairs of matching images.

To play again and rescramble the board, reload the web page.

Figure 5-42 Completed Project 5-5 *Photo images from Joan Carey; Tile image by Patrick Carey*

5. After the board is scrambled, the page will run the `playConcentration()` function to set up the game play and event handlers. There are seven errors in this function that prevent the game from running or running correctly. Locate and fix the errors.
6. When two tiles have been clicked, the page will run the `flipBack()` function after a 1-second delay. There is an error in the `flipBack()` function. Locate it and correct it.
7. Save your changes to the file and then open **project05-05.html** in your web browser. Verify that you can play the game by clicking the tiles to view their images. You should be able to only click two tiles at a time and only when the tile is face down. Matching tiles should remain face up. Reloading the page should reorder the tiles. If you still have errors in the code, use the browser debugger tools to assist you in locating and fixing the errors.

Case Projects

Individual Case Project

Add a page to your individual website that educates visitors about web security. Report the values of at least six properties from Figures 5-36 and 5-37 to illustrate the breadth of information about a user's computer that a web app can access. Perform a web search on practices for using the web safely, and include links to at least three sources, along with a one-sentence summary of each.

Team Case Project

In this project, your team will draw the DOM tree for an HTML document.

To start, break into pairs, with each pair responsible for a different HTML document in your team website. With your partner, sketch the DOM tree for the selected document. Your tree should show the hierarchy of the site, including elements, attributes, and text content, similar to Figure 5-4.

When all the pairs are finished creating their DOM trees, assemble as a full group and compare your trees. Identify and discuss any differences between trees. Make any changes necessary to your own tree based on feedback from the rest of the team.

CHAPTER 6

Enhancing and Validating Forms

When you complete this chapter, you will be able to:

- Use JavaScript to reference form and form elements
- Retrieve values from selection lists
- Retrieve values from option buttons
- Format numeric values and currency values based on local standards
- Write scripts that respond to form events
- Store values in hidden fields
- Understand how web forms are submitted for validation
- Validate web form fields using customized tools
- Test a field value against a regular expression
- Create a customized validation check for credit card data
- Manage the form validation process

In this chapter you will learn how to use JavaScript to manage web forms, perform calculations based on data from those forms, report the results, and validate data entry to catch user error.

Exploring Forms and Form Elements

You have been given two web pages containing commonly used forms: an order form for calculating the cost of a purchase and a payment form for entering credit information to complete the purchase. The general code for the order form web page has already been created for you. Open the files for that page now.

To open the files for the order form:

1. Go to the js06 ▶ chapter folder of your data files.
2. Use your code editor to open the **js06a_txt.html** and **js06a_txt.js** files. Enter your name and the date in the comment section of each file and then save them as **js06a.html** and **js06a.js**, respectively.

3. Return to the **js06a.html** file in your code editor. Within the head section, add the following code to run the js06a.js script, deferring the loading the script file until after the entire page has loaded.

```
<script src="js06a.js" defer></script>
```

4. Take some time to scroll through the contents of the HTML file, noting that a web form containing several `input` elements has been enclosed within a web table.
5. Close the file, saving your changes.
6. Open the **js06a.html** file in your web browser. **Figure 6-1** shows the current layout and contents of the page.

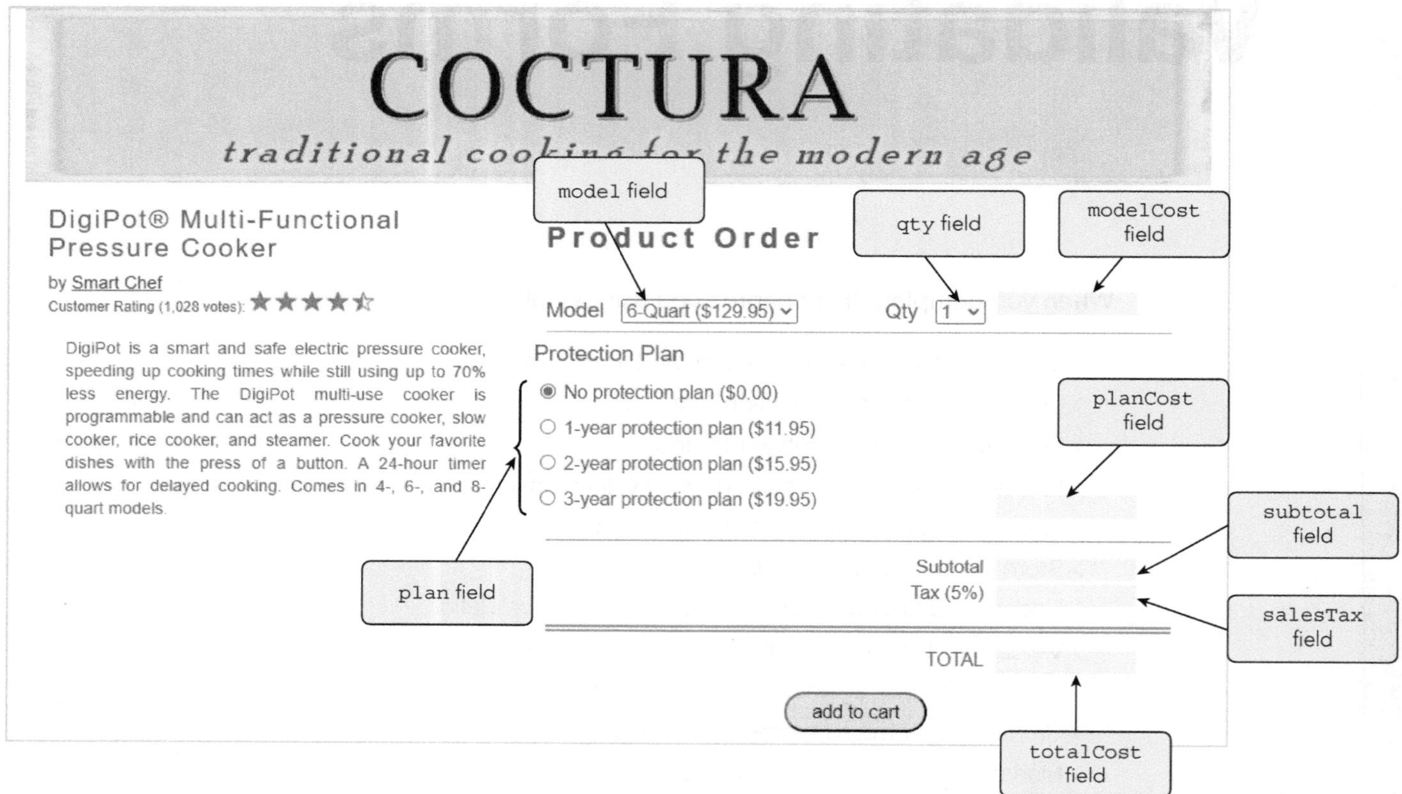

Figure 6-1 Product order form

The order form contains the following fields:

- The `model` field displayed as a selection list from which customers can choose a model to order
- The `qty` field displayed as another selection list from which customers specify the amount of the selected model to order
- The `plan` field displayed as a collection of option buttons from which customers choose the protection plan, if any, for the selected model
- The `modelCost` field calculating the cost of the model times the quantity ordered
- The `planCost` field calculating the cost of the protection plan times the quantity ordered
- The `subtotal` field calculating the sum of the `modelCost` and `planCost` fields
- The `salesTax` field calculating a 5% sales tax on the subtotal
- The `totalCost` field adding the values of the `subtotal` and `salesTax` fields

Note that some of these fields are entered by the customer and some are automatically calculated by the web form using the script you will write. Currently no calculations have been done on the web form data.

The Forms Collection

To program a web form, you work with the properties and methods of the `form` object and the elements it contains. Because a page can contain multiple web forms, JavaScript organizes forms into the following HTML collection:

```
document.forms
```

The first several forms listed in the page are referenced using the expressions `document.forms[0]`, `document.forms[1]`, and so forth. You can also reference a form using the value of the form's `name` attribute using either of the following expressions:

```
document.forms[fname]
document.forms.fname
```

where *fname* is the form's name. As always, you can reference a form using the `document.getElementById()` method if the form has been assigned an id. **Figure 6-2** describes some of the properties and methods associated with individual form objects.

PROPERTY OR METHOD	DESCRIPTION
form.action	Sets or returns the `action` attribute of the web *form*
form.autocomplete	Sets or returns the `autocomplete` attribute; allows the browser to automatically complete form fields
form.enctype	Sets or returns the `enctype` attribute
form.length	Returns the number of elements in the form
form.method	Sets or returns the `method` attribute
form.name	Sets or returns the `name` attribute
form.noValidate	Sets or returns whether the form should be validated upon submission. Use `true` for no validation, `false` to apply validation.
form.target	Sets or returns the `target` attribute
form.reset()	Resets the web form
form.submit()	Submits the web form
form.requestAutocomplete()	Triggers the browser to initiate autocompletion of those form fields that have autocomplete activated

Figure 6-2 Form properties and methods

For example, the following statement resets the form with the name `orderForm` in the current document:

```
document.forms.orderForm.reset()
```

Resetting a form will replace all current values and selections in the form with their default values and selections.

Working with Form Elements

A form and its elements are organized into a hierarchy like the one shown in **Figure 6-3**.

To reference specific elements within that hierarchy, use the following HTML collection:

```
form.elements
```

where *form* is the reference to the web form.

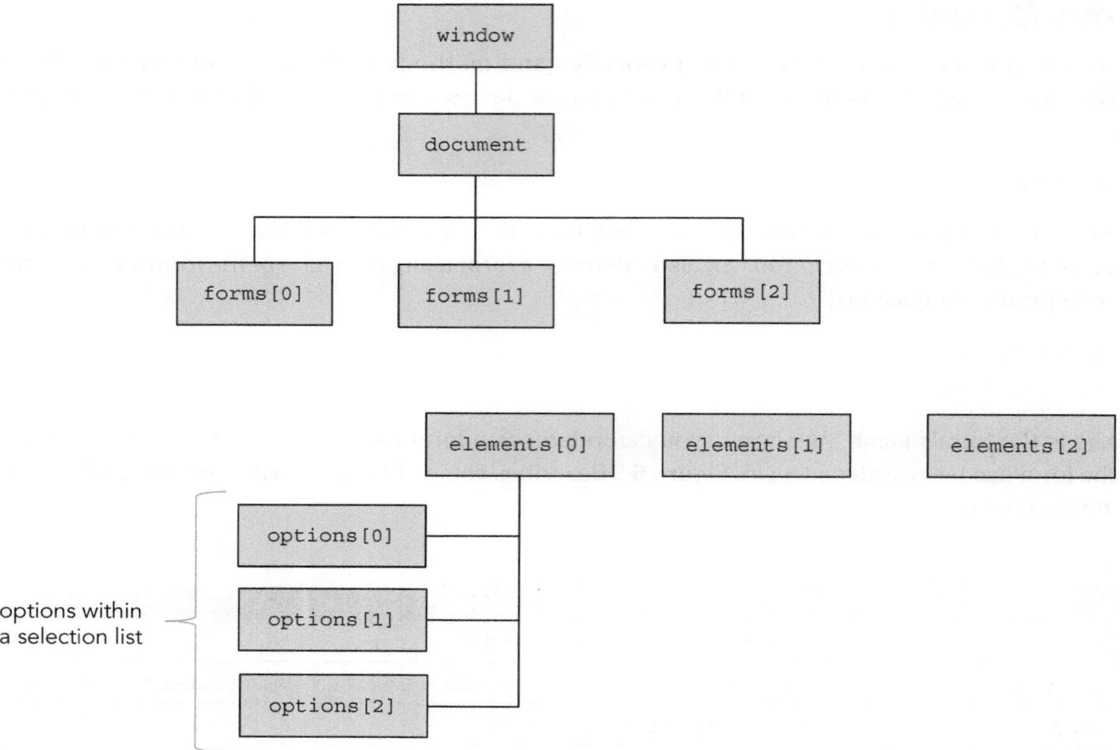

Figure 6-3 Web form hierarchy

You can reference an element using the value of the element's name attribute using the following expression:

```
form.elements[ename]
form.elements.ename
```

where *ename* is name of a field contained within the web form or the index number of the element within the `elements` collection. Fields are always associated with a web form control like an input box or selection list. For example, to reference the `model` field from the `orderForm` form, apply either of the following object references:

```
document["orderForm"].elements["model"]
document.orderForm.elements.model
```

As with the form itself, you can always reference the control associated with a field using the `document.getElementById()` method.

> **Note** The `id` attribute for a web form element references the control that the user interacts with; the `name` attribute references the field in which the element's value is stored.

Properties and Methods of `input` Elements

A common form element is one marked with the HTML `<input>` tag. Every attribute that is associated with the `<input>` tag is mirrored by a JavaScript property. **Figure 6-4** lists some of the properties and methods associated with `input` boxes.

Thus, to set the value of the `username` field within the `orderForm` web form, apply the statement:

```
document.orderForm.username.value = "John Smith";
```

and the text string "John Smith" will appear within the input box control and stored as the value of the `username` field.

PROPERTY OR METHOD	DESCRIPTION
input.autocomplete	The value of the input box's autocomplete attribute
input.defaultValue	The default value for the input box
input.form	The form containing the input box
input.maxLength	The maximum number of characters allowed in the input box
input.name	The name of the field associated with the input box
input.pattern	The value of the input box's pattern attribute
input.placeholder	The value of the input box's placeholder attribute
input.readOnly	Returns whether the input box is read-only or not
input.required	Returns whether the input box is required or not
input.size	The value of the input box's size attribute
input.type	The data type associated with the input box
input.value	The current value displayed in the input box
input.blur()	Removes the focus from the input box
input.focus()	Gives focus to the input box
input.select()	Selects the contents of the input box

Figure 6-4 Properties and methods of input boxes

Navigating Between Input Controls

You might need your script to manage how users navigate between the controls on your form. A form control like an input box, text area box, or selection list receives the focus of the browser when it becomes active, either by moving the cursor into the control or by clicking it. A control that has received the focus is ready for data entry. To use JavaScript to give focus to a form element, apply the following property to the element:

```
element.focus()
```

where *element* is a reference to the web form control that will become active in the document. To remove focus from a form element, apply the following blur() method:

```
element.blur()
```

Note that using the blur() method to remove the focus from an element doesn't give any other element the focus. To speed up data entry, many web forms will open with an input control automatically given the focus. You will program the order form on the Coctura website to give the focus to the selection list from which a customer selects a product model to order.

To give the focus to the selection list:

1. Return to the **js06a.js** file in your code editor.
2. Directly below the initial comment section, add the following code to be run when the page is initially opened in the browser window (see **Figure 6-5**):

```
window.addEventListener("load", function() {
   let orderForm = document.forms.orderForm;
   let model = orderForm.elements.model;

   // Select Model selection list when form opens
   model.focus();
});
```

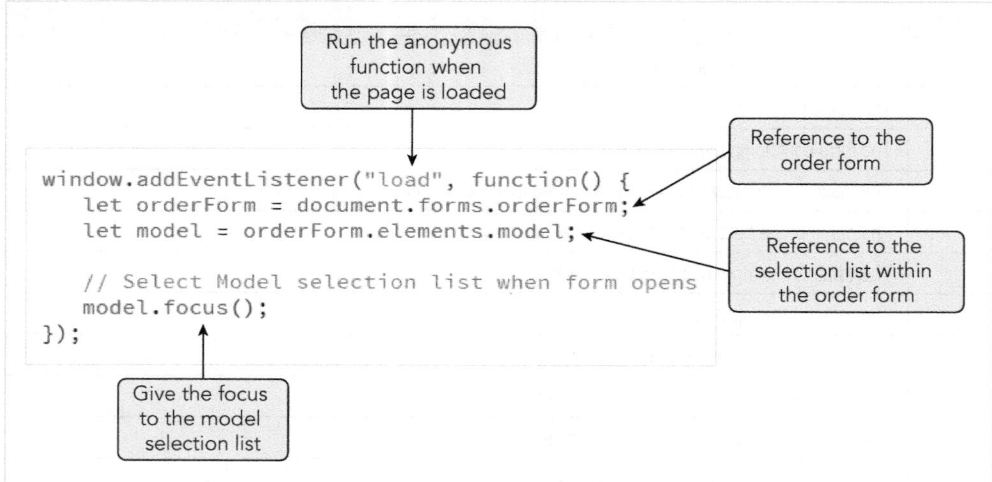

Figure 6-5 Giving the focus to the Model selection list

3. Save your changes to the file and then reload **js06a.html** in your browser.
4. Verify that the selection list box for the model field has the focus, by pressing the up and down arrows on your keyboard to change the selected mode option without having to select the selection list first.

In the rest of the form, you will calculate the cost of a customer's order. This involves (1) determining the price of the order (equal to the price of the selected model multiplied by the quantity ordered); (2) adding the cost of the protection plan, if any, for the quantity of models ordered; (3) calculating the sales tax; and (4) adding all these costs to determine the grand total. Start with a function to calculate the cost of ordering a model.

> **Note** You can also ensure that a field gets the focus when the page loads by adding the `autofocus` attribute to element's markup tag in the HTML file.

Working with Selection Lists

Extracting a value from a form control like an input box is very straightforward: You only need to reference the `value` property of the input box. Selection lists, however, do not have a `value` property because they contain a multitude of possible options each with a different value. **Figure 6-6** describes some of the properties associated with selection lists that you will use in your program.

PROPERTY OR METHOD	DESCRIPTION
select.length	The number of options in the selection list, *select*
select.multiple	Returns `true` if more than one option can be selected from the list
select.name	The selection list field name
select.options	The object collection of the selection list *options*
select.selectedIndex	The index number of the currently selected option
select.size	The number of options displayed in the selection list
select.add(*option*)	Adds *option* to the selection list
select.remove(*index*)	Removes the option with the index number, *index*, from the selection list

Figure 6-6 Properties and methods of selection lists

The value of the field associated with a selection list is the value of the option selected by the user. Selection list options are organized into the following HTML collection:

```
select.options
```

where *select* is the reference to a selection list within the web form. As with other HTML collections, an individual option is referenced either by its index value within the collection or by the value of its `id` attribute. **Figure 6-7** describes the properties associated with individual selection list options within the `options` collection.

PROPERTY OR METHOD	DESCRIPTION
option.defaultSelected	Returns true if *option* is selected by default
option.index	The index number of *option* within the options collection
option.selected	Returns `true` if the option has been selected by the user
option.text	The text associated with *option*
option.value	The field value of *option*

Figure 6-7 Properties and methods of selection list options

To return the value from a selection list field, you must first determine which option has been selected using the `selectedIndex` property and then reference the `value` property of that selected option to determine the field's value. The following code demonstrates how to return the cost of the product chosen from the model selection list box:

```
let mIndex = model.selectedIndex;
let mValue = model.options[mIndex].value;
```

Note | If no option is selected, the `selectedIndex` property returns a value of −1.

The initial cost of the customer's order is equal to the price of the selected model multiplied by the quantity of items ordered. Because both the `model` and `qty` fields are entered as selection lists, you will retrieve the values of the two selected options. Add the code into the `calcOrder()` function, which will be nested and called within the anonymous function you created in the previous set of steps.

To create the `calcOrder()` function:

1. Return to the **js06a.js** file in your code editor.
2. Within the anonymous function add the following statement to call the `calcOrder()` function:

```
// Calculate the cost of the order
calcOrder();
```

3. Next, add the following initial code for the `calcOrder()` function described in **Figure 6-8**.

```
function calcOrder() {
   // Determine the selected model
   let mIndex = model.selectedIndex;
   let mValue = model.options[mIndex].value;

   // Determine the selected quantity
   let qIndex = orderForm.elements.qty.selectedIndex;
   let quantity = orderForm.elements.qty[qIndex].value;

   // Model cost = model cost times quantity
   let modelCost = mValue*quantity;
   orderForm.elements.modelCost.value = modelCost;
}
```

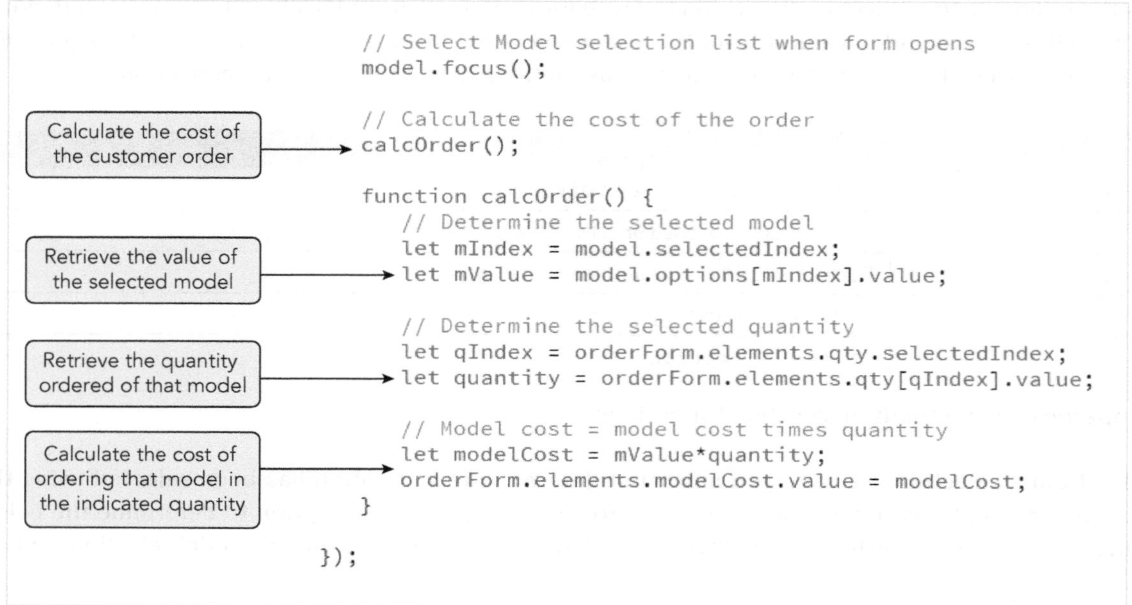

Figure 6-8 Calculating the cost of models ordered

4. Save your changes to the file and then reload **js06a.html** in your browser. As shown in **Figure 6-9**, a cost of $129.95 appears in the input box as the result of multiplying the selected product (the 6-Quart pressure cooker for $129.95) by the select quantity (1).

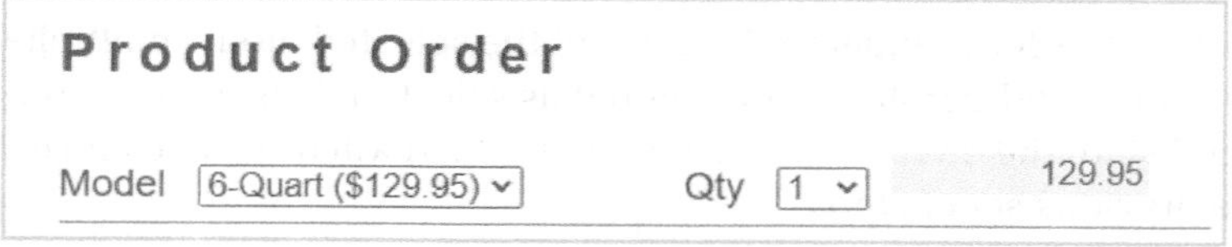

Figure 6-9 Cost of one 6-Quart pressure cooker

To the cost of the order, add the cost of the protection plan, if any, selected by the customer. To retrieve the cost of the protection plan, you will work with the values stored in option buttons associated with the different protection options.

Programming Concepts | Selection List with Multiple Values

Some selection lists allow multiple selections. In those cases, the `selectedIndex` property returns the index of the first selected item. To determine the indices of all the selected items, create a `for` loop that runs through the options in the list, checking each to determine whether the `selected` property is `true` (indicating that the option was selected by the user). If the option is selected, it can then be added to an array of the selected options using the `push()` method. The general structure of the `for` loop is:

```
let selectedOpt = new Array();
for (let i = 0; i < select.options.length; i++) {
   if (select.options[i].selected) {
      selectedOpt.push(select.options[i]);
   }
}
```

where *`select`* is a selection list object. After this code runs, the `selectedOpt` array will contain all the selected options. To extract the values of the selected options, create another `for` loop that iterates through the items in the `selectedOpt` array to extract the `text` and `value` properties of each.

Working with Option Buttons

Option or radio buttons are grouped together when they share a common field name stored in their `name` attribute. For example, the four protection plan options shown in the order form all share the common name of "plan". Option buttons associated with a common field are placed within the following HTML collection:

```
form.elements.options
```

where *form* is the reference to the web form and *options* is the common field name. To reference a specific option from the collection use either the index number or the id value of the option button control. Thus, the first option button for the `plan` field from the customer order form would have the reference:

```
document.forms.orderForm.elements.plan[0]
```

Figure 6-10 describes some of the properties associated with individual option buttons.

PROPERTY	DESCRIPTION
option.checked	Boolean value indicating whether the option button, *option*, is currently checked by the user
option.defaultChecked	Boolean value indicating whether *option* is checked by default
option.disabled	Boolean value indicating whether *option* is disabled or not
option.name	The field name associated with *option*
option.value	The field value association with *option*

Figure 6-10 Properties of option buttons

Locating the Checked Option

The option selected by the user will be indicated by the presence of the `checked` property. The following code uses a `for` loop to go through each option button associated with the `plan` field, storing the value of the selected option in the `pCost` variable, and breaking off the `for` loop and storing the option button value once the checked button has been found:

```
let orderForm = document.forms.orderForm;
let plan = orderForm.elements.plan;
for (let i = 0; i < plan.length; i++) {
   if (plan[i].checked) {
      planValue = plan[i].value;
      break;
   }
}
```

In place of a `for` loop, you can use the following CSS selector, which references the checked option button from the `plan` field:

```
input[name="plan"]:checked
```

By placing this selector within a `querySelector()` method, you can retrieve the value of the checked option without the need for a `for` loop as the following code demonstrates:

```
let planValue =
document.querySelector('input[name="plan"]:checked').value;
```

Note that these techniques will return a value only if an option has been selected from the option button collection. Use this method now to retrieve the cost of the selected protection plan.

To retrieve the cost of the selected plan:

1. Return to the **js06a.js** file in your code editor.
2. Within the `calcOrder()` function add the following code described in **Figure 6-11**.

```
// Retrieve the cost of the protection plan
let planValue =
document.querySelector('input[name="plan"]:checked').value;

// Charge the plan to each item ordered
let planCost = planValue * quantity;
orderForm.elements.planCost.value = planCost;
```

Value of the plan selected by the customer
Calculate the cost of applying the plan to every item ordered

```
    // Model cost = model cost times quantity
    let modelCost = mValue*quantity;
    orderForm.elements.modelCost.value = modelCost;

    // Retrieve the cost of the protection plan
    let planValue = document.querySelector('input[name="plan"]:checked').value;

    // Charge the plan to each item ordered
    let planCost = planValue * quantity;
    orderForm.elements.planCost.value = planCost;
}
```

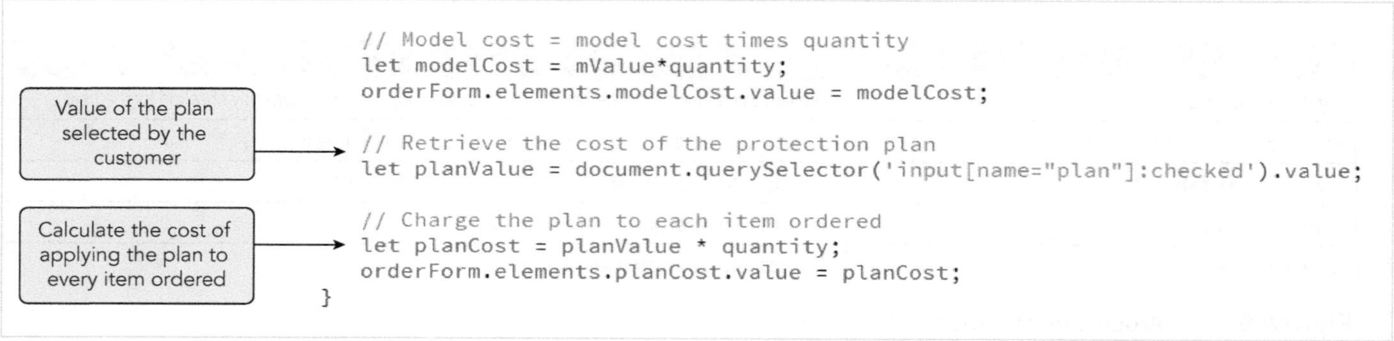

Figure 6-11 Calculating the cost of the protection plan

3. Save your changes to the file and then reload **js06a.html** in your browser. A 0 should now appear in the `planCost` field because no protection plan ($0.00) is selected by default.

> **Note**
>
> Checkbox controls work the same way as option buttons because the `checked` property indicates whether the box is checked and the field value associated with a checked box is stored in the `value` property of the checkbox object. However, this value is applied only when the checkbox is checked; otherwise there is no field value associated with the element.

To complete the order form calculations, add commands to the `calcOrder()` function to calculate the subtotal, taxes due, and the total cost of the order.

To complete the cost calculations:

1. Return to the **js06a.js** file in your code editor.
2. Add the following statements to the `calcOrder()` function to calculate and display the order subtotal:

```
// Calculate the order subtotal
let subtotal = modelCost + planCost;
orderForm.elements.subtotal.value = subtotal;
```

3. Add the following statements to `calcOrder()` to calculate the 5% sales tax:

```
// Calculate the 5% sales tax
let salesTax = subtotal * 0.05;
orderForm.elements.salesTax.value = salesTax;
```

4. Finally, add the following statements to calculate the total cost of the order by adding the subtotal and sales tax:

```
// Calculate the total cost of the order
let totalCost = subtotal + salesTax;
orderForm.elements.totalCost.value = totalCost;
```

5. **Figure 6-12** describes the newly added code in the function.

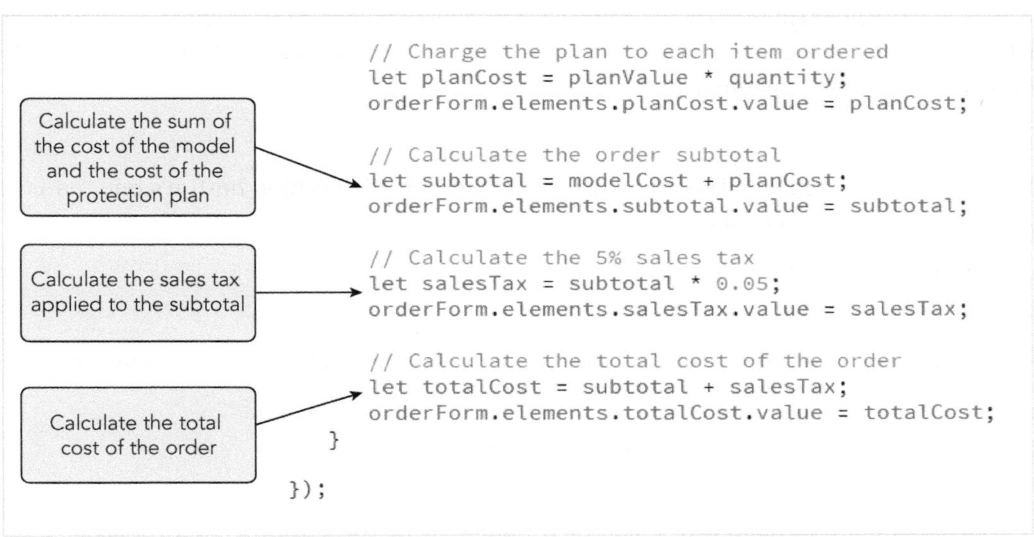

Figure 6-12 Calculating the subtotal, sales tax, and total order cost

6. Save your changes to the file and then reload **js06a.html** in your browser. **Figure 6-13** shows the calculated values from the initial state of the order form.

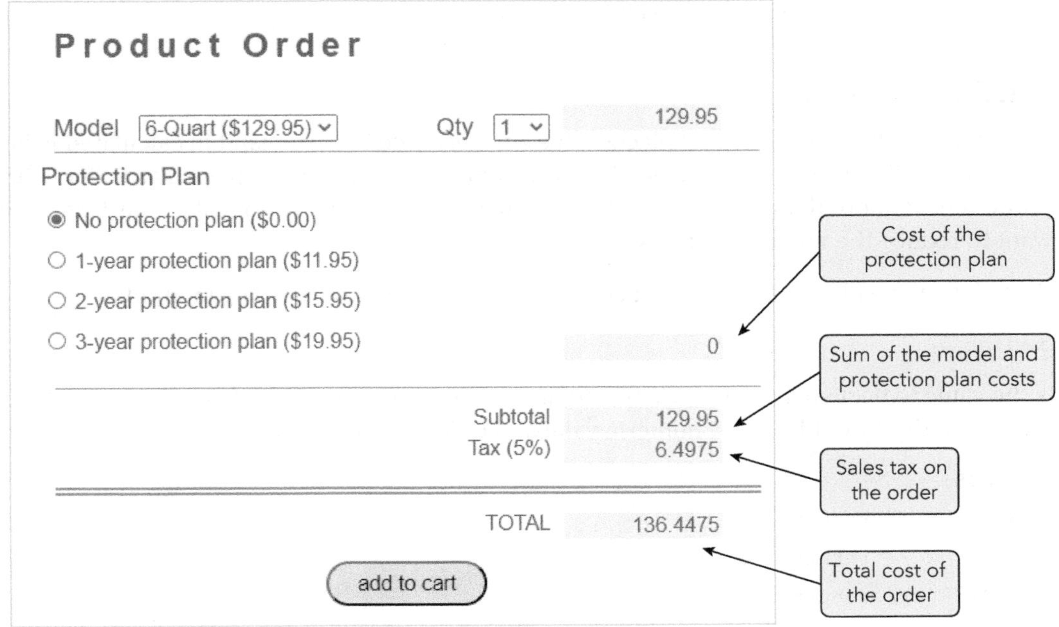

Figure 6-13 Initial order calculations

Accessing the Option Label

A challenge with option buttons is that the text associated with the button is not part of the <input> tag but instead is displayed alongside the button. HTML deals with this challenge with the <label> tag, which marks text associated with a specified form control. For example, the order form contains the following code for the No Protection Plan option button and its label:

```
<input type="radio" id="plan_0" name="plan" value="0" checked />
<label for="plan_0">No protection plan ($0.00)</label>
```

The value of the input control's `id` attribute (plan_0) is the same as the value of label's `for` attribute, associating the input control with the label. Because an input control can be associated with more than one label, JavaScript supports the following `labels` node list for any `input` element:

```
input.labels
```

where *`input`* is a reference to an `input` element. The text of the No Protection Plan option button's one (and only) label would be retrieved using the following commands:

```
let noProtection = document.getElementById("plan_0");
let planLabel = noProtection.labels[0].textContent;
```

You can also use the `querySelector()` method to retrieve the text of the label associated with the checked option button using the code:

```
let plan = document.querySelector('input[name="plan"]:checked');
let planLabel = plan.labels[0].textContent;
```

If the label contains HTML code in addition to plain text, it can be retrieved using the `innerHTML` property.

Formatting Data Values in a Form

The content of a form needs to be simple and clear. The numeric values shown in the order form, while calculated correctly, are difficult to read. Currency values should be displayed to two decimal places with commas used as thousands separators. In some cases, you may want to preface the value with a currency symbol, such as $ or €. You can use JavaScript's formatting methods to format calculated values as currency.

The `toFixed()` Method

JavaScript stores numeric values to 16 decimal places. This level of precision can result in calculated values displayed with a long string of digits. For example, a value such as 1/3 would be stored and displayed as 0.3333333333333333. It is rare that you would need more than a few decimal places in any calculation, so to make your forms more readable you will often want to reduce the number of digits.

To set the number of digits displayed by the browser, apply the following `toFixed()` method:

```
value.toFixed(n)
```

where *`value`* is the value to be displayed and *`n`* is the number of decimal places. The following examples demonstrate how the `toFixed()` method would display numeric values to different levels of precision:

```
let total = 2.835;
total.toFixed(0);    // returns "3"
total.toFixed(1);    // returns "2.8"
total.toFixed(2);    // returns "2.84"
```

Notice that the `toFixed()` method converts a numeric value to a text string and rounds the last digit in the expression rather than truncating it. Do not apply this method until your script has finished all calculations. Prior to that, you should keep the complete 16-digit level of accuracy in your calculations.

Formatting Values Using a Locale String

The `toFixed()` method is limited to setting the decimal place accuracy; it does not format numbers as currency or separate groups of thousand with the comma symbol. To do those tasks, apply the following `toLocaleString()` method:

```
value.toLocaleString(locale, {options})
```

where *`locale`* is a comma-separated list of location and language codes that indicate the locale for displaying numeric values, and *`options`* is a comma-separated list of formatting options for numeric values. With no arguments, the `toLocaleString()` method displays a numeric value using the computer's own local standards. The following code demonstrates the format applied to a sample number in which the user's computer employs standard English United States formatting:

```
let total = 14281.478;
total.toLocaleString();   // returns "14,281.478"
```

Different locales have different formatting standards. In France, the convention is to use spaces to separate groups of a thousand and commas to mark the decimal place. A French locale applied to the same test value would appear as:

```
let total = 14281.478;
total.toLocaleString("fr");   // returns "14 281,47"
```

To create your own standards, customize the appearance of the formatted text using the *`options`* argument of the `toLocaleString()` method. **Figure 6-14** describes the options that provide for complete control over number formatting.

OPTION	DESCRIPTION
`style:` *`type`*	Formatting style to use where *`type`* is "decimal", "currency", or "percent"
`currency:` *`code`*	Currency symbol to use for currency formatting where *`code`* designates the country or language
`currencyDisplay:` *`type`*	Currency text to display where *`type`* is "symbol" for a currency symbol, "code" for the ISO currency code, or "name" for the currency name
`useGroup:` *`Boolean`*	Indicates whether to use a thousands grouping symbol (`true`) or not (`false`)
`minimumIntegerDigits:` *`num`*	The minimum number of digits to display where *`num`* ranges from 1 (the default) to 21
`minimumFractionDigits:` *`num`*	The minimum number of fraction digits where *`num`* varies from 0 to 20; 2 digits are used for currency and 0 digits are used for plain number and percentages
`maximumFractionDigits:` *`num`*	The maximum number of fraction digits where *`num`* varies from 0 to 20; 2 digits are used for currency and 0 digits are used for plain number and percentages
`minimumSignficantDigits:` *`num`*	The minimum number of significant digits where *`num`* varies from 1 (the default) to 21
`maximumSignificantDigits:` *`num`*	The maximum number of significant digits where *`num`* varies from 1 (the default) to 21

Figure 6-14 Options of the `toLocaleString()` method

The following code demonstrates how to display a numeric value as currency using U.S. dollars by setting the locale to U.S. English, the number style to currency, and the currency symbol to "USD" (the $ symbol):

```
let total = 14281.5;
total.toLocaleString("en-US", {style: "currency", currency: "USD"})
// returns "$14,281.50"
```

To display the same currency amount in Euros under a French locale, apply the following commands:

```
let total = 14281.5;
total.toLocaleString("fr", {style: "currency", currency: "EUR"})
// returns "14 281,50€"
```

You can set the *`locale`* value to `undefined` to apply a format based on whatever is set on the user's computer.

> **Note** | The `toLocaleString()` method can be used with date values as well. By applying the method to a date value, you can display a date or time in a wide variety of standard formats.

Use the `toLocaleString()` method to display every calculated value in the order form as U.S. currency prefaced with the $ symbol and with commas separating each group of one thousand.

To apply the `setLocaleString()` method:

1. Return to the **js06a.js** file in your code editor.
2. Go to the `calcOrder()` function and locate the statement that stores the value of the `modelCost` variable in the `modelCost` field of the order form. Append the `toLocaleString()` method to the statement changing it from `orderForm.elements.modelCost.value = modelCost` to:

```
orderForm.elements.modelCost.value = modelCost.toLocaleString("en-US", {style: "currency",
currency: "USD"})
```

3. Repeat Step 2 to the four statements displaying the values of the `planCost`, `subtotal`, `salesTax`, and `totalCost` fields. You can use the copy and paste feature of your code editor to duplicate the code for each field. **Figure 6-15** highlights the changed code in the file.

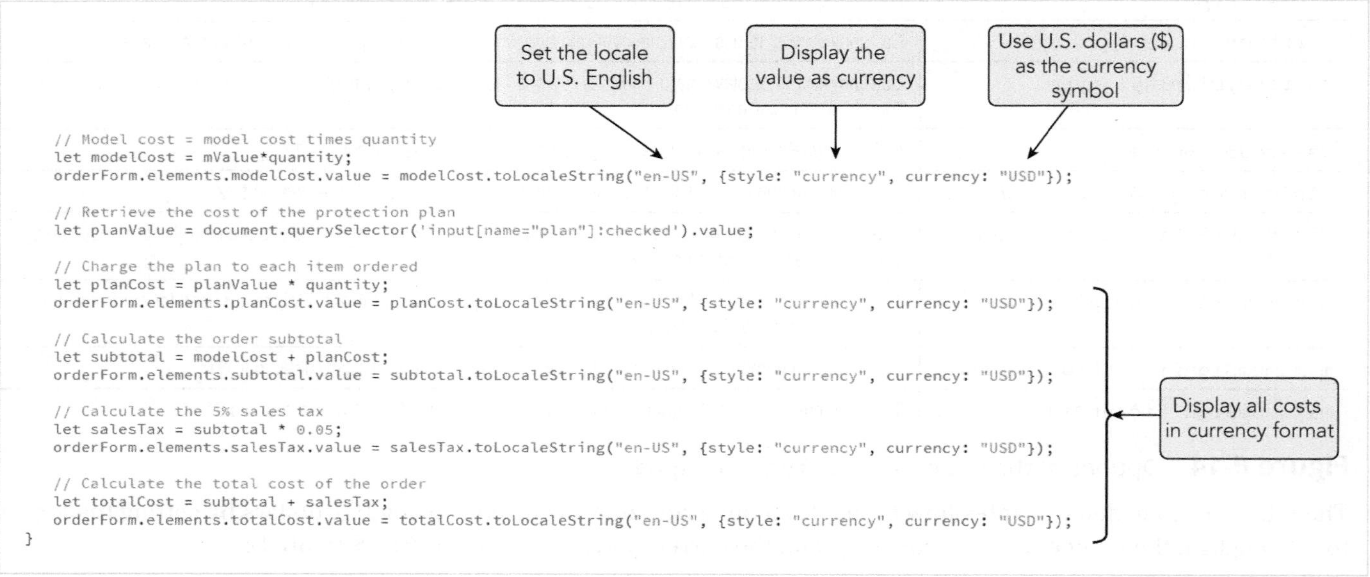

Set the locale to U.S. English

Display the value as currency

Use U.S. dollars ($) as the currency symbol

```
   // Model cost = model cost times quantity
   let modelCost = mValue*quantity;
   orderForm.elements.modelCost.value = modelCost.toLocaleString("en-US", {style: "currency", currency: "USD"});

   // Retrieve the cost of the protection plan
   let planValue = document.querySelector('input[name="plan"]:checked').value;

   // Charge the plan to each item ordered
   let planCost = planValue * quantity;
   orderForm.elements.planCost.value = planCost.toLocaleString("en-US", {style: "currency", currency: "USD"});

   // Calculate the order subtotal
   let subtotal = modelCost + planCost;
   orderForm.elements.subtotal.value = subtotal.toLocaleString("en-US", {style: "currency", currency: "USD"});

   // Calculate the 5% sales tax
   let salesTax = subtotal * 0.05;
   orderForm.elements.salesTax.value = salesTax.toLocaleString("en-US", {style: "currency", currency: "USD"});

   // Calculate the total cost of the order
   let totalCost = subtotal + salesTax;
   orderForm.elements.totalCost.value = totalCost.toLocaleString("en-US", {style: "currency", currency: "USD"});
}
```

Display all costs in currency format

Figure 6-15 Applying the `toLocaleString()` method

4. Save your changes to the file and then reload **js06a.html** in your browser. **Figure 6-16** shows the values in the order form formatted as U.S. currency.

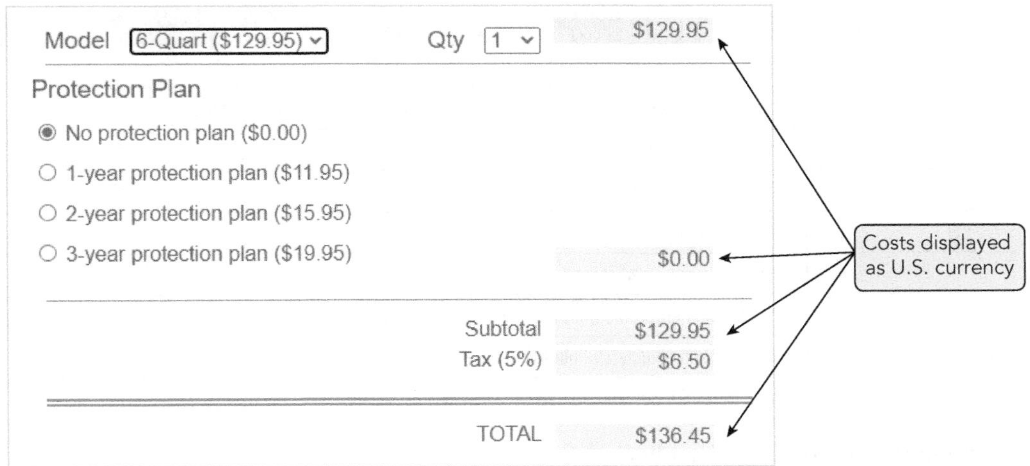

Figure 6-16 Displaying numeric values as currency

Next, add code to recalculate the costs whenever the customer changes a selection in the order form.

Skills at Work | Making a Website International Friendly

On the World Wide Web, your customers and associates can come from anywhere. You need to plan your website for international visitors as well as domestic clients. Consider the following tips as you plan to go "international":

- Support international conventions for dates, times, numbers, and currency using country and language codes in your HTML content and JavaScript programs.
- Avoid images that contain text strings. A picture is a worth a thousand words but not if that picture includes language foreign to your audience.
- Make your layout flexible. The translated version of your content might contain more words or fewer words than your web page. Ensure that the page layout can adapt to different text content. Remember that in some countries, text is read from right to left.
- Optimize your site for international searches, including using country-specific domain names and keywords tailored to international customers.
- Provide customers with a way to convert their payments into their own currency or provide information on exchange rates.
- Be aware of cultural differences: Color, working hours, holidays, and so forth have different meanings in different countries.

Once you have established an international website, monitor its usage with various analytical tools such as Google Webmaster and Analytics. A poor traffic report might indicate a problem with the international content of your website.

Responding to Form Events

Web forms need to be able to respond instantly to changes made to data values and form selections. JavaScript supports provides this interactivity using the event handlers described in **Figure 6-17**.

To run the `calcOrder()` function when the user selects a different model to order, apply the following `onchange` event handler to the `model` field:

```
orderForm.elements.model.onchange = calcOrder;
```

EVENT HANDLER	DESCRIPTION
element.onblur	The form *element* has lost the focus
element.onchange	The value of *element* has changed, and *element* has lost the focus
element.onfocus	The *element* has received the focus
element.oninput	The *element* has received user input
element.oninvalid	The *element* value is invalid
form.onreset	The *form* has been reset
element.onsearch	The user has entered something into a search field
element.onselect	Text has been selected within the *element*
form.onsubmit	The *form* has been submitted

Figure 6-17 Form and element event handlers

Edits made to an input field do not invoke a change event until field loses the focus, signifying that the changes to the field are completed. This is to avoid the event firing while the user is typing values into the input control.

In contrast, the input event is fired whenever the user changes a value within a control even if the control has not lost the focus. If a script needs to respond immediately to changes made while typing a field's value, use the oninput event handler or listen for the input event. Note that the input event does not apply to selection lists or option buttons because no content is changed.

Add an event listener for the change event to every element within the order form, running the calcOrder() function in response.

To add an event listener to every element in the order form:

1. Return to the **js06a.js** file in your code editor.
2. Directly below the statement that gives the focus to the model field, add the following for loop that adds event listeners to every item in the elements collection of the order form (see **Figure 6-18**):

```
// Add an event listener for every form element
for (let i = 0; i < orderForm.elements.length; i++) {
   orderForm.elements[i].addEventListener("change", calcOrder);
}
```

```
window.addEventListener("load", function() {
   let orderForm = document.forms.orderForm;
   let model = orderForm.elements.model;

   // Select Model selection list when form opens
   model.focus();

   // Add an event listener for every form element
   for (let i = 0; i < orderForm.elements.length; i++) {
      orderForm.elements[i].addEventListener("change", calcOrder);
   }
```

Run the calcOrder() function when any order form element changes its value

Figure 6-18 Adding event listeners to a form

3. Save your changes to the file and then reload **js06a.html** in your browser.
4. Test the event listeners by changing the model to **8-Quart ($159.95)**, the quantity to **8** and the protection plan to **3-year protection plan ($19.95)**. **Figure 6-19** shows the updated cost estimate for the order.

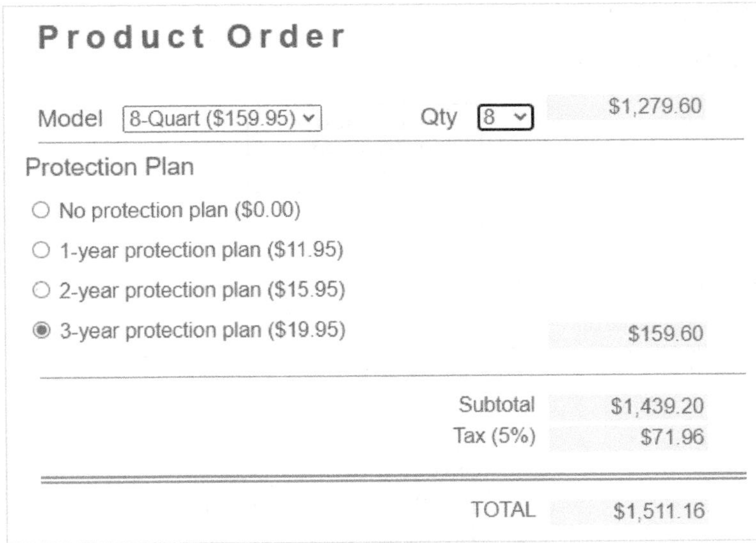

Figure 6-19 Order costs recalculated for different customer choices

Working with Hidden Fields

In many web forms, important data is stored within hidden fields making that data available to the server processing the form but hiding that data from the user. The product order page contains the following hidden fields to store the model and protection plan chosen by the consumer:

```
<input type="hidden" id="modelName" name="modelName" />
<input type="hidden" id="planName" name="planName" />
```

To store values in these two hidden fields extract the name of the model chosen in the Model selection list and the name of the plan chosen from the list of protection plan option.

The model name is contained in the text of the selected option and can be stored in the `modelName` field using the `text` attribute in the following command:

```
orderForm.elements.modelName.value =
orderForm.elements.model.options[mIndex].text;
```

where the `mIndex` variable provides the index of the option chosen from the model selection list.

The text of the selected plan must be retrieved from the text of the `label` element associated with that option button. Retrieve that text using the following statements:

```
let planOpt = document.querySelector('input[name="plan"]:checked');
orderForm.elements.planName.value = planOpt.labels[0].textContent;
```

Add these two sets of commands to the `calcOrder()` function.

To store a value in a hidden field:

1. Return to the **js06a.js** file in your code editor.

2. At the bottom of the `calcOrder()` function add the following code as shown in **Figure 6-20**:

```
orderForm.elements.modelName.value = model.options[mIndex].text;
let selectedPlan =
document.querySelector('input[name="plan"]:checked');
orderForm.elements.planName.value =
selectedPlan.labels[0].textContent;
```

```
    // Calculate the total cost of the order
    let totalCost = subtotal + salesTax;
    orderForm.elements.totalCost.value = totalCost.toLocaleString("en-US", {style: "currency", currency: "USD"});

    orderForm.elements.modelName.value = model.options[mIndex].text;
    let selectedPlan = document.querySelector('input[name="plan"]:checked');
    orderForm.elements.planName.value =  selectedPlan.labels[0].textContent;
  }
});
```

Store the text of the selected option in a selection list

Store the text of the label associated with the checked option in a set of option buttons

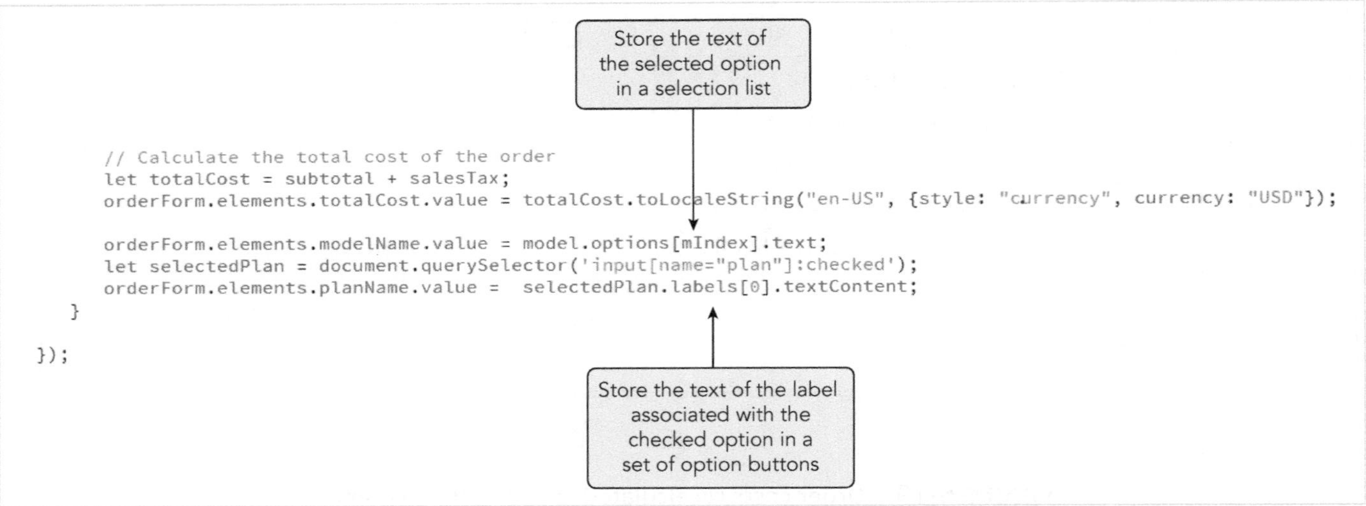

Figure 6-20 Setting the value of hidden fields

3. Save your changes to the file and then reload **js06a.html** in your browser.
4. Open the browser debugger and verify that no errors in the code are noted by the debugger.
5. Close the debugger window when you are satisfied that the code is working without error; otherwise return to your code editor to fix any reported mistakes.

You have completed the coding for the order form report. At this point a customer could click the Add to Cart button and submit the order to the web server for processing. However, because the focus of this book is client-side JavaScript, this form will submit the data to another HTML document named ordersubmit.html located in the same folder as the js06a.html file. The only purpose of the ordersubmit.html document is to display the form data that would be submitted to a server. However, you can view the submitted information to verify that the form is working correctly.

To submit the completed order:

1. Enter the following data in the order form as displayed in your browser: Model = **8-Quart ($159.95)**, Quantity = **6** and Protection Plan = **1-year protection plan ($11.95)**.
2. Click the **add to cart** button to submit the completed form. The browser opens the submitorder.html file with your choices and the calculated values already filled in. See **Figure 6-21**.

Your Order

8-Quart ($159.95)	Qty: 6	$959.70
1-year protection plan ($11.95)		$71.70
	Subtotal	$1,031.40
	Tax (5%)	$51.57
	TOTAL	$1,082.97

Figure 6-21 Contents of the shopping cart

Notice in the browser's address box that the address for the ordersubmit.html file is appended with a long text string called a query string containing field names and values from the product order form. The script embedded in the ordersubmit.html file extracts these field names and values and formats for them for the order summary shown in Figure 6-21. Techniques for extracting data from a query string are beyond the scope of this chapter.

Next you will learn how to use JavaScript and web forms to validate the payment information for this order.

Quick Check 1

1. Provide the object reference to the second element within the first web form on the web page.
2. Provide code to retrieve the value of the selected option in the selection list with the id "state", storing the value in the `stateName` variable.
3. Provide code to retrieve the value of the checked option in the option group for the `shipping` field.
4. Provide code to display the value of the `payment` variable as United States currency.
5. Provide code to run the `calcShipping()` function when the value of the `state` field in the `shoppingCart` form is changed.

Exploring Form Submission

When the user has completed a web form, the data can be submitted for processing as you did with the product order form. Forms are submitted when the user clicks (or otherwise interacts) with a submit button. Submit buttons are marked using `<input>` or `<button>` tags with the attribute `type="submit"`. When a submit button is activated, the following actions occur within the browser:

1. The field values are checked for invalid data.
2. If no invalid data is found, a `submit` event is fired indicating that the form is being submitted.
3. If no errors occur in the form submission, a request is sent to the server or other resource handling the form data.

Once the request has been sent to the server or other resource, the action of the form is completed until another submit button is activated.

Using the `submit` Event

The submission of a form by clicking a submit button creates a `submit` event after a successful validation. A form can also be submitted via JavaScript using the following `submit()` method:

```
form.submit()
```

where *`form`* is a reference to the web form. Note that submitting a form in this fashion bypasses a validation of the form's contents and does not fire the `submit` event of the `form` object.

Resetting a Form

Forms are reset whenever the user clicks a reset button, marked within an `<input>` or `<button>` tag containing the `type="reset"` attribute. When a form is reset, all fields are set back to their default values. Clicking a reset button fires the `reset` event which also be initiated using the `reset()` method:

```
form.reset()
```

In general, avoid resetting a form because restoring all fields to their default values can be confusing to the user.

Validating Form Data with JavaScript

A big part of any form submission is checking the form for invalid data in a process known as validation. When this validation is done using the user's own computer, it is known as client-side validation as opposed to server-side validation, which is handled by the web server.

The product order form you worked on earlier used selection lists and option buttons to limit data to a predetermined list of options. In so doing, the form reduced the possibility of data entry error, making it more likely that any information sent to the server was complete and accurate.

Not every form can be so constructed. Many fields cannot be so easily confined to a list of options, such as fields that request a customer name, password, credit card number, or address. In those situations, client-side validation should be applied as much as possible to catch errors and notify the user of the mistake. While some validation still must be done on the web server, it is good practice to do as much validation as possible on the user's own computer to reduce server load.

HTML provides attributes to restrict what data the user can and cannot enter within a form, and CSS provides style rules that highlight data entry errors. You will want to take advantage of these browser-based validation or native validation tools whenever possible but in other situations you may need to augment these features with a validation script of your own.

A payment form for the customer's order has been created for you. Your task is to write a script providing validation checks and feedback not covered by the built-in browser validation tools. Open the web page form and the script file now.

To open the files for the payment form:

1. Go to the js06 ► chapter folder of your data files.
2. Use your code editor to open the **js06b_txt.html** and **js06b_txt.js** files. Enter your name and the date in the comment section of each file and then save them as **js06b.html** and **js06b.js**, respectively.
3. Return to the **js06b.html** file in your code editor. Within the head section, add a `script` element to run the js06b.js script file, deferring the loading the script file until after the entire page has loaded.
4. Take some time to scroll through the contents of the HTML file, studying the elements used for the input controls on the payment form and the field names associated with each control.
5. Open the **js06b.html** file in your web browser. **Figure 6-22** describes the fields contained within the payment form.

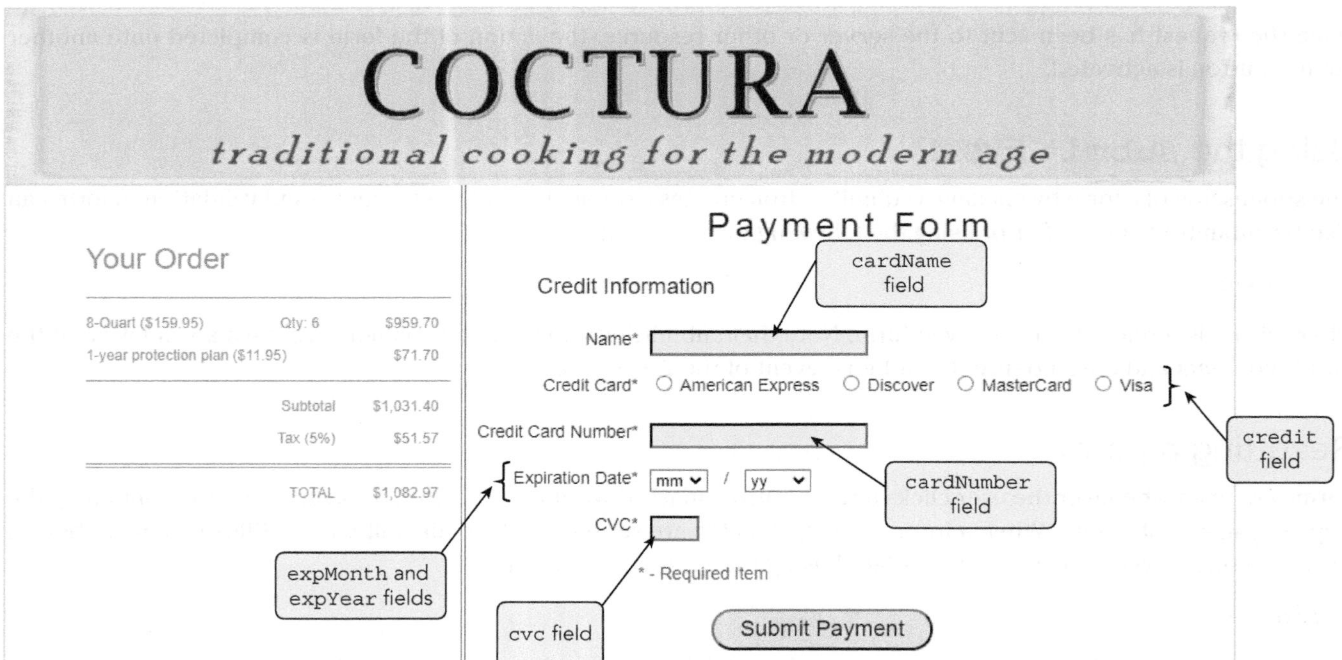

Figure 6-22 Payment form

Before creating your own validation tests, explore the validation features built into the HTML and CSS code.

To explore a validation check:

1. With no data in the payment form, click the **Submit Payment** button on the payment form.
2. The browser returns an error bubble requesting that the Name field be filled out. See **Figure 6-23**.
3. Reload the page and the web form.

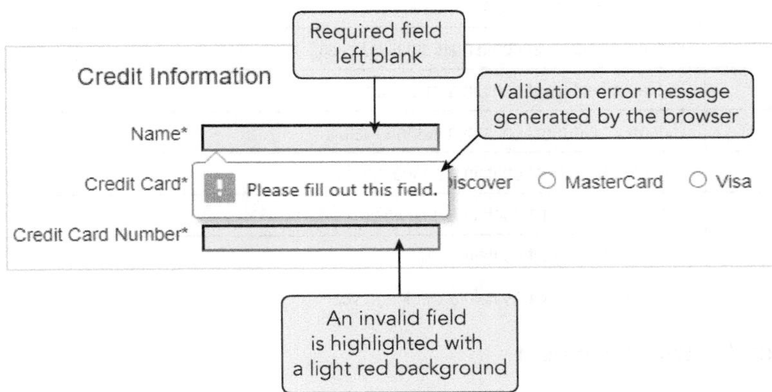

Figure 6-23 Browser validation message and highlighting

The error bubble displayed by the browser occurs because `cardName` is a required field as indicated by the following `<input>` tag in the js06b.html file:

```
<input name="cardName" id="cardName" required type="text" />
```

The other data fields in the form also have the `required` attribute so that a payment cannot be submitted unless data is entered in each field. The appearance and content of the error bubble is determined by the browser.

CSS styles highlight those form fields that are invalid for one reason or another. In this example, input boxes containing invalid data are displayed with a semi-transparent red background based on the following CSS style rule:

```
input:invalid {
   background-color: rgba(221,147,148,0.2);
}
```

where the `invalid` pseudo-class selects those input elements containing invalid data. **Figure 6-24** describes some of the other HTML attributes that can be added to `input` elements to help mark invalid data.

For example, to ensure that a data for an age field must fall between 18 and 35, include the following `min` and `max` attributes with the `<input>` tag:

```
<input name="age" min="18" max="35" type="number" />
```

As much as possible, use these HTML attributes as the first line of defense against invalid data. However, browser-generated validation checks and CSS styles have some important limitations in protecting against invalid data:

- The validation error message is generic and might not contain specific information about the source of the error.
- The validation tests are based on a single field value and do not allow for tests involving multiple fields.
- The validation tests are limited to what was entered (or not entered) into the data field and, thus, cannot be generalized to work with calculated items or functions.

ATTRIBUTE	DESCRIPTION
`maxlength="value"`	Sets the maximum number of characters allowed in an input field
`min="value"`	Sets the minimum allowed value in an input field; can be used with numbers, ranges, dates, and times
`max="value"`	Sets the maximum allowed value in an input field; can be used with numbers, ranges, dates, and times
`pattern="regex"`	Specifies a regular expression pattern that text within an input field must satisfy to be valid
`required`	Makes it a requirement that data be entered into an input field for the field to be valid
`step="value"`	Sets the step interval between values entered into a numeric field
`type="date"`	The input field must contain a date
`type="email"`	The input field must contain an email address
`type="month"`	The input field must contain a month and year
`type="number"`	The input field must contain a numeric value
`type="tel"`	The input field must contain a phone number
`type="time"`	The input field must contain a time value
`type="url"`	The input field must contain a URL
`type="week"`	The input field must contain a week and year

Figure 6-24 Attributes of the `input` element

To supplement the native browser validation tools, use the form validation properties and methods built into JavaScript, which are known collectively as the Constraint Validation API. For this payment form, you will want your script to do the following:

- Provide customized error messages to explain the source of the error.
- Verify that the customer has entered a name for the credit card owner.
- Verify that one of four credit card brands has been selected.
- Verify that a valid credit card number for the user's credit card has been entered.
- Verify that the card's expiration date has been selected from the drop-down lists.
- Verify that a valid CVC number for the user's credit card has been entered.

You will start by exploring how to work with JavaScript's validation properties and methods.

Working with the Constraint Validation API

The Constraint Validation API includes the properties and methods listed in **Figure 6-25**.

For example, the following expression returns the Boolean value `true` if the `cardName` field from the payment form contains valid data:

```
document.forms.payment.elements.cardName.valid
```

You can also test for valid data using the following `checkValidity()` method:

```
document.forms.payment.elements.cardName.checkValidity()
```

The `checkValidity()` method returns a value of `true` for valid data; but, if the field is invalid, the method returns a value of `false` while firing an invalid event. An invalid event is an event that occurs whenever the browser encounters a field whose value does not match the rules specified for its content.

Note The `checkValidity()` method can be applied to a `form` object as well as individual form elements. When applied to a `form` object, if at least one element within that form fails validation, the form fails.

PROPERTY OR METHOD	DESCRIPTION
form.noValidate	Set to true to prevent the native browser tools from validating the web form *form*
form.reportValidity()	Reports on the validation status of *form* using the native browser validation tools
element.willValidate	Returns true if web form element *element* is capable of being validated by the browser (regardless of where the data itself is actually valid)
element.valid	Sets or return the validity of the element where true indicates the element contain valid data and false indicates an invalidate field value
element.validationMessage	Sets or returns the text of the validation message returned by the browser when *element* fails validation
element.validity	Returns a ValidityState object containing specific information about the validation of *element*
element.setCustomValidity(*msg*)	Sets the validity message displayed by the browser where *msg* is the text displayed when *element* fails validation (set *msg* to an empty text string to indicate that the element does not have a validation error)
element.checkValidity()	Returns true if *element* is valid and false if it is not invalid; a false value also fires the invalid event

Figure 6-25 **Constraint Validation API properties and methods**

Exploring the ValidityState Object

There are several reasons why data might be flagged as invalid. Information about the cause of invalid data is stored in the ValidityState object referenced with the expression:

```
element.validity
```

where *element* is a field from a web form. To determine the current validation state of an element, apply the expression

```
element.validity.ValidityState
```

where *ValidityState* is one the validation states described in **Figure 6-26**.

VALIDITY STATE	DESCRIPTION
element.validity.badInput	The field element, *element*, contains data that the browser is unable to convert, such as when an e-mail address lacks the @ character
element.validity.customError	A custom validation message has been set to a non-empty text string using the setCustomValidity() method
element.validity.patternMismatch	The *element* value does not match the character pattern specified in the pattern attribute
element.validity.rangeOverflow	The *element* value is greater than the max attribute
element.validity.rangeUnderflow	The *element* value is less than the min attribute
element.validity.stepMismatch	The *element* value does not match the step attribute
element.validity.tooLong	The *element* character length exceeds the value of the maxLength attribute
element.validity.tooShort	The *element* character length is less than the minLength attribute
element.validity.typeMismatch	The *element* value does not match the data type specified by the type attribute
element.validity.valid	The *element* contains valid data, satisfying all constraints
element.validity.valueMissing	The *element* specified in the pattern does not contain data though it is marked with the required attribute

Figure 6-26 **Properties of a ValidityState object**

In summary, the checkValidity() method will tell you whether a field is invalid; the validity property will tell you why.

In the following code the validity state of the `userMail` field is evaluated to determine whether it contains the correct data type. If the field's data type was set to "mail" and the field did not contain an email address, the `notValid` variable would return a value of `true`, indicating that the `userMail` field does not conform to its specified data type.

```
let email = document.getElementById("userMail");
let notValid = email.validity.typeMismatch;
```

Note that the `typeMismatch` property can only test whether a field's value matches the data type, it does not test whether that field's value is legitimate. Testing an email address only confirms that the text string "looks" like an email address it does not test whether that email address exists.

Creating a Custom Validation Message

You have already seen that when a data field fails validation, the browser displays its own native error bubble notifying the user of the problem. Different browsers may display different messages. For example, Google Chrome displays the message "Please fill out this field" for missing data while Microsoft Edge displays the message "This is a required field." To display the same error message across all browsers, apply the following `setCustomValidity()` method to the element:

```
element.setCustomValidity(msg)
```

where *msg* is the custom message displayed by all browsers, overriding the native browser error message. If an element is valid, store an empty text string for the *msg* parameter, which also marks the element as being valid.

Note You can access the text of the validation error message associated with an invalid data field by using the `element.validationMessage` property where *element* is the form element containing the error.

Use the `setCustomValidty()` method to display the message "Enter your name as it appears on the card" if the user leaves the required field `cardName` blank. Otherwise, store an empty string using the `setCustomValidity()` method so that the `cardName` field is marked as valid.

To create custom validation message:

1. Return to the **js06b.js** file in your code editor.
2. Directly below the initial comment section, add the following `validateName()` function:

```
// Check if the owner's name is entered on the cardfunction
validateName() {
   let cardName = document.getElementById("cardName");
   if (cardName.validity.valueMissing) {
      cardName.setCustomValidity("Enter your name as it appears on the card");
   } else {
      cardName.setCustomValidity("");
   }
}
```

Figure 6-27 describes the code in the function.

By creating your own customized error message, you have provided more specific information to the customer about the nature of the error.

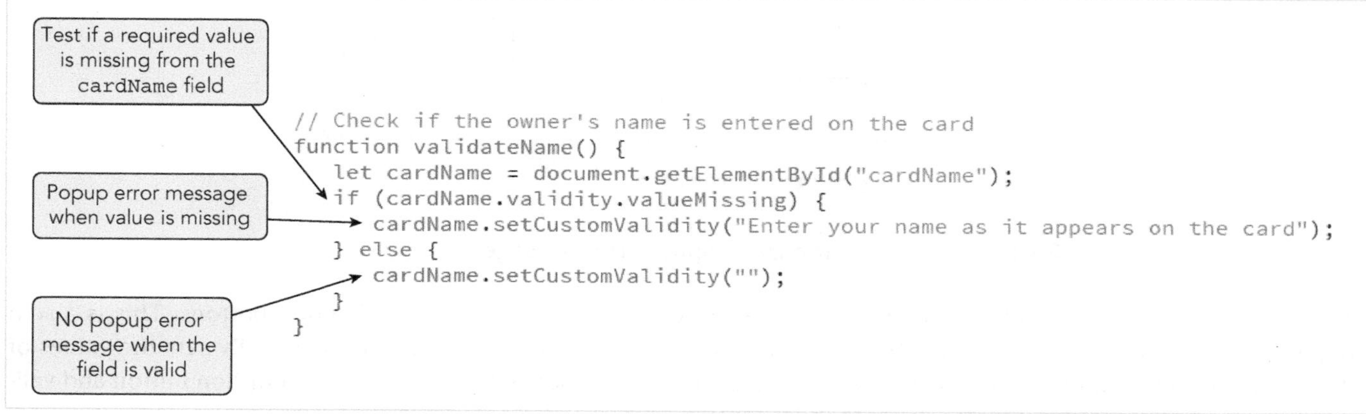

Figure 6-27 Creating the `validateName()` function

Responding to Invalid Data

Form data can be tested after the user enters the data into an input control and when the submit button is clicked to initiate form submission. To check the validity of form data after it is entered, use an event handler or event listener for the `change` event. To catch invalid data before the form is submitted, add an event handler or event listener for the `click` event of the form's submit button.

There are reasons for both approaches. If you want users to be notified immediately of invalid data so that mistakes can be corrected before continuing with the form, validate the data after it is entered. If such constant prompting would annoy and frustrate the user, save all the validation checks until the entire form has been completed and submitted. For the payment form you save all validation checks until the submit button is clicked.

Add an event listener now to run the `validateName()` function when the submit button is clicked.

To add the event listener for the `click` event:

1. Directly above the `validateName()` function add the following statement as described in **Figure 6-28**:

```
let subButton = document.getElementById("subButton");

// Validate the payment when the submit button is clicked
subButton.addEventListener("click", validateName);
```

```
*/

let subButton = document.getElementById("subButton");

// Validate the payment when the submit button is clicked
subButton.addEventListener("click", validateName);
```

Run the `validateName()` function when the submit button is clicked

Figure 6-28 Calling the `validateName()` function

2. Save your changes to the file and then reload **js06b.html** in your web browser.
3. Without entering any data, click the **Submit Payment** button. Verify that the revised error message appears next to the empty `cardName` field. See **Figure 6-29**.
4. Enter a sample name into the `cardName` field and click the **Submit Payment** button again. Verify that no error bubble appears next to the `cardName` field.

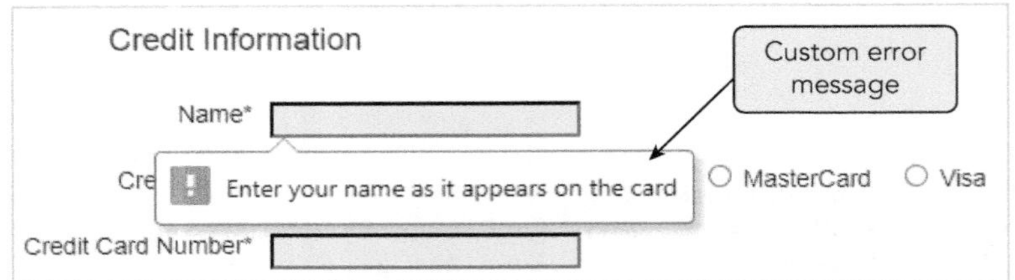

Figure 6-29 Customized popup error message

The next field on the payment form is the `credit` field, which is laid out as a set of option buttons. This is also a required field; however, with option buttons clicking one option button from the list automatically sets the values of the remaining option buttons; therefore, the `required` attribute is needed only with the first option button and validation tests need to be performed only on that first option button.

Create the `validateCredit()` function to test whether the user has selected an option button from the group and if no option button is selected, display the custom validation message "Select your credit card".

To create the `validateCredit()` function:

1. Return to the **js06b.js** file in your code editor.
2. Directly below the event listener for the `click` event, add the following event listener to add another function to the `click` event:

```
subButton.addEventListener("click", validateCard);
```

3. Directly below the `validateName()` function add the following function as described in **Figure 6-30**:

```
// Check if a credit card has been selected
function validateCard() {
   let card = document.forms.payment.elements.credit[0];
   if (card.validity.valueMissing) {
      card.setCustomValidity("Select your credit card");
   } else {
      card.setCustomValidity("");
   }
}
```

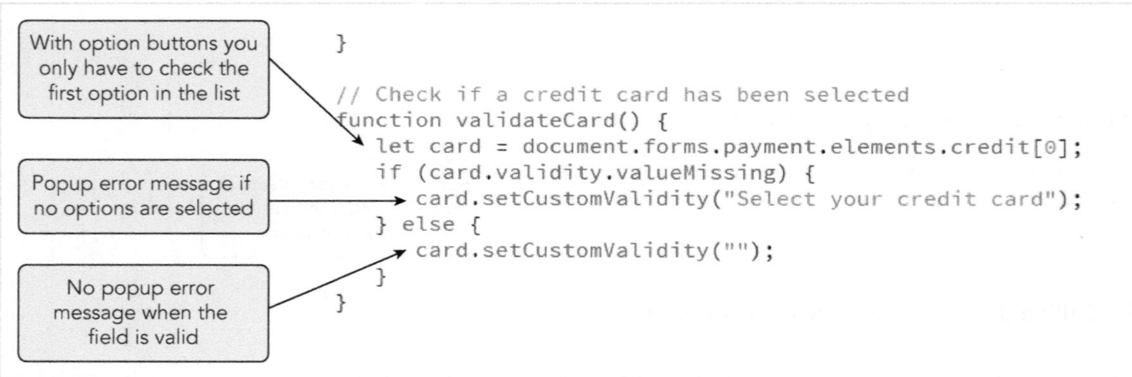

Figure 6-30 Creating the `validateCard()` function

4. Save your changes to the file and then reload **js06b.html** in your web browser.
5. Enter a sample name in the Name box, but do not select a credit card from the list of options.

6. Click the **Submit Payment** button. Verify that the error message "Select your credit card" appears next to the list of unselected credit card options.
7. Click one of the credit card option buttons and click the **Submit Payment** button again. Verify that the next error bubble appears alongside the empty Credit Card Number input box.

The next field in the payment form is the `cardNumber` field in which not only must a value be entered but the value must also be a string of numbers fitting a recognized credit card number pattern.

Validating Data with Pattern Matching

The content of a text string can be validated against a regular expression, which is concise code describing the general pattern and content of the characters within a text string. For example, the regular expression:

```
^\d{5}5$
```

matches any text string containing exactly 5 digits, such as "12345", "80517", or "00314", but not "abcde" or "123456".

It is beyond the scope of this chapter to discuss the syntax of regular expressions, but they are an important tool in the validation of any form, especially forms used in e-commerce. Regular expressions can be long and complicated to accommodate a wide range of possible character patterns, such as would be used to validate a credit card number. The following rather imposing regular expression pattern has already been entered in the `<input>` tag for the `cardNumber` field:

```
pattern = "^(?:4[0-9]{12}(?:[0-9]{3})?|5[1-5][0-9]{14}|6(?:011|5[0-9][0-9])[0-9]{12}|3[47]
[0-9]{13}|3(?:0[0-5]|[68][0-9])[0-9]{11}|(?:2131|1800|35\d{3})\d{11})$"
```

This long and complicated expression matches the valid credit card number patterns associated with the four types of credit cards listed in the payment form. Though you don't have to duplicate this expression in your script file, you want to display a customized error message if the number entered by the customer does not match this regular expression pattern or if no credit card number is entered at all.

Create a function named `validateNumber()` that displays the error message "Enter your card number" if the customer leaves the `cardNumber` field blank or the error message "Enter a valid card number" if the customer enters a number that does not match an approved credit card number pattern. You will use the `valueMissing` property to test for a missing value and the `patternMismatch` property to test for a card number that does not follow the prescribed character pattern.

To create the `validateNumber()` function:

1. Return to the **js06b.js** file in your code editor.
2. Directly below the event listener for the `click` event, add the following event listener to run the `validateNumber()` function in response to the `click` event:

```
subButton.addEventListener("click", validateNumber);
```

3. Directly below the `validateCard()` function add the following function as described in **Figure 6-31**:

```
// Check if the card number is valid
function validateNumber() {
   let cNum = document.getElementById("cardNumber");
   if (cNum.validity.valueMissing) {
      cNum.setCustomValidity("Enter your card number");
   } else if (cNum.validity.patternMismatch) {
      cNum.setCustomValidity("Enter a valid card number");
   } else {
      cNum.setCustomValidity("");
   }
}
```

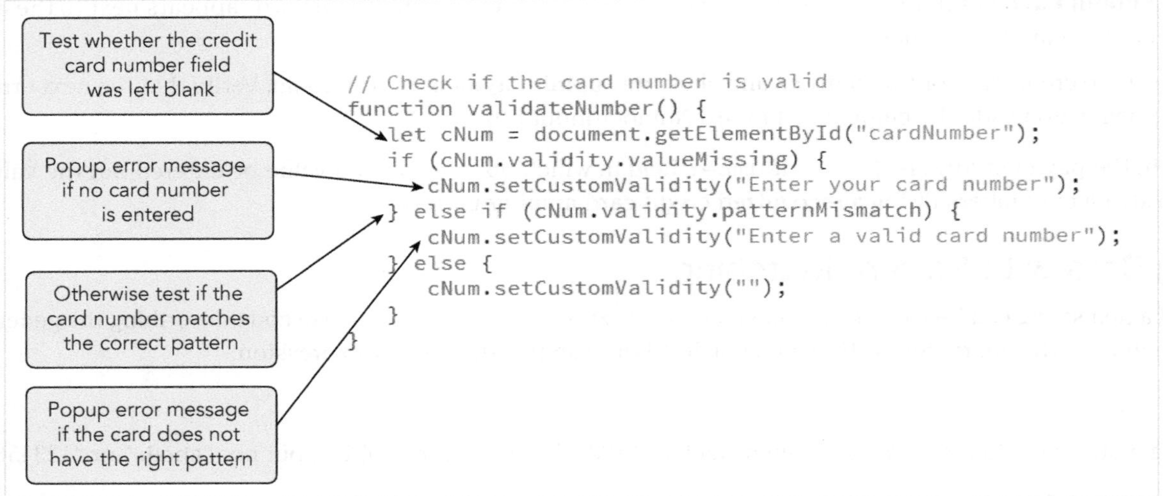

Figure 6-31 Creating the `validateNumber()` function

4. Save your changes to the file and then reload **js06b.html** in your web browser.
5. Enter a sample name in the Name box and select the **MasterCard** credit card.
6. Click the **Submit Payment** button. Verify that the error message "Enter your card number" appears next to the Credit Card Number box.
7. Enter the invalid credit card number **1234567890** into the `cardNumber` field and click the **Submit Payment** button. Verify that the browser displays the message "Enter a valid card number", as shown in **Figure 6-32**.

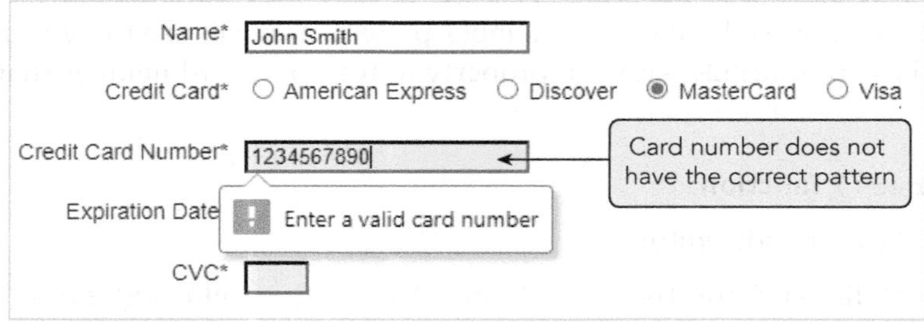

Figure 6-32 Popup error message for an invalid card number

8. Enter the valid credit card number **6011485077126974** into the `cardNumber` field and click the **Submit Payment** button. Verify that the browser accepts this number and does not display an error bubble.

The next part of the payment form contains two drop-down list boxes for the month and year of the credit card expiration date.

Validating a Selection List

The payment form has placed the possible expiration date values of the credit card in two selection lists named `expMonth` and `expYear`. The first entry in each of the two selection lists is "mm" and "yy", respectively. You must validate these two fields so that if either "mm" or "yy" is left selected, their respective fields will be flagged as invalid. Use the `selectedIndex` property to determine if the selected index is 0 (the first entry). If the index is 0, then the browser will declare the field value as invalid, otherwise it will accept the selected month or year as valid.

To validate the expiration date:

1. Return to the **js06b.js** file in your code editor.
2. Directly below the event listeners for the `click` events, add the following event listeners:

```
subButton.addEventListener("click", validateMonth);
subButton.addEventListener("click", validateYear);
```

3. Directly below the `validateNumber()` function add the following function to validate the expiration month:

```
// Check that a month is selected for the expiration date
function validateMonth() {
   let month = document.getElementById("expMonth");
   if (month.selectedIndex === 0) {
      month.setCustomValidity("Select the expiration month");
   } else {
      month.setCustomValidity("");
   }
}
```

4. Add the following `validateYear()` function to validate the expiration year:

```
// Check that a year is selected for the expiration date
function validateYear() {
   let year = document.getElementById("expYear");
   if (year.selectedIndex === 0) {
      year.setCustomValidity("Select the expiration year");
   } else {
      year.setCustomValidity("");
   }
}
```

Figure 6-33 describes the newly added code.

If the first option in the selection list is selected, the month is invalid

```
// Check that a month is selected for the expiration date
function validateMonth() {
   let month = document.getElementById("expMonth");
   if (month.selectedIndex === 0) {
      month.setCustomValidity("Select the expiration month");
   } else {
      month.setCustomValidity("");
   }
}
```

If the first option in the selection list is selected, the year is invalid

```
// Check that a year is selected for the expiration date
function validateYear() {
   let year = document.getElementById("expYear");
   if (year.selectedIndex === 0) {
      year.setCustomValidity("Select the expiration year");
   } else {
      year.setCustomValidity("");
   }
}
```

Figure 6-33 Creating the `validateMonth()` and `validateYear()` functions

5. Save your changes to the file and then reload **js06b.html** in your web browser.
6. Verify that unless you select a month and a year from the selection lists, validation error messages appear when you submit the payment form.

The last field remaining in the payment form is the `CVC` field, which is the card verification code printed on credit cards to provide additional security in financial transactions.

Testing a Form Field Against a Regular Expression

Credit card CVC numbers are either 3- or 4-digit numbers depending on the card being used. American Express cards use 4-digit CVC numbers while Discover, MasterCard, and Visa use 3-digit numbers. The regular expression that matches the 4-digit CVC numbers used by American Express is:

```
/^\d{4}$/
```

while for the other cards, the regular expression is

```
/^\d{3}$/
```

You can determine whether a text string conforms to a regular expression pattern using the following `test()` method:

```
regExp.test(text)
```

where *`regExp`* is the regular expression pattern and *`text`* is the text string containing the characters to be tested. If the text matches the regular expression pattern, the `test()` method returns the value `true`, otherwise it returns `false`. For example, the following code returns a Boolean value indicating whether the value in the `cardCVC` field matches the 4-digit pattern:

```
let cvc = document.getElementById("cvc");
let isValid = /^\d{4}$/.test(cvc.value)
```

To test whether the CVC is valid for American Express cards, use the following expression:

```
if ((card === "amex") && !(/^\d{4}$/.test(cvc.value)))
```

which returns `false` if the card is American Express and not a 4-digit number. For cards that are not American Express and require a 3-digit CVC code, use the `if` condition:

```
if ((card !== "amex") && !(/^\d{3}$/.test(cvc.value)))
```

which returns `false` if the card is not American Express and not a 3-digit number. You will use both of these `if` conditions in the `validateCVC()` function testing whether the customer has entered a valid CVC based on their selected credit card.

To create the `validateCVC()` function:

1. Return to the **js06b.js** file in your code editor.
2. Directly below the event listener statements, add the following statement to run the `validateCVC()` function when the submit button is clicked.

```
subButton.addEventListener("click", validateCVC);
```

3. Directly below the `validateYear()` function add the following code the for `validateCVC()` function:

```
function validateCVC() {
   // Determine which card was selected
   let card =
document.querySelector('input[name="credit"]:checked').value;
```

```
    let cvc = document.getElementById("cvc");

    // Validate the CVC value
    if (cvc.validity.valueMissing) {
       cvc.setCustomValidity("Enter your CVC number");
    } else if ((card === "amex") && !(/^\d{4}$/.test(cvc.value))) {
       cvc.setCustomValidity("Enter a 4-digit number");
    } else if ((card !== "amex") && !(/^\d{3}$/.test(cvc.value))) {
       cvc.setCustomValidity("Enter a 3-digit number");
    } else {
       cvc.setCustomValidity("");
    }
}
```

See **Figure 6-34**.

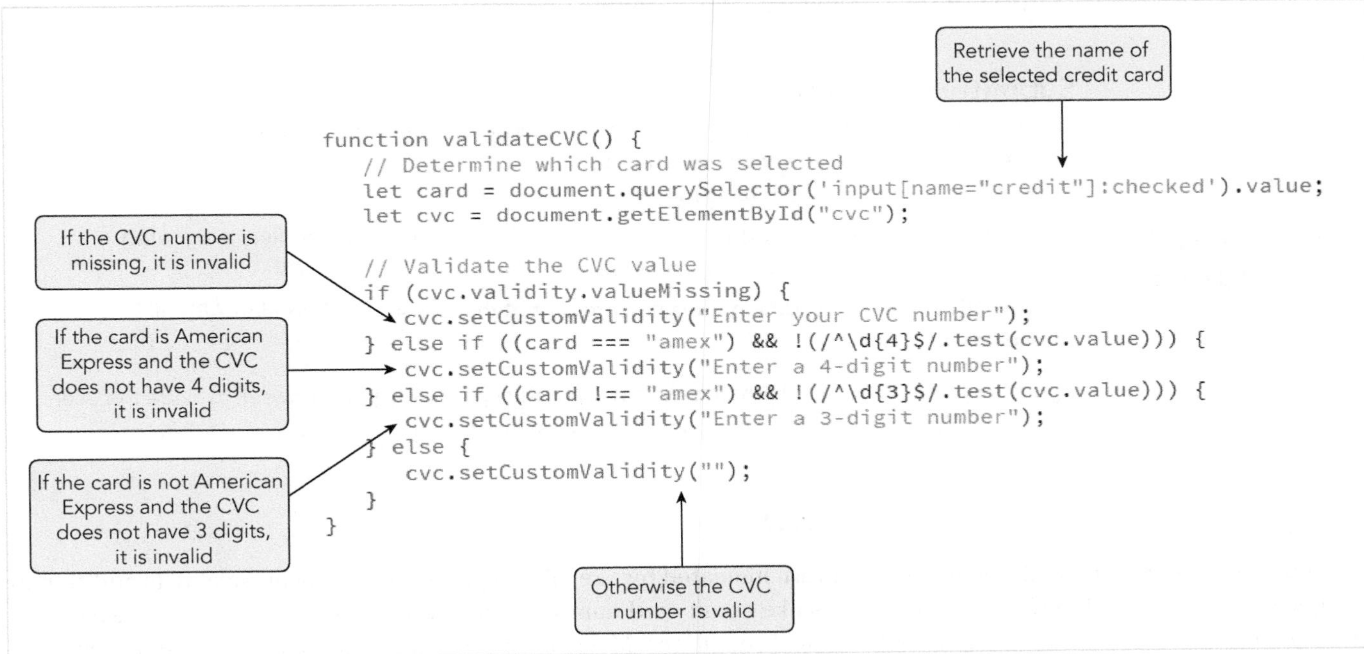

Figure 6-34 Creating the `validateCVC()` function

4. Save your changes to the file and then reload **js06b.html** in your web browser.
5. Complete the payment form by entering a sample name in the Name box, click the **American Express** option button, select **04/2026** as the expiration date, and enter **6011485077126974** as the credit card number.
6. Enter **123** as the CVC number for the card and click the **Submit Payment** button. Verify that the form rejects the CVC number as shown in **Figure 6-35**.
7. Change the CVC number to **1234** and click the **Submit Payment** button again. Verify that the form is successfully submitted and a web page confirming this fact is displayed.

If your form does not work, use the debugger tools on your browser to examine the code and compare your code to that shown in Figure 6-35. The statements in this function are very complicated, and it is easy to misplace a parenthesis or quotation mark.

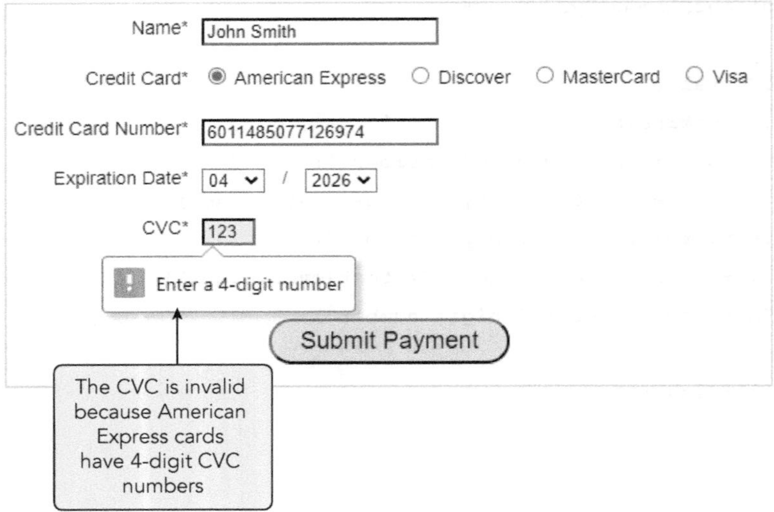

Figure 6-35 Validating the CVC number

Common Mistakes

Submitting a Form

You can submit a form using the method `form.submit()` where *form* is a reference to the web form. A common mistake is to assume that this method is equivalent to clicking a submit button. It is not. The key differences are as follows:

- The `submit` event is not triggered, so any event listeners or event handlers associated with the `submit` event will not be accessed.
- The native browser validation tools that are part of the Constraint Validation API will be bypassed.

If your script needs to use the native validation tools supplied by your browser, provide the user with a submit button and run your code in response to its use.

Creating a Custom Validity Check

A credit card number might fit the numeric pattern indicated by a regular expression but still be invalid. In addition to a specified pattern of characters, numerical ids like credit card numbers employ a checksum algorithm in which the sum of the digits must satisfy specific mathematical conditions. Most credit card numbers use the checksum algorithm known as the Luhn algorithm or the mod 10 algorithm, which calculates the sum of the digits in the credit card number after doubling every other digit going backwards from the end of the number. If the sum of the digits is a multiple of 10, the credit card number is legitimate, otherwise it is not.

A function named `luhn()` has been created for you and saved in the js06b.js file. The function performs the necessary calculations on the digits in a numerical id to determine if those digits satisfy the conditions of the Luhn algorithm. If they do, the function returns a value of `true`, otherwise it returns `false`. You will use this function as one last test of the customer's credit card number, verifying that not only is the pattern of the digits in the credit card number correct but also that the digits satisfy the Luhn algorithm.

To validate the expiration date:

1. Return to the **js06b.js** file in your code editor and go to the `validateNumber()` function.
2. Add the following condition directly before the final `else` condition in the function:

```
} else if (luhn(cNum.value) === false) {
   cNum.setCustomValidity("Enter a legitimate card number");
```

Figure 6-36 shows the complete code of the `validateNumber()` function.

```
// Check if the card number is valid
function validateNumber() {
   let cNum = document.getElementById("cardNumber");
   if (cNum.validity.valueMissing) {
      cNum.setCustomValidity("Enter your card number");
   } else if (cNum.validity.patternMismatch) {
      cNum.setCustomValidity("Enter a valid card number");
   } else if (luhn(cNum.value) === false) {
      cNum.setCustomValidity("Enter a legitimate card number");
   } else {
      cNum.setCustomValidity("");
   }
}
```

If the card number fails the Luhn algorithm, display a validation error

Figure 6-36 Validating the credit card number

3. Save your changes to the file and then reload **js06b.html** in your browser.
4. Enter a sample name in the Name box, click the **Discover** option button, select **04/2026** as the expiration date, enter **6011280768434850** as the credit card number and enter **123** as the CVC number.
5. Click the **Submit Payment** button.

   As shown in **Figure 6-37**, the credit card number is rejected because it fails the Luhn algorithm even though it has the correct general pattern.

Figure 6-37 Reporting an illegitimate credit card number

6. Edit the credit card number by changing the last digit from 0 to 6 so that it reads **6011280768434856** and click the **Submit Payment** button. Verify that the form now passes validation as the credit card number fits the correct pattern and satisfies the Luhn algorithm.

You have completed your work on the validation of the payment form. At this point further validation would be done by the web server to verify that the credit card information matches a real account; but in doing some of the validation on the customer's own computer, you would have weeded out faulty data and reduced the workload on the server.

Managing Form Validation

In completing the payment form, you took advantage of the native browser tools for managing invalid data. With some applications, you might want to disable the native browser validation tools altogether and supply your own validation framework. Such a situation might occur if you need to support older browsers that do not supply native validation. It might also be the case that you do not want to use error bubbles to notify users of errors but would prefer to highlight validation errors in a different way such as with side notes or overlays.

To disable the built-in validation tools supplied by your browser, apply the following statement:

```
form.noValidate = true;
```

where *form* is the reference to the web form. You can achieve the same effect by adding the `novalidate` attribute to the `<form>` tag in the HTML file or by adding the attribute `formnovalidate` to the tag for the form's submit button.

Another way to control the native browser validation is by preventing the default browser actions associated with an `invalid` event (such as displaying an error bubble), which are fired whenever the browser notes an invalid data value. The following code uses the `addEventListener()` method to listen for an occurrence of an invalid event within a form element, running an anonymous function in response:

```
element.addEventListener("invalid", function(evt) {
   evt.preventDefault();
   commands;
});
```

The `evt` parameter in this code is an example of the event object, which is the object associated with an event captured by the script. Every event creates an event object. The anonymous function in this example applies the `preventDefault()` method to this event object to prevent the browser's default action of reporting the error. Having prevented the default actions associated with the event, the script is free to run a set of custom commands to respond to the invalid event.

Note You can determine which form element reported the invalid data by using the `evt.target` property where *evt* is the name of the event object variable.

You can also turn off the built-in validation tools and write your own set of validation procedures and run them in response to the `submit` event occurring within the web form. The general code using an event handler is as follows:

```
form.onsubmit = myValidation;
function myValidation(e) {
   e.preventDefault();
   commands to determine if form passes validation
   if (form is valid) {
      commands run when form passes validation
      return true;
   } else {
      commands run when form doesn't pass validation
      return false;
}
```

The `myValidation()` function runs when the form is submitted, prevents the default actions associated with the submit event and then runs a different set of commands whether the form is valid or not. Notice that the function returns a value of `true` for valid forms and `false` for invalid forms, thus, indicating whether the submission was successful or not.

Using any of these approaches, you can create your own framework of validation tools customized to meet the specific needs of your application and your customers.

Best Practices | Designing an E-Commerce Website

When customers shop online, they are looking for what every customer looks for: good products at a fair price in a shopping experience that is pleasant and easy. While all these things are important, you cannot forget that your competition is only a click away and, if your customers don't have confidence in your website design, they might also not have confidence in the products you sell.

Here are some tips to keep in mind as you build your e-commerce website:

- Do not burden your customers with a long and complicated registration process. Provide guest users with easy access to your catalog because they will be more likely to register after viewing all you have to offer.
- Provide robust search tools. Make it easy to match your customers with the products they are most likely to purchase.
- Make it easy to navigate the purchasing process. Customers should be able to easily move forward and backward in the purchase process so that mistakes can be easily fixed. Provide information to the customer at each step in the process about what is being purchased and how much it will cost. Do not hide fees or taxes until later in the shopping process or you run the risk of irritating your customer.
- Put discount options and membership deals up front so that your customers can take advantage of deals that make a final purchase more likely.
- Use validation tests and security measures to reassure your customers that their credit information is safe and secure.
- Incorporate social media in your e-commerce website, providing your customers the opportunity to discuss with you and other customers your products and services.

Technology and customer tastes are constantly in flux and websites need to respond to a quickly changing market. Evaluate and revaluate your e-commerce design to ensure that it meets the needs of your customers today while you prepare for your customers of tomorrow.

Quick Check 2

1. Provide code to turn off the native browser validation for the web form with the name reviewForm.
2. Provide code to indicate whether there is a type mismatch for data entered in the input box with the id "reviewDate".
3. Provide code to indicate whether the field with the id "reviewRating" has a value greater than allowed by the `max` attribute.
4. Provide code to change the validation message for the reviewRating input box to "Value larger than allowed".
5. Provide code to test whether the value entered in the customerID input box matches the regular expression `/^[A-Z]{3}-\d{2}$/`

Summary

- A web form is a hierarchical structure consisting of `form` object containing form elements.
- Each attribute of a form control is matched by a JavaScript property for an element object.

- Use the `focus()` method to make an input control active on the form. Use the `blur()` method to remove focus from that object.
- Options within a selection are referenced with the options HTML collection. The currently selected option is referenced with the `selectedIndex` property.
- Option buttons that share a common field name belong to the options collection of the `form.elements` object. Reference the currently selected option button using a `for` loop or the `querySelector()` method. Labels associated with an option are referenced using the `labels` collection.
- Numeric values can be displayed to a defined number of decimal places using the `toFixed()` method. Use the `toLocaleString()` method to display numeric values, dates, and currency values according to local and geographic standards.
- When forms are submitted the field values can be validated using native browser validation tools prior to the submit event being triggered. The native browser validation tools are part of the Constraint Validation API.
- Test whether a field value is true using the `checkValidity()` method. To learn the state of a field's value and why it might be invalid, use the `validity` property.
- To create a customized validation error message, use the `setCustomValidity()` method.
- Required elements can be tested using the `validity.valueMissing` property. Values that don't match a specified character pattern can be tested using the `validity.patternMismatch` property.
- A regular expression is code that concisely describes the general pattern and content of characters within a text string. Use the `test()` method to determine whether a text string matches a particular regular expression.
- Checksum algorithms are used to determine whether the digits in a numeric id match specified mathematical conditions. Credit cards use the Luhn or mod 10 algorithm.
- To override the native browser validation tools, apply the `noValidate` property to the web form and then create a customized function that tests for the validity of the data when the submit event of the form is triggered.

Key Terms

browser-based validation
checksum algorithm
client-side validation
Constraint Validation API
event object
focus
invalid event
Luhn algorithm
mod 10 algorithm
native validation
query string
regular expression
server-side validation
validation
`ValidityState` object

Review Questions

1. Objects representing each of the controls in a form are stored in the ________________ collection.
   a. `forms`
   b. `controls`
   c. `inputs`
   d. `elements`
2. To reference elements from the first and only form in the web page with the name `userForm`, which of the following expressions should you not apply?
   a. `document.userForm`
   b. `document["userForm"]`
   c. `document.forms[1]`
   d. `document.forms[0]`

3. Which value of the `selectedIndex` property of a select object corresponds to no selection?
   a. –1
   b. 0
   c. false
   d. 1
4. To remove the focus from a form element, apply which of the following methods?
   a. `focus()`
   b. `delete()`
   c. `step()`
   d. `blur()`
5. Which method do you apply to a selection list to add a new option to the list?
   a. *select*.`insert(`*option*`)`
   b. *select*.`write(`*option*`)`
   c. *select*.`append(`*option*`)`
   d. *select*.`add(`*option*`)`
6. To reference the text associated with an option button, use which of the following HTML collections?
   a. `options`
   b. `elements`
   c. `labels`
   d. `nodes`
7. To display a numeric value to three decimal places, which method should you apply?
   a. *value*.`digits(3)`
   b. *value*.`round(3)`
   c. *value*.`toFixed(3)`
   d. *value*.`float(3)`
8. To display a currency value based on local standards, which method should you apply?
   a. *value*.`toLocaleString()`
   b. *value*.`toCurrency()`
   c. *value*.`toFixed()`
   d. *value*.`test()`
9. When a submit button is clicked in a form, which of the following actions occurs first?
   a. The web form is reloaded.
   b. The field values are validated.
   c. The submit event is fired.
   d. The form is submitted to the server.
10. If a field contains a value that does not match its data type, which value of the `validity` object returns a value of `true`?
   a. `validity.type`
   b. `validity.valid`
   c. `validity.typeMismatch`
   d. `validity.patternMismatch`
11. To test whether a field value is valid, which method should you apply?
   a. *element*.`test()`
   b. *element*.`validity()`
   c. *element*.`submit()`
   d. *element*.`checkValidity()`
12. To display a customized error message for invalid data, which method should you apply?
   a. *element*.`error()`
   b. *element*.`alert()`
   c. *element*.`setCustomValidity()`
   d. *element*.`validityError()`
13. To reference the source of an event where `evt` is the event object variable, use
   a. `evt.src`
   b. `evt.target`
   c. `evt.object`
   d. `evt.alt`
14. Which method do you use to disable the default behavior for an event?
   a. `preventDefault()`
   b. `checkValidity()`
   c. `select()`
   d. `cancelEvent()`
15. To override the native browser tools for managing form validation, which statement should you apply?
   a. *form*.`validate = false`
   b. *form*.`noValidate = true`
   c. *form*.`submit(false)`
   d. *form*.`checkValidity(false)`
16. Describe how to retrieve the value of a field that is entered using a selection list.
17. Under what circumstances would you use the `toLocaleString()` method?
18. Why would you use hidden fields within a web form?
19. If your code submits a form using the expression *form*.`submit()`, what will happen with the browser's native validation tools?
20. When would you choose not to use the native browser validation tools for validating a web form?

Hands-On Projects

Hands-On Project 6-1

In this project you will program the actions of a sign-up form in which users must supply a user name, email address, and password for a new account. Passwords must be at least eight characters long and contain at least one letter and one number. As a validation test, the password must be entered twice to confirm that the user did not inadvertently mistype the password. If the password does not match the required pattern or if the two passwords are not identical, the password field should be flagged as invalid. A preview of the form in which the passwords are mismatched is shown in **Figure 6-38**.

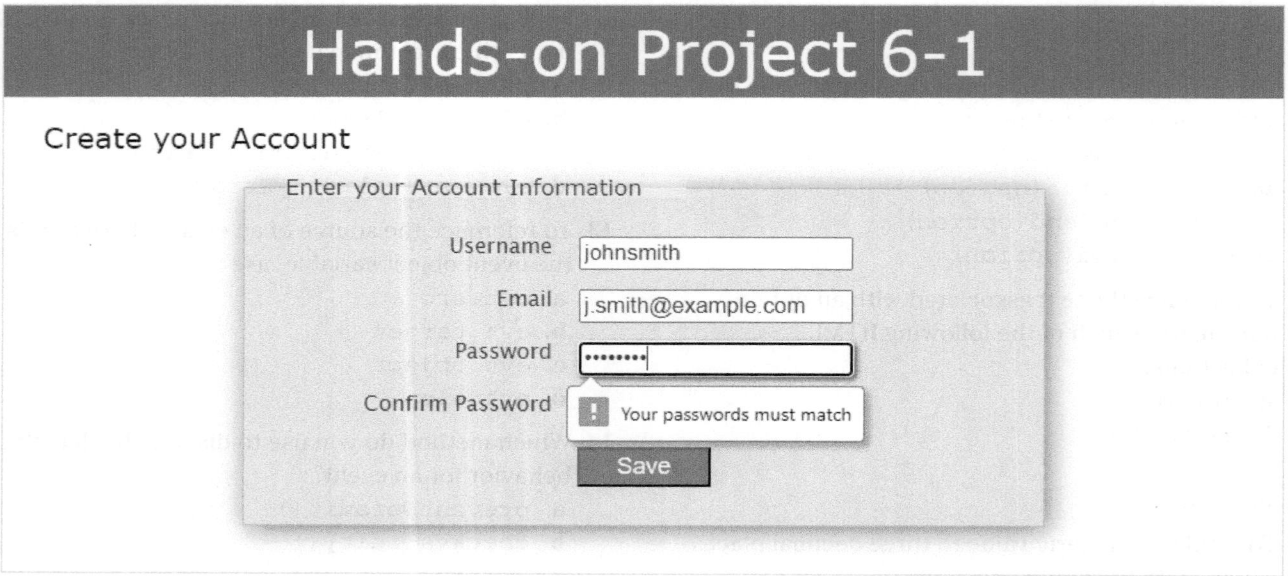

Figure 6-38 Completed Project 6-1

Do the following:

1. Use your code editor to open the **project06-01_txt.html** and **project06-01_txt.js** files from the js06 ▶ project01 folder. Enter your name and the date in the comment section of each file and save them as **project06-01.html** and **project06-01.js**, respectively.
2. Go to the **project06-01.html** file in your code editor and link the page to the project06-01.js file, deferring the script from loading until after the page loads. Take some time to study the sign-up form. Note that the `pwd` field contains a regular expression pattern that will be used to verify that the password is in the proper format. Save your changes to the file.
3. Go to the **project06-01.js** file in your code editor. Below the comment section declare the following variables: `submitButton` referencing the element with the id "submitButton", `pwd` referencing the element with the id "pwd", and `pwd2` referencing the element with the id "pwd2".
4. Create an event listener for the `click` event occurring with the `submitButton` that runs an anonymous function.
5. Within the anonymous function add the following `if else` structure:
   a. If the `pwd` field fails the pattern match, display the validation message "Your password must be at least 8 characters with at least one letter and one number".
   b. Else if the value of the `pwd` field does not equal the value of the pwd2 display the validation message "Your passwords must match".
   c. Otherwise, set the validation message to an empty text string.

6. Save your changes to the file and then open **project06-01.html** in your web browser.
7. Verify that you cannot submit the form if your password is less than eight characters long and does not include at least one number and one letter.
8. Verify that you cannot submit the form if the two passwords do not match.

Hands-On Project 6-2

In this project you will use selection lists to store long lists of hypertext links that might overwhelm a page if displayed within a navigation list. The name of a linked page is displayed as the text of a selection list option while the URL is stored as that option's value. By selecting an item from one of the selection list options, the browser will open the web page with that selected URL. To script this action, you will use the `event` object. One of the properties associated with the `event` object is as follows:

```
evt.target
```

where *`evt`* is the variable name assigned to event object and `target` is the object that received the event. In this project the target is the option selected by the user from one of the selection lists. The event will be the `change` event. A preview of the page is shown in **Figure 6-39**.

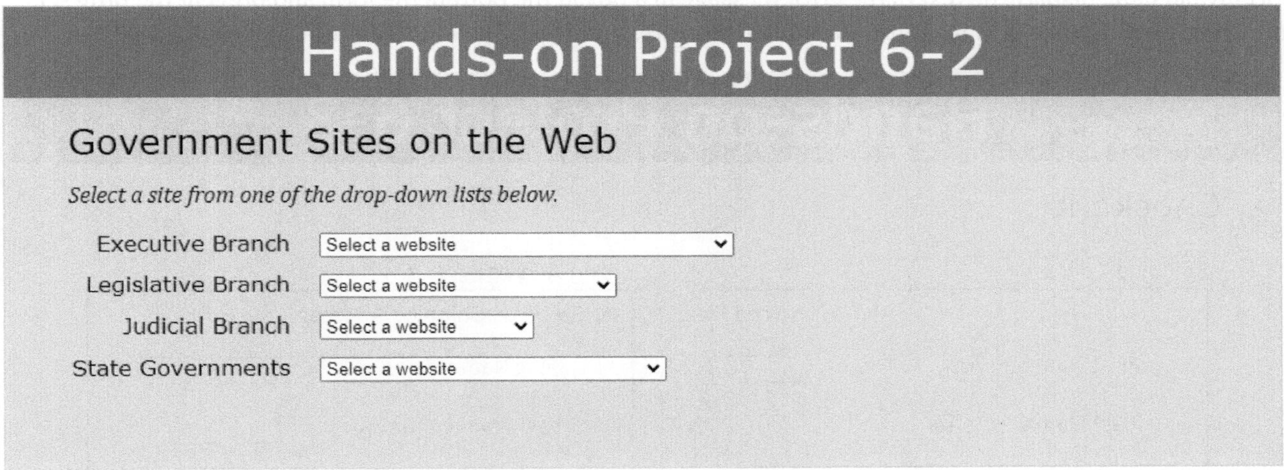

Hands-on Project 6-2

Government Sites on the Web

Select a site from one of the drop-down lists below.

Executive Branch Select a website

Legislative Branch Select a website

Judicial Branch Select a website

State Governments Select a website

Figure 6-39 Completed Project 6-2

Do the following:

1. Use your code editor to open the **project06-02_txt.html** and **project06-02_txt.js** files from the js06 ► project02 folder. Enter your name and the date in the comment section of each file and save them as **project06-02.html** and **project06-02.js**, respectively.
2. Go to the **project06-02.html** file in your code editor and link the page to the project06-02.js file, deferring loading of the script. Study the contents of the file and note that with each option the URL address is stored as the options value. Save your changes to the file.
3. Go to the **project06-02.js** file in your code editor. Add an event listener that runs an anonymous function when the page loads.
4. Within the anonymous function, add a statement that uses the `querySelectorAll()` method to create a node list of all elements matching the CSS selector `form#govLinks select`. Store the node list in the `allSelect` variable.

5. Also, within the anonymous function: Insert a `for` loop that iterates through all of the contents of the `allSelect` node list. At each iteration of the `allSelect` node list do the following:
   a. Apply the `onchange` event handler to `allSelect[i]` to run an anonymous function when the selection list option is changed. Add the parameter `evt` to the anonymous function.
   b. Within the nested anonymous function retrieve the value property of `evt.target` and store it in the `linkURL` variable.
   c. Within the nested anonymous function: Use the `window.open()` method to open a new browser window with `linkURL` as the url of the window. You do not have to set a name for the window or any window options. Store the window under the `newWin` variable.
6. Save your changes to the file and then open **project06-02.html** in your web browser.
7. Verify that by selecting an entry from one of three selection lists, the web page for that entry opens in a new browser tab or window.

Hands-On Project 6-3

In this project you complete the script for a web form that collects billing and shipping information. Because the shipping address and billing address are often the same, this form will include a checkbox to copy the shipping address values into the corresponding billing address fields. Also, instead of using browser error bubbles to report invalid data, display the text of the error message in a box at the bottom the form and prevent the browser from showing error bubbles in response to validation errors. A preview of the form is shown in **Figure 6-40**.

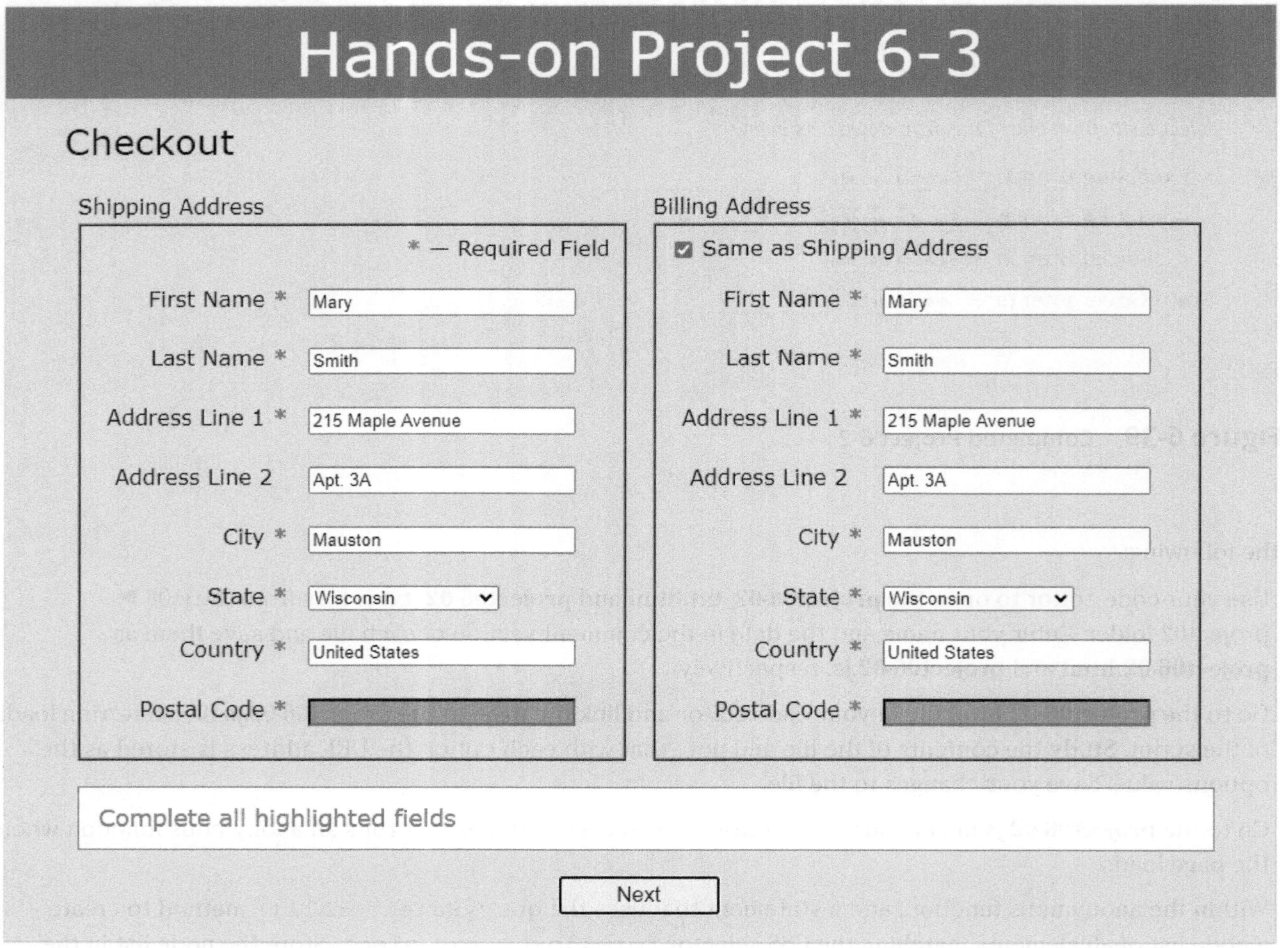

Figure 6-40 Completed Project 6-3

Do the following:

1. Use your code editor to open the **project06-03_txt.html** and **project06-03_txt.js** files from the js06 ▶ project03 folder. Enter your name and the date in the comment section of each file and save them as **project06-03.html** and **project06-03.js**, respectively.
2. Go to the **project06-03.html** file in your code editor and link the page to the **project06-03.js** file, deferring loading of the script. Study the contents of the file and note field names associated with each input element within the form Save your changes to the file.
3. Go to the **project06-03.js** file in your code editor. Below the comment section declare the `useShip` variable to reference the element with the id "useShip". Add an event listener to `useShip` to run the `copyShippingToBilling()` function when clicked.
4. Create the `copyShippingToBilling()` function that copies values from the shipping fields to corresponding billing fields. Within the function, insert an `if` statement that tests whether `useShip` is checked and if it is, do the following:
   a. Set the value of the `firstnameBill` field to the value of the `firstnameShip` field.
   b. Repeat the previous step to set the value of the `lastnameBill`, `address1Bill`, `address2Bill`, `cityBill`, `countryBill`, `codeBill` fields to the values of their corresponding fields in the shipping part of the form.
   c. Set the `selectedIndex` property of the `stateBill` field to the value of the `selectedIndex` property of the `stateShip` field.
5. Below the `copyShippingToBilling()` function do the following:
   a. Declare the `formElements` variable and using the `querySelectorAll()` method store within it a node list corresponding to elements selected with "`input[type='text']`".
   b. Declare the `fieldCount` variable with a value equal to the length of the `formElements` node list.
   c. Declare the `errorBox` referencing the element with the id "errorBox".
6. Create a `for` loop that iterates through each element in the `formElements` node list and for each element apply an event listener that calls the `showValidationError()` function in response to the `invalid` event.
7. Create the `showValidationError(evt)` function and add the following commands to it:
   a. For the event object, `evt`, apply the `preventDefault()` method to prevent the browser from applying the native browser tools to respond to invalid data.
   b. Set the `textContent` property of `errorBox` to the text string "Complete all highlighted fields".
8. Save your changes to the file and then open **js06-03.html** in your browser.
9. Verify that you can copy shipping address information to the billing fields by clicking the Same as Shipping Address box.
10. Verify that you cannot submit the form until all data fields are completed (aside from the second address fields) and that validation errors appear in the error box below the form.

Hands-On Project 6-4

In this project you will explore how to filter the contents of one selection list based on an option chosen in another selection list. The web form you are given contains three selection lists with the make, model, and trim of cars that one might consider purchasing. Your script will link the three selection lists so that selecting a car make will filter the list of car models and selecting a car model will filter the list of car trims. A preview of the completed form in which a single car is chosen from a combination of makes, models, and trims, is shown in **Figure 6-41**.

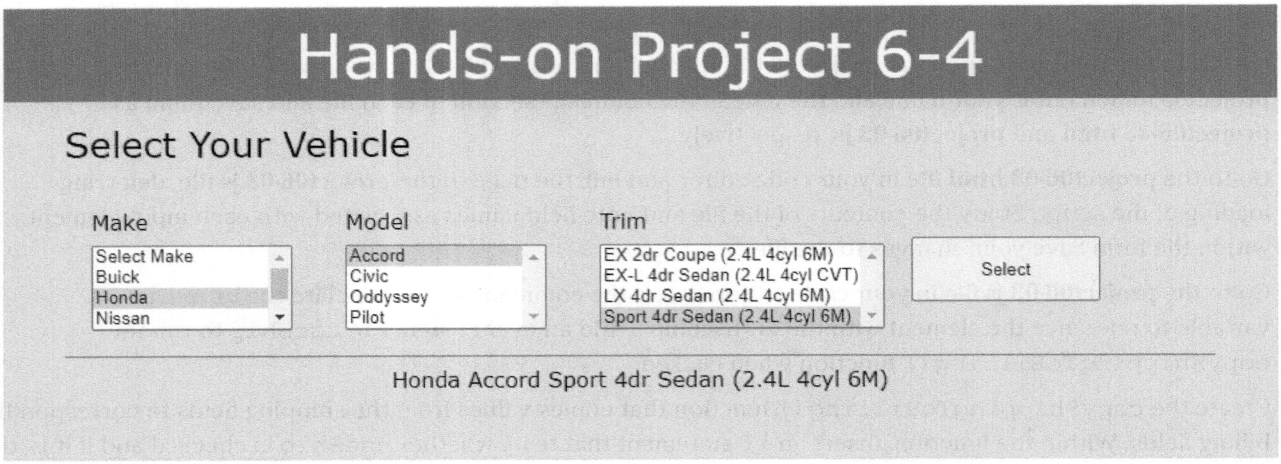

Hands-on Project 6-4

Select Your Vehicle

Make	Model	Trim	
Select Make Buick Honda Nissan	Accord Civic Oddyssey Pilot	EX 2dr Coupe (2.4L 4cyl 6M) EX-L 4dr Sedan (2.4L 4cyl CVT) LX 4dr Sedan (2.4L 4cyl 6M) Sport 4dr Sedan (2.4L 4cyl 6M)	Select

Honda Accord Sport 4dr Sedan (2.4L 4cyl 6M)

Figure 6-41 Completed Project 6-4

Do the following:

1. Use your code editor to open the **project06-04_txt.html** and **project06-04_txt.js** files from the js06 ► project04 folder. Enter your name and the date in the comment section of each file and save them as **project06-04.html** and **project06-04.js**, respectively.
2. Go to the **project06-04.html** file in your code editor and link the page to the project06-04.js file, deferring loading of the script. Study the contents of the form. Note that the class value of each option in the Model selection list corresponds to a car company listed in the Make selection list and that the class value of each option in the Trim selection list corresponds to a model name in the Model selection list. You will use this correspondence in writing a script that filters each selection list based on the option chosen from the previous selection list. Save your changes to the file.
3. Go to the **project06-04.js** file in your code editor. Some of the variables and the event handlers have already been created for you but the script is not complete. You will need to create two functions: one to show all the options within a selection list and the other to filter the options within a selection list to show only those options that match a previously chosen car make or car model.
4. Create the `showAll()` function. The function has a single parameter named `selectList` that will represent one of the selection lists shown in the web form. Within the function do the following:
   a. Declare a variable named `options` that references the collection of `option` elements within `selectList`.
   b. Declare a variable named `optionLength` equal to the length of the `options` node list.
   c. Add a `for` loop that iterates through the items in the `options` node list. For each item in the collection change the value of the `style.display` property to "block" in order to display the option within the selection list.
5. Create the `filterSelect()` function. The function has two parameters named `selectList` and `category`, where `selectList` will represent one of the selection lists in the web form and `category` will determine which options within that selection list will be displayed on the web page. Within the function do the following:
   a. Declare a variable named `options` that references the collection of `option` elements within `selectList`.
   b. Declare a variable named `optionLength` equal to the length of the `options` node list.
   c. Add a `for` loop that iterates through the items in the `options` node list. For each item in the `options` collection, insert an `if else` statement that sets the `style.display` property of the item to "block" if the `className` property of the option equals the `category` variable, otherwise set the `style.display` property to "none" (to hide the option).

6. Create an `onclick` event handler for the `selectVehicle` button to run an anonymous function when clicked. Within the anonymous function, insert a command that writes the text "*make model trim*" to the `vehicle` paragraph in the web page, where *`make`*, *`model`*, and *`trim`* are the text values of the selected options from the three selection lists. (Hint: You will have to use the `text` property of the selected option from each selection list to return the text of the option.)
7. Save your changes to the file and then open **js06-04.html** in your browser.
8. Verify that as you select options from the Make selection list, the options in the Model selection list are filter to show only cars from that make. Verify that as you select options from the Model selection list, the Trim selection list is filtered to show only trim options for that selected model.
9. Verify that when you click the Select button, the text of the make, model, and trim are displayed at the bottom of the web page.

Hands-On Project 6-5

Debugging Challenge

You have been given a web form that is to be used to register attendees at a conference. However, there are errors in the JavaScript program that calculates and reports the total cost of the registration. You have been asked to locate and fix the errors in the code. A preview of the completed form is shown in **Figure 6-42**.

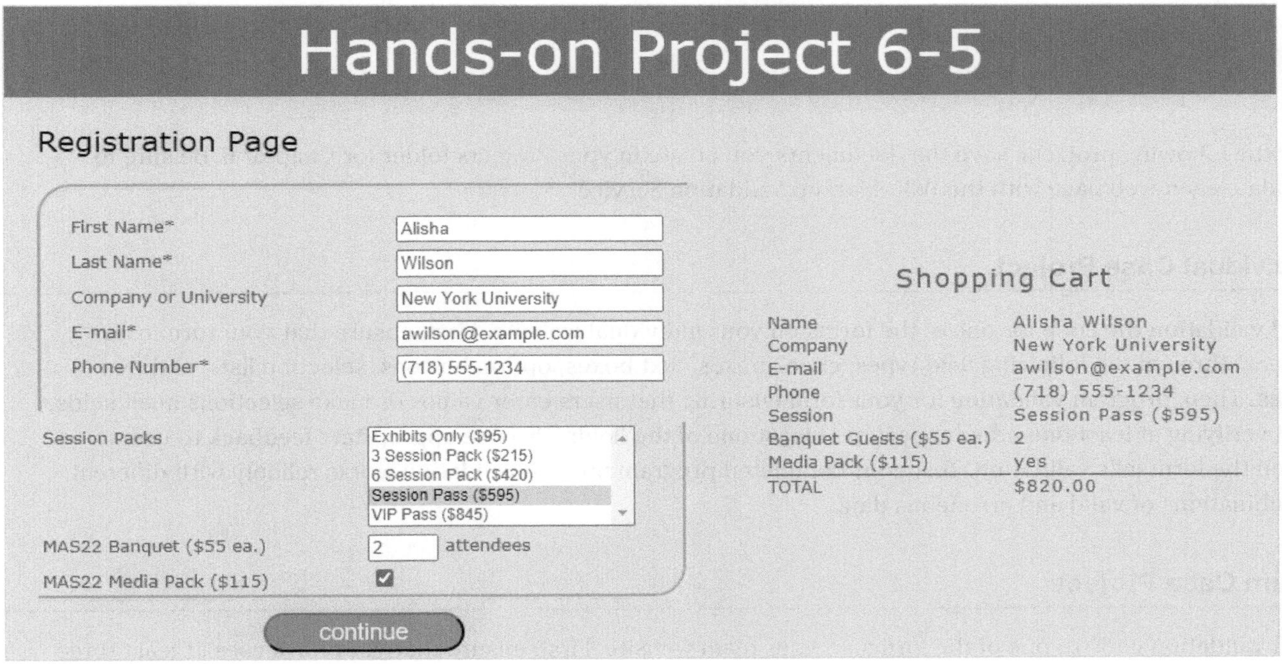

Figure 6-42 Completed Project 6-5

Do the following:

1. Use your code editor to open the **project06-05_txt.html** and **project06-05_txt.js** files from the js06 ▶ project05 folder. Enter your name and the date in the comment section of each file and save them as **project06-05.html** and **project06-05.js**, respectively.
2. Go to the **project06-05.html** file in your code editor and in the head section add a `script` element to load the project06-05.js file, deferring it until the entire page is loaded. Study the contents of the file to become familiar with the structure of the HTML code. Save your changes to the file.

3. Return to the **project06-05.js** file in your code editor. Comments have been added to help you interpret the code in the file.
4. The first part of the code uses an anonymous function to load several event handlers to calculate and recalculate the shopping cart as different form fields lose the focus. There are several errors in this anonymous function.
5. The `sessionTest()` function is used to confirm that the user has selected a session to attend at the conference. If the user did not select a session, the form should be invalid. Locate and fix two errors in setting up the custom validation message.
6. The `calcCart()` function is used to generate the contents of the shopping cart and calculate the total cost of registration. Within this function there are errors in determining the index of the chosen session, whether the user checked the media checkbox, and in the display of the total cost of the registration. Locate and fix all three errors.
7. Save your changes to the file and then open **project06-05.html** in your web browser. Verify the following:
   a. When you enter text into the form fields and tab out of the input boxes, the shopping cart text automatically updates to show your data entry.
   b. As you select different conference options, the total cost of the conference automatically updates.
   c. The total cost of the conference is displayed in U.S. currency.
   d. If you attempt to submit the form without entering all required data, the form will be rejected.

Case Projects

For the following projects, save the documents you create in your Projects folder for Chapter 6. Be sure to validate each web page with the W3C Markup Validation Service.

Individual Case Project

Add validation the code for one of the forms on your individual website. First, ensure that your form uses at least three of the following field types: check boxes, text boxes, option buttons, selection lists, and text areas. Then, program validation for your form ensuring that users enter values or make selections in all fields, and verifying at least one other aspect of at least one of the fields. Provide appropriate feedback to users when the form fails validation. Test your completed program until all validation works reliably with different combinations of valid and erroneous data.

Team Case Project

Add validation code to one of the forms on your team website. First, ensure that your form uses at least three of the following field types: check boxes, text boxes, option buttons, selection lists, and text areas. Next, as a team, plan validation for each field in the form. Your validation should require a value in each field, and should verify at least one other aspect of at least one field. Divide your team into two groups—one that will write code to verify that all fields have values, and the other to write code to verify another aspect of the entered data. Each group's code should also incorporate appropriate feedback to users when it encounters validation errors. When both groups are done, work as a team to integrate the code into the document. Strategize as a team about how to test for all possible validation scenarios. Test and debug the code until your completed program until all validation works reliably with different combinations of valid and erroneous data.

CHAPTER 7

Manipulating Data in Strings, Arrays, and Other Objects

When you complete this chapter, you will be able to:

- Read information from a text file
- Read and write content into a text string
- Interpret the language of regular expressions
- Create a regular expression object and use it in a program
- Sort an array using the `sort()` method with a compare function
- Work with the properties and methods of the `Math` object
- Work with the properties and methods of the `Date` object
- Explore text strings using template literals

Retrieving Content from a Text File

Many web apps need to load and process information from text files or information contained within text strings. This chapter will focus on the JavaScript properties and methods for working with textual data to create a Word Cloud app. A word cloud is a graphical representation of the words and phrases used within a document in which the size and style of each word indicates its frequency and importance. Word clouds are often used in textual analysis to highlight important themes in documents and speeches. **Figure 7-1** shows a preview of the word cloud you will create as applied to the text of Abraham Lincoln's first presidential inaugural address in 1861. Without reading any of the 3600 words of the speech, you can determine that the main themes involve a discussion of the constitution, the union, the government, the states, and their relation to people, with less coverage of slaves or slavery and little to no mention of an impending civil war.

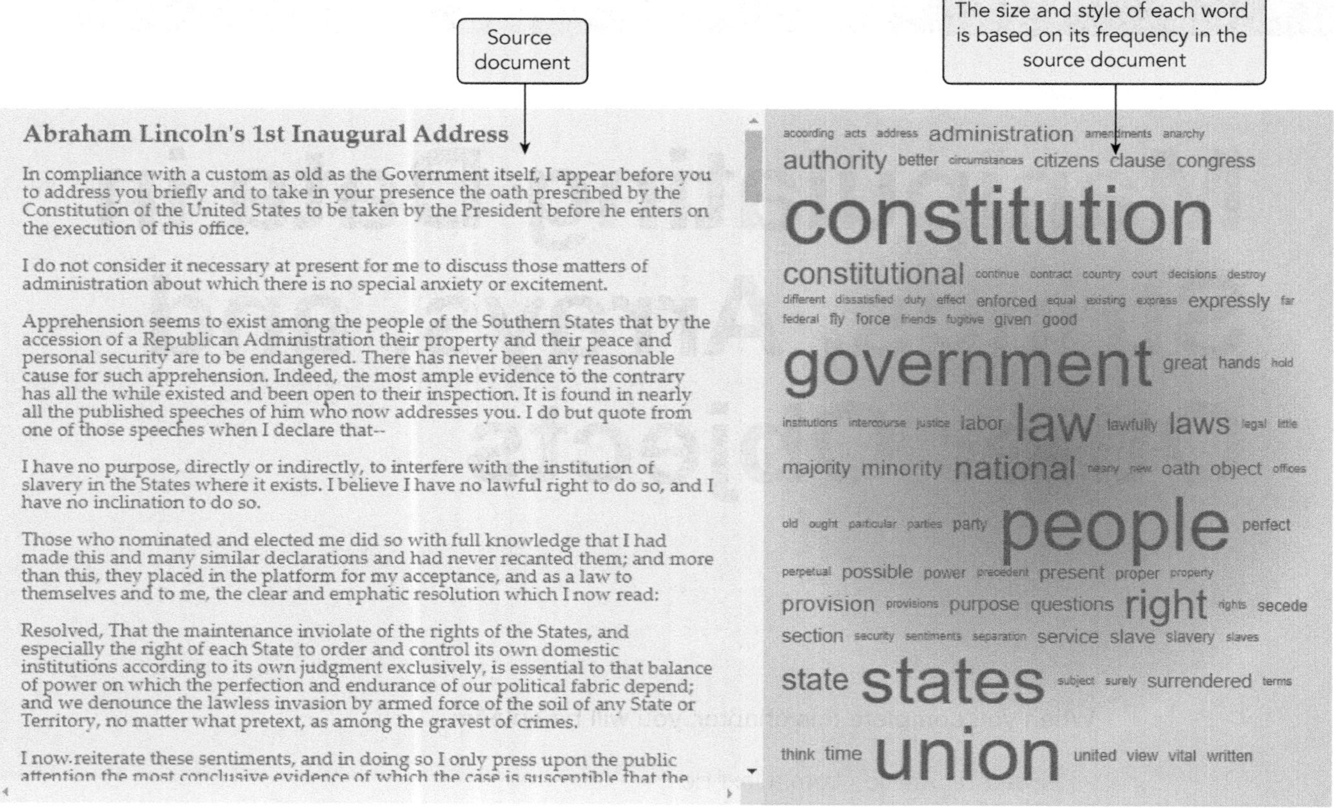

Figure 7-1 A sample word cloud

To create this word cloud, your app will need to do the following:

1. Load the contents of text document and convert it to a text string.
2. Remove all extraneous characters from the text string such as punctuation marks.
3. Remove all extraneous words from the text string, including articles such as “the”, “an”, and “a”.
4. Calculate the frequency of the remaining words.
5. Highlight the words with the greatest frequency in the largest font presented in a word list alongside the complete text of the document.

Ideally, the Word Cloud app should work with any HTML or text document and be flexible enough to allow the user to choose the document to analyze. Files containing the initial code for the app have been created for you. Open those files now.

To open the files for the order form:

1. Go to the js07 ▶ chapter folder of your data files.
2. Use your code editor to open the **js07_txt.html** and **js07_txt.js** files. Enter your name and the date in the comment section of each file and then save them as **js07.html** and **js07.js**, respectively.
3. Return to the **js07.html** file in your code editor. Within the head section, add a `script` element to run the js07.js script, deferring the loading the script file until after the entire page has loaded.
4. Review the contents of the document and then close the file, saving your changes.

The `file` Object

The app has the following `input` element to enable users to select a text file to view:

```
<input id="getFile" type="file" />
```

When a file input control is clicked, the browser displays a File Open dialog box. Once a file is selected, it can be accessed using the JavaScript File API, an API introduced with HTML5 that retrieves the contents of selected files from the local computer or network.

> **Note** | To enable the user to select more than one file, add the `multiple` attribute to the `<input>` tag.

Because the File Open dialog box allows for multiple files to be selected, input boxes of the `file` data type support the following **`files`** collection:

```
element.files()
```

where *`element`* is a reference to an `input` element of the `file` data type. Each item in the `files` collection represents a **`file`** object with information about a specific file. The properties of the `file` object are described in **Figure 7-2**.

PROPERTY	DESCRIPTION
file.lastModified	Returns the date and time that the file was last modified
file.name	Returns the name of the file without the file path
file.size	Returns the size of the file in bytes
file.type	Returns the MIME type of the file

Figure 7-2 Properties of the `file` object

Add an `onchange` event handler to the `getFile` input box to retrieve information about the first (and only) file selected by the user. Use the `this` keyword to reference the input box that initiated the `change` event and store information about the file in the `userFile` variable.

To create an `onchange` event handler:

1. Return to the **js07.js** in your code editor.
2. Directly below the initial comment section, insert the following code to run an anonymous function in response to the change event (see **Figure 7-3**):

```
document.getElementById("getFile").onchange = function() {
   // Retrieve information about the selected file
   let userFile = this.files[0];
};
```

```
document.getElementById("getFile").onchange = function() {
   // Retrieve information about the selected file
   let userFile = this.files[0];
};
```

File object selected by the user

Files collection contains the files selected by the user

Figure 7-3 Retrieving a selected file

Having stored information about the selected file, you will next read its contents.

The File Reader API

To read the contents of an external file JavaScript provides the File Reader API. File readers are JavaScript objects created using the following `new FileReader()` object constructor:

```
let reader = new FileReader()
```

where *reader* is a variable that stores a `FileReader` object. `FileReader` objects support the properties and methods described in **Figure 7-4**.

PROPERTY OR METHOD	DESCRIPTION
reader.abort()	Aborts the read operation
reader.readAsArrayBuffer()	Reads the file contents, storing the result in a raw binary file as a text string
reader.readAsDataURL()	Reads the file contents, storing the result in a data URI
reader.readAsText()	Reads the file contents, storing the result in a text string
reader.error	Returns an error code for failed reads
reader.readyState	Returns the state of the reader as 0 (EMPTY) — no data has been loaded yet; 2 (LOADING) — data is currently being loaded; 3 (DONE) — the read request is completed
reader.result	Returns the contents of the file after the read operation is complete

Figure 7-4 Properties and methods of the **`FileReader`** object

A `FileReader` object works asynchronously so that the rest of the script will continue to run as the external file is read. For that reason, you should not attempt to do anything with the file contents until the reader has completely loaded the file. As the file reader progresses through the document the following events are triggered:

- `loadstart` — The reader is starting to read the file.
- `progress` — The reading is progressing.
- `load` — The reading is complete with no errors.
- `abort` — The reading is aborted.
- `error` — An error has occurred during the reading.
- `loadend` — The reading is complete either successfully or with an error.

If the document is successfully read and loaded, its contents can be accessed with the `result` property of the `FileReader` object.

Create a file reader for the word cloud script to load and read the contents of the `userFile` document. Once the `load` event for the document has occurred (indicating a successful reading), create an `onload` event handler to write the contents of the `userFile` document to the web page.

To load a document using the file reader:

1. Within the anonymous function add the following commands to create a `FileReader` object and to load the contents of the `userFile` object as a text file.

```
// Read the contents of the selected file
let fr = new FileReader();
fr.readAsText(userFile);
```

2. Next, apply the `onload` event handler to the file reader so when the document is complete and successfully loaded, its contents will be written to the web page.

```
// Once the file has finished loading, display in the page
let sourceDoc = document.getElementById("wc_document");
fr.onload=function(){
   sourceDoc.innerHTML = fr.result;
}
```

Figure 7-5 describes the newly added code to the anonymous function.

Create a `FileReader` object

Load userFile as a text file

When the document is loaded, write its contents to the web page

```
document.getElementById("getFile").onchange = function() {
   // Retrieve information about the selected file
   let userFile = this.files[0];

   // Read the contents of the selected file
   let fr = new FileReader();
   fr.readAsText(userFile);

   // Once the file has finished loading, display in the page
   let sourceDoc = document.getElementById("wc_document");
   fr.onload=function(){
      sourceDoc.innerHTML = fr.result;
   }
};
```

Figure 7-5 Reading and loading the contents of a text file

3. Save your changes to the file and then load **fig07.html** in your browser.
4. Click the **Choose File** button to open the File Open dialog box.
5. Locate and open the **lincoln1.html** file from the js07 ▶ chapter folder.

As shown in **Figure 7-6**, the contents of Lincoln's first inaugural address should appear within the web page.

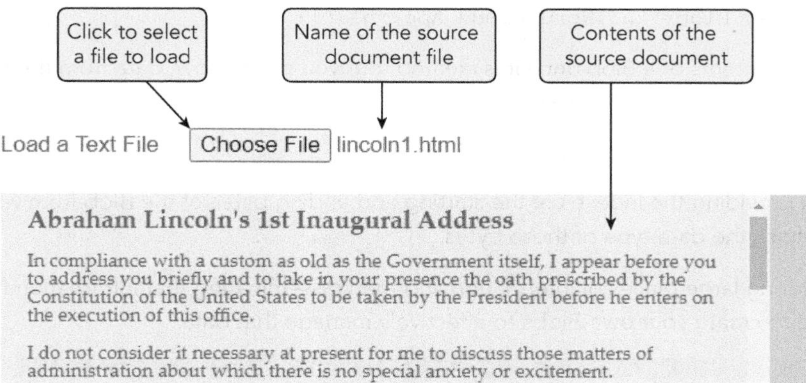

Click to select a file to load
Name of the source document file
Contents of the source document
Load a Text File
Choose File
lincoln1.html
Abraham Lincoln's 1st Inaugural Address
In compliance with a custom as old as the Government itself, I appear before you to address you briefly and to take in your presence the oath prescribed by the Constitution of the United States to be taken by the President before he enters on the execution of this office.
I do not consider it necessary at present for me to discuss those matters of administration about which there is no special anxiety or excitement.

Figure 7-6 External text loaded into the Word Cloud app

In this chapter you will use the lincoln1.html file to develop and test the Word Cloud app. The content of that file includes HTML tags marking the speech's main heading and paragraphs. HTML tags are not included in a word cloud, so you will strip them out, storing only the text content of the speech in a variable named `sourceText`.

To create the `sourceText` variable:

1. Return to the **js07.js** file in your code editor.
2. Within the anonymous function for the `onload` event handler, add the following code to store the text of the source document (see **Figure 7-7**):

```
// Store the text of the document, removing HTML tags
let sourceText = sourceDoc.textContent;
```

3. Save your changes to the file, load **fig07.html** in your browser and then load the **lincoln1.html** file into the web page.
4. Open your browser's debugger console and confirm that no errors are reported by the debugger.

```
      // Once the file has finished loading, display in the page
      let sourceDoc = document.getElementById("wc_document");
      fr.onload=function(){
         sourceDoc.innerHTML = fr.result;

         // Store the text of the document, removing HTML tags
         let sourceText = sourceDoc.textContent;
      }
   };
```

Store the text of the source document without the HTML tags

Figure 7-7 Extracting text content from the source document

Programming Concepts | Blobs and Files

A file is an example of a Blob or Binary Large Object. Blobs are used for data storage in which the data is stored as a chunk of bytes. Like a computer file, a Blob has a `size` property and a `type` property. It is either stored as part of the computer's file system or resides in computer memory. To create a Blob, apply the following new `Blob()` object constructor:

```
let blob = new Blob(blobParts, options);
```

where *`blobParts`* are data source or text string values stored in the Blob and *`options`* define the Blob's data type. For example, the following statement creates a Blob that stores a string of HTML code:

```
let myHeading = new Blob("<h1>Word Cloud App</h1>");
```

You cannot change the contents of a Blob once it is created, but you can remove data from the Blob to create new Blob objects using the following `slice()` method:

```
blob.slice(start, end, contentType)
```

where *`start`* and *`end`* providing the indexes of the starting and ending bytes of the Blob from which to extract data and *`contentType`* defines the data type of those bytes.

If your app involves storing large pieces of information and then disseminating that information for reports and analyses you will need to create your own Blobs to effectively manage that data.

Working with Text Strings

A text string is a JavaScript object, created implicitly by storing or retrieving text. Text string objects can also be created explicitly using the following `new String()` object constructor:

```
let string = new String(text);
```

where *`text`* is the text string that is stored in the *`string`* variable. Both of the following statements create an object containing the text "Abraham Lincoln":

```
let author = "Abraham Lincoln";
let author = new String("Abraham Lincoln");
```

The `new String()` object constructor is often used to reserve space for an empty string whose content is to be determined later by the app.

Because text strings are objects, they are associated with wide variety of JavaScript methods and properties. The fundamental property for any text string is the `length` property, which returns the number of characters in the string. The `length` property is often used with web form apps that need to confirm that an input field such as a user name or password field has the required number of characters to be valid.

Searching for Substrings within a Text String

Apps that manage text often need to determine whether the text string contains a group of characters known as a substring. For example, an app that analyzes email addresses may need to determine whether a text string contains the @ character or ends with a three-letter domain like ".org" or ".com". **Figure 7-8** describes the JavaScript properties and methods for searching text strings to determine whether they contain a specified substring.

PROPERTY OR METHOD	DESCRIPTION
string.length	Returns the number of characters in *string*.
string.endsWith(*text* [,*length*])	Returns true if *string* ends with the substring *text*; the optional *length* property specifies the length of the string to search
string.includes(*text* [,*start*])	Returns true if *string* contains the substring *text*; the optional *start* property specifies the index of the starting character for the search
string.indexOf(*text* [,*start*])	Returns the first index of substring *text* within the text string, *string*; a value of -1 is returned if text is not present within *string*
string.lastIndexOf(*text* [,*start*])	Returns the last index of substring *text* within the text string, *string*
string.startsWith(text [,*start*])	Returns true if *string* starts with the substring *text*

Figure 7-8 Properties or methods for text string characters

The `startsWith()`, `endsWith()`, and `includes()` methods indicate whether a text string contains a specified substring located at the beginning of the string, at the end, or somewhere in-between. Thus, the statement

```
sourceText.includes(" union ")
```

returns `true` if the `sourceText` variable contains the word "union" anywhere within the string and `false` if otherwise. Note that this substring starts and ends with a blank space. A blank space is a whitespace character—a term that refers to any blank or nonprintable character such as a space, tab, or line break. Whitespace characters are important in separating printable characters. This statement would return `true` only if the word "union" is found, but not for words like "unions" or "disunion" in which the "union" substring is not surrounded by whitespace.

To determine exactly where a substring is located within a larger string, apply the `indexOf()` and `lastIndex()` methods. The following two statements apply these methods to locate the first and last occurrence of a blank space within the text string "First Inaugural Address":

```
"First Inaugural Address".indexOf(" ");     // returns 5
"First Inaugural Address".lastIndexOf(" "); // returns 15
```

The first text string character has an index number of 0 and therefore the index of the first blank space in this example is 5, indicating that the blank space is the sixth character in the string. The index value of 15 indicates that the last blank space is the sixteenth character. If the substring is not found within the larger string, both the `indexOf()` and `lastIndex()` methods return an index value of -1.

The Word Cloud app needs to confirm that the user has selected a text file for processing and not a non-text file like an image or video. The `type` property of the `file` object indicates the content of the file by returning file's MIME type. Text files have MIME types starting with the substring "text", such as "text/plain", "text/html", or "text/javascript". Thus, you can confirm that the user selected a text file by checking whether the file's MIME type starts with the "text" substring.

Add a `try catch` statement to the Word Cloud app that uses the `startsWith()` method to verify that a text file has been selected by the user, throwing an error if it has not.

To test that the user has selected a text file:

1. Return to the **js07.js** file in your code editor.
2. Directly below the statement declaring the `userFile` variable, add the following initial code for a `try catch` statement:

```
// Verify that a text file is selected
try {
   let isText = userFile.type.startsWith("text");
   if (!isText) {
      throw userFile.name + " is not a text file";
   }
```

3. Scroll down and directly after the `onload` anonymous function, insert the following code closing the `try` statement and adding a `catch` statement for catching the thrown error.

```
}
// Alert the user to select a text file
catch(err) {
   window.alert(err);
}
```

4. Indent the content of the `try` statement to make your code easier to read. **Figure 7-9** describes the revised code in the file.

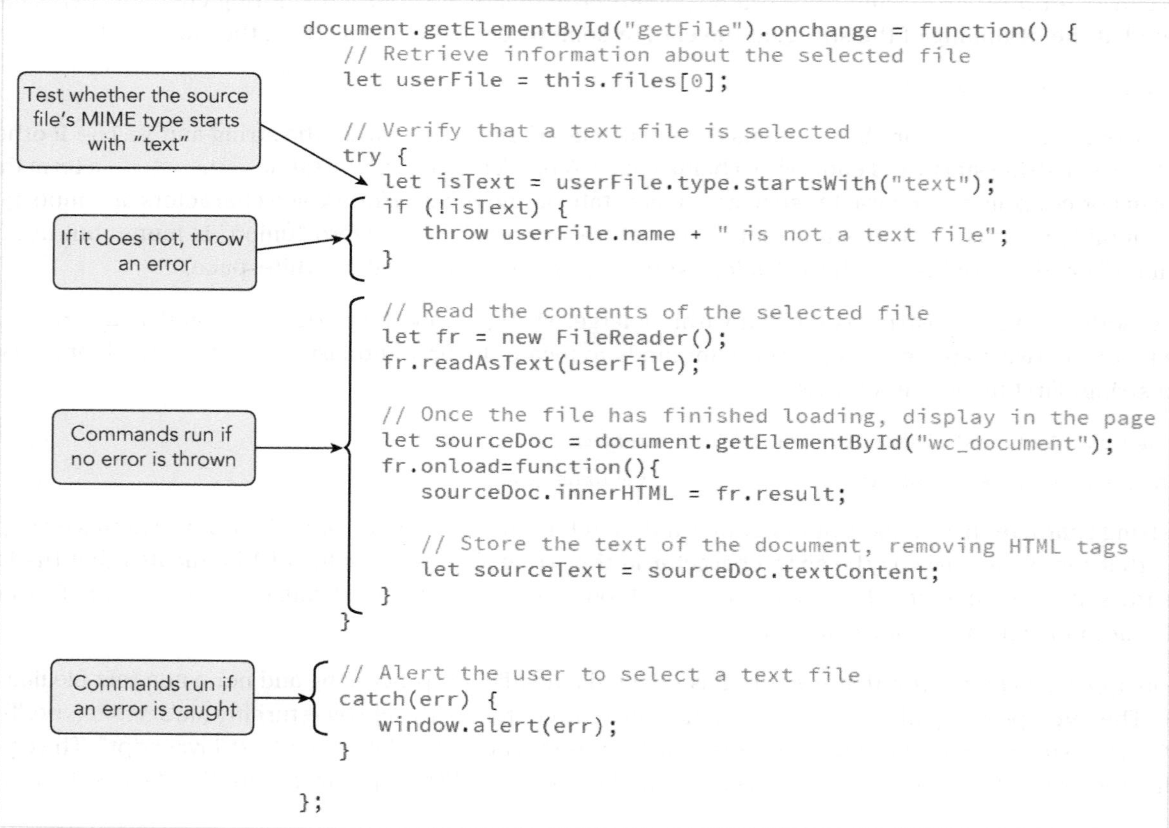

Figure 7-9 Verifying that the user selects a text file

5. Save your changes to the file and then load **fig07.html** in your browser.
6. Click **Choose File** and select the **wordcloud.png** file. Verify that the page displays an alert box indicating that wordcloud.png is not a text file.
7. Click **Choose File** again and select **lincoln1.html**, verifying that the contents of that file load without error.

If your program does not work correctly, check your code against that shown in Figure 7-9. A common mistake is omitting an opening or closing curly brace within the `try catch` statement. Having confirmed that the user has selected a text file, you can begin building the commands that generate a word cloud for the document. You will start by modifying the text within the file.

Modifying Text Strings

An important point to remember with text strings is that they are immutable and cannot be changed, only replaced. Any JavaScript method you apply to a text string will not change that string but instead will return a new string that includes your modifications. **Figure 7-10** lists some of the JavaScript methods that return a new text string from modifying the contents of a source text string.

METHOD	DESCRIPTION
string.toLowerCase()	Converts *string* to lowercase characters
string.toLocaleLowerCase(locale)	Converts string to lowercase characters based on the user's locale
string.toUpperCase()	Converts *string* to uppercase characters
string.toLocaleUpperCase(locale)	Converts string to uppercase characters based on the user's *locale*
string.trim()	Removes whitespace characters from the start and end of *string*

Figure 7-10 Methods to manipulate text strings

You will make the following changes to the text of the source document:

- Convert all characters to lowercase letters to remove the distinction between words like "Nation" and "nation".
- Strip out any leading or trailing whitespace characters from the text so that the text begins and ends with a printable character.

To create a new string containing only lowercase characters apply the following `toLowerCase()` method to the `sourceText` variable:

```
sourceText = sourceText.toLowerCase();
```

To strip out leading and trailing whitespace characters apply the `trim()` function:

```
sourceText = sourceText.trim();
```

Add both of these commands to the `wordCloud()` function running them after the file is successfully read by the browser.

To modify the source text:

1. Return to the **js07.js** file in your code editor.
2. Directly after the statement declaring the `sourceText` variable, add the following command to call the `wordCloud()` function:

```
// Generate the word cloud
wordCloud(sourceText);
```

3. After the closing brace of the `catch` statement, add the following initial code for the `wordCloud()` function:

```
function wordCloud(sourceText) {
   // Convert the source text to lowercase
   // and remove leading and trailing whitespace
   sourceText = sourceText.toLowerCase();
   sourceText = sourceText.trim();

   console.log(sourceText);
}
```

The app writes the content of the `sourceText` to the debugger console so you can view the changing value of that variable as you develop the Word Cloud app. See **Figure 7-11**.

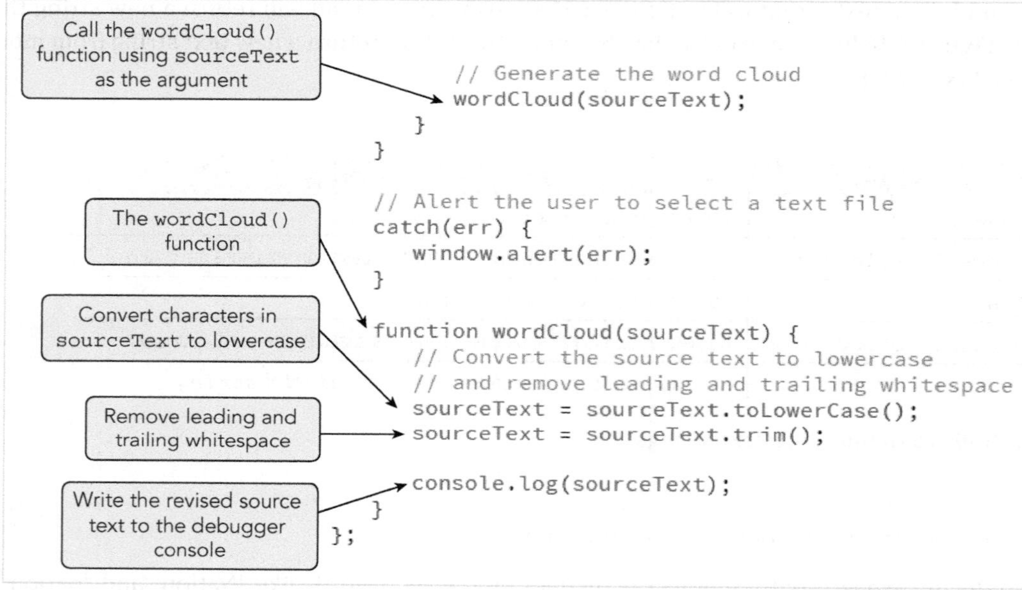

Figure 7-11 Modifying the source text

4. Save your changes to the file and then reload **js07.html** in your browser and load **lincoln1.html** in the web page.
5. View the console log in the browser debugger and verify that content of the `sourceText` variable is displayed in lowercase characters. See **Figure 7-12**.

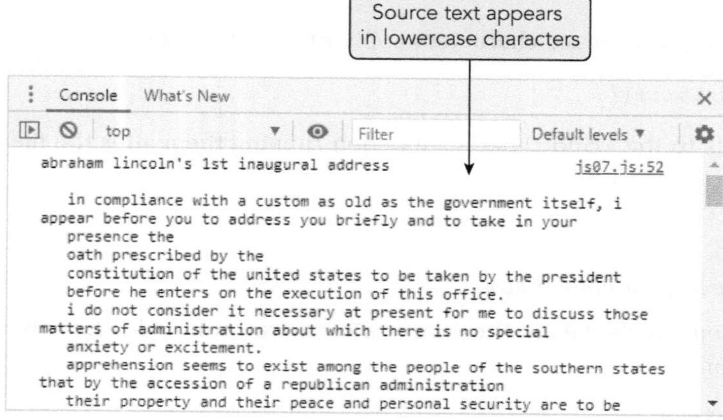

Figure 7-12 Source text in the debugger console

Not all locales use the same rules for displaying uppercase and lowercase letters. For that reason JavaScript also provides the `toLocaleLowerCase()` and `toLocaleUpperCase()` methods to allow for regional differences in character case.

> **Note** Because text strings are immutable it is a mistake to apply a method like `toLowerCase()` to a string thinking that it will modify the string. It won't. To modify a text string, you must completely replace its content with the new string.

Extracting Characters and Substrings

In addition to searching for substrings within larger text strings, JavaScript supports methods for extracting substrings. **Figure 7-13** describes some of the JavaScript substring methods.

METHOD	DESCRIPTION
string.charAt(*i*)	Returns the character at index, *i*, where the first character has index 0, the second character has index 1, ...
string.charCodeAt(*i*)	Returns the Unicode of the character at index, i
string.slice(*start* [,*end*])	Extracts a substring from *string*, between the *start* and *end* index values, if no end value is specified the substring extends to the end of the string.
string.split(*text* [,*limit*])	Splits *string* into an array of string values for each occurrence of text; the optional limit attribute specifies an upper limit for the length of the array
string.substr(*start* [,*length*])	Extracts a substring from *string*, starting at the index value *start* and continuing for the next length characters; if no length value is specified the substring extends to the end of the string
string.substring(*start* [,*end*])	Extracts a substring from *string*, between the *start* and *end* index values; if no *end* value is specified the substring extends to the end of the string

Figure 7-13 Methods to extract characters and substrings

To extract a single character from a text string, apply the following `charAt()` method:

```
string.charAt(i)
```

where *string* is the string object and *i* is the index value of the character starting from 0 for the first character in the string. For example, the following expression returns the fifth character from the text string "Abraham Lincoln".

```
"Abraham Lincoln".charAt(4) // returns "h"
```

To extract substrings longer than a single character, use the `slice()`, `substr()`, or `substring()` methods. All three methods accept either one or two arguments: the first argument specifying where the extraction begins, and the second optional argument specifying where the extraction ends. For the `slice()` and `substring()` methods the second argument specifies the character position directly *after* the end of the extraction so that all characters up to but not including that index are extracted. For the `substr()` method the second argument specifies the number of characters to be extracted. If no second argument is provided, all three methods extract a substring starting from the initial index to the end of the text.

The following code shows the substring extracted from a sample text string starting from the fifth character using each method. With the `slice()` and `substring()` methods, a substring up to the eleventh character is extracted. With the `substr()` method, a substring of 10 total characters is extracted.

```
"Abraham Lincoln".slice(4,10)      // "ham Li"
"Abraham Lincoln".substring(4,10) // "ham Li"
"Abraham Lincoln".substr(4,10)     // "ham Licol"
```

The index can be negative in which case substrings are extracted counting backwards from the end of the text string; however this is true only for the `slice()` and `substr()` methods. The `substring()` method treats negative indexes as zero. The following examples show the result of applying a negative index with each method. Both the `slice()` and `substr()` methods start the extraction seven characters from the end of the text and move forward. The `substring()` method treats the negative index as 0 and extracts the entire string.

```
"Abraham Lincoln".slice(-7, -3) // "Linc"
"Abraham Lincoln".substring(-7) // "Abraham Lincoln"
"Abraham Lincoln".substr(-7, 4) // "Linc"
```

Extraction methods are often used in conjunction with `indexOf()` and `lastIndexOf()` to extract substrings up to a specified character within the text. The following code demonstrates how to extract the user name and domain from a sample email address by first finding the index of the @ character to create substrings of the text before and after that character.

```
let email = "lincoln@example.com";
let atIndex = email.indexOf("@"); // returns 7
email.slice(0, atIndex);          // returns "lincoln
email.slice(atIndex + 1);         // returns "example.com"
```

The first `slice()` method extracts a substring up to (but not including) the @ character. The second `slice()` method extracts a substring starting after the @ character through the end of the text.

Another way to achieve the same result is to split the text string using the following `split()` method:

```
let array = string.split(text)
```

where *`array`* is an array of substrings, *`string`* is the text to be split, and *`text`* is a delimiter character marking where the text should be split. The following code uses the `split()` method to create the `parts` array where `parts[0]` contains the username and `parts[1]` contains the domain.

```
let email = "lincoln@example.com";
let parts = email.split("@");
// parts[0] = "lincoln"
// parts[1] = "example.com"
```

Notice that the delimiter character is not included in either substring because it marks where the substrings begin and end. The `split()` method is very effective for text strings that need to be broken up into multiple substrings based on the placement of several delimiters. Later you will apply the `split()` method to create an array of the words in the Lincoln speech.

Combining Text Strings

New text strings can also be generated by combining two or more existing text strings. **Figure 7-14** describes JavaScript functions for combining text strings.

METHOD	DESCRIPTION
string.concat(*str1*, *str2*, ...)	Appends the substrings *str1*, *str2*, ... to the text string, *string*
string.fromCharCode(*n1*, *n2*, ...)	Constructs a *String* object using the Unicode character codes *n1*, *n2*, ...
string.repeat(*n*)	Repeats the text string, *string*, *n* times

Figure 7-14 Methods to generate new strings

For example, the `concat()` method can be employed to append one or more text strings to an existing string as in the following example in which the `speech` variable stores the text string "four score and seven years".

```
let firstWord = "four";
let speech = firstWord.concat(" score and seven years")
// Returns "four score and seven years"
```

The `concat()` method does the same thing as the + and += operators, so there is no reason to use it in preference to those much more direct approaches.

Comparing Text Strings

Text strings can be compared using JavaScript operators such as the comparison operator === which tests whether two strings are identical in content and type. Text strings can also be compared based on lexicographical order, which indicates the order of characters within a language. In the United States where English is the standard language, the letter "A" is listed before the letter "L" so that "A" is less than "L". The following expressions indicate the ordering of two text strings:

```
"Abraham" < "Lincoln"    // Returns true
"Abraham" > "Lincoln"    // Returns false
```

Note that uppercase letters come before lowercase letters so that if two letters have the same case, then alphabetic order is used to compare them, but if the two strings are identical aside from case, the one starting with an uppercase letter comes first.

Note Lexicographical order is related to Unicode value. The characters A through Z have Unicode values of 65 to 90 and, thus, are "less than" the characters a through z, which have Unicode values of 97 to 122.

Another way of comparing two text strings is with the following `localeCompare()` method:

```
string.localeCompare(compare)
```

where *`string`* and *`compare`* are text strings to compare. The `localeCompare()` method returns the following values:

−1 or a negative number	If *`string`* comes before *`compare`* in lexicographical order
0	If *`string`* equals *`compare`*
1 or a positive number	If *`string`* comes after *`compare`* in lexicographical order

The following statement returns a value of −1 because "a" comes before "z" in lexicographical order:

```
"a".localeCompare("z")   // returns -1
```

Because lexicographical order might differ across locales, JavaScript provides the following `localeCompare()` method:

```
string1.localeCompare(string2, locale, {options})
```

where *`locale`* defines the locale and *`options`* provides optional parameters for determining order. The following statement returns a value of -1 indicating that A comes before Ä under the German (de) language.

```
"A".localeCompare("Ä", "de") // returns -1
```

You have completed the coverage of the JavaScript methods and properties associated with text strings. In the next section you will learn to combine these methods with regular expressions.

Quick Check 1

1. Provide code to create a `FileReader` object named `fReader`.
2. Provide code to read the file memo.txt in the `fReader` object as text.
3. What value is returned by the expression `"Daily Memo".indexOf(" ")`?
4. What text string is returned by the expression `"Daily Memo".slice(3, 8)`?
5. What value is returned by the expression `"Daily".localeCompare("Memo")`?

Introducing Regular Expressions

Many of the techniques and methods used with text strings can also be applied to regular expressions. Before continuing with the development of the Word Cloud app, you will explore the terse language of regular expressions using an interactive demo page.

Regular expressions have the following general form:

```
/pattern/
```

where *pattern* is a regular expression code defining a character pattern. For example, the following regular expression defines a character pattern in which 5 digits are followed by a dash and another 4 digits:

```
/\d{5}-\d{4}/
```

A text string such as "13472-0912" would match this pattern, but text strings such as "13472" or "134720912" do not.

Matching a Substring

The most basic regular expression is simply a substring of characters entered as follows:

```
/chars/
```

where *chars* is the substring text. To help you understand regular expressions, you will apply this regular expression pattern in a demo page that has been created for you.

To open the regular expression demo:

1. Use your browser to open the **demo_regexp.html** file from the js07 ▶ chapter folder.
2. Type **There is the place we shall gather.** in the text area box located in the upper-left corner of the page.
3. Click the **Or enter one directly** text box located directly below the drop-down list box and type **/the/** as the regular expression
4. Click the **Pattern Test** button. The first occurrence of the "the" substring is highlighted and the Pattern Test Result field displays the word "match", indicating that a matching character pattern has been found in the text string. See **Figure 7-15.**

Note | Spaces are part of a regular expression substring. The regular expression `/the/` is different from the regular expression `/ the /`.

Notice that the substring match is case-sensitive and does not match the substring "The" found at the beginning of the sample text.

Regular expressions use the anchors ^ and $ to mark the beginning and end of a text string. The following expression matches the substring "land" but only if it comes at the start of the sample text.

```
/^land/
```

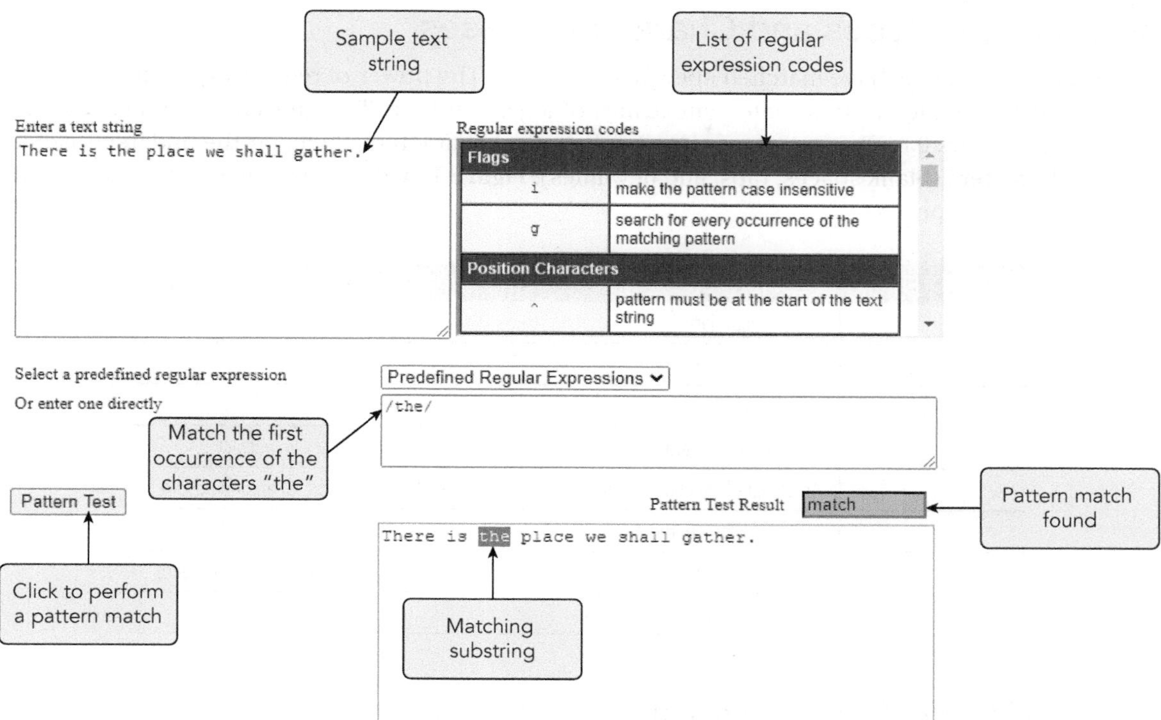

Figure 7-15 Matching a substring

The regular expression

```
/land$/
```

matches the substring "land" only if it comes at the end of the text string. Finally, the expression

```
/^land$/
```

only matches text strings that contain the word "land" and nothing else.

Setting Regular Expression Flags

By default, pattern matching stops with the first match. To override this default behavior, add a modifier character or flag to end of the regular expression. To perform global searches, add the `g` flag to the regular expression

```
/pattern/g
```

To make a regular expression insensitive to case, add the `i` flag:

```
/pattern/i
```

Test these flags in the regular expression demo by matching all occurrences of the substring "the" regardless of case.

To open the regular expression demo:

1. Within the regular expression demo, change the regular expression pattern to `/the/ig`.
2. Click the **Pattern Test** button and verify that all occurrences of the substring "the" are highlighted regardless of the case of the letters.

You can enter the regular expression flags in any order. Thus, `ig` will be treated the same as `gi`.

Defining Character Types and Character Classes

So far, your regular expressions have matched specific characters. The power of regular expressions comes with the introduction of special characters that match substrings of a general type. The four charter types are alphabetical characters; digits (numbers 0 to 9); word characters (alphabetical characters, digits, or the underscore character _) and whitespace characters (blank spaces, tabs, and new lines). **Figure 7-16** describes the regular expression symbols used for these character types.

CHARACTER	DESCRIPTION
`\b`	A word boundary
`\B`	Not a word boundary
`\d`	A digit from 0 to 9
`\D`	Any non-digit character
`\w`	An alphabetical character (in upper- or lowercase letters), a digit, or an underscore
`\W`	Any non-word character
`\s`	A whitespace character (a blank space, tab, new line, carriage return, or form feed)
`\S`	Any non-whitespace character
`.`	Any character

Figure 7-16 Regular expression character types

A regular expression word is any substring containing only word characters. The string "R2D2" is considered a single word, but "R2D2&C3PO" is considered two words, with the & symbol acting as a boundary between the words. Word boundaries are indicated by the `\b` symbol. The following pattern matches any word starting with "art", such as "artful", "artist", or "article".

```
/\bart/
```

On the other hand, the following pattern matches any word that ends with "art" such as "smart", "dart", or "heart".

```
/art\b/
```

Finally, the following pattern places word boundaries around "art" so that it matches only the word "art" and nothing else.

```
/\bart\b/
```

> **Note** Regular expression symbols have opposite meanings when expressed in uppercase letters. The symbol `\B` means the absence of a word boundary, and the symbol `\W` means the absence of a word character.

To apply a word boundary to a regular expression:

1. Within the regular expression demo, change the regular expression pattern to **`/\bthe\b/ig`** to match only the word "the" and nothing else.
2. Click the **Pattern Test** button and verify that only "the" is matched from the text string.
3. Change the regular expression pattern to **`/\Bthe\B/ig`** to match only "the" only when it is *not* surrounded by word boundaries.
4. Click the **Pattern Test** button again and verify that only the string "the" within the word "gather" is selected.
5. Change the regular expression pattern to **`/\bthe\B/ig`** to match only "the" only when it starts a word but does not finish it.
6. Click the **Pattern Test** button and verify that only the string "The" within the word "There" is selected. See **Figure 7-17**.

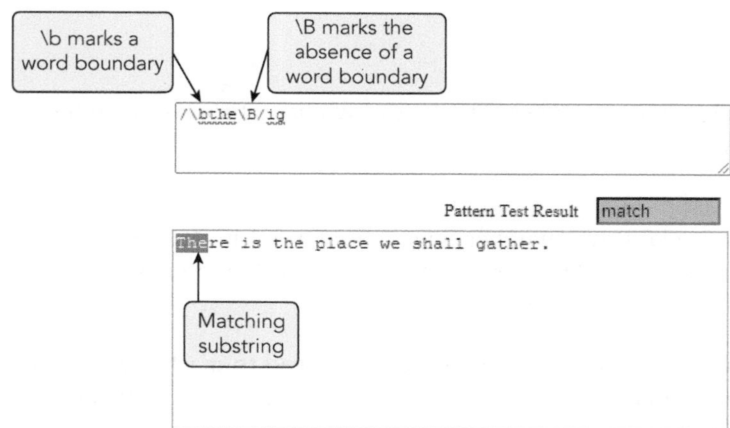

Figure 7-17 Using word boundaries in a regular expression

Digits are represented by the `\d` character. To match any occurrence of a single digit, apply the regular expression

```
/\d/
```

which finds matches in text strings such as 105, 6, or U2 because these examples all contain at least one digit. To match several consecutive digits, repeat the `\d` symbol. The following regular expression matches a substring consisting of 5 consecutive digits:

```
/\d\d\d\d\d/
```

To match words consisting of exactly 5-digit numbers, mark the word boundaries with the `\b` character as follows:

```
/\b\d\d\d\d\d\b/
```

Finally, to match entire text strings that contain a 5-digit number and nothing else, anchor the regular expression pattern with the `^` and `$` characters:

```
/^\d\d\d\d\d$/
```

Test this pattern now on the demo page.

To apply a word boundary to a regular expression:

1. Within the regular expression demo, change the text in the Enter a text string box to **51523**.
2. Change the regular expression pattern to **`/^\d\d\d\d\d$/`** and click the **Pattern Test** button. The demo page highlights all the digits in the test indicating a complete match.
3. Change the sample text string to **51,523** and click the **Pattern Test** button. The demo reports no match because the text string does not consist of 5 digits and no other characters.

There is no character type that matches only alphabetical characters. However, you can specify a collection of characters known as a character class to limit the regular expression to a select group of characters. The regular expression pattern for a character class is:

```
[chars]
```

where *`chars`* are characters in the class. For example, to create a character class matching all vowels in a text string regardless of case, apply the following regular expression pattern

```
/[aeiou]/gi
```

Because characters have a lexicographical order, a character class can also be defined by a range of characters. To create a character class for all lowercase letters, use the following:

```
[a-z]
```

for uppercase letters, use the following:

```
[A-Z]
```

A character class can contain multiple ranges. The following character class matches digits, lowercase letters, and uppercase letters but nothing else:

```
[0-9a-zA-Z]
```

To create a negative character class that matches any character not in the class, preface the list of characters with the caret symbol (^). The following regular expression matches all characters that are not vowels, regardless of case:

```
/[^aeiou]/gi
```

Note that the negative character set uses the same ^ symbol used to mark the beginning of a text string. Although the symbol is the same, the meaning is very different in this context. **Figure 7-18** summarizes the syntax for creating regular expression character classes.

PATTERN	DESCRIPTION
`[chars]`	Match any character in the `chars` list
`[^chars]`	Do not match any character in the `chars` list
`[char1-charN]`	Match characters in the range `char1` through `charN`
`[^char1-charN]`	Do not match any characters in the range `char1` through `charN`
`[a-z]`	Match any lowercase letter
`[A-Z]`	Match any uppercase letter
`[a-zA-Z]`	Match any lower- or uppercase letter
`[0-9]`	Match any digit
`[0-9a-zA-Z]`	Match any digit or letter

Figure 7-18 Character classes

Use the demo page now to explore the workings of character classes.

To create a character class pattern:

1. Within the regular expression demo, change the text in the Enter a text string box to **With malice towards none**.
2. Change the regular expression pattern to `/[aeiou]/gi` and click the **Pattern Test** button. All the vowels in the text string are highlighted.

   Next, select only the consonants in the text string.
3. Change the regular expression pattern to `/[^aeiou]/gi` and click the **Pattern Test** button. The regular expression selects all the characters which are not vowels. See **Figure 7-19**.

Specifying Repeating Characters

Rather than repeating the same character in a regular expression, you can indicate the repetition of a character using the following regular expression code:

```
{n}
```

where *n* is the number of repetitions. The following regular expression defines a character pattern consisting of 5 digits and nothing else:

```
/^\d{5}$/
```

In place of a number, use the symbol `*` for 0 or more repetitions, `+` for 1 or more repetitions, or `?` for 0 or 1 repetitions. **Figure 7-20** describes these and other repetition symbols in the regular expression language.

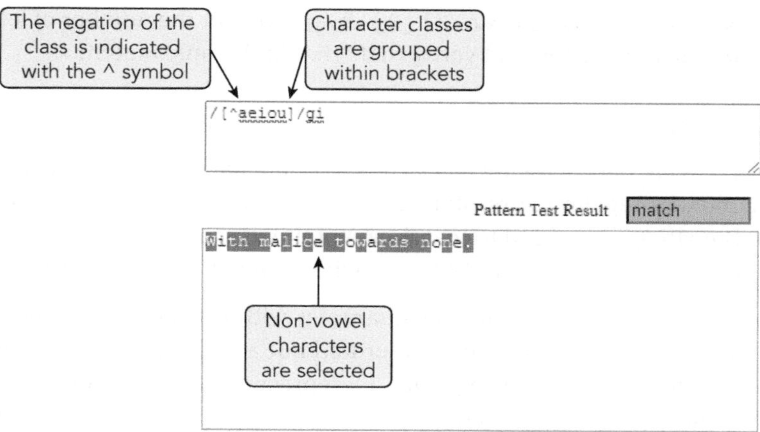

Figure 7-19 Regular expression for non-vowels

REPETITION CHARACTERS	DESCRIPTION
*	Repeat 0 or more times
?	Repeat 0 or 1 time
+	Repeat 1 or more times
{*n*}	Repeat exactly *n* times
{*n*,}	Repeat at least *n* times
{*n*,*m*}	Repeat at least *n* times but no more than *m* times

Figure 7-20 Repetition symbols

To apply a repetition pattern:

1. Within the regular expression demo, change the text in the Enter a text string box to **To be or not to be. That is the question.**
2. Change the regular expression pattern to `/\bt[a-zA-Z]+\b/gi` to match all words that begin with the letter "t" followed by one or more letters.
3. Click the **Pattern Test** button. **Figure 7-21** shows the words matched by the regular expression pattern.

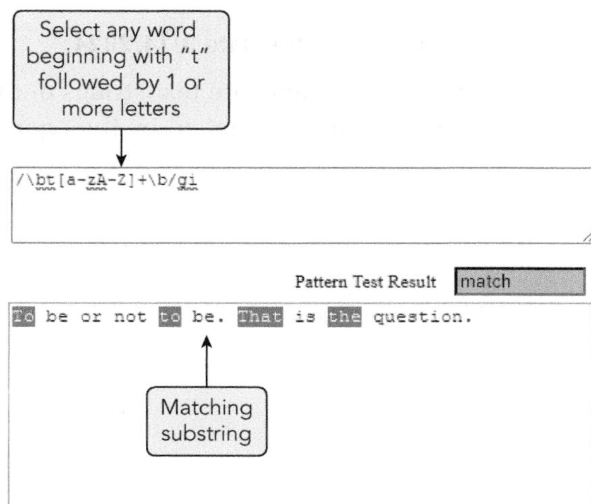

Figure 7-21 Regular expression with repetitive characters

4. Change the regular expression to `/\bt[a-zA-Z]{2}\b/gi` to limit the number of letters after the initial letter "t" to two. Click the **Pattern Test** button and verify that "the" is the only match.

Using Escape Sequences

Many commonly used characters are part of the regular expression language. The forward slash character / is reserved to mark the beginning and end of a regular expression and the ?, +, and * characters specify the number of times a character can be repeated. But what if you need to match one of those characters? For example, how do you create a regular expression matching the date pattern mm/dd/yyyy when the / character is already reserved for other uses?

In such cases, use an escape sequence by prefacing the character with the backslash character \ indicating that the character that follows should be interpreted as a character and not a command. For example, the escape sequence \$ represents the $ character, while the escape sequence \\ represents a single \ character. **Figure 7-22** provides a list of escape sequences for other special characters.

ESCAPE SEQUENCE	REPRESENTS
\/	/
\\	\
\.	.
*	*
\+	+
\?	?
|	|
\(\)	( )
\{ \}	{ }
\^	^
\$	$
\n	A new line
\r	A carriage return
\t	A tab

Figure 7-22 Escape sequences

To apply an escape sequence:

1. Within the regular expression demo, change the text in the Enter a text string box to the date **3/14/2024**.
2. Change the regular expression pattern to `/^\d{1,2}\/\d{1,2}\/\d{4}$/` to match date text strings of the form *mm/dd/yyyy*. Click the **Pattern Test** button. **Figure 7-23** shows that the date is matched by the regular expression pattern.

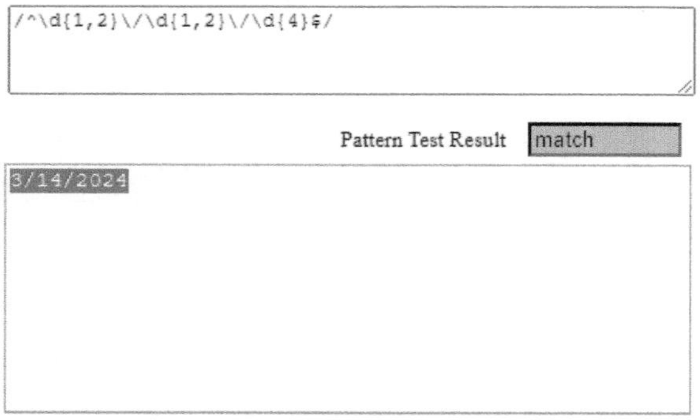

Figure 7-23 Regular expression with an escape sequence

3. Test the regular expression against other data strings; note that the regular expression matches invalidate date strings such as **23/99/0007** or **0/0/0000**.

> **Note** Explore the date expressions available from the selection list on the demo page to learn about other regular expressions involving dates.

Specifying Alternate Patterns and Grouping

Your regular expression will often need to involve several different character patterns. Those patterns can be combined with the | character as follows:

```
pattern1|pattern2
```

where *pattern1* and *pattern2* are two distinct patterns. For example, the following expression matches text strings containing either 5 digits or 5 digits followed by a dash and another 4 digits:

```
/^\d{5}$|^\d{5}-\d{4}$/
```

Explore how to use the alternate character on the demo page by creating a regular expression that matches the abbreviations St., Ave., or Ln.

To specify alternate regular expressions:

1. Within the regular expression demo, change the text in the Enter a text string box to **815 Maple St**.
2. Change the regular expression pattern to `/St.|Ave.|Ln./g` Click the **Pattern Test** button to verify that the regular expression matches "St.".
3. Change the address to **815 Maple Ave**. and then to **815 Maple Ln**. and verify that with each street address, the regular expression matches the street abbreviation.

Another useful technique in regular expressions is to group characters so they can be treated as a single unit. The syntax to create a group is:

```
(pattern)
```

where *pattern* is a regular expression pattern. Groups are often used with the | character to create regular expressions that match different variations of the same text. For example, a phone number might be entered with or without an area code. The pattern for the phone number without an area code, such as 555-1234, is:

```
/^\d{3}-\d{4}$/
```

but if an area code is included in the number, such as 800-555-1234, the pattern for the phone number would be:

```
/^\d{3}-\d{3}-\d{4}$/
```

To treat the area code as optional, place it within a group using the `()` symbols and apply the ? repetition character to the entire area code group. The regular expression is:

```
/^(\d{3}-)?\d{3}-\d{4}$/
```

matching either 555-1234 or 800-555-1234. Test this regular expression now in the demo page.

To create a regular expression group:

1. Within the regular expression demo, change the text in the Enter a text string box to **555-1234**.
2. Change the regular expression pattern to `/^(\d{3}-)?\d{3}-\d{4}$/` and then click the **Pattern Test** button to verify that phone number matches the regular expression pattern. See **Figure 7-24**.

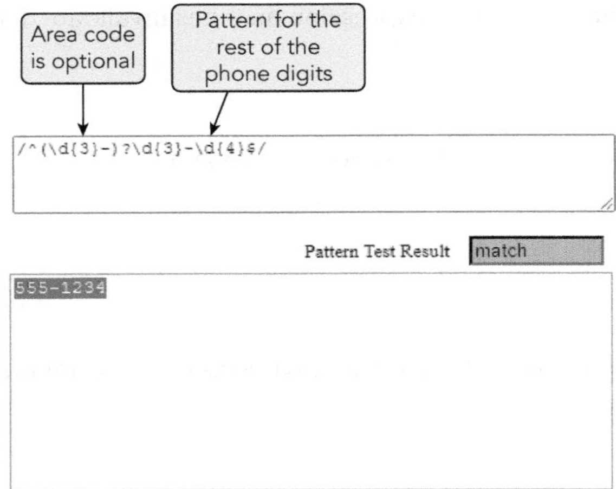

Figure 7-24 Regular expression with grouping

3. Change the phone number text string to **800-555-1234** and click the **Pattern Test** button to verify that this phone number is also matched by the regular expression.
4. Continue to explore other text strings and regular expression patterns and then close the demo page when finished.

Having completed this overview of regular expressions, you are ready to return to the development of the Word Cloud app.

Common Mistakes

Avoiding Mistakes with Regular Expressions

The language of regular expressions is beautifully compact, but it is easy to make mistakes in syntax. Here are some typical errors that may creep into your regular expressions:

- **Including spaces in the regular expression.** In JavaScript, whitespace can make your code more readable, but a blank space in a regular expression is treated as a character and will be evaluated as such.
- **Forgetting to escape special characters.** Characters like `(` and `)` have special meanings in a regular expression so they must be escaped if they are part of the character pattern.
- **Forgetting the ^ and $ characters.** If your regular expression is designed to match the entire text string, you must anchor it with the `^` and `$` characters.
- **Excessive backtracking.** Backtracking occurs when the regular expression contains quantifiers such as the * or + characters, which force the parser to examine each possible substring within a larger text string. A text string consisting of no more than 20 characters might result in millions of individual searches, slowing down the program's execution. You can avoid such catastrophic backtracking by not overusing quantifiers and tightly writing your regular expressions to limit the number of possible matches.

Always test your regular expressions before committing them to your code. There are several free and fee-based regular expression testers available on the web that can highlight syntax errors and help you avoid catastrophic backtracking .

Programming with Regular Expressions

A regular expression can be directly entered into your JavaScript code as a regular expression literal. For example, the following command stores a regular expression literal in the `regx` variable:

```
let regx = /\d{5}-\d{4}/g;
```

Note that the regular expression is *not* enclosed within quotes (it's not a `String` object!)

A regular expression can also be defined using the following `new RegExp()` object constructor:

```
new RegExp(pattern, flags);
```

where *pattern* is the text of the regular expression (enclosed in quotes) and *flags* are the text of any modifiers added to that pattern. The following command stores a regular expression in the `regx` variable using an object constructor:

```
let regx = new RegExp("\d{5}-\d{4}", "g");
```

One of the advantages of using an object constructor is that it can read a variable containing a regular expression. For example, the following code creates a regular expression based on the value of the `patternTest` variable:

```
let patternTest = "\d{5}-\d{4}";
let regx = new RegExp(patternTest, "g");
```

Regular Expression Methods

Because regular expressions are another type of JavaScript object, they have their own collection of methods. For example, you can search a text string to determine whether a character pattern defined by a regular expression is present within the text. You can replace or remove characters within the text string that match a regular expression pattern. You can also split a text string into several substrings at each occurrence of a regular expression character pattern. **Figure 7-25** describes some of the JavaScript methods associated with regular expressions.

METHOD	DESCRIPTION
re.exec(*str*)	Searches the text string, *str*, for the character pattern expressed in the regular expression *re*, returning data about the search results in an array
re.test(*str*)	Searches *str* for the character pattern *re*; if a match is found returns the Boolean value true
re.toString()	Converts the regular expression *re* to a text string
str.match(*re*)	Searches *str* for the character pattern expressed in the regular expression *re*, returning the search results in an array
str.search(*re*)	Searches *str* for a substring matching the regular expression *re*; returns the index of the match, or -1 if no match is found
str.replace(*re*, *newsubstr*)	Replaces the characters in *str* defined by the regular expression re with the text string *newsubstr*
str.split(*re*)	Splits *str* at each point indicated by the regular expression *re*, storing each substring as an item in an array

Figure 7-25 Regular expression methods

One method often used with regular expressions is the following `test()` method to determine whether the contents of a text string match a regular expression pattern:

```
re.test(str)
```

where *re* is a regular expression and *str* is the text string to be tested. The `test()` method returns `true` if a match is found and `false` otherwise. For example, the following code uses the `test()` method to compare the text string stored in the `zipCode` variable with the regular expression object stored in the `regx` variable:

```
let digits = "12345";
let regx = /^\d{5}$/;
let testValue = regx.test(digits); // returns true
```

To determine where the match occurs within the text string, apply the following `search()` method:

```
str.search(re)
```

The `search()` method returns the index of the first matching substring from the string. If no match is found, it returns the value -1, just like the `indexOf()` method discussed earlier. However, unlike the `indexOf()` method, the `search()` method always starts from the beginning of the text string.

Replacing Text with Regular Expressions

Regular expressions can locate and replace substrings within a larger text string using the following `replace()` method:

```
str.replace(re,newsubstr)
```

where *`str`* is a text string containing text to be replaced, *`re`* is a regular expression defining the character pattern of the substrings that need replacing, and *`newsubstr`* is the replacement substring. The following code shows how to apply the `replace()` method to replace "1st" with "First" in a sample text string:

```
let oldtext = "1st Inaugural";
oldtext.replace(/1st/g, "First"); // returns First Inaugural
```

Use the `replace()` method to move all punctuation marks and digits from the Word Cloud app's source text, replacing them with empty text strings. The regular expression to match all characters that are not alphabetic and not whitespace is:

```
/[^a-zA-Z\s]/g
```

Add your code to the `wordCloud()` function now.

To remove non-alphabetic characters from the source text:

1. Return to the **js07.js** file in your code editor.
2. Go to the `wordCloud()` function and directly before the statement writing `sourceText` to the debugger console, add the following code as described in **Figure 7-26**:

```
// Leave only alphabet characters and whitespace in the text
let alphaRegx = /[^a-zA-Z\s]/g;
sourceText = sourceText.replace(alphaRegx, "");
```

```
function wordCloud(sourceText) {
   // Convert the source text to lowercase
   // and remove leading and trailing whitespace
   sourceText = sourceText.toLowerCase();
   sourceText = sourceText.trim();

   // Leave only alphabet characters and whitespace in the text
   let alphaRegx = /[^a-zA-Z\s]/g;
   sourceText = sourceText.replace(alphaRegx, "");

   console.log(sourceText);
}
```

Select characters that are not alphabetic nor whitespace
Replace those characters with an empty text string

Figure 7-26 Removing non-alphabetic characters

3. Save your changes to the file and then reload **js07.html** in your browser and load **lincoln1.html** in the app.
4. View the console log to confirm that the source text no longer contains punctuation marks or digits, but only alphabetic characters and blank spaces. See **Figure 7-27**.

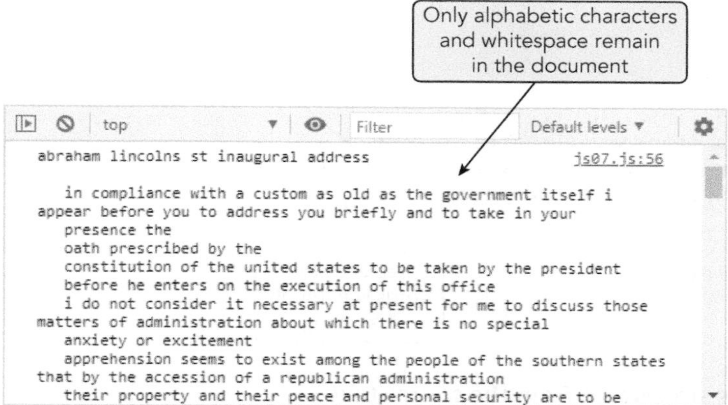
Only alphabetic characters and whitespace remain in the document
top
Filter
Default levels
abraham lincolns st inaugural address
js07.js:56
in compliance with a custom as old as the government itself i
appear before you to address you briefly and to take in your
presence the
oath prescribed by the
constitution of the united states to be taken by the president
before he enters on the execution of this office
i do not consider it necessary at present for me to discuss those
matters of administration about which there is no special
anxiety or excitement
apprehension seems to exist among the people of the southern states
that by the accession of a republican administration
their property and their peace and personal security are to be

Figure 7-27 Source text with only alphabetic characters

The Word Cloud app also needs to remove stop words from the source text. A stop word is a word not normally included within a word cloud because it provides no meaning, including articles such as “and”, “if”, “is”, and “the”. An array of stop words has been created for you and stored at the bottom of the js07.js file. **Figure 7-28** shows a portion of the `stopWords` array.

```
/*----------------------------------------------*/
/* Array of words to NOT include in the word cloud */
/*----------------------------------------------*/

let stopWords = ["a", "about", "above", "across", "after", "afterwards", "again", "against",
                 "ago", "all", "almost", "alone", "along", "already", "also", "although",
                 "always", "am", "among", "amongst", "amoungst", "amount", "an", "and",
                 "another", "any", "anyhow", "anyone", "anything", "anyway", "anywhere",
                 "are", "around", "as", "at", "back", "be", "became", "because", "become",
                 "becomes", "becoming", "been", "before", "beforehand", "behind", "being",
```

Figure 7-28 Part of the `stopWords` array

To remove the stop words from the source text, the Word Cloud app will examine every entry in the `stopWords` array and apply the `replace()` method to replace the stop word in the source text with an empty text string. The `for` loop is:

```
for (let i = 0; i < stopWords.length; i++) {
   let stopRegx = new RegExp("\\b"+stopWords[i]+"\\b", "g");
   sourceText = sourceText.replace(stopRegx, "");
}
```

Note that the regular expression using `\b` to mark the word boundaries around each stop word and the global flag, `g`, to do the replacement throughout the source text. Add this `for` loop to the `wordCloud()` function now.

To remove stop words from the source text:

1. Return to the **js07.js** file in your code editor.
2. Directly before the statement writing `sourceText` to the debugger console, add the following `for` loop as described in **Figure 7-29**.

```
// Remove stop words from the text
for (let i = 0; i < stopWords.length; i++) {
   let stopRegx = new RegExp("\\b"+stopWords[i]+"\\b", "g");
   sourceText = sourceText.replace(stopRegx, "");
}
```

```
   // Remove stop words from the text
   for (let i = 0; i < stopWords.length; i++) {
      let stopRegx = new RegExp("\\b"+stopWords[i]+"\\b", "g");
      sourceText = sourceText.replace(stopRegx, "");
   }

   console.log(sourceText);
}
```

Select all stop words in the document

Replace stop words with empty text string

Figure 7-29 Removing stop words from the source text

3. Save your changes to the file and then reload **js07.html** in your browser and load **lincoln1.html** in the app.
4. View the console log to confirm that stop words have been removed from the source text. See **Figure 7-30**.

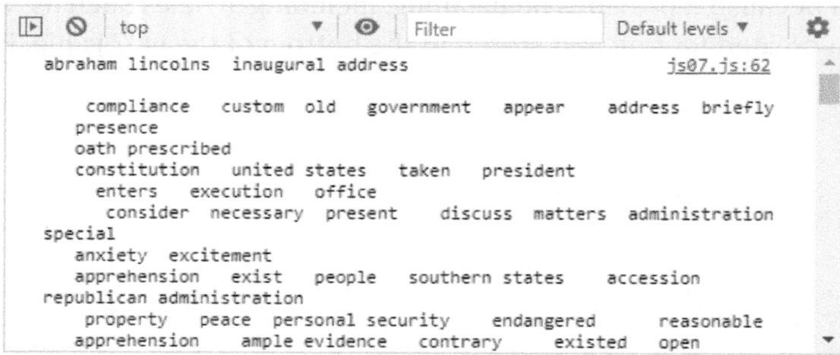

Figure 7-30 Source text without stop words

Having removed the stop words from the source text, you will next place the remaining words into an array.

Splitting a Text String into an Array

To create an array of substrings from a text string, use the following `match()` method:

```
let array = str.match(re)
```

where *`str`* is the text string, *`re`* is the regular expression indicating which substrings to match, and *`array`* contains each matched substring. For example, the following command extracts the individual words from the text string, placing each word as a separate item in the `words` array:

```
let words = "with malice towards none".match(/\b\w+\b/g);
// words = ["with", "malice", "towards", "none"]
```

Note | The global flag must be set to locate all matches in the text string. Without the g flag, only the first match is returned.

Similar to the `match()` method is the `split()` method, which breaks a text string into substrings at each location where a pattern match is found, placing the substrings as individual items in an array. You saw how to use the `split()` method earlier in the session when it was applied with a text string as a delimiter. It can also be used with regular expressions. The following command splits a text string at every occurrence of one or more whitespace characters, creating an array of individual words:

```
words = "with malice towards none".split(/\s+/g);
// words = ["with","malice","towards","none"]
```

Use the `split()` method now to split the source text as every occurrence of one or more whitespace characters, creating an array of words from the source text.

To place the source text words into an array:

1. Return to the **js07.js** file in your code editor.
2. Directly after the `for` loop that removes stop words from the source text, add the following code.

```
// Place the remaining words in array
let words = sourceText.split(/\s+/g);
```

3. Change the statement that writes to the debugger console from `console.log(sourceText)` to **`console.log(words)`**. See **Figure 7-31**.

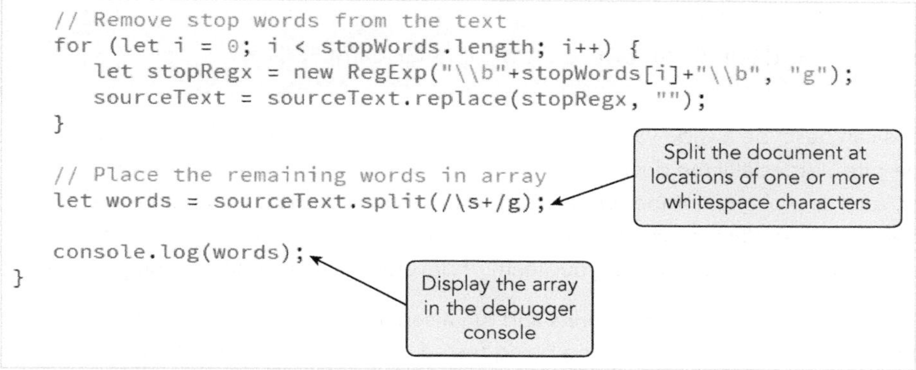

// Remove stop words from the text
for (let i = 0; i < stopWords.length; i++) {
let stopRegx = new RegExp("\\b"+stopWords[i]+"\\b", "g");
sourceText = sourceText.replace(stopRegx, "");
}
// Place the remaining words in array
let words = sourceText.split(/\s+/g);
console.log(words);
}
Split the document at locations of one or more whitespace characters
Display the array in the debugger console

Figure 7-31 Splitting a text string to an array

4. Save your changes to the file and then reload **js07.html** in your browser and load **lincoln1.html** in the app.
5. View the console log to examine the contents of the words array. See **Figure 7-32**.

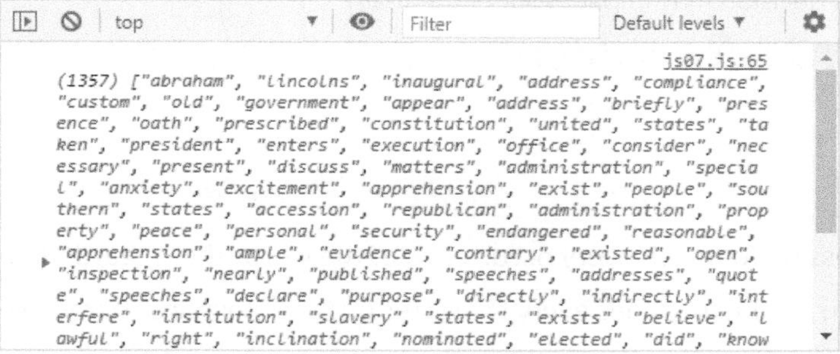

top
Filter
Default levels
js07.js:65
(1357) ["abraham", "lincolns", "inaugural", "address", "compliance", "custom", "old", "government", "appear", "address", "briefly", "pres ence", "oath", "prescribed", "constitution", "united", "states", "ta ken", "president", "enters", "execution", "office", "consider", "nec essary", "present", "discuss", "matters", "administration", "specia l", "anxiety", "excitement", "apprehension", "exist", "people", "sou thern", "states", "accession", "republican", "administration", "prop erty", "peace", "personal", "security", "endangered", "reasonable", "apprehension", "ample", "evidence", "contrary", "existed", "open", "inspection", "nearly", "published", "speeches", "addresses", "quot e", "speeches", "declare", "purpose", "directly", "indirectly", "int erfere", "institution", "slavery", "states", "exists", "believe", "l awful", "right", "inclination", "nominated", "elected", "did", "know

Figure 7-32 Contents of the `words` array

After removing the stop words, there are 1357 words left in the speech, many of which are duplicates.

Referencing Substring Matches

Whenever a method is applied to a regular expression, information about the matched substrings is stored in a JavaScript `RegExp` object using properties labeled `$1` through `$9`. The `$1` property returns the first group of matching substrings, the `$2` property returns the second matching substring and so forth. By using these properties, you can restructure a text string using substrings selected by the regular expression.

For example, in the following code a text string contains the first and last names of several individuals with the names separated by commas. By creating a regular expression that identifies the grouping of the first name and the last name, the ordering of the names can be switched so that the last name comes before the first name followed by a semicolon.

```
let names = "Travis Lee, Darius Green, Alisha Draves";
let re = /(\w+)\s(\w+),?/g;
let names2 = names.replace(re, '$2, $1; ');
// returns "Lee, Travis; Green, Darius; Draves, Alisha"
```

In this code the `$1` property represents the first name group entered as `(\w+)` in the regular expression and `$2` represents the second name group `(\w+)` placed after the whitespace `\s` character. By properly constructing your regular expression you can rearrange the contents of a text string in a wide variety of ways.

You have completed your study of text strings and regular expressions. In the next section you will explore how to retrieve the unique words from the `words` array and tabulate the frequency of each word from the Lincoln speech.

Skills at Work | Balancing Readability and Efficiency in Regular Expressions

The language of regular expressions can describe a wide variety of patterns in a minimal amount of code. However, it is important to consider the trade-offs—especially the decreased readability of complex regular expressions by other programmers. In some cases, such as a phone number or email address, single, compact expressions are standardized and widely used. However, especially for custom regular expressions, it is important to stop and consider which is a higher priority for your organization and/or your team of developers: readability or compactness.

In many cases, you can break a regular expression into smaller units and run a separate test on each. This has the side benefit of enabling you to identify specific issues with a string being tested, rather than simply learning that it does not meet all the requirements coded into a single complex regular expression. In other words, do not try to be too clever and fit several levels of matching into one expression.

On the other hand, breaking a test into multiple statements results in more code, which can take longer to execute and download, and those factors can negatively impact user experience. For these reasons, it is important to understand whether compact code or self-documenting code is a higher priority when creating regular expressions for a project, and that this decision may impact your entire team.

Quick Check 2

1. Provide a regular expression to match every occurrence of the word "the" regardless of case.
2. What regular expression symbol matches every character but a whitespace character?
3. Social security numbers can be entered as either 9 digits in a row or in the form `ddd-dd-dddd`. Write a regular expression to match either pattern.
4. Provide code to test whether the value of the `userID` variable matches a character pattern of 3 digits followed by a dash followed by another 4 digits.
5. Provide code to split the text string stored in the `orderDate` variable at every occurrence of the / character, storing the values in the array `dateArray`.

Exploring Array Methods

To complete the Word Cloud app you will need to work with the properties and methods associated with arrays. JavaScript arrays include methods that change an array's content, order, and size. There are also methods to combine multiple arrays into a single array and to convert the contents of an array into a text string.

Reversing and Sorting an Array

Items are placed in an array either in the order in which they are defined or explicitly by index number. You can alter that order by using the `reverse()` and `sort()` methods. The `reverse()` method reverses the order of the array items, making the last items first and the first items last. In the following set of commands, the `reverse()` method changes the order of the values in the `cards` array:

```
let cards = ["Ace", "King", "Queen", "Jack"];
cards.reverse();
// returns ["Jack", "Queen", "King", "Ace"]
```

The `sort()` method rearranges array items by lexicographical order. Applied to the `cards` array, the `sort()` method produces the following array:

```
cards.sort();
// returns ["Ace", "Jack", "King", "Queen"]
```

Use the `sort()` method to sort the contents of the `words` array in alphabetical order.

To sort the contents of the `words` array:

1. Return to the **js07.js** file in your code editor and go to the `wordCloud()` function.
2. Directly after the statement to create the `words` array, add the following statement to sort the contents of that array (see **Figure 7-33**):

```
// Sort the words in alphabetical order
words.sort();
```

```
   // Place the remaining words in array
   let words = sourceText.split(/\s+/g);

   // Sort the words in alphabetical order
   words.sort();

   console.log(words);
}
```

Sort the array content in alphabetical order

Figure 7-33 Applying the `sort()` method

3. Save your changes to the file and then reload **js07.html** in your browser and load **lincoln1.html** in the app.
4. Use the debugger console to verify that the contents of the array are sorted in alphabetical order. See **Figure 7-34**.

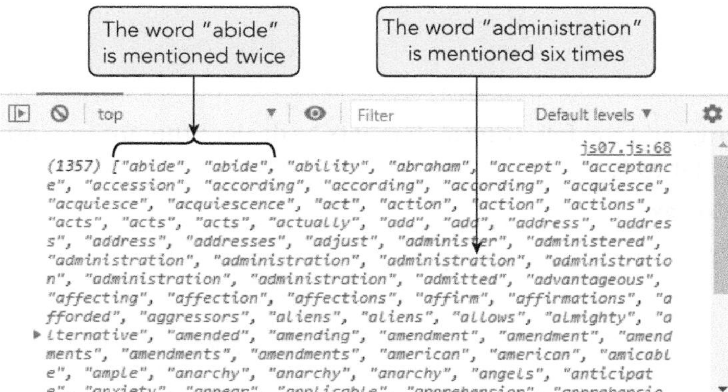

The word "abide" is mentioned twice
The word "administration" is mentioned six times
top
Filter
Default levels
js07.js:68
(1357) ["abide", "abide", "ability", "abraham", "accept", "acceptance", "accession", "according", "according", "according", "acquiesce", "acquiesce", "acquiescence", "act", "action", "action", "actions", "acts", "acts", "acts", "actually", "add", "add", "address", "address", "address", "addresses", "adjust", "administer", "administered", "administration", "administration", "administration", "administration", "administration", "administration", "admitted", "advantageous", "affecting", "affection", "affections", "affirm", "affirmations", "afforded", "aggressors", "aliens", "aliens", "allows", "almighty", "alternative", "amended", "amending", "amendment", "amendment", "amendments", "amendments", "amendments", "american", "american", "amicable", "ample", "anarchy", "anarchy", "anarchy", "angels", "anticipate", "anxiety", "appear", "applicable", "apprehension", "apprehensio

Figure 7-34 The `words` array sorted in alphabetical order

With the words array sorted, it is easier to see the duplicates. For example, the word "abide" appears twice in Lincoln's speech, "according" appears three times, and "administration" appears six times. You will store this information in a multidimensional array named unique in which each item in the array is itself an array consisting of two entries: the first containing the text of the word and the second storing the number of times that word was used.

Note | For an overview of multidimensional arrays, see Chapter 3.

Figure 7-35 shows a preview of this "array of arrays" for a selection of words.

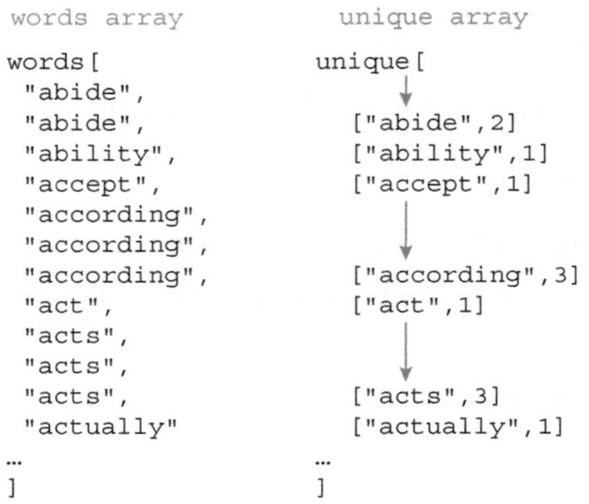

```
words array              unique array

words [                  unique [
  "abide",
  "abide",                 ["abide",2]
  "ability",               ["ability",1]
  "accept",                ["accept",1]
  "according",
  "according",
  "according",             ["according",3]
  "act",                   ["act",1]
  "acts",
  "acts",
  "acts",                  ["acts",3]
  "actually"               ["actually",1]
...                      ...
]                        ]
```

Figure 7-35 The `unique` multidimensional array

To create the unique array, use a for loop that iterates through the items in the words array. If the current word is different from the previous word, add it to the unique array and set the duplicate count to 1, but if it is the same as the previous word, increase the duplicate count by 1 without adding a new array item.

The name of each word in this multidimensional array can be referenced with the expression `unique[i][0]` where *i* is the index of the word in the unique array. The duplicate count is referenced with the expression `unique[i][1]`. For example, the first word "abide" from Figure 7-35 is referenced as `unique[0][0]` and its duplicate count is referenced as `unique[0][1]`. The seventh word "actually" is referenced with the expression `unique[6][0]` and its duplicate count with `unique[6][1]`.

Add code to the `wordCloud()` function to generate the unique array.

To sort the contents of the `words` array:

1. Return to the **js07.js** file in your code editor.
2. Directly after the statement to sort the words array, add the following statements to declare the unique array and enter its initial word and set that duplicate count to 1.

```
// Create an 2D array in which each item is array
// containing a word and its duplicate count
let unique = [ [words[0], 1] ];
```

3. As you generate the `unique` array, you will need to keep track of the index of the current item in the array. Add the following code to declare that variable:

```
// Keep an index of the unique words
let uniqueIndex = 0;
```

4. Add the following `for` loop to iterate through each item in the `words` array, adding new words as they are found or increasing the duplicate count for words previously discovered.

```
for (let i = 1; i < words.length; i++ ) {
   if (words[i] === words[i-1] ) {
      // Increase the duplicate count by 1
      unique[uniqueIndex][1]++;
   } else {
      // Add a new word to the unique array
      uniqueIndex++;
      unique[uniqueIndex] = [words[i], 1];
   }
}
```

5. Delete the `console.log(words);` statement because you will no longer be needing it.

Figure 7-36 describes the newly added code in the file.

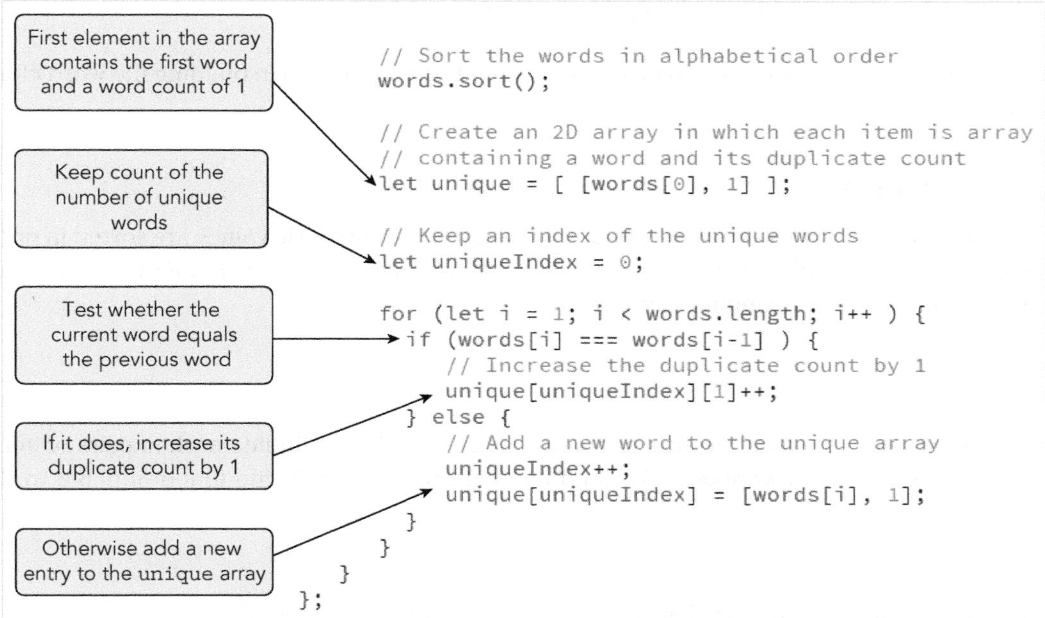

Figure 7-36 Code to generate the array of unique words

Verify that the `unique` array has been properly constructed by viewing its contents in the Scope window of your browser's debugger.

To view the contents of the `unique` array:

1. Save your changes to the file and then reload **js07.html** in your browser.
2. In your browser debugger set a breakpoint at the last line of the `wordCloud()` function directly before the final line of the anonymous function for the `onload` event hander.
3. Click the **Choose File** button and open the **lincoln1.html** file.
4. Go to the Scope window in your browser debugger and examine the contents of the unique array as shown in **Figure 7-37**.

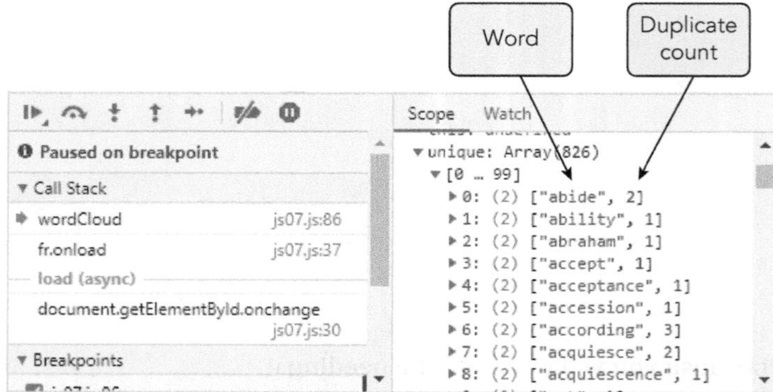

Figure 7-37 Contents of the `unique` array

5. Continue executing the script and then remove the breakpoint from the debugger.

The words in the `unique` array are sorted in alphabetical order but it would be more useful in building the word cloud if the most often-used words were listed first.

Sorting with a Compare Function

The `sort()` method sorts everything in lexicographical order, and because of this, numeric values are sorted in order of their leading digits and *not* their values. Applying the `sort()` method to the following array of numeric values would result in an array that is *not* sorted by increasing numeric value.

```
let x = [45, 3, 1234, 24];
x.sort(); // returns [1234, 24, 3, 45]
```

To sort by numeric value, a compare function must be applied to the `sort()` method to indicate when pairs of items within the array should be swapped (or not swapped). To call a compare function, add the function name to the `sort()` method as follows:

```
sort(compare)
```

where *`compare`* is the name of the compare function. The general form of a compare function is:

```
function compare(a, b) {
   return compareValue;
}
```

where *a* and *b* are parameters representing two items within the array and *`compareValue`* is a value that determines the ordering of those two items.

- If *`compareValue`* is negative, `a` is moved before `b`.
- If *`compareValue`* is positive, `a` is moved after `b`.
- If *`compareValue`* is zero, `a` and `b` retain their original positions.

The compare function determines the relative positions of every item pair within the array. The following compare function can be used to sort numbers by increasing order of value:

```
function ascending(a, b) {
   return a - b;
}
```

When a is less than b, the expression a - b is negative, causing a (the smaller number) to be placed before b (the larger number). If a is greater than b then a - b is positive, causing a to be placed after b. If a - b is zero, the two items have equal value and retain their original array positions. When this compare function is applied to an array of numbers, the smaller numbers will be moved towards the front of the array:

```
let x = [45, 3, 1234, 24];
x.sort(ascending); // Returns [3, 24, 45, 1234]
```

To sort numbers in descending order, use a compare function that returns the difference b - a so that a is placed after b when it is smaller and before b when it's bigger.

```
function descending(a, b) {
   return b - a;
}
```

Note You can embed the compare function as an anonymous function within the sort() method using the following general form:

```
array.sort(function(a, b) {return compareValue;});
```

Use a compare function to sort the unique array by descending order of duplicate count. The code for the compare function is:

```
function byDuplicate(a, b) {
   return b[1] - a[1];
}
```

Note that in this code b[1] and a[1] refer to the duplicate counts for each word, placing the word with the greater duplicate count first. Add this compare function to the Word Cloud app and sort the words in the unique array.

To sort the unique array by duplicate count:

1. Return to the **js07.js** file in your code editor and add the following code to the wordCloud() function as described in **Figure 7-38**:

```
// Sort by descending order of duplicate count
unique.sort(byDuplicate);
function byDuplicate(a, b) {
   return b[1]-a[1];
}
```


Figure 7-38 Using sort() with a compare function

2. Save your changes to the file and then reload **js07.html** in your web browser.
3. In your browser debugger set a breakpoint at the last line of the `wordCloud()` function.
4. Click the **Choose File** button and open the **lincoln1.html** file.
5. Go to the Scope window in your browser debugger. **Figure 7-39** shows the sorted contents of the `unique` array.

   Based on your analysis, "constitution" is most-repeated word in the Lincoln speech with 22 mentions, followed by "people", "union", "government", and "states".

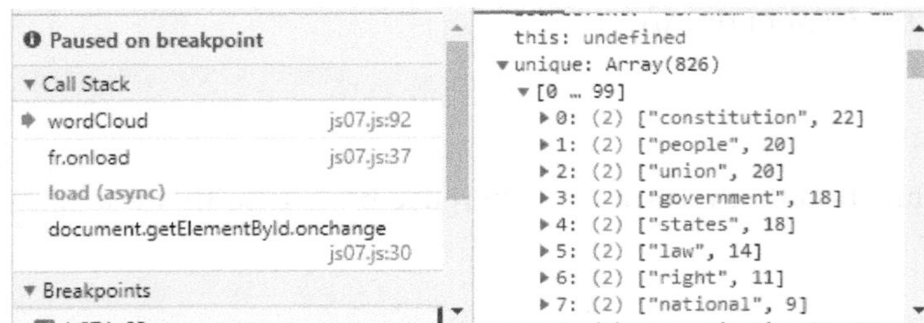

Figure 7-39 Content of the `unique` array sorted by descending order of duplicate count

6. Continue executing the script and then remove the breakpoint from the debugger.

There are 826 unique words in the Lincoln speech, which is too many for a word cloud. You will reduce the array to the 100 most-repeated words.

Extracting and Inserting Array Items

In some scripts, you will need to extract a section of an array, known as a subarray. One way to create a subarray is with the following `slice()` method:

```
array.slice(start, stop)
```

where *start* is the index value of the array item at which slicing begins and *stop* is the index before which slicing ends. The *stop* value is optional; if it is omitted, the array is sliced to its end. The original contents of the array are unaffected after slicing, but the extracted items can be stored in another array. For example, the following command slices three items from the middle of the `months` array and stores them as a new array named `summerMonths`:

```
let months = ["Jan", "Feb", "Mar", "Apr", "May", "Jun",
              "Jul", "Aug", "Sep", "Oct", "Nov", "Dec"];
summerMonths = months.slice(5, 8);
// returns ["Jun", "Jul", "Aug"]
```

Remember that arrays start with the index value 0, so the sixth month of the year (Jun) has an index value of 5, and slicing is applied up to (but not including) array index 8 (Sep).

Related to the `slice()` method is the `splice()` method, a general-purpose method for removing and inserting array items:

```
array.splice(start, size, values)
```

where *start* is the starting index in the array, *size* is the number of array items to remove after the start index, and *values* is an optional comma-separated list of values to insert into the array. If no *size* is specified, the array is spliced to its end. If no *values* are specified, the `splice()` method removes items without replacement. The following statement employs the `splice()` method to remove three names from the middle of the `emp` array while inserting three new names into the same location.

```
let emp = ["Drew", "Lee", "Grant", "Li", "Rao", "Yang"];
emp.splice(1,3,"Evans", "Greer", "Smith");
// emp = ["Drew", "Evans", "Greer", "Smith", "Rao", "Yang"];
```

Note An important difference between the `slice()` and `splice()` methods is that the `splice()` method removes items from the original array, while the `slice()` method returns a new array with the items removed.

Use the `slice()` method to retain the first 100 words in the `unique` array, removing the rest.

To apply the `splice()` method:

1. Return to the **js07.js** file in your code editor and add the following code to the `wordCloud()` function as described in **Figure 7-40**.

```
// Keep the Top 100 words
unique = unique.slice(0, 100);
```

```
      // Sort by descending order of duplicate count
      unique.sort(byDuplicate);
      function byDuplicate(a, b) {
         return b[1]-a[1];
      }

      // Keep the Top 100 words
      unique = unique.slice(0, 100);

   }
};
```


Figure 7-40 Slicing an array

2. Save your changes to the file and then reload **js07.html** in your web browser.
3. In your browser debugger set a breakpoint at the last line of the `wordCloud()` function.
4. Click the **Choose File** button and open the **lincoln1.html** file.
5. Go to the Scope window in your browser debugger and verify that the size of the unique array is reduced to the 100 most-used words.
6. Continue executing the script and then remove the breakpoint from the debugger.
7. Close the browser debugger.

Using Arrays as Data Stacks

Arrays can also store information in a data structure known as a stack in which new items are added to the top of the stack—or to the end of the array—much like a person clearing a dinner table adds dishes to the top of a stack of dirty plates. A stack data structure employs the last-in first-out (LIFO) principle in which the last items added to the stack are the first ones removed. Stack data structures are employed with the Undo feature of some software applications, in which the last command performed is the first command undone.

JavaScript supports several methods for stack data structures. The following `push()` method appends new items to the end of an array:

```
array.push(values)
```

where *values* is a comma-separated list of values to be appended to the end of the array. To remove—or unstack—the last item, apply the following pop() method:

```
array.pop()
```

The following set of commands demonstrates how to employ the LIFO principle with the push() and pop() methods to add and remove items from a data stack:

```
let x = ["a", "b", "c"];
x.push("d", "e"); // x = ["a", "b", "c", "d", "e"]
x.pop();          // x = ["a", "b", "c", "d"]
x.pop();          // x = ["a", "b", "c"]
```

Another type of data structure is the queue, which employs the first-in-first-out (FIFO) principle in which the first item added is the first item removed. You see the FIFO principle in action with a line of people waiting to be served. For array data that should be treated as a queue, use the shift() method to remove the first array item and the unshift() to insert a new first item. The following code demonstrates how to apply these methods to insert and remove items from the start of an array:

```
let x = ["c", "d", "e"];
x.unshift("a", "b"); // x = ["a", "b", "c", "d", "e"]
x.shift();           // x = ["b", "c", "d", "e"]
x.shift();           // x = ["c", "d", "e"]
```

Figure 7-41 summarizes several other array methods. Arrays are a powerful and useful feature of the JavaScript language and can be applied to a wide variety of tasks.

METHOD	DESCRIPTION
array.copyWithin(*target*, *start*, *end*])	Copies items within *array* from the *start* to *end* indexes and pastes those values starting at the target index
array.concat(*array1*, *array2*,...)	Joins *array* to other arrays, creating a single array
array.fill(*value*, *start*, *end*)	Fills *array* with the value *value*, starting from the *start* index through the *end* index
array.indexOf(*value*, *start*)	Returns the index number of the first element equal to *value*, starting from the optional *start* index
array.join(*separator*)	Converts *array* to a text string with array values separated by the *separator* character (if no *separator* is specified, a comma is used)
array.lastIndexOf(*value*, *start*)	Searches backward through *array*, returning the index number of the first element equal to *value*, starting from the optional *start* index
array.pop()	Removes the last item from *array*
array.push(*values*)	Appends *array* with new items, where *values* is a comma-separated list of item value
array.reverse()	Reverses the order of items in *array*
array.shift()	Removes the first item from *array*
array.slice(*start*, *stop*)	Extracts items starting with the *start* index up to the *stop* index, returning a new subarray
array.splice(*start*, *size*, *values*)	Extracts *size* items starting with the item with the index start; to insert new items into the array, specify the array items in a comma-separated *values* list
array.sort(*compare*)	Sorts *array* where *compare* is the name of a function that returns a positive, negative, or 0 value; if no compare function is specified, *array* is sorted in alphabetical order
array.toString()	Converts *array* to a text string with the array values in a comma-separated list
array.unshift(*values*)	Inserts new items at the start of *array*, where *values* is a comma-separated list of new values

Figure 7-41 Array methods

The last part of the Word Cloud app is to display the top 100 words with the font size of each word proportional to the number of times it was repeated. The word with the most duplicates will have the largest size; the word with the fewest duplicates will have the smallest. To size these words correctly, the app will the need count of the word with the most duplicates. Because the `unique` array has been sorted in descending order of duplicate count, the first item in the array will also be the most repeated and, thus, the top count can be stored using the following expression:

```
let maxCount = unique[0][1];
```

Apply this command to the `wordCloud()` function and then sort the `unique` array back into alphabetical order.

To store the maximum duplicate count:

1. Return to the **js07.js** file in your code editor.
2. Directly below the command that slices the `unique` array, add the following commands to the function as shown in **Figure 7-42**.

```
// Find the duplicates of the most-repeated word
let maxCount = unique[0][1];
// Sort the word list in alphabetic order
unique.sort();
```

```
      // Keep the Top 100 words
      unique = unique.slice(0, 100);

      // Find the duplicates of the most-repeated word
      let maxCount = unique[0][1];

      // Sort the word list in alphabetic order
      unique.sort();
   }
};
```

Figure 7-42 Determine the count of the most-repeated words

To display the word list sized proportional to each word's use, create a `for` loop that iterates through every word in the `unique` array. For each word, set its size in `em` units as a fraction of the size of the word with the most repetitions. The most-used word will be displayed with a font size of 1em. A word that appears half as often will have a font size to 0.5em. A word that appears a tenth as often has a font size of 0.1em, and so forth. The font size represented by 1em is set in the CSS style sheet used with this project and could be changed the web designer based on the website design without affecting the script code.

To display each word in a size proportional to its use:

1. Return to the **js07.js** file in your code editor.
2. Directly below the command to sort the `unique` array, add the following commands to reference the element that will contain the word cloud and set its initial content to an empty string.

```
// Reference the word cloud box
let cloudBox = document.getElementById("wc_cloud");
cloudBox.innerHTML = "";
```

3. Add the following `for` loop to add each word to the cloudBox, sized proportional to the number of times it appears in the document.

```
// Size each word based on its usage
for (let i = 0; i < unique.length; i++) {
   let word = document.createElement("span");
   word.textContent = unique[i][0];
   word.style.fontSize = unique[i][1]/maxCount + "em";
   cloudBox.appendChild(word);
}
```

Figure 7-43 describes the code in the file.

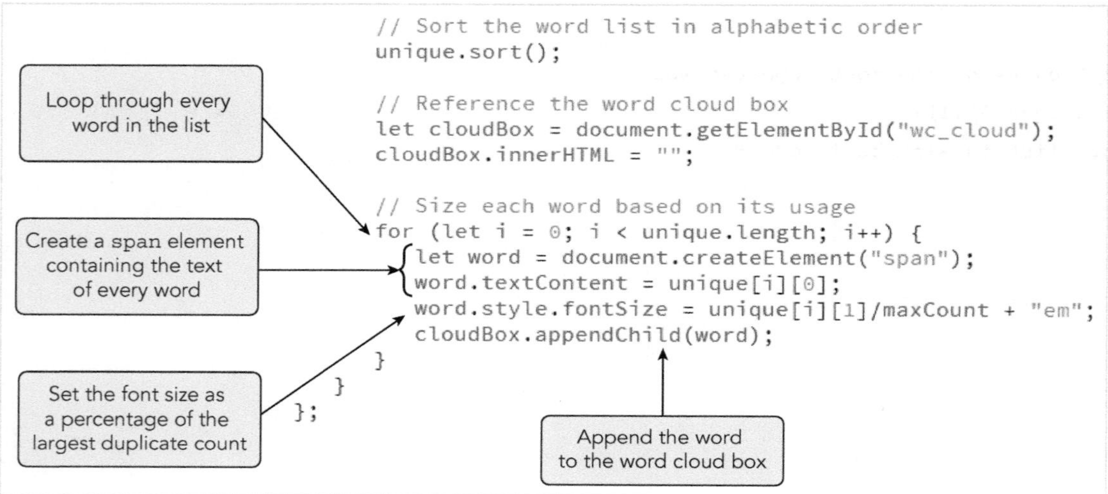

Figure 7-43 Sizing the words in the word cloud

4. Close the js07.js file, saving your changes.
5. Reload the **js07.html** file in your browser.
6. Click the **Choose File** button and load the **lincoln1.html** file. A word cloud is generated for the content of Lincoln's speech shown earlier in **Figure 7-1**.
7. Click the **Choose File** button again and load the **lincoln2.html** speech for Lincoln's second inaugural address given near the end of the Civil War. See **Figure 7-44**.

   You can compare the word cloud in Figure 7-44 with the one shown earlier in Figure 7-1, to see how the tone and emphasis of Lincoln's speech changed between the First and Second Inaugural addresses.
8. Use the Word Cloud app to open the **fdr3.html**, **jkf1.html**, and **reagan1.html** files for those presidential inaugural addresses. What do the word clouds tell you about the content and theme of those speeches?
9. Close the js07.html file.

You have completed your work on the Word Cloud app. The app can be used with almost any text file to generate a word cloud highlighting the most important themes and concepts. By modifying the style sheet, you can create a wide variety of word cloud designs and styles.

Load a Text File [Choose File] lincoln2.html

Abraham Lincoln's 2nd Inaugural Address

Fellow countrymen: at this second appearing to take the oath of the presidential office there is less occasion for an extended address than there was at the first. Then a statement somewhat in detail of a course to be pursued seemed fitting and proper. Now, at the expiration of four years during which public declarations have been constantly called forth on every point and phase of the great contest which still absorbs the attention and engrosses the energies of the nation little that is new could be presented. The progress of our arms, upon which all else chiefly depends is as well known to the public as to myself and it is I trust reasonably satisfactory and encouraging to all. With high hope for the future no prediction in regard to it is ventured.

On the occasion corresponding to this four years ago all thoughts were anxiously directed to an impending civil war. All dreaded it all sought to avert it. While the inaugural address was being delivered from this place devoted altogether to saving the Union without war insurgent agents were in the city seeking to destroy it without war seeking to dissolve the Union and divide effects by negotiation. Both parties deprecated war but one of them would make war rather than let the nation survive, and the other would accept war rather than let it perish. And the war came.

One eighth of the whole population were colored slaves not distributed generally over the union but localized in the southern part of it. These slaves constituted a peculiar and powerful interest. All knew that this interest was somehow the cause of the war. To strengthen perpetuate and extend this interest was the object for which the insurgents would rend the Union even by war while the government claimed no right to do more than to restrict the territorial enlargement of it. Neither party expected for the war the magnitude or the duration which it has already attained. Neither anticipated that the cause of the conflict might cease with or even before the conflict itself should cease. Each looked for an easier triumph and a result less fundamental and astounding. Both read the same Bible and pray to the same God and each invokes His aid against the other.

It may seem strange that any men should dare to ask a just God's assistance in

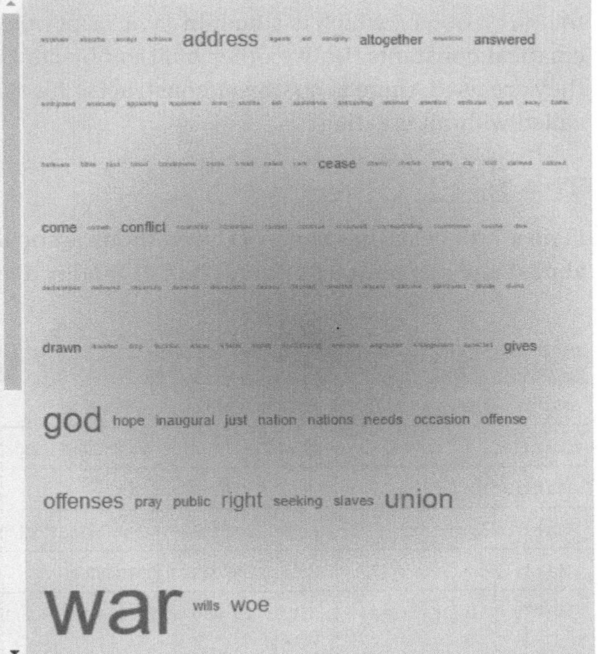

Figure 7-44 Word cloud for Lincoln's second inaugural address

Quick Check 3

1. Provide code to sort the `username` array based on the `byOrders()` compare function.
2. What will be the contents of the totals array after the following command?

```
let totals = [12, 55, 128, 25, 437];
totals.sort();
```

3. What will be the contents of the x array after the following command?

```
let x = ["a", "b", "c", "d", "e", "f", "g"];
let sliced = x.slice(2, 4);
```

4. What will be the contents of the x array after the following command?

```
let x = ["a", "b", "c", "d", "e", "f", "g"];
x.splice(2, 3, "h", "i", "j");
```

5. What will be the contents of the x array after the following command?

```
let x = ["a", "b", "c", "d", "e", "f", "g"];
x.pop();
```

Exploring the `Math` Object

In this final section you will explore two other important objects used in many JavaScript applications. The first is the `Math` object, which is a built-in JavaScript object used for performing mathematical operations and storing mathematical constants. Unlike other built-in objects like the `String` and `Array` objects, which must be created before they are used, there is no object constructor for `Math` objects. All properties and methods of the `Math` object can be called without creating it.

The `Math` Object

Figure 7-45 describes some of the methods associated with the `Math` object. Using these methods, you can construct almost any mathematical expression or modify a numeric value through rounding or truncating fractional digits.

METHOD	DESCRIPTION	EXAMPLE	RETURNS
`Math.abs(x)`	Returns the absolute value of *x*	`Math.abs(-5)`	5
`Math.ceil(x)`	Rounds *x* up to the next highest integer	`Math.ceil(3.58)`	4
`Math.exp(x)`	Raise *e* to the power of x	`Math.exp(2)`	e^2 (approximately 7.389)
`Math.floor(x)`	Rounds *x* down to the next lowest integer	`Math.floor(3.58)`	3
`Math.log(x)`	Returns the natural logarithm of *x*	`Math.log(2)`	0.693
`Math.max(values)`	Returns the largest of a comma-separated list of values	`Math.max(3, 5)`	5
`Math.min(x, y)`	Returns the smallest of a comma-separated list of values	`Math.min(3, 5)`	3
`Math.pow(x, y)`	Returns *x* raised to the power of *y*	`Math.pow(2,3)`	2^3 (or 8)
`Math.rand()`	Returns a random number between 0 and 1	`Math.rand()`	Random number between 0 and 1
`Math.round(x)`	Rounds *x* to the nearest integer	`Math.round(3.58)`	4
`Math.sqrt(x)`	Returns the square root of *x*	`Math.sqrt(2)`	approximately 1.414
`Math.trunc(x)`	Returns the integer portion of *x*, removing any fractional digits	`Math.trunc(13.85)`	13

Figure 7-45 Methods of the `Math` object

In addition to the methods shown in Figure 7-45, the `Math` object also supports trigonometric functions. For example, to calculate the sine, cosine, or tangent of a given angle `x`, you would enter the following commands:

```
Math.sin(x)
Math.cos(x)
Math.tan(x)
```

Note that trig calculations are performed for angles in radians, not degrees. To calculate the inverse of the trig functions, use the `Math.asin()`, `Math.acos()`, and `Math.atan()` methods.

`Math` Object Properties

Many mathematical expressions require the use of constants such as π or e. Rather than entering the numeric values of these constants directly into your code, you can reference the built-in constants stored as properties of the `Math` object. The general syntax for any built-in constant is:

```
Math.CONSTANT
```

where *`CONSTANT`* is the name of one of the mathematical constants described in **Figure 7-46**.

CONSTANT	DESCRIPTION
`Math.E`	The base of the natural logarithms (2.71828...)
`Math.LN10`	The natural logarithm of 10 (2.3026...)
`Math.LN2`	The natural logarithm of 2 (0.6931...)
`Math.LOG10E`	The base 10 logarithm of e (0.4343...)
`Math.LOG2E`	The base 2 logarithm of e (1.4427...)
`Math.PI`	The value of p (3.14159...)
`Math.SQRT1_2`	The value of 1 divided by the square root of 2 (0.7071...)
`Math.SQRT2`	The square root of 2 (1.4142...)

Figure 7-46 `Math` constants

You can use the `Math.PI` constant with the built-in trig functions to do calculations of sine, cosine, and tangent on angles measured in degrees. The following commands show the form for calculating trig values for an angle stored in the `deg` variable:

```
Math.sin(deg*Math.PI/180)
Math.cos(deg*Math.PI/180)
Math.tan(deg.Math.PI)
```

Applying a `Math` Method to an Array

In the Word Cloud app you took advantage of the fact that the `unique` array was sorted in descending order to quickly retrieve the maximum value of the duplicate counts (as it would have to be the first item in the array). Sorting an array is certainly one of way of determining the maximum or minimum array value, but if you don't want to sort the array, you can apply the `max()` or `min()` methods. However, those methods only apply to comma-separated lists of numeric values and not items within an array. There are two approaches to using them with arrays.

One approach is to use the `apply()` method, which applies a method from object to another object. The general syntax for the `max()` and `min()` methods is as follows:

```
Math.max.apply(null, array)
Math.min.apply(null, array)
```

where *`array`* is the array of item values. The following code uses this approach to calculate the maximum and minimum values from a sample array.

```
Math.max.apply(null, [3, 8, 2, 4, 6]) // returns 8
Math.min.apply(null, [3, 8, 2, 4, 6]) // returns 2
```

Another approach is to use the spread operator. The spread operator, written as an ellipsis of three dots, spreads out the items within an array into a comma-separated list of values. The following statements show how to apply the spread operator to calculate the maximum and minimum values from an array without sorting:

```
Math.max(...[3, 8, 2, 4, 6]) // returns 8
Math.min(...[3, 8, 2, 4, 6]) // returns 2
```

The spread operator can be used with any JavaScript method or function that requires a comma-separated list of values. For example, in the following code the spread operator is used to concatenate the contents of two arrays into a single array:

```
let x1 = [1, 2, 3];
let x2 = [4, 5];
let allX = [...x1, ...x2]
// returns [1, 2, 3, 4, 5]
```

The spread operator can also be used with text strings in which each individual character of a string is spread out into separate characters, as in the following example in which the text string "bcd" is spread into separate characters:

```
let chars = ["a", …"bcd ", "e"]
// returns ["a","b","c","d","e"]
```

Note that the spread operator is not supported in early editions of many browsers, so check the compatibility of your users' browsers before committing to its use.

Random Numbers and Random Sorting

Many applications, particularly games, involve working with random numbers. JavaScript generates random numbers using the `Math.random()` method, which returns a random number between 0 and 1. To return a random value from a different range, apply the following expression:

```
lowest + size*Math.random()
```

where *`lowest`* is the lower boundary of the range and *`size`* is the size of the range. For example, to generate a random number from 20 to 30, apply the following expression:

```
20 + 10*Math.random();
```

Many applications need to limit random numbers to integers. To do so, enclose the random value within the `Math.floor()` method, which rounds a number down to the next-lowest integer. The following statement generates random integers from 21 to 30:

```
Math.floor(21 + 10*Math.random());
```

Some applications, such those that simulate games of chance like poker, need to randomly sort the contents of an array. To randomly sort an array, create a compare function that randomly selects a positive, negative, or zero value. The following compare function employs a simple approach to this challenge:

```
function randOrder(){
  return 0.5 - Math.random();
}
```

When applied with the `sort()` method in the following code, the contents of the x array will be randomly sorted:

```
let x = ["a", "b", "c", "d", "e", "f", "g"];
x.sort(randOrder); // x sorted in random order
```

Note that this is the simplest compare function for generating random order, but it may not always be the best. In some simulations it might bias the random sorting to the earliest array items. The study of generating "true" random numbers is broad and complex with various tests to compare the randomness of different approaches. You can find other compare functions and algorithms on the web that perform a similar task but with fewer built-in biases.

Exploring the `Date` Object

Another important object used in scripts that involve calendars and scheduling is the `Date` object, which stores date and time values. `Date` objects are created using the following `new Date()` object constructor:

```
new Date("month day, year hrs:mins:secs")
```

where *month*, *day*, *year*, *hrs*, *mins*, and *secs* provide the `Date` object's date and time. For example, the following statement creates a `Date` object storing a date of May 23, 2024, at a time of 2:35:05 p.m.:

```
let orderDate = new Date("May 23, 2024 14:35:05");
```

Note that time values are based on a 24-hour clock so that a time of 2:35:05 p.m. would be entered as 14:35:05. Dates and times can also be specified as numeric values in the form:

```
new Date(year, month, day, hrs, mins, secs)
```

where each parameter is a numeric equivalent of a date or time. Month values are entered as integers ranging from 0 (January) up to 11 (December) and hour values once again use a 24-hour clock. Thus, the following expression also stores a date of May 23, 2024, at 2:35:05 p.m.:

```
let orderDate = new Date(2024, 4, 23, 14, 35, 5);
```

If no time value is specified, it is assumed that the time is 0 hours, 0 minutes, and 0 seconds of the specified day, in other words midnight of the specified day. If neither day nor time is specified as in the following expression, JavaScript will store the current date and time using information drawn from the system clock.

```
let today = new Date()
```

Extracting Information from Dates and Times

JavaScript dates are stored as numbers equal to the number of milliseconds between the specified date and January 1, 1970, at midnight. For example, the date May 23, 2024, at 2:235:05 p.m. is stored internally as 1,716,492,905,000 milliseconds. Because dates are stored as numbers, the interval between two dates is expressed as the difference in milliseconds. Because there are 1000 milliseconds in one second, 60 seconds in one minute, 60 minutes in one hour, and 24 hours in one day; to express a time difference in days; you must divide the time difference by 1000*60*60*24 as in the following statement:

```
let day1 = new Date("May 23, 2024");
let day2 = new Date("June 1, 2024");
let days = (day2 - day1)/(1000*60*60*24);   // returns 9
```

JavaScript also supports several methods for extracting date and time information from a `Date` object. **Figure 7-47** describes these methods.

DATE	METHOD	DESCRIPTION	RESULT
`let today = new Date("May 23, 2024 14:35:05");`	`today.getSeconds()`	Seconds (0 – 59)	5
	`today.getMinutes()`	Minutes (0 – 59)	35
	`today.getHours()`	Hours (0 – 23)	14
	`today.getDate()`	Day of the month (1 – 31)	23
	`today.getMonth()`	Month (0 – 11), where January = 0, February =1, etc.	4
	`today.getFullYear()`	4-digit year value	2024
	`today.getDay()`	Day of the week (0 – 6), where Sunday = 0, Monday = 1, etc.	4
	`today.toLocaleString()`	Text of the date and time using local conventions	"5/23/2024 2:35:05 PM"
	`today.toLocaleDateString()`	Text of the date using local conventions	"5/23/2024"
	`today.toLocateTimeString()`	Text of the time using local conventions	"2:35:05 PM"

Figure 7-47 Methods of the `Date` object

All these methods will extract time information based on local time as specified on the user's computer. In some applications, especially those involving international data exchanges, you will need to base your date and time values on Universal Time Coordinated (UTC) time or Greenwich Mean Time (GMT) corresponding to the current date and time in Greenwich, England. Each of the methods described in Figure 7-47 has an equivalent method using UTC time. For example, the following code retrieves the current clock hour based on the user's own computer and on Greenwich:

```
let today= new Date();
localHour = today.getHours ()   // returns the local hour
GMTHour = today.getUTCHours()   // returns the hour in Greenwich
```

In same fashion, the `getUTCDate()` returns the date in Greenwich, `getUTCDay()` returns the day of the month in Greenwich, and so forth.

Setting Date and Time Values

JavaScript also supports methods to change the date or time stored within a `Date` object. Changing these values is often used with apps that involve setting a future date or time based on a current value, such as setting the expiration date for an online membership or for orders placed within a shopping cart. **Figure 7-48** summarizes the methods supported by `Date` objects for setting date and time values.

DATE METHOD	DESCRIPTION
`date.setDate(value)`	Sets the day of the month, where *value* is an integer, ranging from 1 up to 31 (for some months)
`date.setFullYear(value)`	Sets the 4-digit year value where *value* is an integer
`date.setHours(value)`	Sets the 24-hour value, where *value* is an integer ranging from 0 to 23
`date.setMilliseconds(value)`	Sets the millisecond value where *value* is an integer between 0 and 999
`date.setMinutes(value)`	Sets the minutes value where *value* is an integer ranging from 0 to 59
`date.setMonth(value)`	Sets the month value where *value* is an integer ranging from 0 (January) to 11 (December)
`date.setSeconds(value)`	Sets the seconds value where *value* is an integer ranging from 0 to 59
`date.setTime(value)`	Sets the time value where *value* is an integer representing the number of milliseconds since midnight on January 1, 1970

Figure 7-48 Setting date and time values

For example, the following code uses the `setFullYear()` method to store a date that is one year after the current date (whatever that may be):

```
let date = new Date();
let year = date.getFullYear();   // stores the year
date.setFullYear(year + 1);      // increases year by 1
```

The different `set` methods overlap so that applying the method `setHours(48)` to a `date` object will increase the day value by two. Also note that you can use the `setHours()` method with hours, minutes, seconds, and milliseconds. The expression

```
setHours(5, 30, 15, 4)
```

will set a time value equal to 5 hours, 30 minutes, 15 seconds, and 4 milliseconds. This technique also applies to the `setMinutes()` and `setSeconds()` methods so you can always set a time value for any time unit as well as smaller intervals of that unit using a single method.

Best Practices | Writing Dates and Times for a Global Marketplace

Be careful with your dates and times or you run the risk of confusing your international readers. For example, the text string 10/1/2024 is interpreted as October 1, 2024 in some countries, and as January 10, 2024 in others. Some countries express times in a 12-hour (AM/PM) format while others use the 24-hour clock.

If you expect your dates and times to be read by an international audience, ensure that your text corresponds to local standards. One way to do this is to spell out the month portion of the date, expressing a date as "October 1, 2024". Other designers suggest that a date format with the year expressed first (for example, 2024-10-1) is less likely to be misinterpreted. With JavaScript, you can write dates and times in the user's own local format with the following method:

```
date.toLocaleString()
```

which returns the date and time formatted as a text string based on the local conventions. Thus, date values such as October 1, 2024, at 2:45 p.m. would be displayed on a computer in the United States as:

Tue, October 1, 2024 2:45:00 PM

While a computer in France would display the same date and time as:

mardi 1 octobre 2018 1714:45:00

To display only the date or only the time, use the `toLocaleDateString()` and `toLocaleTimeString()` methods.

Exploring Template Literals

As you continue to work with text strings and arrays, you might find it easier to store your text strings as template literals. A template literal encloses the text string within a backtick character (`), located on your keyboard's tilde key, rather using a single or double quote. Replacing single or double quotes with the backtick character has several advantages: (1) Template literals can be extended across multiple lines without using the + operator; (2) Characters like single and double quotes can be placed directly within the text string; and (3) whitespace characters including line breaks are preserved as part of the text string.

Adding Placeholders to Template Literals

Another advantage of a template literal is that variables and expressions can be inserted directly within the text string using the following placeholder:

```
${placeholder}
```

where *`placeholder`* is the name of a variable or expression that returns a value. For example, the following code inserts the text of the `group1` and `group2` variables directly into the text string:

```
let group1 = "none";
let group2 = "all";
`With malice towards ${group1} and charity for ${group2}`
// Returns "With malice towards none and charity for all"
```

If you place an expression within the placeholder, the JavaScript interpreter will evaluate the expression's value and insert it directly into the text string.

Tagging a Template Literal

Template literals do more than allow you to easily insert variables and expressions into a text string. They also break up the text string into an implicit array of literal substrings between the placeholders. In the example in the previous section, the template literal created an array containing two items: "With malice towards" and "and charity for". The placeholders themselves form a set of arguments called substitutions.

Template literals can be tagged with a function that accesses the values stored within the literal substrings and placeholder values, and modifies the text *before* it is stored in a variable. The general form of a function that tags a template literal is:

```
function {literals, ...substitutions}
  commands
    return value;
}
```

where `literals` is the array of substrings within the template literal and `substitutions` are the placeholder values. The value returned by the function is then passed to the variable. For example, the following `highlight` function goes through the array of literal substrings and placeholder values to return a text string in which each substitution is displayed in uppercase letters:

```
function highlight(literals, ...substitutions) {
   let result = "";
   for (let i = 0; i < substitutions.length; i++) {
      result += literals[i];
      result += substitutions[i].toUpperCase();
   }
      return result;
}
```

To tag the template literal with this function, place the function name directly before the template literal. The function is applied to the text string modifying it in place as follows:

```
highlight`With malice towards ${group1} and charity for ${group2}`;
// Returns "With malice towards NONE and charity for ALL"
```

You might find it disconcerting to apply a function to a text string without formally calling the function or referencing an array that only exists within the template literal. However, once mastered, tagged template literals can greatly increase the speed and efficiency of your work with text strings and arrays.

Quick Check 4

1. Provide a JavaScript expression to return the value of sin (45°).
2. Provide two ways of calculating the maximum value of the items from the `sales` array without sorting or using a `for` loop.
3. Provide code to store the current date and time in the `trialStart` variable.
4. Provide code to store a date and time in the `expireDate` variable that is one month after the `trialStart` variable.
5. Provide code to store the text string "Four score and 7 years ago" as a template literal in a variable named `preamble`, tagging the template literal with the `revise()` function.

Summary

- The File API is used to retrieve the contents of selected files on the local computer or network.
- File reader objects are created using the new `FileReader()` object constructor. Use the `readAsText()` method to read files containing text content.
- To determine the placement of a character within a text string, use the `indexOf()` or `lastIndexOf()` methods.
- You can change the case of a text string using the `toLowerCase()` and `toUpperCase()` methods of the `String` object.
- To extract substrings from a text string, use the `slice()`, `substring()`, or `substr()` methods.
- To break a text string into an array of separate substrings, use the `split()` method of the `String` object.
- Regular expressions are written in a terse language to provide the description of a text string character pattern. The general form of a regular expression is */pattern/*.
- A flag can be added to regular expressions to indicate whether matching should be done for the entire text string and whether matching should be case sensitive.
- In a regular expression, word characters indicated the by `\w` symbol match all alphabetical characters, digits, and the underscore (`_`) character. Words are those substrings consisting only of word characters. Word boundaries are indicated by the `\b` symbol.
- Select groups of characters in a regular expression can be enclosed within a character class using the square bracket symbols `[` and `]`.
- Repetition in a regular expression is indicating by a numeric value enclosed within the brace symbols { and }.
- To create a regular expression object, use the new `RegExp()` object constructor.
- To test whether a regular expression matches a sample text string, use the `test()` method. To determine where within the sample text string a match occurs, use the `search()` method. To replace a substring with a new substring, use the `replace()` method.
- To sort an array in alphabetical order, apply the `sort()` method. To create a custom sort, include a compare function within the `sort() method` in the form `sort(compare)` where `compare` is the name of the function. The compare function should return either a positive, negative, or zero value to determine the sorting order.
- To create subarrays from an array, use the `slice()` or `splice()` methods. To add or remove items from the end of an array use the `push()` and `pop()` methods. To insert or remove items from the start of an array use the `shift()` and `unshift()` methods.
- The `Math` object can be used to store mathematical functions and constants.
- To generate a random number between 0 and 1, use the `Math.rand()` method.
- Functions that require comma-separated values can be applied to an array of values by using the `apply()` method or the spread operator (entered as an ellipsis ...).
- Dates can be created and stored using the `new Date()` object constructor. To store the current date and time, apply the command `new Date()`.
- Text strings can be stored in template literals with variables or expressions entered directly into the text string. Template literals can be tagged with the functions that modify the text string before it is saved to a variable.

Key Terms

anchor
backtracking
Binary Large Object (Blob)
Blob
character class
compare function
`Date` object
escape sequence
File API
`file` object
File Reader API
`files` collection
first-in-first-out (FIFO)
flag
immutable
last-in-first-out (LIFO)
lexicographical order
`Math` object
MIME type
queue
regular expression literal
spread operator
stack
stop word
subarray
substring
whitespace character
word
word character
word cloud

Review Questions

1. To allows users to select one or more text files to be read into web form, which attribute do you add to the `input` element?
   a. `type="text"`
   b. `type="files"`
   c. `type="file"`
   d. `type="reader"`
2. What event is triggered when the File Reader object completes reading a file with no errors?
   a. load
   b. write
   c. loadend
   d. submit
3. What value is returned by the following expression?
   ```
   "In the course of events".indexOf("course")
   ```
   a. 5
   b. 6
   c. 7
   d. 8
4. What is the value of the `introTxt` variable after the following commands?
   ```
   let introTxt = "Four Score and Seven";
   introText.toLowerCase();
   ```
   a. "Four Score and Seven"
   b. "four Score and seven"
   c. "FOUR SCORE AND SEVEN"
   d. "fourscoreandseven"
5. What substring is generated by applying the following command?
   ```
   "When in the course of events".
   slice(5, 11);
   ```
   a. "in the course"
   b. "the course"
   c. " in the "
   d. "in the"
6. What is the regular expression that matches a text string consisting of 6 digits and no other characters?
   a. `/\d{6}/`
   b. `/^\d{6}$/`
   c. `/\d{6}/g`
   d. `/^d(6)$/`
7. To match any non-word character, which symbol should be used in a regular expression?
   a. `\w`
   b. `\b`
   c. `\W`
   d. `\B`
8. Provide the regular expression symbols to match at least 5 consecutive digits in a text string.
   a. `\d{5, }`
   b. `\d{5}`
   c. `\d{5+}`
   d. `\d{5*}`

9. Provide the regular expression to match any occurrence of "Tim", "Timothy", or "Timmy" in a text string, but nothing else.
   a. `/Tim*/g`
   b. `/Tim+/g`
   c. `/Tim?/g`
   d. `/Tim|Timothy|Timmy/g`

10. Which of the following creates a variable named `userID`, for regular expression for the pattern `/\d{6}/g`?
    a. `let userID = regex("/\d{6}/g");`
    b. `let userID = new reg(/\d{6}/g);`
    c. `let userID = new RegExp(/\d{6}/g);`
    d. `let userID = new RegExp("/\d{6}/", "g");`

11. What is the value of the x array after the following command?

```
let x = [8, 45, 1, 32, 12, 5];
x.sort();
```

    a. `[1, 12, 32, 45, 5, 8]`
    b. `[1, 5, 8, 12, 32, 45]`
    c. `[12, 32, 45, 1, 5, 8]`
    d. `[45, 32, 12, 8, 5, 1]`

12. Which of the following expressions in a compare function could be used to sort an array in descending order?
    a. `a - b`
    b. `b - a`
    c. `-1`
    d. `+1`

13. What is the value of the x array after the following code?

```
let x = [1, 3, 5, 7, 9];
x.splice(2, 3, 9, 11, 12);
```

    a. `[2, 4, 9, 11, 12]`
    b. `[1, 3, 5]`
    c. `[1, 3, 9, 11, 12]`
    d. `[9, 11, 12, 5, 7, 9]`

14. Which method removes the last item in an array?
    a. `pop()`
    b. `push()`
    c. `shift()`
    d. `unshift()`

15. To round the value of x up to the next highest integer, which expression should be entered?
    a. `round(x)`
    b. `Math.round(x)`
    c. `Math.ceil(x)`
    d. `floor(x)`

16. What feature does the File Reader API provide to the programmer?

17. What is the difference between the `indexOf()` and `lastIndex()` methods?

18. Describe how to insert a variable or expression directly into a text string using a template literal.

19. When are compare functions necessary for sorting arrays?

20. Provide the code to store the current date and time in a variable named `today`.

Hands-On Projects

Hands-On Project 7-1

In this project, you will use regular expressions to verify that a password passes validation before it is accepted. In this web form, all proposed passwords must (1) be at least eight characters long, (2) have at least one uppercase letter, (3) have at least one digit, and (4) have at least one of the following symbols !, @, #, or $. If the password fails validation, a message indicating the reason for failure should appear in the web form. A preview of the completed project is shown in **Figure 7-49**.

Do the following:

1. Use your code editor to open the **project07-01_txt.html** and **project07-01_txt.js** files from the js07 ► project01 folder. Enter your name and the date in the comment section of each file and save them as **project07-01.html** and **project07-01.js**, respectively.

Hands-on Project 7-1

Create your Account

Enter your Account Information

Username john.smith@example.com

Password ••••••••

Your password must include one of the following: !$#%.

Save

Figure 7-49 Completed Project 7-1

2. Go to the **project07-01.html** file in your code editor and link the page to the project07-01.js file, deferring the script from loading until after the page loads. Save your changes to the file.
3. Go to the **project07-01.js** file in your code editor. Within the event listener for the `submit` event add the commands specified in steps 4 through 6.
4. Add the **`e.preventDefault()`** command to prevent the browser from responding to the `submit` event.
5. Create the following variables containing regular expressions:
   - **a.** Create the **`regex1`** variable containing a regular expression literal with a character class that matches any uppercase letter A through Z.
   - **b.** Create the **`regex2`** variable containing a regular expression literal that matches any single digit.
   - **c.** Create the **`regex3`** variable containing a regular expression with a character class containing the symbols !$#%. (Hint: you will have to use \$ for the $ symbol.)
6. Create an `if else` statement that with the following conditions and outcomes:
   - **a.** If the length of `pwd` is less than 8, set the text content of the `feedback` object to "Your password must be at least 8 characters."
   - **b.** Else if the `test()` method with the `regex1` regular expression applied to the `pwd` variable returns a false value, set the text content of the `feedback` object to "Your password must include an uppercase letter."
   - **c.** Else if the `test()` method with the `regex2` regular expression applied to `pwd` returns `false`, set the text of `feedback` to "Your password must include a number."
   - **d.** Else if the `test()` method with the `regex3` regular expression applied to `pwd` returns false, set the text of `feedback` to "Your password must include one of the following: !$#%".
   - **e.** Otherwise, apply the `submit()` method to the `signupForm` object to submit the form for processing.
7. Save your changes to the file and then load **project07-01.html** in your web browser. Verify that the form cannot be submitted unless a password is provided that has at least eight characters with at least one uppercase letter, one digit, and one of the following characters !$#%. Also verify that if an invalid password is provided, a text message appears on the web form indicating the reason for failure.

Hands-On Project 7-2

In this project you will generate a poker hand containing five cards randomly selected from a deck of cards. The names of the cards are stored in a text string that will have to be converted into an array. The array will be randomly sorted to "shuffle" the deck. Each time the user clicks a Deal button, the last five cards of the array will be removed, reducing the size of the deck size. When the size of the deck drops to zero, a new randomly sorted deck will be generated. A preview of the completed project with a randomly generated hand is shown in **Figure 7-50**.

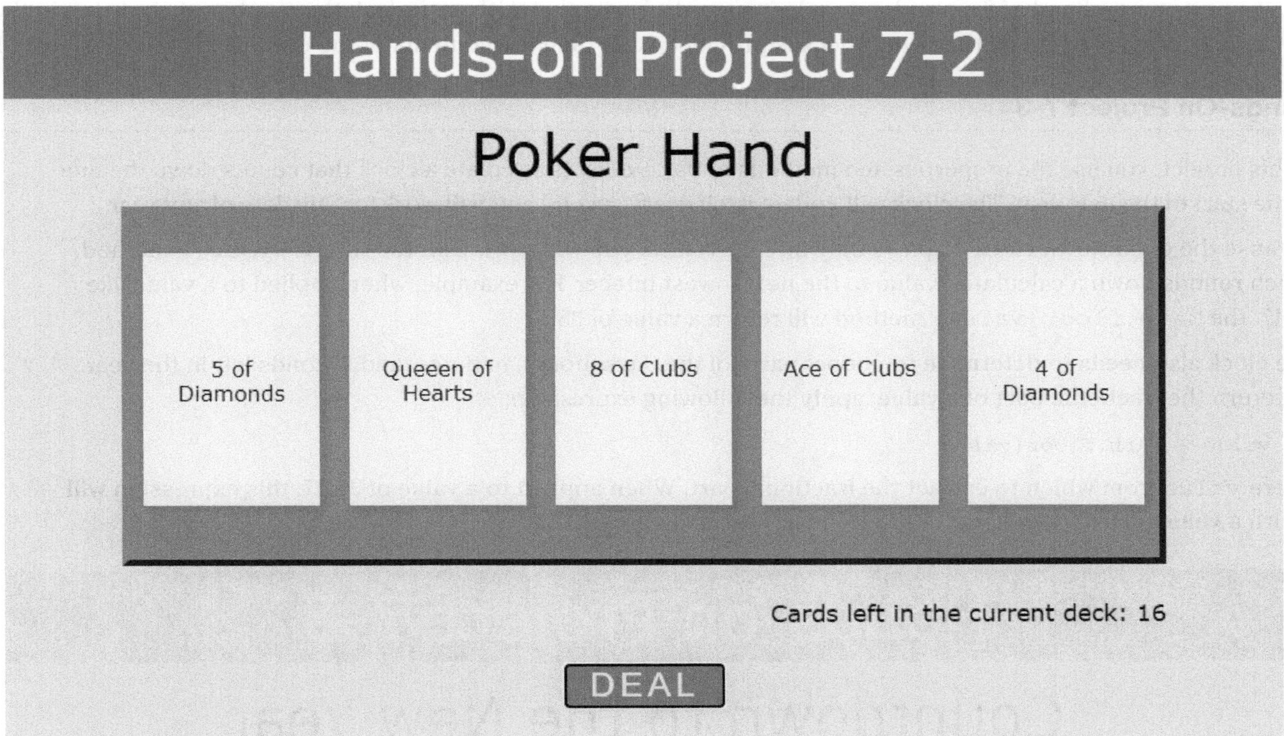

Figure 7-50 Completed Project 7-2

Do the following:

1. Use your code editor to open the **project07-02_txt.html** and **project07-02_txt.js** files from the js07 ▶ project02 folder. Enter your name and the date in the comment section of each file and save them as **project07-02.html** and **project07-02.js**, respectively.
2. Go to the **project07-02.html** file in your code editor and link the page to the project07-02.js file, deferring the script from loading until after the page loads. Save your changes to the file.
3. Go to the **project07-02.js** file in your code editor. Within the `onclick` event hander, add the commands described in Steps 4 through 5.
4. Create a function named **`newDeck()`**. The purpose of this function is to generate a new shuffled array of poker cards. Add the following commands to the function:
   a. Split the contents of the `deckStr` variable at each occurrence of the "," character. Store the substrings generated by the `split()` method in the deck array.
   b. Sort the contents of the deck array using the `shuffle()` function as the compare function.
   c. Create the `shuffle()` function with 2 parameters named `a` and `b`. Return the value of 0.5 minus a randomly-generated number created with the `Math.random()` method.

5. Below the `newDeck()` function add a `for` loop that iterates through the contents of the `cards` node list. For each item in the node list do the following:
   a. If the length of the deck array is 0, call the `newDeck()` function.
   b. Use the `pop()` method to remove the last item from the `deck` array and store the popped item as the text content of the current item in the `cards` node list.
   c. Change the value of the text content of the `cardsLeft` object to the value of the length of the `deck` array.
6. Save your changes to the file and then load **project07-02.html** in your web browser. Click the Deal button to generate a new hand of five randomly selected cards. Verify that with each deal, the number of cards left in the deck decreases by 5 and that a new deck is provided each time the contents of the current deck are exhausted.

Hands-On Project 7-3

In this project, you use the properties and methods of `Date` objects to create a clock that counts down the time to the start of the new year. The clock will update itself every second and will work for any date of any year.

Because the countdown clock displays only integer values, you will work with the `Math.floor()` method, which rounds down a calculated value to the next lowest integer. For example, when applied to a value like 38.47, the `Math.floor(value)` method will return a value of 38.

The clock also needs to determine fractional parts of the days, hours, minutes, and seconds left in the year. To return the fractional part of a value, apply the following expression:

```
value - Math.floor(value)
```

where *`value`* from which to extract the fractional part. When applied to a value of 38.47, this expression will return a value of 0.47. A preview of the clock is shown in **Figure 7-51**.

Figure 7-51 Completed Project 7-3

Do the following:

1. Use your code editor to open the **project07-03_txt.html** and **project07-03_txt.js** files from the js07 ▶ project03 folder. Enter your name and the date in the comment section of each file and save them as **project07-03.html** and **project07-03.js**, respectively.

2. Go to the **project07-03.html** file in your code editor and link the page to the project07-03.js file, deferring the script from loading until after the page loads. Save your changes to the file.
3. Return to the **project07-03.js** file in your code editor and add a command that uses the `setInterval()` method to run the `countdown()` function every 1000 milliseconds.
4. Create the **`countdown()`** function and within the function add the commands specified in steps 5 through 11.
5. Declare the **`now`** variable and use the `new Date()` object constructor to store within it the current date and time.
6. Apply the `toLocaleString()` method to the now variable to display the text of the current date and time in the `currentTime` object.
7. Declare the **`newYear`** variable and using the `new Date()` object constructor store the date "January 1, 2024".
8. Use the `getFullYear()` to retrieve the 4-digit year value from the now variable, increase that value by 1 and store the result in the **`nextYear`** variable.
9. Use the `setFullYear()` method to change the year value of `newYear` to the value of the `nextYear` variable.
10. Perform the following calculations to determine the days, hours, minutes, and seconds left until the New Year:
    a. Calculate the days left by calculating the difference between `newYear` and `now` and dividing that difference by 1000*60*60*24. Store the result in the **`daysLeft`** variable.
    b. Multiply the fractional part of the `daysLeft` variable by 24 and store the result in the **`hrsLeft`** variable.
    c. Multiply the fractional part of the **`hrsLeft`** variable by 60 and store the result in the **`minsLeft`** variable.
    d. Mulitply the fractional part of the **`minsLeft`** variable by 60 and store the result in the **`secsLeft`** variable.
11. Display the following results in the web page clock:
    a. Apply the `Math.floor()` method to the `daysLeft` variable and write the result to the text content of the `daysLeftBox` object.
    b. Repeat the previous step for the `hrsLeft`, `minsLeft`, and `secsLeft` variables, storing their results in the `hrsLeftBox`, `minsLeftBox`, and `secsLeftBox` objects.
12. Save your changes to the file and open **project07-03.html** in your web browser. Verify that the web page shows the current date and time and updates the time left in the current year every second.

Hands-On Project 7-4

In this project you will explore how to apply array methods to add, remove, and search for entries within the array of customer names. A web page has been created for you containing web form buttons to enable the different array features. Your task is to create event handlers for those buttons. A preview of the completed page is shown in **Figure 7-52**.

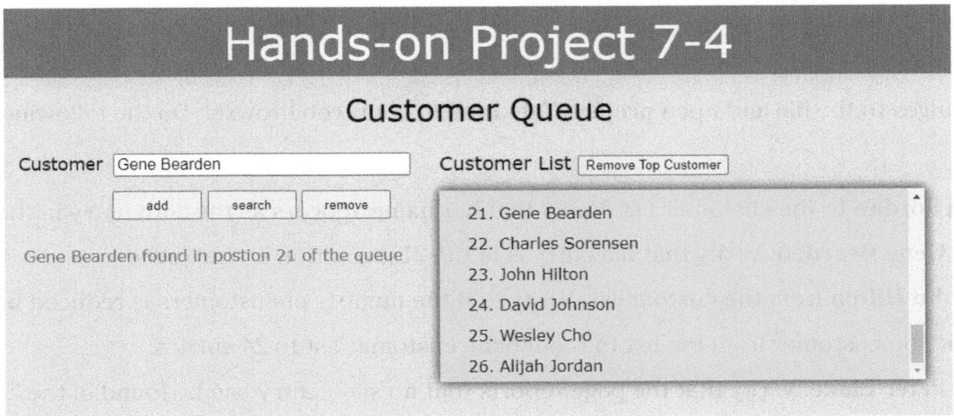

Figure 7-52 Completed Project 7-4

Do the following:

1. Use your code editor to open the **project07-04_txt.html** and **project07-04_txt.js** files from the js07 ▶ project04 folder. Enter your name and the date in the comment section of each file and save them as **project07-04.html** and **project07-04.js**, respectively.
2. Go to the **project07-04.html** file in your code editor and link the page to the project07-04.js file, deferring the script from loading until after the page loads. Take some time to study the content and structure of the document. There are four buttons you will need to program for adding, searching for, and removing customer names and another button for removing the top customer from the queue. Save your changes to the file.
3. Return to the **project07-04.js** file in your code editor. Add an `onclick` event handler for the `addButton` object. Within the event handler do the following:
   a. Use the `push()` method to add the value of the `customerName` object to the end of the `customers` array.
   b. Run the `generateCustomerList()` function to update the contents of the ordered list that appears on the web page.
   c. Change the text of the `status` paragraph to "*customer* added to the end of the queue" where *customer* is the value of the `customerName` object.
4. Add an `onclick` event handler for the `searchButton` object. Within the event handler do the following:
   a. Use the `indexOf()` method to locate the index of the array item whose value equals the value of the `customerName` object. Add 1 to the index value and store the result in the **place** variable.
   b. If `place` is equal to 0, change the text of the `status` paragraph to "customer is not found in the queue" where *customer* is the value of the `customerName` object; otherwise change the text of the `status` paragraph to "*customer* found in position *place* of the queue" where *place* is the value of the `place` variable.
5. Add an `onclick` event handler for the `removeButton` object. Within the event handler do the following:
   a. Use the `indexOf()` method to locate the index of the array item whose value equals the value of the `customerName` object. Store the index in a variable named **index**.
   b. If `index` is not equal to –1 then (i) use the `splice()` method to remove one item from the customers array whose index equal the value of the index variable, (ii) change the text of the `status` paragraph to "customer removed from the queue", and (iii) call the `generateCustomerList()` function to recreate the ordered list of customer names. Otherwise, change the text of the `status` paragraph to "*customer* is not found in the queue".
6. Add an `onclick` event handler for the `topButton` object. Within the event handler do the following:
   a. Apply the `shift()` method to remove the first item from the `customers` array, storing the value returned by the `shift()` method in the `topCustomer` variable.
   b. Change the text of the `status` paragraph to "*Top customer* from the queue" where *Top Customer* is the value of the `topCustomer` variable.
   c. Call the `generateCustomerList()` function.
7. Save your changes to the file and open **project07-04.html** in your web browser. Do the following tasks to test your code:
   a. Add **Alijah Jordan** to the customer list. Verify that her name appears as the 26th entry in the list.
   b. Search for **Gene Bearden**. Verify that his entry is in the 21st position in the queue.
   c. Remove **John Hilton** from the custom list. Verify that the number of customers is reduced back to 25.
   d. Remove the top customer from the list to reduce the customer list to 24 entries.
   e. Search for **Peter Blake**. Verify that the page reports that no such entry can be found in the customer list.

Hands-On Project 7-5

Debugging Challenge

Stylometry is the statistical analysis of the variation in literary style between one author and another. By examining the types of words authors use and their frequency, statisticians can attribute authorship to disputed texts. In this project you will work with a JavaScript app that compares two authors based on the frequencies of words of different lengths. A preview of the completed page is shown in **Figure 7-53**, comparing the word length frequency of Ernest Hemmingway and H.P. Lovecraft based on excerpts from two of their short stories.

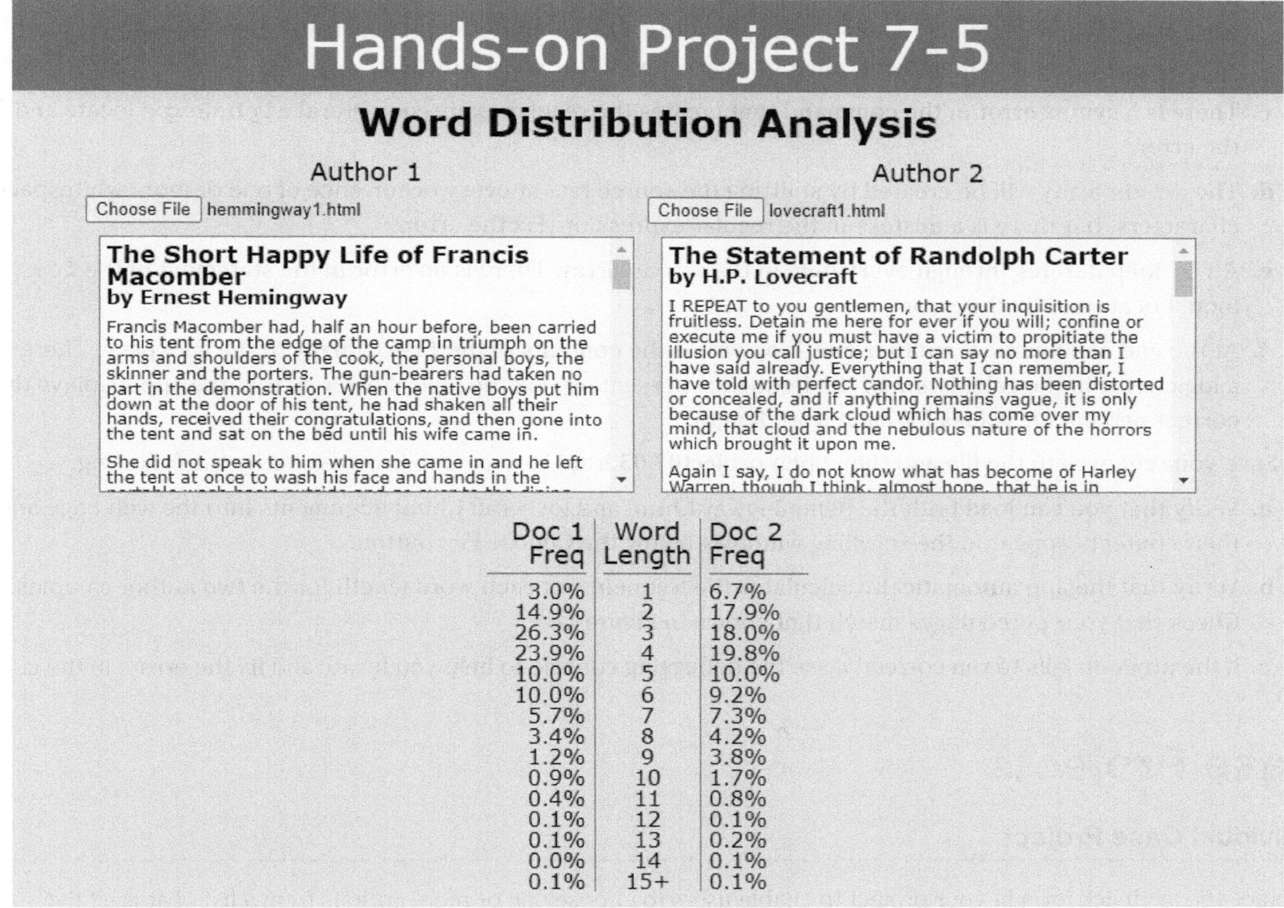

Figure 7-53 Completed Project 7-5

This app has already been written for you, but there are several errors scattered throughout the program that need to be fixed. Study the code and fix the app.

Do the following:

1. Use your code editor to open the **project07-05_txt.html** and **project07-05_txt.js** files from the js07 ► project05 folder. Enter your name and the date in the comment section of each file and save them as **project07-05.html** and **project07-05.js**, respectively.
2. Go to the **project06-05.html** file in your code editor and in the head section add a script element to load the project07-05.js file, deferring it until the entire page is loaded. Take some time to study the contents of the file to become familiar with its structure. Save your changes to the file.

3. Return to the **project07-05.js** file in your code editor. Comments have been added to help you interpret the code in the file.
4. The code starts with two anonymous functions that run in response to button1 and button2 being clicked. There is an error in both anonymous functions. Locate and fix the error.
5. The main part of the program is done in the `generateWordFreq()` function. There are several errors in this function that need to be fixed.
   a. The code initially reads the content of the `inputFile` document but there are two syntax errors that need to be fixed before the files can be read.
   b. In the command that stores the text of the output document in the `sourceText` variable there is a logical error that will cause the word lengths to appear longer than they should be. Fix the error in the command that causes the app to include extraneous characters in the source text.
   c. There is a syntax error in the command that creates the regular expression literal `alphaRegx`, locate and fix the error.
   d. The `words` array will be created by splitting the source text at every occurrence of one or more whitespace characters, but there is a mistake in the regular expression. Fix the error.
   e. A `for` loop iterates through every item in the `words` array. There is an error in the statement of the `for` loop. Locate and fix the error.
   f. At the end of a function, another `for` loop writes the contents of the `freqs` array to the web page. There is a logic error in the calculation of the frequency percentage. Fix the logical error so that the app displays the correct percentage values for each word length.
6. Save your changes to the file and then open **project07-05.html** in your web browser. Verify the following:
   a. Verify that you can load both the hemmingway1.html and lovecraft1.html documents into the web page and their contents appear in the scrolling windows below the Choose File button.
   b. Verify that the app automatically calculates the frequency of each word length for the two author samples. Check that your percentages match that shown in Figure 7-53.
   c. If the program fails to run correctly, use the debugging console to help you locate and fix the errors in the code.

Case Projects

Individual Case Project

Enhance the feedback form in your project to enable users to choose one or more options from a list of at least five options. Include code that adds user selections to either an array or an object and ensure that if a user deselects one of the options, it is removed from the array or object. Add code to convert the array or object to a string.

Team Case Project

Have each group member demonstrate the enhancements they created for the Individual Case Project to the group, including reviewing the code. From the different group members' implementations, decide on what information would be most useful to collect on the group feedback form and whether to store it in an array or an object. Then write the code together to add these features to the group site, ensuring that the code removes an option from the array or object if a user deselects it. Add code to convert the array or object to a string.

CHAPTER 8

Creating Customized Objects, Properties, and Methods

When you complete this chapter, you will be able to:

- Describe the fundamentals of object-oriented programming
- Create an object literal
- Define a method for a customized object
- Apply a method to an object class using a prototype
- Create and apply a closure
- Work with public, private, and privileged methods
- Create a prototype chain to combine objects
- Work with associative arrays to store data in JSON format

In this chapter, you will work with self-contained pieces of code and data called objects. You already have some experience with object-oriented programming with JavaScript built-in objects such as the `String`, `Date`, and `Array` objects. In this chapter you will learn how to create customized objects with their own collections of properties and methods that can be used and reused in your apps.

Understanding Object-Oriented Programing

The JavaScript code you have written so far has been tailored for specific situations. Most of your variables, statements, and functions were specific to one document and one application. That approach limits your code's usefulness. For example, code that calculates the total cost of sales for one brand of products is similar to code used for other products. Rather than recreating the same code structure, it would be more efficient to have structures that can be reused and applied to a variety of applications. That kind of reusability is the goal of object-oriented programming.

Reusing Software Objects

Object-oriented programming (OOP) refers to the creation of reusable software objects that can be easily incorporated into multiple programs. Objects involve programming code and data that can be treated as an individual unit and reused in a wide variety of contexts. An object can be as compact as a single input button or as wide-ranging as an entire program such as a database application. Object-oriented programming, therefore, would consist in describing how these different objects interact with each other in presenting a finished application.

In your JavaScript programs, you deal with three kinds of objects. Native objects, such as the `Date` or `Array` objects, are objects that are part of the JavaScript language. Host objects are objects provided by the browser for use in interacting with the web document and browser, such as the `Window`, `Document`, or `Form` objects. Custom objects, also known as user-defined objects, are objects created by the user for specific programming tasks. For example, a developer might create a "chart object" that provides properties and methods associated with graphical charts. A developer could then include the chart object as another object within an application. **Figure 8-1** illustrates the basic idea behind object-oriented programing in which objects from different sources come together to create a finished product.

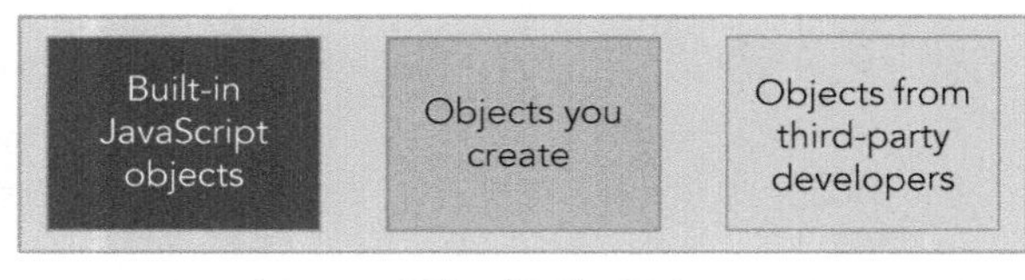

Figure 8-1 Combining objects within an application

Understanding Encapsulation

Objects use a process called encapsulation by which all code (primarily properties and methods) and data needed for the object are completely contained within the object itself. The code and data are hidden so they cannot be read or modified by other programs. The inner workings of the object are instead accessed through an interface that consists of the programmatic elements accessible to other programs and scripts. By hiding the object's inner mechanisms, encapsulation reduces complexity, allowing programmers to concentrate on the task of integrating the object into their own programs. Encapsulation also prevents other programmers from accidentally introducing programming errors into the object.

Encapsulated objects are like the workings of a handheld calculator. You interact with the calculator by pressing digits and calculation buttons (the "properties and methods" of the calculator) but you don't need to know how the calculator works to achieve its results. JavaScript's built-in `Document` object is another example of encapsulation. You work with the `Document` object through its interface, consisting of methods like the `getElementById()` method or properties like the `title` property; but you do not work directly with the `Document` object's inner code.

In this chapter you will create the following four objects for an online card game:

- A card object containing properties and methods associated with a single card
- A hand object containing a collection of card objects held by a player
- A deck object containing the complete collection of card objects used in a game
- A game object containing properties and methods associated with game play

You will work with two JavaScript source files: one that creates the objects you need and another that applies those objects to a specific application; in this case, an online version of the Draw Poker game. Some of the preparatory work in developing your application has been done for you. Open the files that will be used by this application now.

To open the files for Draw Poker application:

1. Go to the js08 ▶ chapter folder of your data files.
2. Use your code editor to open the **js08a_txt.html**, **js06a_txt.js**, and **objects_txt.js** files. Enter your name and the date in the comment section of each file and then save them as **js08.html**, **js08.js**, and **objects.js**, respectively.
3. Return to the **js08a.html** file in your code editor. Within the head section, add the following code to run the js08.js and objects.js script files, deferring the scripts until the entire page has loaded.

```
<script src="objects.js" defer></script>
<script src="js08.js" defer></script>
```

4. Examine the contents of the file, noting the structure, ids, and class names of the elements used to create the Draw Poker web page.
5. Close the file, saving your changes.
6. Open the **js08.html** file in your web browser. **Figure 8-2** shows the current layout and contents of the page.

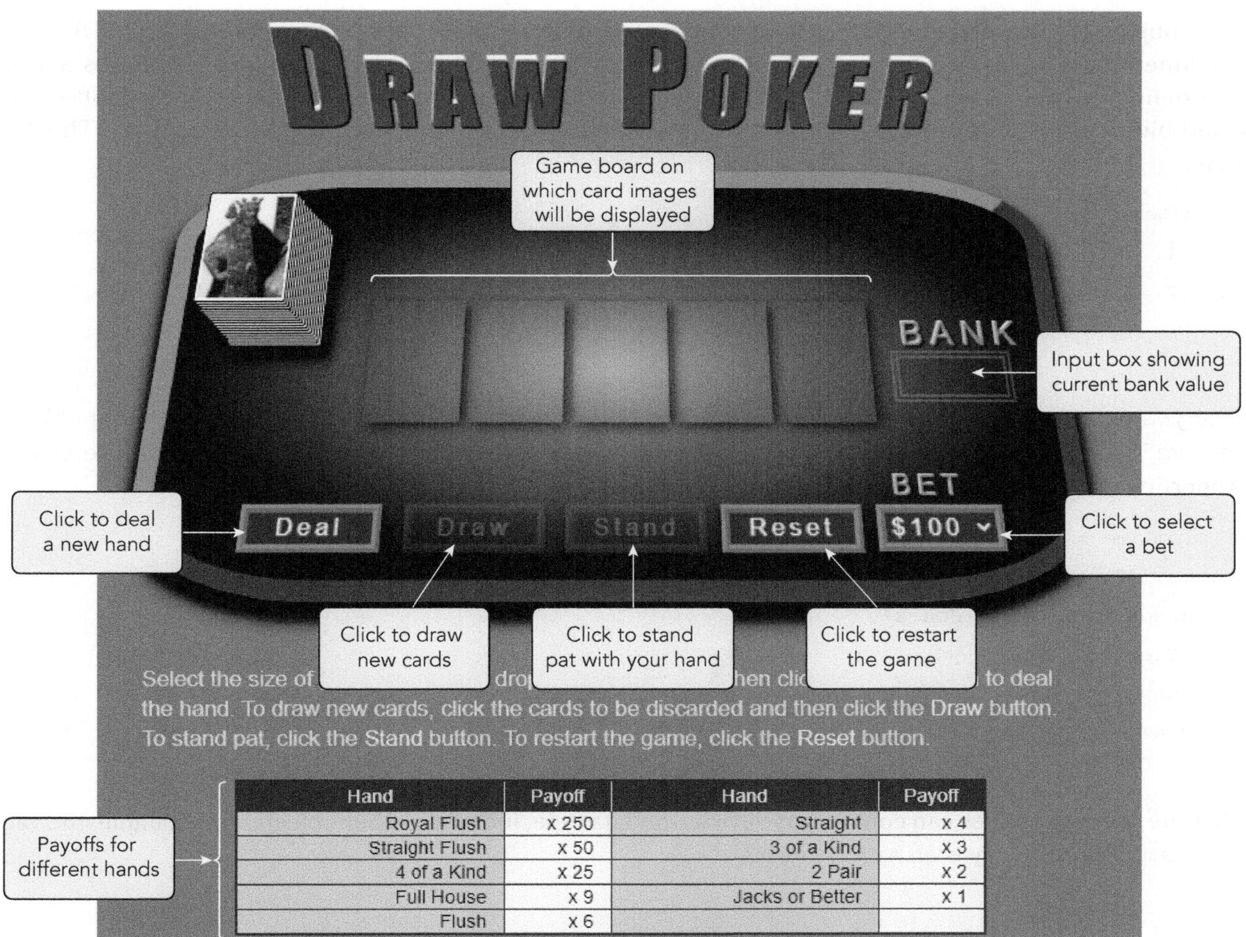

Hand	Payoff	Hand	Payoff
Royal Flush	x 250	Straight	x 4
Straight Flush	x 50	3 of a Kind	x 3
4 of a Kind	x 25	2 Pair	x 2
Full House	x 9	Jacks or Better	x 1
Flush	x 6		

Figure 8-2 Starting Draw Poker page

The page displays the poker table on which users will play a game of draw poker. Note that the Draw and Stand buttons are disabled. They will not be enabled until a game has started. The game play has the following conditions:

- The player will start with $500 (play money) in the bank.
- Before each hand is dealt, the player chooses an amount to bet from the selection list. The bank is reduced by the amount bet.
- The player clicks the Deal button and is dealt five cards from a randomly shuffled poker deck.
- The player can replace any or all cards in the hand with new cards by clicking the Draw button.
- After the draw, the hand is evaluated. To win back the bet, the hand needs to contain at least a pair of jacks or better. Higher-valued hands result in higher payoffs.
- After the player's winnings (if any) are added to the bank, a new hand is dealt. The game continues until the bank is empty or the player quits.

The initial code for the Deal, Draw, and Stand buttons has already been created for the page. What has not been created is code that defines objects used by the game and how those objects interact with the game play. You will start by creating an object for the Draw Poker game itself.

Creating an Object Literal

A custom object can be defined either as an instance of an object class or as an object literal. An object literal is a standalone object used once for a single purpose. Within the object literal you can add properties and methods that define the object and its behavior. To create an object literal, provide the object's name followed by a command block that stores object properties within a comma-separated list of `name:value` pairs. The general syntax is:

```
let objName = {
  name1: value1,
  name2: value2,
...
};
```

where *objName* is the name of the object, *name1*, *name2*, and so on are properties associated with that object, and *value1*, *value2*, etc. are the property values. The following code creates an object named `cardGame` containing five properties named `title`, `createdBy`, `yearCreated`, `lastRevised`, and `programmers`.

```
let cardGame = {
  title: "Draw Poker",
  createdBy: "Ronnell Jones",
  yearCreated: 2024,
  lastRevised: null,
  programmers: ["Tom Devlan", "Chanda Bhasin"]
};
```

Note that the property values can contain any JavaScript data type, including other objects. For example, the value of the `programmers` property is an `Array` object.

Note | A property can be assigned the `null` value if no initial value has been set.

Objects can be nested within one another. In the following code the `creators` property is also an object literal nested within the `cardGame` object:

```
let cardGame = {
   title: "Draw Poker",
   creators: {
      supervisor: "Ronnell Jones",
      programmers: ["Tom Devlan", "Chanda Bhasin"]
   }
   yearCreated: 2024,
   lastRevised: null
};
```

For the Draw Poker app, the `pokerGame` object will contain two properties: `currentBank` storing the amount currently in the player's bank, and `currentBet` storing the size of the player's wager. You will set the initial values of both properties to `null`. Place the code for this object in the objects.js file so that it can be available to other apps involving poker games.

To create the `pokerGame` object:

1. Return to the **objects.js** file in your code editor.
2. Directly below the initial comment section, insert the following code to create the `pokerGame` object as described in **Figure 8-3**:

```
/* Object defining the poker game */
let pokerGame = {
   currentBank: null,
   currentBet: null
};
```

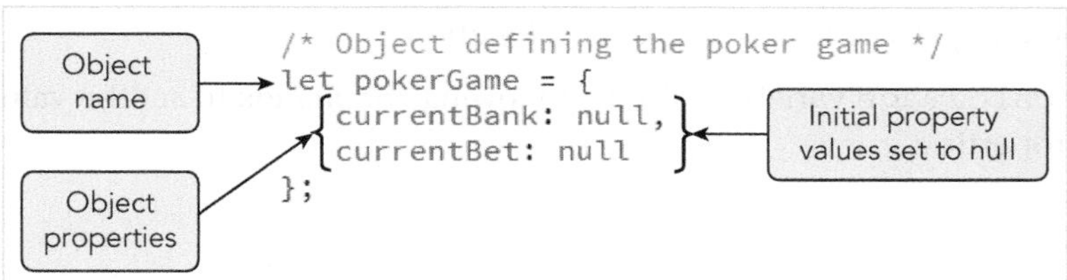

Figure 8-3 Creating the `pokerGame` object literal

3. Save your changes to the file.

Dot Operators and Bracket Notation

Accessing a custom object property uses the by-now familiar *object.property* notation involving a dot operator connecting the object name with an object property. Object properties can also be referenced using the following bracket notation:

```
object["property"]
```

where *object* is the object name and *property* is the object property. The value of the `currentBank` property of the `pokerGame` object could be set with either of the following statements:

```
pokerGame.currentBank = 500;
pokerGame["currentBank"] = 500;
```

One of the advantages of bracket notation is the property name itself can be referenced as a variable. For example, consider the following object literal:

```
let employee = {
   name: "Ronnell Jones",
   position: "manager"
};
```

The following statements could be used to specify which property to display:

```
let prop = "name";
window.alert(employee[prop]);
```

and the browser would display an alert box with the name of the employee, "Ronnell Jones". This kind of flexibility would be important in a database application involving dozens of properties associated with an object, but it cannot be easily done with the dot operator notation.

> **Note** | Nested object properties are referenced using the dot operator notation `object.prop1.prop2`... or the bracket notation `object["prop1"]["prop2"]`...

Built-in JavaScript objects also support both the dot operator and the bracket notation. You may recall that the `id` property of the `forms` object element could be referenced either as `document.forms.id` or `document.forms["id"]`. As you develop in your skill with JavaScript programming, you might switch between the two notations based on the needs of your code.

In the Draw Poker game, players start with $500 in the bank and have a default betting size of $25. Set these values now using the dot operator format.

To set values for the `currentBank` and `currentBet` properties:

1. Return to the **js08.js** file in your code editor and go to `playDrawPoker()` function.
2. Directly below the command declaring the `cardImage` variable, add the following commands to set the values of the `currentBank` and `currentBet` properties:

```
// Set the initial bank and bet values
pokerGame.currentBank = 500;
pokerGame.currentBet = 25;
```

3. Add the following command to display the `currentBank` value in the `bankBox` element:

```
// Display the current bank value
bankBox.value = pokerGame.currentBank;
```

4. Finally, the `currentBet` value should be updated every time the user changes the selected option in the `betSelection` list box. Add the following event listener to the code:

```
// Change the bet when the selection changes
betSelection.onchange = function() {
   pokerGame.currentBet = parseInt(this.value);
}
```

   Note that the `parseInt()` function is used to store the numeric value of the selected bet in the `currentBet` property. **Figure 8-4** describes the newly added code.

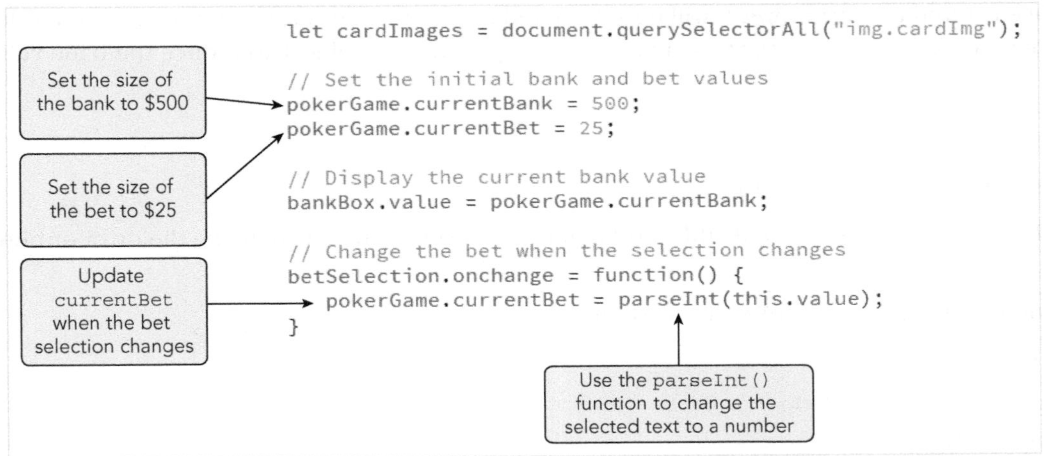
let cardImages = document.querySelectorAll("img.cardImg");
// Set the initial bank and bet values
pokerGame.currentBank = 500;
pokerGame.currentBet = 25;
// Display the current bank value
bankBox.value = pokerGame.currentBank;
// Change the bet when the selection changes
betSelection.onchange = function() {
pokerGame.currentBet = parseInt(this.value);
}
Set the size of the bank to $500
Set the size of the bet to $25
Update currentBet when the bet selection changes
Use the parseInt() function to change the selected text to a number

Figure 8-4 Setting values for `currentBank` and `currentBet`

5. Save your changes to the file and then reload **js08.html** in your browser. Verify that a bank value of 500 appears in the BANK box and a value of 25 appears in the BET box.

Next, you will add custom methods to the `pokerGame` object.

Creating a Custom Method

Methods are added to a custom object by including a function name and its commands as part of the object definition. The general syntax to add a method to an object literal is:

```
let objName = {
   method: function() {
      commands
   }
};
```

where *method* is the name of the method and *commands* are commands associating with the method. For example, the following code adds the `placeBet()` method to the `pokerDeck` object:

```
let pokerDeck = {
   currentBank: null,
   currentBet: null,
   placeBet: function() {
      this.currentBank -= this.currentBet;
      return currentBank;
   }
};
```

Note that the `placeBet()` method uses the `this` keyword to reference the current object, which in this case is the `pokerDeck` object itself. The `-=` assignment operator subtracts the value of the current bet from the current bank value. The method concludes by returning the value of the `currentBank` property.

Methods for custom objects are called in the same way they are for built-in JavaScript objects. Thus, to apply the `placeBet()` method to the `pokerDeck` object, run the expression:

```
pokerDeck.placeBet()
```

and whatever value has been stored in `currentBet` will be subtracted from `currentBank` and the new bank value will be returned by the method. Add the `placeBet()` method to the `pokerGame` object to reduce the bank value by the size of the bet.

To define the `placeBet()` method:

1. Return to the **objects.js** file in your code editor.
2. Go to the code for the `pokerGame` object and add a `,` (comma) to the end of the line defining the `currentBet` property.
3. Add the following code defining the `placeBet()` method:

```
placeBet: function() {
   this.currentBank -= this.currentBet;
   return this.currentBank;
}
```

Figure 8-5 describes the code for the `placeBet()` method.

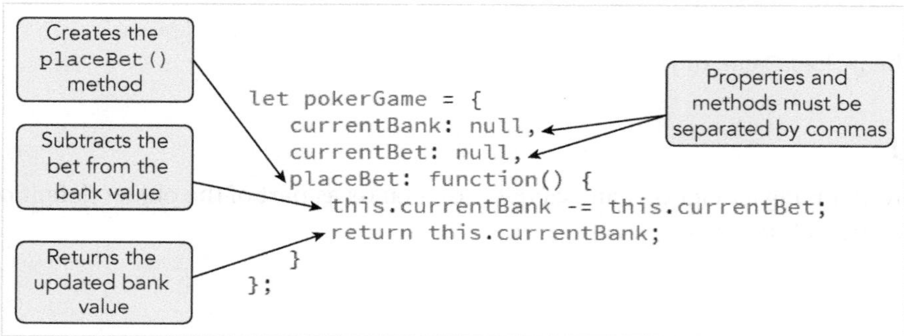

Figure 8-5 Creating the `placeBet()` method

4. Save your changes to the file.

The `placeBet()` method will be applied whenever the player starts a new hand by clicking the Deal button, but only if the player's bank has sufficient funds to cover the bet. Add an `if else` condition to the event listener for the Deal button that reduces the value of the player's bank, but only if the bank has sufficient funds to cover the bet.

To apply the `placeBet()` method:

1. Return to the **js08.js** file in your code editor.
2. At the top of the anonymous function for the `click` event of the Deal button, insert the following `if` condition:

```
if (pokerGame.currentBank >= pokerGame.currentBet) {
```

3. Indent the next six statements that enable or disable the buttons on the poker game page.
4. On the line after the six lines you indented, add the following statement to change the bank value based on the size of the bet placed by the user:

```
// Reduce the bank by the size of the bet
bankBox.value = pokerGame.placeBet();
```

5. Complete the `if else` structure by adding the following code warning the player that their bank cannot cover their bet:

```
} else {
   statusBox.textContent = "Insufficient Funds";
}
```

Figure 8-6 shows the newly added code to the anonymous function.

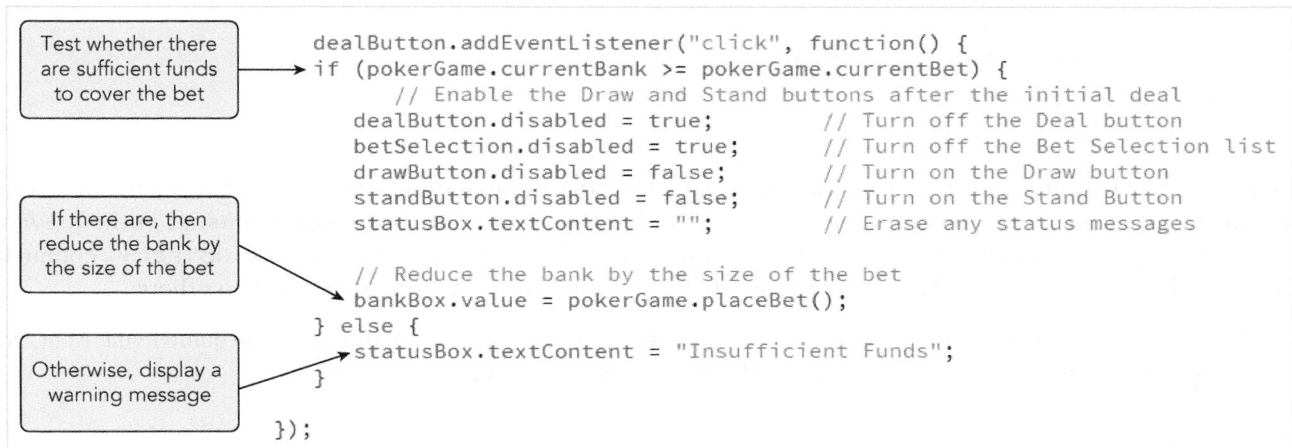

Figure 8-6 Applying the `placeBet()` method

6. Save your changes to the file.

Test the buttons used in the Draw Poker game. Whenever you click the Deal button, your bank should be reduced by the size of the bet and the Deal button should be disabled as you choose whether to draw new cards or stand pat. Of course, currently you have no cards; that feature will come later! Finally, the program should warn you if you attempt to place a bet larger than the size of your bank.

To test the buttons in the Draw Poker game:

1. Reload the **js08.html** file in your browser.
2. Select **100** from the Bet selection list and click the **Deal** button. Verify the bank is reduced to $400 and the Deal button is disabled.
3. Click either the **Draw** or **Stand** button to re-enable the Deal button and prepare the game for another hand.
4. Continue to click the **Deal** button followed by the **Draw** or **Stand** button to reduce the bank amount to $0.
5. Verify that when you attempt a bet that exceeds your bank account, an Insufficient Funds message appears on the poker table.
6. Click the **Reset** button to reload the game, restoring the bank balance to $500.

Creating an Object with the `new` Operator

Another way to create an object literal is with the following `new Object()` command:

```
let objName = new Object();
objName.property = value;
objName.method = function() {
   commands
};
```

where *objName* is the object name, *property* is a property defined for that object, and *method* is a method assigned to that object. The following code defines the `pokerGame` object and its properties and methods using the `new Object()` operator:

```
let pokerGame = new Object();
pokerGame.currentBank = null;
pokerGame.currentBet = null;
pokerGame.placeBet = function() {
   this.currentBank -= this.currentBet;
   return this.currentBank;
};
```

The `new Object()` statement creates a generic object using with the initial properties and methods of the JavaScript base object. Any other properties or methods must be added in separate JavaScript statements, as in the previous example. The biggest limitation of an object created either as an object literal or with the `new Object()` command is that the object is not reusable. Any custom properties or methods apply to that object and no others.

You have completed the initial work on the Draw Poker game by creating a custom object for the game itself. Next, you will study how to create object classes for the cards, hands, and deck used in the game.

Quick Check 1

1. What is object-oriented programming?
2. Provide code to create an object literal named `pokerCard` containing a `suit` property with a value of "Spades" and a `rank` property with a value of 12.
3. Provide code that adds a `dropRank()` method to the `pokerCard` object that decreases the value of the `rank` property by 1.
4. Provide code to return the value of the `rank` property of the `pokerCard` object in bracket notation.

Working with Object Classes

Using an object literal to create the `pokerGame` object was an appropriate choice because there would only be one game object within any application. However, when an application requires several copies of the same type of object, you need to create an object class.

Understanding Object Classes

An object class acts as a template or blueprint for the creation of new objects all sharing a common collection of properties and methods. For each new object based on a class, an object instance is created. For example, the `Array` object represents a class of objects containing properties and methods associated with arrays, but the specific array used for a program is an instance of that class. Creating an instance of a class is also known as instantiating a class.

Object Constructors and Literals

Objects are instantiated using an object constructor having the general form:

```
new Class(parameters)
```

where *Class* is the name of an object class and *parameters* are the values passed to the object class used in creating an instance of that class. **Figure 8-7** lists some of the classes built into JavaScript from which you can instantiate an object. Many of these classes will be familiar to you from your experience developing other applications.

An object constructor can also be applied to customized object classes to instantiate new objects. In this section you will develop your own object classes to be used with any card game app such as the Draw Poker game.

OBJECT CLASS	DESCRIPTION
`Arguments`	Retrieves and manipulates arguments within a function
`Array`	Creates new array objects
`Boolean`	Creates new Boolean objects
`Date`	Retrieves and manipulates dates and times
`Error`	Returns run-time error information
`Function`	Creates new function objects
`Global`	Stores global variables and contains various built-in JavaScript functions
`JSON`	Manipulates objects formatted in JavaScript Object Notation (JSON)
`Map`	Stores key-value pairs, remembering the original insertion order of the keys
`Math`	Contains methods and properties for performing mathematical calculations
`Number`	Contains methods and properties for manipulating numbers
`Object`	The base class for all built-in JavaScript classes
`Promise`	Represents the completion of an asynchronous operation and its resulting value
`RegExp`	Contains methods and properties for a regular expressions
`Set`	Contains a collection of unique values of any type
`String`	Contains methods and properties for manipulating text strings
`WeakSet`	Contains a collection of unique objects of any type

Figure 8-7 Built-in JavaScript object classes

Constructor Functions

Object constructors are defined with the following constructor function:

```
function Class(parameters) {
   this.prop1 = value1;
   this.prop2 = value2;
...
   this.method1 = function1;
   this.method2 = function2;
...
}
```

where *`Class`* is the name of the object class; *`parameters`* are the parameters used by the constructor function; *`prop1`*, *`prop2`*, etc. are the properties associated with that object class; and *`method1`*, *`method2`*, etc. are the methods. The `this` keyword refers to any object instance of this particular object class.

For example, the constructor function for an object class of poker cards might appear as follows:

```
function pokerCard(cardSuit, cardRank) {
  this.suit = cardSuit;
  this.rank = cardRank;
  this.showCard() function() {
     return "Your card is a " + this.rank + " of " + this.suit;
  };
}
```

The `suit` and `rank` properties store the suit and rank of `pokerCard` objects based on the values specified by the `cardSuit` and `cardRank` parameters. The `showCard()` function returns a text string describing the card.

Once the constructor function for the object class is defined, instances of the object are created with the command

```
let object = new Class(parameters);
```

where *`object`* is an instance of the object, *`Class`* is the object class as defined by the constructor function, and *`parameters`* are parameter values. The following code instantiates two `pokerCard` objects: one for the king of hearts and the other for the seven of spades:

```
let card1 = new pokerCard("hearts", "king");
let card2 = new pokerCard("spades", "7");
```

The `showCard()` method attaches to both objects so that the statement `card1.showCard()` returns the text string "Your card is a king of hearts".

Create a constructor class for poker cards in the objects.js file defining properties for the `suit` and `rank` properties.

To create the class of poker card objects:

1. Return to the **objects.js** file in your code editor.
2. Directly below the object literal for the `pokerGame` object, insert the following constructor for the class of poker card objects as described in **Figure 8-8**.

```
/* Constructor function for poker cards */
function pokerCard(cardSuit, cardRank) {
   this.suit = cardSuit;
   this.rank = cardRank;
}
```

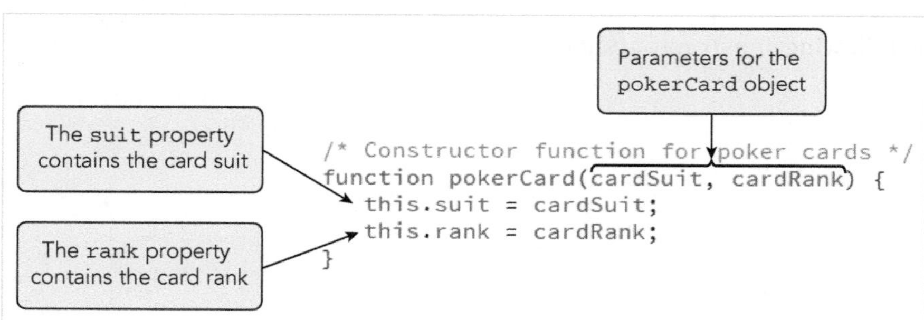

Figure 8-8 Creating the **`pokerCard`** object class

3. Save your changes to the file.

Next, you will create an object class representing an entire deck of cards.

Combining Object Classes

An object class can include objects defined in other classes. For the Draw Poker game, you will create the `pokerDeck` class containing an array of 52 `pokerCard` objects. The code for the constructor function follows:

```
function pokerDeck() {
   let suits = ["clubs", "diamonds", "hearts", "spades"];
   let ranks = ["2", "3", "4", "5", "6", "7", "8", "9",
                "10", "jack", "queen", "king", "ace"];
   this.cards = [];
```

```
   for (let i = 0; i < 4; i++) {
      for (let j = 0; j < 13; j++) {
         this.cards.push(new pokerCard(suits[i], ranks[j]));
      }
   }
};
```

The contents of the `cards` array are generated with a nested `for` loop that iterates through each combination of four possible suits and 13 possible ranks to create an array of 52 `pokerCard` objects containing the following items:

```
[
   pokerCard {suit: "clubs", rank: "2"},
   pokerCard {suit: "clubs", rank: "3"},
   pokerCard {suit: "clubs", rank: "4"},
   pokerCard {suit: "clubs", rank: "5"},
...
   pokerCard {suit: "spades", rank: "ace"}
]
```

The following command instantiates an object from the `pokerDeck` class, storing it in the `myDeck` variable:

```
let myDeck = new pokerDeck();
```

A specific card within the deck can then be referenced using the `cards` array property along with an index number representing the position of the card within the deck. Thus, to retrieve the fourth card from `myDeck`, apply the following expression:

```
myDeck.cards[3]  // Returns the 5 of clubs
```

Add the constructor function for the `pokerDeck` object class to the objects.js file.

To create the class of poker deck objects:

1. Below the constructor function for the `pokerCard` object class, insert the following constructor for the class of `pokerDeck` objects (see **Figure 8-9**):

```
/* Constructor function for poker decks */
function pokerDeck() {
   // List the suits and ranks
   let suits = ["clubs", "diamonds", "hearts", "spades"];
   let ranks = ["2", "3", "4", "5", "6", "7", "8", "9",
                "10", "jack", "queen", "king", "ace"];
   this.cards = [];

   // Add a card for each combination of suit and rank
   for (let i = 0; i < 4; i++) {
      for (let j = 0; j < 13; j++) {
         // Add a pokerCard object
         this.cards.push(new pokerCard(suits[i], ranks[j]));
      }
   }
};
```

2. Save your changes to the file.

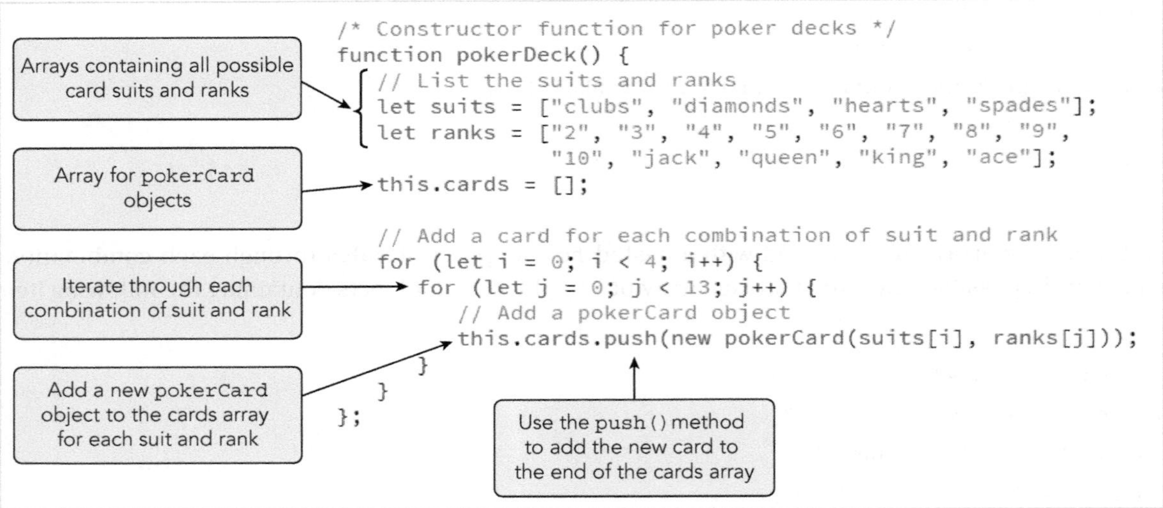

Figure 8-9 Creating the `pokerDeck` object class

Almost all card games require cards to be sorted in random order. You can add the following `shuffle()` method to the `pokerDeck` object class to randomize the order of items in the `cards` array.

```
this.shuffle = function() {
   this.cards.sort(function() {
      return 0.5 - Math.random();
   });
};
```

The code applies the `sort()` method with a compare function to return a random arrangement of each pair of array items. Add the `shuffle()` method to the constructor function of the `pokerDeck` object class.

To create the `shuffle()` method:

1. Add the following method to the constructor function for the `pokerCard` object class as described in **Figure 8-10**:

```
// Method to randomly sort the cards in the deck
this.shuffle = function() {
   this.cards.sort(function() {
      return 0.5 - Math.random();
   });
};
```

```
            // Add a pokerCard object
            this.cards.push(new pokerCard(suits[i], ranks[j]));
         }
      }

      // Method to randomly sort the cards in the deck
      this.shuffle = function() {
         this.cards.sort(function() {
            return 0.5 - Math.random();
         });
      };

};
```

Defines the `shuffle()` method of the `pokerDeck` object class

Compare function that returns a random number between –0.5 and 0.5

Figure 8-10 Creating the `shuffle()` method

2. Save your changes to the file.

With the initial properties and methods of the `pokerDeck` object class defined, add an instance of that object class to the Poker Game app and use the `shuffle()` method to shuffle the contents of the deck.

To instantiate the `pokerDeck` class:

1. Return to the **js08.js** file in your code editor.
2. Directly after the command setting the initial value of the `currentBet` property to 25, insert the following command to create and shuffle a new deck of cards (see **Figure 8-11**):

```
// Create a deck of shuffled cards
let myDeck = new pokerDeck();
myDeck.shuffle();
```

```
pokerGame.currentBet = 25;

// Create a deck of shuffled cards
let myDeck = new pokerDeck();
myDeck.shuffle();
```

Figure 8-11 Creating an instance of the `pokerDeck` object class

3. Save your changes to the file.

Before going further with the development of the Poker Game app, confirm that a shuffled deck of cards is generated by the code. You will use the Scope window within your browser's debugger to check on your progress.

To view the contents of the `myDeck` object:

1. Reload the **js08.html** file in your web browser and open the browser debugger.
2. Put a breakpoint at the line applying the `shuffle()` method to the `myDeck` object.
3. Reload the web page so that it stops at the breakpoint.
4. Go to the browser Scope window.
5. Under the list of objects with Local scope, click and expand the `myDeck` and `cards` objects. As shown in **Figure 8-12**, the `cards` array contains an unshuffled list of poker cards.
6. Click the **Step over next function call** button in the debugger or press **F10** to skip tracing the `shuffle()` method. As shown in **Figure 8-12**, the cards array should now show the poker cards in random order.

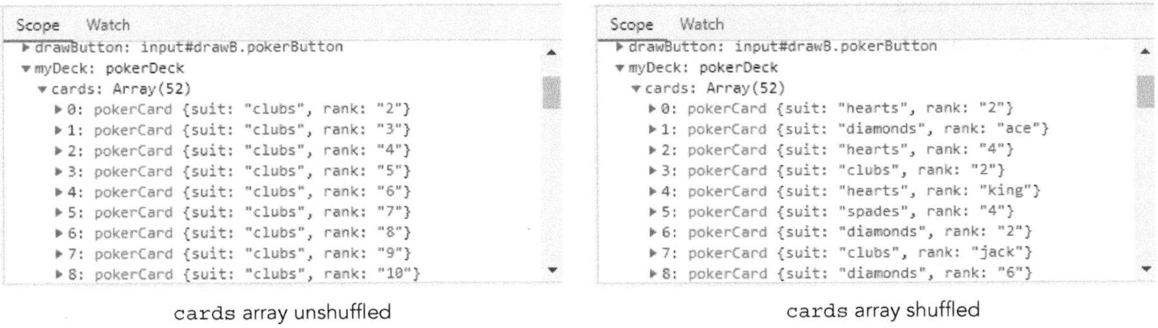

```
Scope   Watch
▶ drawButton: input#drawB.pokerButton
▼ myDeck: pokerDeck
  ▼ cards: Array(52)
    ▶ 0: pokerCard {suit: "clubs", rank: "2"}
    ▶ 1: pokerCard {suit: "clubs", rank: "3"}
    ▶ 2: pokerCard {suit: "clubs", rank: "4"}
    ▶ 3: pokerCard {suit: "clubs", rank: "5"}
    ▶ 4: pokerCard {suit: "clubs", rank: "6"}
    ▶ 5: pokerCard {suit: "clubs", rank: "7"}
    ▶ 6: pokerCard {suit: "clubs", rank: "8"}
    ▶ 7: pokerCard {suit: "clubs", rank: "9"}
    ▶ 8: pokerCard {suit: "clubs", rank: "10"}
```

`cards` array unshuffled

```
Scope   Watch
▶ drawButton: input#drawB.pokerButton
▼ myDeck: pokerDeck
  ▼ cards: Array(52)
    ▶ 0: pokerCard {suit: "hearts", rank: "2"}
    ▶ 1: pokerCard {suit: "diamonds", rank: "ace"}
    ▶ 2: pokerCard {suit: "hearts", rank: "4"}
    ▶ 3: pokerCard {suit: "clubs", rank: "2"}
    ▶ 4: pokerCard {suit: "hearts", rank: "king"}
    ▶ 5: pokerCard {suit: "spades", rank: "4"}
    ▶ 6: pokerCard {suit: "diamonds", rank: "2"}
    ▶ 7: pokerCard {suit: "clubs", rank: "jack"}
    ▶ 8: pokerCard {suit: "diamonds", rank: "6"}
```

`cards` array shuffled

Figure 8-12 Contents of the `myDeck` object before and after shuffling

7. Remove the breakpoint and resume the script without interruption.

The final object class you need for the Draw Poker game is a class for poker hands consisting of poker cards drawn from a poker deck. The constructor function for the `pokerHand` object class is:

```
function pokerHand(handLength) {
   this.cards = new Array(handLength);
}
```

The function has a single parameter, `handLength`, specifying the number of cards in the hand. Like the `pokerDeck` object class, individual `pokerCard` objects will be placed in the `cards` array with an array length equal to the value of the `handLength` parameter. Add this constructor to the objects.js file.

To create the `pokerHand` object class:

1. Return to the **objects.js** file in your code editor.
2. Directly below the constructor for the `pokerDeck` class, insert the following constructor function for the `pokerHand` class as described in **Figure 8-13**:

```
/* Constructor function for poker hands */
function pokerHand(handLength) {
   this.cards = new Array(handLength);
}
```

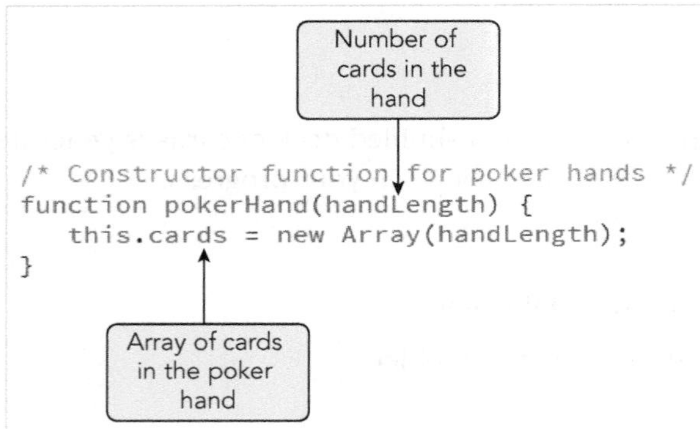

Figure 8-13 Creating the `pokerHand()` object class

3. Save your changes to the file and then return to the **js08.js** file in your code editor.
4. Directly below the command the declares the `myDeck` object and shuffles it, add the following code as described in **Figure 8-14** to create an instance of a five-card poker hand:

```
// Create an empty poker hand object
let myHand = new pokerHand(5);
```

```
// Create a deck of shuffled cards
let myDeck = new pokerDeck();
myDeck.shuffle();

// Create an empty poker hand object
let myHand = new pokerHand(5);
```

Poker hand containing five cards

Figure 8-14 Instantiating a `pokerHand()` object

5. Save your changes to the file.

One of the advantages of object-oriented programming is that it encourages the creation of objects that mimic their real-world counterparts. A poker hand is constructed by dealing cards from a deck into the hand, so the `pokerDeck` object needs a `dealTo()` method in which cards are taken from the deck and moved into a hand by moving items in one `cards` array to the other array. The code for the `dealTo()` method is a follows:

```
function pokerDeck() {
...
   this.dealTo = function(pokerHand) {
   let cardsDealt = pokerHand.cards.length;
   pokerHand.cards = this.cards.splice(0, cardsDealt);
  }
};
```

The `dealTo()` method has a single parameter, `pokerHand`, which references the `pokerHand` object that will receive the cards from the poker deck. The function then uses the `splice()` method to remove items from the `cards` array of the `pokerDeck` object, placing them in the `cards` array of `pokerHand` object. After the application of this method, the number of cards in the poker deck is reduced by the number of cards dealt to the poker hand.

To add the `dealTo()` method to the `pokerDeck` object class:

1. Return to the **objects.js** file in your code editor.
2. Scroll up to the `pokerDeck` constructor in the objects.js file.
3. Within the constructor function, add the following code to define the `dealTo()` method (see **Figure 8-15**):

```
// Method to deal cards from the deck into a hand
this.dealTo = function(pokerHand) {
   let cardsDealt = pokerHand.cards.length;
   pokerHand.cards = this.cards.splice(0, cardsDealt);
}
```

```
      // Method to randomly sort the cards in the deck
      this.shuffle = function() {
         this.cards.sort(function() {
            return 0.5 - Math.random();
         });
      };

      // Method to deal cards from the deck into a hand
      this.dealTo = function(pokerHand) {
         let cardsDealt = pokerHand.cards.length;
         pokerHand.cards = this.cards.splice(0, cardsDealt);
      };
   };
```

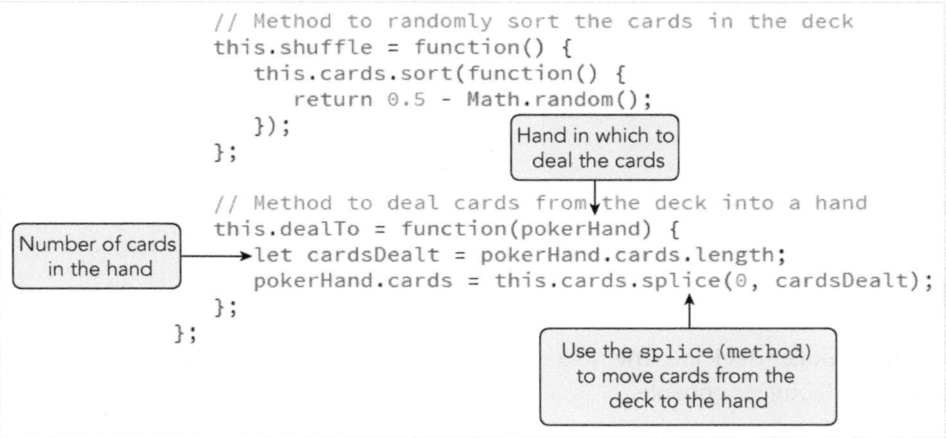

Figure 8-15 Creating the `dealTo()` method of the `pokerDeck` object class

4. Save your changes to the file.

A new hand is created every time the Deal button is clicked. Because the size of the deck is reduced with each deal, the app should verify that the deck has at least 10 cards before dealing a new hand; otherwise create a newly shuffled deck and deal cards from that deck.

Add an instance of the `pokerHand` object to the Draw Poker app, placing the code within the event listener for the `click` event of the Deal button.

To create an instance of the `pokerHand` object:

1. Return to the **js08.js** file in your code editor and go to the event listener for the `click` event of the `dealButton` object.
2. Directly below the command that applies the `placeBet()` method to the `pokerGame` object, add the following code to check whether a new deck is required:

```
// Get a new deck is there are less than 10 cards left
if (myDeck.cards.length < 10) {
    myDeck = new pokerDeck();
    myDeck.shuffle();
}
```

3. Next, add the following code to deal five cards from the poker deck into the poker hand, displaying the contents of both objects in the debugger console (see **Figure 8-16**):

```
// Deal 5 cards from the deck to the hand
myDeck.dealTo(myHand);
console.log(myDeck, myHand);
```

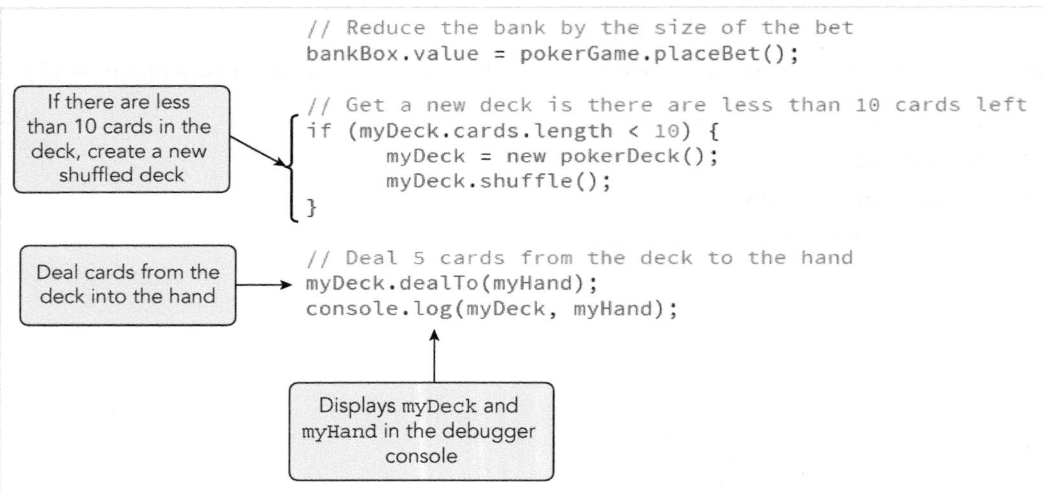

Figure 8-16 Dealing from the deck into a hand

4. Save your changes to the file.

Verify that cards have been dealt from the poker deck into the poker hand by clicking the Deal button and viewing the contents of `myDeck` and `myHand` in your debugger console.

To deal a hand:

1. Reload the **js08.html** file in your browser and open your browser's debugging console.
2. Click the **Deal** button.
3. Click **pokerDeck** in the debugger console to expand its contents for viewing.
4. Click **pokerHand** in the debugger console and then click **cards** to expand its contents. **Figure 8-17** shows the expanded view of the user-created objects.

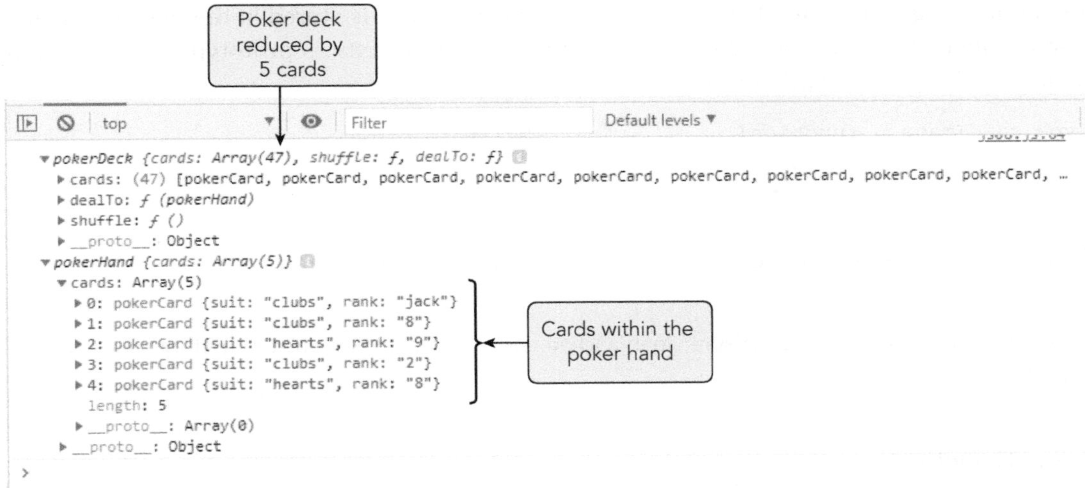

Figure 8-17 Cards in the poker hand

5. Close your browser's debugger.

The Draw Poker game does not yet show the actual cards in the page. You will add this feature using object prototypes.

Working with Object Prototypes

Every JavaScript object has a prototype, which is a template for all the properties and methods associated with the object's class. If the constructor function can be thought of as a machine to instantiate objects, then a prototype is the blueprint for that object. When an object is instantiated from a constructor function, it uses properties and methods defined in the prototype.

However, instantiating new objects can be an inefficient use of memory and resources because the same code is copied from the constructor function into every object instance. Imagine the strain on resources when several methods with dozens of lines of code each are copied from the constructor function into thousands of object instances. A better approach is to place the code for those methods directly into the object's prototype, which is then accessible to the constructor function and all object instances without the need for individual copies.

The Prototype Object

The prototype is itself an object (almost everything in JavaScript is) and is referenced using the expression:

```
Class.prototype
```

where *Class* is the name of the object class. For example, the prototype for the `pokerCard` object class is referenced as follows:

```
pokerCard.prototype
```

To add a method to a prototype, apply the command:

```
Class.prototype.method = function;
```

where *method* is the name of the method and *function* is the function applied by the method. The function can be entered as an anonymous function or it can be a reference to the name of a function created elsewhere in the code.

Images of the 52 poker cards have been created for the Draw Poker app. The file names of the card images follow the convention *rank*_*suit*.png. where *rank* is the card's rank and *suit* is the card's suit. For example, the image for the 5 of hearts is stored in the image file, 5_hearts.png, the queen of hearts image is stored in the queen_hearts.png file, and so forth. The following code adds a `cardImage()` method to the `pokerCard` prototype that returns this file name for every instance of the `pokerCard` object:

```
pokerCard.prototype.cardImage = function() {
   return this.rank + "_" + this.suit + ".png";
}
```

Add this method to the objects.js file so that it can be made available for every poker card.

> **Note** | A general programming practice to ensure clean and efficient code is to add custom methods only to the object prototype.

To create the `cardImage()` method:

1. Return to the **objects.js** file in your code editor.
2. Directly below the constructor function for the `pokerCard` object class, add the following code to create the `cardImage()` method for the `pokerCard` prototype (see **Figure 8-18**):

```
// Method to reference the image of the poker card
pokerCard.prototype.cardImage = function() {
   return this.rank + "_" + this.suit + ".png";
}
```

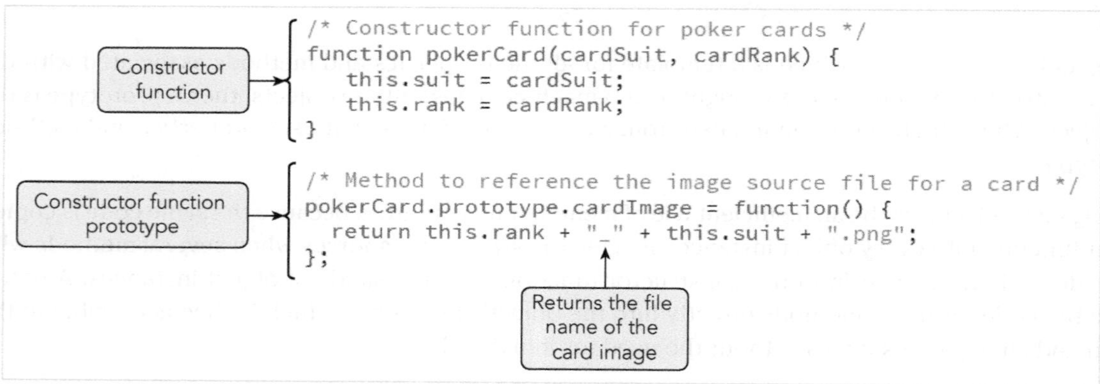

Figure 8-18 Creating the `cardImage()` method

3. Save your changes to the file.

Card images are displayed in the Draw Poker web page using `img` elements belonging to the `cardImg` class. The web page contains five such `img` elements, all displaying the empty contents of the blank.gif image file. Replace those images with the images of the five cards in the poker hand, using the image files as specified by the `cardImage()` method.

To display card images:

1. Return to the **js08.js** file in your code editor.
2. Scroll down to the event listener for the `click` event with the Deal button. Replace the `console.log(myDeck, myHand)` statement with the following code:

```
// Display the card images on the table
for (let i = 0; i < cardImages.length; i++) {
   cardImages[i].src = myHand.cards[i].cardImage();
}
```

Note that the `cardImages` object is a node list that references all `img` elements belonging to the `cardImg` class. **Figure 8-19** describes the new code in the file.

```
// Deal 5 cards from the deck to the hand
myDeck.dealTo(myHand);

// Display the card images on the table
for (let i = 0; i < cardImages.length; i++) {
   cardImages[i].src = myHand.cards[i].cardImage();
}
```

Replace the blank card image with images determined by the `cardImage()` method

Figure 8-19 Displaying card images for a dealt hand

3. Save your changes to the file.
4. Reload the **js08.html** file in your browser.
5. Click the **Deal** button and verify that the images of the cards in the dealt hand are displayed on the table (your card images will differ). See **Figure 8-20**.

Figure 8-20 Card images from the dealt hand

6. Continue clicking the **Draw** button followed by the **Deal** button to generate new poker hands.

One of the advantages of this approach in generating the card images is that developers can supply their own card images if they follow the naming conventions for the Draw Poker app.

Extending Built-in JavaScript Objects

Another feature of prototypes is the ability to add new methods to existing objects, which is what you did with the `pokerCard` object. However, this feature also applies to built-in JavaScript objects. Native objects such as the `Array`, `Date`, and `String` objects can be extended with new methods added to those object's prototypes. For example, to make the `shuffle()` method, defined earlier for the `pokerDeck` object, available to all arrays, apply the following expression:

```
Array.prototype.shuffle = function() {
   this.sort(function() {
      return 0.5 - Math.random();
   });
}
```

Now, any array can be sorted in random order by applying the `shuffle()` method. Use caution and restraint when adding new custom properties and methods to native objects because poorly formed code can "break" the object, making the code unusable for all native objects of that class.

Best Practices | Making your Object-Oriented Code SOLID

There are many benefits to object-oriented programming but only if you follow some very important principles. The developer Robert C. Martin laid out those principles under the acronym SOLID:

- **Single Responsibility Principle:** Every object class should be designed with a single purpose. Do not create complex objects that serve multiple purposes; instead, split the duty among several different object classes.
- **Open/Close Principle:** Object classes should be open for extensions (adding new features) but closed for modifications (changing existing features). Your objects should be able to be extended without having to be modified.
- **Liskov's Substitution Principle:** Introduced by Barabara Liskov in 1987, the principle states that "*Derived classes must be substitutable for their base or parent classes.*" In other words, if an object class is based on another class or parent class, that object should be able to be substituted for its parent. A lower-order object class should not operate in a way that is incompatible with the general object class in which it resides.
- **Interface Segregation Principle:** Objects should not require a particular interface to perform. The design of the interface should be left to the developer and a properly constructed object should fit into any interface that the developer needs for a particular project or application.
- **Dependency Inversion Principle:** Objects defined in higher-order modules should not be affected by changes in lower-order modules or objects. For example, the operation of a coffee machine (a higher-order object) should not be affected the choice of coffee grind (a lower-order object).

You can read more about the SOLID principles and other best practices for object-oriented programming on the web.

You programmed the actions of the Deal button. In the next section you will program the actions of the Draw button to enable players to discard useless cards in a quest to get the best possible hand.

Quick Check 2

1. How does an object class differ from an object literal?
2. Provide code for a construction function named `bounceBall` with two parameters named `x` and `y` and properties named `speedX` and `speedY` with initial values equal to the `x` and `y` parameter values.
3. Provide code to instantiate an object variable named `myBall` created from the `bounceBall` class with initial `x` and `y` values of 50 and 100.
4. What is an object prototype and what is its relationship to a constructor function?
5. Provide code to add the `moveBall()` method to the prototype of the `bounceBall` constructor function.

Introducing Closures

Players improve their hands in Draw Poker by replacing one or more cards with new cards from the deck. To mimic this action, you will add the following `replaceCard()` method to the `pokerHand` prototype:

```
pokerHand.prototype.replaceCard = function(index, pokerDeck) {
   this.cards[index] = pokerDeck.cards.shift();
};
```

The `replaceCard()` method has two parameters: the `index` parameter identifying which card to replace and the `pokerDeck` parameter specifying from which deck the new card should be drawn. The `shift()` method moves the first card from the `cards` array in the `pokerDeck` object into the appropriate location within the `cards` array of the `pokerHand` object. Add this method to the objects.js file.

To add the `replaceCard()` method to the `pokerHand` prototype:

1. Return to the **objects.js** file in your code editor.
2. Directly below the constructor function for the `pokerHand` class add the following code described in **Figure 8-21**:

```
// Method to replace a card in a hand with a card from a deck
pokerHand.prototype.replaceCard = function(index, pokerDeck) {
   this.cards[index] = pokerDeck.cards.shift();
};
```

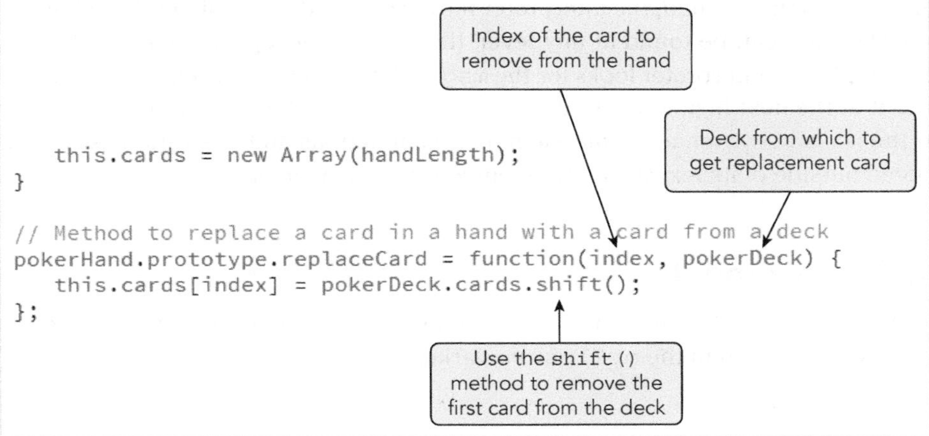

Figure 8-21 Creating the `replace()` method of the `pokerHand` prototype

3. Save your changes to the file.

Players indicate which cards should be replaced by clicking the card image. A selected card is "flipped over" to display the back of the card and then once the Draw button is clicked all flipped-over cards will be replaced with cards from the deck. The code needs to remember which card images were flipped and match them to corresponding cards in the player's hand. To do that task, the code will use a closure.

Lexical Scope

To understand what closures are and why they are so useful in object-oriented programming, you must start with the concept of variable scope. Recall that scope determines where a variable or function is accessible within the program code. Many scripts involve multiple levels of nested functions in which variables declared at one level are accessible to all functions at a lower level. For example, the following code contains a set of nested functions named appropriately `outer()` and `inner()`. When the `outer()` function is called, it runs itself and the `inner()` function to log two message in the debugger console.

```
function outer() {
   let msg = "ace of spades";
   function inner() {
      console.log(msg);
   }
   inner();
   console.log("is my card");
}
// run the outer() function
outer();
// logs "ace of spades"
// logs "is my card"
```

Note that `inner()` function logs the content of the `msg` variable even though that variable is declared outside of that function. The `inner()` function "knows" what is meant by the `msg` variable because of lexical scope or static scope in which the scope of variables, functions, and other objects is based on their physical location within the source code. In this case, the JavaScript Interpreter recognizes the `msg` variable because it is part the larger context of the `outer()` function that encompasses the declaration of the `msg` variable and the creation of the `inner()` function.

The interpreter applies lexical scope in evaluating all variables it encounters, starting by looking for a matching variable declaration within the innermost function. If none is found, the interpreter moves outward to the higher-level functions until it finds the declaration. If no declaration can be found at any level, the interpreter reports an error due to an unrecognized variable name. In this example, the interpreter looks for the `msg` variable declaration within the `inner()` function, and failing to find it, locates it at the next higher level within the `outer()` function. The interpretation of a variable and its value exists within the lexical environment that encompasses functions and the variables they use. An attempt to use a variable referenced outside of its lexical environment will return an error.

Closures and the Lexical Environment

Now examine the following code in which the `outer()` function doesn't call the `inner()` function but instead returns the function itself as a variable, which is then stored in the `myClosure` variable.

```
function outer() {
   let msg = "ace of spades";
   function inner() {
      console.log(msg);
   }
   return inner;
   console.log("is my card");
}
let myClosure = outer();
myClosure();
// logs "ace of spades
```

When `myClosure()` is called in the last line of the code, it bypasses the `outer()` function completely to run only the `inner()` function. And yet, even though the `msg` variable is referenced outside of its lexical environment, the code still works.

The reason is because of a closure, which is created when a copy is made of a function that includes the lexical environment of variables used within that function. When the `inner()` function was stored in the `myClosure` variable, a closure was created in which the lexical environment that defined the meaning of the `msg` variable was also copied. Closures "enclose" everything about the function, including its context within the larger source code. That is why the `msg` variable still had meaning within the `myClosure` variable.

Because a closure copies a function's lexical environment, it takes more memory. Overuse of closures can lead to excessive memory consumption, impairing system performance. You should use closures only when necessary to achieve a program objective.

Programming Concepts | Functions as Objects and Variables

Functions, like almost everything in JavaScript, are objects with their own collections of properties and methods. For this reason, a function can be copied and stored as a variable to create closures. Function object properties include the following:

- *`function`*`.name` returns the function's name
- *`function`*`.caller` returns the function that called the function
- *`function`*`.length` returns the number of arguments used by the function

For example, the following commands log the number of arguments required by the `myHand()` constructor function, returning a value of 1 because the function has a single argument.

```
let myHand = newPokerHand(5);
console.log(myHand.constructor.length); // logs "1"
```

Because functions are objects, any function can be created using the following `new Function()` object constructor

```
let function = new Function(arg1, arg2, ..., body);
```

where *`function`* is the function's name, *`arg1`*, *`arg2`*, etc. are the function arguments, and *`body`* is the function code. The following code creates the `adder()` function used for returning the sum of two values:

```
let adder = new Function("x", "y", "return x + y");
```

The `adder()` function is equivalent to the following set of statements:

```
function adder(x, y) {
   return x + y;
}
```

One advantage of the `new Function()` constructor is that it can be used to construct dynamic functions whose properties and methods are themselves variables.

Closures with `for` Loops

Closures also appear in the operation of program loops that call functions at each iteration. Consider the following `for` loop that displays the value of a counter variable after a 1-second delay:

```
for (let i=0; i < 3; i++) {
   setTimeout(function() {
      console.log("The counter is " + i);
   }, 1000);
}
// logs "The counter is 0"
// logs "The counter is 1"
// logs "The counter is 2"
```

The `setTimeout()` method delays operation of the `console.log()` until after the loop is finished and counter variable, `i`, removed from memory. Yet, despite this, the value of the counter variable at the time the `setTimeout()` method was called is preserved.

The reason for this behavior is that the program loop copies and encloses the function nested within the `setTimeout()` method and, thus, also copies its lexical environment. The fact that the anonymous function is not actually run until well after the loop finishes changes nothing. Because of closures, the JavaScript interpreter "remembers" the value of `i` at the time it was encountered in the loop.

Closures also appear in program loops involving event handlers that are not run until the event occurs (well after the program loop finishes). Even though the code is run later, the lexical environment surrounding the event handler function is copied because of the closure. You will take advantage of this feature of closures in the following loop that flips over cards displayed on the poker table:

```
for (let i = 0; i < cardImages.length; i++) {
    cardImages[i].onclick = function() {
       if (this.src.includes("cardback.png")) {
          this.src = myHand.cards[i].cardImage();
       } else {
          this.src = "cardback.png";
       }
    }
}
```

The loop adds an `onclick` event handler to every card image on the table. When the player clicks an image, if the card is currently displaying the back of the card, it changes the image to the front, otherwise it displays the card back. Notice that the code within the event handler is not run until the player clicks the card (well after the loop is finished) but because of closures, the value of the index counter `i` is copied as part of the lexical environment so that the correct card is flipped in response to the `click` event.

Note The `includes()` method determines whether the complete file name of the card image includes the substring "cardback.png" indicating that the card is flipped on its back.

To add code to flip the card images:

1. Return to the **js08.js** file in your code editor.
2. Within the `for` loop that displays the five card images, add the following code as described in **Figure 8-22**:

```
// Flip the card images when clicked
cardImages[i].onclick = function() {
   if (this.src.includes("cardback.png")) {
      // Show the front of the card
      this.src = myHand.cards[i].cardImage();
   } else {
      // Show the back of the card
      this.src = "cardback.png";
   }
}
```

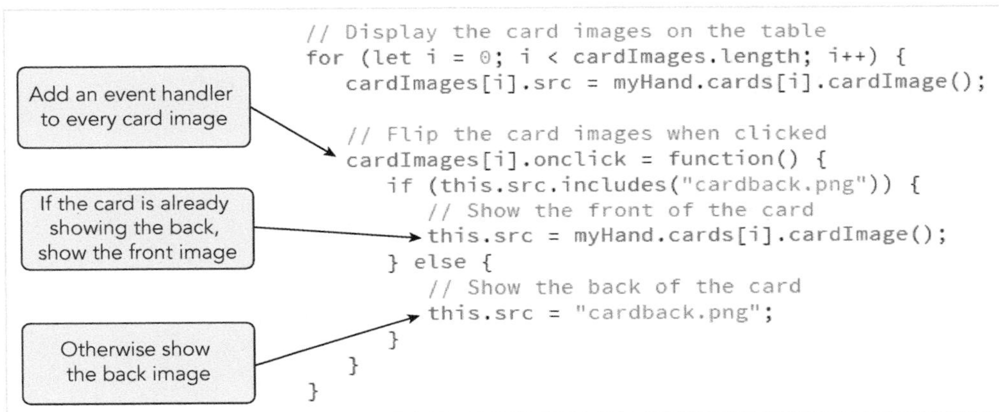

Figure 8-22 Switching the card images between the back and front

3. Save your changes to the file and then reload **js08.html** in your browser.
4. Click the **Deal** button to deal a new hand to the table.
5. Verify that you can switch each card image between its front and back by clicking it. See **Figure 8-23**.

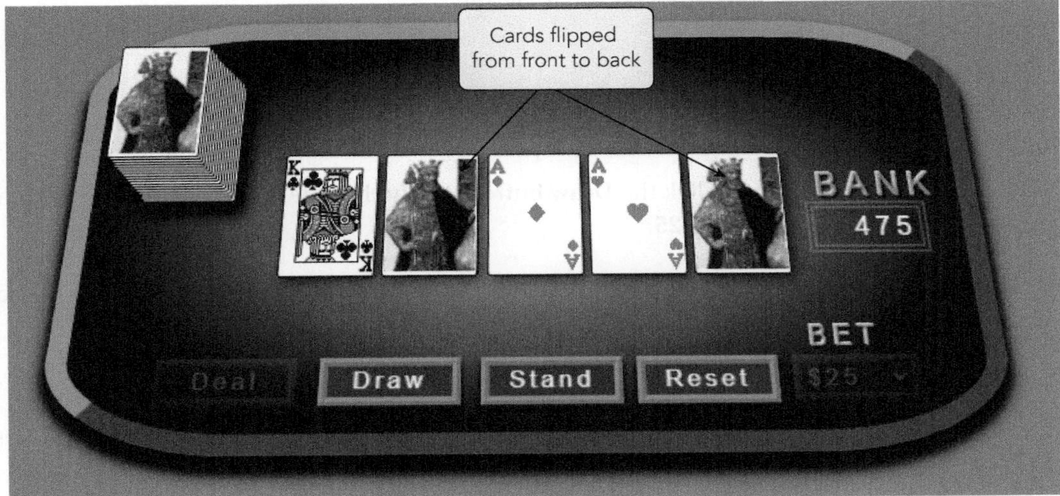

Figure 8-23 Cards flipped on the table

After the Draw button is clicked, cards that have been flipped over are replaced with new cards from the deck. Add code to the Draw button's `onclick` event handler to check each card to determine if it has been flipped over, and if so, replace it with a new card from the deck.

To program the Draw button:

1. Return to the **js08.js** file in your code editor.
2. Scroll down to the `onclick` event handler for the Draw button and directly below the statement that turns off the Stand button, add the following `for` loop:

```
// Replace cards marked to be discarded
for (let i = 0; i < cardImages.length; i++) {
   if (cardImages[i].src.includes("cardback.png")) {
      // Replace the card and its image on the table
      myHand.replaceCard(i, myDeck);
      cardImages[i].src = myHand.cards[i].cardImage();
   }
}
```

   Figure 8-24 describes the newly added code.

Event listener for the click event in the Draw button
Loop through the list of card images
If the card is showing the back image, replace it with a new card from the deck

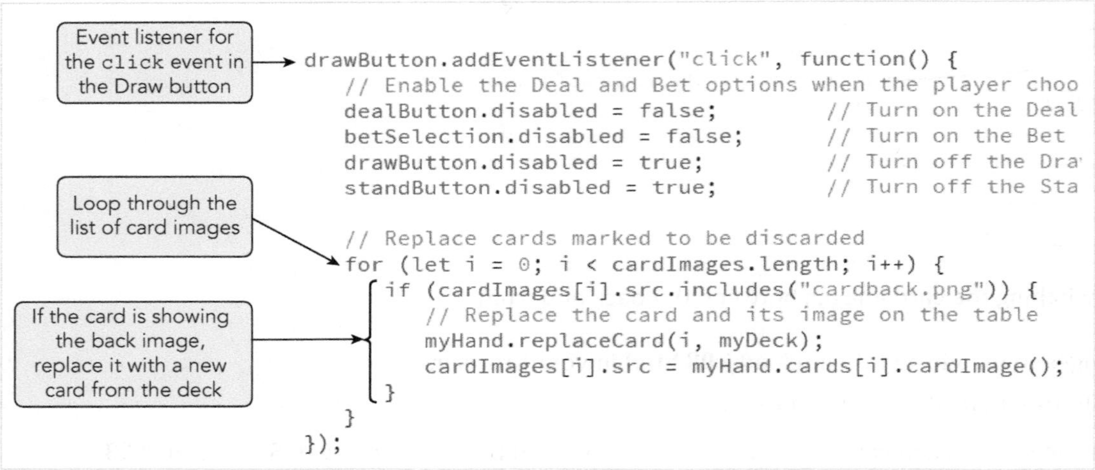

```
drawButton.addEventListener("click", function() {
   // Enable the Deal and Bet options when the player choo
   dealButton.disabled = false;        // Turn on the Deal
   betSelection.disabled = false;      // Turn on the Bet
   drawButton.disabled = true;         // Turn off the Dra
   standButton.disabled = true;        // Turn off the Sta

   // Replace cards marked to be discarded
   for (let i = 0; i < cardImages.length; i++) {
      if (cardImages[i].src.includes("cardback.png")) {
         // Replace the card and its image on the table
         myHand.replaceCard(i, myDeck);
         cardImages[i].src = myHand.cards[i].cardImage();
      }
   }
});
```

Figure 8-24 Replacing marked cards when the Draw button is clicked

3. Save your changes to the file and then reload **js08.html** in your browser.
4. Click the **Deal** button to deal a new hand to the table.
5. Click cards from the table to flip them and then click the **Draw** button. Verify that the flipped cards are replaced with new cards drawn from the deck. See **Figure 8-25**.

Notice that the correct card is replaced in the player's hand because the closure "remembers" the index value associated with the event handler and uses it with the `replaceCard()` method.

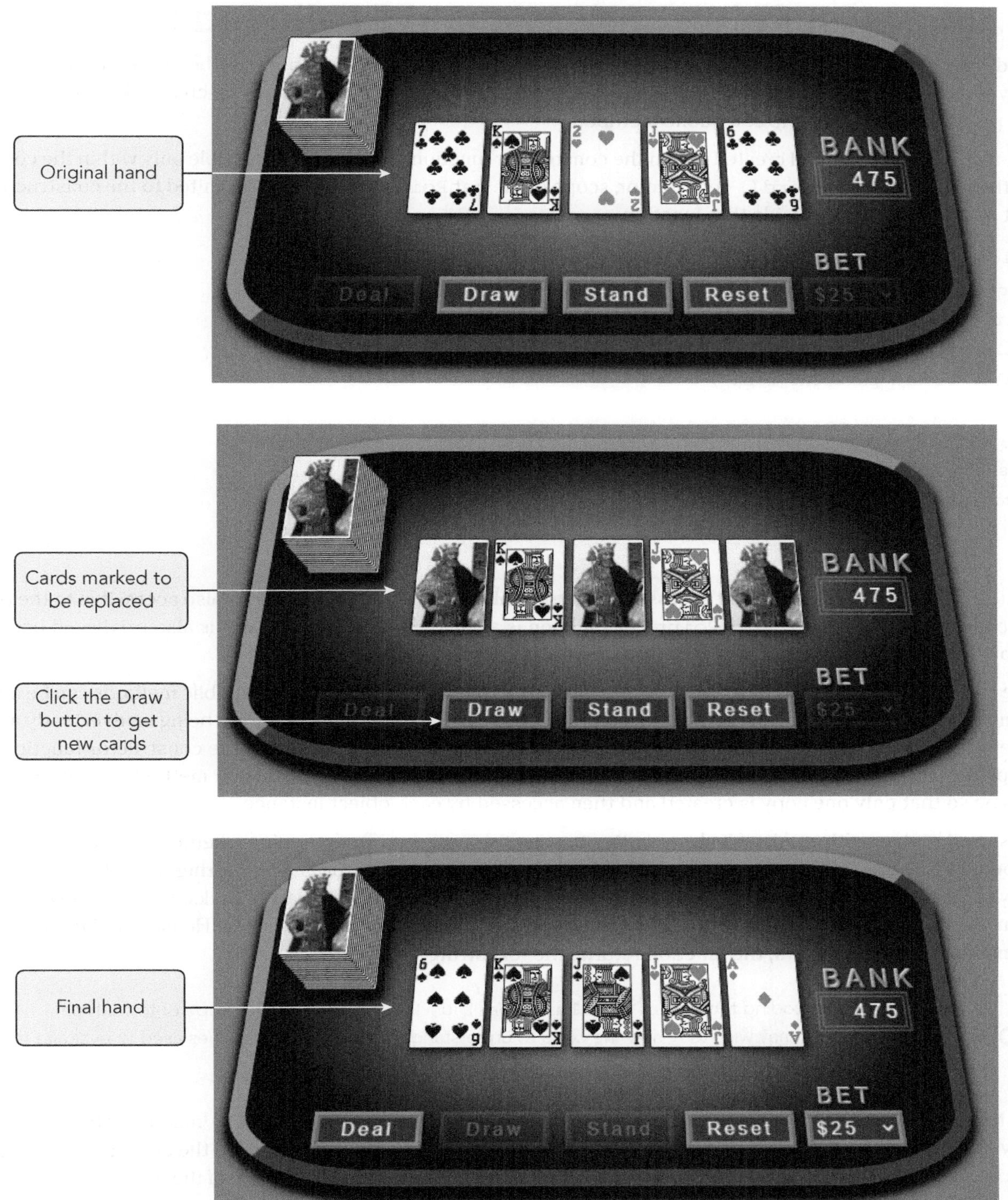

Figure 8-25 Marking and replacing cards from the hand

Working with Public, Private, and Privileged Methods

Methods associated with custom objects can be public, private, or privileged. A public method is defined for the object prototype and, thus, can be called outside of the object. The `replaceCard()` method you created for the `pokerHand` object prototype is an example of a public method.

A private method is a method created within the constructor function and, thus, is accessible only within the constructor. In the following `pokerCard()` constructor, scope of the `getPoints()` function is limited to the constructor and cannot be accessed from outside that function:

```
function pokerCard(rank) {
   function getPoints() {
      if (rank === "ace") return 11;
      else if ("king,queen,jack".includes(rank)) return 10;
      else return parseInt(rank);
   }

   this.showPoints = function() {
      console.log(rank + " is worth " + getPoints());
   }
}
```

A privileged method is a method that accesses private variables and methods but that is also accessible to the public. In the code sample above, the `showPoints()` function is available to the public, but it is also privileged because it relies on the value returned by calling the private `getPoints()` function.

Private and privileged methods can be made only within the constructor function itself. Public methods can be made at any time using the object's prototype. Private methods are essential to protect code from being inadvertently altered, but they come at a cost in system resources. Because the methods are placed within the constructor function, they are copied each time a new object is instantiated. Thus, you should always place such methods within the object prototype so that only one copy is created and then accessed by each object instance.

Players must end up with a pair of jacks or better to win at draw poker. To determine whether a player is a winner, a function named `handType()` has been provided for you. The function returns a text string describing the player's hand with text values such as "Jacks or Better" for winning hands that have a pair of Jacks, Queens, Kings, or Aces. The function also returns the text of other winning hands such as Flushes, Straights, Full Houses, and Royal Flushes. For hands that are not winners, the function returns the text string "No Winner".

> **Note** Some of the coding techniques in the `handType()` function are beyond the scope of this tutorial; however, you may wish to review the code to understand some of the approaches used to evaluate the contents of a poker hand.

To use this function in your app, you will copy the function code into the `getHandValue()` method of the `pokerHand` prototype. The `getHandValue()` method will then be public and available to any users of the `pokerHand` object, but the `handType()` function and its nested functions will be private and inaccessible outside of the `pokerHand` prototype.

To add the `getHandValue()` method:

1. Return to the **objects.js** file in your code editor.
2. Directly below the `replaceCard()` method of the `pokerHand` prototype, add the following code to create the `getHandValue()` method:

```
// Method to determine the value of the pokerHand
pokerHand.prototype.getHandValue = function() {
   return handType(this);
}
```

3. Scroll to the bottom of the file. The complete code of the `handType()` function is placed between a pair of opening and closing comments.
4. Use your code editor to cut the code of the function and paste it directly below the `return handType(this)` statement within the `getHandValue()` method you just entered. **Figure 8-26** shows part of the newly pasted code.

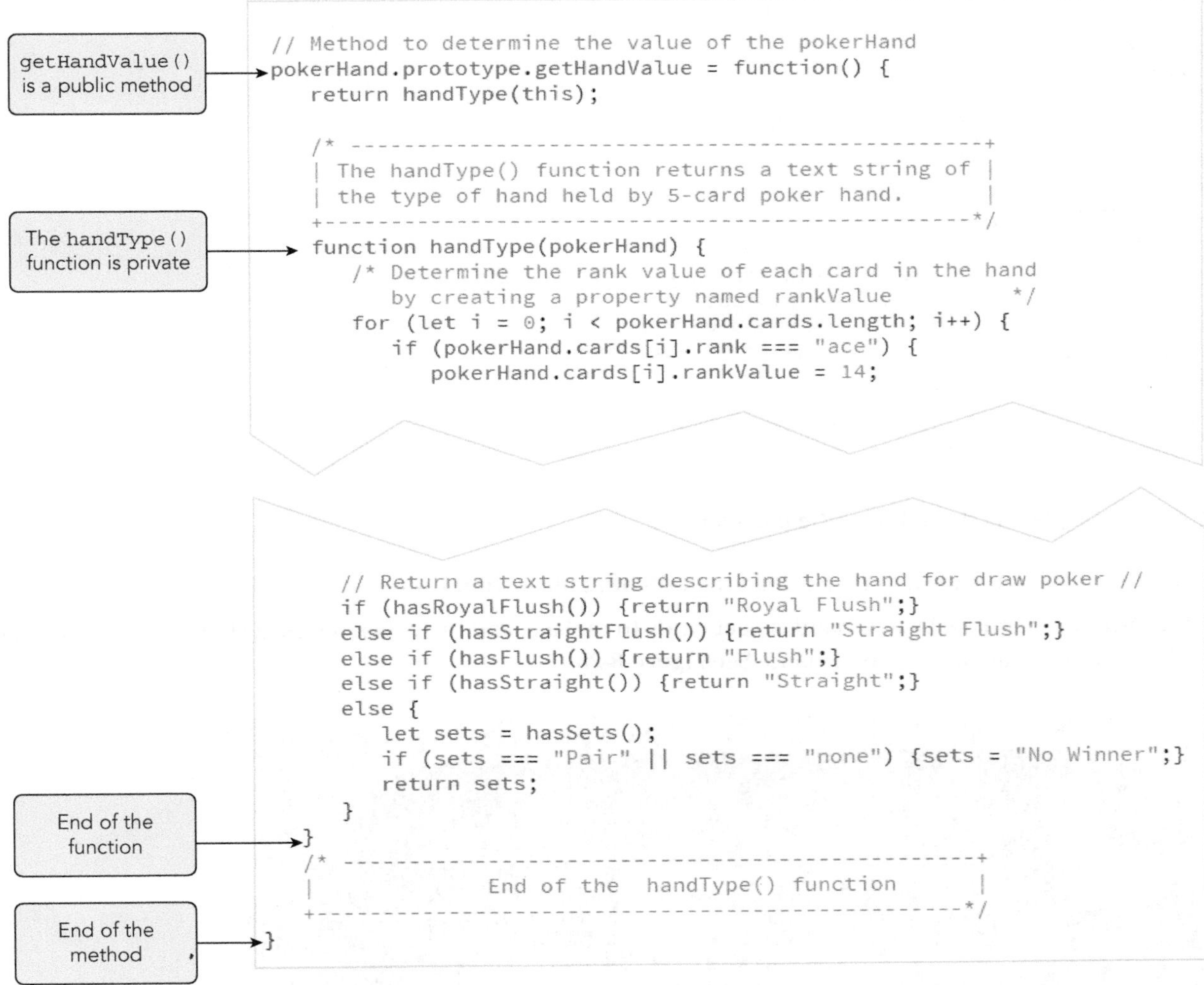

getHandValue() is a public method
The handType() function is private
End of the function
End of the method
// Method to determine the value of the pokerHand
pokerHand.prototype.getHandValue = function() {
return handType(this);
/* ---+
| The handType() function returns a text string of |
| the type of hand held by 5-card poker hand. |
+---*/
function handType(pokerHand) {
/* Determine the rank value of each card in the hand
by creating a property named rankValue */
for (let i = 0; i < pokerHand.cards.length; i++) {
if (pokerHand.cards[i].rank === "ace") {
pokerHand.cards[i].rankValue = 14;
// Return a text string describing the hand for draw poker //
if (hasRoyalFlush()) {return "Royal Flush";}
else if (hasStraightFlush()) {return "Straight Flush";}
else if (hasFlush()) {return "Flush";}
else if (hasStraight()) {return "Straight";}
else {
let sets = hasSets();
if (sets === "Pair" || sets === "none") {sets = "No Winner";}
return sets;
}
}
/* ---+
| End of the handType() function |
+---*/
}

Figure 8-26 Adding the `getHandValue()` public method

5. Save your changes to the file.

Apply the `getHandValue()` method to report the value of the player's final hand after the Draw or Stand button is clicked.

To apply the `getHandValue()` method:

1. Return to the **js08.js** file in your code editor and go to the event listener for the Draw button's click event.
2. Directly below the `for` loop that replaces cards from the hand add the following statements to display the value of the hand in the status box:

```
// Evaluate the hand drawn by user
statusBox.textContent = myHand.getHandValue();
```

3. Add the following statements to the Stand button's `click` event listener to cover the condition when the player continues play without drawing any new cards.

```
// Evaluate the hand drawn by user
statusBox.textContent = myHand.getHandValue();
```

Figure 8-27 describes the newly added code in the file.

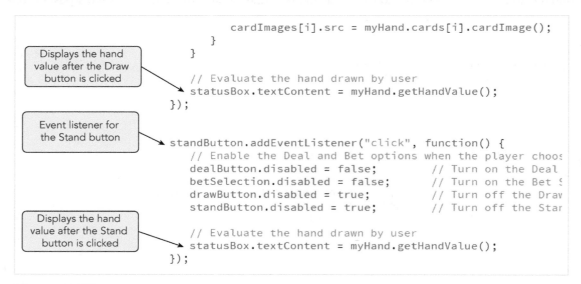

```
                  cardImages[i].src = myHand.cards[i].cardImage();
               }
            }

            // Evaluate the hand drawn by user
            statusBox.textContent = myHand.getHandValue();
         });

         standButton.addEventListener("click", function() {
            // Enable the Deal and Bet options when the player choos
            dealButton.disabled = false;        // Turn on the Deal
            betSelection.disabled = false;      // Turn on the Bet S
            drawButton.disabled = true;         // Turn off the Drav
            standButton.disabled = true;        // Turn off the Star

            // Evaluate the hand drawn by user
            statusBox.textContent = myHand.getHandValue();
         });
```

Displays the hand value after the Draw button is clicked

Event listener for the Stand button

Displays the hand value after the Stand button is clicked

Figure 8-27 Displaying the value of the played hand

4. Save your changes to the file and then reload the **js08.html** file in your browser.
5. Click the **Deal** button to deal a new hand, select cards to replace, and then click the **Draw** button. Verify that the table displays the value of the played hand. See **Figure 8-28**.

Figure 8-28 Results of a played hand

6. Click the **Deal** button followed by the **Stand** button to play the hand as originally dealt. Verify that the table once again displays the value of the hand.

The only task remaining is to update the bank value for winning hands. Recall that different hands provide different payouts. For example, a Pair of Jacks or Better repays the original bet while Two Pair pays back double the bet, Three of a Kind plays back triple, and Royal Flush (if you can get one) pays back 250× the bet. Add a new method named `payBet()` to the `pokerGame` object literal to calculate the amount of the payout and update the value of the player's bank.

To create the payBet() method:

1. Return to the **objects.js** file in your code editor and scroll up to the `pokerGame` object literal at the top of the page.
2. Type a comma, at the end of the `placeBet()` method and add the following statement to begin the `payBet()` method:

```
payBet: function(type) {
   let pay = 0;
   switch (type) {
      case "Royal Flush": pay = 250; break;
      case "Straight Flush": pay = 50; break;
      case "Four of a Kind": pay = 25; break;
      case "Full House": pay = 9; break;
      case "Flush": pay = 6; break;
      case "Straight": pay = 4; break;
      case "Three of a Kind": pay = 3; break;
      case "Two Pair": pay = 2; break;
      case "Jacks or Better": pay = 1; break;
   }
```

   The `switch case` statement examines the value of the type parameter, returning the `pay` multiplier for each possible hand or 0 if there is no winning hand.
3. Add the following commands to update the value of the player's bank and return it:

```
this.currentBank += pay*this.currentBet;
return this.currentBank;
```

4. Type } to close the `payBet()` method. **Figure 8-29** describes the complete code of the method.

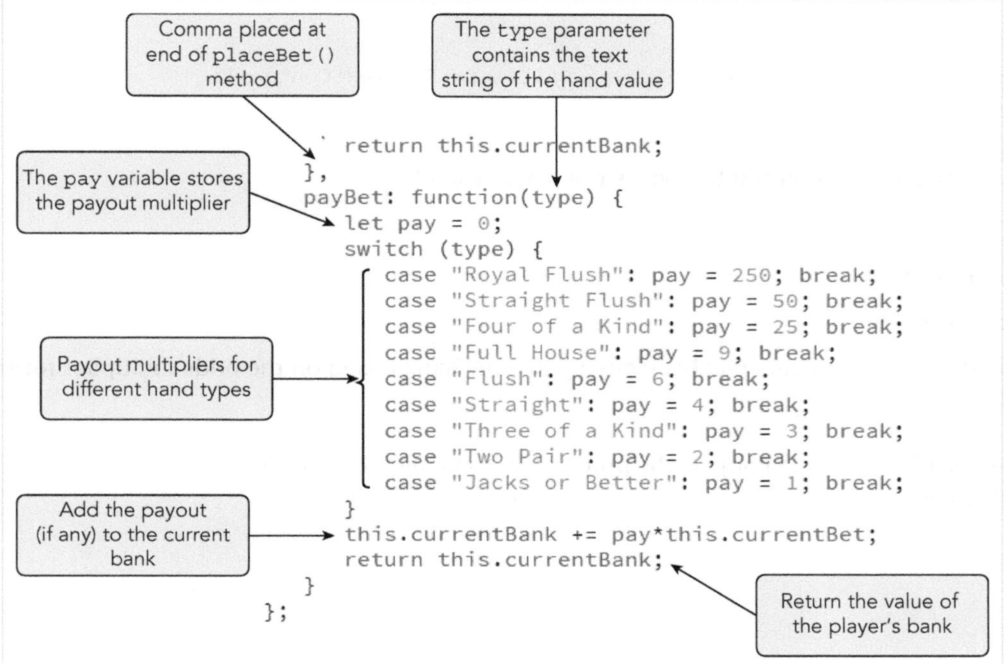

Figure 8-29 Calculating the payout for a winning hand

5. Close the file, saving your changes.

Apply the `payBet()` method to update the player's bank after the Draw or Stand button is clicked.

To apply the `payBet()` method:

1. Return to the **js08.js** file in your code editor and scroll down to the `click` event listener for the Draw button.
2. Add the following code to the event listener:

```
// Update the bank value
bankBox.value = pokerGame.payBet(statusBox.textContent);
```

3. Go to the `click` event listener for the Stand button and add the following statement:

```
// Update the bank value
bankBox.value = pokerGame.payBet(statusBox.textContent);
```

   Figure 8-30 shows the newly add code in the file.

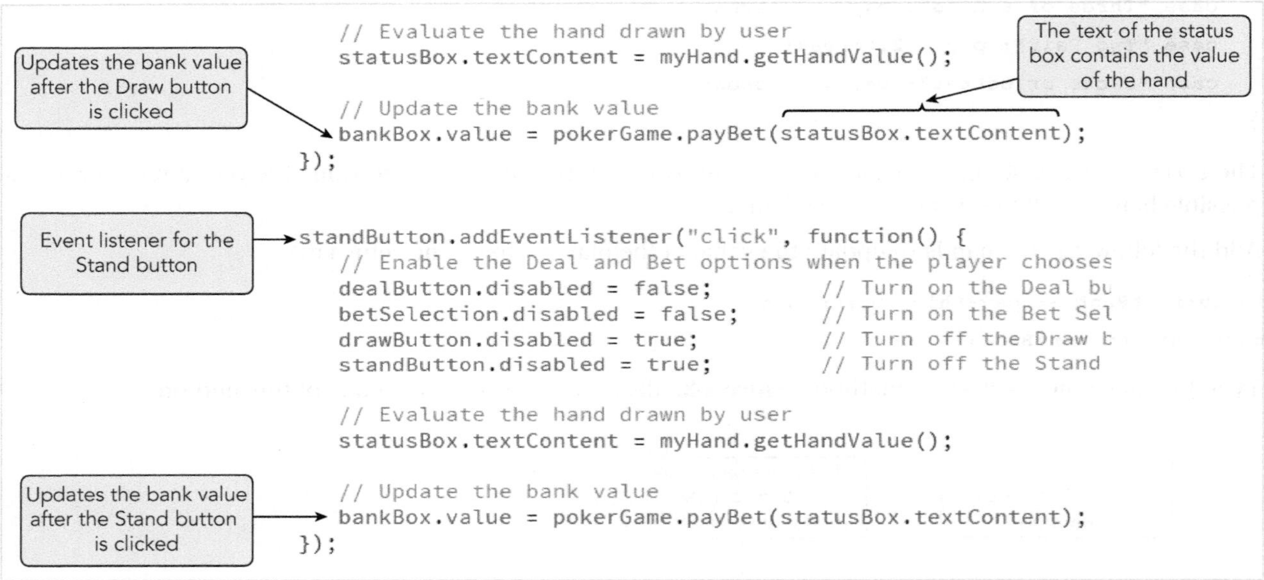

```
   // Evaluate the hand drawn by user
   statusBox.textContent = myHand.getHandValue();

   // Update the bank value
   bankBox.value = pokerGame.payBet(statusBox.textContent);
});

standButton.addEventListener("click", function() {
   // Enable the Deal and Bet options when the player chooses
   dealButton.disabled = false;        // Turn on the Deal bu
   betSelection.disabled = false;      // Turn on the Bet Sel
   drawButton.disabled = true;         // Turn off the Draw b
   standButton.disabled = true;        // Turn off the Stand

   // Evaluate the hand drawn by user
   statusBox.textContent = myHand.getHandValue();

   // Update the bank value
   bankBox.value = pokerGame.payBet(statusBox.textContent);
});
```

Updates the bank value after the Draw button is clicked
The text of the status box contains the value of the hand
Event listener for the Stand button
Updates the bank value after the Stand button is clicked

Figure 8-30 Applying the `payBet()` method to update the player's bank

4. Close the file, saving your changes.
5. Reopen **js08.html** in your browser.
6. Play the game, verifying that winning hands pay back money to your bank based on the odds multiplier for the different types of hands.

You have completed your work on the Draw Poker app. In the process of designing this app, you created custom objects that can be used in other poker card games.

Skills at Work | Guiding User Choices with Interface Cues

Ensuring that the logic of your JavaScript programs works is, of course, essential. However, you also need to make sure users intuitively understand how to use your programs. A judicious use of visual formatting can go a long way toward showing users how to interact with a program. In the Draw Poker game, buttons that were not applicable at certain points in the game were disabled and grayed out. For example, a player would not be able to click the Draw or Stand buttons until the Deal button had already been clicked. This visual cue removed distracting information from the player and guided the player to fewer legitimate choices.

Although you do not need to be an expert in design to be a successful JavaScript programmer, it can be useful to pay attention to the visual aspects of interfaces that you encounter on other websites and apps and draw lessons from them to make your application easier to work with.

Quick Check 3

1. What is the lexical environment of a variable or function?
2. What is a closure?
3. What is a disadvantage of creating a closure?
4. What is the difference between a public method and a private method?
5. What is a privileged method?

Combining Objects with Prototype Chains

Object classes can inherit properties and methods from other object classes. **Figure 8-31** shows a diagram of three object classes named `Person`, `Employee`, and `Staff`. The `Person` object class contains properties and methods that describe individuals, such as the individual's name and age. The `Employee` object inherits those properties and methods and adds others unique to employees, such as an employee's date of employment or annual salary. Finally, the `Staff` object class inherits properties and methods from the `Employee` object, adding properties and methods specific to staff members, such as information on current projects or membership in different working groups.

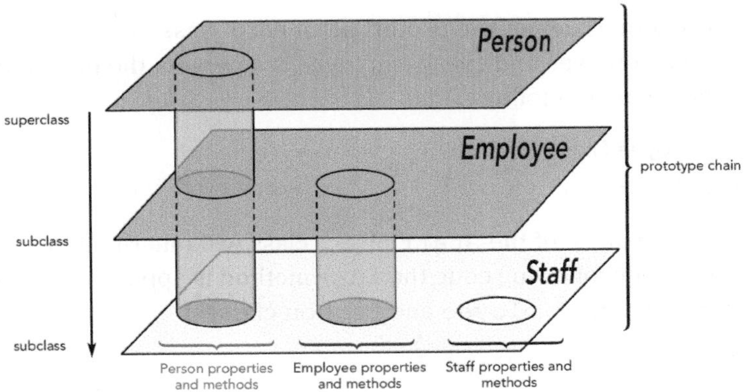

Figure 8-31 Prototypal inheritance

These object classes form a hierarchy or prototype chain ranging from a base object class, known as the superclass, down to the lower classes or subclasses. The process by which the properties and methods of an object class at one level are shared with an object class at the next level is called prototypal inheritance.

Creating a Prototype Chain

To demonstrate how prototypal inheritance works in JavaScript, consider the following code that creates the object classes for `Person`, `Employee`, and `Staff`. In this example, methods within each class build upon methods from the other classes. The `name()` method of the `Person` class returns the text string *`firstName.lastName`* and the `email()` method of the `Employee` class builds upon that method to return the text string *`firstName.lastName`*`@example.com`. Finally, the `id()` method of the `Staff` class uses the `email()` method to return the text string *`firstName.lastName`*`@example.com [`*`title`*`]`.

```
function Person(fName, lName) {
   this.firstName = fName;
   this.lastName = lName;
   this.name = function() {
      return this.firstName + "." + this.lastName;
   }
}
function Employee(fName, lName) {
   this.firstName = fName;
   this.lastName = lName;
   this.email = function() {
      return this.name() + "@example.com";
   }
}
function Staff(fName, lName) {
   this.firstName = fName;
   this.lastName = lName;
   this.title = null;
   this.id = function() {
      return this.email() + " [" + this.title + "]";
   }
}
```

To chain these object classes together, define the prototype of each class as an instance of a higher-order class. Because every staff member is an employee and every employee is a person, the prototype chain from staff member to employee to person would be defined as follows:

```
Staff.prototype = new Employee();
Employee.prototype = new Person();
```

Once the chain is established, an instance of the `Staff` object class will inherit all properties and methods defined throughout the prototype chain. In the following code the `id()` method is applied to a new hire showing a text string that relies on methods inherited from the `Employee` and `Person` classes:

```
let hire = new Staff("Keisha", "Adams");
hire.title = "Programmer";
console.log(hire.id());
// logs Keisha.Adams@example.com [Programmer]
```

Order is important when defining a prototype chain. Start at the lowest subclass and move up the chain to the superclass. When the JavaScript interpreter encounters a reference to a property or method, it attempts to resolve it in the following order:

1. Check for the property or method within the current object instance.
2. Check for the property or method with the object's prototype.
3. If the prototype is an instance of another object, check for the property or method in that object.
4. Continue moving through the prototype chain until the property or method located or the end of the chain is reached.

All prototype chains ultimately find their source in the base object.

Using the Base Object

The base object or `Object` is the fundamental JavaScript object whose properties and methods are shared by all native, host, and custom objects. All objects are ultimately subclasses of `Object`. **Figure 8-32** describes some of the properties and methods that all objects inherit from the `Object` prototype.

PROPERTY OR METHOD	DESCRIPTION
object.constructor	References the constructor function that creates *object*
object.hasOwnProperty(*prop*)	Returns `true` if *object* has the specified property, *prop*
object.isPrototypeOf(*obj*)	Returns `true` if *object* exists in object *obj* prototype chain
object.propertyIsEnumerable(*prop*)	Returns `true` if the *prop* property is enumerable
object.toLowerString()	Returns a text string representation of *object* using lower standards
object.toString()	Returns a text string representation of *object*
object.valueOf()	Returns the value of *object* as a text string, number, Boolean value, `undefined`, or `null`

Figure 8-32 Common object properties and methods

For example, to determine whether an object supports a particular property use the `hasOwnProperty()` method. Thus, the following code returns `true` to confirm that the `hire` object contains the `title` property but `false` for the `email` property because that property is inherited from a higher-order object class:

```
hire.hasOwnProperty("title");  // true
hire.hasOwnProperty("email");  // false
```

The constructor for `Object` also supports methods to retrieve and define properties for any custom or native object. **Figure 8-33** lists some of the methods associated with the `Object` constructor.

METHOD	DESCRIPTION
Object.assign(*target, sources*)	Copies all of the enumerable properties from the *sources* objects into the *target* object
Object.create(*proto, properties*)	Creates an object using the prototype, *proto*; where properties is an optional list of *properties* added to the object
Object.defineProperty(*obj, prop, descriptor*)	Defines or modifies the property, *prop*, for the object, *obj*; where *descriptor* describes the property
Object.defineProperties(*obj, prop*)	Defines or modifies the properties, *prop*, for the object, *obj*
Object.freeze(*obj*)	Freezes *obj* so that it cannot be modified by other code
Object.getPrototypeOf(*obj*)	References the prototype of the object, *obj*
Object.isFrozen(*obj*)	Return `true` if *obj* is frozen
Object.keys(*obj*)	Returns an array of the enumerable properties found in *obj*

Figure 8-33 Methods of the base object

As the hierarchy of objects and classes becomes more complex, it is often important to know which objects are associated with which prototypes. To reference the prototype of an object instance, apply the `getPrototypeOf()` method to the base object as in the following command that returns the prototype for the `hire` object, which in this example is the `Person` object (the last link in the prototype chain created above).

```
Object.getPrototypeOf(hire)  // returns the Person object
```

The following `Object.create()` method provides another way to create objects based on existing prototypes:

```
let newObject = Object.create(prototype);
```

where *`newObject`* is an instance of a new object based on the object class *`prototype`*. The following code creates an instance of a new object based on the `Staff` prototype and then uses the `name()` method from that prototype to return the full name of that staff member:

```
let hire2 = Object.create(Staff.prototype);
hire2.firstName = "Sandi";
hire2.lastName = "Ghang";
hire2.name();  // Returns the text string "Sandi.Ghang"
```

Note You can also view an object's prototype in your browser's debugger by using the `__proto__` property of the object.

Using the `apply()` and `call()` Methods

You can share methods between objects without defining one object as an instance of another. In the following code, the `showRank()` method is defined for the `pokerCard` object prototype to display the `rank` property in the debugger console:

```
function pokerCard(rankValue) {
   this.rank = rankValue;
}
pokerCard.prototype.showRank = function() {
   console.log(this.rank);
};
```

This method of logging rank values would be useful for any type of card game. To borrow a method from one object class and apply it with objects of a different class, use the following `apply()` method:

```
function.apply(thisObj [,argArray])
```

where *`function`* is a reference to a function, *`thisObj`* is the object that receives the actions of the function, and *`argArray`* is an optional array of argument values sent to the function. Thus, to apply the `showRank()` function to cards of `UnoCard` class, use the following `apply()` method:

```
function UnoCard(rank) {
   this.rank = rank;
}
let myUno = new UnoCard("8 green");
pokerCard.prototype.showRank.apply(myUno);
// logs "8 green"
```

One of the advantages of copying and applying a method like `showRank()` is that if the developer needs to make modifications to that method's code, those edits will be automatically shared with all objects that rely upon it.

Another way of sharing a method between objects is the `call()` method. The `call()` method is similar to the `apply()` method except that the argument values are placed in a comma-separated list of values instead of an array, as follows:

```
function.call(thisObj, args)
```

where *args* is a comma-separated list of argument values for function.

Note The `apply()` method is used with arrays (think "a" for "array"), while the `call()` method is used for a comma-separated list of values (think "c" for "comma").

This chapter has only scratched the surface of the study of prototypes and the organization of JavaScript objects. Just as you can build a complex lexical environment of nested functions and variables, you can create a complex hierarchical structure of objects and object prototypes. As you expand your knowledge and application of customized objects, you will need to adopt strategies for managing those objects to ensure integrity of your data and to keep your code lean and efficient.

Data Storage with Associative Arrays

Objects can also be used for storing and organizing data. The JavaScript object literal structure is also used as an associative array with data values defined using *key*:*value* pairs in which a key term is paired with a data value. The general structure is:

```
let array = {key1:value1, key2:value2, …}
```

where *key1*, *key2*, etc. are the keys and *value1*, *value2*, etc. are the values associated with each key. For example, the following structure defines several key values describing the properties of an employee:

```
let employee = {
  name: "Keisha Adams",
  position: "programmer",
  dept: "sales"
};
```

where the `Array` object uses an index to reference an item, an associative array uses a key. To reference the employee name, use the bracket notation `employee["name"]`, which for this object returns the value "Keisha Adams".

Despite the name, associative arrays are, strictly speaking, *not* arrays and do not support the JavaScript `Array` object properties and methods. There is no `length` property for associative arrays nor is there a `sort()` method for sorting the array contents.

Note Associative arrays are called hash tables or hashes in other programming languages.

The `for in` and `for of` Loops

Because associative arrays do not use indexes, you cannot examine their contents using a program loop with a counter variable. Instead of using a `for` loop, apply the following `for in` loop:

```
for (let prop in object) {
  commands
}
```

where *prop* references the properties or keys within the associative array and *object* is the object containing the data structure. For example, the following `for in` loop iterates through each key in the employee data structure, writing the key value to the console log:

```
for (let prop in employee) {
   console.log(prop + " is " + employee[prop];
}
// logs "name is Keisha Adams"
// logs "position is programmer"
// logs "dept is sales"
```

If an object inherits properties from other objects, all those properties will be included in the `for in` loop. The following `for in` loop iterates through properties in the `person` object as well as properties inherited from the `employee` object.

```
let person = {
   name: "Keisha Adams"
}
let employee = Object.create(person);
employee.position = "programmer";
for (let prop in employee) {
   console.log(prop + " is " + employee[prop]);
}
// logs "name is Keisha Adams"
// logs "position is programmer"
```

Note that `for in` loops do not follow a specific order because keys can be listed and read out in any order. For item collections in which order is important, use an `Array` object with array values assigned index numbers. Only properties that are countable or enumerable are accessible to `for in` loops. You can determine whether a property is enumerable using the following `propertyIsEnumerable()` method:

```
obj.propertyIsEnumerable(prop)
```

where *obj* is the object and *prop* is the property.

Similar to the `for in` loop is the `for of` loop, which is used for items that are enumerable. The syntax of the `for of` loop is:

```
for (let items of list) {
  commands
}
```

where *items* references the values within an enumerable list such as an array, node list, or HTML collection. For example, the following `for of` loop iterates all the items within the `pokerCards` array, writing the value of the `rank` property to the debugger console:

```
for (let items of pokerCards) {
  console.log(items.rank);
}
```

The `for of` loop is an efficient way to loop through the contents of a list without using a counter variable.

Storing Object data in JSON

The general structure of JavaScript objects was quickly seen as a useful vehicle for storing and organizing data. Douglas Crockford, one of JavaScript's pioneering architects, advocated a similar data structure called JavaScript Object Notation or JSON that could be used for storing structured data in a text-based format. JSON files are often used in web applications that need to transfer data between the server and the client.

JSON is not part of JavaScript, though it employs a similar syntax, nor is it used solely by JavaScript. A JSON file can be parsed and interpreted by programming languages such as PHP and Python. JSON is an example of a data interchange format, which is a text format that almost all systems have agreed upon as a common standard for information exchange. Another such language is XML. In fact, Crockford advocated for JSON as an alternate data interchange format to XML.

Note | JSON data is often stored in text files with the file name extension ".json".

The following is an example of employee data saved in the JSON format. This data could be stored in its own JSON text file, sent from the server to the client via a data stream, or stored as a text string in a JavaScript variable.

```
{
  "name" : "Keisha Adams",
  "age" : 27,
  "address" : {
    "street" : "41 Maple Avenue",
    "city" : "Ithaca",
    "state" : "New York",
    "postal code" : "14850"
  },
  "phone" : [
    {
      "type" : "work",
      "number" : "607-555-7812"
    },
    {
      "type" : "mobile",
      "number" : "607-555-0048"
    }
  ],
  "spouse" : null
}
```

Data written in JSON is organized as a comma-separated list of *`key`*`:` *`value`* pairs, though with JSON the key names must always be enclosed within double quotation marks. JSON supports three data types:

- **Simple values** such as numeric values, text strings, Boolean values, and null
- **Objects** with contents written as *`key`*`:` *`value`* pairs
- **Arrays** containing an array literal of simple values or objects

Although JSON data appears in the form of an object literal, it is not an object. It is a text string. However, a JSON text string can be converted to an object using the following `parse()` method:

```
let object = JSON.parse(JSONtxt)
```

where *`object`* is an object storing the JSON data and *`JSONtxt`* is the text of the JSON data structure. Once converted into an object, values from the JSON data structure can be referenced as any other JavaScript object. For example, if the `parse()` method were applied to the above JSON text string and then stored in a variable named `employee`, its values could be referenced using the following statements:

```
employee["name"]              // returns "Keisha Adams
employee.age                  // returns 27
employee.address.city         // returns "Ithaca"
employee["phone"][1].type     // returns "mobile"
```

As with all JavaScript objects, properties are referenced using either the bracket or the dot notation and nested objects are referenced by enclosing on object name within another. A JSON data structure might have several of these data values nested within one another. Notice that the Keisha Adams data includes a phone key with an array of objects listing work and mobile numbers.

> **Note** Because JSON key names must be enclosed within double quotes, use single quotes to enclose the JSON data structure. For longer data structures that span several lines, store the text string as template literals using the backtick (`) character to mark the beginning and end of the string.

Many applications need to convert JavaScript objects into JSON text strings so that the information contained within the object can be exchanged with a server or database application. To convert a JavaScript object into the JSON format use the following `stringify()` method:

```
JSON.stringify(object, [replacer [, space]]);
```

where *`string`* stores the JSON text string, *`object`* is the JavaScript object to be converted, *`replacer`* is an optional function is an array of text strings and numeric values for filtering the object, and *`space`* is an optional argument to insert spaces into the output string for readability. The following are some examples of applying the `stringify()` method to custom and built-in JavaScript objects:

```
JSON.stringify(27)
// returns '27'
JSON.stringify(false)
// returns 'false'
JSON.stringify({name: "Keisha Adams", age: 27})
// returns '{"name":"Keisha Adams","age",27}'
JSON.stringify(new Date(2024, 5, 4, 13, 15, 8))
// returns '2024-06-04T18:15:08.000Z'
```

Note that applying the `stringify()` method to a `Date` object returns a text of the date value in Greenwich time.

You may not want to write all the properties of an object into a text string, so you can specify the list of properties to include in the array as part of the `replacer` argument. The following expression returns only the `name` property of the object, dropping the `age` property:

```
JSON.stringify({name: "Keisha Adams", age: 27}, ['name'])
// returns '{"name":"Keisha Adams"}'
```

In developing applications to communicate with server scripts and programs, you may need to use JSON as the data format. Many applications use the `stringify()` method to convert object data into a suitable format for transferring to a server.

Common Mistakes

Catching Syntax Errors in JSON Data

JSON is an excellent format for data exchange and because it builds upon the structure of JavaScript objects, it should be a very familiar format. However, despite its appearance, there are some important differences in the code for JSON data and JavaScript objects. Keep these syntax issues in mind when you write your JSON data:

- Key names should always be enclosed within double quotes. An error will result if you use single quotes or avoid using quotes at all.
- The collection of *`key`*`:` *`value`* pairs must be placed in a comma-separated list. Failure to separate these pairs with a comma or using a semicolon in place of a comma will result in an error.
- All nested objects within the JSON data structure must include the opening and closing braces.
- JSON data is entered as a text string; therefore, it should be enclosed within single quotes when written on one line. If the code extends over several lines, enter it as a template literal with the opening and closing marked with the backtick character (`).

By catching these errors, you can avoid problems with writing data in JSON format.

Quick Check 4

1. Provide code to specify that the `Clothing` object class is a subclass of the `Merchandise` class.
2. Provide an expression to test whether the `myCard` object contains a property named "suit".
3. Which command should be used to loop through properties of an associative array?
4. When would you use the `call()` method with an object?
5. How do you convert a JSON text string into a JavaScript object? How do you convert a JavaScript object into a JSON text string?

Summary

- Object-oriented programming (OOP) refers to the creation of reusable software objects that can be easily incorporated into multiple programs.
- An object literal is a standalone object used once for a single purpose. Within the object literal you can add properties and methods that define the object and its behavior.
- Properties are added to a custom object with *`name`*`:` *`value`* pairs within a command block. Methods are added as nested functions within the command block.

- Object properties can be referenced using either the dot operator or bracket notation.
- An object literal can be created with the `new Object()` constructor.
- An object class acts as a template or blueprint for the creation of new objects all sharing a common collection of properties and methods. Each new object based on a class creates an instance of that class.
- An object constructor function is used to create a new class of objects.
- Every JavaScript object has a prototype, which is a template for all the properties and methods associated with the object's class. Object prototypes are referenced using the `prototype` property.
- Prototypes can be used to add methods to existing object classes.
- A closure is a copy of a function that also copies the lexical environment of variables within the function.
- Methods associated with custom objects can be public, private, or privileged. A public method is defined for the object prototype and, thus, can be called outside of the object. A private method is a method created within the constructor function and, thus, is accessible only within the constructor. A privileged method is a method that accesses private variables and methods but that is also accessible to the public.
- Object classes can be combined with prototype chains in which the property and methods of one object are inherited by other objects in the chain. All native and custom objects are connected ultimately to the base object.
- Methods in one object class can be applied to another object class using the `apply()` and `call()` methods.
- Data can be stored within associative arrays in which data values are matched to key names. A `for in` loop can be used to loop through the contents of an associative array. A `for of` loop can be used to loop through lists that are enumerable.
- JavaScript Object Notation or JSON is a text-based data structure used for storing data using the general structure of *`key`*`:`*`value`* pairs within an object.

Key Terms

associative array
base object
bracket notation
closure
constructor function
custom object
data interchange format
dot operator
encapsulation
enumerable
host object
instantiating
interface
JavaScript Object Notation
JSON
lexical environment
lexical scope
native object
object class
object constructor
object instance
object literal
object-oriented programming (OOP)
private method
privileged method
prototypal inheritance
prototype
prototype chain
public method
static scope
subclass
superclass
user-defined object

Review Questions

1. **Why are objects encapsulated?**
   a. So that they can act as templates for other objects
   b. To create an interface for an app
   c. To share their code in a prototype chain
   d. So that the code and data are hidden from other programs
2. **What is an object literal?**
   a. A template for the creation of other objects
   b. A native object built into JavaScript
   c. A host object used by the web browser
   d. A standalone object used for a single purpose
3. **Provide the reference to the `dateHired` property of the employee object in bracket notation.**
   a. `employee.dateHired`
   b. `employee[dateHired]`
   c. `employee["dateHired"]`
   d. `employee:dateHired`
4. **The `new Object()` command ____________.**
   a. creates a new object from the JavaScript base object
   b. is used to create an object class
   c. is used to create a closure
   d. creates a new native object
5. **An object class is used ____________.**
   a. to create standalone objects built for a single purpose
   b. to create native objects
   c. as a template for new objects sharing the same properties and methods
   d. to create host objects
6. **To create an object class, you need a(n) __________.**
   a. JavaScript framework
   b. constructor function
   c. object literal
   d. closure
7. **Provide code to instantiate an object from the `Employee` object class, storing the object in the `myEmp` variable.**
   a. `let myEmp = new Employee;`
   b. `let myEmp = Employee();`
   c. `let myEmp : Employee();`
   d. `let myEmp = new Employee()`
8. **What is an object prototype?**
   a. A literal object used for a single purpose
   b. A template for all properties and methods associated with an object class
   c. A constructor function used to create an object class
   d. A host object built into the web browser
9. **Provide code to add the `review()` method to the prototype of the `Employee` class.**
   a. `Employee.review = function()`
   b. `Employee.prototype.review() = function`
   c. `Employee.prototype.review = function`
   d. `Employee.review.prototype = function`
10. **A closure is a ____________.**
    a. command block that encloses an object's properties and methods
    b. copy of a variable that encloses that variable's value
    c. closed chain of object prototypes
    d. copy of a function along with the lexical environment of variables within that function
11. **What is a privileged method?**
    a. A method that takes precedence over other methods in the script
    b. A method created that access private variables and methods but is also accessible to the public
    c. A method associated with an object prototype
    d. A method associated with a native or host object
12. **The hierarchy of objects connected via their prototypes is known as a(n) ____________.**
    a. prototype chain
    b. prototype tree
    c. object list
    d. object tree
13. **Which object method references the prototype of an object instance?**
    a. `Object.prototype()`
    b. `Object.getPrototype()`
    c. `Object.getPrototypeOf()`
    d. `Object.loadPrototype()`

14. A `for in` loop is used to ____________.
   a. iterate through the contents of an associative array
   b. determine whether an object contains a specified property
   c. iterate through the contents of any array
   d. write the contents of an object in JSON format

15. Which method should be used to convert text written in JSON to a JavaScript object?
   a. `JSON.toObject()`
   b. `JSON.stringify()`
   c. `JSON.construct()`
   d. `JSON.parse()`

16. What are some advantages of creating custom objects using object-oriented programming?

17. Provide code to create an object class named `realEstate` containing two properties named `salesPrice` and `squareFoot`, setting both of those property values to `null`.

18. Why should you add a method to the prototype of an object class rather than adding the method to the constructor function of the object class?

19. What are the advantages and disadvantages of closures?

20. Why would you place object data in the JSON format?

Hands-On Projects

Hands-On Project 8-1

In this project you will build the object class for a countdown timer. The `timer` object will have properties to record the minutes and seconds remaining, and to record the id value used with for the `windows.setInterval()` method. The timer object will also have a method that runs the timer, updating its value once per second or pausing the timer. A preview of the interface that controls the actions of the `timer` object is shown in **Figure 8-34**.

Figure 8-34 Completed Project 8-1

Do the following:

1. Use your code editor to open the **project08-01_txt.html** and **project08-01_txt.js** files from the js08 ► project01 folder. Enter your name and the date in the comment section of each file and save them as **project08-01.html** and **project08-01.js**, respectively.
2. Go to the **project08-01.html** file in your code editor and link the page to the project08-01.js file, deferring the script until after the page loads. Take some time to study the code of the file and then close it, saving your changes.

3. Return to the **project08-01.js** file in your code editor. Directly below the Object Code comment add a constructor function for the `timer` object containing two parameters named `min` and `sec`. Set the `timer.minutes` property equal to `min`, the `timer.seconds` property equal to `sec`, and the `timer.timeID` property equal to `null`.
4. Directly below the `timer()` constructor function, add the `runPause()` method to the `timer` object class prototype. The `runPause()` method has three parameters named `timer`, `minBox`, and `secBox`. Within the anonymous function for the `runPause()` method add the tasks described in Steps 5 through 6.
5. Insert an `if else` statement testing whether `timer.timedID` is truthy (has a value). If it does, you will pause the timer by applying the `window.clearInterval()` method using `timer.timeID` as the parameter value; set `timer.timeID` equal to null. Otherwise, run the `window.setInterval()` method to start the timer, running the `countdown()` function every 1000 milliseconds; store the id of the `setInterval()` method in the `timer.timeID` property.
6. Add the `countdown()` function that updates the timer every second. Within the function, add an `if else` statement that does the following:
   a. If `timer.seconds` is greater than 0, decrease the value of `timer.seconds` by 1.
   b. Else, if `timer.minutes` is greater than 0, decrease the value of `timer.minutes` by 1 and set the value of `timer.seconds` to 59.
   c. Else the timer has reached 0:0; stop the timer by running the `window.clearInterval()` method with `timer.timeID` as the parameter value and then set the value of `timer.timeID` to `null`.
   d. After the `if else` statement, write the value of `timer.minutes` to `minBox.value` and `timer.seconds` to `secBox.value`
7. Scroll to the bottom of the file. Declare an instance of the `timer` object and name it `myTimer` using `minBox.value` and `secBox.value` as the parameter values for the initial value of the timer.
8. Create an `onchange` event handler for `minBox` that sets `myTimer.minutes` to `minBox.value`. Create an `onchange` event handler for `secBox` that sets `myTimer.seconds` to `secBox.value`.
9. Create an `onclick` event handler for the `runPauseTimer` button that runs an anonymous function that applies the `runPause()` method to `myTimer` using `myTimer`, `minBox`, and `secBox` as the parameter values.
10. Save your changes to the file and then load **project08-01.html** in your web browser.
11. Verify that clicking the RUN/PAUSE button alternately starts and pauses the timer and that the timer correctly updates itself every second, stopping when it reaches 0:0.

Hands-On Project 8-2

In this project you will write code defining objects for balls bouncing within a container. When a ball hits the container side it will rebound, and the container will shift in the direction of the ball's velocity. Each instance of the ball object includes properties for the ball's radius, horizontal and vertical position, and horizontal and vertical velocity. The container object will have properties defining its width, height, and position. New balls with random velocity are added to the center of the container by clicking a New Ball button. A preview of the completed project is shown in **Figure 8-35**.

Do the following:

1. Use your code editor to open the **project08-02_txt.html** and **project08-02_txt.js** files from the js08 ► project02 folder. Enter your name and the date in the comment section of each file and save them as **project08-02.html** and **project08-02.js**, respectively.
2. Go to the **project08-02.html** file in your code editor and link the page to the project08-02.js file, deferring the script until after the page loads. Close the file, saving your changes.

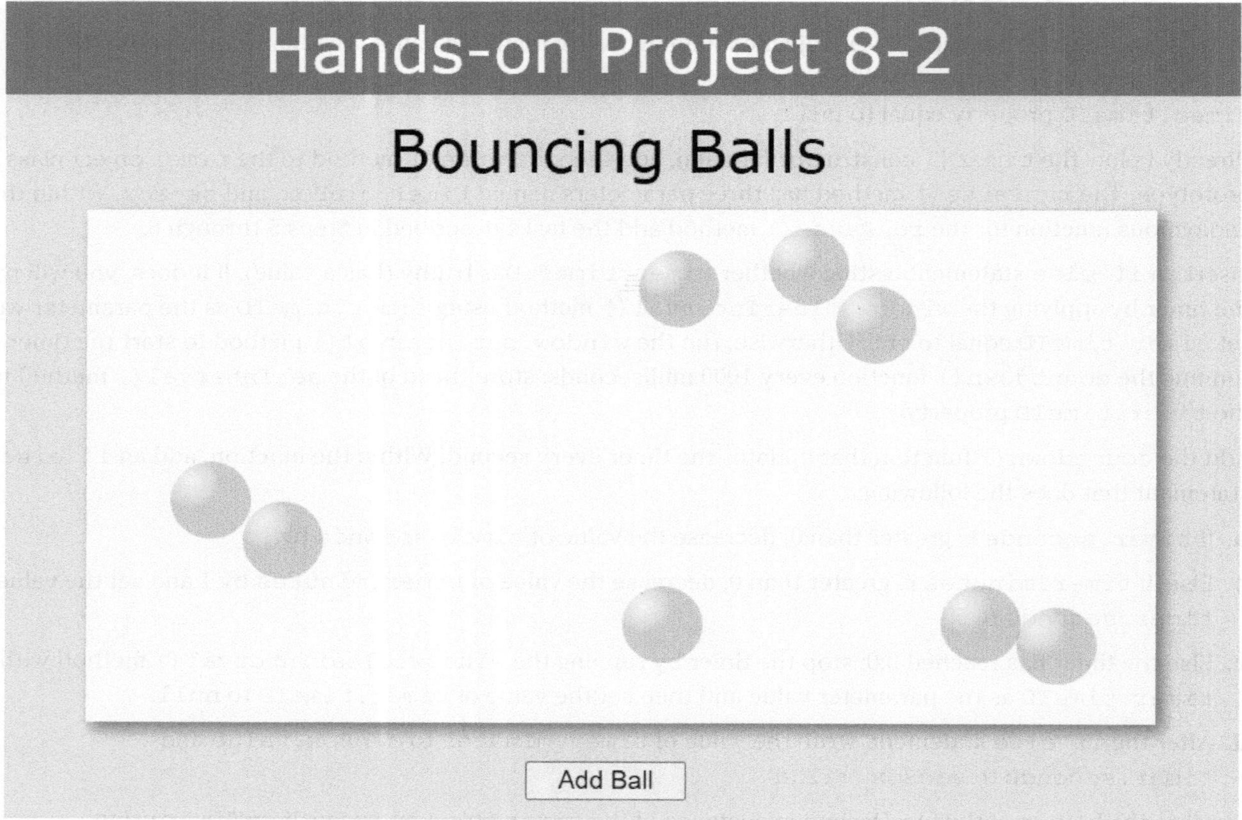

Figure 8-35 Completed Project 8-2

3. Return to the **project08-02.js** file in your code editor. Directly below the Object Code comment create an object literal named `box` with its `width` and `height` properties equal to `BOX_WIDTH` and `BOX_HEIGHT` and its `xPos` and `yPos` properties equal to 0.
4. Create a constructor function for the `ball` class. The constructor function has a single parameter named `size`. Within the constructor function set the value of the `radius` property to `size` and the `xPos`, `yPos`, `xVelocity`, and `yVelocity` properties to `null`.
5. Create the `moveWithin()` method of the ball object class prototype that runs an anonymous function with `container` as its only parameter. The purpose of this method is to move the ball within the container, bouncing it off the container sides. Within the anonymous function do the following:
    a. Set the top and left positions of the ball by creating the `ballTop` variable equal to `this.yPos` and the `ballLeft` variable equal to `this.xPos`.
    b. Set the bottom and left positions of the ball by creating the `ballBottom` variable equal to `this.yPos + this.radius` and the `ballRight` variable equal to `this.xPos + this.radius`.
    c. If `ballTop` is less than zero or `ballBottom` is greater than `container.height`, then bounce the ball vertically by (i) increasing `container.yPos` by the value of `this.yVelocity` and (ii) setting `this.yVelocity = -this.yVelocity`.
    d. If `ballLeft` is less than zero or `ballRight` is greater than `container.width`, then bounce the ball horizontally by (i) increasing `container.xPos` by the value of `this.xVelocity` and (ii) setting `this.xVelocity = -this.xVelocity`.
    e. Move the ball within the container by increasing the value of `this.yPos` by `this.yVelocity` and by increasing the value of `this.xPos` by `this.xVelocity`.

6. Scroll down to the Interface Code section and within the `onclick` event handler for the `addBall` button add the code described in Steps 7 and 8.
7. Create an instance of a ball object with the following properties:
   a. Store an instance of the ball object in a variable named `newBall` with a size value equal to `BALL_RADIUS`.
   b. Center the `newBall` within the container by setting the `yPos` property to `(BOX_HEIGHT - BALL_RADIUS)/2` and the `xPos` property to `(BOX_WIDTH - BALL_RADIUS)/2`.
   c. Give `newBall` an initial random velocity by calling the `rand()` function, setting the value of the `yVelocity` and `xVelocity` properties to `rand(-10, 10)`.
8. Animate the motion of `newBall` by calling the `window.setInterval()` method. Within the method, run the following code in an anonymous function every 25 milliseconds:
   a. Apply the `moveWithin()` method to `newBall` with `box` as the value of the container parameter.
   b. Move the image of the ball by setting `ballImage.style.top` equal to `newBall.yPos + "px"` and `ballImage.style.left` equal to `newBall.xPos + "px"`.
   c. Shake the image of the container by setting `boxImage.style.top` equal to `box.yPos + "px"` and `boxImage.style.left` equal to `box.xPos + "px"`.
9. Save your changes to file and then load **project08-02.html** in your browser.
10. Verify that you can add new balls to the container by clicking the Add Ball button and that the balls bounce off the sides, shaking the container.

Hands-On Project 8-3

In this project you will create objects to describe the contents of a pizza and the contents of a shopping cart. Each pizza is described by its size, crust, and list of toppings. An interface that allows customers to build their pizza by selecting items from a web form has been created for you. Your job will be to write the object code to work with this interface, storing data about the pizzas the customers build. A preview of the completed project is shown in **Figure 8-36**.

Figure 8-36 Completed Project 8-3

Do the following:

1. Use your code editor to open the **project08-03_txt.html** and **project08-03_txt.js** files from the js08 ▶ project03 folder. Enter your name and the date in the comment section of each file and save them as **project08-03.html** and **project08-03.js**, respectively.
2. Go to the **project08-03.html** file in your code editor and link the page to the project08-03.js file, deferring the script until after the page loads. Take some time to study the contents and structure of the web from which customers will make their selections. Close the file, saving your changes.
3. Return to the **project08-03.js** file in your code editor. Directly below the Object Code comment create an object literal named `cart`. The `cart` object has a single property named `items` containing an empty array and a single method named `addItem(foodItem)` Add the command `this.items.push(foodItem)` to this method.
4. Create a constructor function for the `Pizza` object class containing a `size` and `crust` property with no initial values and a `toppings` property containing an empty array.
5. Create a constructor function for the `Topping` object class containing the `name` and `side` property to store the name of the topping and whether covers the entire pizza or is limited to the pizza's left or right side. Do not enter initial values for these properties.
6. Add the `addToCart(cart)` method to the `Pizza` prototype. Within the method run the command `cart.items.push(this)` to add the pizza to the `items` array of a shopping cart.
7. Add the `summarize()` method to the `Pizza` prototype to create a text string summarizing the content of the pizza. Within the function do the following:
   a. Declare a variable named `summary` with the initial value "Pizza: ".
   b. Add the value of `this.size` and `this.crust` to the value of `summary`. Separate the size and crust values with a blank space.
   c. Create a `for` loop that iterates through the `this.toppings` array. For each item in the array add the text string *name* (*side*) to the `summary` variable, where *name* is the value of the `this.toppings[i].name` property and *side* is the value of the `this.toppings[i].side` property.
   d. After the `for` loop, return the value of the `summary` variable.
8. Scroll down to the `buildPizza()` function. This function builds a pizza object based on selections made on the web form. Add the following code to the function.
   a. Create an instance of a `Pizza` object storing it in `myPizza`.
   b. Set the value of `myPizza.size` to `pizzaSizeBox.value`. Set the value of `myPizza.crust` to `pizzaCrustBox.value`.
   c. Add the selected toppings to the pizza by creating a `for` loop that iterates through the contents of the `checkedToppings` node list. Within the loop, (i) create an instance of a `Topping` object named `myTopping`; (ii) set `myTopping.name` equal to `checkedToppings[i].name` and `myTopping.side` equal to `checkedToppings[i]value`; (iii) apply the `addTopping(myTopping)` method to `myPizza`.
   d. After the `for` loop, return the value of `myPizza`.
9. Go to the `updateCart()` function, which adds the pizza to the shopping cart. Add the following commands to the function:
   a. Run the `buildPizza()` function, storing the result in the `myPizza` variable.
   b. Apply the `addItem(myPizza)` method to the `cart` object.
   c. Run the `console.log(cart)` method to write the contents of the `cart` object to the debugger console.
   d. Create a paragraph element containing the value of `summarize(myPizza)`. Use the `appendChild()` method to append the paragraph to the `cartBox` element.
   e. Reset the page for the next pizza by running the `clearPizzaImage()` function followed by the `clearToppings()` function.

10. Save your changes to the file and then load **project08-03.html** in your browser. Verify that you can build a pizza and add it to the shopping cart by clicking controls on the web form. Verify that the debugger console lists all of the pizzas added to the `cart` object.

Hands-On Project 8-4

In this project you will explore how to retrieve text data from a JSON file and display that data in a web table. The first few lines of a JSON file containing a staff directory is shown in **Figure 8-37**.

```
{ "directory" : [
   {
      "id" : "emp850-02",
      "firstName" : "Hyun",
      "lastName" : "Choi",
      "position" : "Accounting Specialist I",
      "dept" : "CU Accounting Services",
      "email" : "hyun.choi@ccul.example.com",
      "phone" : "800-555-8142"
   },
   {
      "id" : "emp300-01",
      "firstName" : "Dan",
      "lastName" : "Moses",
```

Figure 8-37 Staff directory stored in JSON format

In this file, there is single root object named directory containing an array of objects with each object containing `key:value` pairs for the employee id, first name, last name, position, department, email address, and phone number. To iterate through these properties, you will use a `for in` loop with the following general form:

```
for (let prop in object) {
commands
}
```

where prop references the properties associated with *`object`* and commands are the commands applied to each `key:value` pair in the object. **Figure 8-38** shows the final version of the web table you will create for this project.

Do the following:

1. Use your code editor to open the **project08-04_txt.html** and **project08-04_txt.js** files from the js08 ► project04 folder. Enter your name and the date in the comment section of each file and save them as **project08-04.html** and **project08-04.js**, respectively.
2. Go to the **project08-04.html** file in your code editor and link the page to the project08-04.js file, deferring the script until after the page loads. Close the file, saving your changes.
3. Return to the **project08-04.js** file in your code editor. Some of the code to create the app has already been entered for you. Go to the `onload` event handler for the `fr` (file reader) variable and add the following code:
   a. Add a command to convert the contents of the JSON data in `fr.result` into an object named `staff`.
   b. Call the `makeStaffTable()` function using `staff` as the parameter value.
4. Go to the `makeStaffTable()` function and add the commands described in Steps 5 through 7.

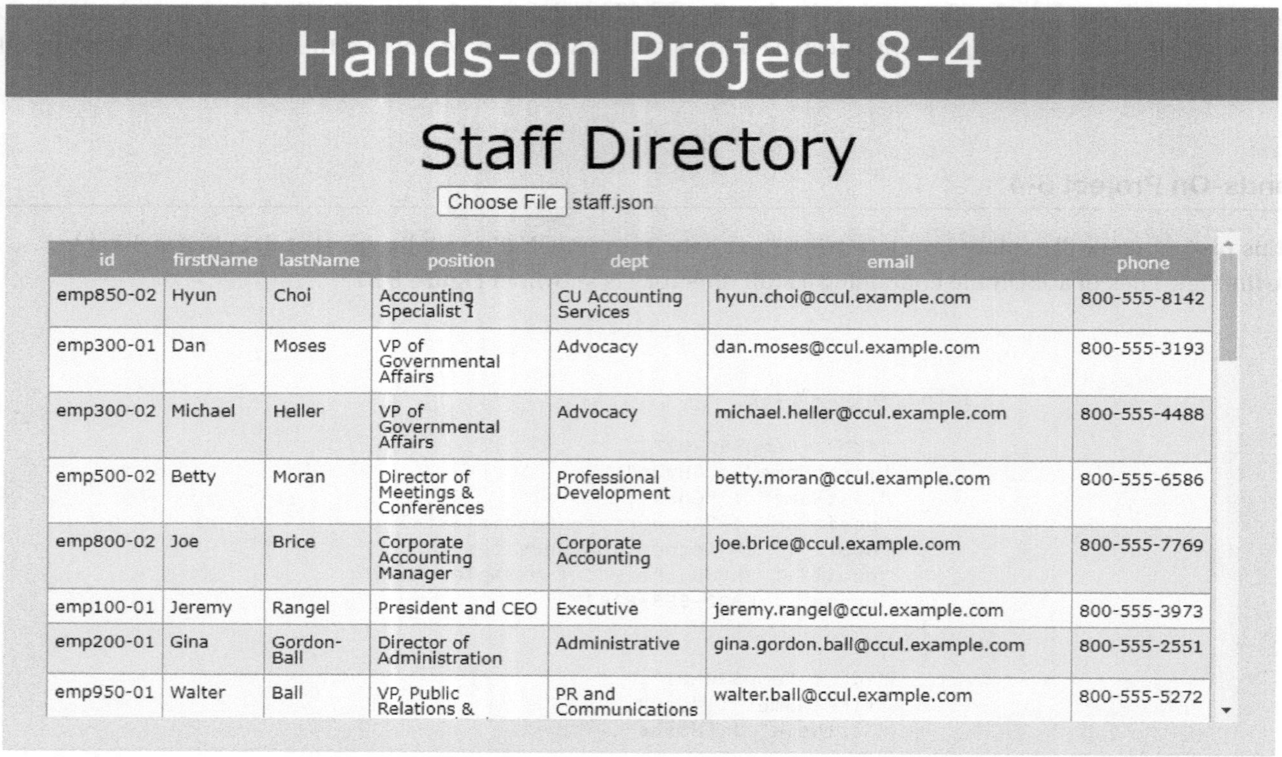

Hands-on Project 8-4

Staff Directory

Choose File staff.json

id	firstName	lastName	position	dept	email	phone
emp850-02	Hyun	Choi	Accounting Specialist 1	CU Accounting Services	hyun.choi@ccul.example.com	800-555-8142
emp300-01	Dan	Moses	VP of Governmental Affairs	Advocacy	dan.moses@ccul.example.com	800-555-3193
emp300-02	Michael	Heller	VP of Governmental Affairs	Advocacy	michael.heller@ccul.example.com	800-555-4488
emp500-02	Betty	Moran	Director of Meetings & Conferences	Professional Development	betty.moran@ccul.example.com	800-555-6586
emp800-02	Joe	Brice	Corporate Accounting Manager	Corporate Accounting	joe.brice@ccul.example.com	800-555-7769
emp100-01	Jeremy	Rangel	President and CEO	Executive	jeremy.rangel@ccul.example.com	800-555-3973
emp200-01	Gina	Gordon-Ball	Director of Administration	Administrative	gina.gordon.ball@ccul.example.com	800-555-2551
emp950-01	Walter	Ball	VP, Public Relations &	PR and Communications	walter.ball@ccul.example.com	800-555-5272

Figure 8-38 Completed Project 8-4

5. First create a table row containing the property names stored in the JSON file using the properties from the first directory entry. Create a `for in` loop for the object stored in `staff.directory[0]` and add the following commands to the loop:

   a. Use the `document.createElement()` method to create a `th` element named `headerCell`.

   b. Store `prop` as the text content of `headerCell`.

   c. Use the `appendChild()` method to append `headerCell` to the `headerRow` object.

   d. After the `for in` loop completes, append `headerRow` to the `staffTable` object.

6. Next, create table rows containing the property values for each entry in the `directory` array. Add a `for` loop that loops through the items of `staff.directory`. Within the `for` loop do the following:

   a. Create an element node for the `tr` element and store it in the `tableRow` variable.

   b. Create a `for in` loop for the properties listed in the `staff.directory[i]`. For each property do the following: (i) Create an element node for the `td` element and store it in the `tableCell` variable; (ii) store the value of `staff.directory[i][prop]` as the text content of `tableCell`; (iii) append `tableCell` to the `tableRow` object.

   c. After the `for in` loop completes, append `tableRow` to the `staffTable` object.

7. After the `for` loop is finished, use the `appendChild()` method to append `staffTable` to the `containerBox` object.

8. Save your changes to the file and then load **project08-04.html** in your web browser.

9. Click the Choose File button and open the **staff.json** file from the js08 ▶ project04 folder. Verify that the contents of the file are converted into a web table with the property names in the first table row and the property values for each directory entry shown in subsequent table rows.

Hands-On Project 8-5

Debugging Challenge

You have been given code for a web page that loads game logs from classic chess games. A preview of the completed project is shown in **Figure 8-39**.

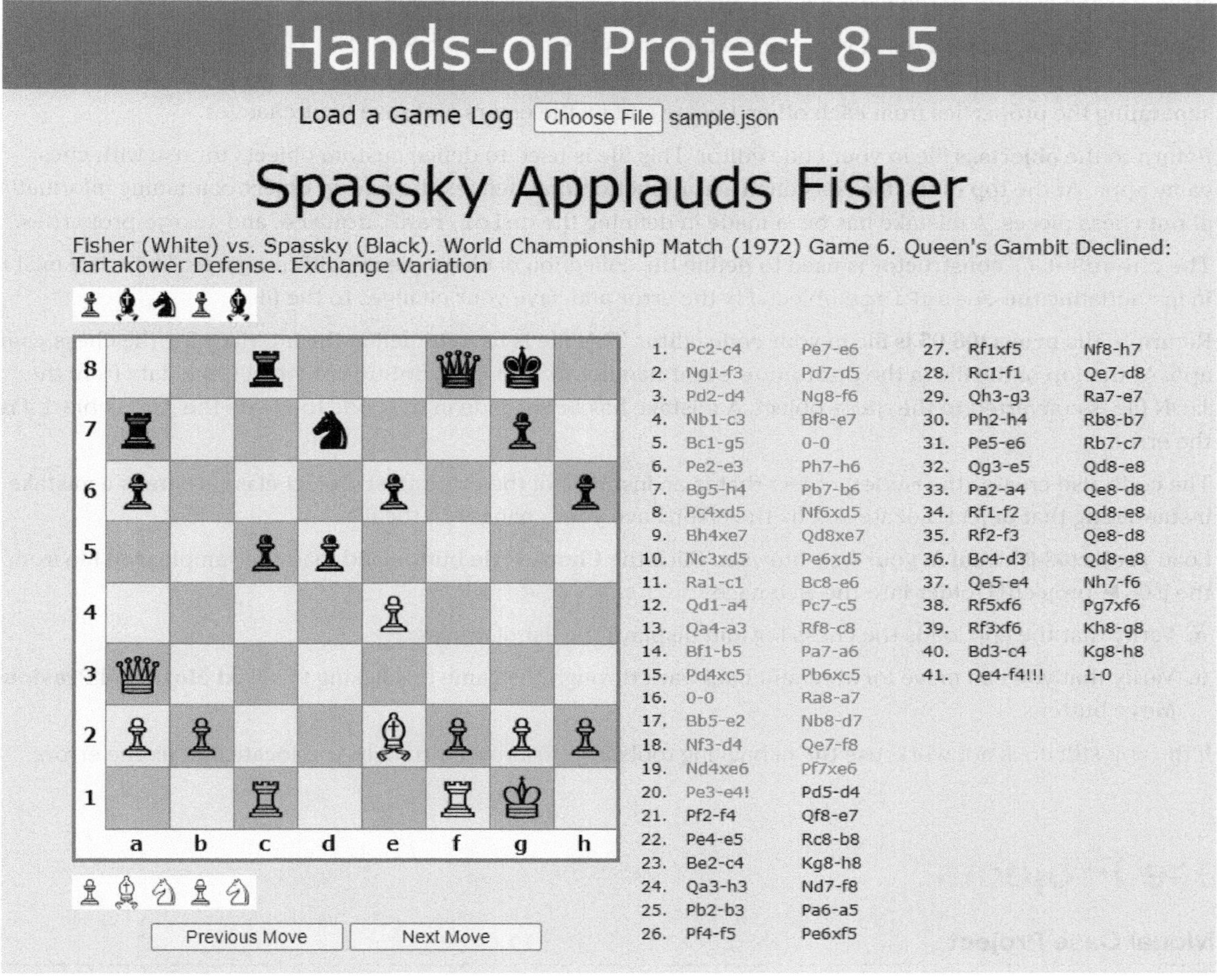

Figure 8-39 Completed Project 8-5

The location of each square on a chess board is identified by a letter and number for the square column and row. For example, the e2 square is placed in the fifth column and second row of the board. One way of logging a chess game is to record the opening and closing positions of pieces as they are moved. The log entry "Pc2-c4" means to move the pawn on square c2 to square c4.

The moves shown in Figure 8-39 are stored in a JSON file. The chess board is created with a web table in which each <td> tag has been assigned an id matching its square. Form buttons have been provided to move forward and backward through the game with the movement of the pieces on the board matching the game log.

The code for this app contains several errors that keep it from running correctly. You have been asked to use your knowledge of object-oriented programming to debug the program.

Do the following:

1. Use your code editor to open the **project08-05_txt.html**, **project08-05_txt.js**, and **objects_txt.js** files from the js08 ▶ project05 folder. Enter your name and the date in the comment section of each file and save them as **project08-05.html**, **project08-05.js**, and **objects.js**, respectively.
2. Go to the **project08-05.html** file in your code editor and link the page to the project08-05.js and objects.js files, deferring the scripts until after the page loads. Study the code in the HTML file to become familiar with the structure and content of the file. Close the document, saving your changes.
3. Go to the **sample_txt.json** file in your code editor and save it as **sample.json**. The JSON file contains information on a sample game, but there are several mistakes in the syntax of the JSON data in naming the properties and separating the properties from each other. Locate and fix the errors and save your changes.
4. Return to the **objects.js** file in your code editor. This file is used to define custom objects for use with chess game apps. At the top of the file is a constructor function that defines the `piece` object containing information about chess pieces. A mistake has been made in defining the `color`, `rank`, `square`, and `image` properties.
5. The `chessSet()` constructor is used to define the collection of chess pieces within a game. There is a mistake in instantiating the `chessPiece` object. Fix the error and save your changes to the file.
6. Return to the **project08-05.js** file in your code editor. This file is used to define the interface for the chess game app. At the top of the file in the `onchange` event handler for the `getLogButton` object, the data from the JSON file is converted to the `game` object. A mistake has been made in the code to create the game object. Fix the error.
7. The code also creates the `mySet` object that is an instance of the `chessSet` object class. There is a mistake in instantiating that object. Locate and fix the error. Save your changes to the file.
8. Load **project08-05.html** in your web browser. Click the **Choose File** button and load the sample.json file from the js08 ▶ project05 folder into the web page.
    a. Verify that the app loads the chess log and displays the list of moves.
    b. Verify that you can move forward and backward through the game by clicking the **Next Move** and **Previous Move** buttons.
9. If the app still does not work, use the debugging tools in your browser to help you locate and fix the errors.

Case Projects

Individual Case Project

Add object-oriented programming techniques to your project by creating custom objects to manage some of the tasks in your project. Store the objects in a separate file. Create a constructor function for a class of objects and then add methods to your object class prototypes. Create instances of each object class in your code. Your objects and object classes should be designed in such a way that they could be used with other applications.

Team Case Project

Have your group members discuss the objects they created for the Individual Case Project to the group, reviewing how they designed the objects so they could be easily used with other applications. Suggest ways that each member's custom objects could be used in other projects that might be designed in the future.

CHAPTER 9

Managing State Information and Security

When you complete this chapter you will be able to:

- Describe the fundamentals of sessions and state information
- Share data between web pages using query strings
- Explain how data is stored using the Web Storage API
- Use browser tools to view and manage web storage contents
- Identify the purpose and structure of a cookie
- Write data into a cookie
- Retrieve data from web storage
- Force the deletion of a persistent cookie
- Describe the fundamental concepts involved in web security

End users often need to store their data in a permanent form that can be accessed whenever they return to a website. For example, customers do not want to reenter the same credit card data and shipping address with each new purchase from an online store. Gamers want to maintain a win/loss record and be able to return to matches that last longer than a single session. An online blog needs to keep a record of ongoing conversations and discussion threads. In this chapter you will learn some techniques to store data that persists from one website session to the next and explore ways in which that data is made safe and secure.

Understanding Sessions and State Information

A session is begun each time the user visits a website within a browser window or tab. During that session data called state information is transferred between the client computer and the web server via the Hypertext Transfer Protocol (HTTP), which is a set of rules defining how data is to be read and interpreted between the client and server.

HTTP was originally designed to be stateless so that data would not be maintained between sessions. A stateless design is a static design because the server treats all clients equally, saving no information about the client's previous sessions. Stateless designs can be very efficient because the server does not have to retrieve data for individual users and clients, but they are also extremely limiting because they do not allow information and actions from one session to be preserved for future sessions. There are many applications that require storing state information, during and between sessions, such as:

- Shopping carts that store the items selected by a customer while visiting an online store
- User profile pages maintained by companies and organizations for their customers and members
- Web forms spanning multiple web pages in which data entered in one form must be accessible to other pages and other forms
- Website designs that allow users to choose customized colors and fonts based on their accessibility needs

State information that needs to be maintained between and during individual sessions can be stored either remotely on the web server or locally on the client device. There are reasons for both approaches. Storing the data on the web server makes it accessible to any of the user's client devices, so that data follows the user from one device to the next. However, storing a lot of information on the server can strain server resources, slowing down the connection between the server and the client. That load can be lessened by storing some of the data on the client device. The best designs often involve both server-side and client-side storage. Note that client-side storage should only be used for data that is applicable to a specific client device or for data that is only required for the current browser session.

Programming Concepts | Encryption

The main protocol used to encrypt data on websites is Secure Sockets Layer (SSL). The use of SSL encryption is widespread on the web. However, the SSL standard is being replaced by Transport Layer Security (TLS), which will eventually replace SSL. Both SSL and TLS encryption can be used to prevent a man-in-the-middle attack, in which data being exchanged between two parties is read and potentially changed in transit. SSL and TLS encrypt data between the client and the server, making it essentially impossible for anyone who might intercept that data in transit to read or change it.

This chapter focuses on storing and retrieving state information stored on the client side, covering the following methods for storing client-side data:

- Data appended as a text string to a website address
- Data saved to a storage file created and stored on the client device
- Data placed within a cookie created and stored on the client device

You will explore these techniques using the website *Eating Well in Season* (EWS), developed for a company delivering quality produce from local farms directly to paid subscribers. Web designers for EWS have created a member sign-up form that extends across two pages. The first page collects contact information for new subscribers and the second page records the subscriber's membership options. Because the sign-up form covers two pages, data entered on the first page must be accessible to the second page.

To access the files for Eating Well in Season website:

1. Go to the js09 ▶ chapter folder of your data files.
2. Use your code editor to open the **js09a_txt.html**, **js09b_txt.html**, and **js09b_txt.js**, files. Enter your name and the date in the comment section of each file and then save them as **js09a.html**, **js09b.html**, and **js09b.js**, respectively.
3. Open the **js09a.html** file in your browser.

The initial page in the web form contains fields for entering the new member's name, email address, phone number, and mailing address. The second page contains fields for membership options. When users submit the first form, they will be automatically redirected to the second. Thus, the first technique you will explore involves transferring data from the first form to the second.

Sharing Data Between Forms

Each time the web server and client exchange data, an HTTP request is generated, consisting of two parts: a header with metadata about the browser and its capabilities, and a body with information necessary to process the request. When a user submits a web form, data from that form is sent to the server using either the `post` method or the `get` method. The `post` method appends the form data to the body of the HTTP request, while the `get` method appends the data as a query string added to a website's URL. One reason to use the `get` method is that the query string can be read and parsed by a JavaScript program running on the client device and thus does not require the browser to store data in a separate file for retrieval.

> **Note** To retrieve data from a form submitted using the `post` method, you must run a script on the server written in a server-side language like PHP that can access data stored in the HTTP request.

To append form data within a query string, add the following `method` and `action` attributes to the `form` element:

```
<form method="get" action="url">
```

where *`url`* is the website address or file name of the resource that will be opened when the form is submitted. For the EWS website, the form stored in the js09a.html file will open the web form stored in the js09b.html file. Edit the `form` element in the js09a.html so that it opens the js09b.html file using the `get` method, appending the form data as a query string.

To set the form's `method` and `action` properties:

1. Return to the **js09a.html** file in your code editor.
2. Scroll down to the `<form>` tag within the body of the HTML file and insert the following attributes as shown in **Figure 9-1**:

```
action="js09b.html" method="get"
```

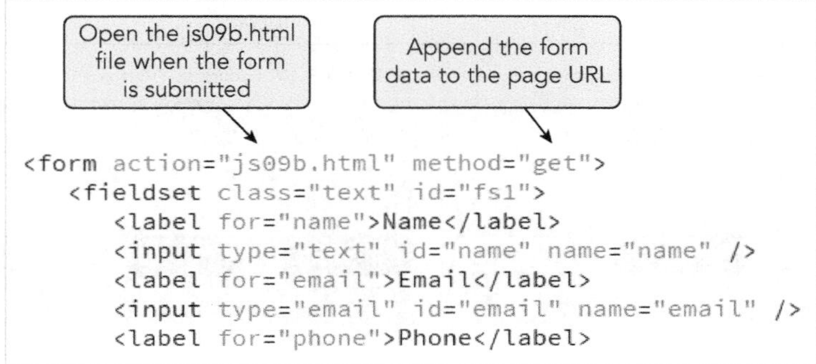

Figure 9-1 Applying the `get` method to a form

3. Close the file, saving your changes.

Next, submit a completed registration form, verifying that it opens the js09b.html file with the data fields and values appended to the URL shown in your browser's address bar.

To submit the form:

1. Open the **js09a.html** file in your browser.
2. Complete the web form using your contact information if you are working on your own computer or a fictitious contact if you are sharing a device with others. See **Figure 9-2**.

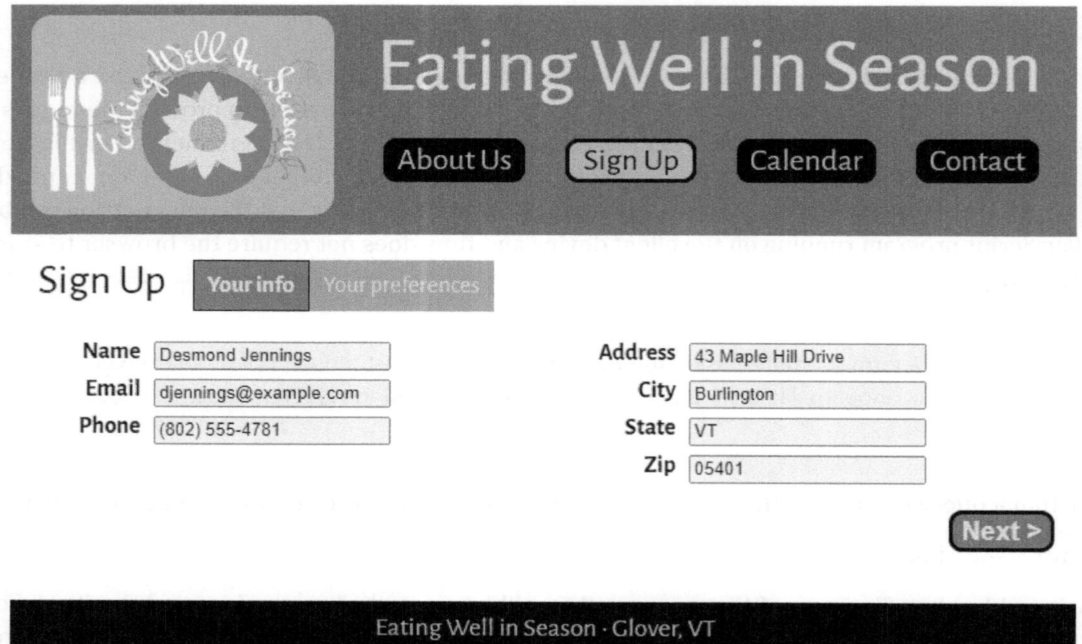

Figure 9-2 Entering sample data into a form

3. Click the **Next** button to submit the form and open the **js09b.html** file.

   As shown in **Figure 9-3**, the browser's address bar shows the URL for the js09b.html file appended with a query string containing field names and values.

Figure 9-3 Viewing the query string

A URL containing a query string has the general format

```
http://server/path/file?field1=value1&field2=value2...
```

where `server` and `path` are the server and path names for the web page and `file` is the file name of the web page. The query string starts with the `?` character and contains data stored as `field=value` pairs with each pair separated by the & character. The following text string contains sample text of a query string appended to the URL of the js09b.html file:

```
?name=Desmond+Jennings&email=djennings%40example.com&phone=%28802%29
+555-4781&address=43+Maple+Hill+Drive&city=Burlington&state=VT&zip=0
5401
```

To retrieve data from a query string, split the text string into separate substrings for each *name=value* pair, yielding the following text for the name, email, phone, address, city, state, and zip fields:

```
name=Desmond+Jennings
email=djennings%40example.com
phone=%28802%29+555-4781
address=43+Maple+Hill+Drive
city=Burlington
state=VT
zip=05401
```

You will use JavaScript string methods to automate the process of retrieving the field names and values.

Retrieving the Query String Text using the `Location` object

Recall that the URL for the current web page is stored within JavaScript's `Location` object. The text of the query string is referenced with the `location.search` property, which returns the entire query string including the initial `?` character. Because you don't need that first `?` character you will use the `slice()` method to extract a substring from the query string starting from the second character.

To extract the field names and values from the query string:

1. Open the **js09b.html** file in your code editor and add a `script` element to run the js09b.js file, deferring the running of the script until after the web page is loaded. Close the file, saving your changes.
2. Open the **js09b.js** file in your code editor. After the initial comment section, add the following code to store the text of the query string in the `qString` variable:

```
// Retrieve the text of the query string
let qString = location.search.slice(1);
console.log(qString);
```

Figure 9-4 describes the code in the file.

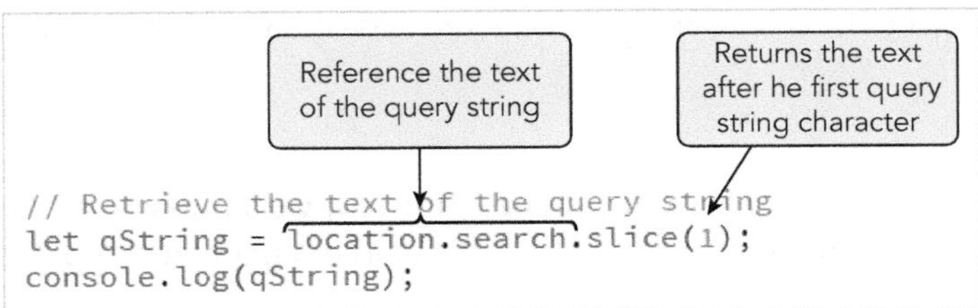

Figure 9-4 Viewing the query string

3. Save your changes to the file and then reload the current **js09b.html** file with its appended query string in your web browser. If you need to reenter the form data, return to the **js09a.html** file and resubmit the form with your contact information.
4. Open your browser debugger and view the contents of the console log to confirm that the text of the query string has been stored in the `qString` variable.

With the text of the query string stored in the `qString` variable, you can begin the process of extracting its data.

Replacing URI Encoding Characters

Before data can be placed within a query string it must be encoded. Website addresses cannot contain blank spaces, so any blanks within a data value must be replaced with the + character. There are other characters not allowed within a query string. The / and : characters are not allowed because they are used in the URL pathname. Including those characters within the query string will confuse the browser as it attempts to load the website. Under the Hypertext Transfer Protocol, a character that cannot be used within a query string is replaced with a URI-encoded character. A list of some of the reserved characters and their corresponding URI character codes is displayed in **Figure 9-5**.

CHARACTER	URI CHARACTER CODE	CHARACTER	URI CHARACTER CODE
space	%20	/	%2F
!	%21	:	%3A
#	%23	;	%3B
$	%24	<	%3C
&	%26	=	%3D
'	%27	>	%3E
(	%28	?	%3F
)	%29	@	%40
*	%2A	[	%5B
+	%2B	]	%5D
,	%2C	^	%5E

Figure 9-5 URI character codes

Under URI-encoding, a text string like "phone=(802) 555-4781" is replaced by "phone=%28802%29+555-4781". To decode the text string back into its original form, apply the following `decodeURIComponent()` function:

```
decodeURIComponent(string)
```

where *`string`* is a text string containing URI-encoded characters. The following statement restores data stored as a query string to its original text:

```
decodeURIComponent("phone=%28802%29%20555-4781")
// returns "phone=(802) 555-4781"
```

To convert a text string from its original form into URI code, apply the `encodeURIComponent()` method to the string.

Use the `replace()` method to replace every occurrence of the + character in the `qString` variable with a blank space and apply the `decodeURIComponent()` method to the query string text to replace other encoded characters.

To replace encoded characters in the query string text:

1. Return to the **js09b.js** file in your code editor. Directly after the line that declares the `qString` variable add the following statements to modify the contents of that text string:

```
// Replace the encoded characters in the query string
qString = qString.replace(/\+/g, " ");
qString = decodeURIComponent(qString);
```

See **Figure 9-6**.

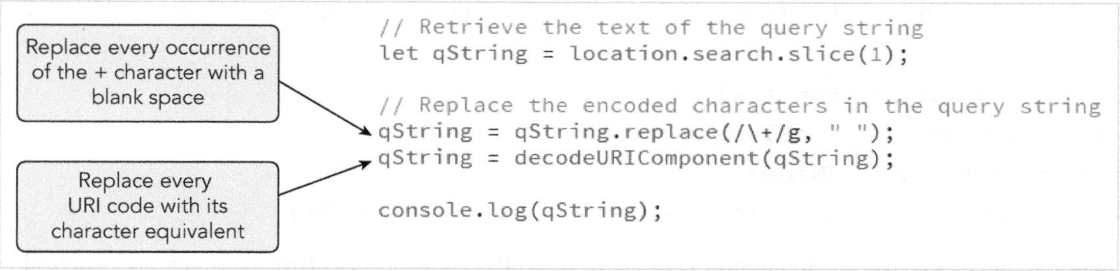

Replace every occurrence of the + character with a blank space
Replace every URI code with its character equivalent
// Retrieve the text of the query string
let qString = location.search.slice(1);
// Replace the encoded characters in the query string
qString = qString.replace(/\+/g, " ");
qString = decodeURIComponent(qString);
console.log(qString);

Figure 9-6 Replacing characters from a query string

2. Save your changes to the file and reload the **js09b.html** file in your browser using the form data you have entered.
3. Verify that the debugger console shows the text of the `qString` variable without the encoded characters. See **Figure 9-7**.

Figure 9-7 Revised query string text

4. Close your browser's debugger.

The final task of transferring data from the js09a.html file involves writing the field names and values into the web form on the js09b.html web page. To create the form elements, the script will split the query string at each location of the `&` character, creating an array of *`name=value`* pairs. The script will then use a `for of` loop to iterate through those pairs, writing a form label for the field name and an input box for the field value. Add the code to create these form elements now.

To create form elements from the query string:

1. Delete the `console.log()` statement and add the following command to create the `formData` array by splitting the query string at each occurrence of the `&` character:

```
// Split the field=name pairs into separate array items
let formData = qString.split(/&/g);
```

2. Add the following initial code for the `for of` loop to iterate through each item in the `formData` array

```
for (let items of formData) {
```

3. Enter the following code to extract the field name and value from each *`name=value`* pair and store them in the `fieldname` and `fieldValue` variables:

```
// Extract the field names and values
let fieldValuePair = items.split(/=/);
let fieldName = fieldValuePair[0];
let fieldValue = fieldValuePair[1];
```

4. Enter the following code to create a `label` element containing the field name and append it to the `contactInfo` box from the web page:

```
// Create a label containing the field name
let fieldLabel = document.createElement("label");
fieldLabel.textContent = fieldName;
document.getElementById("contactInfo").appendChild(fieldLabel);
```

5. Enter the following code to create an input box containing the field value. Use the `fieldname` variable as the input box's id and name. Disable the input box so that its contents may be viewed but not edited in this web form.

```
// Create an disabled input box with the field value
let inputBox = document.createElement("input");
inputBox.id = fieldName;
inputBox.name = fieldName;
inputBox.value = fieldValue;
inputBox.disabled = true;
```

6. Add the following code to append the input box to the `contactInfo` element and close the `for of` loop.

```
document.getElementById("contactInfo").appendChild(inputBox);
}
```

Figure 9-8 describes the complete code to display the field names and values in the web form.

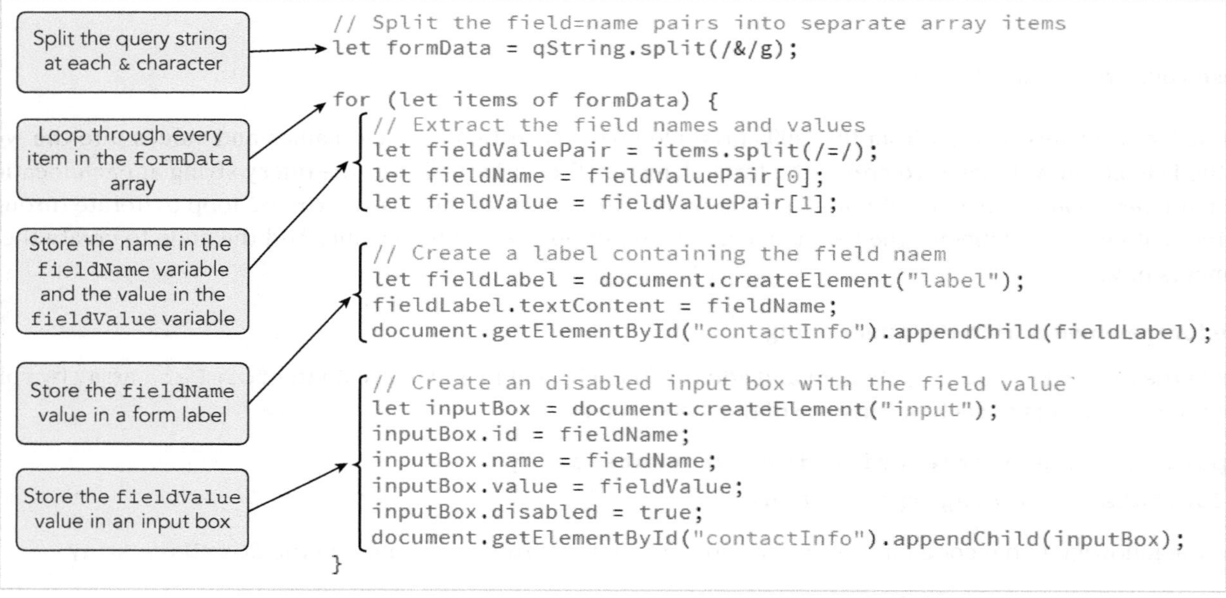

Figure 9-8 Extracting data from a field name/value pair

7. Save your changes to the file and reload the **js09b.html** file in your browser using the form data you have entered. Verify that the field names and values from the query string appear in the web page. See **Figure 9-9**.

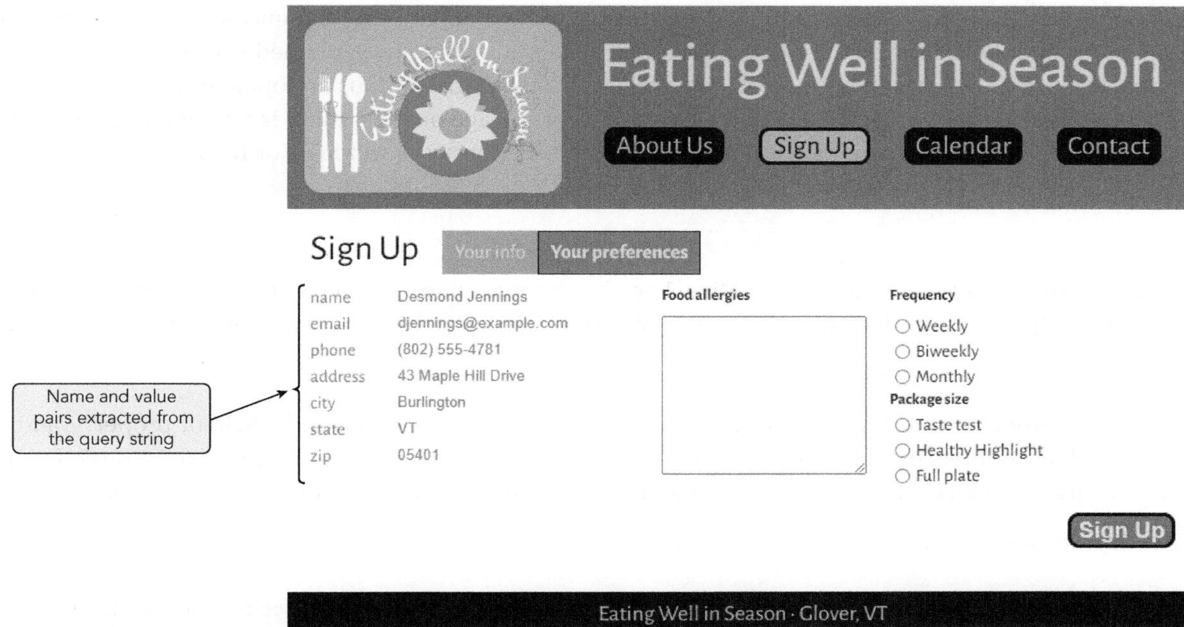

Figure 9-9 Field names and values displayed in a web page

You have completed your work copying data from one web form to another using query strings. Next you will explore how to store data in a file on your computer.

Quick Check 1

1. What is the difference between the `post` method and the `get` method?
2. Why do you apply the `decodeURIComponent()` method to data value enclosed within a query string?
3. What character is used within a query string to separate *`name=value`* pairs?

Introducing Web Storage

Storing data in a query string works well for multipart forms in which data needs to be accessed only for the current session and only as the user moves between forms. For applications that involve data that is not part of a sequential set of forms or needs to be available for future sessions, you need web storage.

The Web Storage API

The Web Storage API is a JavaScript specification enabling browsers to store data as an associative array within a file that can be read by the browser. Web storage is easy to use and can store large amounts of textual data (though currently it cannot store non-textual data) and is supported by all current browsers. However, it is not supported in older browsers, so you may need to examine other storage options, such as cookies, if you need to support legacy browsers and operating systems.

There are two types of storage supported in the Web Storage API: local storage and session storage. Both storage objects map field names and values in into *`key`*`:`*`value`* pairs of an associative array. The difference between session storage objects and local storage objects is based on the data's scope and how long it is stored.

Local Storage and Session Storage Objects

With a local storage object, the data is permanently stored by the browser and can be accessed at any time. The data cannot be removed until it is explicitly removed by a web app or by the browser's built-in tools for managing web storage.

When data is stored within a session storage object, it is accessible only during the current session. Moreover, the storage object exists only as long as the browser window or tab in which it was defined is open. Once that browser tab or window is closed, the session storage object is deleted. If two browser tabs are open to the same website location, they create separate session storage objects. With session storage objects, there is no communication between different locations and from the same location if opened in different browser windows or tabs.

Storing Data in Web Storage

Local storage is referenced with JavaScript's native `localStorage` object. Session storage is referenced using the `sessionStorage` object. To store data within either local storage or session storage, apply the following `setItem()` method:

```
storage.setItem(key, value)
```

where *`storage`* is either `localStorage` or `sessionStorage`, *`key`* is the name of the field or property, and *`value`* is the key's value. For example, the following statement stores the value "Desmond Jennings" into the `name` key, placing the *`key=value`* pair into local storage to be available whenever that website location is accessed again:

```
localStorage.setItem("name", "Desmond Jennings");
```

Note To temporarily save the `name` key and value in web storage, replace `localStorage` in the statement with `sessionStorage`.

Previously, you reached a point in the js09b.html file where the member preferences were stored within fields on the page's web form. You will complete the script for that page by writing that form data into local storage. Membership data was stored in the following form controls:

- Input boxes nested within the contactInfo `div` element containing the member's contact information
- Radio buttons containing membership options
- A `textarea` box in which members describe their allergies

You will reference these input controls using the `querySelectorAll()` method and then write the name of each field and the field's value to local storage.

To store field values in local storage:

1. Return to the **js09b.js** file in your code editor.
2. At the bottom of the file add the following statement to create an `onclick` event handler for the Sign Up button:

```
// Store data to local storage when the user signs up
document.getElementById("signupBtn").onclick = function() {
}
```

3. Within the event handler's anonymous function, add the following statement to define a node list of the data fields to be saved to local storage:

```
// data fields to be saved to local storage
let formFields = document.querySelectorAll("#contactInfo input,
input[type=radio], textarea");
```

4. Within the anonymous function, add the following `for of` loop to iterate through the node list of fields, writing the field name and value to local storage:

```
// write each field name and value to local storage
for (let fields of formFields) {
   localStorage.setItem(fields.name, fields.value);
}
```

5. Directly after the `for of` loop, insert the following command to display the contents of the `localStorage` object in the debugger console:

```
console.log(localStorage);
```

Figure 9-10 describes the newly added code.

```
// Store data to local storage when the user signs up
document.getElementById("signupBtn").onclick = function() {
   // data fields to be saved to local storage
   let formFields = document.querySelectorAll("#contactInfo input, input[type=radio], textarea");

   // write each field name and value to local storage
   for (let fields of formFields) {
      localStorage.setItem(fields.name, fields.value);
   }

   console.log(localStorage);
}
```

Select the fields containing data to be stored

Place each field and value in local storage

Write the local storage contents to the debugger console

Figure 9-10 Writing data to local web storage

6. Save your changes to the file and then reload **js09b.html** using the sign-up data you previously entered.
7. Complete the web form by entering a food allergy in the Food allergies box and selecting a Frequency option and Package size option from the radio buttons.
8. Click the **Sign Up** button.
9. Open your browser's debugger and view the console to confirm that the field names and values have been added to local storage. See **Figure 9-11**.

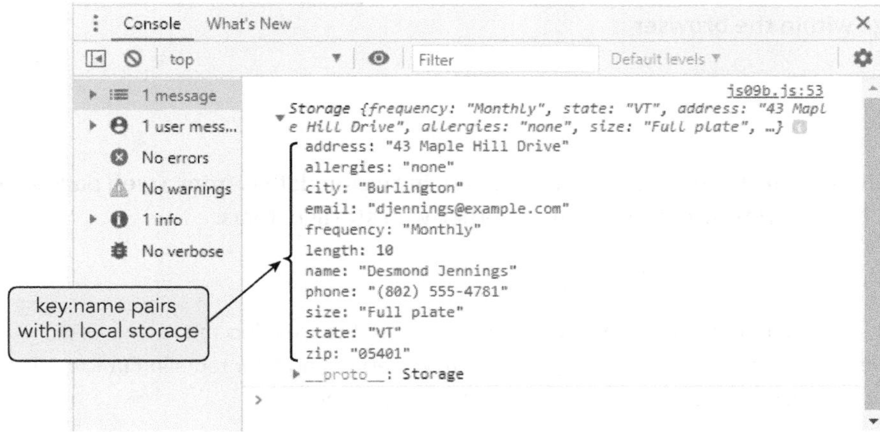

Figure 9-11 Contents of local web storage

The order of the items within local storage do not necessarily match the order of items in the web form. As with other associative arrays, the keys within the `localStorage` and `sessionStorage` objects are not enumerable.

Note The number of keys saved in web storage is referenced in the `length` property of the `localStorage` or `sessionStorage` objects.

Viewing Web Storage Items in your Browser

Your browser provides tools to view and manage web storage contents so you can edit or remove storage objects that no longer serve a purpose. Explore this feature of the Google Chrome browser now.

To view the web storage contents:

1. With the browser debugger still open, click **Application** from the menu list at the top of the debugger pane. You might have to click » to view hidden menu options.
2. Double-click **Local Storage** from the list of storage options to expand the Local Storage menu.
3. Click **file://** to display the list of fields stored in local storage from web pages that originate on your device. See **Figure 9-12**.

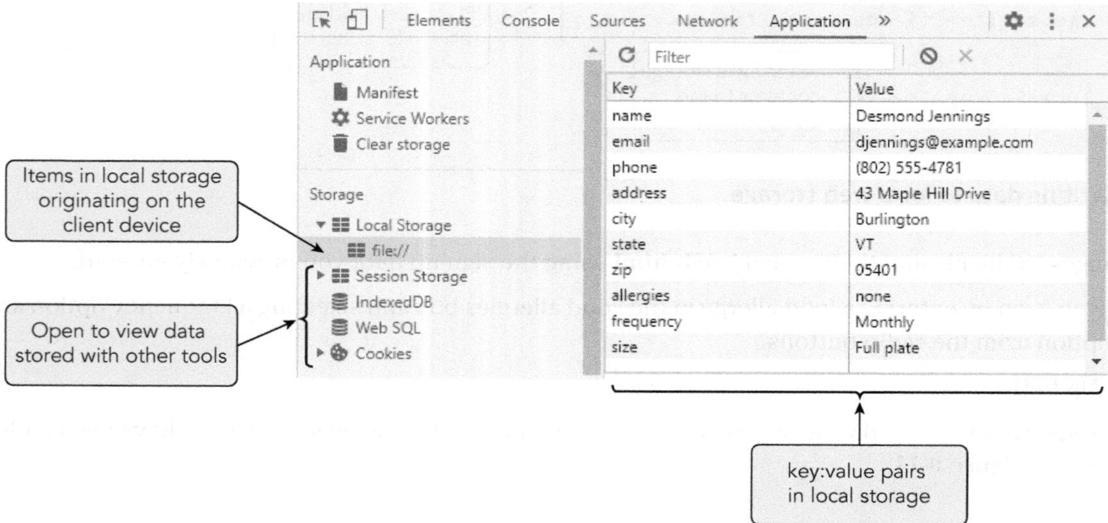

Figure 9-12 Viewing web storage within the browser

4. Close your browser debugger.

The browser organizes web storage values by origin. Because the Eating Well in Season data is from a web page stored on the client computer, its origin is `file://`. Your browser might list other web storage items.

> **Note** To view web storage data on Safari, click Show JavaScript Console from the Develop tab menu. Click Storage from the menu list in the JavaScript Console pane. To view web storage contents in Firefox, click Web Developer from the Firefox menu, click Application, and then click Storage.

Retrieving Items with the `getItem()` Method

Data stored within local or session storage can be retrieved using the following `getItem()` method:

```
storage.getItem(key)
```

where *`key`* is the key whose value is to be retrieved and *`storage`* is either `localStorage` or `sessionStorage`. For example, the following statement retrieves the value of the `name` key from local storage:

```
localStorage.getItem("name") // returns Desmond Jennings
```

Because web storage is saved as an associative array, a stored key value can also be accessed as a property using either of the following:

```
storage.key
storage["key"]
```

The following statement returns the stored value for the name key by accessing the name property of the localStorage object:

```
localStorage.name // returns Desmond Jennings
```

Finally, a key can be referenced with the key() method:

```
key(index)
```

where *index* represents the index number of the key within the storage object. The following statement returns the ninth key from local storage, which in this example is the name key.

```
localStorage.key(8) // returns "name"
```

Use the getItem() method to retrieve the local storage keys for the Eating Well website and display them in a web page listing your membership preferences.

To retrieve values from local storage:

1. Use your code editor to open the **js09c_txt.html** and **js09c_txt.js**, files from js09 ▶ chapter folder of your data files. Enter your name and the date in the comment section of each file and then save them as **js09c.html** and **js09c.js**, respectively.
2. Return to the **js09c.html** file in your code editor and add a script element to run the js09c.js file, deferring the running of the script until after the web page is loaded. Close the file, saving your changes.
3. Go to the **js09c.js** file in your code editor and add the following code, creating an array of key names:

```
// Eating Well Preference Keys
let keys = ["name", "email", "phone", "address", "city", "state",
           "zip", "allergies", "frequency", "size"];
```

4. Add the following for of loop to iterate through each item in the keys array, creating a table row for each entry.

```
for (let item of keys) {
   let newRow = document.createElement("tr");
}
```

5. Within the for of loop, add the following code to create and append a table cell containing the name of each key from the keys array:

```
// Display the storage key
let keyCell = document.createElement("td");
keyCell.textContent = item;
newRow.appendChild(keyCell);
```

6. Add the following code to create and append a table cell containing key values:

```
// Display the key value
let keyValue = document.createElement("td");
keyValue.textContent = localStorage.getItem(item);
newRow.appendChild(keyValue);
```

7. Complete the `for of` loop by appending the new table row to the table element with the id "prefTable".

```
// Append each key=name pair as a table row
document.getElementById("prefTable").appendChild(newRow);
```

Figure 9-13 describes the completed code.

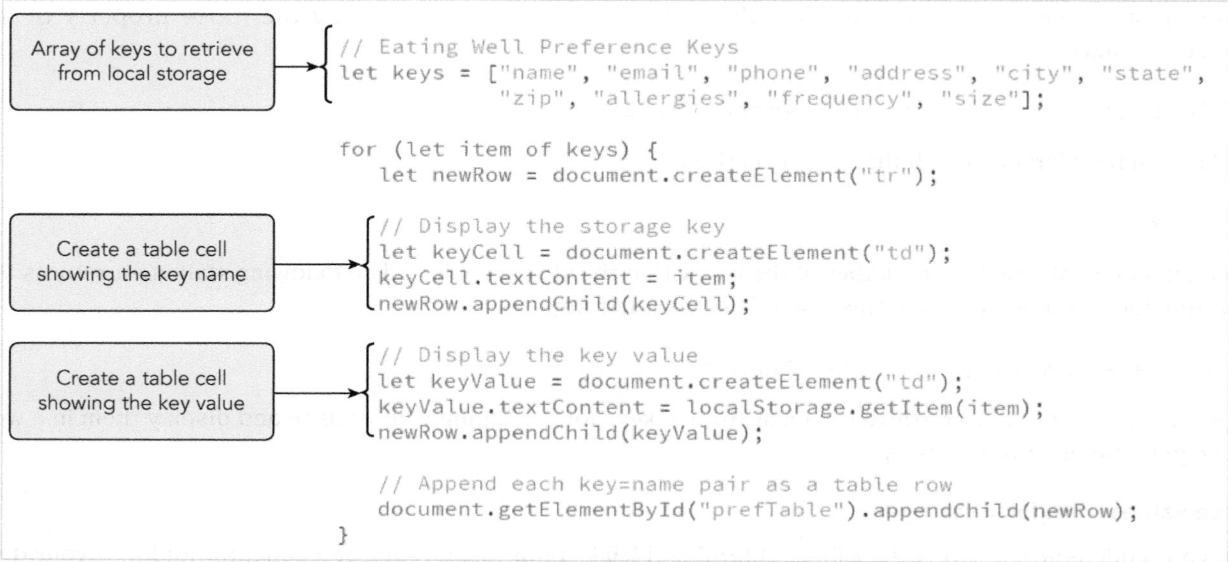

Array of keys to retrieve from local storage
Create a table cell showing the key name
Create a table cell showing the key value
// Eating Well Preference Keys
let keys = ["name", "email", "phone", "address", "city", "state",
"zip", "allergies", "frequency", "size"];
for (let item of keys) {
let newRow = document.createElement("tr");
// Display the storage key
let keyCell = document.createElement("td");
keyCell.textContent = item;
newRow.appendChild(keyCell);
// Display the key value
let keyValue = document.createElement("td");
keyValue.textContent = localStorage.getItem(item);
newRow.appendChild(keyValue);
// Append each key=name pair as a table row
document.getElementById("prefTable").appendChild(newRow);
}

Figure 9-13 Getting values from web storage

8. Save your changes to the file and then load **js09c.html** in your web browser. As shown in **Figure 9-14**, the page shows the current user preferences read from local storage.

Your Eating Well Preferences

name	Desmond Jennings
email	djennings@example.com
phone	(802) 555-4781
address	43 Maple Hill Drive
city	Burlington
state	VT
zip	05401
frequency	Monthly
size	Full plate

Figure 9-14 Web storage values displayed in a web table

With the keys saved under local storage, anytime you access a page from that website you will be able to access the keys and their values. However, you might not want to have your browser cluttered with keys which are no longer of use. If that is the case, you can remove them.

Removing Items from Web Storage

Data in session storage is erased when the session ends with the closing of the browser window or tab. Data in local storage must be manually erased using the browser tools or the following `removeItem()` method:

```
storage.removeItem(key)
```

where *key* is the name of a web storage key from the current page. To remove all keys from storage in the current page apply the following `clear()` method:

```
storage.clear()
```

Use the `removeItem()` method to remove all local storage keys for Eating Well website.

To remove items from local storage:

1. Return to the **js09c.js** file in your code editor.
2. At the bottom of the file add the following code to loop through the content of the `keys` array, removing each key from local storage (see **Figure 9-15**):

```
// Remove Eating Well keys when the Remove Preference button is clicked
document.getElementById("removePrefBtn").onclick = function() {
   for (let item of keys) {
      localStorage.removeItem(item);
   }
}
```

```
// Remove Eating Well kyes when the Remove Preference button is clicked
document.getElementById("removePrefBtn").onclick = function() {
   for (let item of keys) {
      localStorage.removeItem(item);
   }
}
```

Remove the item from local storage

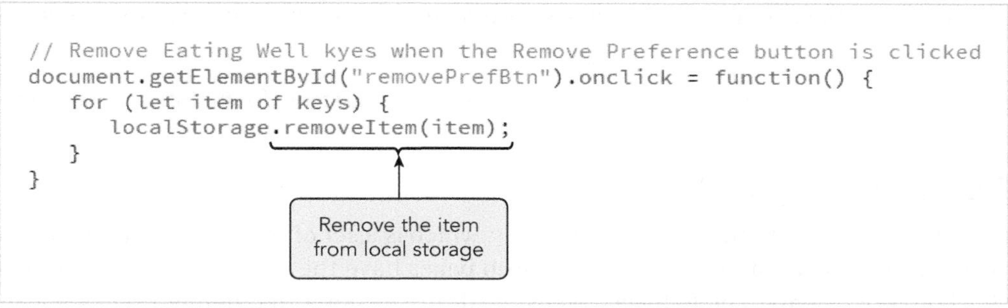

Figure 9-15 Removing items from local storage

3. Close the file, saving your changes.
4. Reload the **js09c.html** file in your browser and click the **Remove Preferences** button.
5. Reload the page and verify that values for the `name` through `size` fields no longer appear in the web table indicating that those keys have been removed from local storage.

If you need to add the Eating Well preferences back to local storage you will have to complete the data entry forms in the js09a.html and js09b.html files.

Exploring Storage Events

Saving data to web storage triggers a `storage` event within the active browser window or tab. If two pages are open to the same location and one of the pages stores data to local or session storage, the other page will be notified via the `storage` event. The event handler to respond to that event is:

```
window.onstorage = function(event) {
   commands
}
```

where *`event`* is the `event` object representing the storage event and *`commands`* are commands run in response to a change in the values saved to web storage. The `event` object supports the properties described in **Figure 9-16**.

PROPERTY	DESCRIPTION
`key`	Returns the name of the key that was changed
`newValue`	Returns the value of the changed key
`oldValue`	Returns the original value of the changed key
`storageArea`	Returns the storage object (`localStorage` or `sessionStorage`) that was changed
`url`	Returns the URL of the document whose key was changed

Figure 9-16 Properties of the storage `event` object

For example, the following code writes text to the debugger console indicating which storage key was changed and how it was changed from its previous value to its current value:

```
window.onstorage = function(e) {
   console.log("The " + e.key + " value was
   changed from " + e.oldValue + " to " + e.newValue);
}
```

Web apps with data spread across several browser windows or tabs can broadcast changes made to web storage in one page to all other pages. For example, an online game might be spread across several browser tabs with one tab displaying the game interface and another tab containing game statistics that are constantly updated during game play.

Note | You can also respond to changes in local or system storage using an event listener for the `storage` event.

Web Storage and the Same-Origin Policy

Web storage ensures data integrity by adhering to the same-origin policy, which is a set of security standards restricting the transfer of data between web pages of different origins. Two web pages have the same origin if the protocol, port, and host are the same for both documents. The following website addresses point to different origins because they do not share the same protocol, port, and host:

```
http://www.example.com
http://store.example.com       // different hostname
http://www.example.com:8080    // different port number
https://www.example.com        // different protocol
```

Data stored in one origin is not accessible to websites from other origins. The same-origin policy does not include the origin's path, which is a storage folder on the web server. Addresses that differ only in their paths are part of the same origin and thus do not violate the same-origin policy. The following addresses are part of the same origin and thus could share data:

```
http://www.example.com/members/login.html
http://www.example.com/store/order.html
http://www.example.com/cart/purchase.html
```

The same-origin policy applies only to the content of scripts and APIs such as the Web Storage API. Other resources such as images and CSS style sheets are not affected.

Note | If the same-origin policy did not exist, then a web page in one browser window or tab could alter pages displayed in other browser windows or tabs. A malicious program could insert advertising, or simply redirect the browser to a new website. The security of private networks and intranets would be at risk without the same-origin policy as content on the private network would be accessible to any other website opened by the user.

You have completed your work on the Eating Well website. In the next sections you will explore other techniques for storing data that persists within a single session or across sessions.

Quick Check 2

1. What is the same-origin policy?
2. What are two types of web storage objects?
3. Provide code to create a session storage object named `orderQty` that stores a value of 5.
4. Provide code to retrieve the value of the `orderQty` key from session storage.
5. Provide code to delete the `orderQty` key from session storage.

Introducing Cookies

Prior to the Web Storage API, cookies were the only way to save web session data. A cookie is a small piece of information, stored as a text string, exchanged via an HTTP request between the web server and the client device. **Figure 9-17** illustrates the process by which session data is exchanged using cookies.

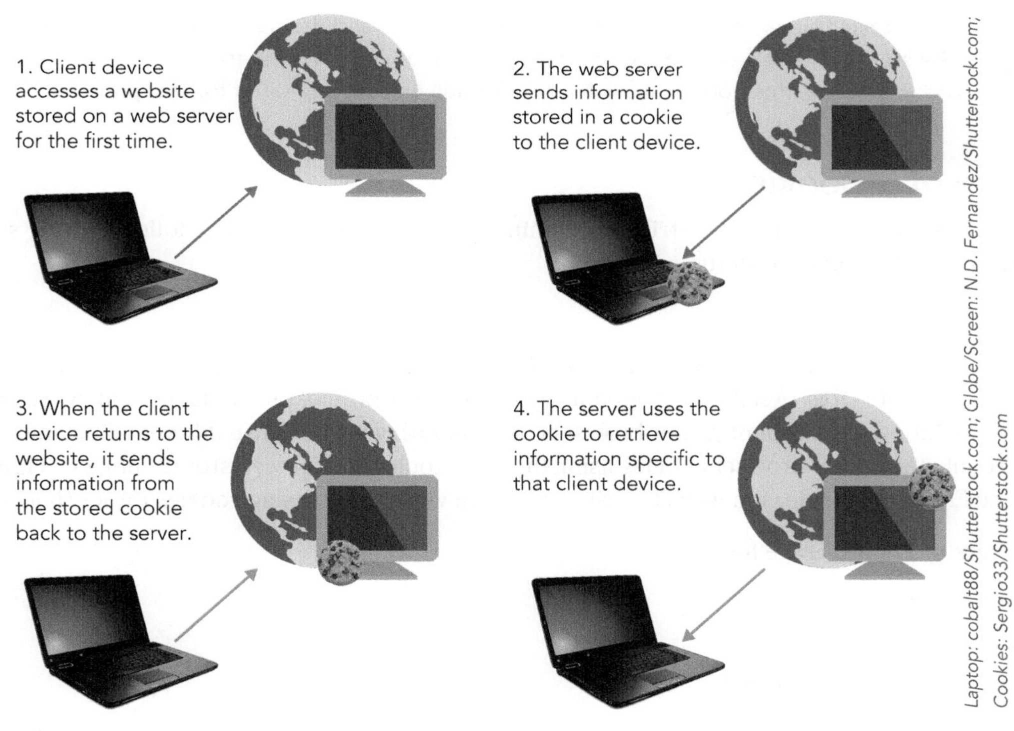

Figure 9-17 Cookies and web servers

Cookies adhere to the same-origin policy so that data cannot be exchanged using cookies from different origins.

Cookies vs. Web Storage

Web storage and cookies should be considered complementary approaches. While it is easier to save and retrieve data from web storage, cookies are better integrated with scripts running on the web server. **Figure 9-18** lists some of the important differences between cookies and web storage.

COOKIES	WEB STORAGE
An old standard introduced in 1995, supported by legacy browsers and apps	A newer standard introduced in 2012 and supported by almost all browsers
Stored on the client device and transferred to the web server as part of an HTTP header	Stored on the client device but not transferable to the web server
Requires access to a web server for testing and development	Does not require a web server for testing and development
Each domain can store a maximum of 20 cookies and the largest cookie size is generally limited to 4KB	Each domain can save 5 MB in web storage with no practical limit on the number of stored keys
Can be set to expire automatically without user or browser intervention	Unless session storage is used, items must be removed manually either through a JavaScript command or via the browser interface
Data must be parsed from a text string using JavaScript string methods	Data can be read directly using the Web Storage API
Data can be accessed directly on both the server side and the client side	Data can be accessed directly only on the client side

Figure 9-18 Comparing cookies and web storage

Websites support two types of cookies: session cookies, which exist only for the current browser session, and persistent cookies, which are available beyond the current session. A session cookie might be used within an online store to allow customers to save their selected items in a shopping cart while continuing to shop. A persistent cookie might be used to help those customers retrieve their purchase history or access delivery information on previously purchased items.

> **Note** Because cookies are exchanged between the client device and the web server via HTTP, the web page must be stored on a server for development and testing. There are several free web servers, such as Apache and Nginx, that you can download and install on your computer for that purpose.

The Structure of a Cookie

In its simplest form, a cookie is just a text string containing a `name=value` pair. The following text string defines a cookie storing the value "Burlington" in the `city` field:

```
city=Burlington
```

Cookies are stored in a protected file on your computer. The Google Chrome browser stores cookies in the Cookie file located in the folder C:\Users*Your User Name*\AppData\Local\Google\Chrome\User Data\Default, where *Your User Name* is the name of your Windows 10 account. Other browsers and operating systems use different file names and locations. You can view the contents of your browser cookies using the same tools used for web storage objects. **Figure 9-19** shows the contents of the Eating Well in Season website if the site's data were stored using cookies rather than web storage.

In general, browsers provide storage for:

- 20 cookies per website domain
- 300 cookies from all websites
- 4 kilobytes of space for each cookie

In practice, browsers are more generous in what they allow. Chrome, for example, supports up to 180 cookies per website domain while Safari allows 600 cookies. Most browsers support at least 50. If the limit per domain is exceeded, the oldest cookie is automatically deleted by the browser. If a cookie exceeds the 4K limit, it will be ignored by the browser and not saved.

> **Note** Avoid overloading your server and clients with cookies. A long list of cookies will slow down the connection between the server and the client device, impairing performance.

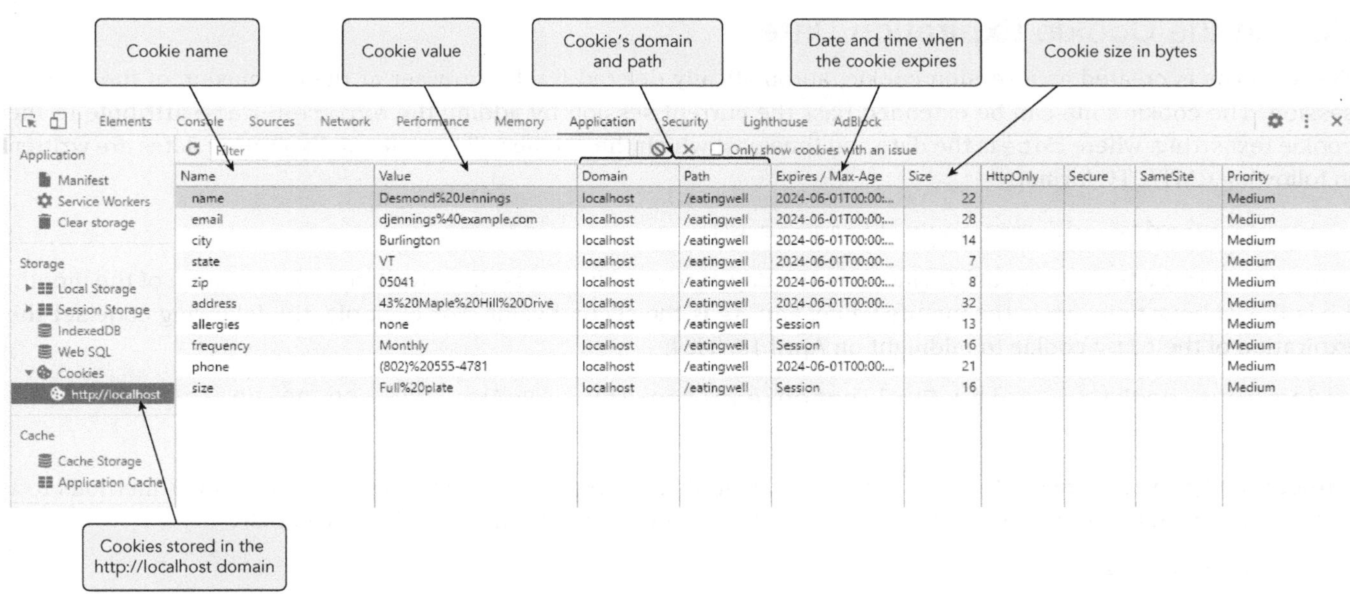

Figure 9-19 Cookies listed in the Application window of the Chrome Developer pane

Writing Data into a Cookie

A cookie is created by writing the cookie text into the following `document.cookie` object:

```
document.cookie = string;
```

where *`string`* defines the cookie for a particular field. The following code creates three cookies, storing data for the `city`, `state`, and `zip` fields:

```
document.cookie = "city=Burlington";
document.cookie = "state=VT";
document.cookie = "zip=05401";
```

A single cookie can contain multiple *`name=value`* pairs. For example, the following cookie contains values for all three fields separated by the `&` symbol:

```
document.cookie = "city=Burlington&state=VT&zip=05401";
```

Combining fields within a single cookie is a way of getting around limits placed on the total number of cookies per website. If that is not an issue, it is usually easier to place only a single *`name=value`* pair within the `document.cookie` object.

As with query strings, the text of the *`name=value`* pair cannot contain spaces, semicolons, commas, or other non-alphanumeric characters. To store a value containing those characters, apply the `encodeURIComponent()` method to the data value prior to writing the cookie as in the following code that writes the text "Desmond Jennings" into a cookie:

```
let username = "Desmond Jennings";
let nameCode = encodeURIComponent(username);
document.cookie = "name=" + nameCode;
```

The cookie stores the text string `name=Desmond%20Jennings` with the `%20` code, replacing the blank space within the user's name.

Setting the Cookie Expiration Date

Every cookie is created as a session cookie, automatically deleted by the browser at the conclusion of the current session. The cookie's life can be extended past the current session by adding the `expires=`*`date`* attribute to the cookie text string, where *`date`* is the date and time past which the cookie will be deleted. Expiration dates are written in following GMT/UTC format:

```
;expires=wday, dd-mmm-yyyy hh:mm:ss GMT
```

where *`wday`* is the three-letter abbreviation of the day of the week, *mmm* is the three-letter abbreviation of the month, *`hh`* is the 24-hour time, *mm* is the minute value, and *`ss`* is the second value. For example, the following code set the expiration of the `city` cookie to midnight on April 18, 2024:

```
document.cookie = "city=Burlington;expires=Thu, 18 Apr 2024 00:00:00
GMT";
```

Rather than typing the complete date string, you can apply the `toGMTString()` or `toUTCString()` methods to a `Date` object as in the following code, which adds an expiration date of June 1, 2024 to the cookie:

```
let username = "Desmond Jennings";
let nameCode = encodeURIComponent(username);
let expire = new Date("June 1, 2024");
let expireCode = expire.toUTCString();
document.cookie = "name=" + nameCode + ";expires=" + expireCode;
```

Note Do not encode the `expires` attribute using the `encodeURIComponent()` method. JavaScript will not recognize a UTC date when it is encoded.

Expiration dates can also be set relative to the current date. For example, to set a cookie to expire in six months, add 6 to the current month by using the `setMonth()` and `getMonth()` methods:

```
let expire = new Date();
let expire = setMonth(expire.getMonth() + 6);
```

Cookies also support the following `max-age` attribute to set an expiration date relative to the date and time on which the cookie was created:

```
;max-age=seconds;
```

where *`seconds`* is the number of seconds before the cookie will expire. The following code sets the cookie to expire 365 days after its creation:

```
let username = "Desmond Jennings";
let nameCode = encodeURIComponent(username);
let maxAge = 60*60*24*365;
document.cookie = "name=" + nameCode + ";max-age=" + maxAge;
```

A cookie is not deleted until the browser accesses it past its expiration date. At that point, the cookie will be removed from the browser and the server.

Note There is no attribute to make a cookie permanent. To make a cookie practically permanent, set the `expires` date or the `max-age` value far into the future.

Setting the Cookie Path

Just as web storage items are associated with specific locations, so too are cookies associated with specific website domains and folders within those domains. By default, a cookie is associated with the same website and folder of the web page in which it was defined as well as any subfolders of that folder. A cookie created for the *www.example.com/orders/order.html* web page will be accessible to the web page *www.example.com/orders/cart.html* but not to *www.example.com/members/myaccount.html* because that page lies on a completely different path even if it is on the same server.

With some applications you might want to specify the path so that all cookies are associated with the same folder regardless of the page's location on the server. To define the cookie path, add the following `path` attribute to the cookie text:

```
;path=directory
```

where *`directory`* is the directory path on the web server where the cookie is stored and read. The following code defines the cookie for the `city` field, placing it within the `members` folder of the website:

```
document.cookie = "city=Burlington;path=/members";
```

Any page stored within the members folder or a subfolder will be able to access this cookie. To make all cookies accessible regardless of their folder location, set the `path` attribute to the root folder as in the following statement that makes the `city` field available to any page within any folder on the website:

```
document.cookie = "city=Burlington;path=/";
```

Using the root folder has the disadvantage that all cookies within a website must have unique names. A cookie named `title` cannot be used to describe a product in one web page and store an employee title in another page. For this reason, it is considered best practice to confine cookies to those folders and subfolders on the web server where they are needed, freeing the cookie name for use elsewhere on the website.

Setting the Cookie Domain

Cookies are also restricted to a particular web domain. A cookie created for *www.example.com* is not accessible to any page from any other domain. A cookie created for a page at *www.example.com* cannot be read from *www.microsoft.com* or another other domain. This security feature prevents other domains from "snooping" on cookies that do not belong to them.

However, many sites use multiple domains and subdomains. The Eating Well website might employ domains such as *www.example.com*, *news.example.com*, and *members.example.com*. Although these separate domain names help organize the website contents, cookies created under one domain are not accessible to pages in the other domains. To avoid this problem, specify the cookie's domain by adding the following `domain` attribute to the cookie string:

```
;domain=domain-name
```

where *`domain-name`* is the name of the domain on the sever in which the cookie resides. The cookie will then be available to any page within domain-name or any of its subdomains. The following statement makes the `city` cookie available to all domains on the *example.com* website:

```
document.cookie = "city=Burlington;domain=example.com";
```

Under the same-origin policy you cannot set the domain of a cookie to a domain other than a domain found on your web server.

Defining Cookie Security

The final attribute that can be added to a cookie is the `secure` attribute, specifying whether the cookie must be exchanged over a secure HTTPS connection as opposed to a less secure HTTP connection. The following statement makes the `city` cookie secure, requiring the web server and the client device to communicate over HTTPS:

```
document.cookie = "city=Burlington;secure";
```

Best Practices | Providing Persistent Logins

Websites and applications that require users to log into a server commonly can keep a user logged in for weeks or months at a time without compromising the security of the user's login information. Such sites often display a checkbox with the label "Remember me" or "Keep me logged in" as part of the login form and enable you to continue to access customized content in the future without repeatedly providing your login information. Because cookies store data in plain text, they can be read from a user's drive by malicious applications; for this reason, sensitive information such as passwords should never be stored in cookies.

In a system that supports persistent logins, when a user logs into the system, the web server provides the browser a string of random characters known as a token. The token is stored in a cookie, which the web server uses to verify the user's identity the next time the user requests access. Because the token is a random string, malicious programs cannot anticipate its value to log into a user's account from another location. A web server stores the token value and compares it to the username to verify the user's identity. At that time, the server generates a new token, which is stored in a cookie on the user's machine.

Because cookies are stored unencrypted on the client device's hard drive, where they could be read by malicious programs, sensitive information should never be stored in a cookie. Adding the `secure` attribute to all cookies is an important part of an comprehensive plan for site security.

A Function to Write the Cookie Value

Putting all these attributes together can result in a long and complex cookie string. The following statement defines the `address` cookie, setting the cookie to expire on Thursday April 18, 2024 at midnight, confining the cookie to the members folder on the *example.com* domain, and restricting transmission of the cookie to a secure HTTPS connection:

```
document.cookie = "city=Burlington;expires=Thu, 18 2024 00:00:00
GMT;path=/members;domain=example.com;secure;
```

Many apps employing cookies include a customized function to write the cookie value without the need for typing a long and complicated text string. **Figure 9-20** shows an example of a function to construct a cookie based on values supplied for the cookie's name, value, expiration date, path, domain, and secure attributes.

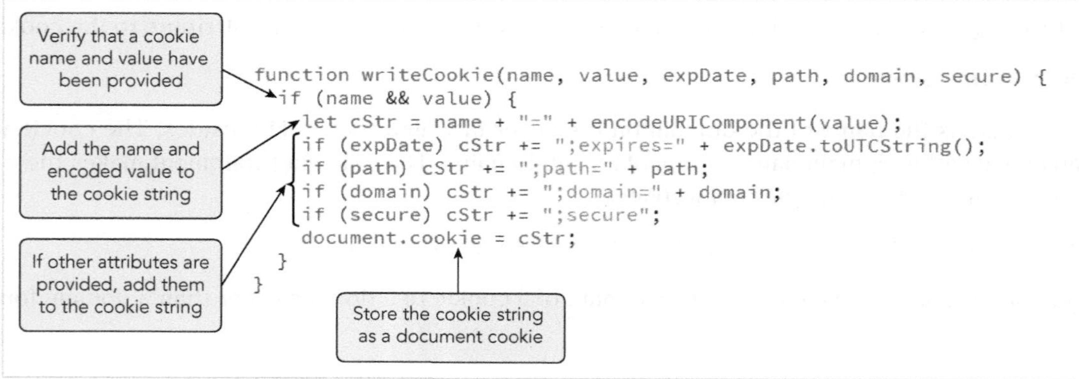

Figure 9-20 Function to write a cookie

The following statements apply this function to create a cookie for the `age` field, setting its expiration date to May 15, 2024 at midnight and placing the cookie in the `members` folder:

```
let expDate = new Date("May 15, 2024");
writeCookie("age", 18, expDate, "/members");
```

Once a cookie has been created its value can only be changed by writing the cookie again with a new value but under the same name, path, and domain. The revised cookie will overwrite the original cookie within both the browser and the web server.

Note | Cookies are transferred automatically between the browser and the server via the HTTP or HTTPS protocols. Once you have defined a cookie, you only need to open the page on the web server to enable it.

Reading a Cookie

All *name=value* pairs that have been previously saved as cookies for the current web page can be retrieved using the `document.cookie` object. If the *name=value* pairs for the Eating Well in Season website had been saved as cookies, the value of the `document.cookie` object would be:

```
name=Desmond%20Jennings; email=djennings%40example.com;
phone=(802)%20555-4781; address=43%20Maple%20Hill%20Drive;
city=Burlington; state=VT; zip=05041; allergies=none;
frequency=Monthly; size=Full%20plate
```

Each *name=value* pair is separated from the others with a semicolon and a blank space. The `document.cookie` value does not contain any information about the cookie's `expires`, `max-age`, `domain`, `path`, or `secure` attributes. Those attributes are treated as commands to be run by the browser and web server and are not directly accessible to JavaScript.

To extract the field names and values from `document.cookie`, apply the same approach used to access *name=value* pairs from a query string:

1. Apply the `split()` method to `document.cookie`, creating an array of *name=value* pairs for each stored cookie.
2. Loop through the array, saving each *name=value* pair as a separate item.
3. Extract the cookie name and cookie value from those pairs.
4. Apply the `decodeURIComponent()` method to the cookie value, replacing URI codes with their character equivalents.

You can organize your cookie values by placing them within a custom object so that each cookie name appears as a property of that object and the cookie value appears as a property value. **Figure 9-21** displays the code in the `readCookie()` function, which returns an object containing the names of each cookie as a separate object property.

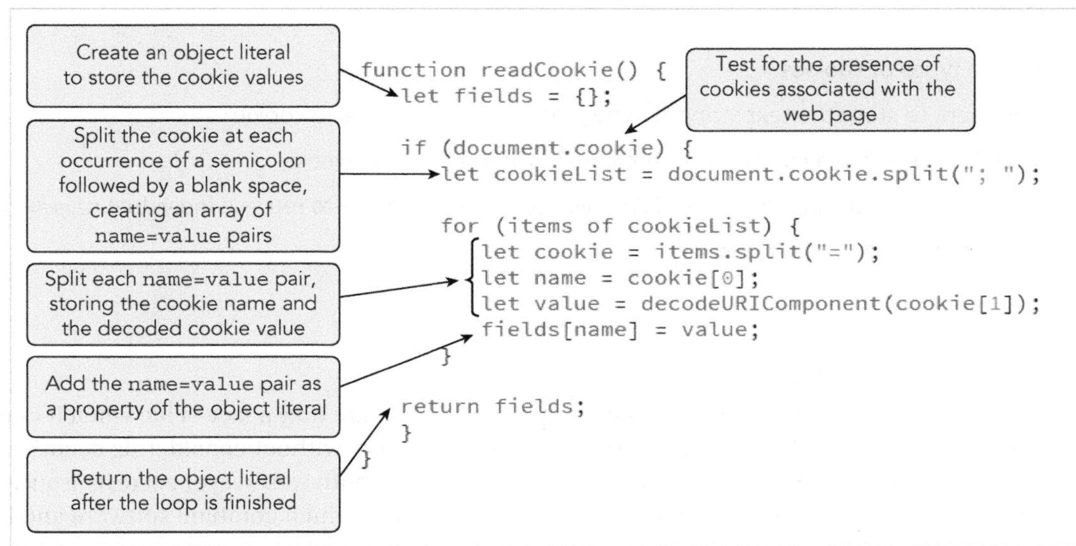

Figure 9-21 Function to read a cookie

To apply this function to the cookies created for a website like Eating Well in Season, you can use the following code, which retrieves each cookie value as a property of the `myPreferences` object:

```
let myPreferences = readCookie();
myPreferences.name   // returns "Desmond Jennings"
myPreferences.email  // returns "djennings@example.com"
myPreferences.phone  // returns "(802) 555-4781"
...
```

Functions like `writeCookie()` and `readCookie()` can make it easier to read and write cookies in your website application.

Deleting a Cookie

A session cookie is automatically deleted whenever a browser window or tab associated with that cookie is closed. Persistent cookies remain until they expire. To force the deletion of a persistent cookie, change the `expires` date to a past date or change the value of the `max-age` attribute to zero. The following statement deletes the `city` cookie from the `members` folder by setting its age to zero seconds:

```
document.cookie = "city=;max-age=0;path=/members";
```

If the cookie was created with defined values for the `path` and `domain` attributes, those attributes need to be included in any statement removing the cookie. Some browsers will not delete a cookie if you do not include the `path` attribute.

Cookies can also be deleted manually within your browser by:

1. Opening the Application or Storage window within your browser's developer tools (shown in Figure 9-19 for the Google Chrome browser).
2. Selecting Cookies from the list of storage options.
3. Selecting the origin of the cookies you wish to delete.
4. Selecting the cookies to be removed and pressing the Delete key on your keyboard.

Once the cookie is removed from your browser it will be automatically deleted on the web server as well.

Quick Check 3

1. What are the two types of cookies?
2. Provide a statement to store the text string "Jolene Jones" in the `username` cookie.
3. What attribute do you add to a cookie to set the cookie's lifetime to one week?
4. At what substring should you split the value of `document.cookie` object to retrieve individual *`name=value`* pairs?
5. How do you delete a cookie with JavaScript?

Exploring Security Issues

Viruses, worms, data theft by hackers, and other types of security threats are now a fact of life when it comes to web-based applications. If you put an application into a production environment without considering security issues, you are asking for trouble. To combat security violations, you need to consider both web server security issues and secure coding issues. Web server security involves technologies such as firewalls, which combine software and hardware to prevent access to private networks connected to the Internet. One very important technology is the Secure Sockets Layer (SSL) protocol, which encrypts data and transfers it across a secure connection. This type of security technology works well in the realm of the Internet. However, JavaScript programs are downloaded and executed locally within the web browser of a client computer and are not governed by security technologies such as firewalls and SSL.

This section discusses security issues that relate to web browsers and JavaScript.

Note Although web server security issues are critical, they are properly covered in books on Apache, Nginx, Internet Information Services, and other types of web servers. Be sure to research security issues for your web server and operating system before putting your website online.

Secure Coding with JavaScript

The terms secure coding and defensive coding refer to writing code in a way that minimizes any intentional or accidental security issues. Secure coding has become a major goal for many information technology companies, primarily because of the exorbitant cost of fixing security flaws in commercial software. According to one study, it is 100 times more expensive to fix security flaws in released software than it is to apply secure coding techniques during the development phase. The National Institute of Standards & Technology estimates that tens of billions of dollars per year is spent identifying and correcting software errors.

Basically, all code is insecure unless proven otherwise. Unfortunately, there is no magic formula for writing secure code, although there are various techniques that you can use to minimize security threats in your scripts. Your first line of defense in securing your JavaScript programs is to validate all user input. You have studied various techniques in this book for validating user input, including how to validate data with regular expressions and how to use exceptions to handle errors as they occur in your scripts. Be sure to use these techniques in your scripts, especially scripts that run on commercial websites. The remainder of this section discusses security issues that relate to web browsers and JavaScript.

JavaScript Security Concerns

The web was originally designed to be read-only, which is to say its primary purpose was to locate and display documents that existed on other areas of the web. With the development of programming languages such as JavaScript, web pages can now contain programs in addition to static content. This ability to execute programs within a web page raises several security concerns. The security areas of most concern to JavaScript programmers are:

- Protection of a web page and JavaScript program against malicious tampering
- Privacy of individual client information
- Protection of the local file system of the client or website from theft or tampering.

JavaScript code that is not written securely is vulnerable to a code injection attack, in which a program or user enters code that changes the function of the web page. For instance, a malicious program could open a web page containing a form and enter JavaScript code in one of the form fields designed to retrieve sensitive information from the server. Such a program could then relay this information to a person other than the owner.

Validating forms before submission is an important part of preventing injection attacks. In addition, it is important to escape characters in form field values that could be part of malicious code, which involves converting the characters to their character code equivalents, as you do when URI-encoding cookie data. For form input, escaping is generally performed by the web server before processing user input.

Another security concern is the privacy of individual client information in the web browser window. Your contact information and browsing history are valuable pieces of information that many advertisers would like to access to tailor their advertising based on your personal tastes. Without security restrictions, a JavaScript program could read this information from your web browser. One of the most important JavaScript security features is its lack of certain types of functionality. For example, many programming languages include objects and methods that make it possible for a program to read, write, and delete files. To prevent mischievous scripts from stealing information or causing damage by changing or deleting files, JavaScript does not allow any file manipulation aside from cookies, web storage, and a few other emerging standards, which are site specific. Similarly, JavaScript does not include any sort of mechanism for initiating a network connection, preventing JavaScript programs from infiltrating a private network or intranet from which information may be stolen or damaged. Another helpful limitation is the fact that JavaScript cannot run system commands or execute programs on a client. The ability to read and write cookies is the only type of access to a client JavaScript allows, and browsers strictly govern cookies and do not allow access to cookies from outside the domain that created them through the same-origin policy.

Common Mistakes

Storing Sensitive Information in Cookies

Cookies are stored on a user's computer as plain text files. If a user's computer is infected with malware, any data, including the contents of cookies, is vulnerable to being stolen and used fraudulently by a third party. For this reason, your programs should never place sensitive information, such as a password or credit card information, in a cookie. All modern browsers offer secure storage of logins and other personal information, which users can choose to enable; note that this information is not stored in cookies, but instead it is stored using a separate browser-specific mechanism. For more information on the hazards of storing sensitive information in cookies, use a search engine to search on "storing passwords in cookies."

Using Third-Party Scripts

Although the same-origin policy is an important part of web browser security, in some cases you want scripts from other domains, known as third-party scripts, to be able to run on your web pages. For instance, some companies provide widgets, which are programs that you can add to your web pages but that run from the provider's web server, rather than from your own. Another common situation requiring third-party scripts is the use of a content delivery network (CDN), which is a company that maintains web servers optimized for fast delivery of content. CDNs are commonly used by large organizations, and generally provide content from their own domain rather than from the client's domain.

To enable a third-party script in a web document, include a `script` element with a `src` value pointing to the third-party content. The same-origin policy limits scripts to those referenced by HTML documents from the original web server; this enables web pages to use third-party scripts.

Skills at Work | Using the Web Securely

When you access the web at home, school, or work, there are a couple steps you can take to keep your personal information secure. When your browser asks if you would like to save your login information, or a website you are visiting offers to remember you for next time, you should say yes only if you are using a computer whose users you trust, such as a computer owned by you or a friend or family member. You should never allow a browser or website to save any information you enter when using a public or shared computer, as the information can be accessed by anyone else using the computer.

When connected to a public wireless network—like at a café or at your school—you should transmit sensitive data only when you are connected to a server using an encrypted connection (using the HTTPS protocol). For instance, if you are using a wireless network at a café and you want to log into a website, ensure that your login will be handled with HTTPS. Taking these steps can help ensure the security of your personal information when you use the web.

Quick Check 4

1. What is secure coding or defensive coding?
2. What is a code injection attack?
3. What are third-party scripts?

Summary

- Websites can be either stateless so that information is not maintained between one session and the next or they can be designed to store information from previous sessions for the needs and convenience of the user.
- Information from a web form can be appended to the URL of a web page as a query string by adding the `get` method to the `form` element in the HTML file.
- Data in a query string is encoded using URI codes and placed within *`name=value`* pairs which are separated with the `&` symbol. Extract data from a query string using JavaScript's string methods and decode the data values using the `decodeURIComponent()` method.
- Data can be stored on the client device between sessions using the Web Storage API, which places data temporarily in session storage or permanently in local storage referenced with the `sessionStorage` and `localStorage` objects.
- Each web storage item is entered as a text string the form of a *`name=value`* pair.
- To place data in web storage, use the `setItem()` method. To retrieve item from web storage use the `getItem()` method. To delete a web storage item, use the `removeItem()` method.
- Data can be stored on the web server and client device between sessions using cookies, which are text strings containing *`name=value`* pairs. Cookies are either session cookies, which are automatically deleted at the end of each session, or persistent cookies, which expire at a specified date and time.
- To store data in a cookie, write the cookie text string to the `document.cookie` object.
- The expiration date for a cookie can be set using the `expires` or `max-age` attribute. The cookie's domain and path can be set using the `domain` and `path` attributes. The cookie can be set to be transmitted over a secure HTTPS connection by adding the `secure` attribute to the cookie text.
- Data can be retrieved from stored cookies by splitting the cookie string at each occurrence of the `"; "` substring.
- JavaScript includes safeguards such as the same-origin policy to guard against security breaches. However, it is still important to write code with an eye toward security and to avoid other potential problems such as code injection attacks.

Key Terms

code injection attack
content delivery network (CDN)
cookie
encoding
escape
`get` method
HTTP request
Hypertext Transfer Protocol (HTTP)
local storage object
man-in-the-middle attack
origin
path
persistent cookie
`post` method

query string
same-origin policy
secure (or defensive) coding
Secure Sockets Layer (SSL)
session
session cookie
session storage object
state information
stateless
third-party scripts
token
Transport Layer Security (TLS)
URI-encoded character
Web Storage API

Review Questions

1. HTTP was originally designed to be ______________, which means that web browsers store no persistent data about a visit to a website.
   a. hidden
   b. encrypted
   c. stateless
   d. stateful
2. What attribute should be added to the `<form>` element to submit the form data appended to a query string?
   a. `post`
   b. `get`
   c. `action`
   d. `src`
3. What method should be applied to decode data values within a query string?
   a. `decode()`
   b. `parse()`
   c. `decodeString()`
   d. `decodeURIComponent()`
4. What method should be applied to a query string to extract the *`name=value`* pairs from the string text?
   a. `query_string.split(/&/g)`
   b. `query_string.extract(/&/g)`
   c. `query_string.substring(/&/g)`
   d. `query_string.subst(/&/g)`
5. Which of the following addresses has the same origin as http://www.example.com?
   a. https://www.example.com
   b. http://www.example.com/members
   c. http://members.example.com
   d. http://example.com:8080
6. What is the object reference to a web storage object that is retained after the current session concludes?
   a. `localStorage`
   b. `sessionStorage`
   c. `webStorage`
   d. `permanentStorage`
7. Provide code to store the `username` key with value "user301x" in session storage.
   a. `sessionStorage = "username=user301x"`
   b. `sessionStorage[username] = "user301x"`
   c. `sessionStorage.setItem(username, user301x)`
   d. `sessionStorage.setItem("username", "user301x")`
8. To extract a key based on its index within the storage object, which method should you use?
   a. `extract()`
   b. `split()`
   c. `key()`
   d. `storage()`
9. To remove all keys from web storage for the current origin, which method should you apply?
   a. `removeItem()`
   b. `removeItems()`
   c. `clear()`
   d. `clearAll()`
10. Which of the following is not a difference between web storage and cookies?
    a. Cookies can be stored permanently; web storage items have an expiration date.
    b. Cookies are the older standard used with legacy browsers; web storage represents a newer standard.
    c. Cookies require a web server for development and testing; web storage does not.
    d. Cookie values must be parsed using JavaScript's String methods; web storage values can be read directly.
11. Provide code to save the text string "user301x" in the `username` cookie.
    a. `cookie.username = "user301x"`
    b. `document.cookie = "username=user301x"`
    c. `cookie["username"] = "user301x"`
    d. `username.cookie = "user301x"`

12. Which attribute should be added to the cookie text string to set the date on which a cookie should be removed?

a. `max-age`
b. `deleteBy`
c. `removeBy`
d. `expires`

13. What attribute should be added to a cookie string to specify the folder in which the cookie should be stored on the server?

a. `folder`
b. `directory`
c. `dir`
d. `path`

14. What attribute should be added to a cookie string to transfer the cookie over HTTPS?

a. `https`
b. `secure`
c. `secure=high`
d. `safety`

15. To separate the value of `document.cookie` into individual *`name=value`* pairs, split the text at every occurrence of what substring?

a. `";"`
b. `"&"`
c. `" & "`
d. `"; "`

16. When would you use query strings to store user data?

17. How does the same-origin policy keep web data safe and secure?

18. What is the difference between session storage and local storage?

19. Why should a password never be stored in a cookie?

20. Explain what a code injection attack is, and one step you can take to prevent such attacks.

Hands-On Projects

Hands-On Project 9-1

In this project you will work on a web page in which customers attach greeting messages to gifts purchased for friends and family. The contents of the greeting message will be entered on one web page form and then displayed as part of a shopping cart on a separate page. Data will be transferred from one page to the next by appending data to a query string. A preview of the shopping cart page with a sample gift card message is shown in **Figure 9-22**.

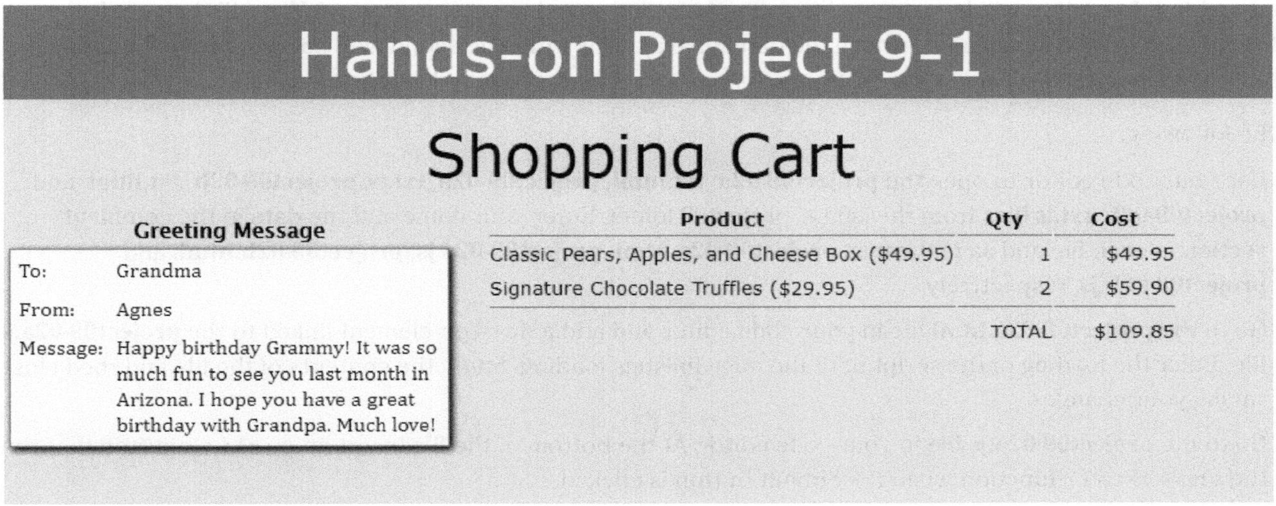

Figure 9-22 Completed Project 9-1

Do the following:

1. Use your code editor to open the **project09-01a_txt.html**, **project09-01b_txt.html**, and **project09-01b_txt.js** files from the js09 ▶ project01 folder. Enter your name and the date in the comment section of each file and save them as **project09-01a.html**, **project09-01b.html**, and **project09-01b.js**, respectively.
2. Go to the **project09-01a.html** file in your code editor. Edit the `form` element so that submitting the form opens the project09-01b.html file using the `get` method. Close the file, saving your changes.
3. Go to the **project09-01b.html** file in your code editor and add a `script` element linked to the project09-01b.js file. Defer the loading of the script until the page finishes loading. Take some time to study the contents of the HTML file and then close the file, saving your changes.
4. Go to the **project09-01b.js** file in your code editor. Apply the `slice()` method to the `location.search` object, storing the text after the first character in the **`query`** variable.
5. Use the `replace()` method to replace very occurrence of the + character in the `query` variable with a blank space. Apply the `decodeURIComponent()` method to replace every URI-encoded character in `query` with the matching character.
6. Appy the `split()` method to the query string to split the text at every occurrence of the `&` character, placing each *`name=value`* pair as a separate item in the **`cardFields`** array.
7. Create a `for of` loop that loops through every item in the `cardFields` array. At each iteration of the loop do the following:
   a. Split each item at the location of the = character, store the substrings in the `nameValue` array variable.
   b. Store the first item in the `nameValue` array in the `name` variable. Store the second item in the `nameValue` array in the `value` variable.
   c. Store the value of the `value` variable as the text content of the document element with an id equal to the `name` variable.
8. Save your changes to the file and then load **project09-01a.html** in your web browser. Enter sample greeting text in the field of the web form and then click the Submit button. Verify that the browser opens the **project09-01b.html** file with the text of the greeting message displayed in the page.

Hands-On Project 9-2

In this project you will use web storage to store information from a membership form of a cycling group. The membership information will be extracted from the form and saved to session storage. You will then confirm that the data has been saved and retrieve the data, displaying it within a second web page. **Figure 9-23** shows a preview of membership data retrieved from session storage and presented within a web table.

Do the following:

1. Use your code editor to open the **project09-02a_txt.html**, **project09-02a_txt.js**, **project09-02b_txt.html**, and **project09-02b_txt.js** files from the js09 ▶ project02 folder. Enter your name and the date in the comment section of each file and save them as **project09-02a.html**, **project09-02a.js**, **project09-02b.html**, and **project09-02b.js**, respectively.
2. Go to the **project09-02a.html** file in your code editor and add a `script` element linked to the **project09-02a.js** file. Defer the loading of the script until the page finishes loading. Study the contents of the file and then close it, saving your changes.
3. Go to the **project09-02a.js** file in your code editor. At the bottom of the file insert an `onclick` button that runs the `showData()` function when the Submit button is clicked.

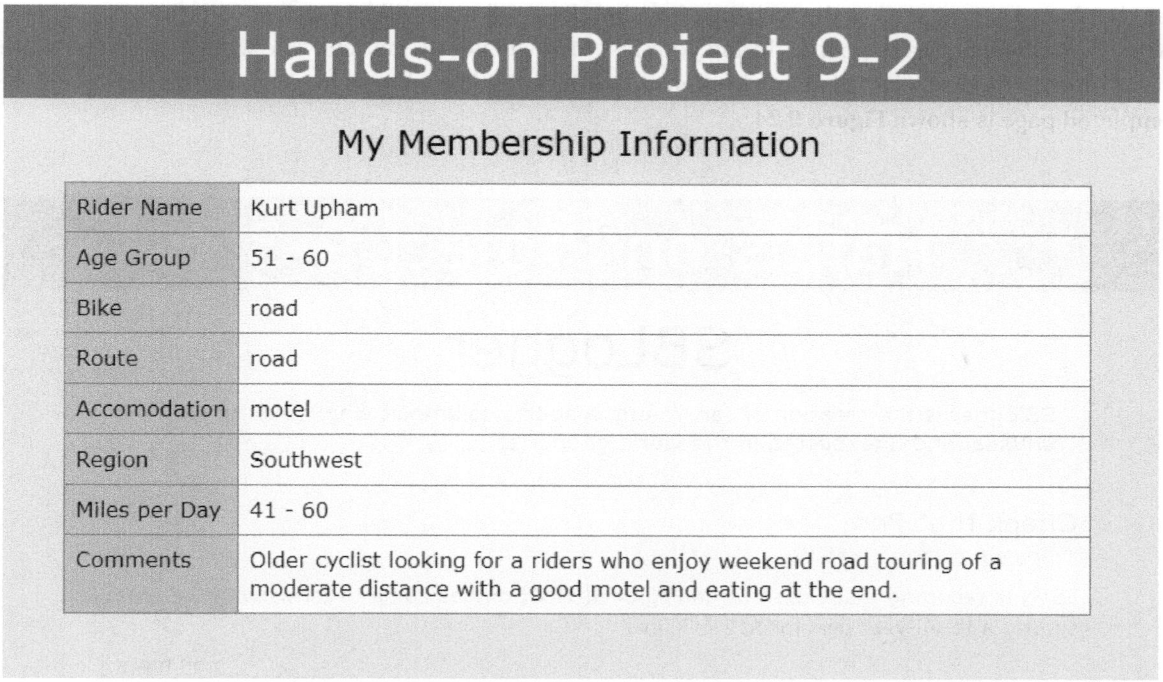

Hands-on Project 9-2

My Membership Information

Rider Name	Kurt Upham
Age Group	51 - 60
Bike	road
Route	road
Accomodation	motel
Region	Southwest
Miles per Day	41 - 60
Comments	Older cyclist looking for a riders who enjoy weekend road touring of a moderate distance with a good motel and eating at the end.

Figure 9-23 Completed Project 9-2

4. Add the `showData()` function and within the function insert the following commands:
   a. Insert a command to the store the value of the `riderName` object in a session storage object named `riderName`.
   b. Repeat the previous step for the `ageGroup`, `bikeOption`, `routeOption`, `accOption`, `region`, `miles`, and `comments` objects.
   c. Add a command that changes the value of the `location.href` object to the project09-02b.html file.
5. Close the file, saving your changes.
6. Go to the **project09-02b.html** file in your code editor and add a `script` element linked to the project09-02b.js file. As before, defer the loading of the script until the page loads. Review the contents of the file and then close it, saving your changes.
7. Go to the **project09-02b.js** file in your code editor. At the bottom of the file insert a command to retrieve the value of the `riderName` key from session storage and store that value in the text content of the `riderName` object in the web page.
8. Repeat Step 7 for the `ageGroup`, `bikeOption`, `routeOption`, `accOption`, `region`, `miles`, and `comments` keys.
9. Save your changes to the file and then load **project09-02a.html** in your web browser. Enter sample membership data in the web form and then click the Submit button. Verify that the project09-02b.html opens and that the membership information you entered is displayed in the web table.

Hands-On Project 9-3

In this project you will use web storage on a blogging site that posts news commentary and articles from the world of sports. The website will record the date and time of your last visit in a local storage item. Links to articles that have been posted to the website after that date and time will be marked with the text string "New". Articles that were already posted during your last visit will not be marked. The website will also store the date and time of the user's last visit in a local storage object with the key named "sbloggerVisit". A preview of the completed page is shown **Figure 9-24**.

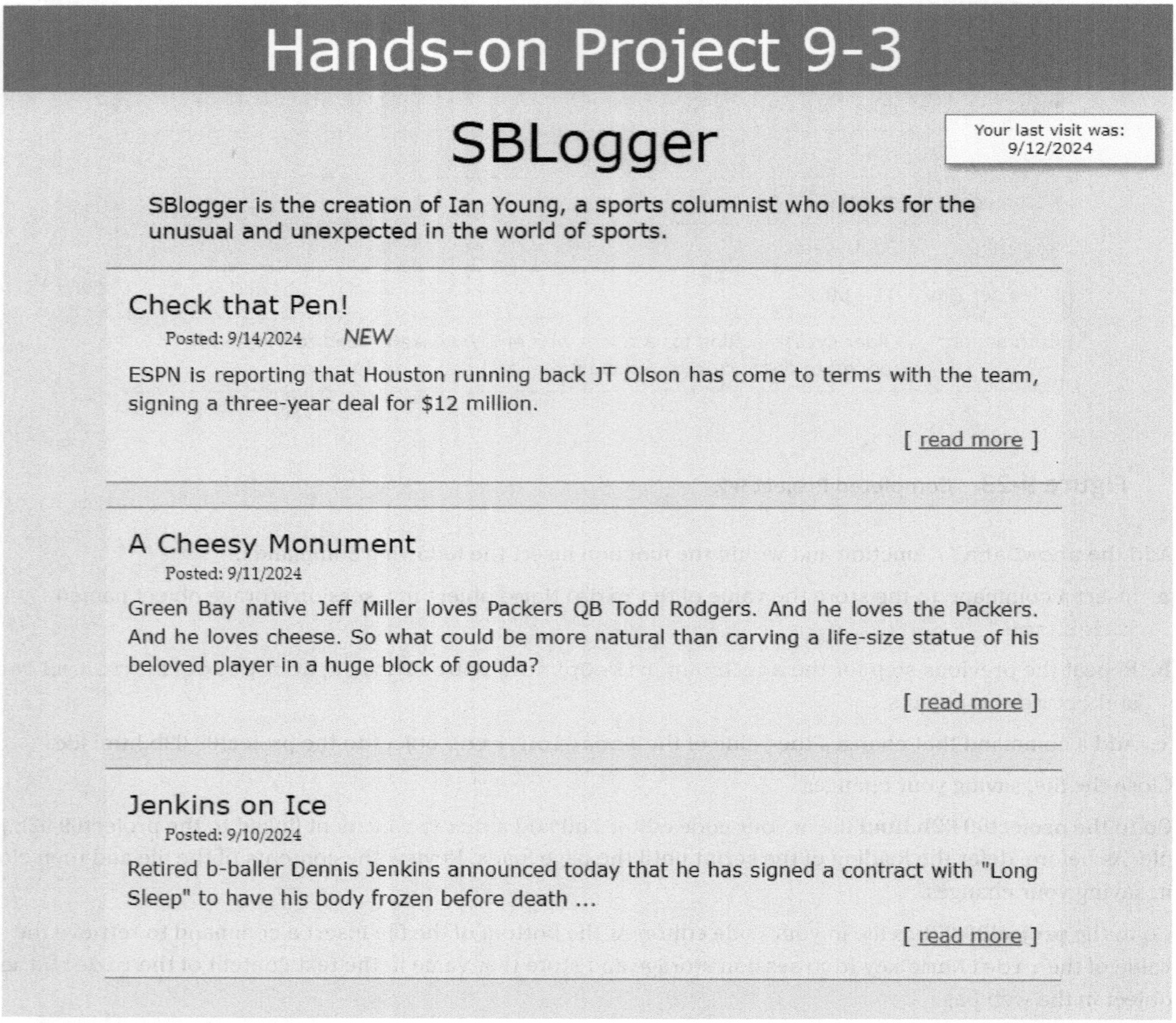

Hands-on Project 9-3
SBLogger
Your last visit was: 9/12/2024
SBlogger is the creation of Ian Young, a sports columnist who looks for the unusual and unexpected in the world of sports.
Check that Pen!
Posted: 9/14/2024 NEW
ESPN is reporting that Houston running back JT Olson has come to terms with the team, signing a three-year deal for $12 million.
[read more]
A Cheesy Monument
Posted: 9/11/2024
Green Bay native Jeff Miller loves Packers QB Todd Rodgers. And he loves the Packers. And he loves cheese. So what could be more natural than carving a life-size statue of his beloved player in a huge block of gouda?
[read more]
Jenkins on Ice
Posted: 9/10/2024
Retired b-baller Dennis Jenkins announced today that he has signed a contract with "Long Sleep" to have his body frozen before death ...
[read more]

Figure 9-24 Completed Project 9-3

Do the following:

1. Use your code editor to open the **project09-03_txt.html** and **project09-03_txt.js** files from the js09 ► project03 folder. Enter your name and the date in the comment section of each file and save them as **project09-03.html** and **project09-03.js**, respectively.
2. Go to the **project09-03.html** file in your code editor and add a `script` element linked to the **project09-03.js** file. Defer the loading of the script until the page finishes loading. Take some time to study the contents of the HTML file. Note the date of the user's last visit will be displayed in a `span` element with the id "lastVisitDate" and the date of each posted article is stored in a `span` element belonging to the "posttime" class. Save your changes to the file.

3. Go to the **project09-03.js** file in your code editor. Create an `if` statement that tests whether the object `localStorage.sbloggerVisit` exists. If it does exist, add the commands described in Steps 4 through 7.
4. Retrieve the value of the `sbloggerVisit` key from local storage and save the key value to the **`storedLastDate`** variable.
5. Display the value of `storedLastDate` as the text content of the `lastVisitDate` object to show the date of the user's last visit to the website.
6. Declare the **`lastDate`** variable, storing within it a `Date` object using the value of the `storedLastDate` variable.
7. Create a `for of` loop that iterates through each item in the `articleDates` collection. Each time through the loop do the following for every posted article on the website:
    a. Declare the **`articleDate`** variable storing within it a `Date` object containing the date text of the current item in the loop.
    b. If `articleDate` is greater than `lastDate` (meaning that the article was posted after the user's last visit) then add `"<strong>new</strong>"` to the HTML content of the current item in the `articleDates` collection.
8. If `localStorage.sbloggerVisit` does not exist (meaning this is the user's first visit to the website), then do the following:
    a. Change the text content of the `lastVisitDate` object to "Welcome to SBlogger!"
    b. Create a `for of` loop that iterates through each item in the `articleDates` collection. Each time through the loop add `"<strong>new</strong"` to the HTML content of the current date item.
9. After the `if else` statement, run the following code to update the stored date value in the `sbloggerVisit` key:
    a. Declare the **`currentDate`** variable and store within it a `Date` object containing the date "9/12/2024". (Note that this is just a test date you will use to verify that the application is working properly.)
    b. Apply the `toLocaleDateString()` method to `currentDate` and store the date string in `sbloggerVisit` key of local storage.
10. Save your changes to the file and then load the **project09-03.html** file in your web browser. Verify the following:
    a. The first time the page loads, the Date of Last Visit box should display the message "Welcome to SBlogger!" and all three articles should be marked as "New" because this is your first visit to the website.
    b. The second time you reload the page, the Date of Last Visit box should display the date "9/12/2024" and only the first article should be marked as "New".
11. If you need to reset the website to correct your errors, delete the `sbloggerVisit` key from the saved items in local storage using the Developer Tools in your web browser. When you have completed the project, delete the `sbloggerVisit` key from local storage so that it is not saved permanently within your browser.

Hands-On Project 9-4

In this project you will work with cookies that stores the fastest time to complete a sliding block puzzle. Much of the code for the puzzle has already been written. Your task is to write the code that records the user's best time and stores it within a persistent cookie with a 90-day lifetime.

To complete this task you will have to load your project onto a web server placed on a remote site or installed on your own computer. If you need to install your own server, you can download free server software like XAMPP from the web or you can use software supplied by your instructor.

NOTE: If you are unable to get access to a server, you can complete this project using local web storage by modifying the steps to store data in the `localStorage` object rather than in a cookie. A preview of the completed page is shown in **Figure 9-25**.

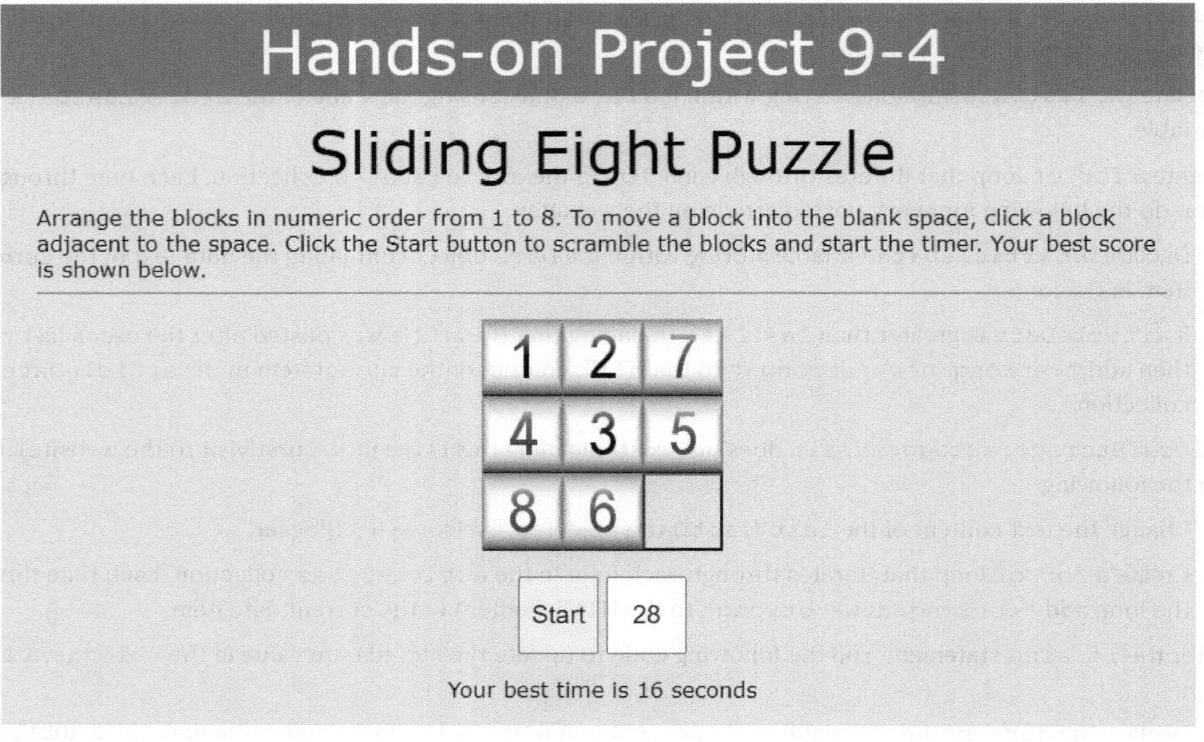
Hands-on Project 9-4
Sliding Eight Puzzle
Arrange the blocks in numeric order from 1 to 8. To move a block into the blank space, click a block adjacent to the space. Click the Start button to scramble the blocks and start the timer. Your best score is shown below.
1
2
7
4
3
5
8
6
Start
28
Your best time is 16 seconds

Figure 9-25 Completed Project 9-4

Do the following:

1. Use your code editor to open the **project09-04_txt.html** and **project09-04_txt.js** files from the js09 ▶ project04 folder. Enter your name and the date in the comment section of each file and save them as **project09-04.html** and **project09-04.js**, respectively.
2. Go to the **project09-04.html** file in your code editor. A `script` element linked to the library.js file has already been added to the page to provide the interface to the puzzle. Add another `script` element linked to the **project09-04.js** file to provide code for the cookie will you create. Defer the loading of that script file until the page finishes loading. Review the contents of the file and then save your changes.
3. Go to the **project09-04.js** file in your code editor. Within the anonymous function for the event listener of the browser window's `load` event, add the following code:
   a. Insert an `if` statement testing whether the `document.cookie` object exists for this page.
   b. If the `if` statement is true, change the text content of the `bestText` object to the text string "*`best`* `seconds`" where *`best`* is the value returned by the `getBestTime()` function.
4. Create the `getBestTime()` function. The purpose of this function is to retrieve the user's current best time to solve the sliding block puzzle. Add the following code to the function:
   a. If the `document.cookie` object exists then i) Declare the `cookieArray` variable containing the text of the document cookie split at the occurrence of the `"="` character. ii) Convert the cookie value to an integer by applying the `parseInt()` function to the value of `cookieArray[1]` and return it from the function.
   b. If the `document.cookie` object does not exist, return a value of 9999.

5. Create the `updateRecord()` function. The purpose of this function is to replace the user's best time with the time of their recent attempt if that attempt was better. Add the following commands to the function:
   a. Declare the `solutionTime` variable, storing within it value of the document element with the id "timer". Apply the `parseInt()` function to that value to convert it from a text string to an integer.
   b. Call the `getBestTime()` function and store the returned value in the `bestTime` variable.
   c. If `solutionTime` is less than `bestTime` then let `bestTime` equal `solutionTime`.
   d. Change the text content of the `bestText` object to "*best* seconds" where *best* is the value of the `bestTime` variable.
   e. Write the following text string to the `document.cookie` object, setting the max age of the cookie to 90 days:

      puzzle8Best=*best*

      where *best* is the value of the `bestTime` variable.
6. Save your changes to the file and then load all the web page files for this project to a folder on your web server.
7. Start your server software if necessary, and then use your browser to open the **project09-04.html** from the folder on your server. Verify the following:
   a. When you initially open the page, the page footer should display the message "Your best time is not yet recorded".
   b. Click the Start button and begin sliding the block pieces by clicking blocks adjacent to the open square. The timer will automatically stop when the blocks are in the correct order. Verify that the footer shows the updated best time.
   c. Close the web page and your browser. Verify that when you reopened the web page in your browser the updated best time is displayed in the page footer.
   d. Attempt to solve the puzzle several times, verifying that the page always shows the best time from all your attempts.
   e. If you need to retest the web page, delete the `puzzle8Best` cookie using the tools in your browser.

Hands-On Project 9-5

Debugging Challenge

You have been given code to add items to a shopping cart in a website for winter clothing company. There are four pages describing different winter gloves. Each page contains a web form and a form button to add the selected product to a shopping cart. Information about the selected product will be added to session storage in the text string:

product & *price* & *quantity* & *size* & *color*

where *product* is the name of the glove style, *price* is the glove's price, *quantity* is the quantity ordered, *size* is the glove size, and *color* is the glove's color. The first item added to the cart will have the key name `cartItem1`, the second `cartItem2`, and so forth.

However, there are several mistakes in the code that need to be corrected before the shopping cart works properly. A preview of a completed shopping cart is shown in **Figure 9-26**.

Do the following:

1. Use your code editor to open the **order_txt.js** and **cart_txt.js** files from the js09 ▶ project05 folder. Enter your name and the date in the comment section of each file and save them as **order.js** and **cart.js**, respectively.

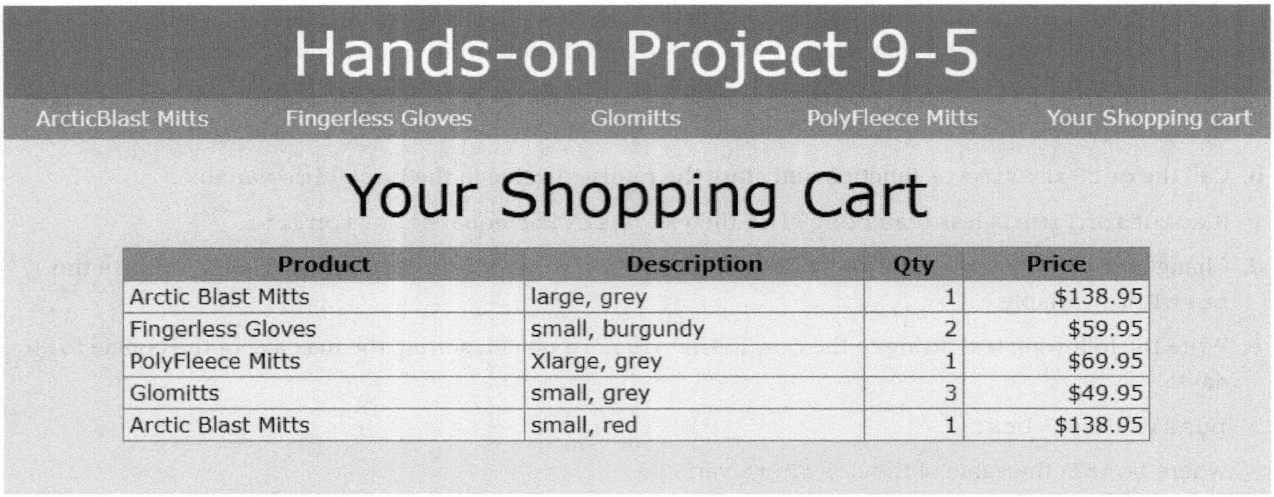

Hands-on Project 9-5

ArcticBlast Mitts Fingerless Gloves Glomitts PolyFleece Mitts Your Shopping cart

Your Shopping Cart

Product	Description	Qty	Price
Arctic Blast Mitts	large, grey	1	$138.95
Fingerless Gloves	small, burgundy	2	$59.95
PolyFleece Mitts	Xlarge, grey	1	$69.95
Glomitts	small, grey	3	$49.95
Arctic Blast Mitts	small, red	1	$138.95

Figure 9-26 Completed Project 9-4

2. There are four HTML products for the four different sample products for the shopping cart. Open the **product01.html** through **product04.html** files in your code editor to review their content and structure. Each is already linked to the order.js script file to add items to the shopping cart. Close the file after your review, you do not have to make any changes to the file.
3. Open the **cart.html** file in your code editor. This page will display the contents (if any) of the shopping cart. The page is already linked to the cart.js file to display shopping cart items. Close the file after reviewing the page contents. You do not need to make any changes to the file.
4. Go to the **order.js** file in your code editor. Fix the following mistakes in the file:
   a. When the customer adds an item to the shopping cart, the app should create or update a session storage key named `itemsInCart` containing the number of cart items. However, there are several mistakes in storing values in this key. Locate and fix the errors.
   b. The app will also store information about the selected item which each piece of information separated by the `" & "` substring. Fix the mistake in writing the text string.
   c. The app concludes by the text string of the production summary to a session storage item named `cartItem`*n* where *n* is the number of the cart item. There is a mistake in the statement that writes the text string to session storage. Fix the error.
5. Save your changes to the file and then go to the **cart.js** file in your code editor. Fix the following mistakes:
   a. To display the shopping cart the app extracts the value of the `itemInCart` session storage key. Fix the errors in the code to retrieve information about the number items to display in the shopping cart.
   b. The code extracts information about each product from the `cartItem`*n* key; however, there is a mistake in retrieving that information and writing that data to the `productArr` array. Fix the errors in those lines.
6. Save your changes to the file and then load the **product01.html** file in your browser. Verify that the app works correctly as follows:
   a. Using the **product01.html** through **product04.html** web page forms, click the Add to Shopping Cart button to add new items to your shopping cart.
   b. Click the link to the Shopping Cart page to verify that the items you selected are displayed in the shopping cart.
   c. If the app does not work, view the contents of your session storage using the web storage tools in your browser.

Case Projects

Individual Case Project

Enhance the personal website you have created in the preceding chapters of this book to include state information that will be retained from one session to the next. You can use either web storage or cookies depending on the tools available to you. Remember that if you use cookies you need to place your website on its own server. If your website contains web forms that span several pages, show your mastery of query strings by adding code to store data within query strings as users navigate from one form to the next.

Team Case Project

Have each group member solicit feedback from other group members on security issues with the team website. Discuss ways of ensuring data validity and privacy. Discuss ways in which state information on the team website could be maintained between sessions and how long that information should be retained. After all group members have presented their sites and received feedback, implement any suggestions for your site that your group generally felt would be good additions. Document your discussions and your conclusions.

CHAPTER 10

Programming with Event Objects and Third-Party APIs

When you complete this chapter, you will be able to:

- Write code for event objects and event properties
- Work with events for mice, touchscreens, and pointer devices
- Program a drag and drop action using pointer events
- Create drag and drop interfaces using the Drag and Drop API
- Write code that responds to keyboard events
- Create interactive maps using the Google Maps API
- Locate your position using geolocation
- Add routes and directions to a Google Map using the Google Directions and Renderer services
- Use the Device Orientation API to detect changes in client device speed and position
- Create more efficient code for mobile devices by reducing script numbers and sizes

---

As you gain experience in developing your own web apps you will have to consider the needs of users who will access your app from a wide variety of devices from desktop computers to laptops to mobile devices and tablets. In supporting those devices, you will need to consider how users will interact with your app. Will they use a keyboard or a mouse or a touchscreen? Will you need to consider their geographic location if they are using a mobile device? In this chapter you will examine some of the tools and techniques for managing events occurring between the user and your website.

Working with Events as Objects

In this chapter you will work with a website for the Oak Top House, a conference center in Columbus, Ohio. Meeting rooms at the Oak Top House are available for daily or multiday rental and are commonly used for wedding receptions, graduation parties, conferences, and other special events. You have been asked to work on a web page in which customers design a room layout suitable for their event. Open the web page for Oak Top House's Rose Room now.

To open the files for the Oak Top House website:

1. Go to the js10 ▶ chapter folder of your data files.
2. Use your code editor to open the **js10a_txt.html** and **js10a_txt.js** files. Enter your name and the date in the comment section of each file and then save them as **js10a.html** and **js010a.js**, respectively.
3. Take some time to study the contents of the js10a.html file to become familiar with its contents and its code.
4. Open the **js10.html** file in your web browser. **Figure 10-1** shows the initial layout of the page.

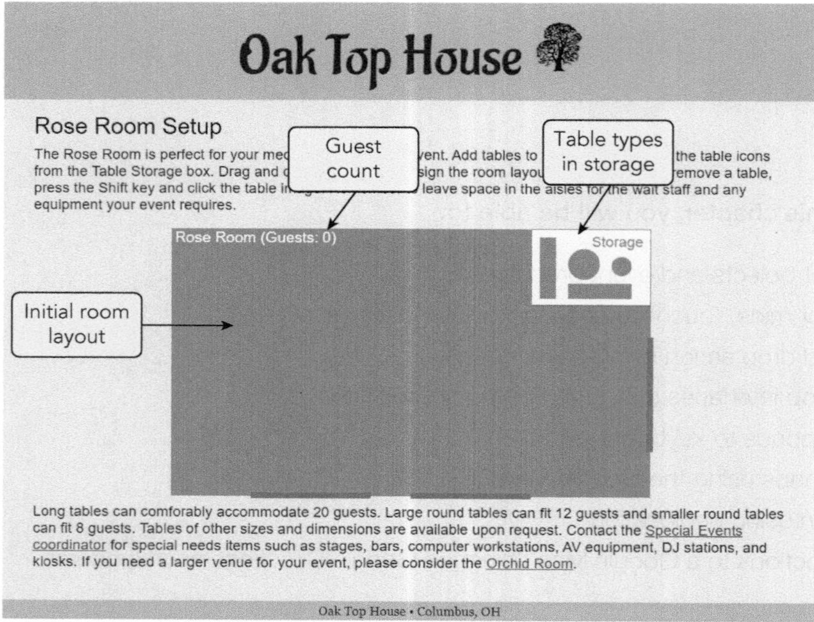

Figure 10-1 Rose Room Banquet Hall Setup page

In the upper-right corner of the room layout is Table Storage containing icons of four different types of tables ranging from round tables that can accommodate 8 to 12 guests to long tables that can accommodate 20 guests. The layout of the Rose Room will show positions of the tables for the event and will include an estimate of the number of guests that the layout can accommodate. Table positions can be set by dragging and dropping the table images.

The `Event` Object

All interactions between the user and a web app take place in the context of events. If the user strikes a keyboard key while working with a web page or web form, that action creates an event. If the user clicks the mouse button or drags the cursor across the web page or touches a point on the screen, those actions also create events. Because of the object-oriented nature of JavaScript, an event is just another type of object to be managed by your code.

An event object contains information about the event occurring within the web page or browser. Initiating an event such as clicking a mouse button generates an event object describing which mouse button was clicked, what object on the web page was clicked, the exact location of the cursor when the mouse button was clicked, and so forth. The event object is passed as parameter of the function managing the event as in the following command in which an event object included as a parameter of `userClick()` function:

```
myButton.onclick = userClick;
function userClick(event) {
   commands
}
```

The *event* parameter can be assigned any name, but the general practice is to name it `event`, `evt`, `ev`, or simply `e` (a practice we will follow in this chapter). Once the event object has been named, it can be referenced within the function to return information about the event. In the following code the event object is named `e` and uses the `button` property to provide information about the button clicked by the user:

```
function userClick(e) {
   console.log("The " + e.button + " button was clicked.");
}
```

Figure 10-2 describes some of the properties and methods common to many of the events supported by JavaScript.

PROPERTY	DESCRIPTION
`e.bubbles`	Returns a Boolean value indicating whether the event is bubbling up through the object hierarchy
`e.cancelable`	Returns a Boolean value indicating whether the event can have its default action canceled
`e.currentTarget`	Returns the object that is currently experiencing the event
`e.defaultPrevented`	Returns a Boolean value indicating whether the `preventDefault()` method was called for the event
`e.eventPhase`	Returns the phase of the event propagation the event object is currently at, where 0 = NONE, 1 = CAPTURING_PHASE, 2 = AT_TARGET, and 3 = BUBBLING_PHASE
`e.isTrusted`	Returns a Boolean value indicating whether the event is trusted by the browser
`e.target`	Returns the object in which the event was initiated
`e.timeStamp`	Returns the time (in milliseconds) when the event occurred
`e.type`	Returns the type of the event
`e.view`	Reference the browser window in which the event occurred
METHOD	**DESCRIPTION**
`e.preventDefault()`	Cancels the default action associated with the event
`e.stopImmediatePropagation()`	Prevents other event listeners of the event from being called
`e.stopPropagation()`	Prevents further propagation of the event through the object hierarchy

Figure 10-2 Event object properties and methods

Event Capturing and Bubbling

A property common to all events is the `target` property indicating which object initiated the event. When an element is clicked by a mouse or pointer device, the expression

```
event.target
```

returns a reference to that object. It might not always be clear which object is associated with an event. Consider the act of clicking a table cell nested within a table row, inside of a table that is part of a `div` element placed within a web page displayed in a browser window. Within that hierarchy of objects, which one is associated with the click?

The answer is based on the way that events propagate through a web document. Events move down the object hierarchy from the window to the innermost object during the capture phase, reach the innermost object at the target phase, and then move back up the hierarchy during the bubbling phase. The target of the event is the innermost object in that hierarchy. **Figure 10-3** shows the propagation of an event as it moves through these phases.

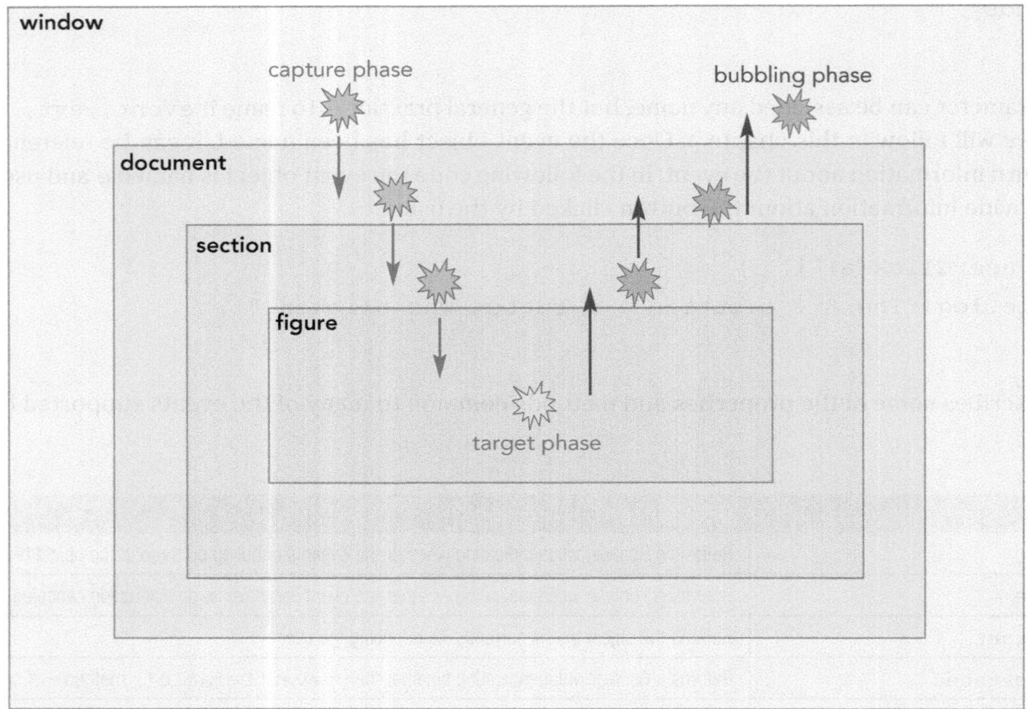

Figure 10-3 Capturing and bubbling of events

By default, event listeners listen for events during the bubbling phase. Event handlers do not support capturing or bubbling, so they respond to the event at the target phase.

> **Note** To listen for events during the capture phase, apply the method `addEventlistener(event_name, true)` to the event. To keep an event from propagating to the next object, apply the `stopPropagation()` method to the event object.

Event listeners allow for greater flexibility in responding to events. A web app could respond to the same event with different actions depending on which object within the hierarchy is currently experiencing the event and whether the event occurs during the capture phase or during the bubbling phase. You can determine which event in the hierarchy is currently experiencing the event using the `currentTarget` property. In most cases you do not need to consider event propagation in your scripts, but it does become useful in some gaming apps. For the Oak Top House website, you will focus on events associated with mice and other pointing devices.

The first feature you will add to the app will give users the ability to add tables to the room by clicking one of the four icons in table storage. For each table in storage, you will create an `onclick` event handler that copies the clicked table and appends it as a new child element of the room.

Because tables might overlap, you will specify the table stacking with the CSS `zIndex` property, which determines how overlapping page objects are displayed. An element with a higher z-Index value will appear on top of objects with lower z-index values. As each new table is added to the room, it will be given the highest z-index value.

Some of the code to complete this project has already been created for you. Your first task is to enter the event handlers to add tables from storage to the Rose Room.

To create `onclick` event handlers for the tables in storage:

1. Return to the **js10a.js** file in your code editor.
2. When the page initially loads it will run the `setupRoom()` function to establish the functions and variables used by the app. Directly below the `countSeats()` function add the following `for of` loop that adds `onclick` event handlers to each table in storage:

```
// Add tables from storage to the banquet hall
for (let items of storageTables) {
   items.onclick = function() {
      let storageCopy = items.cloneNode(true);
      room.appendChild(storageCopy);
```

3. Within the anonymous function add the following commands to increase the value of the `zIndexCounter` so that newly copied tables will be displayed on top of any other table in the room:

```
zIndexCounter++;
storageCopy.style.zIndex = zIndexCounter;
```

4. Complete the anonymous function and the loop by adding the following commands to run the `countSeats()` function, updating the room's guest count:

```
      countSeats();
   }
}
```

   Be sure to close off the command blocks in the `for of` loop and the anonymous function. **Figure 10-4** describes the newly added code in the file.

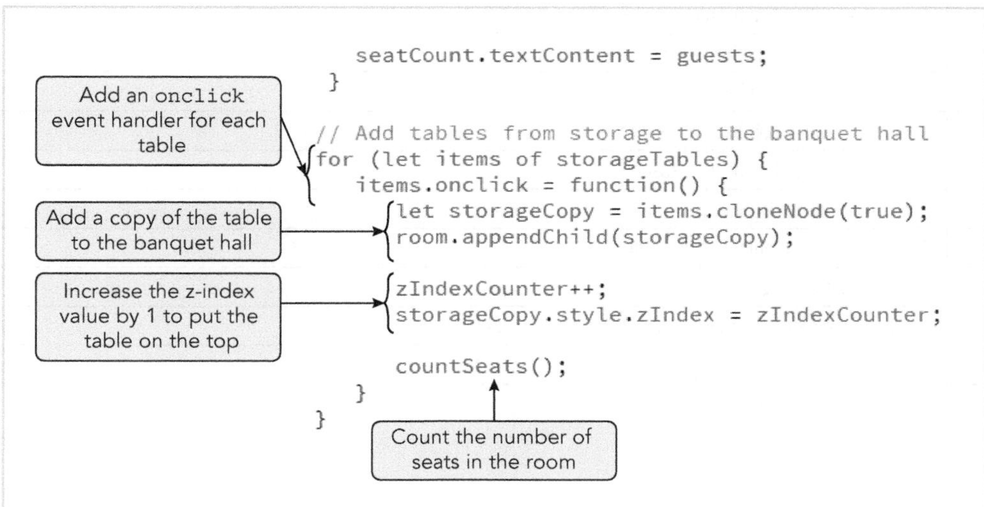

Figure 10-4 Creating event handlers for the tables in storage

5. Save your changes to the file and then reload **js10a.html** in your browser.
6. Click each icon in table storage, verify that a copy of the table is added to the room and the guest count increases by the number of seats at the table. See **Figure 10-5**.

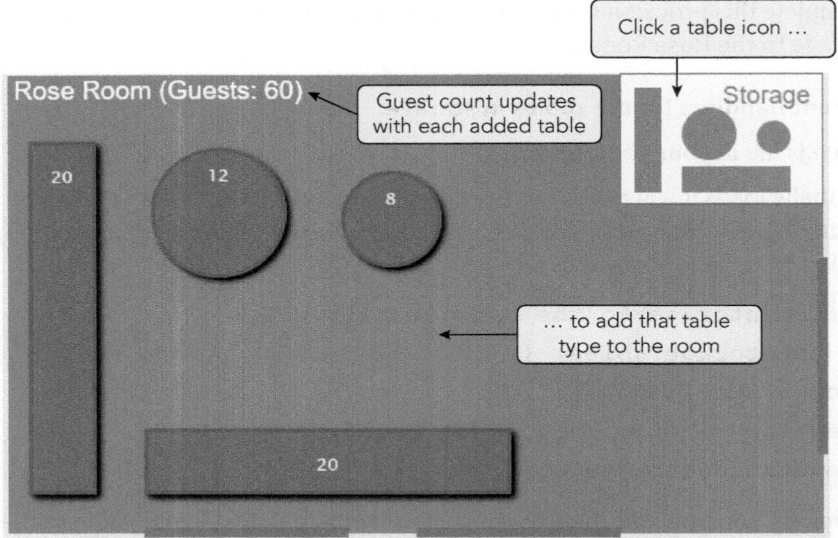

Figure 10-5 Adding tables to the Rose Room

Your next task is to give customers the ability to move tables around within the banquet hall using their mouse or pointing device.

Exploring Mouse, Touch, and Pointer Events

Thus far your work with mice and other pointing devices has been limited to the `click` event. However, there are several other actions associated with mice such as moving the mouse cursor across the web page, pressing the mouse button down and then releasing it, double-clicking the mouse button, or opening a context menu by right-clicking the mouse. **Figure 10-6** describes some of the other events associated with mice and other pointing devices.

EVENT	DESCRIPTION
`click`	The mouse button has been pressed and released on an element
`contextmenu`	The right mouse button has been pressed and released
`dblclick`	The mouse button has been double-clicked
`mousedown`	The mouse button has been pressed down
`mouseup`	The mouse button has been released
`mousemove`	The mouse pointer is moving
`mouseover`	The mouse pointer enters an element
`mouseout`	The mouse pointer leaves an element
`mouseenter`	Similar to the mouseover event except that it does not bubble
`mouseleave`	Similar to the mouseout event except that it does not bubble
`wheel`	The mouse scroll wheel has been rotated

Figure 10-6 Mouse events

A mouse action can combine several events in quick succession. The action of clicking the mouse button combines three events fired in the following order:

1. `mousedown` (the button is pressed down)
2. `mouseup` (the button is released)
3. `click` (the button is pressed and released)

Other events are fired more than once during an action. Moving the mouse pointer across an element causes the `mousemove` event to be fired continuously with each new pointer position triggering a new `mousemove` event.

The event object for mouse events has its own set of properties that return specific information about the condition of the mouse and its buttons. **Figure 10-7** describes some of the properties specific to mice events.

EVENT PROPERTY	DESCRIPTION
`e.button`	Returns the pressed button where: 0 = primary (usually left), 1 = middle or wheel, 2 = secondary (usually right), 3 = 4th button (usually back), 4th = 5 button (usually forward)
`e.buttons`	Returns the pressed button or buttons where: 0 = no button, 1 = primary (usually left), 2 = secondary (usually right), 4 = middle or wheel, 8 = 4th button (usually back), 16 = 5 button (usually forward). If more than one button is pressed the numeric sum is returned
`e.detail`	Returns a number describing the event. For `click` and `dblclick` this is the current click count. For `mousedown` and `mouseup` this is the current click count plus 1.
`e.relatedTarget`	Returns the secondary target of the event. For `mouseenter,` this is the element that the mouse is leaving, for `mouseleave`, this is the element that the mouse is entering.

Figure 10-7 Mouse event object properties

You can create scripts that respond differently depending on which mouse button was clicked by the user as determined by the `button` or `buttons` property. Be aware, however, that some buttons are reserved by the browser for specific tasks. The right mouse button is reserved for context menus. Thus, if your application requires the use of that button, you must prevent the display of a context menu by running a function for the `contextmenu` event that returns a value of `false`. The following code demonstrates this technique by first disabling the context menu for a specified element and then writing text to the debugger console if the secondary (right) button is clicked within that element:

```
element.oncontextmenu = function() {
   return false;
}
element.onmouseup = function(e) {
   e.preventDefault();
   e.stopPropagation();
   if (e.button === 2) {
      console.log("Right mouse button clicked");
   }
}
```

Note that the anonymous function for the `mouseup` event also prevents the default action associated with the event and halts the propagation of the event through the object hierarchy.

> **Note** The `click` event responds to the click of any mouse button, though for secondary mouse buttons you may have to prevent the browser's default response to the button click before supplying your own code.

Exploring Touch Events

Users are increasingly visiting websites with tablets and mobile devices that utilize touch in place of a mouse. Touch events share some of the same characteristics as mouse events but there are important differences. A mouse event consists of a single point of contact; touchscreens allow for multiple simultaneous contact points. A mouse event is a single interface involving the action of the button; touch events consist of the three following interfaces:

- In the Touch interface the user touches the screen at a single contact point called a touchpoint.
- In the TouchList interface the user creates several touchpoints simultaneously, such as the act of "pinching" with two fingers to zoom into or out of a window.
- In the TouchEvent interface the state of touchpoints on the touch surface changes, such as would occur when touchpoints move or change their pressure on the touch surface.

Within each interface there are four primary touch events, described in **Figure 10-8**.

EVENT	DESCRIPTION
`touchstart`	A touch point is placed on the touch surface
`touchmove`	A touch point is moved along the touch surface
`touchend`	A touch point is removed from the touch surface
`touchcancel`	A touch point has been disrupted by the device or operating system and is no longer available

Figure 10-8 Touch events

Touchscreen browsers emulate mouse events so that a tap on the screen initiates a touch cascade consisting of touch and mouse events. See **Figure 10-9**.

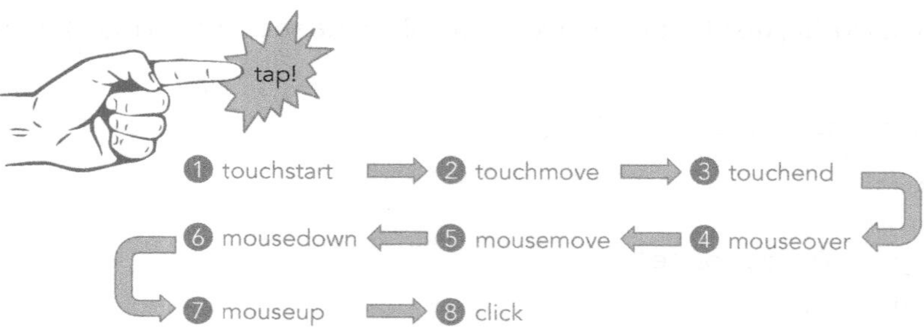

Figure 10-9 The touch cascade for a tap action

Associating the same action with multiple events can be a problem if the script includes event handlers for several events within the cascade. One way of managing the cascade is to apply the `preventDefault()` method to the event so that the browser's default method emulating mouse events is not invoked. The general code structure is:

```
element.ontouchstart = function(e) {
    commands for the touchstart event
    e.preventDefault();
}
```

One drawback to this approach is that it can result in complicated scripts that include code for every possible touch and mouse event.

Finally, a browser might have its own actions associated with touch events. The CSS `touch-action` property can be used to disable those default actions. The following JavaScript command disables all default touch actions associated with the element by setting the value of the `touch-action` property to "none":

```
element.style.touchAction = "none";
```

Other values of the touch-action property include pan-x, pan-y, and pinch-zoom to enable only those actions on the element. You can read more about touch-action on the web.

Managing Multiple Touchpoints

Touchscreens allow for multiple touchpoints such as the pinch gesture in which two fingers are used to zoom into an element. Multiple touchpoints are stored in a TouchList object. Every touchpoint within that list is referenced using the touches property, which returns an array of touchpoints related to a single touch action. Thus, touches [0] references the first touchpoint in the action, touches [1] references the second, and so forth. The total number of touchpoints within any action is returned by the touches.length property.

Because not all touchpoints change with each touch event, the changedTouches object returns an array of touchpoints whose properties have changed. If there are two points on the screen but one point moves in a zoom-out gesture, there would be two items in the touches array, but only one item in changeTouches, and that item would be referenced with changedTouches [0]. Thus, index numbers in the touches array do not necessarily correspond to indexes in the changeTouches array.

Finally, not all touchpoints will be in contact with the same target. The targetTouches object returns an array of touchpoints within a specified element. In some apps there might be two touchpoints, each associated with a different target and thus the length of targetTouches for each target element would be 1. Using the targetTouches array you can focus only on those touchpoints in contact with the target and ignore touchpoints placed elsewhere.

As you add more touchpoints to an app, the level of complexity increases. Some game apps require managing multiple touchpoints and gestures, but for the Oak Top House app, you only need to worry about one touchpoint.

Using Pointer Events

Originally JavaScript only supported mouse events because they were the primary means of interacting with the document. Touch events were added later with the rising popularity of touchscreens. Other types of devices such as stylus pens were introduced a bit later still. Any action that involves using a device to point at an object on the screen is called a pointer event.

JavaScript uses pointer events to organize mice, touch, and other similar events under one roof. Rather than writing separate code for each device, the goal is to write one set of code for all pointers. **Figure 10-10** lists some of the pointer events supported by JavaScript. Note the similarity between these events and the mouse events in Figure 10-6.

EVENT	DESCRIPTION
pointerdown	The pointer has become active such as when a mouse button is pressed down, or physical contact is made with a touch surface
pointerup	The pointer is no longer active
pointermove	The pointer has changed coordinates
pointerover	The pointer has moved over a specified element
pointerout	The pointer has moved out of a specified element
pointerenter	Similar to pointerover except that it does not bubble
pointerleave	Similar to pointerout except that it does not bubble
pointercancel	The pointer is no longer able to generate events

Figure 10-10 Pointer events

Pointer events include properties that are not supported by mice but are supported by other pointers. For example, a pen stylus has properties such as the pressure of the pen on the screen surface or the pen's tilt angle. **Figure 10-11** describe some of pointer's "non-mouse" properties.

POINTER EVENT PROPERTY	DESCRIPTION
`e.pointID`	Returns a unique identifier for devices that allow multiple pointers
`e.width`	The width of the contact point along the horizontal axis
`e.height`	The height of the contact point along the vertical axis
`e.pressure`	The pressure of the pointer on the device surface ranging from 0 (no pressure) to 1 (maximum pressure)
`e.tangentialPressure`	The pressure of the pointer tangent to the device surface, ranging from 0 to 1
`e.tiltX`	The angle of the pointer with the device surface along the horizontal axis, ranging from -90 to 90
`e.tiltY`	The angle of the pointer with the device surface along the vertical axis, ranging from -90 to 90
`e.twist`	The clockwise rotation of the pointer with respect to the device surface
`e.pointerType`	The type of pointer (mouse, touch, pen, etc.)
`e.isPrimary`	Returns `true` if the pointer is the primary pointer of the device

Figure 10-11 Pointer event properties

For apps that need to accommodate both mouse and touch events, the following events are treated by the browser as equivalent:

```
pointerdown = mousedown = touchstart
pointerup = mouseup = touchend
pointermove = mousemove = touchmove
```

Thus, the following event handler would be interpreted as a `mousedown` event for a mouse and a `touchstart` event for a touchscreen:

```
element.onpointerdown = function
```

You will use the `pointerdown`, `pointmove`, and `pointerup` events in your code to provide drag and drop functionality to the Oak Top House website.

Programming a Drag and Drop Action

A drag and drop action proceeds through the following phases:

- The **grab phase** in which an element is selected at the `pointerdown` event
- The **move phase** in which the element follows the motion of the pointer during the `pointermove` event
- The **drop phase** in which the element is released at the `pointerup` event

Add an event listener to initiate the grab phase in response to a `pointerdown` event for tables in the Rose Room.

To add an event listener for the `pointerdown` event:

1. Return to the **js10a.js** file in your code editor.
2. Go to the anonymous function in the `for of` loop, and add the following statement after the command to run the `countSeats()` function. See **Figure 10-12**.

```
// Grab the table in response to the pointerdown event
storageCopy.addEventListener("pointerdown", grabTable);
```

```
        zIndexCounter++;
        storageCopy.style.zIndex = zIndexCounter;

        countSeats();

        // Grab the table in response to the pointerdown event
        storageCopy.addEventListener("pointerdown", grabTable);
    }
}
```

Run the `grabTable()` function in response to the `pointerdown` event

Figure 10-12 Listening for the `pointerdown` event

Next you will begin writing the code of the `grabTable()` function.

Finding Event Coordinates

During a drag and drop action the selected object follows the pointer around the screen, matching its coordinates to the change in the pointer's coordinates. Coordinates are measured relative to the top-left corner of a container, such as a page element, the browser window, the web page, or the screen. **Figure 10-13** describes four sets of JavaScript properties that return event coordinates.

HORIZONTAL	VERTICAL	EVENT COORDINATES
`e.offsetX`	`e.offsetY`	Measured relative to the top-left corner of the element in which the event occurred
`e.clientX`	`e.clientY`	Relative to the top-left corner of the browser viewport or window
`e.pageX`	`e.pageY`	Relative to the top-left corner of the web page
`e.screenX`	`e.screenY`	Relative to the top-left corner of the screen

Figure 10-13 Event coordinates

Every coordinate property returns the pointer's relative location in pixels. If a pointer event occurs 100 pixels to the right and 50 pixels down from the top-left corner of the browser window, the value of `e.clientX` will be 100 and `e.clientY` will be 50. The pointer's position relative to other containers would be measured by the other properties.

Note If the entire page is visible within the browser window, `e.pageX` and `e.pageY` return the same values as `e.clientX` and `e.clientY`.

Use the `clientX` and `clientY` properties to store the initial position of the pointer during the `pointerdown` event.

To save the pointer's initial position:

1. Scroll to the top of the js10a.js file and directly below the statement that sets the initial value of `zIndexCounter` to 0, add the following statement to declare the `startingX` and `startingY` variables:

```
let startingX, startingY; // initial pointer coordinates
```

2. Scroll down and below the `for of` loop, insert the following `grabTable()` function:

```
// Grab a table from the banquet hall
function grabTable(e) {
}
```

3. Within the `grabTable()` function insert the following command to store the initial position of the pointer:

```
startingX = e.clientX;
startingY = e.clientY;
```

4. Add the following command to disable the browser's default touch actions around the target of the `pointerdown` action:

```
e.target.style.touchAction = "none";
```

5. Finally, apply the following commands to increase the `z-index` value of the table so that it will be on top of the other tables during the subsequent drag and drop action:

```
zIndexCounter++;
e.target.style.zIndex = zIndexCounter;
```

Figure 10-14 describes the newly added code in the file.

```
      // Grab the table in response to the pointerdown event
      storageCopy.addEventListener("pointerdown", grabTable);
   }
}

// Grab a table from the banquet hall to begin drag and drop
function grabTable(e) {
   startingX = e.clientX;
   startingY = e.clientY;
   e.target.style.touchAction = "none";
   zIndexCounter++;
   e.target.style.zIndex = zIndexCounter;
}
```


Figure 10-14 The `grabTable()` function

The script also needs to store the table's initial position. The horizontal and vertical coordinates of an element within its parent can be retrieved with the following properties:

```
elem.offsetLeft
elem.offsetTop
```

As with the event coordinates, `offsetLeft` and `offsetTop` return the element's position in pixels. The element must be placed within its parent with its CSS `position` property set to `absolute` and the `position` property of the parent element set to `relative` or `absolute`.

Create the `tableX` and `tableY` variables to store the initial position of the table and then add event handlers to the table for the `pointermove` and `pointerup` events.

To save the table's initial position:

1. Scroll to the top of the js10a.js file and directly below the statement declaring the `startingX` and `startingY` variables, declare the following variables:

```
let tableX, tableY; // initial table coordinates
```

2. Add the following commands to the `grabTable()` function to store the table's initial position with the room layout:

```
tableX = e.target.offsetLeft;
tableY = e.target.offsetTop;
```

3. Add the following event listeners to the function:

```
e.target.addEventListener("pointermove", moveTable);
e.target.addEventListener("pointerup", dropTable);
```

See **Figure 10-15**.

```
function grabTable(e) {
   startingX = e.clientX;
   startingY = e.clientY;
   e.target.style.touchAction = "none";
   zIndexCounter++;
   e.target.style.zIndex = zIndexCounter;

   tableX = e.target.offsetLeft;
   tableY = e.target.offsetTop;

   e.target.addEventListener("pointermove", moveTable);
   e.target.addEventListener("pointerup", dropTable);
}
```

Store the table's initial position
Add event listeners to the table

Figure 10-15 Storing the table's starting position

Next you will write code that moves the table following the pointer.

Dragging and Dropping an Element

Dragging is accomplished by calculating the change in position of the pointer during the `pointermove` event and moving the selected object by the same amount. Because the pointer and the object move by the same distance and direction, the object will appear to be dragged by the pointer. Create the `moveTable()` function to (1) determine the pointer's current position, (2) calculate the distance and direction the pointer has traveled, and (3) move the table by the same amount.

To calculate the table's new position:

1. Directly below the `grabTable()` function add the following `moveTable()` function:

```
// Move the table along with the pointer
function moveTable(e) {
}
```

2. Within the `moveTable()` function add the following code to determine the pointer's current location and the distance it has traveled in the horizontal and vertical direction:

```
let currentX = e.clientX;
let currentY = e.clientY;
let deltaX = currentX - startingX;
let deltaY = currentY - startingY;
```

3. Finally, add the following code to move the table in the horizontal and vertical direction by the same amount that the pointer has traveled:

```
// Calculate the table's new position
e.target.style.left = tableX + deltaX + "px";
e.target.style.top = tableY + deltaY + "px";
```

Note that the table is placed within the room using the CSS `left` and `top` properties. **Figure 10-16** shows the completed code of the `moveTable()` function.

Determine the pointer's current position

Calculate the distance the pointer traveled horizontally and vertically

Move the table the same distance as the pointer

```
// Move the table along with the pointer
function moveTable(e) {
   let currentX = e.clientX;
   let currentY = e.clientY;
   let deltaX = currentX - startingX;
   let deltaY = currentY - startingY;

   // Calculate the table's new position
   e.target.style.left = tableX + deltaX + "px";
   e.target.style.top = tableY + deltaY + "px";
}
```

Figure 10-16 The `moveTable()` function

Once a table has been dropped it should no longer follow the pointer. Thus, the drop action needs to remove the event listeners for the `pointermove` and `pointerup` events, leaving the table at its final recorded position.

To drop an element:

1. Directly below the `moveTable()` function add the following `dropTable()` function:

```
function dropTable(e) {
   e.target.removeEventListener("pointermove", moveTable);
   e.target.removeEventListener("pointerup", dropTable);
}
```

   Figure 10-17 describes the newly added code.

```
// Drop the table onto the banquet hall
function dropTable(e) {
   e.target.removeEventListener("pointermove", moveTable);
   e.target.removeEventListener("pointerup", dropTable);
}
```

After the table is dropped, remove the event listeners so the table no longer moves with the pointer

Figure 10-17 The `dropTable()` function

2. Save your changes to the file and then reload **js10a.html** in your web browser.
3. Add tables to the Rose Room and then use your pointer to drag and drop each table to a new location within the room. **Figure 10-18** shows a sample room layout that can accommodate up to 128 guests.

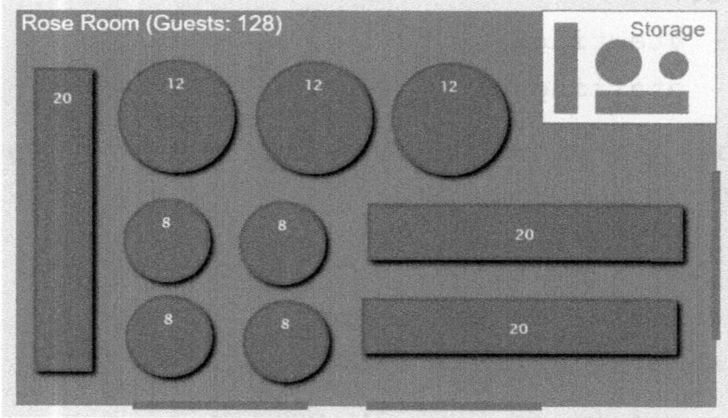

Figure 10-18 A table layout created with drag and drop

Browser Tools for Touchscreen Emulation

The app you created should work equally well with mice and touchscreens. If you do not have a touchscreen device, you can still test the touch by using the device emulator with your browser's developer tools.

For Chrome, Edge, and Firefox, display the emulator by opening your browser's Developer Pane and clicking the device icon or press `Ctrl+Shift+M` to enter Responsive Design Model. For Safari, open the Develop menu and click Enter Responsive Design Model or press `Shift+Cmd+R`. Under Chrome and Edge, the pointer will appear as a blurry circle to indicate that touch emulation is active (see **Figure 10-19**).

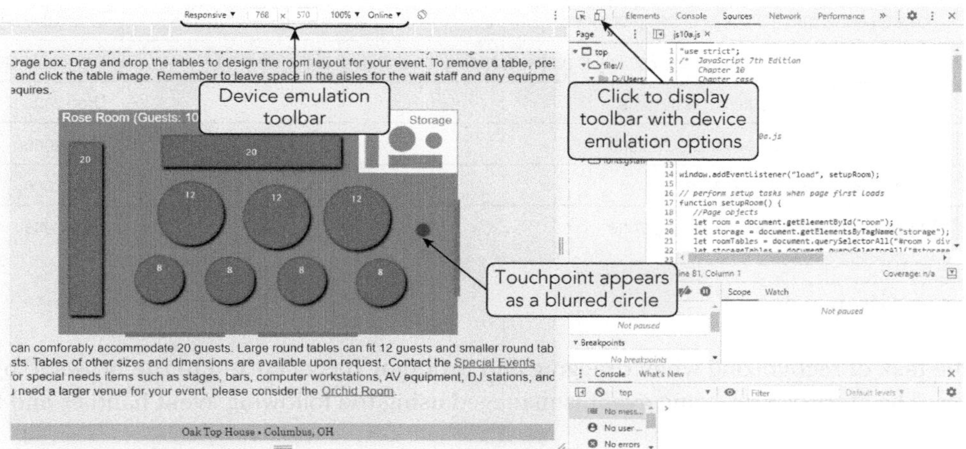

Figure 10-19 Touchscreen emulation within Google Chrome

From the device toolbar you can choose different devices to emulate or define the properties of a new device. Note that device emulation cannot replace testing on the actual device, so you should always test your app on a variety of platforms and browser versions before releasing it to the public.

Quick Check 1

1. What is the difference between the `target` property and the `currentTarget` property?
2. What sequence of events is initiated during a mouse click and in what order?
3. What event properties provide the coordinates of the pointer relative to the web page?
4. What is the touch cascade?
5. What two events are treated by the browser as equivalent to the `pointerdown` event?

Exploring the Drag and Drop API

There are some elements that support drag and drop without JavaScript. A hypertext link can be opened by dragging and dropping the link into the browser's address bar. Text can be added to a web form by dragging and dropping it into a text box control. Other elements can be given this feature by adding the following attribute to their element tag:

```
<element draggable = "true">
```

Adding the `draggable` attribute only makes the element capable of being dragged. To define the browser response does requires JavaScript.

Note You can also make an element draggable by running the command `elem.draggable = "true"` in your JavaScript code.

The HTML Drag and Drop API

JavaScript manages draggable elements using the Drag and Drop API (DnD API), defining what elements can be dragged and where they can be dropped. The API supports two types of events: events targeted to draggable elements and events targeted to an element, called a drop zone, that will receive dragged items. **Figure 10-20** describes both types of events and their targets.

EVENT	DESCRIPTION	EVENT TARGET
`dragstart`	A draggable element starts being dragged by the user	Draggable element
`drag`	The element is in the process of being dragged	Draggable element
`dragend`	A pointer button is released, or the Esc key is pressed, ending the dragging of the element	Draggable element
`dragenter`	A draggable element enters a drop zone	Drop zone
`dragover`	The element is hovering over a drop zone	Drop zone
`dragleave`	The element leaves a drop zone	Drop zone
`drop`	The element is released onto a drop zone	Drop zone

Figure 10-20 Drag and drop events

The DnD API leaves the task of recognizing when dragging and dropping has occurred to the browser, bypassing the need for pointer events. The start of a dragging event is managed using the following event handler and listener:

```
dragElem.ondragstart = function;
dragElem.addEventListener("dragstart", function);
```

where *dragElem* references an element whose `draggable` attribute has been set to "`true`" and that has started being dragged by the user. As the drag commences the browser supplies an image of the dragged element tethered to the pointer. There is no need to store the pointer's coordinates during the drag operation or to move the element using pointer events.

As the image of the element is dragged, it will pass over other elements on the page. To enable one of those elements to act as a drop zone, add the following event handler or listener to it:

```
dropZone.ondragover = function;
dropZone.addEventListener("dragover", function);
```

where *dropZone* is an element that can receive the draggable element. Elements that are not drop zones will display the ⃠ symbol alongside the pointer to indicate that the element cannot be dropped there.

Note | When an element is enabled as a drop zone, all children of that element also act as drop zones.

Elements are released into the drop zone by applying an event handler or listener to the `drop` event:

```
dropZone.ondrop = function;
dropZone.addEventListener("drop", function);
```

To avoid conflicts with pointer and touch events that might fire during the drag and drop, functions for the `dragover` and `drop` events should start with the command:

```
event.preventDefault();
```

where *event* is the event object for the function. Any commands associated with pointer or touch events will be superseded by the function. You can also have the function return the value `false` to prevent further handling of the drag and drop action.

Note When dragging and dropping an element using the DnD API, it is easy to forget that the event target is based on the event and not the element being moved. For the `dragstart` event, `e.target` references the dragged item; for the `dragover` and `drop` events, `e.target` references the drop zone.

Transferring Data with Drag and Drop

Once the image of the element has been dropped, there can be several results, including:

- The draggable element is moved from its original location into the drop zone.
- A copy of the draggable element is added to the drop zone.
- Data from the draggable element is written into the drop zone.

Unlike with pointer events in which the element is physically moved across the page, the DnD API transfers information about the element. This information is stored in a `dataTransfer` object. **Figure 10-21** describes some of the `dataTransfer` methods for storing and retrieving data from the drag and drop operation.

METHOD	DESCRIPTION
`dataTransfer.setData(mime, data)`	Store data in the *`dataTransfer`* object where *`mime`* is the mime-type of the data and *`data`* is a text string containing the data value
`dataTransfer.setDragImage(`*`image, xOffset, yOffset`*`)`	Defines a semi-transparent image to displaying during the drag operation where *`image`* is the image to display, and *`xOffset`* and *`yOffset`* set the horizontal and vertical distance from the pointer to the image
`dataTransfer.getData(`*`mime`*`)`	Retrieves data stored in the `dataTransfer` object method
`dataTransfer.clearData()`	Clears all data from the `dataTransfer` object

Figure 10-21 Methods of the **`dataTransfer`** object

For example, to store the id of the dragged item, apply the following `setData()` method during the `dragstart` event:

```
e.dataTransfer.setData("text", e.target.id)
```

where `e.target` references element being dragged. To retrieve that id value during a `drop` event, apply the following `getData()` method to the `dataTransfer` object:

```
e.dataTransfer.getData("text")
```

Figure 10-22 demonstrates the complete sequence of moving an element into a drop zone by setting and getting data from the `dataTransfer` object.

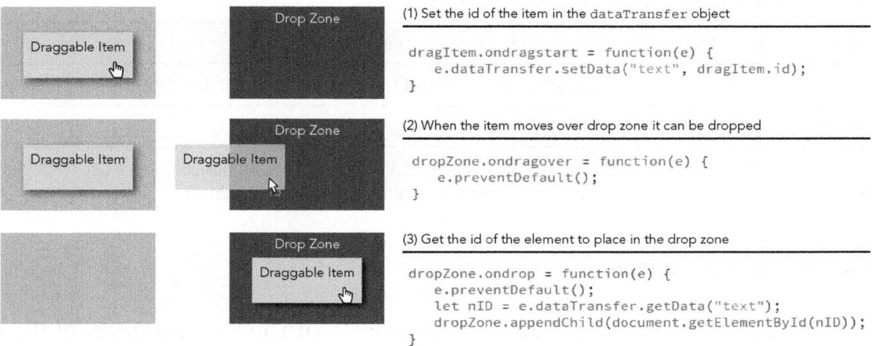

Figure 10-22 Moving an object using the Drag and Drop API

The sequence starts by storing the id of the element in the `dataTransfer` object and concludes by retrieving the id to move that element using the `appendChild()` method. The code to copy the element into the drop zone is similar except that a clone of the dragged element would be placed in the drop zone.

> **Note** You can store HTML code within the `dataTransfer` object, using the "text/html" mime-type along with the inner or outer HTML code of the dragged element. To transfer an object, use the `JSON.stringify()` method to convert the object into a text string that can be stored in the `dataTransfer` object and the `JSON.parse()` method to convert it once the element has been dropped.

The Drag and Drop API can simplify the drag and drop process, but currently it is not well supported on touch devices. If you need to support such devices you will have to work with pointer events. Also note that the browser's default drag and drop behavior for naturally draggable objects like images can conflict with pointer events. To manage those kinds of objects using only pointer events, set the object's `draggable` attribute to `"false"`.

Working with Keyboard Events

Your app for the Oak Top House does not provide a way for removing tables from the room layout. You have been asked to give users the ability to remove a table by clicking the table while the Shift key is pressed down. To add this feature, you will have to work with keyboard events.

When a user presses a key on the keyboard, the following events occur in order:

1. `keydown` The key is pressed down.
2. `keypress` The key is pressed down and released, resulting in a character.
3. `keyup` The key is released.

The distinction between the `keydown`/`keyup` events and the `keypress` event lies in the difference between the physical keyboard and the generated character. The `keydown`/`keyup` events are fired in response to the physical act of pressing and releasing a keyboard key, while `keypress` is fired in response to the creation of a character. **Figure 10-23** describes some of the properties associated with keyboard events.

EVENT PROPERTY	DESCRIPTION
`e.altKey`	Returns a Boolean value indicating whether the Alt key was used in the keyboard event
`e.ctrlKey`	Returns a Boolean value indicating whether the Ctrl key was used
`e.shiftKey`	Returns a Boolean value indicating whether the Shift key was used
`e.metaKey`	Returns a Boolean value indicating whether the meta key (the Command key on Mac keyboards or the Windows key on PC keyboards) was used
`e.code`	Returns a text string of the physical key that was pressed
`e.key`	Returns the text containing the value of the key that was pressed
`e.charCode`	Returns the Unicode value of the character generated by the `keypress` event (this property has been deprecated)
`e.keyCode`	Returns the value of the physical key that was pressed (deprecated)
`e.location`	Returns the location number of the key, where 0 = key located in the standard position, 1 = a key on the keyboard's left edge, 2 = a key on the keyboard's right edge, and 3 = a key on the numeric keypad (deprecated)

Figure 10-23 Keyboard event properties

To determine which key was pressed, use either the `code` property or the `key` property of the keyboard event. The `code` property provides the name of the key and the `key` property provides the character generated. **Figure 10-24** demonstrates that these are not always the same thing.

ACTION	E.CODE	E.KEY
Pressing the "a" through "z" keys	"KeyA" through "KeyZ"	"a" through "z"
Pressing the "0" through "9" keys	"Digit0" through "Digit9"	"0" through "9"
Pressing the Spacebar	"Space"	" "
Pressing the Shift key	"ShiftLeft" or "ShiftRight"	"Shift"
Pressing the Ctrl key	"ControlLeft" or "ControlRight"	"Control"
Pressing the Alt key	"AltLeft" or "AltRight"	"Alt"
Pressing the Command key	"MetaLeft" or "MetaRight"	"Meta"
Pressing the Tab, Enter, Backspace Insert, Delete, Home, End, Page Up, and Page Down keys	"Tab", "Enter", "Backspace", "Insert", "Delete", "Home", "End", "PageUp", "PageDown"	"Tab", "Enter", "Backspace", "Insert", "Delete", "Home", "End", "PageUp", "PageDown"
Pressing the arrow keys	"ArrowUp", "ArrowDown", "ArrowLeft", "ArrowRight"	"ArrowUp", "ArrowDown", "ArrowLeft", "ArrowRight"

Figure 10-24 Comparing the values of `e.code` and `e.key`

> **Note** The `keypress` event only fires when a character is generated, thus there is no `code` or `key` value for `keypress` events of keys like Shift, Alt, or Tab.

The cursor does not have to be within a form field for a keyboard action to be recognized. Keyboard events can also be associated with the browser window or document. The following statement fires whenever the user presses down a key within the active browser window:

```
window.onkeydown= function(e) {
  commands
}
```

In addition to character keys, JavaScript supports the modifier keys Alt, Ctrl, Shift, and Command using the `altKey`, `ctrlKey`, `shiftKey`, and `metaKey` properties, which return `true` if the key is pressed down during an event. These properties can be combined with pointer events, so that event handlers and listeners can be written for actions that involve both pointers and keyboard modifiers.

Use the `shiftKey` property with the Oak Top House app to determine whether the user is pressing down the Shift key during the `pointerdown` event. If the key is pressed, remove the table from the room layout and update the guest count.

To remove a table from the room layout:

1. Return to the **js10a.js** file in your code editor.
2. Scroll down to the `grabTable()` function.
3. At the start of the function insert the following `if` command block to test whether the Shift key was pressed and if it has, remove the table from the web page and update the guest count:

```
if (e.shiftKey) {
   // Remove the table from the room
   e.target.parentElement.removeChild(e.target);
   countSeats();
}
```

4. Enclose the rest of the code in the function within an `else` command block, indenting the code to make it easier to read. **Figure 10-25** shows the completed code of the `grabTable()` function.

If the Shift key is pressed down remove the table and update the guest count

Place the remaining code within an `else` command block

```
// Grab a table from the banquet hall to begin drag and drop
function grabTable(e) {
   if (e.shiftKey) {
      // Remove the table from the room
      e.target.parentElement.removeChild(e.target);
      countSeats();
   } else {
      startingX = e.clientX;
      startingY = e.clientY;
      e.target.style.touchAction = "none";
      zIndexCounter++;
      e.target.style.zIndex = zIndexCounter;

      tableX = e.target.offsetLeft;
      tableY = e.target.offsetTop;

      e.target.addEventListener("pointermove", moveTable);
      e.target.addEventListener("pointerup", dropTable);
   }
}
```

Figure 10-25 Responding to a keyboard event

5. Close the file, saving your changes.
6. Reload the **js10a.html** file in your web browser. Verify that you can add tables to the Rose Room, move them around to create new room layouts, and remove tables by holding down the Shift key as you click the table image.

You have completed your work on the room layout page by giving customers the ability to add, move, and remove tables from the banquet hall. In the next session you will explore other events and APIs that will be useful to the Oak Top House website.

Best Practices | Making Drag and Drop User-Friendly

Drag and drop interfaces are so common it is easy to forget that you still need to design them to be easy for the end user. Here are some tips to make your drag and drop apps user-friendly.

- Create visual clues for objects that are draggable. This can be as simple as changing the cursor style when the pointer hovers over the object or adding an outline or drop shadow to draggable objects.
- During the drag, choose a cursor style that reflects the action. If the action involves moving the object, choose a move cursor. If the action involves copying, choose a copy cursor. You can view cursor styles as part the CSS cursor property or you can create your own customized cursor.
- Provide visual clues for the drop zones so that users understand where the object can be dropped and where it cannot.
- It can be difficult to drop an item in an exact location. Give your dropped items the ability to "snap to" a point when the object is close rather than requiring precision dropping.
- Touchscreens can be difficult to use with drag and drop because fingers are not as precise as pointers. Provide your touchscreen users with at least a one square centimeter of space for grabbing an item. During the drag, make sure that user's finger does not cover any important information needed for the drag and drop.

- Drag and drop is traditionally a mouse or touchscreen activity. Make your app accessible to all users by enabling keyboard events so that users can move an item using the keyboard arrow keys and drop objects pressing the Enter or Spacebar keys. Provide messages to screen readers explaining exactly how to do drag and drop with keyboard keys.

A drag and drop interface can be fun to create and use, but it must meet the needs of the user. Do not choose a drag and drop interface if you can accomplish the same thing with a simpler more straightforward approach. The flashiest interface is of no use if it leaves a frustrated customer.

Quick Check 2

1. What must be added to an HTML element to make it draggable?
2. What event handler is applied to an element when it starts being dragged?
3. What property and method can be used to store data associated with a drag and drop action?
4. What is the difference between the `keypress` and `keydown` events?
5. How do you determine if the Ctrl key is pressed down during a pointer event?

Creating an Interactive Map

Another page in the Oak Top House website provides a driving map with directions to the conference center. To complete this page, you will work with the Google Maps API.

Getting Started with the Google Maps API

The Google Maps API is one of the most popular third-party APIs available for JavaScript, allowing developers to supplement their websites with maps of almost any place on the globe and to augment those maps with pins highlighting points of interest or to show travel routes connecting one location with another.

To use the Google Maps API, go to the Google Console at *https://console.cloud.google.com/* and do the following:

1. Pick a product to purchase, such as the Google Maps API.
2. Set up a billing account for your product.
3. Create and enable a project to access the Google Maps API.
4. Create an API key to allow your website to access the Google Maps API.

Google provides step-by-step instructions for setting up the Google Maps platform at *https://developers.google.com/maps/gmp-get-started.* Although you have to provide Google with payment information to set up your account, at the time of this writing Google provides $200 in free monthly usage of Google Cloud products. Under their current pricing structure, Google charges $7 for every 1000 map requests and $5 for every 1000 requests for map directions. Unless you generate a lot of requests for maps and directions, it is unlikely you will exceed the free monthly allowance.

If you do not wish to set up a billing account on Google Cloud at this time, review the material in this section for future reference.

After setting up a billing account and a project, you must get an API key from Google Maps. An API Key is a string of characters passed from your application to an API platform, verifying you are the owner of an account and project that has access to the tools built into the API. You can safeguard your API key so that it only works with specific website domains or IP addresses. Look under the Credentials menu on Google Cloud for more information about setting up access restrictions to your API key.

> **Note** | To restrict the use of the API key to pages hosted on your own local network, you will need your network's IP address. You can retrieve that address by going to the *google.com* website and searching for the phrase "my ip".

Once you have secured an API key for your Google Maps account, you are ready to add maps to your website. The Google Maps API is made accessible to your web page by including the following `script` element:

```
<script src="https://maps.googleapis.com/maps/api/js?key=keyID&callback=function">
</script>
```

where *`keyID`* is a key obtained from Google Cloud for your project and *`function`* is a callback function called by the API to generate a map. The API key is a long and complex string of characters, but you can copy the key value from your project account on Google Cloud and paste it directly into your code.

Add the Google Maps API to a web page for the Oak Top House web page that provides customers with directions to the conference center.

To add the Google Maps API:

1. Set up a billing account on Google Cloud and create a project.
2. Within the project add the Google Maps API for JavaScript and set up a Google Maps API key.
3. Go to the js10 ▶ chapter folder of your data files.
4. Use your code editor to open the **js10b_txt.html** and **js10b_txt.js** files. Enter your name and the date in the comment section of each file and then save them as **js10b.html** and **js010b.js**, respectively.
5. Go to the **js10b.html** file in your code editor and within the document head, add the following command to link to your script file:

```
<script src="js10b.js" defer></script>
```

6. Add the following `script` element to access the Google Maps API, copying the API key from your project account:

```
<script defer
 src="https://maps.googleapis.com/maps/api/js?key=keyID &callback=initMap">
</script>
```

   where *`keyID`* is the text of your API key. **Figure 10-26** shows the code with the API key text blurred out. You will have to copy and insert your own key within the indicated place in the `src` attribute.

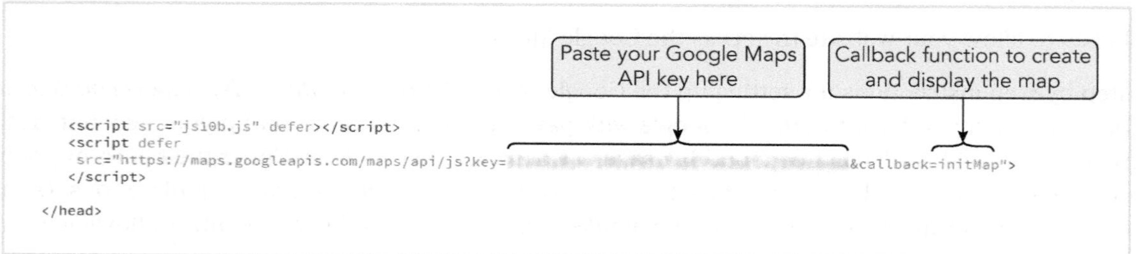

Figure 10-26 Linking to the Google Maps API

7. Review the contents of the rest of the document and then close the file, saving your changes.

Now that your page can access the Google Maps API, you will begin creating the `initMap()` callback function showing the location of the Oak Top House within the city of Columbus, Ohio. (This is a fictional convention center; the "location" is provided for instructional purposes only.)

The map Object

All Google maps are treated as objects with a large library of properties and methods. To create a `map` object, apply the following `new google.maps.Map()` object constructor:

```
let map = new google.maps.Map(element, mapOpt);
```

where *map* is the variable name given to the map, *element* references a page element in which the map is displayed, and *mapOpt* is an object literal of map options and properties.

There are dozens of options for defining the appearance and behavior of the map but only two are required: a zoom value to set the map's level of magnification and a center value to determine where the map is centered. The *mapOpt* object literal has the following structure:

```
mapOpt = {
   zoom: zoomValue,
   center: LatLng,
   other map properties
}
```

where *zoomValue* ranges from 0 (showing the entire globe) up to 20 (individual buildings), and *LatLng* sets the coordinates of the map center by latitude and longitude. Latitude and longitude values are specified as an object literal in the following format:

```
{lat: latitude, lng: longitude}
```

with *latitude* ranging from –90 to 90 and *longitude* ranging from –180 to 180. Latitude and longitude can also be set using following `LatLng()` method of the `maps` object:

```
new google.maps.LatLng(latitude, longitude)
```

Once a latitude and longitude value has been defined, it cannot be modified. To use different coordinates, you must define a new set of latitude and longitude values.

The following code demonstrates how to create a Google Map centered at Oak Top House (latitude 39.9118° latitude, longitude –82.99879°). The rendered map will be displayed without map controls for street view, map type, and full screen view.

```
let map = new google.maps.Map(elem, {
   zoom: 11,
   center: { lat: 39.96118, lng: -82.99879}
   streetViewControl: false,
   mapTypeControl: false,
   fullscreenControl: false
});
```

Add code to the js10b.js file to create a map for the Oak Top House and then view the rendered map in your web browser.

To create a Google map:

1. Return to the **js10b.js** file in your code editor.
2. Add the following statement to the `initMap()` function to store the global coordinates of the Oak Top House convention center:

```
// Create a map to the Oak Top House
let oakTopHouse = {lat: 39.96118, lng: -82.99879};
```

3. Add the following command to create a map centered at Oak Top House with a zoom level of 11 and the full screen control turned off:

```
let myMap = new google.maps.Map(displayMap, {
   zoom: 11,
   center: oakTopHouse,
   fullscreenControl: false,
});
```

The map will be displayed within the `displayMap` element, which has been previously defined for you. **Figure 10-27** describes the newly added code.

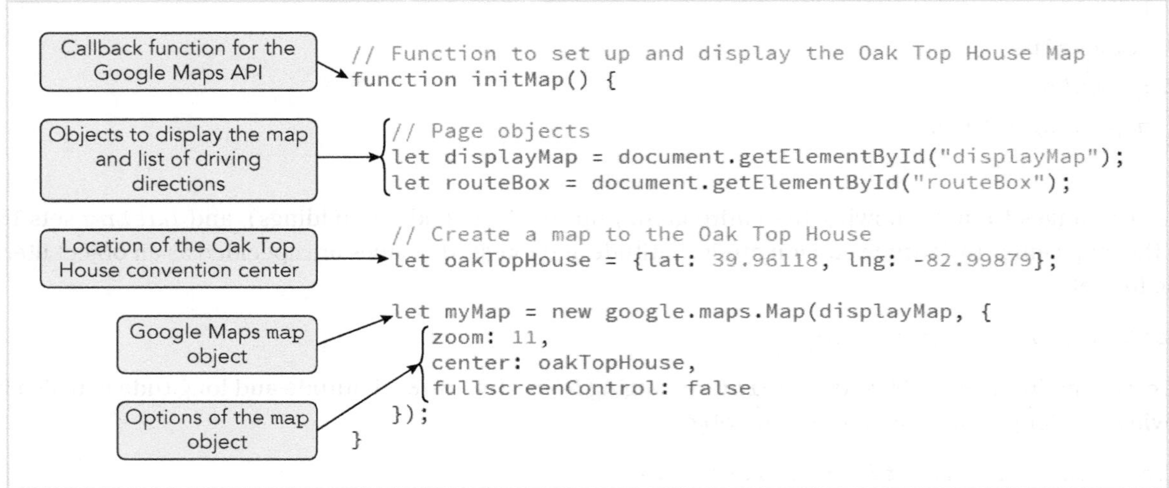

Figure 10-27 Creating a `map` object

4. Save your changes to the file and then open **js10b.html** in your web browser. As shown in **Figure 10-28**, the page displays a map centered on downtown Columbus, Ohio—the fictional home of the Oak Top House.

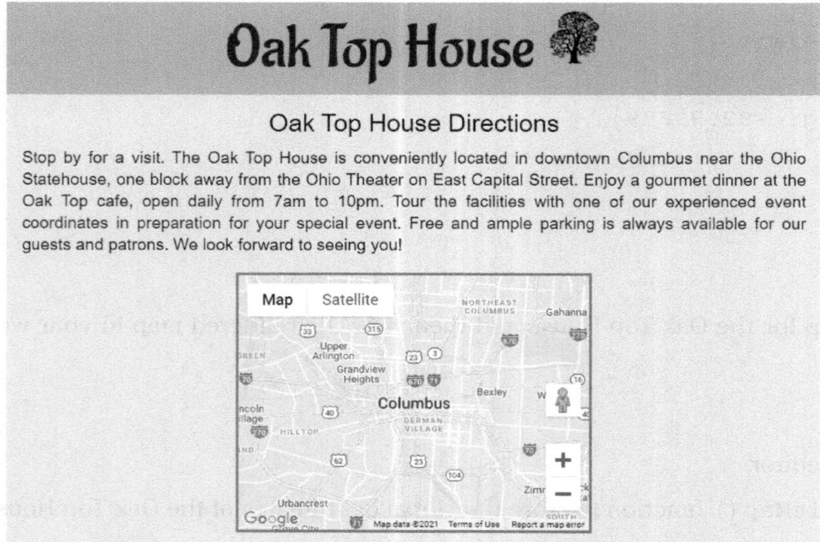

Figure 10-28 Google map of the Oak Top House location

If your web page did not render the map shown in **Figure 10-28**, first check the debugger to verify that you do not have any syntax errors in the code. If the map still fails to load, verify that you have a valid Google Maps API key and that your network is not blocking any connections from Google Cloud.

Adding Map Pins

Map objects provide detail information on streets, cities, countries, and terrain, but you will often need to add content specific to your application. A map pin or marker can be used to highlight a specific location on the map such as a home or business. Map markers are created with the following object constructor:

```
marker = new google.maps.Marker(markerOpt)
```

where *markerOpt* is an object literal containing marker properties. Among the properties supported by *markerOpt* are the following:

```
markerOpt = {
   position: LatLng,
   map: map,
   title: "title"
   icon: image,
   label: text
}
```

where *LatLng* is a latitude and longitude object, *map* is a map object, *title* is the text that appears as a tooltip when users hover over the marker pin, *image* is an image file to be used to represent the marker pin, and *text* is text that appears as a label within the marker pin. If you do not specify an icon or label, Google Maps will apply its own defaults in rendering the marker pin. It is a good idea in a map with multiple pins to supply a different label for each pin. Labels should not be more than one character to fit within the pin image.

> **Note** | Markers can also be added to maps using the command `marker.setMap(map)` where *marker* is a marker object and *map* is a map object. To remove a marker from its map, run `marker.setMap(null)`.

Add a pin to the Oak Top House map to identify the location of the conference center. You will reference the coordinates using the latitude and longitude values previously stored in the `oakTopHouse` variable and use the default pin markers supplied by Google Maps.

To add a marker to a map:

1. Return to the **js10b.js** file in your code editor.
2. Add the following commands to the `initMap()` function to create a marker for the Oak Top House location:

```
// Add a marker for the Oak Top House
new google.maps.Marker({
   position: oakTopHouse,
   map: myMap,
   title: "Oak Top House"
});
```

   Figure 10-29 displays the added code to generate the marker.

```
      let myMap = new google.maps.Map(displayMap, {
         zoom: 11,
         center: oakTopHouse,
         fullscreenControl: false
      });

      // Add a marker for the Oak Top House
      new google.maps.Marker({
         position: oakTopHouse,
         map: myMap,
         title: "Oak Top House"
      });
   }
```

Marker position

Map in which to place the marker

Tooltip title

Figure 10-29 **Adding a marker to a map**

3. Save your changes to the file and then open **js10b.html** in your web browser. The map will reopen with a marker placed at the center of Columbus, Ohio. Hover your pointer over the pin to display the tooltip. See **Figure 10-30**.

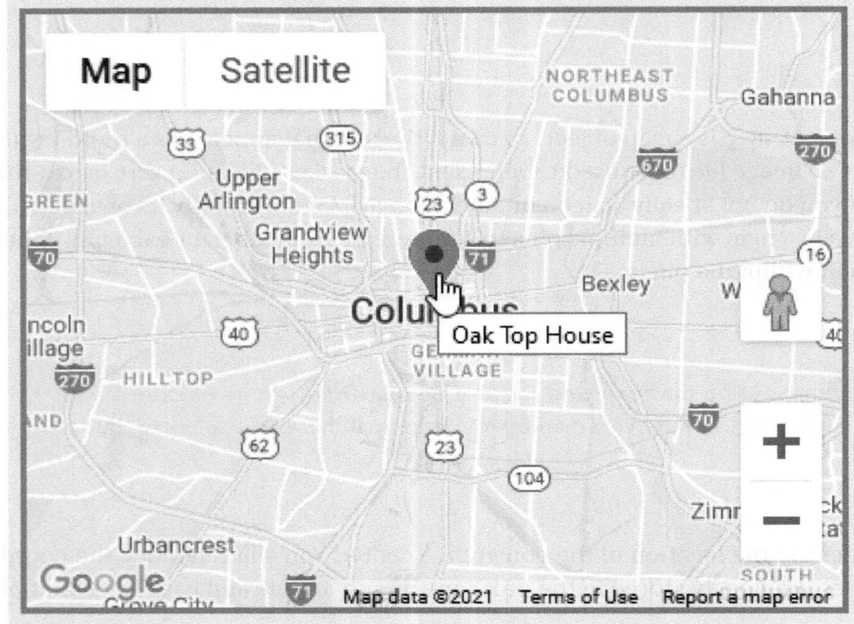

Figure 10-30 **Marker with tooltip**

Another feature that can be added to a map are directions connecting two or more locations. You can use geolocation to give Oak Top House customers driving directions to the conference center from their current position.

Mapping Your Position with Geolocation

Geolocation is the process that determines the position of the client device using either a built-in GPS receiver or information drawn from the client's network IP address. Not every client device supports geolocation, so you must verify that the device's position can be determined and provide workarounds if it cannot.

The Geolocation API provides information on the global position of the client device, using the `getCurrentPosition()` method of the `navigator.geolocation` object:

```
navigator.geolocation.getCurrentPosition(success, fail, opt)
```

where *success* is a callback function run if the browser successfully retrieves the device's global position, *fail* is an optional callback function handling geolocation failures, and *opt* are optional geolocation parameters. Only the callback function for a successful geolocation is required and has the following structure:

```
function success(position) {
  Commands involving the position object
}
```

The *position* parameter provides the **position object** containing data on the device's position. **Figure 10-31** lists some of the properties associated with the `position` object. Note that some properties require a GPS sensor.

PROPERTY	DESCRIPTION
pos.coords.latitude	Returns the latitude of the client device
pos.coords.longitude	Returns the client device's longitude
pos.coords.altitude	Returns the altitude in meters (GPS required)
pos.coords.heading	Returns the device's heading in degrees, where 0° indicates a heading due North, 90° is East, 180° is South, and 270° is West (GPS required)
pos.coords.speed	Returns the device's speed in meters per second (GPS required)

Figure 10-31 Properties of the `Position` object

Sometimes the `getCurrentPosition()` function is not successful, which can occur if geolocation is not supported by the client or the device fails to make a connection to a GPS server. To cover those situations, call the following failure function so that the failure can be gracefully managed by your app:

```
function fail(error) {
    Commands involving the error object
}
```

The *error* object supports two properties: the `code` property containing the error number and the `message` property containing a description of the error. Possible error codes are:

1. PERMISSION_DENIED (the position was not determined because the page was not given permission)
2. POSITION_UNAVAILABLE (an internal source of error in the client prevented the acquisition of the device's position)
3. TIMEOUT (the position was not retrieved with the allotted time)

The following code calls the `getCurrentPosition()` function and, if successful, writes the device's current latitude and longitude to the debugger console, but if unsuccessful logs the reason:

```
navigator.geolocation.getCurrentPosition(getPos, handleError);
function getPos(pos) {
    console.log("Latitude = " + pos.coords.latitude);
    console.log("Longitude = " + pos.coords.longitude);
}
function handleError(err) {
    console.log("Unable to get location.");
    console.log("Error Code: " + err.code);
    console.log("Reason : " + err.message);
}
```

The optional *opt* parameter of the `getCurrentPosition()` method supports the following properties and values to set whether the current position should be retrieved with high accuracy (`true` or `false`), the amount of time in milliseconds before a timeout error is triggered, and the maximum age in milliseconds allowed to the device to use a cached position rather than querying for a current position.

```
{
    enableHighAccuracy: Boolean,
    timeout: value,
    maximumAge: value
}
```

Unless your app has special need for these options, you can use the default geolocation options.

Add code to retrieve your device's current position, saving the latitude and longitude in the `myPosition` object. In case of failure, display the error message in the debugger console.

To access the device's global position:

1. Return to the **js10b.js** file in your code editor.
2. Directly below the code to create the map marker, add the following command to get the device's current location:

```
// Get the device's current position
navigator.geolocation.getCurrentPosition(getPos, handleError);
```

3. Add the `getPos()` function to store your device's current location:

```
function getPos(pos) {
    let myPosition = {
        lat: pos.coords.latitude,
        lng: pos.coords.longitude
    }
    console.log(myPosition);
}
```

4. Add the `handleError()` function to handle errors from the Geolocation API:

```
// In case of geolocation error
function handleError(err) {
    console.log("Geolocation error: " + err.message);
}
```

Figure 10-32 describes the newly added code.

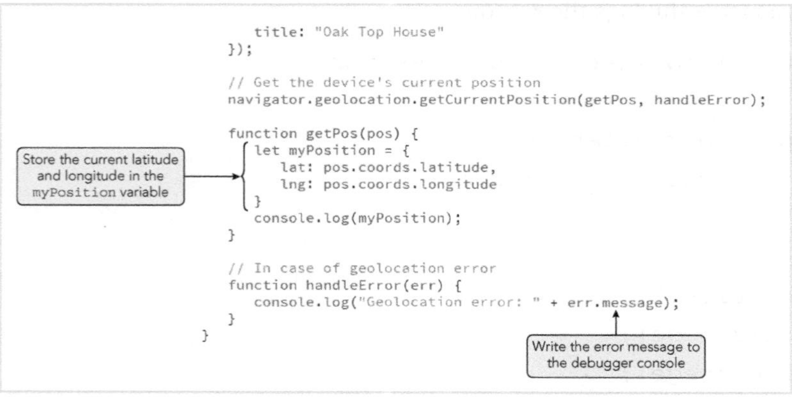

```
        title: "Oak Top House"
    });

    // Get the device's current position
    navigator.geolocation.getCurrentPosition(getPos, handleError);

    function getPos(pos) {
        let myPosition = {
            lat: pos.coords.latitude,
            lng: pos.coords.longitude
        }
        console.log(myPosition);
    }

    // In case of geolocation error
    function handleError(err) {
        console.log("Geolocation error: " + err.message);
    }
}
```

Store the current latitude and longitude in the `myPosition` variable

Write the error message to the debugger console

Figure 10-32 Getting the device's current position

5. Save your changes to the file and then reload **js10b.html** in your browser. When requested, click the **Allow** button to allow the page to know your location.
6. Open the debugger console and verify your device's latitude and longitude are displayed. See **Figure 10-33**.

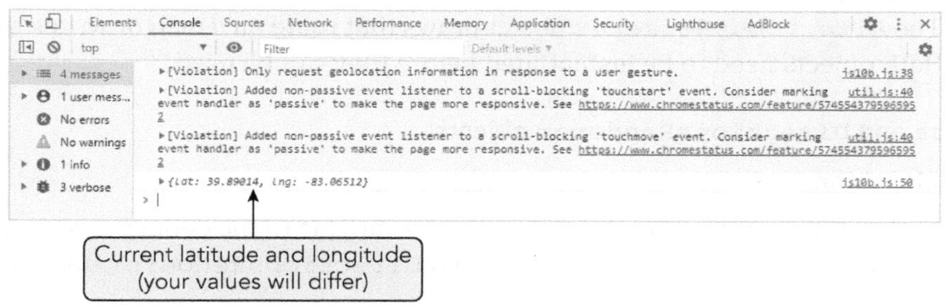

Figure 10-33 The device's current position

7. Close the browser debugger console.

> **Note** If the Geolocation API displays violation warnings like those in Figure 10-33, it is because the `getCurrentPosition()` function is best run in direct response to a user action such as clicking a form button, rather than run automatically when the page loads. However, the function will operate either way.

For devices in constant motion, the Geolocation API also supports the following `watchPosition()` method to continually update position data in response to movement:

```
id = navigator.geolocation.watchPosition(success, fail, opt)
```

where *`success`*, *`fail`*, and *`opt`* have the same meaning they have with the `getCurrentPosition()` function and *`id`* is a timer ID registering the repeated invocations of the function, as it is called every time the device changes location. To clear the function, apply the following method:

```
navigator.geolocation.clearWatch(id)
```

The `watchPosition()` function can be very resource-intensive, so only use it when you need to track a device in constant motion.

Common Mistakes

Handling Errors with Geolocation

Geolocation has come a long way since its early days. Almost every browser and device will be able to retrieve information about its current global location. If your app reports an error in determining its location, here are some possible fixes:

- Use a modern browser version. If you are using Internet Explorer, make sure it is Internet Explorer 9 or higher.
- Enable location services on your browser or mobile devices when requested.
- There may be access restrictions on a school or business network. Talk with a network administrator to determine if you need clearance.

If you are still having trouble, try loading the page with a different browser or network. Sometimes simply rebooting your computer will fix the problem.

Finally, do not overlook the possibility that you have made a mistake in your code. Use your debugger to locate any syntax, runtime, or logical errors that may be keeping your program from working.

Adding Directions to a Map

Once you have determined the device's location, you can augment the Oak Top House map with traveling directions from your location to the conference center. The Google Maps API provides two objects to manage directions. The `DirectionsService` object queries the Google Maps Directions Service to find the most efficient route between two locations for a given mode of travel. The `DirectionsRenderer` object draws that route on a map or writes the turn-by-turn directions to the web page. Both objects need to be instantiated before they can be used.

To instantiate the `DirectionsService` and `DirectionsRenderer` objects:

1. Return to the **js10b.js** file in your code editor.
2. Within the `getPos()` function below the statement to write the `myPosition` variable to the debugger console, add the following two statements to instantiate `DirectionsService` and `DirectionsRenderer` objects:

```
// Set up direction service and rendering
let routeFind = new google.maps.DirectionsService();
let routeDraw = new google.maps.DirectionsRenderer();
```

Figure 10-34 shows the new code in the file.

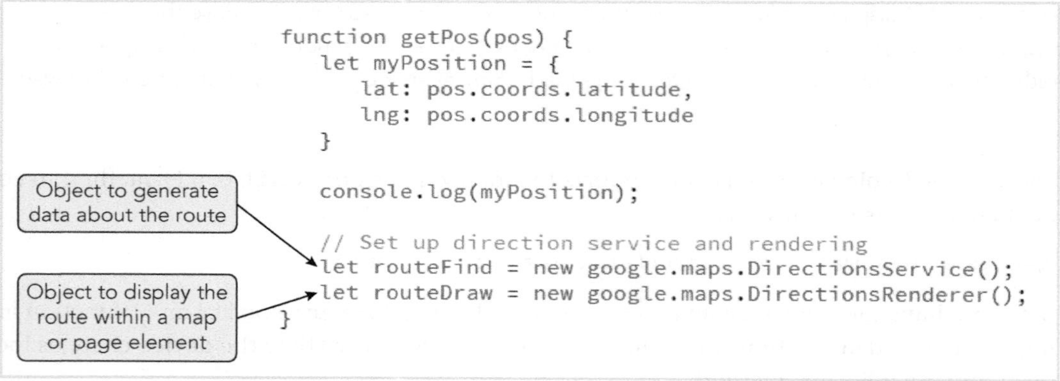

```
function getPos(pos) {
   let myPosition = {
      lat: pos.coords.latitude,
      lng: pos.coords.longitude
   }

   console.log(myPosition);

   // Set up direction service and rendering
   let routeFind = new google.maps.DirectionsService();
   let routeDraw = new google.maps.DirectionsRenderer();
}
```


Figure 10-34 The device's current position

The `routeFind` variable will be used to query the directions service and generate directions to the Oak Top House and the `routeDraw` variable will be used to display that route on the map.

The `route` Object

Routes submitted to the directions service are described in the following object:

```
route ={
   origin: location,
   destination: location,
   travelMode: type
}
```

where *`location`* is either a latitude and longitude object, or a named location such as street, city, state, or country; while `travelMode` describes the travel conveyance using one of the follow types:

- DRIVING For routes based on standard driving directions (the default)
- BICYCLING For cycling routes using bike paths and preferred streets
- TRANSIT For routes that use public transportation
- WALKING For walking routes using pedestrian paths and sidewalks

The following cycling route starts from a specified latitude and longitude and ends at the Mount Rushmore National Monument:

```
route = {
   origin: {lat: 43.932652, lng: -103.576607},
   destination: "Mount Rushmore, SD",
   travelMode: "BICYCLING"
}
```

A route can also include fields for departure or arrival time, driving preferences (such as avoiding toll roads), public transit type, or waypoints on the way to the destination. You can learn more about creating detailed route requests using the Google Maps documentation on the Google Console website.

For the Oak Top House website, you will define a driving route starting from your location and ending at the convention center.

To define a driving route:

1. Directly below the command declaring the `routeDraw` variable, add the following object specifying the route:

```
// Drive from current location to Oak Top House
let myRoute = {
   origin: myPosition,
   destination: oakTopHouse,
   travelMode: "DRIVING"
}
```

   See **Figure 10-35**.

```
      // Set up direction service and rendering
      let routeFind = new google.maps.DirectionsService();
      let routeDraw = new google.maps.DirectionsRenderer();

      // Drive from current location to Oak Top House
      let myRoute = {
         origin: myPosition,
         destination: oakTopHouse,
         travelMode: "DRIVING"
      }
   }
```

Figure 10-35 Route object from your location to the convention center

2. Save your changes to the file.

Having defined a route, you will next generate driving directions from your location to the Oak Top House.

Displaying the Driving Route

Directions between an origin and a destination are generated by calling the directions service using the following `route()` method:

```
directionsService.route(routeObj, callback);
```

where *`routeObj`* is the route object and *`callback`* is a callback function processing the results returned from the directions service.

The first parameter of the callback function stores the response from the service; the second parameter stores the final status of the request. A status value of "OK" indicates that the service successfully found driving directions for the route; any other status value indicates failure. With the two parameters, the callback function has the general form:

```
function callback(result, status) {
   if (status === "OK") {
      display the result
   } else {
      report an error
   }
}
```

If the status of the request is "OK", store the directions in a `DirectionsRenderer` object using the following `setDirections()` method:

```
directionsRenderer.setDirections(result)
```

otherwise, alert the user that directions could not generated. Add this code structure to your script.

To generate directions between the origin and the destination:

1. Directly below the command creating the `myRoute` object, add the following:

```
// Generate directions for the route
routeFind.route(myRoute, function(result, status) {
   if (status == "OK") {
      routeDraw.setDirections(result);
   } else {
      routeBox.textContent = "Directions Unavailable: " + status;
   }
});
```

   See **Figure 10-36**.

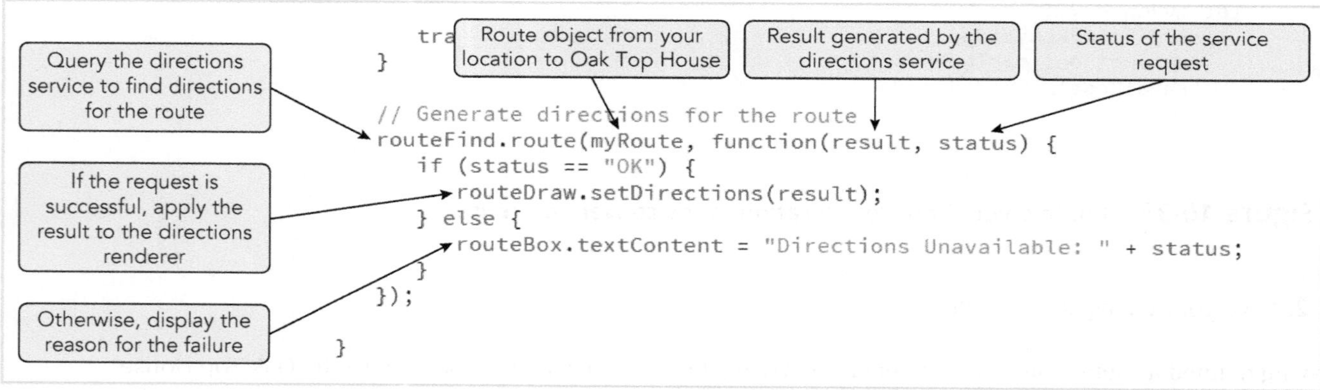

Figure 10-36 Generating directions for the route

2. Save your changes to the file and then reload the **js10b.html** file in your browser. Allow the browser to use your location and verify that no error message is generated the directions service.

This project assumes a driving path exists between your current location and the convention center in Columbus, Ohio. If the browser displays an alert box with the message "ZERO_RESULTS", it indicates that no such driving path exists (which might be the case if you are not located within North America). Revise the code to provide a different destination that would be drivable for you.

Programming Concepts | Synchronous and Asynchronous Callbacks

The `route()` method uses a callback function to retrieve direction information. A callback is any executable code that is called to complete a task or return a value, such as generating a driving direction for a given route and mode of travel.

A synchronous callback is a callback that accomplishes its task before returning control to the caller. If the task is a long one or if there is some difficulty in completing the task, the script stalls, waiting for the response. The compare functions used with the `sort()` method are an example of a synchronous callback because sorting cannot proceed until the results of the callback are returned.

An asynchronous callback releases the program execution as it works on its task so that the callback and the rest of the code are working in parallel. The problem with an asynchronous callback is that there is no guarantee that tasks in the callback will be finished before the rest of the code needs the result. Thus, the code must ensure that a result has been provided before working on outcome. That is why the `route()` method included a *`status`* parameter to ensure that the callback function had completed its task (either successfully or unsuccessfully). Asynchronous callbacks are often used with calls to external resource such as third-party APIs and scripts running on a web server.

When directions have been successfully retrieved from the directions service, the route is placed on the map using the following `setMap()` method of the `directionsRenderer` object:

```
directionsRenderer.setMap(map)
```

Turn-by-turn directions are displayed within a web page element using the following `setPanel()` method:

```
directionsRenderer.setPanel(elem)
```

Add both methods to your code, completing the page that shows both the route to the Oak Top House and the turn-by-turn directions.

To show the route to the Oak Top House:

1. Return to the **js10b.js** file in your code editor.
2. Directly below the command applying the `setDirections()` method, add the following two statements to draw the route and show the direction list:

```
// Display route and directions
routeDraw.setMap(myMap);
routeDraw.setPanel(routeBox);
```

Figure 10-37 shows the completed code.

```
// Generate directions for the route
routeFind.route(myRoute, function(result, status) {
   if (status == "OK") {
      routeDraw.setDirections(result);
      // Display route and directions
      routeDraw.setMap(myMap);
      routeDraw.setPanel(routeBox);
   } else {
      routeBox.textContent = "Directions Unavailable: " + status;
   }
});
```

Draw the route on the map using a polyline
Display the turn-by-turn directions in the routeBox element

Figure 10-37 Displaying the travel route

3. Close the file, saving your changes, and then reload **js10b.html** in your browser. Verify that the page now shows the route and the driving directions between your location and the Oak Top House. See **Figure 10-38**.

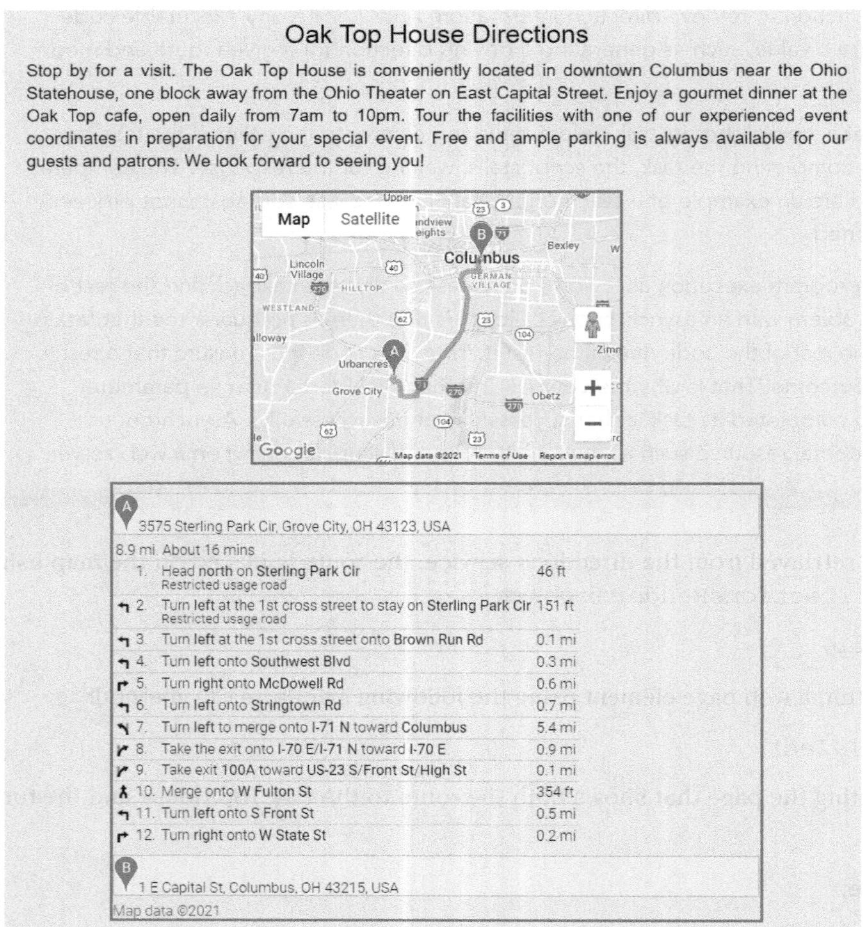

Figure 10-38 Route and directions to the Oak Top House

You have completed your work on the Oak Top House Directions map. The Google Maps API is a broad and powerful set of tools for creating interactive maps, and you have only scratched the surface of what it can do. For example, you can develop maps that respond to pointer events with content that can be modified by the user in real time. The API is extensively documented at the Google Console website.

Introducing the Device Orientation API

For some apps you will need information about the movements of the client device, but not on a global scale. The Device Orientation API provides access to data from specialized hardware in many mobile devices for detecting changes in position and speed. A device's gyroscope detects its orientation in space, and its accelerometer detects changes in speed. The Device Orientation API lets your apps react to changes in the data provided by this hardware through the `deviceorientation` and `devicemotion` events.

The `deviceorientation` event reports a set of coordinates with the property names `alpha`, `beta`, and `gamma`. Each property corresponds to one of the three dimensions, analogous to the *x*, *y*, and *z* axes used in geometry. By comparing changes in orientation mathematically, your code can respond to user actions including tilting a device. For example, you could use the `deviceorientation` event to create a game that simulates a marble on a flat board, with the user tilting the device back and forth and side to side to get the marble into a center hole without falling off one of the edges. Based on changes in the orientation of the device, your app would run code changing the direction of the marble's movement.

The `devicemotion` event reports values for acceleration and rotation. You could use this event in an app that provides the user with continuous information on their direction and speed, determining if the user is moving or standing still.

Preparing an App for Mobile Use

When you create an app with mobile users in mind, it is important to account for some of the limitations of handheld devices. In this section, you will explore a few development practices that can make your apps work better and more reliably for mobile users.

Testing Tools

Mobile devices run different browsers than desktop computers. Even though Chrome, Firefox, Safari, and Internet Explorer all make mobile versions available for different mobile operating systems, the mobile versions are distinct from the desktop versions, and may have different capabilities, limitations, and even bugs. For all these reasons, it is important to test your apps on the mobile platforms that you expect your users to be running.

The quickest and easiest way to test your code is to use the device emulation features built into your web browser; however, emulation does not always capture all the subtleties of the actual device. A professional web development department or studio often maintains a large collection of mobile devices for testing mobile apps on various operating systems and with different screen sizes and resolutions. Because most developers do not have the resources to maintain a collection of mobile devices, other options exist. Several services are available online that enable developers to interact with virtual versions of many mobile devices. You can locate some of these services by searching on "mobile device testing service." In addition, the makers of mobile operating systems and browsers all provide free programs that simulate interactions with their devices or software.

Minimizing Download Size

The amount of data required by a mobile app and how it is handled is an important consideration for developers. Although mobile devices can connect to the Internet via a fast local network, many mobile users access the web through the wireless provider's mobile network. While mobile speeds are increasing on a regular basis, speed limitations and the cost of bandwidth can impair performance. Therefore, to ensure that users can effectively make use of your app, you should design the app to download as little data as possible.

Web developers have come up with several strategies for minimizing download size, including loading scripts responsively and minifying files. For small web apps, it is common to include all JavaScript code in a single external JavaScript file. However, as your web apps become more complex, they will include code that is not needed unless a user chooses a specific option. In those cases, you can reduce the amount of code that needs to be downloaded by dividing up the JavaScript code into multiple files and downloading each file only when requested.

Minifying Files

You have learned that adding indents and line breaks makes it easier for you and others to interpret your code. A JavaScript processor does not care about that. The code will run the same way with or without those features. In a large web app that will be used by mobile devices, it is important for developers to remove every unneeded character, reducing the download size as much as possible. One commonly used method is minifying files, by removing comments, indents, and line breaks, and tweaking the code in other ways to make the file size smaller.

Figure 10-39 shows an example of a JavaScript program before and after minifying.

Figure 10-39 Minifying a JavaScript file

Before minifying, the file contained 1,769 characters. After removing all line breaks, indents, and comments the minified version contained 708 characters—a 60 percent reduction! There are several free minifying programs on the web for reducing the file size of your HTML, CSS, and JavaScript programs. Many code editors also include minifying tools.

Minifying is the last thing you should do with your code prior to publishing, and only after you have ensured all errors have been found and fixed and the code has been vetted by colleagues and customers. Always keep a non-minified version of the file available for future revisions. Remember that once you minify a file, all comments, line returns, and indents will be forever lost if you have not saved the original.

Skills at Work | Making your App Transparent

Apps that use geolocation require the user's permission before acquiring geolocation data. This part of the specification is implemented by browsers, so no additional steps are required by app developers to carry it out. However, it serves as a useful model of data transparency, which is the process of making it clear to users what information your app wants to collect from them and how you intend to use it. The more transparent you are with your data requests and use, the more trust you build with the users of your apps. Data transparency also helps your colleagues as your app will clearly document: (a) What it is doing, (b) why it is doing it, and (c) what is required of the end user. It will help everyone if you are clear and complete in all your coding.

Quick Check 3

1. Provide code for a map options object named `mapOpt` that is centered at 43.992722° latitude and -102.241509° longitude with a zoom level of 15.
2. Provide code to create a new marker named `cityMarker` using options defined in the object literal, `cityOptions`.
3. What does it mean if the Geolocation API returns an error code of 3?
4. What is the difference between the `DirectionsService` object and the `DirectionsRenderer` object?
5. Why would you minify a file?

Summary

- Events are objects with their own collections of properties and methods.
- Events propagate through the object hierarchy either by bubbling up the object hierarchy or by capturing down the object hierarchy.
- Pointer events can be used to respond to mouse and touch events as well as events associated with other pointer devices.
- To create a drag and drop action using pointer events, capture the object during a `pointerdown` event, move the object during the `pointermove` event, and release the object during the `pointerup` event.
- You can determine the pointer's location within the browser window using the `e.clientX` and `e.clientY` event properties.
- The Drag and Drop API simplifies the drag and drop process by making object draggable using tools built into the browser.
- `DataTransfer` objects are used with the Drag and Drop API to transfer data from dragged elements into the drop zone.
- Keyboard actions can be captured using the `keydown`, `keypress`, and `keyup` events. The `keydown` and `keyup` events capture the physical act of typing on a keyboard; the `keypress` event captures the act of generating a character.
- The Google Maps API can be used to create interactive maps embedded into a web page. To use the API, you need to set up a billable account with Google and establish an API key for the app.
- Google maps are generated by centering the map at a specified latitude and longitude and setting the zoom level for the map view.
- Pin markers can be placed on a map using the `new google.maps.Marker()` method with each pin being given a position and title.
- To add a route between two points on the map, create a `DirectionsService` object to determine the directions between the points and a `DirectionsRenderer` object to display the route on the map or within a box containing turn-by-turn directions.
- You can make an app more suitable for mobile devices by reducing the number of script files that must be loaded and by minifying the script file contents to remove extraneous content.

Key Terms

accelerometer
API key
asynchronous callback
bubbling phase
callback
capture phase
`dataTransfer` object
data transparency
Device Orientation API
`DirectionsRenderer` object
`DirectionsService` object
Drag and Drop API (DnD API)
drop zone
Geolocation API
geolocation
Google Maps API
gyroscope
minifying
modifier keys
pointer event
`position` object
synchronous callback
target phase
touch cascade
Touch interface
TouchEvent interface
TouchList interface
touchpoint

Review Questions

1. The object that initiated an event is referenced using which of the following?
   a. `e.currentTarget`
   b. `e.origin`
   c. `e`
   d. `e.target`
2. The part of event propagation in which events from the event target up the browser window is ______________.
   a. the target phase
   b. the bubbling phase
   c. the capture phase
   d. the event phase
3. What is the order of events triggered during a mouse click action?
   a. just `click`
   b. `mousedown`, `mouseup`, and then `click`
   c. `mousedown`, `click`, and then `mouseup`
   d. `mousedown` and then `mouseup`
4. Touch events begin with which event?
   a. `touchstart`
   b. `touch`
   c. `touchdown`
   d. `tap`
5. An array of touchpoints that have changed during an event is referenced with which object?
   a. `touches`
   b. `newtouches`
   c. `changedTouches`
   d. `touchList`
6. Which of the following events is interpreted as being equivalent to the `pointerup` event?
   a. `touchstart`
   b. `touchend`
   c. `touchmove`
   d. `touchoff`
7. The horizontal distance between a pointer event and the containing element is given with which property?
   a. `e.clientX`
   b. `e.offsetX`
   c. `e.screenX`
   d. `e.pageX`
8. To make an element draggable, what attribute should be added to the element tag?
   a. `dragstart = "true"`
   b. `drag = "true"`
   c. `drag = "on"`
   d. `draggable = "true"`
9. Which statement will store data during the `dragstart` event?
   a. `e.drag.setData()`
   b. `e.dragstart.setData()`
   c. `e.setData()`
   d. `e.dataTransfer.setData()`
10. Which of the following events will return the character generated by a keyboard action?
    a. `keydown`
    b. `keypress`
    c. `keyup`
    d. `key`
11. Which of the following object constructors creates a Google Maps object?
    a. `new google.maps.Map()`
    b. `new maps()`
    c. `new maps.Map()`
    d. `new google.Map()`
12. Which of the following objects defines a global position at 45° latitude and -80° longitude?
    a. `{lat: 45; long: -80}`
    b. `{lat = 45, long = -80}`
    c. `{lat: 45, lng: -80}`
    d. `{lat: 45; lng: -80}`
13. Which statement returns the device's global position?
    a. `navigator.position()`
    b. `navigator.getCurrentPosition()`
    c. `navigator.geolocation.getCurrentPosition()`
    d. `navigator.gelocation.getPosition()`
14. You wish to use Google Maps to show a public bus route between two locations. What value should you enter for the route's travelMode field?
    a. BUS
    b. TRANSIT
    c. DRIVE
    d. PUBLIC
15. What method is used to apply a set of directions to a *directionsRenderer* object?
    a. *directionsRenderer*`.setMap()`
    b. *directionsRenderer*`.setPanel()`
    c. *directionsRenderer*`.setDirection()`
    d. *directionsRenderer*`.route()`
16. How do event listeners and event handlers manage event propagation?

17. What is a touch cascade?

18. How does the Drag and Drop API differ from drag and drop effects created using pointer events?

19. What do you need to set up before you can use the Google Maps API in your web app?

20. What does minifying do to a code file?

Hands-On Projects

Hands-On Project 10-1

In this project you will use pointer events to add drag and drop functionality to a jigsaw puzzle page. The page already contains code that generates and randomizes the placement of 48 jigsaw pieces. Your task will be to complete the page by writing code to enable users to drag and drop individual pieces. The code in this page closely resembles the code used to add drag and drop capability to the Oak Top House room layout page. A preview of the puzzle page is shown in **Figure 10-40**.

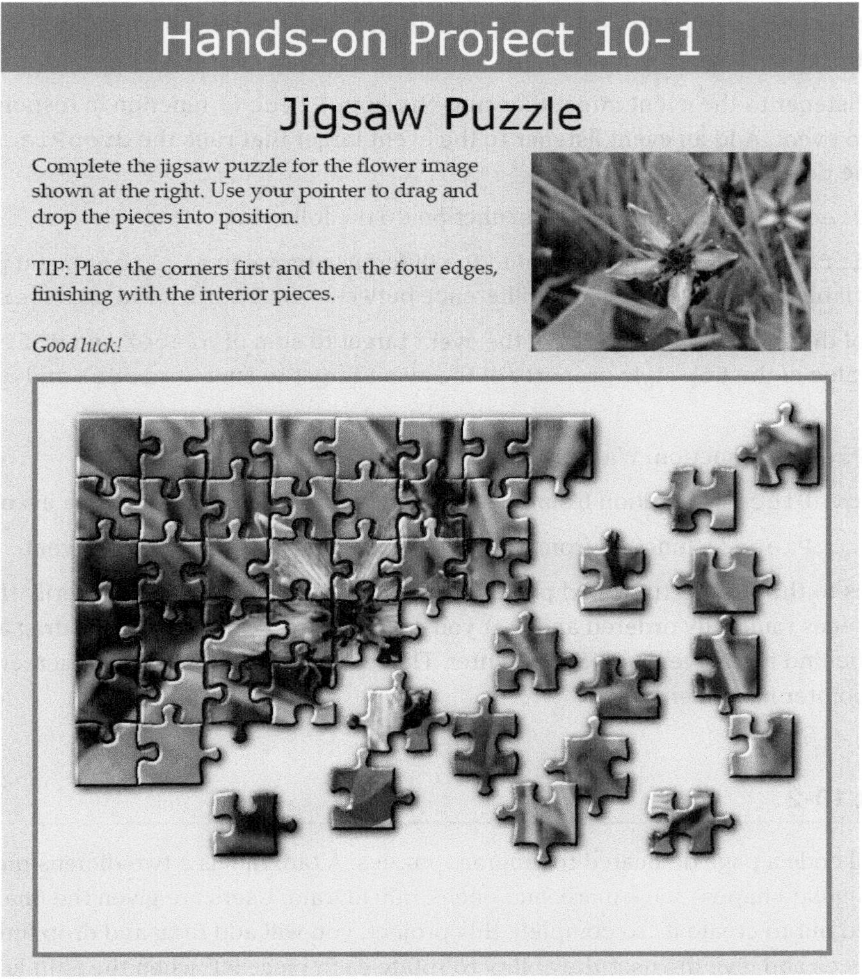

Figure 10-40 Completed Project 10-1

Do the following:

1. Use your code editor to open the **project10-01_txt.html** and **project10-01_txt.js** files from the js10 ▶ project01 folder. Enter your name and the date in the comment section of each file and save them as **project10-01.html** and **project10-01.js**, respectively.
2. Go to the **project10-01.html** file in your code editor. Add a `script` element linked to the project10-01js file. Defer the loading of the script until after the page is loaded. Close the file, saving your changes.
3. Go to the **project10-01.js** file in your code editor. At the bottom of the file create a `for` loop that iterates through every item in the `pieces` node list. For each item, add an event listener that runs the `grabPiece()` function in response to the `pointerdown` event.
4. Create the `grabPiece()` function. Within the function do the following:
   a. Set the value of the `pointerX` and `pointerY` variables to the values of the `clientX` and `clientY` properties of the event object.
   b. Set the value of the `touchAction` style for the event target to "none".
   c. Increase the value of the `zCounter` variable by 1 and apply that value to the `zIndex` style of the event target.
   d. Set the value of the `pieceX` and `pieceY` variables to the values of the `offsetLeft` and `offsetTop` properties of the event target.
   e. Add an event listener to the event target that runs the `movePiece()` function in response to the `pointermove` event. Add an event listener to the event target that runs the `dropPiece()` function in response to the `pointerup` method.
5. Create the `movePiece()` function. Within the function do the following:
   a. Declare the `diffX` variable, setting it equal to the difference between `e.clientX` and `pointerX`. Declare the `diffY` variable setting it equal to the difference between `e.clientY` and `pointerY`.
   b. Set the value of the `left` style property of the event target to sum of `pieceX` and `diffX` plus the text string "px". Set the value of the `top` style property of the event target to sum of `pieceY` and `diffY` plus the text string "px".
6. Create the `dropPiece()` function. Within the function do the following:
   a. Remove the `movePiece()` function from the event listener for the `pointermove` event.
   b. Remove the `dropPiece()` function from the event listener for the `pointerup` event.
7. Save your changes to the file and then load **project10-01.html** in your web browser. Verify that the page loads with the puzzle pieces randomly ordered and that you can move pieces around using drag and drop. The puzzle pieces might lag behind the movement of the pointer. This is an effect of the browser screen's refresh not keeping up with pointer movements.

Hands-On Project 10-2

In this project you will code a page dedicated to tangram puzzles. A tangram is a two-dimensional shape that is created by five triangular shapes, one square, and one parallelogram. Users are given the final shape but not how the pieces are laid out to create it. To complete this project, you will add drag and drop functionality to the seven tangram pieces and give the user the ability to rotate each piece 90° when the Shift key is held down as the shape is clicked. A preview of the page is shown in **Figure 10-41**.

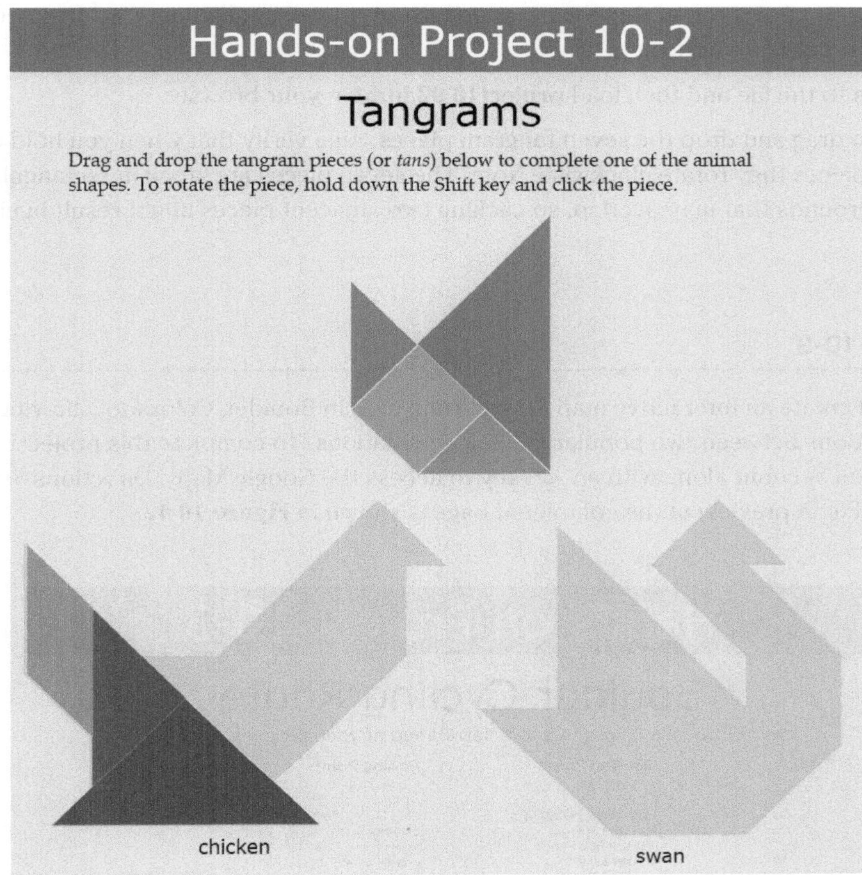

Figure 10-41 Completed Project 10-2

Do the following:

1. Use your code editor to open the **project10-02_txt.html** and **project10-02_txt.js** files from the js10 ► project02 folder. Enter your name and the date in the comment section of each file and save them as **project10-02.html** and **project10-02.js**, respectively.
2. Go to the **project10-02.html** file in your code editor. Add a `script` element linked to the project10-02js file. Defer the loading of the script until after the page is loaded. Close the file, saving your changes.
3. Go to the **project10-02.js** file in your code editor. Below the `rotateTan()` function add a `for` loop that iterates through all the pieces in the tans node list. For each piece add an event listener that runs the `grabTan()` function in response to the `pointerdown` event.
4. Create the `grabTan()` function. Within the function do the following:
    a. If the Shift key has been pressed down, call the `rotateTan()` function using the event target and a value of 15 as the parameter values.
    b. Otherwise, store the `e.clientX` and `e.clientY` values in the `eventX` and `eventY` variables. Set the `touch-action` style to "none". Increase the `zCounter` variable by 1 and apply it to the `zIndex` style of the event target.
    c. Add an event listener to run the `moveTan()` function in response to the `pointermove` event. Add an event listener to run the `dropTan()` function in response to the `pointerup` event.
5. Create the `moveTan()` function. Within the function calculate the distance horizontally and vertically that the pointer has moved from its initial position and move the event target the that same amount.

6. Create the `dropTan()` function. Within the function remove that event listeners you created for the `pointermove` and `pointerup` events.
7. Save your changes to the file and then load **project10-02.html** in your browser.
8. Verify that you can drag and drop the seven tangram pieces. Also verify that when you hold down the Shift key and click the pieces they rotate clockwise. Note: The seven pieces are stock in rectangular images with transparent backgrounds that may overlap, so clicking two adjacent pieces might result in either piece being selected.

Hands-On Project 10-3

In this project you will create an interactive map for a cycling club in Boulder, Colorado, allowing cyclists to view a map with directions between two popular cycling destinations. To complete this project, you will need to set up a Google Cloud account along with an API key to access the Google Maps, Directions Service, and Directions Renderer APIs. A preview of the completed page is shown in **Figure 10-42**.

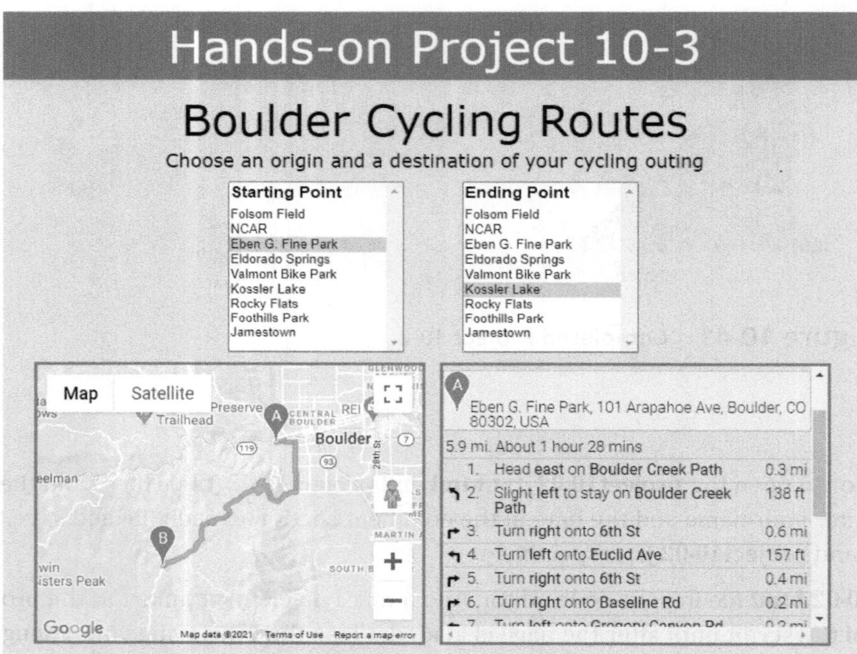

Figure 10-42 Completed Project 10-3

Do the following:

1. Use your code editor to open the **project10-03_txt.html** and **project10-03_txt.js** files from the js10 ▶ project03 folder. Enter your name and the date in the comment section of each file and save them as **project10-03.html** and **project10-03.js**, respectively.
2. Go to the **project10-03.html** file in your code editor. Add a `script` element linked to the project10-03js file. Defer the loading of the script until after the page is loaded.
3. Add another script element with the following `src` attribute: **`https://maps.googleapis.com/maps/api/js?key=`*`key`*`&callback=showMap`** where *`key`* is your Google Maps API key. Also defer this script until after the page is loaded.

4. Close the file, saving your changes and then go to the **project10-03.js** file in your code editor. Steps 5 through 10 should all be down within the `showMap()` function. Several variables have already been declared for you.
5. Use the `new google.maps.DirectionsService()` object constructor to create a `DirectionsService` object named **`bikeFind`**.
6. Use the `new google.maps.DirectionsRenderer()` object constructor to create a `DirectionsRenderer` object named **`bikeDraw`**.
7. Create a *`LatLng`* object named **`Boulder`** storing within it a latitude of 40.01753° and a longitude of -105.26496°.
8. Use the `new google.maps.Map()` object constructor to instantiate a new Google map named **`myMap`**. Set the zoom level to 12 and center the map on Boulder.
9. Create event listeners for the `startingPoint` and `endingPoint` selection lists, running the `drawRoute()` function in response to the `change` event.
10. Create the `drawRoute()` function. Within the function insert an `if` statement that tests whether the selected index for the `startingPoint` and `endingPoint` selection lists are both not equal to 0. If true, then do the following:
    - **a.** Define a route object named **`bikeRoute`** with an origin at `startingPoint.value` and a destination at `endingPoint.value`. Set the travelMode option to BICYCLING.
    - **b.** Apply the `route()` method to the `bikeFind` object generating directions between the starting and ending points. If the status of the request is "OK" then (i) apply the `setDirections()` method to `bikeDraw` object request directions from the directions service, (ii) apply the `setMap()` method to `bikeDraw` to display the route within `myMap`, and (iii) apply the `setPanel()` method to `bikeDraw` to display the turn-by-turn directions within the `bikeDirections` object.

      If the status is not "OK" then change the text content of the `bikeDirections` object to "Directions Unavailable: *status*".
11. Save your changes to the file and then load **project10-03.html** in your browser. Verify that a map of Boulder, Colorado appears in the left box. Verify that when you select starting and ending points from the two list boxes, a route is drawn on the map and turn-by-turn directions are provided between the two points.

Hands-On Project 10-4

In this project you will explore how to use the Drag and Drop API to move chess pieces onto and around a chess board. Refer to Figure 10-22 for help in coding this project.

Dropping a piece onto a square moves the element from its current location (either in the chess board or on the board), appending it as a child element of the square. In some cases, the square may already be occupied by another piece. If that is case, that occupying piece will be removed and returned to its box. To determine whether another piece is already in the drop zone, you will use the *`node`*`.tagName` property, which returns the tag name of an element node in uppercase letters. A preview of the completed page is shown in **Figure 10-43**.

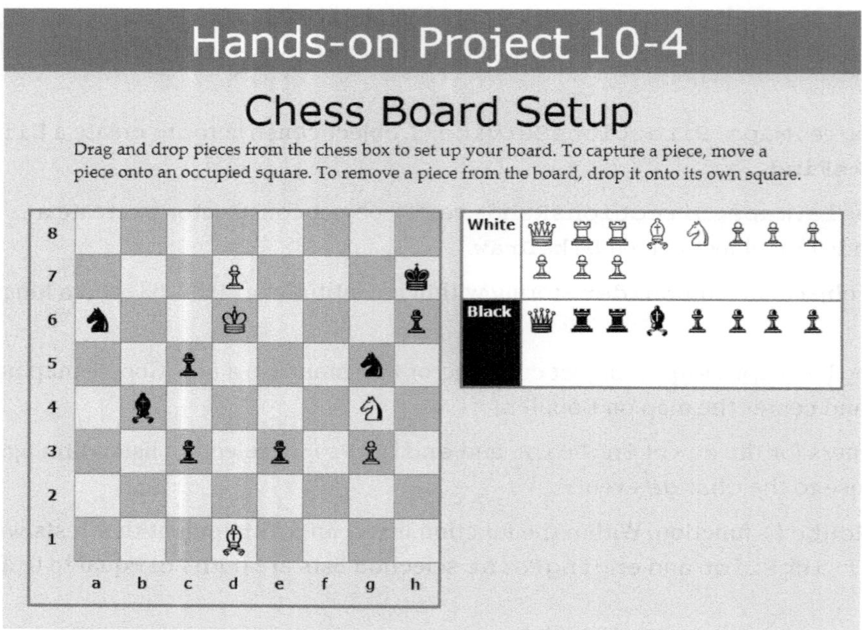

Figure 10-43 Completed Project 10-4

Do the following:

1. Use your code editor to open the **project10-04_txt.html** and **project10-04_txt.js** files from the js10 ▶ project04 folder. Enter your name and the date in the comment section of each file and save them as **project10-04.html** and **project10-04.js**, respectively.
2. Go to the **project10-04.html** file in your code editor. Add a `script` element linked to the project10-04js file. Defer the loading of the script until after the page is loaded. Take some time to study the contents of the file. Note that every chess piece is marked with a span element and given a unique id. White pieces belong to the white class, while black pieces belong to the black class. After you have become familiar with the content and structure of the document, close the file saving your changes.
3. Go to the **project10-04.js** file in your code editor. Create a `for` loop that iterates through all the contents of the pieces collection. For each piece do the following:
   a. Set the value of the piece's `draggable` property to "true".
   b. Create an event handler for the `dragstart` event that sets the text of event target's id in the `dataTransfer` object.
4. Create a `for` loop that iterates through all the items in the `boardSquares` node list. Add the tasks described in Steps 5 through 11 to this `for` loop.
5. For each item create an event handler for the `dragover` event. In the anonymous function associated with the event, add a command that prevents the default actions associated with the `dragover` event.
6. For each item create an event handler for the `drop` event that runs an anonymous function. Add the tasks described in Steps 7 through 11 to the function.
7. Insert a command to prevent the default action associated with the `drop` event.
8. Declare the **`pieceID`** variable that gets the id value from the `dataTransfer` object.
9. Declare the **`movingPiece`** variable that references the document element with that id.
10. If the tag name of the event target equals "TD" (indicating that you are dropping the piece onto an empty square), append `movingPiece` as a child of the event target.

11. Otherwise, if the tag name equals “SPAN” (indicating the you are dropping the piece onto another piece), do the following:
    a. Store the event target in a variable named **`occupyingPiece`**.
    b. Store the parent element of `occupyingPiece` in a variable named **`square`**.
    c. Use the `appendChild()` method to append `movingPiece` as a child of `square`.
    d. Move the occupying piece back to the chess box. If the class name of `occupyingPiece` equals “white” then use the `appendChild()` method to append `occupyingPiece` to the `whiteBox` object; otherwise append `occupyingPiece` to the `blackBox` object.
12. Save your changes to the file and then load **project10-04.html** in your web browser. Verify that you can move pieces from the chess box onto the board. Also verify that moving a piece onto a square that is occupied by another piece, moves the occupying piece back to its box.

Hands-On Project 10-5

Debugging Challenge

You have been given a web app for a crossword puzzle game. The page is designed to accept pointer and keyboard input. From the keyboard, players can type their answers, move to a different space using the Arrow, Tab, and Enter keys or delete letters using the Delete and Backspace keys. Finally, they can toggle the typing direction between across and down by pressing the Spacebar key. While the pointer actions are working correctly, the keyboard actions are not. You have been asked to debug the code for keyboard actions. A preview of the page is shown in **Figure 10-44**.

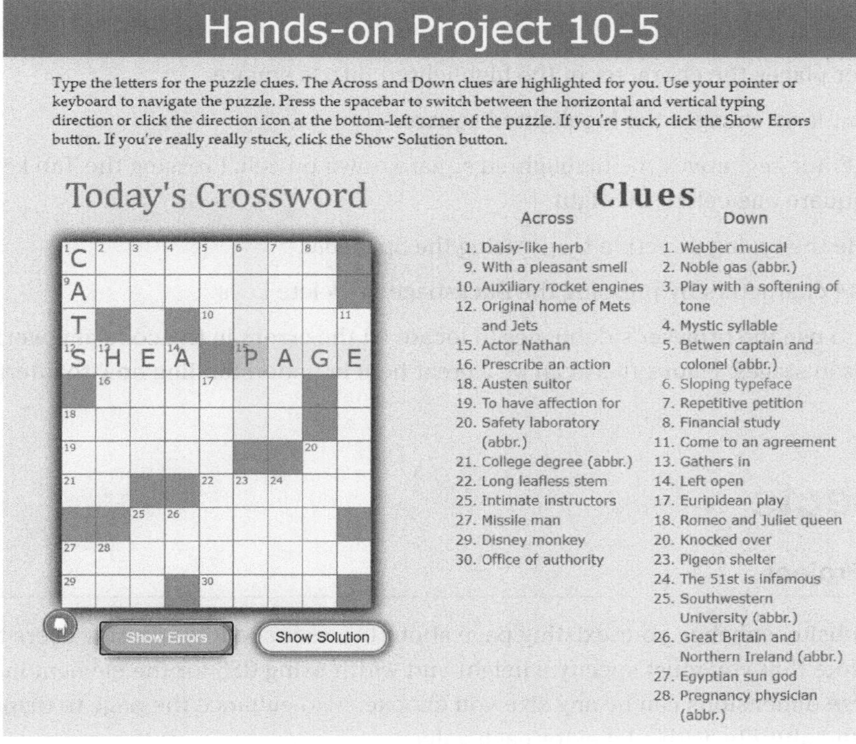

Figure 10-44 Completed Project 10-5

Do the following:

1. Use your code editor to open the **project10-05_txt.html** and **project10-05_txt.js** files from the js10 ► project05 folder. Enter your name and the date in the comment section of each file and save them as **project10-05.html** and **project10-05.js**, respectively.
2. Go to the **project10-05.html** file in your code editor and add script elements to link the file the cross.js and project10-05.js files, deferring both scripts until is page is loaded. Take some time to study the contents of document and then close, the file saving your changes.
3. Go to the **cross.js** file in your code editor. This file contains many variables and functions used in the operation of the crossword puzzle. While there are no errors in this file, take some time to study the code so you have a better grasp of the project. Close the file without saving your changes you might have made.
4. Go to the **project10-05.js** file in your code editor. Fix the following mistakes in the file:
   a. The first statement in the file calls the `selectLetter()` function when the user types a keyboard key in the document. Keyboard actions will control the actions of this program, but there is a mistake in the statement.
   b. Default actions associated with the keyboard should be prevented. A line has been added to the `selectLetter()` function to do this, but it is causing an error.
   c. The value of the key typed by the user will be stored in the `userKey` variable, but there is a mistake in declaring this variable.
   d. When the user presses the Spacebar, the typing direction should toggle between across and down. However, there is an error in the `else if` statement that calls the `switchTypeDirection()`.
   e. If the user types a letter from "a" to "z", the character should be added to the puzzle in uppercase. Fix the line that write the character so that it does this.
5. Save your changes to the file and then load **project10-05.html** in your web browser.
6. Test the page by typing answers into the crossword puzzle. Verify the following:
   a. Typing a letter places the character in the highlighted puzzle square.
   b. Pressing arrow keys changes the highlighted square.
   c. Pressing the Enter key moves the highlighted square down on cell. Pressing the Tab key moves the highlighted square one cell to the right.
   d. You can toggle the typing direction by pressing the Spacebar.
   e. You can delete characters by pressing the Backspace or Delete keys.

   You might have to use the browser's debugger to locate all the errors in the code and work through the debugging issues in stages. Figure 10-24 can be a great help in understanding how to interpret keyboard entries.

Case Projects

Individual Case Project

In your individual website, enhance your existing page about browser security to show users their current location on a map. Note that you must specify a height and width using CSS for the element in which you display the map; these dimensions can be any size you choose. Also enhance the page to display the user's latitude, longitude, and altitude, with a label for each value.

Team Case Project

Divide into two or three subgroups, with each group taking responsibility for downloading, installing, and becoming familiar with the testing tool for a touchscreen or mobile operating system under Google Android and Apple iOS. Note that the testing tools for Apple iOS can be installed only on an Apple Mac computer, so ensure that the subgroup responsible for this OS includes at least one member with the necessary hardware.

In your group, download your group's tool using the appropriate URL:

- Android: *https://developer.android.com/sdk/index.html*
- iOS: *https://developer.apple.com/xcode/downloads/*

Read the documentation at the same URL or included with the tool to learn how to open and test a web app using the tool. Open your Group Case Project web app in your subgroup's tool and then test the following aspects of your app:

- Appearance on at least three virtual devices with different screen sizes
- Functionality of your navigation interface
- Functionality of your form

Note the results of each test, even if the result is that the app performs the same as on a desktop computer. Share your results with the other subgroups and then as a group create a report describing the following:

- Areas where your app functioned as you expected in each OS
- Areas where your app functioned unexpectedly in each OS
- Aspects of the app that you would have liked to test in each tool, but may have been unable to
- At least two advantages and two disadvantages of each tool

CHAPTER 11

Managing Data Requests with AJAX and Fetch

When you complete this chapter, you will be able to:

- Understand the nature of server requests and responses
- Work with the content of HTTP messages
- Create HTTP request objects using AJAX
- View the status of an HTTP request and response
- Understand the limitations of AJAX and nested callbacks
- Write functions in arrow function syntax
- Create and use promise objects
- Manage requests and responses using the Fetch API
- Retrieve content written in XML
- Create an autocomplete search box
- Work with third-party APIs
- Manage security issues with third-party APIs

When you go to the web to get information such as the current state of the weather, driving conditions, or the stock market, you are making data requests to a server resource. The server resource takes your request and generates a response in the form of a weather forecast, driving directions, or stock quotes. The request/response action takes place entirely within the web page. Because the browser is only retrieving the data it needs and not the entire page, the result is a more efficient and more flexible means of exchanging information with the server. In this chapter you will explore how to use such techniques to augment your own web apps with data requests to server resources.

Note This chapter assumes you will have access to a web server and server scripts provided either by your instructor or set up on your own computer.

Introducing Server Requests

Web pages are a fundamental means of delivering content on the Internet. In this approach, illustrated in **Figure 11-1**, a browser accesses a page via the HTTP protocol with the page's content generated using server-side scripts with content often drawn from server-side databases.

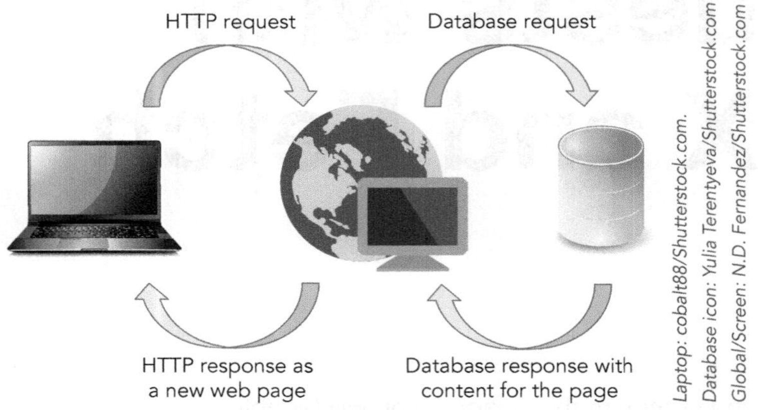

Figure 11-1 Processing a web page

The transfer of data from the server to the web page is synchronous because once the browser has asked for a web page, nothing can be done on the client until the page's content is generated and returned by the server. However, it is inefficient to transfer entire pages when only part of a page needs to be updated. The Google Search box shown in **Figure 11-2** provides a list of suggestions based what the user has typed into a search box and updates that list with each additional character. The only part of the page that needs to be updated is the contents of the suggestion list.

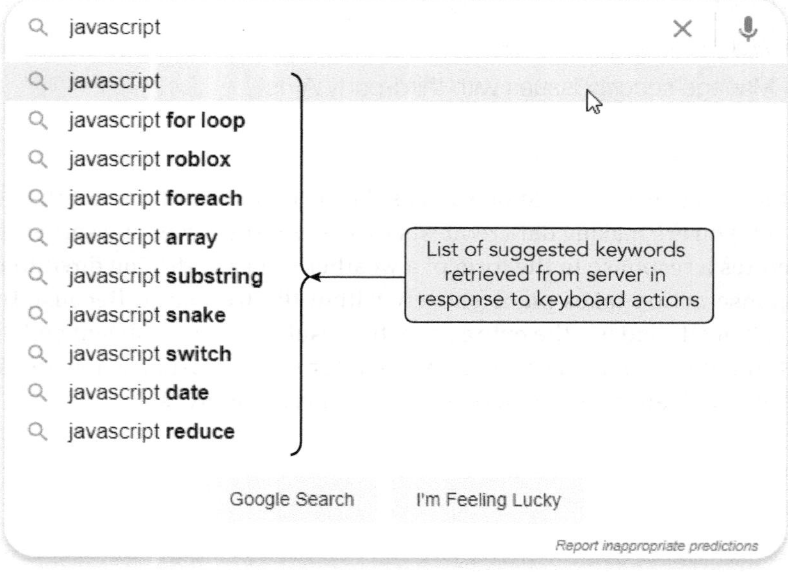

Figure 11-2 Google search suggestions

The approach used by the Google Search box and other similar apps is to send a request to the server, which then operates on that request and returns a response to the client. A request to a weather server could supply information on the client's location and a script running on the server would use that data to generate a forecast, which is then returned to the client. See **Figure 11-3**.

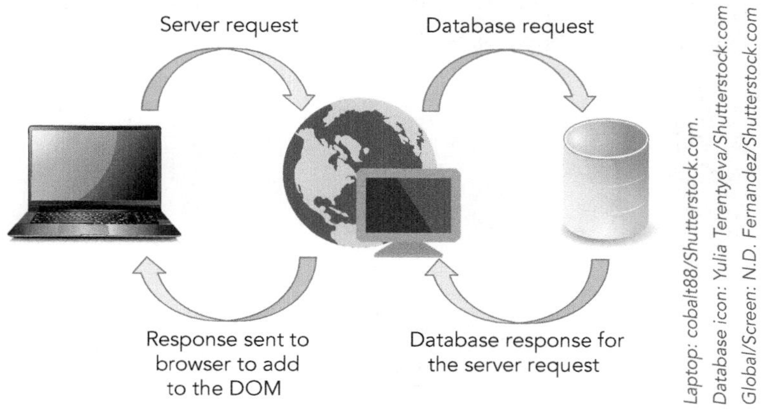

Figure 11-3 Processing a server request

Data transfers of this type between the client and the server are asynchronous, freeing up the client for other tasks while waiting for a response. A single web page might wait on several such asynchronous requests. For weather forecasts or stock market quotes, requests can be automated to repeat at set intervals so that information is constantly streamed between the server and client, but not preventing the client from completing other tasks.

In this chapter you will add asynchronous requests to a web page created by a sports blogger to retrieve news stories, headlines, and commentary from a server. The basic structure and content of the page has already been created for you. Your job will be to write code requesting information from the server and displaying the server's response within the page.

To open the files for the sports blog:

1. Go to the js11 ▶ chapter folder of your data files.
2. Use your code editor to open the **js11_txt.html** and **js11_txt.js** files. Enter your name and the date in the comment section of each file and then save them as **js11.html** and **js11.js**, respectively.
3. Take some time to study the contents of the js11.html file. Note that the only page content currently in the file is the header logo, search box, and list of navigation links. All other content will be generated and returned by the server.

Because you will be interacting directly with a server, you will need to place all files for this project in a web server of your own. You can install local server software on your computer using a free program like XAMPP, or you might have access to a server account provided by your instructor.

Note | See Appendix A for installation instructions for XAMPP.

To place the files on your server:

1. Copy all the files in the chapter folder, except the js11_txt.html and js11_txt.js files, and paste them into a new directory on your server.

   If you are using XAMPP you can place them in a new subfolder of the `htdocs` folder where your version of XAMPP is installed. In Nginx, the folder name is `html`. For IIS, the default folder is `wwwroot`. If you are using a server provided by your instructor or using different server software, consult your instructor or the server documentation to determine the folder in which website pages should be stored.

2. Use your web browser to open the **js11.html** file from its location on your server. If you are using a local server this would be the address: `http://localhost/`*`folder`*`/js11.html` where *`folder`* is the name of the subfolder in which you have stored the project files. **Figure 11-4** shows the initial contents of the page as viewed on a local server.

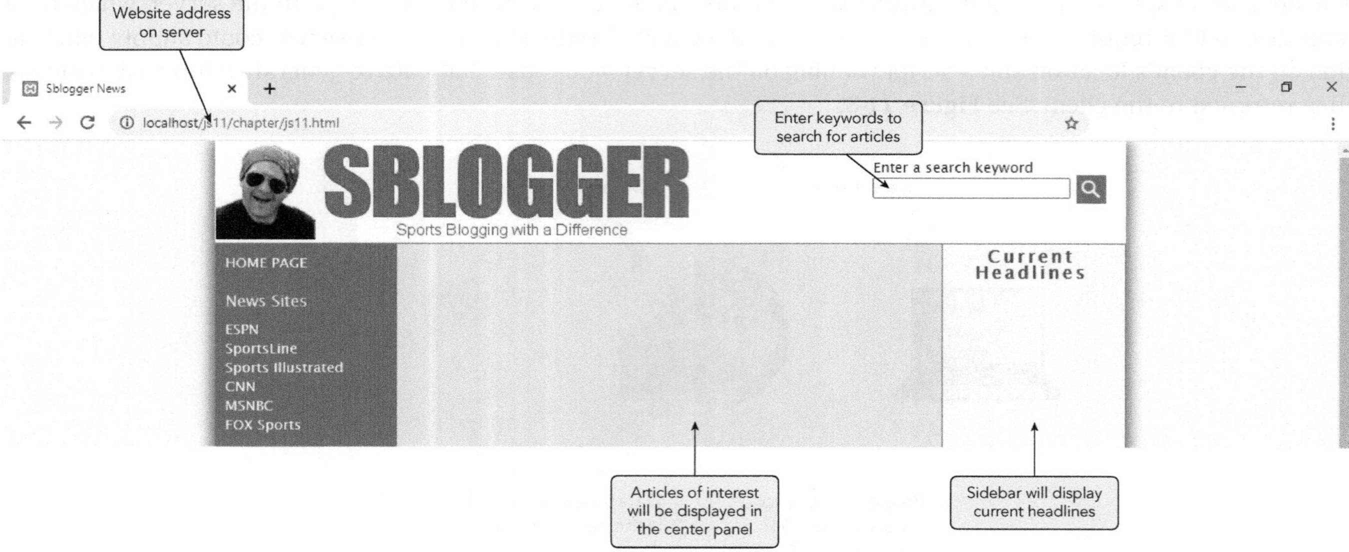

Figure 11-4 Initial blogging page

> **Note** In this chapter, you will always edit the copy of the files placed on your server. When viewing the page in your browser, always use the page's address on the web server and not the location from your computer's disk drive.

The page is currently devoid of content and must be able to retrieve and display content from other sources:

- The daily commentary needs to be retrieved from a file residing on the web server.
- Current headlines will be retrieved from an online newsfeed.
- Archived columns will be retrieved from the server after the user enters a keyword in the search box.
- Suggested keywords will appear in the search box in response to keyboard actions.

Before you begin writing the code for this project, you will review some of the principles of communication via the Hypertext Transfer Protocol.

Exploring HTTP Messages

Hypertext Transfer Protocol (HTTP) is a set of rules defining how requests are made by an HTTP client to an HTTP server and how responses are returned from the server to the client. The term HTTP client refers to the client, usually a web browser, making the request. HTTP server refers to a computer, usually the web server, that receives HTTP requests and returns responses to HTTP clients.

Understanding HTTP Messages

When a request is submitted from a web page, the HTTP client opens a connection to the server and submits a request encapsulated within an HTTP message. The web server then returns a response also encapsulated within a message. The request and response messages have the following general structure:

```
start line
header lines
blank line
message body
```

The *start line* identifies the type of request or response, the resource to access, and the HTTP version. The following is a typical HTTP start line that makes a request to the server resource file submit.cgi using the GET method via the HTTP 1.1 protocol. A query string `topic=Baseball` is attached to the URL of the requested resource.

```
GET submit.cgi?topic=Baseball HTTP/1.1
```

The start line of the response message from the server to the client contains information about the protocol and the response status. The following start line indicates a successful response via the HTTP 1.1 protocol:

```
HTTP/1.1 200 OK
```

After the start line are the header lines. A header can include zero or more lines with each header written in a *name:value* pair:

```
header: value
```

The following `Connection` header specifies that the HTTP connection should close after the web client receives the server response. The `Date` header identifies the date and time of the message in Greenwich Mean Time. The `Cache-Control` header tells the browser that it should not cache any server content it receives.

```
Connection: close
Date: Wed, 26 June 2024 18:32:07 GMT
Cache-Control: no-cache
```

Caching is the temporary storage of data on a local device for faster access. Most web browsers reduce the amount of data that needs to be retrieved from a server by caching retrieved data on a local computer. If caching is enabled in a web browser, the browser will attempt to locate any necessary data in its cache before making a request from a web server. While this technique improves web browser performance, it goes against the goal of dynamically updating portions of a web page with request information from the server. Thus, many apps will set the `Cache-Control` header to `no-cache`.

A blank line separates the message header and the message body. The message body might contain data needed for the request or the data returned with the response. However, message bodies are not required for either request or response messages. With a GET request, no message body is necessary because any form data is appended to the URL as a query string.

Although GET and POST requests are among the most common types of HTTP requests, other methods that can be used with an HTTP request are HEAD, DELETE, OPTIONS, PUT, and TRACE. For example, the HEAD method returns information about a document, but not the document itself. An app might use the HEAD method to determine the last modification date of a web page before requesting it from the web server.

Note

Although HTTP is probably the most widely used protocol on the Internet, it is not the only one. HTTP is a component of a large collection of Internet communication protocols called the Transmission Control Protocol/Internet Protocol (TCP/IP). Other common protocols include the Hypertext Transfer Protocol Secure (HTTPS), which provides secure Internet connections used in web-based financial transactions and other communications that require heightened security and protection, and the Internet Message Access Protocol (IMAP), used for storing and accessing email.

Introducing AJAX

The technology for sending and receiving HTTP messages between the client and the server was first introduced as AJAX (Asynchronous JavaScript and XML), a term coined by Jesse James Garrett in 2005 in an article titled *AJAX: A New Approach to Web Applications*. Garnett's article focused attention on techniques already pioneered by such apps as Google Suggest and Gmail. AJAX is based on the following three foundations:

- **Asynchronous**—The client is free to use the other contents of the website without waiting for a response from the server. All responses are managed in separate data streams.
- **JavaScript**—Programming can be managed on the client side using only the JavaScript language. No other client-side programming language or app is necessary.
- **XML**—Data can be stored in XML, a markup language similar to HTML for creating structured documents using element tags.

There have been several changes since Garnett's principles of AJAX were first articulated. JSON has replaced XML as the preferred language of data exchange and the tools described in Garnett's article to manage server requests have been replaced by better tools; however, the fundamental concepts have not changed.

The `XMLHttpRequest` Object

AJAX is built on the `XMLHttpRequest` (XHR) object, which is used to send asynchronous requests from the client to the server over HTTP. A request object is instantiated using the following object constructor:

```
let xhr = new XMLHttpRequest()
```

where *`xhr`* is the variable that stores the request object. Once a request object has been instantiated, it can open a connection to the server, request data, and process the server response. **Figure 11-5** lists some of the common request object methods.

METHOD	DESCRIPTION
`xhr``.open(`*`method, url, async`*`)`	Specifies the type of request, where `method` is either `GET` or `POST`, `url` is the location of requested resource, `async` is `true` to set up an asynchronous request or `false` to set up a synchronous request
`xhr``.send(`*`content`*`)`	Submits a request using the information specified in the `open()` method; the optional *`content`* argument provides the message body (used only with `POST` requests)
`xhr``.abort()`	Cancels the current request
`xhr``.getAllResponseHeaders()`	Returns a text string containing all the headers in the HTTP message
`xhr``.getResponseHeader(`*`header`*`)`	Returns the text of the specified header in the HTTP message
`xhr``.setRequestHeader(`*`header, value`*`)`	Defines an HTTP header using the header and name arguments

Figure 11-5 Request object methods

Requests begin with the `open()` method defining where to submit a request and how that request should be processed. The following statement uses the GET method to open an asynchronous request between the client and the submit.pl file on the server:

```
let xhr = new XMLHttpRequest();
xhr.open("get", "submit.pl&id=41088")
```

Note that the request data is appended to the URL as a query string. The location of the resource is defined relative to the location of the page. In this case the submit.pl file is assumed to be in the same folder as the web page. For other locations, you will need to specify the complete URL. By default, requests are asynchronous, but you can set the `async` parameter to `false`, establishing a synchronous request as in the following statement, which causes the program to pause as it awaits a response from the server:

```
xhr.open("get", "submit.pl&id=41088", false)
```

In most situations, you will use an asynchronous connection so that app can continue without waiting for a response.

Note Request objects follow the same-origin policy enforced with cookies and other server data streams so that any requested resource must reside on the same domain, port, and path as the requesting page.

Once the request has been defined, it is sent to the server using the following `send()` method:

```
xhr.send(content);
```

where *`content`* is content sent to the resource to be used in processing the request. A *`content`* value is only required if the request uses the POST method that stores data in the body of the request message. The following code uses the POST method to open and send an id value to a server script, storing the text "id=41088" as a line in the message body:

```
xhr.open("post", "submit.pl");
xhr.send("id=41088");
```

If the request uses the GET method or does not need to include data in the message body, set the content value to `null` as in the following expression:

```
xhr.send(null)
```

Daily commentary for the sports blog is stored as an HTML fragment in the commentary.html file located on the server. You will create an AJAX request asking for this file using the GET method and then send the request.

To create a request object:

1. Use your code editor to open the **js11.js** file from the folder on your web server.
2. Within the `init()` function add the following statement to create a request object:

```
// Create a request object
const xhr = new XMLHttpRequest();
```

3. Add the following statement to define the server resource and the method for opening the resource:

```
// Open the request and send it
xhr.open("get", "commentary.html");
```

4. Finally, send the request. Because there is no data to be sent to the server, set the data value to null.

```
xhr.send(null);
```

Figure 11-6 describes the code in the file.

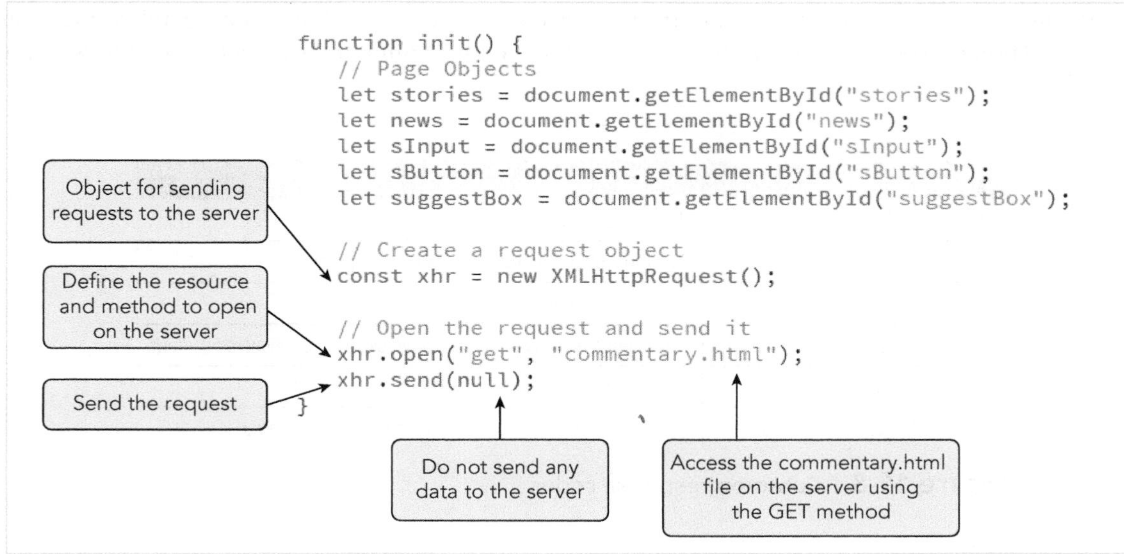

function init() {
// Page Objects
let stories = document.getElementById("stories");
let news = document.getElementById("news");
let sInput = document.getElementById("sInput");
let sButton = document.getElementById("sButton");
let suggestBox = document.getElementById("suggestBox");
// Create a request object
const xhr = new XMLHttpRequest();
// Open the request and send it
xhr.open("get", "commentary.html");
xhr.send(null);
}
Object for sending requests to the server
Define the resource and method to open on the server
Send the request
Do not send any data to the server
Access the commentary.html file on the server using the GET method

Figure 11-6 Creating a request object

Once a request has been defined and sent, the client will wait for a response from the server.

Managing a Response

In the opening, sending, and receiving a response from the server, the request object progresses through these five states:

- **UNSENT (0)**—The request object is created but has not yet been opened.
- **OPENED (1)**—The `open()` method is called to load the request.
- **HEADERS_RECEIVED (2)**—The `send()` method has been called to send the request.
- **LOADING (3)**—The browser has begun receiving a response from the server.
- **COMPLETE (4)**—The response from the server is complete.

Each change in state triggers a `readystatechange` event that can be managed using either an event handler or event listener applied to the request object:

```
xhr.onreadystatechange = function;
xhr.addEventListener("readystatechange", function)
```

Information about the current state of the request object and any contents that it might contain are stored in request object properties. **Figure 11-7** describes some of the properties.

PROPERTY	DESCRIPTION
xhr.readyState	Returns an integer indicating the current state of the request (0 = UNSENT, 1 = OPENED, 2 = HEADERS_RECEIVED, 3 = LOADING, 4 = COMPLETE)
xhr.status	Returns an integer indicating the status of the request (200 = "OK", 404 = "Not Found", etc.)
xhr.statusText	Returns a text string indicating the status of the request ("OK", "Not Found", etc.)
xhr.responseText	Returns the text of the response from the server
xhr.responseXML	Returns the response data as an XML DOM document

Figure 11-7 Request object properties

To determine the current state of the request object, use the `readyState` and `status` properties. If the `readyState` value is 4, the response from the server is complete. However, a complete response does not necessarily mean a successful response, so you also must use the `status` property to confirm that a successful connection with the server was made. **Figure 11-8** lists some of the common status codes contained within the start line of the returned message.

CODE	TEXT	DESCRIPTION
200	OK	The request was successful
301	Moved Permanently	The requested URL has been permanently moved
302	Moved Temporarily	The requested URL has been temporarily moved
304	Not Modified	The client already has the current version of the requested content
404	Not Found	The requested URL was not found
500	Internal Server Error	The request could not be completed due to server error

Figure 11-8 Common response codes

Successful connections will have status codes of 200 to 300. For other status values, write the text of the status message to the debugger console to inform the developer of an issue in creating the connection.

You will create an event handler for the `readystatechange` event that tests whether a complete response and a successful connection has been received from the server.

To create an event handler for changes in request state:

1. Directly below the statement that defines the `xhr` request object, add the following `onreadystatechange` event hander:

```
// Handle the changing request state
xhr.onreadystatechange = function() {
}
```

2. Within the anonymous function, add the following code that first tests whether the response is complete and then tests whether the response is successful. If the response is not successful, log an error message.

```
if (xhr.readyState === 4) {
   if (xhr.status >= 200 && xhr.status < 300) {
      // Manage the response
   } else {
      console.log("Request failed: " + xhr.statusText);
   }
}
```

Figure 11-9 shows the complete code within the event handler.

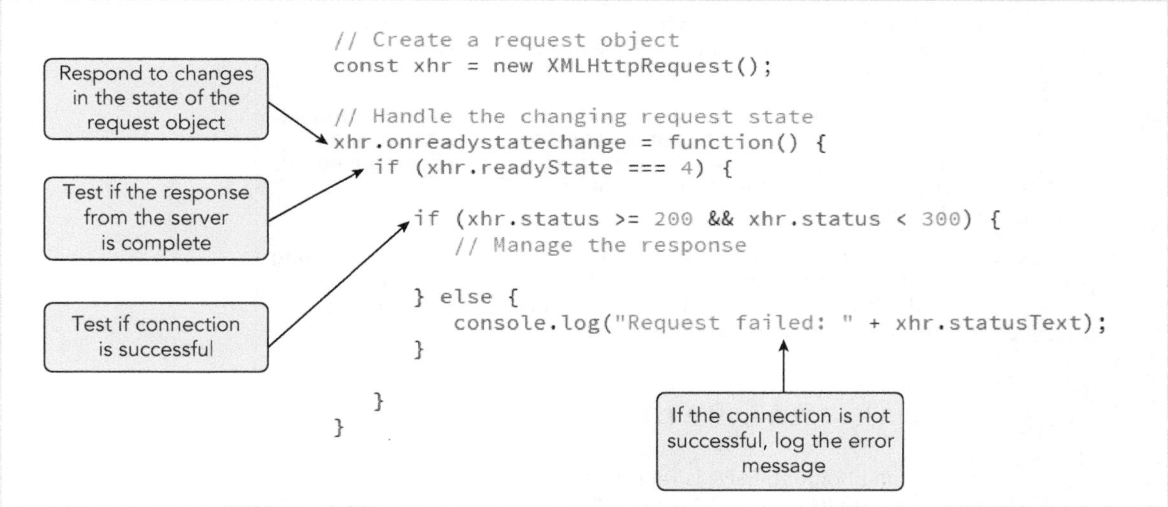

```
// Create a request object
const xhr = new XMLHttpRequest();

// Handle the changing request state
xhr.onreadystatechange = function() {
   if (xhr.readyState === 4) {

      if (xhr.status >= 200 && xhr.status < 300) {
         // Manage the response

      } else {
         console.log("Request failed: " + xhr.statusText);
      }

   }
}
```


Figure 11-9 Handling changes in the ready state

Note Always place the `onreadystatechange` event handler before the statements that open and send the request so that the browser can manage the changing state of the request object.

You can evaluate the server response once you have determined that the response is complete and the connection successful. The text of the response content is stored in the `responseText` property of the request object or in the `responseXML` property if the server resource is returning an XML document as the response.

For the sports blog, the response from the commentary.html file is simply the HTML code of the day's commentary. Store that code within the web page's `stories` object, displaying the current commentary on sports stories of the day.

To write the response text:

1. Directly below the `// Manage the response` comment, insert the following statement as shown in **Figure 11-10**:

```
stories.innerHTML = xhr.responseText;
```

Write the response text to the `stories` element

```
if (xhr.status >= 200 && xhr.status < 300) {
   // Manage the response
   stories.innerHTML = xhr.responseText;

} else {
   console.log("Request failed: " + xhr.statusText);
}
```

Figure 11-10 Displaying the request response text

2. Save your changes to the file and then reload the **js11.html** file from your web server. **Figure 11-11** shows two articles pulled from the server's commentary.html file and placed within the web page.

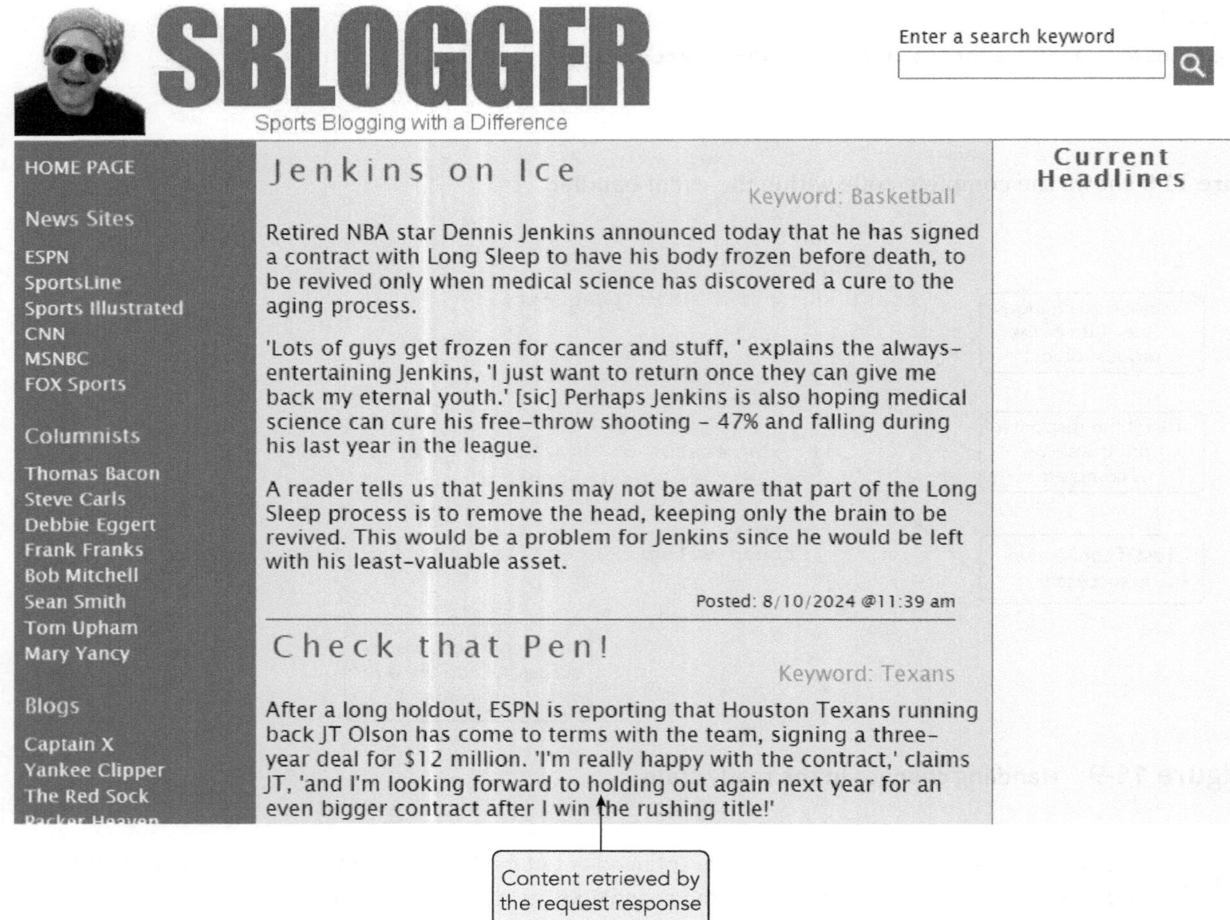

SBLOGGER
Sports Blogging with a Difference
Enter a search keyword
HOME PAGE
News Sites
ESPN
SportsLine
Sports Illustrated
CNN
MSNBC
FOX Sports
Columnists
Thomas Bacon
Steve Carls
Debbie Eggert
Frank Franks
Bob Mitchell
Sean Smith
Tom Upham
Mary Yancy
Blogs
Captain X
Yankee Clipper
The Red Sock
Jenkins on Ice
Keyword: Basketball
Retired NBA star Dennis Jenkins announced today that he has signed a contract with Long Sleep to have his body frozen before death, to be revived only when medical science has discovered a cure to the aging process.
'Lots of guys get frozen for cancer and stuff, ' explains the always-entertaining Jenkins, 'I just want to return once they can give me back my eternal youth.' [sic] Perhaps Jenkins is also hoping medical science can cure his free-throw shooting - 47% and falling during his last year in the league.
A reader tells us that Jenkins may not be aware that part of the Long Sleep process is to remove the head, keeping only the brain to be revived. This would be a problem for Jenkins since he would be left with his least-valuable asset.
Posted: 8/10/2024 @11:39 am
Check that Pen!
Keyword: Texans
After a long holdout, ESPN is reporting that Houston Texans running back JT Olson has come to terms with the team, signing a three-year deal for $12 million. 'I'm really happy with the contract,' claims JT, 'and I'm looking forward to holding out again next year for an even bigger contract after I win the rushing title!'
Current Headlines
Content retrieved by the request response

Figure 11-11 New sports commentary pulled from the server

Viewing the Status of a Request and Response

Most browsers include developer tools to evaluate requests and responses from the server. These tools are useful to gauge the performance of a request/response as well as to locate and fix network connection errors. Use the developer tools in your browser to view the status of the requests and responses associated with the commentary.html file.

To view the request/response status:

1. Open the developer tools for your browser. If you are using Safari click **Show Web Inspector** from the Develop menu.
2. Within the Developer Pane or the Web Inspector Pane, click the **Network** menu located at the top of the pane.
3. The pane shows a network log of browser network activity arranged in chronological order. Click **XHR** from the list of resources to show the request objects currently in use.
4. Reload the **js11.html** file to reload the request and then click **commentary.html** from the list of request objects. A window showing network information associated with the file is opened within the pane.
5. Click **Headers** to view the HTTP content of both the request and response messages. See **Figure 11-12**.

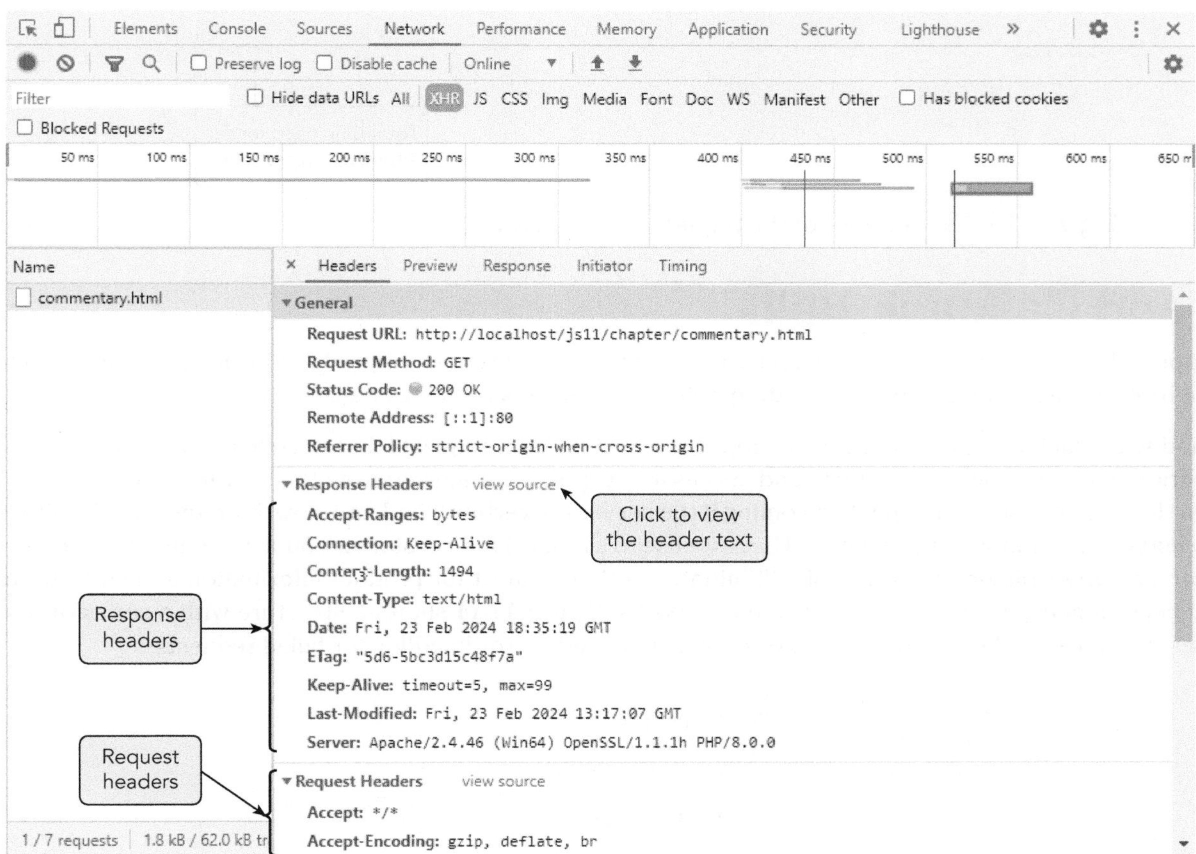

Figure 11-12 HTTP headers for the request and response

6. Click **Timing** to view information on the timings involved with sending the request and receiving a response from the server. See **Figure 11-13**.
7. Close the Developer Pane or the Web Inspector on your browser.

Using the tools shown in Figure 11-13, a developer can track the amount of time required to manage the request and response. In this case the entire process takes a bit more than 40 milliseconds, which does not sound like much, but if an app has several dozen requests even milliseconds can result in unacceptable delays for the end user.

Use the network tools panel when you need to make sure that requests and responses are being transferred as expected or to trace files that may be slowing down your app. By default the network tool uses the online connection resulting in the fastest speeds. To simulate lower bandwidth connections, use the throttling drop-down list box and choose another connection speed for your app.

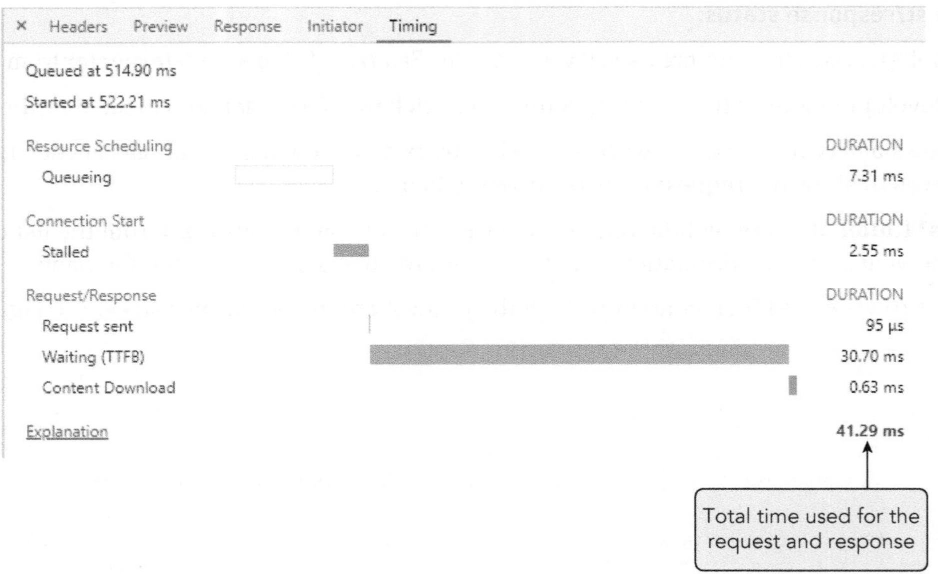

Figure 11-13 Timings of the request and response

AJAX and Callback Hell

The AJAX approach works very well for apps consisting of a few asynchronous requests. It begins to break down for apps with multiple asynchronous requests, creating a situation known as callback hell.

To understand what callback hell is, imagine an app that has dozens of requests. Each request is associated with a callback function that is run once a complete and successful response is received from the server resource. There is no guarantee that a response will be quick in coming if the server is overburdened and slow. Moreover, each callback function can initiate one or more new requests. The response to a request for a customer contact initiates a new request for the customer's order history, which itself will initiate another request for product information and so forth in a growing and near-unmanageable pyramid of nested callbacks. **Figure 11-14** shows a structure with a series of three nested requests with callbacks; and this code does not even include error handling for failed requests.

```
const xhr1 = new XMLHttpRequest();
xhr1.onreadystatechange = function() {
   if (xhr1.readyState === 4 && xhr1.status === 200) {
   // process the response to create a 2nd request
   const xhr2 = new XMLHttpRequest();

      if (xhr2.readyState === 4 && xhr2.status === 200) {
         // process the response to create a 3rd request
         const xhr3 = new XMLHttpRequest();

            if (xhr3.readyState === 4 && xhr3.status === 200) {
            // process the response and generate output

            };
         xhr3.open("get", url3);
         xhr3.send(null);
         };
      xhr2.open("get", url2);
      xhr2.send(null);
   };
};
xhr1.open("get", url1);
xhr1.send(null);
```

Figure 11-14 Nested callbacks resulting in callback hell

That is not to say these situations cannot be handled within AJAX with good coding practices. You can avoid creating large structures of nested callbacks by keeping your code shallow. However, AJAX, with its reliance on callbacks is susceptible to this type of problem. In the next section you will learn another set of tools to manage server request and responses that avoids callback hell.

Quick Check 1

1. What is caching?
2. What are the foundations of AJAX?
3. Provide a statement to create a new request object named `MyReq`.
4. Provide a statement to open the `MyReq` object to the URL *http://www.example.com* using the GET method.
5. What property value indicates that a complete response has been received from the server?

Introducing Arrow Functions

Before discussing other ways of managing asynchronous requests, we first need to discuss functions. So far in your coding you have created functions using function declarations. You can also store a function using a function expression as in the following code which stores the `addValues()` function as a variable:

```
let addValues = function(a, b) {
   let sum = a + b;
   return sum;
}
addValues(3, 5); // returns 8
```

In 2015 with the release of ECMAScript 6, JavaScript introduced arrow function syntax in which extraneous characters are removed from the function expression. Arrow function syntax has the following general form:

```
let functionName = (parameters) => {
   statements
}
```

with the fat arrow => symbol replacing the `function` keyword and *`parameters`* and *`statements`* having the same meaning they would have for a function declaration or function expression. The `addValues()` function can be written in arrow function syntax as:

```
let addValues = (a, b) => {
   let sum = a + b;
   return sum;
}
```

Arrow functions act the same way as function expressions or function declarations. The expression `addValues(4, 6)` would return a value of 10 no matter which of the three approaches was used to define the function.

Note | You can create named functions using the `const` keyword in place of `let` for both a function expression and an arrow function.

Arrow Functions and Parameter Values

The parentheses can be removed around the parameter list for functions that contain a single parameter. The following arrow function applies this approach with the `doubleIt()` function which has only parameter:

```
let doubleIt = a => {
   let double = a*2;
   return double;
}
doubleIt(6); // returns 12
```

If the function contains a single statement, there is no need for the command block or the `return` keyword, resulting in a very terse function expression. For example, the following code that declares the `doubleIt()` function

```
function doubleIt(a) {
   return a*2;
}
```

can be written as a single line in arrow function syntax:

```
let doubleIt = a => a*2;
```

If the function does not contain any parameters, you must still include parentheses as a placeholder separating the = assignment operator from the => fat arrow symbol. The following expression uses this approach to define a function that logs the text "Response Received":

```
let writeEnd = () => console.log("Response Received");
```

The general rule is that if an arrow function contains a single parameter, omit the parentheses, otherwise always include them.

Note You cannot insert a line break between the parameters and the fat arrow symbol. If the parameter list and the fat arrow symbol are not on the same line, a syntax error will result.

Anonymous functions can be written in arrow function syntax as well. The following function declaration

```
function() {
   console.log("Response Received");
}
```

becomes in arrow function syntax the single line:

```
() => console.log("Response Received")
```

Figure 11-15 provides other examples comparing function declarations to their arrow function equivalents.

Aside from the differences in syntax, arrow functions differ from function declarations in how the `this` keyword is handled. In function declarations, the `this` keyword returns the object that called the function, which could be the window object, document object, or a page object, among other things. With arrow functions the `this` keyword always returns the object that defined or owns the function. Thus, arrow functions do not have their own `this`, they always take their meaning from the outside context.

You might find arrow functions confusing at first, but with practice you will be able write them as easily as function declarations. One area where arrow functions are often used is in creating promises.

FUNCTION DECLARATION	ARROW FUNCTION

`function sumTen(x, y) {`
`  let total = x + y + 10;`
`  return total;`
`}`
	`let sumTen (x, y) => {`
	`  let total = x + y + 10;`
	`  return total;`
	`}`

`function sum(x, y) {`
`  return x + y;`
`}`
	`let sum = (x, y) => x + y;`

`function addTen(x) {`
`  return x + 10;`
`}`
	`let addTen = x => x + 10;`

`function randNum() {`
`  return Math.random;`
`}`
	`let randNum = () => Math.`
	`random;`

`function (msg) {`
`  console.log(msg);`
`}`
	`msg => console.log(msg);`

`setTimeout(function() {`
`  alert("hello");`
`}, 2000);`
	`setTimeout(() =>`
	`alert("hello"), 2000);`

`numbers.sort(function(a, b)`
`{`
`  return b-a;`
`});`
	`numbers.sort((a,b) => b-a);`

`form.onclick = function()`
`{`
`  alert("Click");`
`}`
	`form.onclick = () =>`
	`alert("Click");`

Figure 11-15 Arrow function examples

Best Practices When to Use and Not Use Arrow Functions

Arrow functions can make your code more concise; however, they do not entirely replace function declarations or function syntaxes. Here are situations where arrow functions would not be appropriate:

- Do not use arrow functions if it makes your code more difficult to interpret and debug. Being compact is not always a virtue.
- Because arrow functions do not have their own `this` value, they should not be used with event handlers where the `this` value is needed.
- Also, since arrow functions do not have their own `this` value, they should also not be used to define object methods or methods for object classes. Use function declarations instead.
- Function declarations support the `arguments` object that references all arguments used in the function.

Arrow functions work best with functions that have few statements. Their utility is reduced for extended functions comprising several statements.

Exploring the Promise Object

A promise is an object that does not have a value currently but might have one in the future. For example, you might promise to buy groceries for dinner, but whether you do or not depends on future events. A server may promise to respond to a request from the client but has not done so yet. There is no guarantee that a promise will ever be kept, so a promise will exist in one of three states:

- **pending** The promise has been given but not yet fulfilled or rejected.
- **resolved** The promise has been fulfilled.
- **rejected** The promise will not be fulfilled.

Promises operate asynchronously so that while the promise is pending, the script is free to accomplish other tasks.

Defining a Promise Object

A promise object is defined using the following `new Promise()` object constructor:

```
let promise = new Promise((resolve, reject) => {
   // statements defining the promise
   resolve(resolve value);
   reject(rejected value);
});
```

where *`resolve`* and *`reject`* are callbacks that are run once the promise is either resolved or rejected. Nothing happens until the promise is settled. Note that this object constructor uses arrow function syntax but you could have also used a function declaration. The command block contained within the promise is called the executor. The executor's statements are run in the background once the promise is initiated. Once the promise is settled, a value is sent to the *`resolve`* and *`reject`* functions.

The following code defines a promise involving dinner preparations. After a two-second delay, the executor returns a random number between 0 and 1 so that 80% of the time the promise will be resolved with the purchase of groceries and 20% of the time that option will be rejected. But the resolution of the promise will not be known until after 2 seconds has passed.

```
let planDinner = new Promise( (resolve, reject) => {
   setTimeout( ()=>
      if (Math.random() < 0.8)
          resolve("Bought groceries")
      } else {
         reject("Ordered takeout");
      }
   }, 2000);
});
```

To initiate a promise, apply the following statements to the promise object:

```
promise
.then(function)
.catch(function)
```

where *promise* references the promise object, and the `then()` and `catch()` methods run functions depending on whether the promise was resolved or rejected. Both functions reference the `resolve` or `reject` method stored in the promise's executor. The following statements initiate the `planDinner` promise, using arrow function syntax to log the promise's outcome:

```
planDinner
.then(msg => console.log(msg))
.catch(msg => console.log(msg));
console.log("Planning dinner");
```

When the `planDinner` promise is initiated, the debugger console first displays the message "Planning dinner". Over the next two seconds, the promise is pending, after which the promise is settled by logging the message "Bought groceries" if the promise is resolved or "Ordered takeout" if the promise is rejected.

Chaining Promises

One promise might rely on the successful resolution of a prior promise. For example, you might promise to buy groceries, cook a meal, and clean the dishes, but without buying groceries there is no promise to cook and without cooking there are no dirty dishes. A promise chain has the following general structure:

```
promise
.then(function)
.then(function)
...
.catch(function)
```

with each `then()` method returning a promise object with values passed to the next `then()` method. The chain ends with a `catch()` statement handling any rejection that breaks the promise chain. Promise chains avoid callback hell because the promises are not nested within one another but are executed in sequence as each promise is passed off to the next.

The following code shows how multiple `then()` methods can be chained to pass promise values through the chain. As before, "Planning dinner" is immediately written to the log as the promise is initiated. If the promise is resolved successfully, the message "Bought groceries" is logged and the `then()` method returns the text string "Started cooking", which is passed to the next `then()` method where it is also logged. If the initial promise is rejected, only the text "Ordered takeout" is logged.

```
buyGroceries
.then(msg => {
   console.log(msg);
   return "Started cooking";
})
.then(newMsg => console.log(newMsg))
.catch(msg => console.log(msg));

console.log("Planning dinner");
```

Promises can also be nested within the `then()` method to create resolved and rejected functions at each link in the chain. The following code places a promise object within the first `then()` method. The `planDinner` promise is initiated and if it is settled successfully, this second promise is created that resolves after a one-second delay as either "Made dinner" (70% of the time) or "Ordered takeout anyway" (30% of the time). A successful resolution of that promise is returned to the next `then()` method, which logs it in the console. The message from a rejected promise is still caught using the `catch()` method.

```
console.log("Planning dinner");
buyGroceries
.then(msg => {
   console.log(msg);
   return new Promise( (resolve, reject) => {
      setTimeout( () => {
         if (Math.random() < 0.7) {
            resolve("Made dinner");
         } else {
            reject("Ordered takeout anyway");
         }
      }, 1000);
   });
})
.then(newMsg => console.log(newMsg))
.catch(msg => console.log(msg));
```

When this code is run, three possible strings of messages will be logged:

```
Planning dinner > Ordered takeout
Planning dinner > Bought groceries > Ordered takeout anyway
Planning dinner > Bought groceries > Made dinner
```

The log informs the user what promises were kept and if they were not kept, at what point the promise chain was broken. In general, you should avoid nesting promises or you run the risk of duplicating "callback hell" except with promises.

Running Multiple Promises

Multiple promises can be organized in a wide variety of ways. The promises could be independent actions such as with an app that tries to retrieve different data from different servers. Independent promises are managed using the following `Promise.all()` method:

```
Promise.all(array)
.then(function)
.catch(function)
```

where *`array`* is an array of promise objects. The promises run independently from each other. Upon the successful competition of the last pending promise, the `then()` method is invoked. However, if any of the promises fails, the `catch()` method is immediately invoked.

But you might also have promises trying to fulfill the same task, such as with promises retrieving the same data from different servers. The promises are essentially racing each other and the task is completed with the first resolved promise. Such a promise structure is implemented with following `Promise.race()` method:

```
Promise.race(array)
.then(function)
.catch(function)
```

where *`array`* is once again an array of promise objects. In this structure the `then()` method will handle the resolved function associated with promise that finishes first and the `catch()` method will handle the rejection if that promise fails. The other promises are ignored once the first promise either fulfills or fails.

Promises are a powerful feature that was introduced in ES6, and this overview only scratches the surface of what can be accomplished with promises and asynchronous connections. One use of promises is with requesting data using the Fetch API.

Using the Fetch API

The Fetch API uses promises to manage server requests, avoiding some of the problems associated with callback hell. A request is made to a server using the method:

```
fetch(url, options)
```

where *url* is the location of the server resource and *options* is an optional object defining values for the HTTP message. The following statement uses fetch to make a GET request from the submit.pl file on the server. The `fetch()` method creates an asynchronous request, so that the app continues to run while the status of the promise is pending.

```
fetch("submit.pl&id=41088")
```

Figure 11-16 list some of the option properties that can be included with `fetch()` to provide more content with the server request.

FETCH OPTIONS	DESCRIPTION
`body:` *`string`*	Text of the message body placed within the request message
`cache:` *`type`*	Specifies how the browser will interact with the HTTP cache, where `type` is `default`, `no-store`, `reload`, `no-cache`, `force-cache`, or `only-if-cached`
`credentials:` *`type`*	Specifies if and how cookies should be included with the request where `type` is `omitted`, `same-origin`, or `include`
`headers:` *`object`*	Specifies an object instance containing key-value pairs to be placed in the request header
`method:` *`type`*	Specifies the type of request where `type` is `GET` (the default), `POST`, `PUT`, `PATCH`, `DELETE`, `HEAD`, `OPTIONS`, `CONNECT`, or `TRACE`

Figure 11-16 Options of the `fetch()` method

For example, the following statement makes a POST request, providing the header and body content of the message as part of the request:

```
fetch("submit.pl", {
   method: "POST",
   headers: {"Content-Type" : "application/json"},
   body: "{'id':41088}"
})
```

Fetch does not need event handlers or listeners to constantly monitor the request status. Like other promise objects the request is pending until resolved or rejected.

Managing Fetch Responses

The promise initiated by fetch can be managed in the following chain:

```
fetch(url, options)
.then(function)
.then(function)
...
.catch(function)
```

with each `then()` method returning a promise that is passed to the next `then()` method. If the fetch promise is rejected, `catch` handles the rejection. The following code shows how fetch could be used in place of AJAX to retrieve the text of the commentary.html file and write that content to the `stories` element:

```
fetch("commentary.html")
.then(response => response.text())
.then(text => stories.innerHTML = text)
.catch((error) => console.log(error));
```

Fetch goes through the following steps in processing this request:

1. A promise is made to connect to the resource at commentary.html.
2. Once the promise is resolved, it is passed to the first `then()` method where the text of the response object is parsed using the `response.text()` method, creating another promise.
3. That promise is passed to the next `then()` method as the `text` parameter and stored in the inner HTML of the `stories` element.
4. If the promise is rejected at any point in the chain, an error message is written to the console.

Notice that arrow functions are applied in this code sample, but you could also use a function declaration. Arrow functions are preferred because they result in much cleaner code that clearly displays the logic of passing information from one promise to the next in the chain.

The initial promise defined with the `fetch()` method creates a response object containing information about the server's response. **Figure 11-17** describes some of the properties associated with that response object.

PROPERTY	DESCRIPTION
response.headers	Returns an object containing the response header
response.ok	Returns a value indicating the nature of the HTTP code, where a status code of 200 to 299 returns true and false if otherwise
response.status	Returns the status code of the response
response.statusText	Returns a text string describing the response status
response.type	Returns the type of response, where type is `basic`, `cors`, `error`, `opaque`, or `opaquedirect`
response.url	Returns the URL of the response

Figure 11-17 Response object properties

As with AJAX, you can read the status of the server's response using the `status` or `statusText` properties, thus gaining valuable information about why a promise might have been rejected.

Figure 11-18 describes some of the methods associated with fetch's response object.

METHOD	DESCRIPTION
response.error()	Returns a response object associated with a network error
response.arrayBuffer()	Returns a low-level binary data often used with image and multimedia data
response.blob()	Returns a Blob object used file-like objects that contain text or binary data
response.formData()	Returns a promise object that resolves as form data comprised of key-value pairs
response.json()	Returns a promise object that can be parsed as JSON data
response.text()	Returns a promise object that can be parsed as text string data

Figure 11-18 Response object methods

For example, you can read the content the server's response using the `blob()`, `formData()`, `json()`, or `text()` methods.

Error Handling with Fetch

If the promise can get a response from the server, even an error response, fetch counts the promise as being resolved. This means that only network errors, such as failure to connect to the server, are treated as failed promises.

The ok property can be used to catch non-network failures. A `false` value of the ok property indicates a failure on the server to completely process the request as in the following code that catches a server error in attempting to retrieve the commentary.html file:

```
fetch("commentary.html")
.then(response => {
   if (response.ok) {
      return response.text();
   } else {
      return "Commentary not available";
   }
})
.then(text => stories.innerHTML = text)
.catch((error) => console.log(error));
```

If the promised response is not ok, the text "Commentary not available" is passed to the next `then` and displayed in the page. Depending on the app, more robust error handling can be invoked.

Using Fetch to Return a Search

You will use Fetch to request commentary archived on the sports blog server. Each commentary is marked by a keyword that can be entered using a search box on the sports blogger page. The keyword is sent to a server script that returns articles matching that keyword.

The server script is written in Perl, a popular scripting language often used to generate and manipulate text strings. Perl is supported by almost all web servers. However, before you can use the script file, you will need to modify the file so that it can locate the Perl executable files on your server. The perl.exe file is often located in a server's */usr/bin/perl* or */root/bin/perl* folder. If you are running XAMPP or another server on your computer, you will need to specify the path on your computer to the perl.exe file. A common path under XAMPP might be "C:\xampp\perl\bin\perl.exe".

To edit the script file:

1. Use your code editor to open the **archives.pl** file from the js11 ▶ chapter folder on your server.
2. At the top of the page change the first line to

```
#!location
```

   where *`location`* points to the perl.exe file on your server. If you specify a path on your local computer using the XAMPP server, enclose the path and the name of the perl.exe file in quotes. **Figure 11-19** shows a sample path (yours may differ).

Enter the location of the perl.exe file on the server

```
#!/usr/bin/perl

# Confirm that perl is located in the usr/bin/perl folder on the server

#All perl scripts should use strict
use strict;

use CGI;
my $cgi_object = new CGI();
```

Figure 11-19 Specifying the location of the perl.exe file

3. Close the file, saving your changes.

To use the archives.pl script, send the request `archives.pl?skey=`*`keyword`* to the server where *`keyword`* is the name of the keyword associated with an archived commentary. Create a fetch request to this script file now.

To fetch commentaries from the server archive:

1. Use your code editor to open the **js11.js** file stored on your web server.
2. Directly after the `xhr.send(null)` command insert the following event handler for a `click` event associated with the `sButton` element:

```
// Retrieve archived articles from the web server
sButton.onclick = () => {
};
```

3. Within the anonymous function, add the following `fetch()` method to access the archive using the value of the `sInput` element as the keyword. Because the value is appended as a query string, it must be encoded.

```
fetch("archives.pl?skey=" + encodeURIComponent(sInput.value))
```

4. Add the following `then()` method to return the value of the promised response, displaying an error message if the response result contains an HTTP error:

```
.then ( response => {
   if (response.ok) {
      return response.text();
   } else {
      return "Unable to retrieve commentary";
   }
})
```

5. Add the following `then()` method to insert text of the commentary within the `stories` element:

```
.then ( comtext => stories.innerHTML = comtext )
```

6. Catch any network errors by adding the following `catch()` method:

```
.catch (stories.innerHTML = "Network Failure");
```

Figure 11-20 describes the complete code to fetch a response from the archives.pl server script.

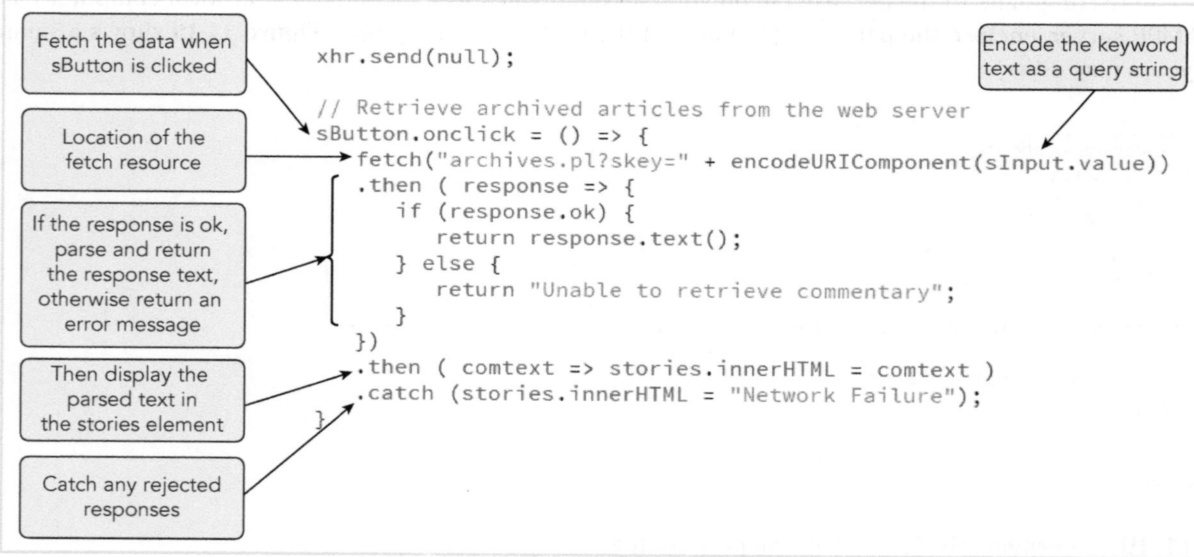
Fetch the data when sButton is clicked
Location of the fetch resource
If the response is ok, parse and return the response text, otherwise return an error message
Then display the parsed text in the stories element
Catch any rejected responses
Encode the keyword text as a query string
xhr.send(null);
// Retrieve archived articles from the web server
sButton.onclick = () => {
fetch("archives.pl?skey=" + encodeURIComponent(sInput.value))
.then (response => {
if (response.ok) {
return response.text();
} else {
return "Unable to retrieve commentary";
}
})
.then (comtext => stories.innerHTML = comtext)
.catch (stories.innerHTML = "Network Failure");
}

Figure 11-20 Fetching archived articles by keyword

7. Save your changes to the file and then open the **js11.html** file from its location on your server.
8. Enter **baseball** into the keyword search box and click the **magnifying glass icon**. As shown in **Figure 11-21**, two commentaries are retrieved from the blog archive.

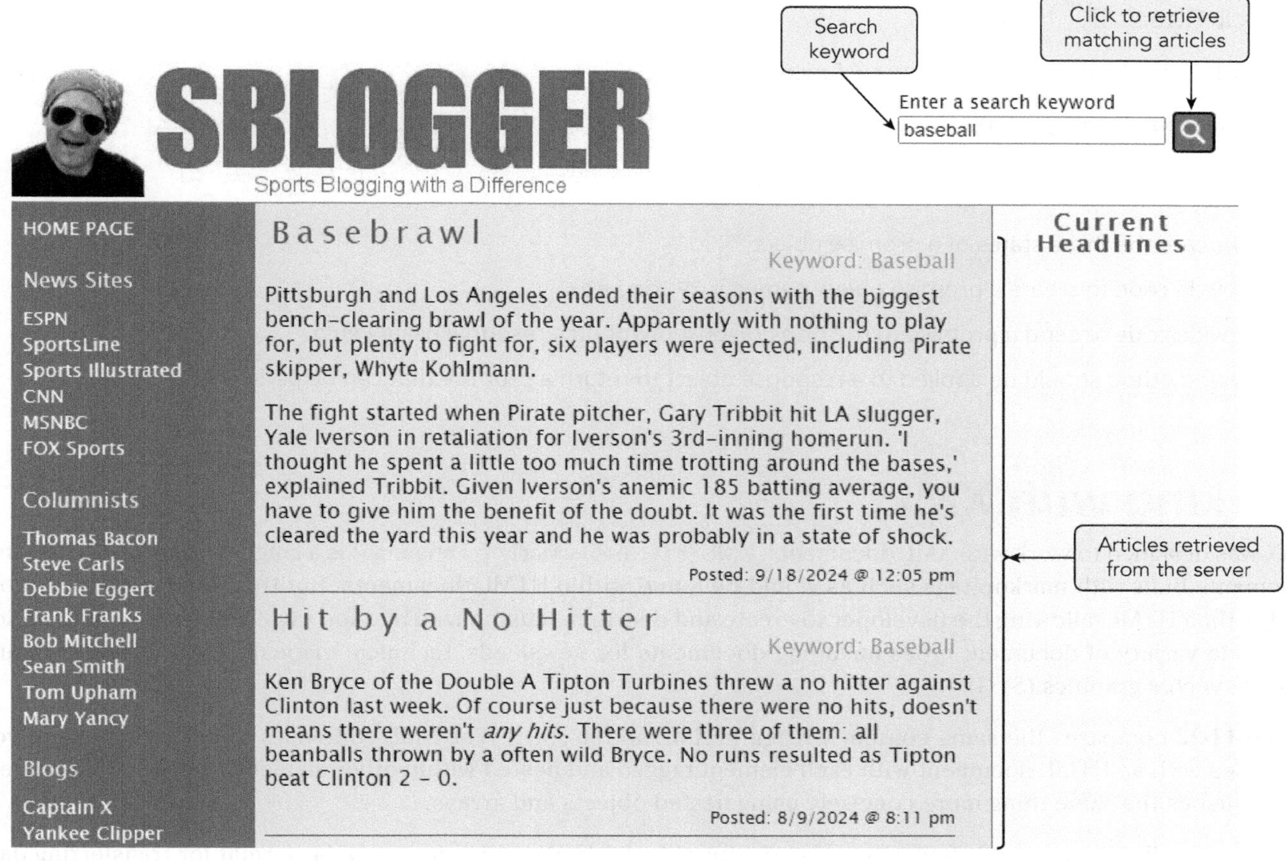

Figure 11-21 Articles retrieved by keyword

If your Fetch request fails, check for the following errors:

- Verify that your server is accessible and running.
- Verify that you have entered the correct path to the perl.exe file in the archives.pl file.
- The archives.pl might not be publicly executable. Check with the instructor or system administrator to verify that you can run the file.
- Check your code against the code shown in Figure 11-20 to verify that you have not made any syntax errors.

In the next session you will explore how to use Fetch to retrieved data stored in XML and JSON format.

Common Mistakes

Working with Fetch

As you use Fetch in designing your own web apps, here are important points to remember when using the `fetch()` method:

- HTTP errors will not be caught with Fetch. The `catch()` method will only catch network errors. To catch other errors, you must examine the properties of the response object.
- The `fetch()` method returns a response object. To extract useful information, the response object needs to be parsed with methods like `text()` and `json()`.
- Be sure to apply the correct parser to the data type. Use `response.json()` for JSON data; use `response.text()` for basic text strings.
- The `fetch()`, `then()`, and `catch()` methods are not separate statements but part of one long statement. The command could be written on a single line as `fetch().then().then().catch()`.

Quick Check 2

1. Write the following function in arrow function syntax:

```
function display(msg) {
   alert(mg);
}
```

2. What are the three states of a promise object?
3. Provide code to create a promise object named `myPromise`.
4. Provide code to send a promise to the https://jsonshow/photos resource using Fetch.
5. What method should be applied to a response object to return a promise that can be parsed as text?

Working with XML

AJAX was designed to work with XML documents. XML (Extensible Markup Language) is a language used for structured documents built with markup tags such as would be found within HTML documents. But the XML language is more flexible than HTML, allowing the developer to create and distribute customized markup tags. XML forms a foundation for a wide variety of document types including documents for newsfeeds, technical manuals, legal documents, and scalable vector graphics (SVG).

Figure 11-22 compares the same content written in XML and in JSON. The XML code uses the same structure you would see with an HTML document with each element tagged and nested within other elements. The JSON document accomplishes the same thing more concisely using nested objects and arrays.

Due to its smaller file size and similarity to JavaScript objects, JSON is the more popular format for transferring data between client and server. However, XML is still widely used in such applications as RSS newsfeeds, that transmit current new stories to media outlets and podcasts. JavaScript provides tools to handle both formats.

The home page of the sports blog displays current headlines drawn from a newsfeed stored in the headlines.xml file on the server. You will write code to fetch that content, displaying it within a sidebar on the sports blog home page.

XML Document

```
<?xml version="1.0" encoding="UTF-8" standalone="yes" ?>
<rss>
   <channel>
      <title>Current Headlines</title>
      <description>Sports News Feed</description>
      <item>
         <title>Carls leads at PGA</title>
         <description>Brett Carls leads in the final round of the PGA Championship</description>
      </item>
      <item>
         <title>Groveney Signs</title>
         <description>Islanders sign Steve Groveney to a 2-year contract</description>
      </item>
  </channel>
</rss>
```

Figure 11-22 Comparing XML and JSON

JSON Document

```
{
  "rss": {
    "channel": {
    "title": "Current Headlines",
    "description": "Sports News Feed",
    "item": [
      {
        "title": "Carls leads at PGA",
        "description": "Brett Carls leads in the final round of the PGA Championship"
       },
      {
        "title": "Groveney Signs",
        "description": "Islanders sign Steve Groveney to a 2-year contract"
       }
      ]
    }
  }
}
```

Figure 11-22 Comparing XML and JSON (Continued)

Parsing XML Content

XML is stored as text within the body of the server response. To convert that text into an XML DOM object, first create the following `parser` object:

```
let parser = new DOMParser();
```

where *`parser`* is an object that supports methods for converting text into a DOM. To create the DOM, apply the following `parseFromString()` method to the parser:

```
parser.parseFromString(text, mimeType)
```

where *`text`* is the text string to be parsed and *`mimeType`* identifies the type of structured data stored in the text string. Mime type values include "text/html", "text/xml", and "image/svg+xml" for working with HTML, XML, and SVG documents. For example, the following expression creates a `parser` object and uses it to convert XML text stored in the headlines.xml file into a DOM:

```
new DOMParser().parseFromString("headlines.xml", "text/xml")
```

Use Fetch to retrieve the text of the headlines.xml document from your server and then parse the retrieved text, creating a node tree.

To fetch the headlines.xml file from the server:

1. Return to the **js11.js** file in your code editor.
2. Directly below the code for the `sButton.onclick` event handler, insert the following code to fetch headlines from the server:

```
// Fetch current headlines from the web server
fetch("headlines.xml")
```

3. Add the following statement to parse the text string from the response object once the promise is resolved:

```
.then (response => response.text())
```

4. Add the following statement to receive the parsed text string and convert it into a DOM:

```
.then (str => new DOMParser().parseFromString(str, "text/xml"))
```

Figure 11-23 describes the newly added code in the file.

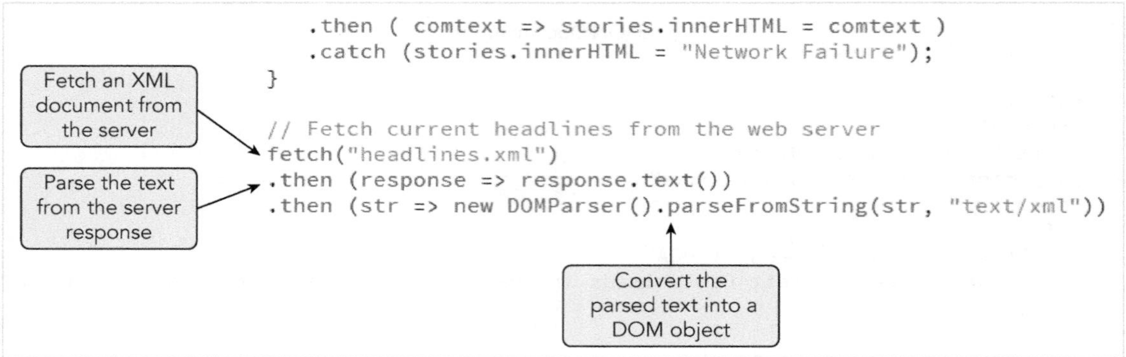

Figure 11-23 Loading and parsing an XML document

The content in the headlines.xml file has the following structure with one or more `item` elements nested within a newsfeed channel. Each item contains a headline, hypertext link, and a summary of a news story.

```
<rss version="2.0">
   <channel>
      <title>Newsfeed title</title>
      <description>Newsfeed description</title>
      <item>
         <title>Story Headline</title>
         <link>Story URL</link>
         <description>Story summary</description>
      </item>
…
   </channel>
</rss>
```

Each new story item needs to be converted to the following HTML structure and then appended to the web page sidebar:

```
<article>
   <h2><a href="Story URL">Story Headline</a></h2>
   <p>Story summary</p>
</article>
```

You can convert this structure by navigating through the nodes within the XML node tree using JavaScript's node properties and methods.

Working with an XML Node Tree

Because XML node trees are DOM objects, they are accessible to the same JavaScript methods used with an HTML DOM. You can create a node list using the `querySelectorAll()` method and use the `appendChild()` methods to create or move element nodes. Use JavaScript's node methods to convert the content of each news item into an HTML article.

To write the headlines into HTML articles:

1. Directly below the `then()` method that parses the XML document, add the following `then()` method to receive the XML DOM:

```
// Write the XML content to HTML
.then (dom => {
});
```

2. Within the anonymous arrow function, add the following statement creating a node list of all `item` elements in the XML DOM:

```
let items = dom.querySelectorAll("item");
```

3. Add the following statement to loop through all the elements in the `items` node list:

```
// Loop through each story item
for (let story of items) {
```

4. Within the `for` loop, add the following statement to extract the headline, link, and summary of each story:

```
// Write the story content and append it to the page
let headline = story.children[0].textContent;
let link = story.children[1].textContent;
let summary = story.children[2].textContent;
```

5. Add the following statement that uses a template literal to write the story content into an HTML fragment (be sure to use the backtick character ` to enclose the text string):

```
let htmlCode = `<article><h2><a href="${link}">${headline}</a></h2>
               <p>${summary}</p></article>`;
```

6. Complete the `for` loop by inserting the HTML code into the news sidebar:

```
news.insertAdjacentHTML("beforeend", htmlCode);
}
```

Figure 11-24 shows complete code of the final `then()` method.

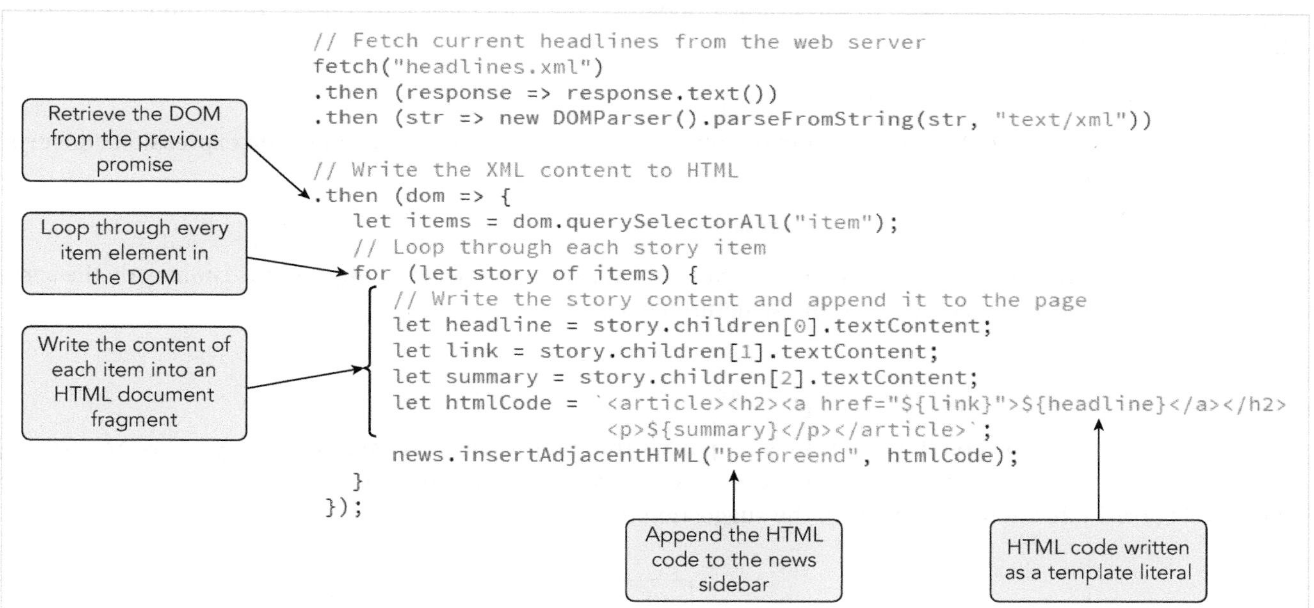

Figure 11-24 Converting XML content to HTML

7. Save your changes to the file and then reload the **js11.html** file from your web server. As shown in **Figure 11-25**, the sidebar displays the headlines retrieved from the headlines.xml document.

Note To keep the headlines current, enclose Fetch within the `setInterval()` method running requests and receiving responses at regular intervals.

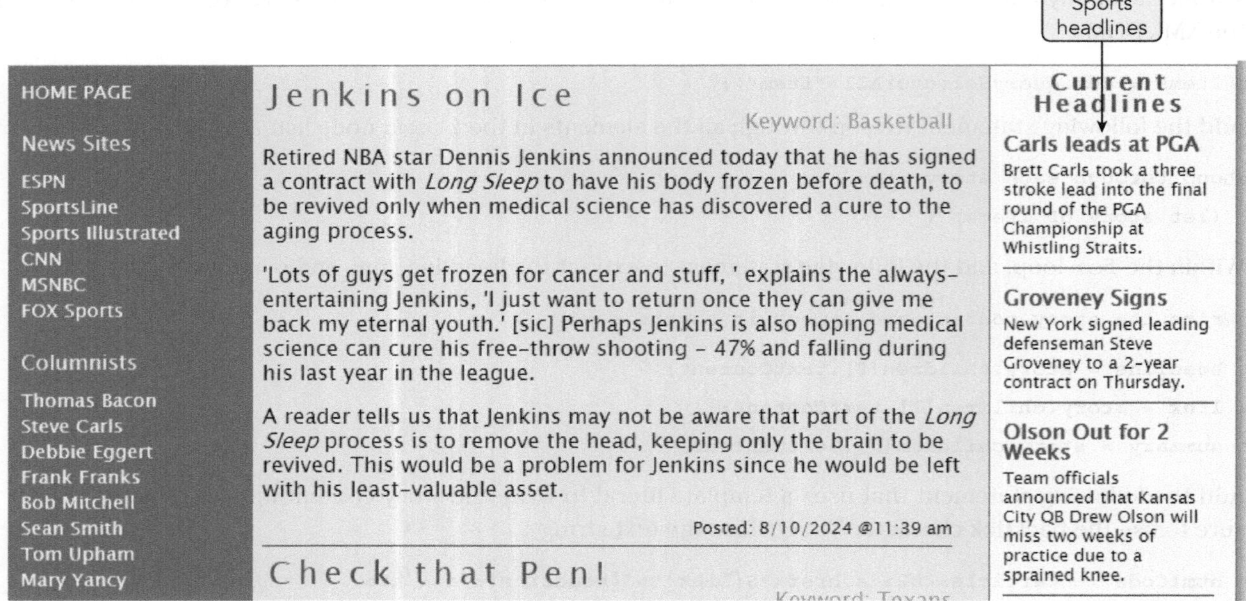
Sports headlines
HOME PAGE
News Sites
ESPN
SportsLine
Sports Illustrated
CNN
MSNBC
FOX Sports
Columnists
Thomas Bacon
Steve Carls
Debbie Eggert
Frank Franks
Bob Mitchell
Sean Smith
Tom Upham
Mary Yancy
Jenkins on Ice
Keyword: Basketball
Retired NBA star Dennis Jenkins announced today that he has signed a contract with Long Sleep to have his body frozen before death, to be revived only when medical science has discovered a cure to the aging process.
'Lots of guys get frozen for cancer and stuff, ' explains the always-entertaining Jenkins, 'I just want to return once they can give me back my eternal youth.' [sic] Perhaps Jenkins is also hoping medical science can cure his free-throw shooting - 47% and falling during his last year in the league.
A reader tells us that Jenkins may not be aware that part of the Long Sleep process is to remove the head, keeping only the brain to be revived. This would be a problem for Jenkins since he would be left with his least-valuable asset.
Posted: 8/10/2024 @11:39 am
Check that Pen!
Current Headlines
Carls leads at PGA
Brett Carls took a three stroke lead into the final round of the PGA Championship at Whistling Straits.
Groveney Signs
New York signed leading defenseman Steve Groveney to a 2-year contract on Thursday.
Olson Out for 2 Weeks
Team officials announced that Kansas City QB Drew Olson will miss two weeks of practice due to a sprained knee.

Figure 11-25 Headlines added to sidebar

JavaScript also supports the opposite operation by taking an XML DOM and converting it to a text string. To create a text string from a DOM, first create an XML Serializer object using the expression:

```
let serializer = new XMLSerializer();
```

where *serializer* is an object used to serializing a DOM. To convert a DOM into a text string, apply the following method to the serializer:

```
serializer.serializeToString(dom)
```

where *dom* is the node tree containing elements to convert to text. For example, the following expression converts a DOM into a text string:

```
new XMLSerializer().serializeToString(dom)
```

Once the DOM has been converted to a text string, it can be sent as text to a server where scripts running on the server can parse the string and work directly with the structured content.

Creating an Autocomplete Search Box

A problem with the search box on the sports blogger page is that there is no list of supported keywords. You will augment the search by adding an autocomplete feature providing a list of keywords based on characters typed into the search box. **Figure 11-26** shows a preview of the suggestion box in action.

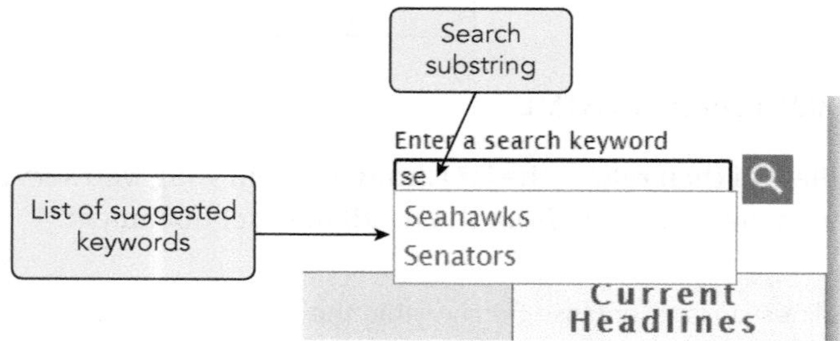
Search substring
Enter a search keyword
se
List of suggested keywords
Seahawks
Senators
Current Headlines

Figure 11-26 Suggested keywords displayed in the search box

The list of keyword suggestions is generated by the keywords.pl script running on the server. The URL to invoke this script is:

```
keywords.pl?suggest=substring
```

where *substring* is a substring of characters used by the script to generate suggestions. Before writing the JavaScript code to fetch this information, you must first edit the keywords.pl file so that it can access the perl.exe executable file on your server.

To edit the keywords.pl file:

1. Use your code editor to open the **keywords.pl** file from the js11 ► chapter folder on your server.
2. At the top of the page, change the first line to

```
#!location
```

   where *location* is the path to the perl.exe file on your server.

3. Close the file, saving your changes.
4. Open your browser and type the following in the following address box:

```
http://domain/path/keywords.pl?suggest=s
```

   where *domain* is the domain name of your server and *path* is the path to the keywords.pl file. The script returns a list of suggested keywords starting with the letter "s". See **Figure 11-27**.

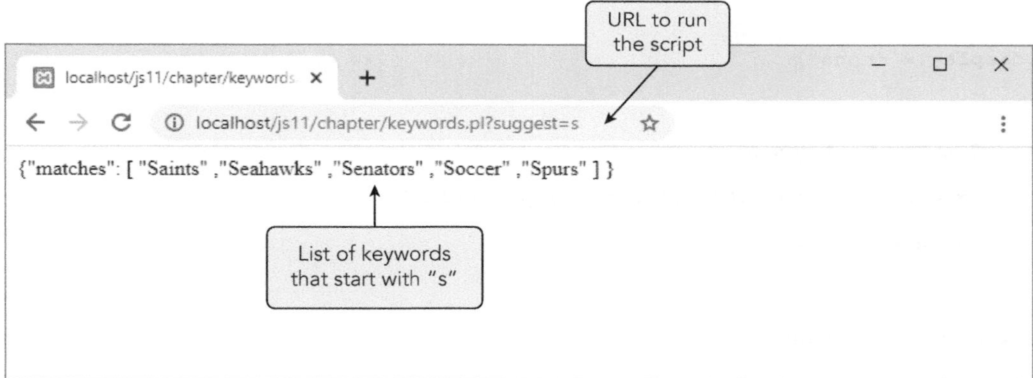

Figure 11-27 Accessing the keywords.pl script

5. Try other character strings to verify that the browser returns keywords starting with the suggested substring. Note that an empty list means that no keywords start with the suggest substrings. Not all character strings are matched by a list of keywords.

If you fail to get search results from the server script or get an error message, verify that you have specified the correct path to the perl.exe program in the keywords.pl file. Also verify that you have access privileges to the file and that your server is operating.

Working with JSON Data

The list of suggested keywords is returned in JSON format with individual suggestions stored in the `matches` array. For example, the substring "se" returns the following JSON string:

```
{
   "matches": ["Seahawks","Senators"]
}
```

To parse JSON text fetched from a server, apply the `json()` method to the Fetch response:

```
response.json()
```

Once parsed, the JSON data can be handled as an object literal. Add commands to the js11.js file to fetch keywords from the keywords.pl script based on characters entered in the search box. The `fetch()` method should be called with each `keyup` event occurring within the box.

To make a request to the keywords.pl file:

1. Return to the **js11.js** file loaded on your server.
2. Below the `then()` method that writes the newsfeed headlines to the web page, add the following `keyup` event handler for the search box:

```
// Suggest keywords as text is entered in the search box
sInput.onkeyup = () => {
}
```

3. Within the anonymous arrow function, add the following `if else` statements testing whether printable characters have been typed into the search box. If there are no printable characters, hide the suggestion box; otherwise fetch a list of keyword matches from the server and parse the response.

```
if (sInput.vaue === "") {
   suggestBox.style.display = "none";
} else {
   // Retrieve a list of matching keywords
   fetch("keywords.pl?suggest=" + encodeURIComponent(sInput.value))
   .then (response => response.json())
}
```

Figure 11-28 describes the code in the file.

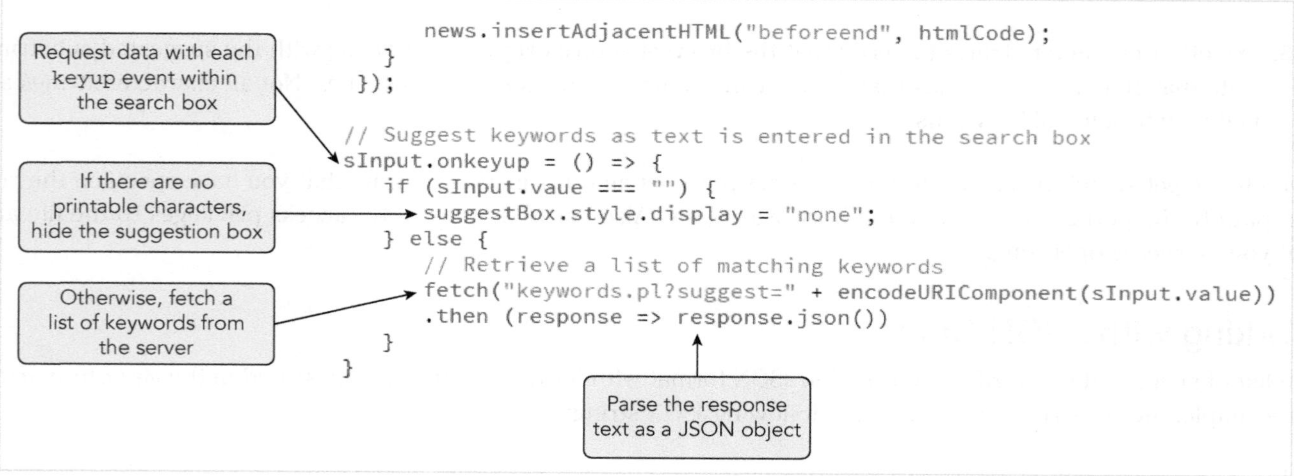

```
      news.insertAdjacentHTML("beforeend", htmlCode);
   }
});

// Suggest keywords as text is entered in the search box
sInput.onkeyup = () => {
   if (sInput.vaue === "") {
      suggestBox.style.display = "none";
   } else {
      // Retrieve a list of matching keywords
      fetch("keywords.pl?suggest=" + encodeURIComponent(sInput.value))
      .then (response => response.json())
   }
}
```


Figure 11-28 Requesting matching keywords from the server

Building the Suggestion Box

Once the JSON data has been retrieved and parsed, the JSON object can be used to write the following HTML code for a suggestion box:

```
<div id="suggestBox">
   <div class="suggestion">json.matches[0]</div>
   <div class="suggestion">json.matches[1]</div>
...
</div>
```

where *json*.matches[0], *json*.matches[1], and so on are the suggested keywords from the matches array. Styles for the div elements have already been defined in the CSS style sheet, you only need to build the structure of the suggestion box and append it to the web page.

To begin building the suggestion box:

1. Below the then() method, add another then() method that receives the keywords object containing the JSON data:

```
// Build the suggestion box
.then(keywords => {
   suggestBox.innerHTML = "";
})
```

2. Directly after the suggestBox.innerHTML statement add the following if else statement that tests whether there are any keyword matches. If there are none, hide the suggestion box; otherwise begin displaying the contents of the box.

```
if (keywords.matches.length === 0) {
   // No suggestions to display
   suggestBox.style.display = "none";
} else {
   // Display suggestions
   suggestBox.style.display = "block";
}
```

3. Within the else condition, add the following for loop writing a div element for every item in the matches array:

```
// Create a list of suggestions
for (let word of keywords.matches) {
   let suggestion = document.createElement("div");
   suggestion.textContent = word;
   suggestBox.appendChild(suggestion);
}
```

Figure 11-29 displays the code to create the box of suggested keywords.

```
// Suggest keywords as text is entered in the search box
sInput.onkeyup = () => {
   if (sInput.vaue === "") {
      suggestBox.style.display = "none";
   } else {
      // Retrieve a list of matching keywords
      fetch("keywords.pl?suggest=" + encodeURIComponent(sInput.value))
      .then (response => response.json())
      // Build the suggestion box
      .then(keywords => {
         suggestBox.innerHTML = "";
         if (keywords.matches.length === 0) {
            // No suggestions to display
            suggestBox.style.display = "none";
         } else {
            // Display suggestions
            suggestBox.style.display = "block";
            // Create a list of suggestions
            for (let word of keywords.matches) {
               let suggestion = document.createElement("div");
               suggestion.textContent = word;
               suggestBox.appendChild(suggestion);
            }
         }
      })
   }
}
```

If there are no suggestions, hide the suggestion box

Otherwise display the box

Write a `div` element for each suggestion

Figure 11-29 Building the suggestion box

4. Save your changes to the file and then reload the **js11.html** file using the server address.
5. Type **b** in the Search box and verify that a list of five matching keywords is displayed (see **Figure 11-30**).

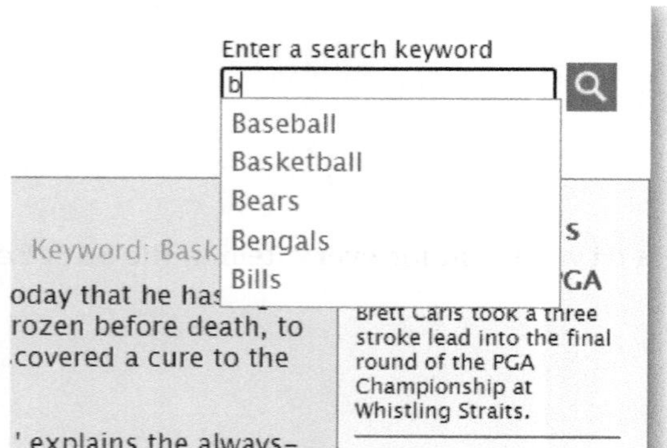

Figure 11-30 Viewing a list of keywords starting with "b"

6. Continue typing **be** and verify that the list is reduced to two entries (Bears and Bengals).
7. Type **ben** and verify that only Bengals is listed as a suggested keyword.

If the program does not display a list of keyword suggestions or reports an error, check your code against that shown in Figure 11-29. Common errors would include neglecting to close a command block with a closing curly brace or neglecting to close a `then()` method with a closing right parenthesis.

If a user clicks a suggested keyword, it should be added to search box and articles matching that keyword should be retrieved from the server. Add this feature to the app.

To add an `onclick` event handler to suggestions:

1. Return to the server's **js11.js** file in your code editor.
2. Directly after the command to append the suggestion to the `suggestBox` element, add the following event handler to (a) insert the word in the Search box, (b) hide the suggestion list, and (c) run the search using the Search box keyword.

```
// Add suggestion to search box when clicked
suggestion.onclick = () => {
   sInput.value = word;
   suggestBox.style.display = "none";
   sButton.click();
}
```

Figure 11-31 displays the final code added to the app.

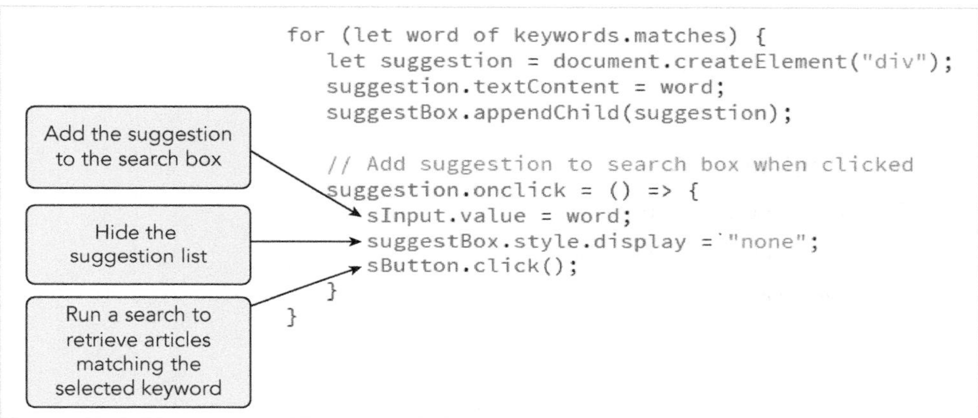

Figure 11-31 Creating an event handler for each picked suggestion

3. Save your changes to the file and then reload the **js11.html** file using the server address.
4. Type **a** in the Search box and then click **Astros** from the list of suggestions. Verify that the word "Astros" is added to the Search box and that the article titled "DL on DL" is retrieved from the server.

You have completed your work on the autocomplete suggestion box. At this stage in development there are only a few articles, but as more are added you will be able to make a more sophisticated tool for locating articles of interest to the reader.

Programming Concepts GET, POST, PUT, PATCH, and DELETE

The most common HTTP methods to use with Fetch are GET, POST, PUT, PATCH, and DELETE. Each method is associated with a specific type of database operation.

- The GET method is the default Fetch option, and it is used to retrieve server data. Because GET is limited to read-only operations there is no risk of modifying server content.
- The POST method sends data to the server, such as uploading the contents of a web form or adding a new user profile.
- The PUT method changes an existing data. PUT could be used to change the contents of an existing user profile.
- The PATCH method is like the PUT method in that it modifies existing data. The difference is that PUT replaces all the data, while PATCH only rewrites part of that data. The PATCH method would be used to modify part of a user profile.
- The DELETE method deletes data on the server, such as removing an entire user profile from an online database.

continued

Other than GET, the name of the method always needs to be included in the message body. For example, the following statement uses Fetch and the DELETE method to call a server script that deletes a user with the id "41088" from an online database:

```
fetch("https://example.com/deleteuser/41088", {
   method: "DELETE"
})
```

The deletion is handled by a server script; the DELETE method only tells that script to do it. Note that each method can return a response to the client. The DELETE method might return a response indicating the successful removal of the user data or it might reject the request to indicate that no such deletion can occur.

If you are building a database app in which clients can read, create, modify, or delete server data, you will rely on these different methods to create a clean and polished app. The Fetch API makes this task much easier.

Quick Check 3

1. Provide code to create an XML parser.
2. What method converts an XML text string into a DOM?
3. What method converts an XML DOM back into a text string?
4. What method parses JSON data received from a response object?
5. When would you use the PUT method in a Fetch request?

Working with Third-Party APIs

So far, the code for the sports blog relied on scripts provided by blog's host server. However, many websites augment their content with content provided by third parties that supply APIs that can be accessed via AJAX or Fetch. Many of these services are known as freemium services in which there is no cost to the developer if the requests are few. A freemium service helps developers evaluate the API without committing financial resources and makes the service available to smaller operations with low request volume. Once the developer's site moves out of the production phase and goes online, such services become premium services with monthly or annual charges based on traffic volume.

Requesting a Random GIF

The owners of the sports blog website want to enhance the site by attaching fun animated GIFs to their articles. Rather than create their own GIFs, they will use the website *Giphy.com* to retrieve a randomly generated GIF. Giphy supports an extensive library of over a million GIFs, stickers, emojis, and animated text indexed by content topic and image size. The Giphy API can be integrating into website apps so that developers can augment their apps with GIFs containing specific content. Giphy's API for developers is currently limited to 42 requests per hour and 1000 requests per day. Higher volumes require a paid subscription once developers move from testing a website to putting it into production for public use.

To request GIFs from *Giphy.com*, set up an account and get a beta API key now.

To set up a Giphy account:

1. Use your browser to open the website **https://developers.giphy.com/** and click the **Get Started** link to start working with the website.
2. Click on the **Login** link a create a new free account, specifying your email address, user name, and password.
3. Go to your dashboard page and create a new app using a beta API for developers to test the service.
4. Explore the Giphy website to learn about how to use the site to access GIFs for your own website.

Third-Party Endpoints

Third–party services like Giphy provide several different APIs organized by endpoint. An endpoint is the point of contact between the client device and a service resource; essentially an endpoint is the URL to which the request is made. Giphy provides endpoints including the following:

- *https://api.giphy.com/v1/gifs/trending* For GIFs trending upward in popularity
- *https://api.giphy.com/v1/gifs/search* For searching for GIFs by a keyword or phrase
- *https://api.giphy.com/v1/gifs/translate* To convert a keyword or phrase into a GIF
- *https://api.giphy.com/v1/gifs/random* To return a random GIF related to a keyword or phrase
- *http://upload.giphy.com/v1/gifs* To upload your own GIFs to the Giphy library

For this project you will use the *https://api.giphy.com/v1/gifs/random* endpoint, retrieving a GIF related to the search keyword entered by the user. The random GIF endpoint includes the following parameters for specifying the type of GIF to request:

- `api_key` The developer's API key required to access the Giphy library
- `tag` A keyword or phrase describing the GIF
- `limit` A numeric value specifying the number of GIFs to be retrieved
- `rating` The content rating of the GIF ranging from "g" (family friendly) to "r" (mature content)

For example, the following code encloses parameter values within a template literal to fetch a single family-friendly GIF related to the topic of golf. Information about the selected GIF is returned to the client as a JSON object.

```
let url = "https://api.giphy.com/v1/gifs/random";
let key = "Ft4wVVyKlRqRyPrsj6jUdDuZmJNcgpQ7";
fetch(`${url}?api_key=${key}&tag=golf&limit=1&rating=pg`)
.then(response => response.json())
```

Note It is good practice to store your API key and the endpoint URL as variables so that they can be used with other Fetch commands. Use template literals to avoid typing mistakes when entering the URL and query string of the requested endpoint.

You will add a function to the js11.js file that uses fetch to retrieve a random GIF on a specified topic.

To create a function for retrieving random GIFs:

1. Return to the **js11.js** file in your code editor.
2. Scroll to the bottom of the page and after the `init()` function insert the following `getGIF()` function to access the Giphy API and return one randomly chosen GIF based on the value of the `topic` parameter. Enter your own API key as the value of the `key` variable in your code.

```
// Fetch a GIF for a given topic from Giphy.com
function getGIF(topic) {
   const url = "https://api.giphy.com/v1/gifs/random";
   const key = "key";
   fetch(`${url}?api_key=${key}&tag=${topic}&limit=1&rating=pg`)
   .then(response => response.json())
}
```

Be sure to enclose the template literal text of the `fetch()` method within backtick (`) characters. See **Figure 11-32**.

Figure 11-32 Accessing the Giphy API

Giphy returns an extensive JSON object with detailed information on the GIF, its file size, dimensions, creation date, and so forth. For this project you only need to reference the URL of the file image, which is contained within the following reference:

```
json.data.images.fixed_height.url
```

where *json* is the name assigned to the JSON object fetched from the API. Add a `then()` method to fetch to create an `img` element with the GIF URL as the value of the `src` attribute and then append that image to the `stories` element.

To create a GIF image:

1. Add the following `then()` method to the `getGif()` function as shown in **Figure 11-33**.

```
.then(obj => {
   let newImg = document.createElement("img");
   newImg.src = obj.data.images.fixed_height.url;
   stories.appendChild(newImg)
})
```

```
// Fetch a GIF for a given topic from Giphy.com
function getGIF(topic) {
   const url = "https://api.giphy.com/v1/gifs/random";
   const key = "";
   fetch(`${url}?api_key=${key}&tag=${topic}&limit=1&rating=pg`)
   .then(response => response.json())
   .then(obj => {
     let newImg = document.createElement("img");
     newImg.src = obj.data.images.fixed_height.url;
     stories.appendChild(newImg)
   })
}
```

Create an img element

Retrieve the URL of the GIF and make it the source of the inline image

Append the image to the stories element

Figure 11-33 Appending the GIF as a page image

2. Scroll up the page to the anonymous function for the `sButton.onclick` event handler.
3. Between the `then()` and `catch()` methods, add another `then()` method that runs the `getGIF()` function using the value of the `sInput` element. Because the Giphy API requires all topic names to be lowercase, apply the `toLowerCase()` method to the keyword.

```
.then (() => {
   let topic = sInput.value.toLowerCase();
   getGIF(topic);
})
```

Figure 11-34 shows the newly added code in the anonymous function.

```
// Retrieve archived articles from the web server
sButton.onclick = () => {
   fetch("archives.pl?skey=" + encodeURIComponent(sInput.value))
   .then (response => {
      if (response.ok) {
         return response.text();
      } else {
         return "Unable to retrieve commentary";
      }
   })
   .then(comtext => stories.innerHTML = comtext )
   .then (() => {
      let topic = sInput.value.toLowerCase();
      getGIF(topic);
   })
   .catch ( stories.innerHTML = "Network Failure");
}
```

Retrieve the topic name in lowercase characters

Call the getGIF() function to display the GIF for that topic

Figure 11-34 Calling the `getGIF()` function

4. Close the file, saving your changes to the file.
5. Reload **js11.html** from its location on your web server. Enter **Golf** into the Search box to retrieve articles related to golf from the archives. Verify that the page also loads an animated GIF, displaying it below the Physician Heal Thyself article. See **Figure 11-35**. Note that your GIF will be different and each time you request the golf article a different GIF will appear.

Figure 11-35 Golf articles with random GIF

If the GIF fails to load, check your code. Common errors include mistakes in the Giphy API key, mistyping the Giphy endpoint, or syntax errors entered into Fetch. Check your debugger console for any network or HTTP error messages.

Exploring Security Issues with APIs

Browsers use the same-origin policy to ensure security in the exchange of data between different domains. However, third-party APIs like the APIs for Giphy or Google Maps do make such content available in an apparent violation of that policy. There are three approaches commonly used to manage the same-origin policy but still allow the transfer of data between websites of differing origins: CORS, JSONP, and XHR proxies.

Working with CORS

One way of allowing requests and responses to bypass their origins is to use Cross Origin Resource Sharing (CORS), which places information with the HTTP message header indicating that such transfers are allowed. To enable cross-origin requests, the CORS standard requires that the server hosting the resource include an `Access-Control-Allow-Origin` header in the HTTP message it sends to the requesting site, specifying that it can access data from the server. For example, the following HTTP header authorizes requests from the *example.com* website.

```
Access-Control-Allow-Origin: https://example.com
```

The *example.com* domain in this example is a fully qualified domain that can receive data without hindrance from the browser. To authorize requests from any domain, the header will employ the * wildcard character as follows:

```
Access-Control-Allow-Origin: *
```

If the API client needs to pass authentication headers or cookies, it must connect as a fully qualified domain. This policy is applied to prevent unauthorized content in the form of cookies from violating the same-origin policy. If the `Access-Control-Allow-Origin` header is missing or does not include the origin of the requesting site, the browser will forbid the request and an error message will appear in the browser console. Both `XMLHttpRequest` objects and the Fetch API follow the same-origin policy so that a web app can only request resources from the application's origin unless the response from the resource includes the required CORS header.

> **Note** If the same-origin policy is violated, the requested data will still be sent, but the browser will not allow JavaScript to access the response.

Using JSONP

CORS represents the newer standard for handling the same-origin problem. Prior to CORS, data transfer across origins was managed using JSONP, otherwise known as JSON with Padding. When developers began looking for ways to work around the same-origin policy for AJAX requests, they looked to one of the few HTML elements that is not subject to that policy: the `script` element. A web document can load a script from another domain, and it is left to the developer to ensure that any script loaded into an app is from a trusted source.

The `script` element calls an API running on a server from a different origin, which then returns request content in JSON format. Because the data is returned within the `script` element, the object is treated as the parameter for a callback function and the same-origin policy is not invoked. The callback function identified in the script receives a JSON object from the server, parses that object, and uses it within the app. The basic syntax of an HTML `script` element that employs the JSONP approach is:

```
<script src="resource?callback=function"></script>
```

where *resource* is the web address of the resource and *function* is the callback function that handles the JSON data returned by that resource. For example, Google Maps uses the JSONP approach to enable developers to access its mapping API via the following `script` element:

```
<script
src="https://maps.googleapis.com/maps/api/js?key=key&callback=func">
</script>
```

where *key* is the user's API key and *func* is the callback function that will receive the data from Google Maps. Many third-party APIs give developers the options of requesting data using AJAX, Fetch, or JSONP depending on the security needs of the developer.

JSONP is a popular solution to the same-origin policy because of its simplicity. However, you are still bringing executable code into your website from another location, so you must ensure that the API is not responding with malicious code. Always verify an API's trustworthiness and integrity before you use it. Another challenge with the JSONP approach is that there is no easy way of determining whether a request has failed and for what reason. Some developers nest the callback function within a `setTimeout()` method so they can notify the user of a failure to connect after a certain time limit has passed. However, such an approach might not consider slow connections due to low bandwidth rather than server failure. Finally, as the name implies, JSONP only works with data in the JSON format. It would not work with data stored as XML.

Using XHR with a Proxy

A final solution to the same-origin policy is to use a proxy server to handle the request for your site. Instead of requesting directly from the resource, make the request to another (proxy) server that *is* a trusted domain for the resource and that can then pass that information onto your app. Under this approach the app would then use an AJAX request object or Fetch to make the request of the proxy server and include parameters indicating the API that will manage the response. You can find proxy servers such as CORS-Anywhere to manage your requests. Be aware, however, that you will probably need to set up an account with the proxy server to utilize its features.

Skills at Work | Web Developer Job Titles and Roles

Web developers who work for large organizations often have a specific focus in both their job skills and responsibilities. The arena of web development can be divided up in several ways, but one of the most common is between developers who focus on client-side code and those who work on server-side code. A web developer who works primarily with HTML, CSS, and client-side JavaScript is known as a front-end developer. A developer who works mainly with server-side languages and libraries such as PHP, Perl, SQL, and Node.js is known as a back-end developer.

Increasingly web developers are sought who have skills and responsibility for both client-side and server-side code. These developers are known as full stack developers. Even if your goal is front-end development, it is important to attain at least basic familiarity with server-side issues and challenges. Both front-end and back-end developers need to be able to communicate to work together effectively and deliver a polished final product.

Quick Check 4

1. What is a freemium service?
2. What is an API endpoint?
3. What are three ways that an app can deal with the same-origin policy?

Summary

- Clients can request data from servers to augment existing web pages, receiving a response asynchronously.
- Information about the request and response is contained within the header and the body of an HTTP message.
- AJAX is an older technology used to create request objects that can be submitted to a server resource, receiving a response that can be parsed and added to a web page.
- A request from a server resource is monitored using the `readystatechange` event, which records when the response is complete, and the connection is successful.
- Apps based on AJAX can sometimes result in "callback hell" in which several asynchronous requests are nested within one another, resulting in confusing and unwieldy code.
- Arrow function syntax is often used to create concise code defining the parameters and statements associated with a function.
- A promise object is an object that does not have a current value but might have one in the future once the promise is settled.
- A promise chain is created by creating a sequence of `then()` methods concluding with a `catch()` method that catches any rejected promises.
- The Fetch API replaces AJAX by using promises to request and receive responses from server resources. Requests are made with the `fetch()` method; responses are handled with the `then()` and `catch()` methods.
- Data stored in an XML document is marked with tags similar to tags used with HTML documents. Data stored in an XML text string can be parsed and transformed into a node tree, at which point it can be manipulated using JavaScript node methods.
- A JSON data object must be parsed using the *`response`*`.json()` method before its contents can be used in a web app where *response* is the variable containing the response from the server.
- Third-party APIs often offer freemium services for which there is no cost to the developer for resource requests if the requests are few.
- To bypass the same-origin policy, third-party apps use Cross Origin Resource Sharing (CORS) to allow websites to access server resources across origins by placing messages in the header to identify fully qualified domains.
- JSON with padding or JSONP places requests for server resources within the `script` element, bypassing challenges with the same-origin policy.

Key Terms

arrow function
Asynchronous JavaScript and XML (AJAX)
asynchronous
back-end developer
caching
callback hell
Cross Origin Resource Sharing (CORS)
endpoint
executor
Extensible Markup Language (XML)
fat arrow
Fetch API
freemium service
front-end developer
fully qualified domain
full stack developer
HTTP function expression client
HTTP message
HTTP server
JSON with Padding (JSONP)
Perl
promise

promise chain
proxy server
request
response
RSS newsfeed
synchronous
XHR object
`XMLHttpRequest` object

Review Questions

1. Data is transferred via query strings using the ______________.
   a. PUT method
   b. POST method
   c. GET method
   d. QUERY method
2. The temporary storage of data on a local device is called ______________.
   a. asynchronous storage
   b. synchronous storage
   c. remote storage
   d. caching
3. Which of the following is not a part of the AJAX standard?
   a. JSON
   b. JavaScript
   c. Asynchronous communication
   d. XML
4. Which of the following methods instantiates a request object under AJAX?
   a. `new Request()`
   b. `new XMLHttpRequest()`
   c. `new XMLRequest()`
   d. `new XHR()`
5. An AJAX request to a server begins with which method?
   a. `send()`
   b. `connect()`
   c. `start()`
   d. `open()`
6. What code value is sent to the client to indicate that a response from the server is complete?
   a. 1
   b. 2
   c. 3
   d. 4
7. What is the arrow function version of the following anonymous function?

```
function(obj) {
   console.log(obj.name);
}
```

   a. `function (obj) => console.log(obj.name)`
   b. `obj => console.log(obj.name)`
   c. `obj => obj.name`
   d. `let obj => console.log(obj.name)`
8. Which of the following is not one of a promise's three states?
   a. Pending
   b. Settled
   c. Resolved
   d. Rejected
9. Resolved promises are managed by which method?
   a. `fetch()`
   b. `then()`
   c. `catch()`
   d. `resolve()`
10. To run several promises simultaneously, accepting only the first response, which method should be applied to the array of promise objects?
    a. `Promise.all()`
    b. `Promise.first()`
    c. `Promise.race()`
    d. `Promise.settled()`
11. What would be the final result of a successful response in the following Fetch code?

```
fetch("https://example.com/report")
.then (response => response.json())
.then (text => console.log(text.msg))
.catch (error => console.error(error))
```

    a. A response is received containing an HTTP message with the text of a JSON object in the message body.
    b. The content of the JSON text is parsed, creating an object literal.
    c. The text of the response message is written to the debugger console.
    d. An error message is sent to the error console.
12. Which method converts XML text into a DOM that is accessible to JavaScript's node methods?
    a. *response*`.json()`
    b. *text*`.stringify()`
    c. *response*`.xml()`
    d. *parser*`.parseFromStringify()`

13. Which method is used in Fetch to parse JSON data retrieved from a server resource?
    a. `response.parse()`
    b. `response.stringify()`
    c. `response.json()`
    d. `response.text()`
14. A service that is essentially free unless the developer exceeds a limit on the number of requests within a specified time is called a ______________.
    a. premium service
    b. freemium service
    c. testing service
    d. beta service
15. Which of the following does JSONP use to bypass the same-origin policy?
    a. A request object
    b. A `script` element
    c. A proxy server
    d. A promise object
16. What is the difference between a standard HTTP request and one that uses an `XMLHttpRequest` object?
17. When would you use arrow function syntax in place of a function declaration in your code?
18. Describe some of the differences between AJAX and Fetch.
19. What is callback hell?
20. Summarize the three methods for managing the same-origin policy between a client and a server resource.

Hands-On Projects

Note In some of the following projects you will have to place your project files on your own server and make modifications to server scripts to match your server's configuration. Talk to your instructor or technical resource desk if you are unsure about how to work with server-side scripts.

Hands-On Project 11-1

In this project you will use Fetch to retrieve the Astronomy Picture of the Day (APOD) from an API on the NASA website. The endpoint for retrieving either a picture or image has the URL:

```
https://api.nasa.gov/planetary/apod?api_key=DEMO_KEY&date=date
```

where *date* is the date of the photo to be retrieved from the NASA APOD archive. The API key, "DEMO_KEY" is free to the public but is limited to 30 requests per hour with a total of 50 requests per day. If you are not sure how many requests you have left, view the `X-RateLimit-Remaining` value in the HTTP header of the response object. The APOD API returns a JSON object in which the name of the picture is given by `json.title`, a description is stored in `json.explanation`, and the picture source is stored in `json.url`. The picture of the day can be either an image file or a video file. The file type is stored in `json.media_type`. **Figure 11-36** shows a preview of the web page with a picture for a specified date.

Do the following:

1. Use your code editor to open the **project11-01_txt.html** and **project11-01_txt.js** files from the js11 ► project01 folder. Enter your name and the date in the comment section of each file and save them as **project11-01.html** and **project11-01.js**, respectively.
2. Go to the **project11-01.html** file in your code editor. Add a `script` element linked to the project11-01js file. Defer the loading of the script until after the page is loaded. Close the file, saving your changes.

Hands-on Project 11-1

Astronomy Picture of the Day

Picture Date 02/08/2021

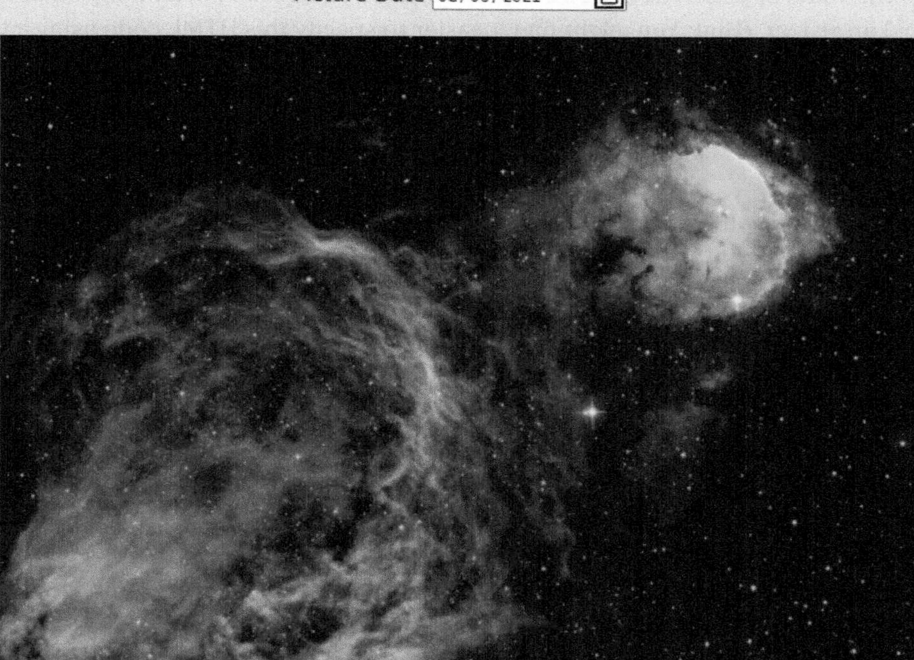

WR23 and Interstellar Clouds in Carina

Stars can be like artists. With interstellar gas as a canvas, a massive and tumultuous Wolf-Rayet star has created the picturesque ruffled half-circular filaments called WR23, on the image left. Additionally, the winds and radiation from a small cluster of stars, NGC 3324, have sculpted a 35 light year cavity on the upper right, with its right side appearing as a recognizable face in profile. This region's popular name is the Gabriela Mistral Nebula for the famous Chilean poet. Together, these interstellar clouds lie about 8,000 light-years away in the Great Carina Nebula, a complex stellar neighborhood harboring numerous clouds of gas and dust rich with imagination inspiring shapes. The featured telescopic view captures these nebulae's characteristic emission from ionized sulfur, hydrogen, and oxygen atoms mapped to the red, green, and blue hues of the popular Hubble Palette. New: APOD now available in Bulgarian from Bulgaria

Figure 11-36 Completed Project 11-1

3. Go to the **project11-01.js** file in your code editor. Within the anonymous function for the `dateBox.onchange` event handler, add the following:

   a. Declare the `dateStr` variable and set it equal to the value of the `dateBox` element.

   b. Use the `fetch()` method to make a request to the following url:

      `https://api.nasa.gov/planetary/apod?api_key=DEMO_KEY&date=`*`dateStr`*

      where *`dateStr`* is the value of the `dateStr` variable.

   c. Add a `then()` method that takes a successful response and applies the `json()` method to the response object to parse the JSON text string.

   d. Add a `then()` method that receives the JSON object and runs the `showPicture()` method with the JSON object as the parameter value.

   e. Add a `catch()` method that displays the text of the rejected promise in the debugger console.

4. Create a function named `showPicture()` with a single parameter named `json`. Within the function create an `if else` structure that tests the following conditions:

   a. If `json.media_type` equals "video" then change the inner HTML of the `imageBox` element to the following:

   ```
   <iframe src="url"></iframe><h1>title</h1><p>explanation</p>
   ```

   where *`url`* is the value of `json.url`, *`title`* is the value of `json.title`, and *`explanation`* is the value of `json.explanation`. (Hint: You might find it easier to specify this HTML code using a template literal.)

   b. If `json.media_type` equals "image" then change the inner HTML of the `imageBox` element to the following:

   ```
   <img src="url"/><h1>title</h1><p>explanation</p>
   ```

   c. Otherwise, change the inner HTML of the `imageBox` element to the text string: "Image not Available".

5. Save your changes to the file and then open **project11-01.html** in your web browser. Select a date from the Picture Date input box and verify that an image or video requested from the NASA APOD service for that date appears in the web page.

Hands-On Project 11-2

In this project you will create an interactive form that retrieves the place name and region for a given country and postal code. The place name and region values are accessed from an API at the following URL:

```
http://api.zippopotam.us/country/postal
```

where *`country`* is the country code and *`postal`* is the postal code. The API returns a JSON object containing information about the place and region corresponding to the postal code. The following is sample JSON output for the United States (US) and the postal code 90210.

```
{
  "post code": "90210",
  "country": "United States",
  "country abbreviation": "US",
  "places": [
    {
      "place name": "Beverly Hills",
      "longitude": "-118.4065",
      "state": "California",
      "state abbreviation": "CA",
      "latitude": "34.0901"
    }
  ]
}
```

Because the places and state names include spaces, you have to use the bracket form in place of the dot form to reference those properties. Use `json.places[0]["place name"]` to reference the place name and `json.places[0]["state abbreviation"]` to reference the state. A preview of the completed project is shown in **Figure 11-37**.

Do the following:

1. Use your code editor to open the **project11-02_txt.html** and **project11-02_txt.js** files from the js11 ► project02 folder. Enter your name and the date in the comment section of each file and save them as **project11-02.html** and **project11-02.js**, respectively.

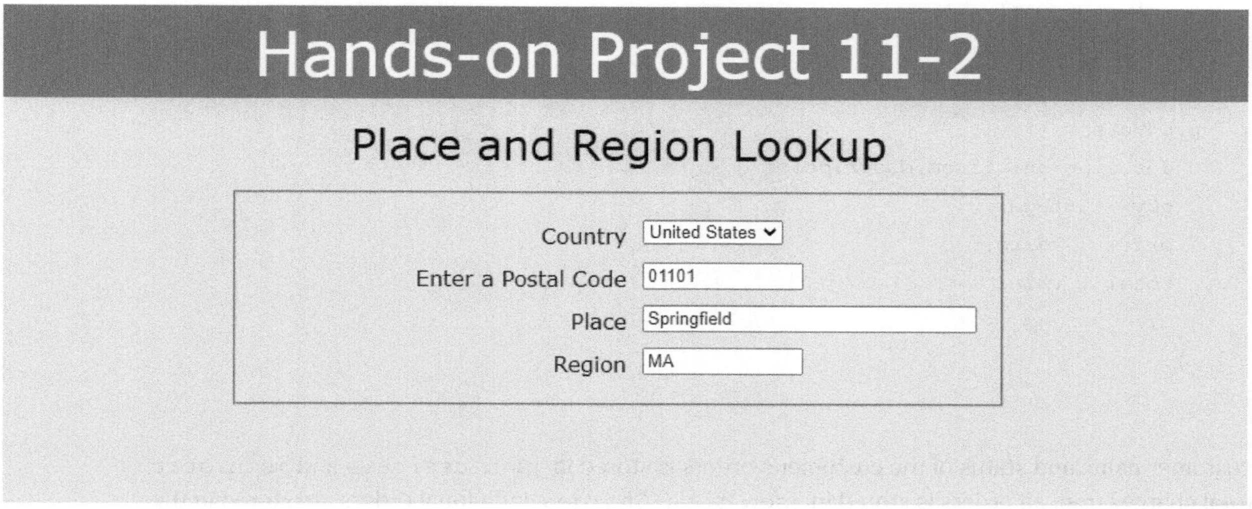

Figure 11-37 Completed Project 11-2

2. Go to the **project11-02.html** file in your code editor. Add a `script` element linked to the project11-02.js file. Defer the loading of the script until after the page is loaded. Take some time to study the content and structure of the document and then close the file, saving your changes.
3. Go to the **project11-02.js** file in your code editor. Within the anonymous function for the `postalCode.onblur` event handler, add the following:
   a. Declare the `codeValue` and `countryValue` variables setting them equal to the value of the `postalCode` and `country` elements, respectively.
   b. Set the value of the `place` and `region` elements to an empty text string.
   c. Use Fetch to access the API at

      `http://api.zippopotam.us/`*`country`*`/`*`code`*

      where *`country`* is the value of the `countryValue` variable and *`code`* is the value of the `codeValue` variable.
   d. When the Fetch promise is returned, add a `then()` method to parse the JSON response object.
   e. Add another `then()` method using an arrow function with a single parameter named json. Set the value of the place element to place property for the postal code and the region element to the state abbreviation property.
   f. If the response is rejected, write the error text to the console log.
4. Save your changes to the file and then open the **project11-02.html** file in your browser. Enter the postal code **01101** in the Postal Code box and press the Tab key. Verify that Springfield, MA, appears as the place and region.
5. Select **Spain** from the Country list box and enter **30151** in the Postal Code box. Verify that Santo Angel, MU, appears as the place and region.

Hands-On Project 11-3

In this project you will complete an app that retrieves customer orders for *Wizard Works*, a manufacturer of brand name fireworks and pyrotechnics. The app connects to a script named wworders.pl on your web server. Customers send user id and password information to the server script and the script responds with the following JSON object containing information on the customer's order:

```
{
  username : "name",
  status :  "order status",
  totalCharges : amount
```

```
    orderHistory : [{
      orderDate : date,
      orderCost : value,
      products : [{
        description: "item description",
        qty : integer,
        price : value,
        total : value
      } ...]
    } ...]
  }
```

The customer name and status of the customer's orders is stored in `json.username` and `json.status`. The total charges from all orders is stored in `json.totalCharges`. Individual orders are stored in the `json.orderHistory` array. Each order in the array contains information about the date of the order and the total cost of the order. Items purchased within each order are stored in the `json.orderHistory.items` array. Each item in that array contains an object with the product's description, quantity ordered, price, and total cost.

You will add this information in table form to the web page. **Figure 11-38** shows a preview of the completed web page for sample customer.

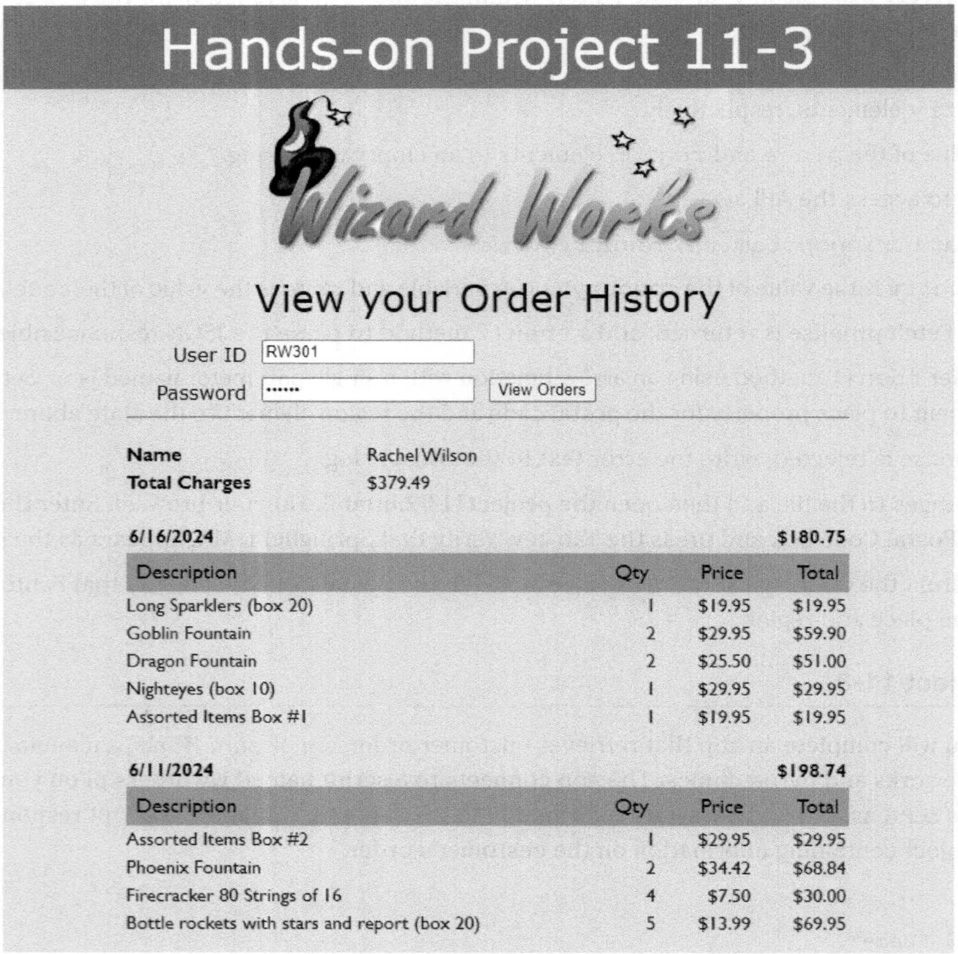

Hands-on Project 11-3

Wizard Works

View your Order History

User ID RW301

Password •••••• View Orders

Name	Rachel Wilson
Total Charges	$379.49

6/16/2024 **$180.75**

Description	Qty	Price	Total
Long Sparklers (box 20)	1	$19.95	$19.95
Goblin Fountain	2	$29.95	$59.90
Dragon Fountain	2	$25.50	$51.00
Nighteyes (box 10)	1	$29.95	$29.95
Assorted Items Box #1	1	$19.95	$19.95

6/11/2024 **$198.74**

Description	Qty	Price	Total
Assorted Items Box #2	1	$29.95	$29.95
Phoenix Fountain	2	$34.42	$68.84
Firecracker 80 Strings of 16	4	$7.50	$30.00
Bottle rockets with stars and report (box 20)	5	$13.99	$69.95

Figure 11-38 Completed Project 11-3

Do the following:

1. Use your code editor to open the **project11-03_txt.html** and **project11-03_txt.js** files from the js11 ▶ project03 folder. Enter your name and the date in the comment section of each file and save them as **project11-03.html** and **project11-03.js**, respectively.
2. Go to the **project11-03.html** file in your code editor. Add a `script` element linked to the project11-03.js file. Defer the loading of the script until after the page is loaded. Close the file, saving your changes.
3. Open the **wworders.pl** file in your code editor. Edit the initial line to read as follows:

```
#!location
```

   where *`location`* is the location and name of the perl.exe executable file on your server. See your instructor or technical support person for assistance in locating the perl.exe file on your server. Close the file, saving your changes.
4. Copy the js11 ▶ project03 folder and upload it to a folder on your server. For XAMPP, place the files in a new subfolder of the `htdocs` folder where your version of XAMPP is installed. In Nginx, the folder name is `html`. For IIS, the default folder is `wwwroot`. If you are using a server provided by your instructor or using different server software, consult the server documentation to determine the folder in which website pages should be stored.

   At this point, the rest of your work should be done with files on the server.
5. Go to the **project11-03.js** file in your code editor. Within the anonymous function for the `viewOrders.onclick` event handler, add the following:
   a. Declare the `user` and `pwd` variables with values equal to the value of the `userIDBox` and `pwdBox` elements, respectively.
   b. Use Fetch to connect to `wworders.pl?id=`*`user`*`&pwd=`*`pwd`* where *`user`* is the value of the `user` variable and *`pwd`* is the value of the `pwd` variable.
   c. When the Fetch promise is returned, add a `then()` method to parse the JSON response object.
   d. Add another `then()` method to run the `buildOrderTable()` function using the json object as the parameter value.
   e. If the response is rejected, write the error text to the console log.
6. Go to the `buildOrderTable()` function. Within the function insert an `if else` structure that tests whether `obj.status` is equal to "Orders Not Found". If it is, change the inner HTML of the `orderResult` element to the text string "No orders found for this user id and password". Otherwise, do the tasks in Steps 7 through 9.
7. Within the `else` condition, declare a variable named `htmlCode` setting its initial value to the following text string.

```
<table id="summary"><tr><th>Name</th><td>username</td>
<tr><th>Total Charges</th><td>totalCharges</td></tr></table>
```

   where *`username`* is the value of `obj.username` and *`totalCharges`* is the value of `obj.totalCharges`.
8. Add a `for` loop to the `else` condition that loops through the contents of the `obj.orderHistory` array, creating a separate table for each order. With each iteration of the loop, do the following:
   a. Add the following text string to the value of the `htmlCode` variable:

```
<table class="orderList"><tr><th colspan="2">date</th>
<th colspan="2">cost</th></tr><tr><th>Description</th>
<th>Qty</th><th>Price</th><th>Total</th></tr>
```

   where *`date`* is the value of `orderDate` property for the current order in the `orderHistory` array and *`cost`* is the value of the `orderCost` property for the current order.

b. Information about the products ordered is displayed in separate rows of the orderList table. Within the `for` loop, nest another `for` loop that iterates through the contents of the `products` array for the current order and for each item in the `products` array, add the following text string to the value of the `htmlCode` variable:

```
<tr><td>description</td><td>qty</td><td>price</td>
<td>total</td></tr>
```

where *`description`*, *`qty`*, *`price`*, and *`total`* are the values of the `description`, `qty`, `price`, and `total` properties for the current item in the `products` array.

c. After the nested `for` loop is finished, add the text string "`</table>`" to the `htmlCode` variable to close off the orderList table.

9. After the outer `for` loop is finished but still within the `else` condition, write the value of the `htmlCode` variable as the inner HTML of the `orderResult` element.

10. Save your changes to the file.

11. Use your browser to open the project11-03.html file from its location on your server.

12. Verify that you can display order history for Wizard Works customers by submitting the following User ID/ Password combinations to the web form: **RW301/kaboom** and **BA684/sparkler**.

13. Verify that if you enter any other combination of user id and password, the page displays the message "No orders found for this user id and password".

Hands-On Project 11-4

In this project you will use your computer's position along with a third-party app to determine the current level of sun safety for your location. The app to return UV and ozone values for your position has the endpoint:

```
https://api.openuv.io/api/v1/uv?lat=lat&lng=lng
```

where *`lat`* is the latitude and *`lng`* is the longitude. The API returns a wealth of solar data related to sun safety and exposure times before burning. The content you are interested is stored within the following JSON object:

```
{result: {
   uv: value,
   uv_max: value,
   ozone: value,
   safe_exposure_time : {
     st1: value,
     st2: value,
     st3: value,
     st4: value,
     st5: value,
     st6: value
   }
}
```

Once you have retrieved and parsed this data and determined your latitude and longitude, you will display the sun safety information in the tables shown in **Figure 11-39**.

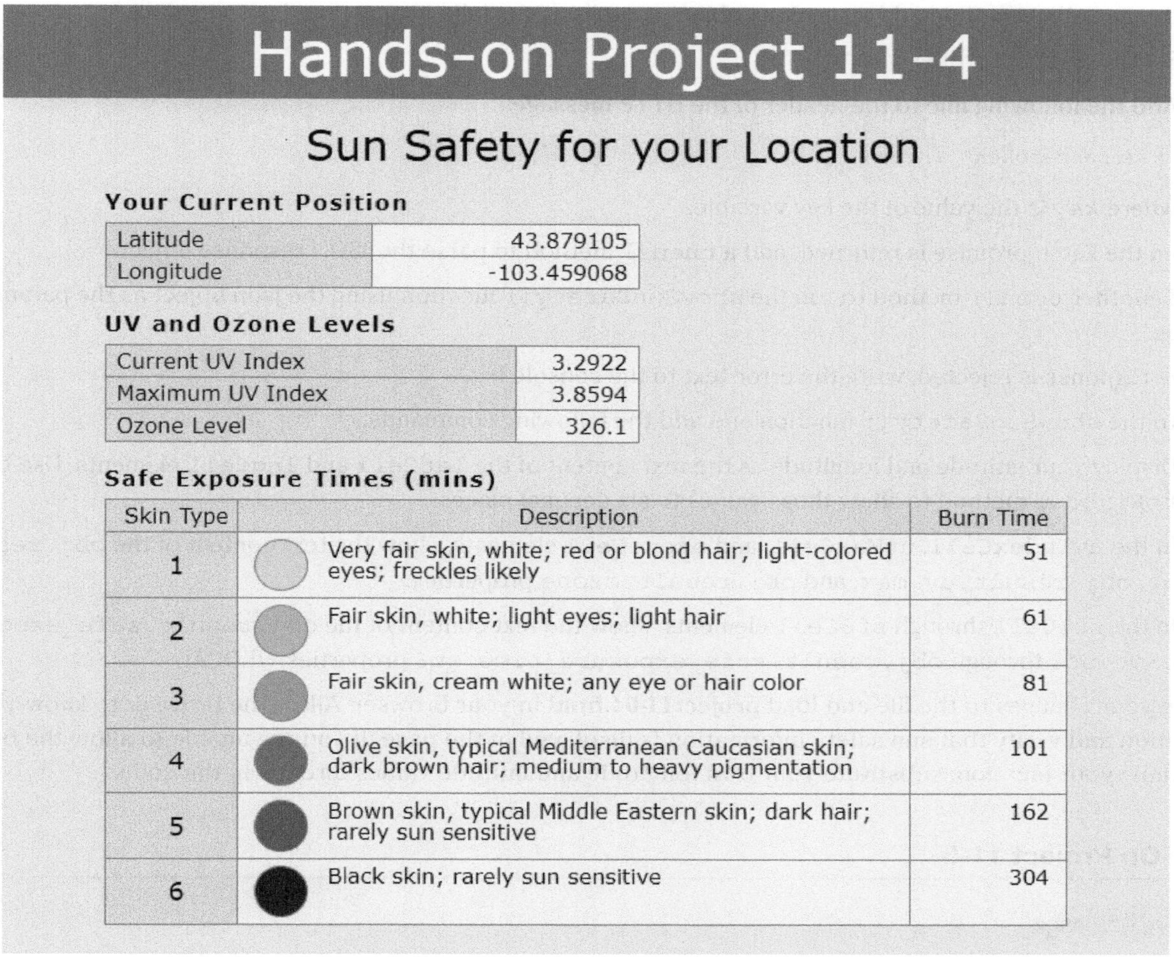

Hands-on Project 11-4

Sun Safety for your Location

Your Current Position

Latitude	43.879105
Longitude	-103.459068

UV and Ozone Levels

Current UV Index	3.2922
Maximum UV Index	3.8594
Ozone Level	326.1

Safe Exposure Times (mins)

Skin Type	Description	Burn Time
1	Very fair skin, white; red or blond hair; light-colored eyes; freckles likely	51
2	Fair skin, white; light eyes; light hair	61
3	Fair skin, cream white; any eye or hair color	81
4	Olive skin, typical Mediterranean Caucasian skin; dark brown hair; medium to heavy pigmentation	101
5	Brown skin, typical Middle Eastern skin; dark hair; rarely sun sensitive	162
6	Black skin; rarely sun sensitive	304

Figure 11-39 Completed Project 11-4

Do the following:

1. Use your code editor to open the **project11-04_txt.html** and **project11-04_txt.js** files from the js11 ▶ project04 folder. Enter your name and the date in the comment section of each file and save them as **project11-04.html** and **project11-04.js**, respectively.
2. Go to the **project11-04.html** file in your code editor. Add a `script` element linked to the project11-04.js file. Defer the loading of the script until after the page is loaded. Take some time to study the contents and structure of the document and then close the file, saving your changes.
3. Go to the Open UV Index API website at *https://www.openuv.io/* and register for an API key. The API key is free but limited to 50 requests per day. You will not need to supply payment information, but you will need an email account to receive the key.
4. Once you have received the key, return to the **project11-04.js** file in your code editor. Go to the `getLocation()` function and within the function complete the tasks in Steps 5 through 10.
5. Declare the `url` variable and set its value equal to "https://api.openuv.io/api/v1/uv". Declare the `key` variable and set its value equal to the key you received from the Open UV Index API website.
6. Use Fetch to connect to request UV data from the endpoint `url?lat=lat&lng=lng` where *`url`* is the value of the `url` variable, *`lat`* is the value of the `myPosition.lat` object and *`lng`* is the value of `myPosition.lng`.

7. To the `fetch()` method add an options object containing the following properties and values:
   a. Set the `method` property to "GET".
   b. Add the following line to the header of the HTTP message:

   ```
   "x-access-token" : key
   ```

   where *key* is the value of the key variable.
8. When the Fetch promise is returned, add a `then()` method to parse the JSON response object.
9. Add another `then()` method to run the `showSunSafety()` function using the json object as the parameter value.
10. If the response is rejected, write the error text to the console log.
11. Go to the `showSunSafety()` function and add the following commands:
    a. Display your latitude and longitude as the text content of the `latCell` and `lngCell` elements. Use the `toFixed()` method to show those values to six decimal places.
    b. In the `uvIndexCell`, `uvMaxCell`, and `ozoneCell` elements, show the text content of the `obj.result.uv`, `obj.result.uv_max`, and `obj.result.ozone` properties.
    c. In the `st1Cell` through `st6Cell` elements, show the text content of the `obj.result.safe_exposure_time.st1` through `obj.result.safe_exposure_time.st6` properties.</EOCAL>
12. Save your changes to the file and load **project11-04.html** in your browser. Allow the browser to know your location and verify that sun safety information is displayed in the page. If you are unable to allow the browser to know your location, substitute your own longitude and latitude values directly in the code.

Hands-On Project 11-5

Debugging Challenge

You have been given a website for a science fiction (SF) author's book review and commentary. The website draws content from three sources on the server: (1) archived book reviews stored as text in the sfreviews.pl file, (2) a list of popular SF authors stored in JSON format in authorlist.json file, and (3) a newsfeed describing recent SF podcasts stored in the sfpod.xml file. Unfortunately, the web page is unable to access the files and render them correctly. Use your knowledge of requests and responses to fix the errors in the code. A preview of the corrected page is shown in **Figure 11-40**.

Do the following:

1. Use your code editor to open the **project11-05.html** and **project11-05.js** files from the js11 ► project05 folder. Enter your name and the date in the comment section of each file and save them as **project11-05.html** and **project11-05.js**, respectively.
2. Go to the **project11-05.html** file in your code editor and add a `script` element linked to the project11-05.js file. Defer the loading of the script until after the page is loaded. Take some time to study the contents and structure of the file, saving your changes.
3. Open the **sfreviews.pl** file in your code editor. Edit the initial line to read as follows:

   ```
   #!location
   ```

   where *location* is the location and name of the perl.exe executable file on your server. See your instructor or technical support person for assistance in locating the perl.exe file on your server. Close the file, saving your changes.
4. Copy the js11 ► project05 folder and upload it to a folder on your server. Consult the server documentation to determine the folder in which website pages should be stored.

Hands-on Project 11-5

Welcome to the SF Control Room

I started this blog in order to share my latest fiction with my readers and to post reviews and comments on the world of Science Fiction and Fantasy. From time to time, we'll have interviews with other great authors in the Sci-Fi and Fantasy markets as well as give you the inside scoop on upcoming conventions.

Archived Reviews by Author

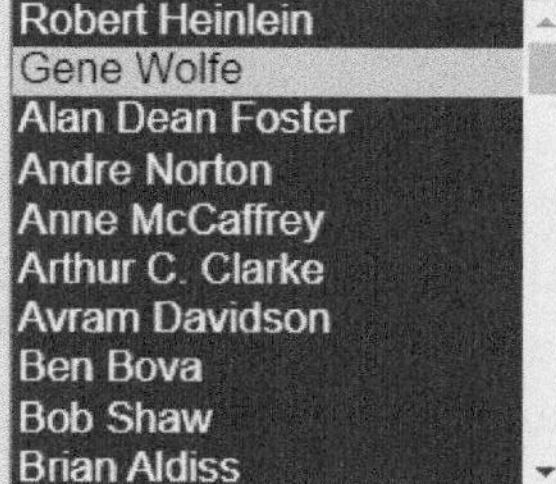

The Shadow of the Torturer
by Gene Wolfe

In Short: The first part of the classic 4-part series set in a distant fantastical future

4 Stars

Set on Earth (Urth) perhaps millions of years into the future; Gene Wolfe introduces us to one of the most interesting characters in the history of science fiction, a young torturer named Severian. Severian serves out his apprenticeship in the Matachin Tower, which astute readers will realize is a grounded spaceship (Severian is unaware of this and unaware of other artifacts of a long-dead powerful civilization.) But the residues of technology are secondary in interest to the journeys of Severian, as he wanders Urth after being exiled for committing the crime of mercy.

Wolfe draws upon a rich literary tradition in constructing his novel. The opening chapter is reminiscent of the opening of Great Expectations and I could spot dozens of classic allusions scattered across each chapter. Wolfe's language is exquisite. With many terms based on Latin or Greek, all with a phenomenal rightness to what they identify or - often - suggest. Badelaire, lansquenet, amchasphand, chrisos, orichalk, pinakothek, salpinx, ephor ... and the tricky thing is that every now and then one of them is a real word . The novel highlights Wolfe's wonderful command of language and enriches the tapestry of this deep and penetrating work.

Don't be put off by that preceding paragraph. The novel is as fun, exciting, and engrossing as any potboiler. Note that this is the first book in the series, The Book of the New Sun. I know of no better or more literate series in the history of science fiction.

Control Room #4
Kevin looks at science fiction in the digital age and the impact on online media on science fiction magazines and fanzines. Kevin will also read the first half of his new novelette, Null Gateway.

Control Room #3
Kevin discusses the early days of the pulps with science fiction historian, critic, and author, Fredric Ogletree.

Control Room #2
Kevin reads an excerpt from his new novelette, The Wages of Sin, and a science essay, I am an Emergent Phenomenom. Kevin will also review the latests novel by K.D. Wilson and the new sf movie, Blaster Force (it stinks).

Control Room #1
Kevin Vinter introduces a new podcast with a packed program of readings and interviews from the world of science fiction. Kevin reads an extended excerpt from his Hugo awarding-winning novel, The Long Sleep and provides backstory on the writing of this sf classic.

Figure 11-40 Completed Project 11-5

5. Go to the **project11-05.js** file in your code editor. Fix the following mistakes in the file:
   a. In the statement that fetches the list of authors from the `authorlist.json` file, there is a mistake in the `fetch()` statement.
   b. Fix the mistake in the `then()` method that uses an arrow function to parse the response from the server.
   c. In the `fetch()` statement that retrieves reviews of books in the `sfreviews.pl` file, there is a mistake in formatting the query string.
   d. The reviews should be returned as text string, but there is a mistake in the `then()` method that parses the text content.
   e. Scroll down to the `then()` statement that parses the XML content from the `sfpod.xml` file, creating a DOM node list. There is a mistake in defining the `Parser` object.
   f. In the `for` loop that writes the summary of the podcasts, there is a mistake in the template literal that writes the HTML code.
6. Save your changes to the file and then load **project11-05.html** in your web browser from your web server location.

7. Verify the following in the completed page:
    a. Verify that a list of SF authors appears in a selection list next to book review.
    b. Verify that four podcast summaries are displayed on the right edge of the page.
    c. Verify that when you click **Robert Heinlein** or **Gene Wolfe** from the list of authors, the page retrieves a review of one of their novels.

Case Projects

Individual Case Project

Identify data provided by an API that you would like to include in your personal website. You should choose a web service other than those used in the chapter and the Hands-on Projects. If you have an idea for data you'd like to access but are unsure what service might provide that data, perform a web search on a description of the data plus "API". For instance, if you were looking for a source of tide tables, you might search for "tide tables API". Use the documentation for the web service to construct a Fetch request and to display selected data from the service on your website.

Team Case Project

Identify data provided by an API that you would like to include in your group website. You should choose a web service other than those used in the chapter, the Hands-on Projects, or the Individual Case Project of any group member. If you have an idea for data you'd like to access but are unsure what service might provide that data, perform a web search on a description of the data plus "API". For instance, if you were looking for a source of tide tables, you might search for "tide tables API". Use the documentation for the web service to construct a Fetch request and to display selected data from the service on your website.

CHAPTER 12

Introducing jQuery

When you complete this chapter, you will be able to:

- Use the jQuery library to apply jQuery methods to a selection of elements
- Modify the contents and structure of the DOM using jQuery
- Manage browser events using jQuery
- Create effects and animations using jQuery methods
- Apply jQuery Plugins, such as jQuery UI, to create specialized animations

---

Developers often find themselves reusing the same sets of code across multiple projects. That code provides a foundation for future projects, saving the developer time and effort. The most useful sets of JavaScript code can be organized into a JavaScript library where they can be quickly applied to a wide variety of projects and applications. Some JavaScript libraries are provided to the public for free. Perhaps the most successful of these free libraries is jQuery, which is a library enabling developers to implement many common JavaScript tasks with minimal coding. In this chapter, you will learn what jQuery can do and how you can use it in your projects.

Getting Started with jQuery

A challenge for developers in the early years of the web was that different browsers implemented JavaScript in different ways. The two competing standards were promoted by the Netscape and Internet Explorer browsers. Among other differences, the two browsers took fundamentally different approaches in referencing page objects, managing events, and handling server requests. For any JavaScript app to be truly compatible across browsers, a way had to be found to reconcile those differences. Several JavaScript libraries were proposed for this purpose. The most popular of these libraries was jQuery.

> **Note** | jQuery was designed to run the same on all browsers, which was the biggest part of its appeal.

The jQuery library is a concise set of tools that simplifies commonly needed tasks with a minimum of coding. The core features supported by jQuery are:

- **DOM manipulation** jQuery makes it easier to navigate the document's node tree, reference elements by their CSS selector, and to create and remove elements from the web page.
- **Event management** jQuery provides tools to handle browser and user events that makes it easier to write event-driven code.
- **Animation effects** jQuery supports a large collection of animation effects to enhance user interaction with any website or web app.
- **Widgets** jQuery provides a collection of widgets such as photo slideshows, calendars, and web form controls that can be incorporated into almost any website.
- **AJAX** jQuery makes it easy to create and apply AJAX requests and responses.

In addition to these core features, there are collections of jQuery plugins created by third-party programmers providing more tools to the frontend developer. There are plugins to support social media forums, run online videos, design flexible page layouts, and create scrolling slideshows, among other things. You can find libraries of jQuery plugins by doing a search on the web or on the jQuery website.

Versions of jQuery

From its initial release in August 2006, jQuery has gone through several releases, some of which are described in **Figure 12-1**.

VERSION	RELEASE DATE	DESCRIPTION
1.0	August 2006	First stable release
1.9	January 2013	Removal of deprecated features and code cleanup
2.0	April 2013	Dropped support for IE 6 through IE8 to improve performance and reduce file size
3.0	June 2016	Support for promises and compatible with HTML5, provided a slim version of the library
3.2	March 2017	Added support for template elements, deprecation of older features
3.4	May 2019	Performance improvements and security fixes
3.5	May 2020	Security fixes, `.even()` and `.odd()` methods, deprecation of older features

Figure 12-1 Versions of jQuery

As of this writing the most current release is jQuery 3.6.0, but new versions with security updates are released every few months. You might not want to always use the most recent version of jQuery. Several plugins are designed to work with earlier jQuery versions and will not work with the more recent versions, so you need to check the documentation of any third-party plugin to ensure that it is compatible with your jQuery version.

Loading jQuery

The jQuery library is accessible either as a .js file downloaded to your website or as a link to a file residing on a Content Delivery Network. A Content Delivery Network (CDN) is a web server that hosts open-source software and is optimized for quick delivery of that software. If your app needs to work offline you should download the library file, but if that is not a concern and you wish to save space, create a link to the file on the CDN. Generally, using the CDN is considered the best practice if network connection is not a concern. jQuery recommends that links to the CDN include Subresource Integrity checking (SRI) to ensure that the resources on the CDN have not been tampered with.

Each release of the jQuery library comes in several versions. An uncompressed version allows programmers to view the JavaScript code that is used in the library. A minified version compresses the library to save space and memory while increasing execution speed but at the expense of readability. Both versions are available in normal and slim builds.

The normal jQuery build includes the full features of the jQuery library. The slim jQuery build removes features such as AJAX and some animation tools, which have been supplanted by Fetch and CSS. As the name implies, the slim build is smaller and thus would execute faster than the normal build.

Note | Use the slim build if you do not need the full jQuery library. If you are not sure which build you need, it is safest to load the slightly larger full build.

Is jQuery Still Relevant?

A question confronting web developers is whether jQuery is still relevant since many of the reasons for jQuery no longer apply. All major browsers now support a common core of JavaScript standards, so coding for cross-browser compatibility is not as much of an issue as it once was. Moreover, several features that jQuery provides are now part of standard JavaScript. For example, jQuery's ability to select elements using CSS selectors can also be accomplished using JavaScript's `querySelector()` and `querySelectorAll()` methods. An argument could be made that there is little need for a JavaScript library that duplicates things JavaScript already does so well.

Nonetheless, a web developer should be familiar with jQuery. At the time of this writing jQuery remains the most popular JavaScript library in the world, used on 77% of the top 1 million websites. Of sites that use jQuery, 55% still use Version 1, which means that a lot of websites are operating under the adage: "If it's not broken, don't fix it." So, you will probably encounter jQuery either maintaining already-existing websites or building your own apps on its established foundations. Full coverage of jQuery would require several chapters of material, so this chapter will serve as an introduction.

You will learn how to use jQuery in a Frequently Asked Questions page for *Bonsai Expression*, a company that sells bonsai trees and supplies for interested arborists. The FAQ page answers several questions about the art of bonsai, but to keep the page at a manageable length, the answers are collapsed until the question is clicked. Clicking the question again collapses the answer. **Figure 12-2** shows a preview of the page in operation.

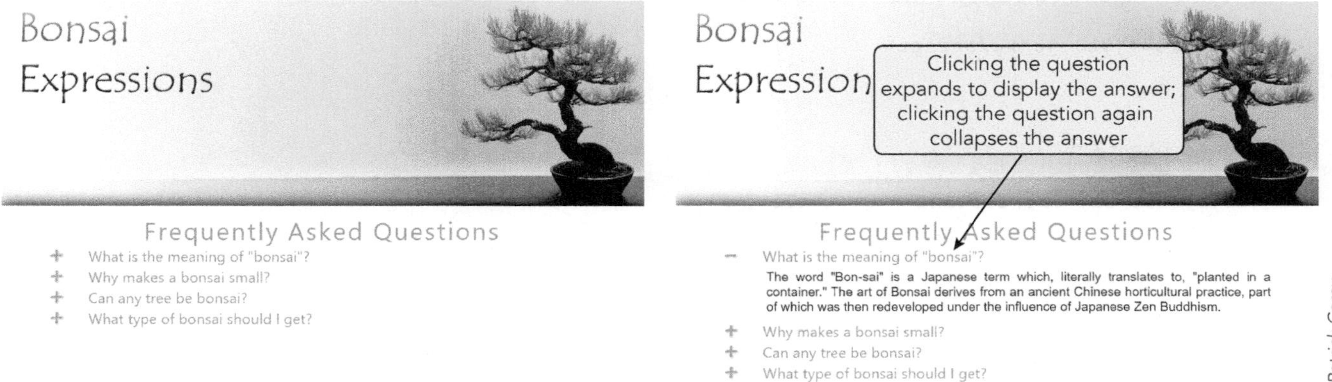

Figure 12-2 Expanding an FAQ answer

While there are ways of completing this assignment using CSS or standard JavaScript, you will complete the page using jQuery. Rather than downloading the jQuery library file, you will link to the latest build on a jQuery CDN.

To set up the files for jQuery:

1. Go to the js12 ► chapter folder of your data files.
2. Use your code editor to open the **js12_txt.html** and **js12_txt.js**, files. Enter your name and the date in the comment section of each file and then save them as **js12.html** and **js12.js,** respectively.
3. Go to **code.jquery.com** website in your browser.

4. Click the link for the minified build of the latest core jQuery release. The website displays the Code Integration overlay shown in **Figure 12-3** with a link to the jQuery file (your overlay might look slightly different).

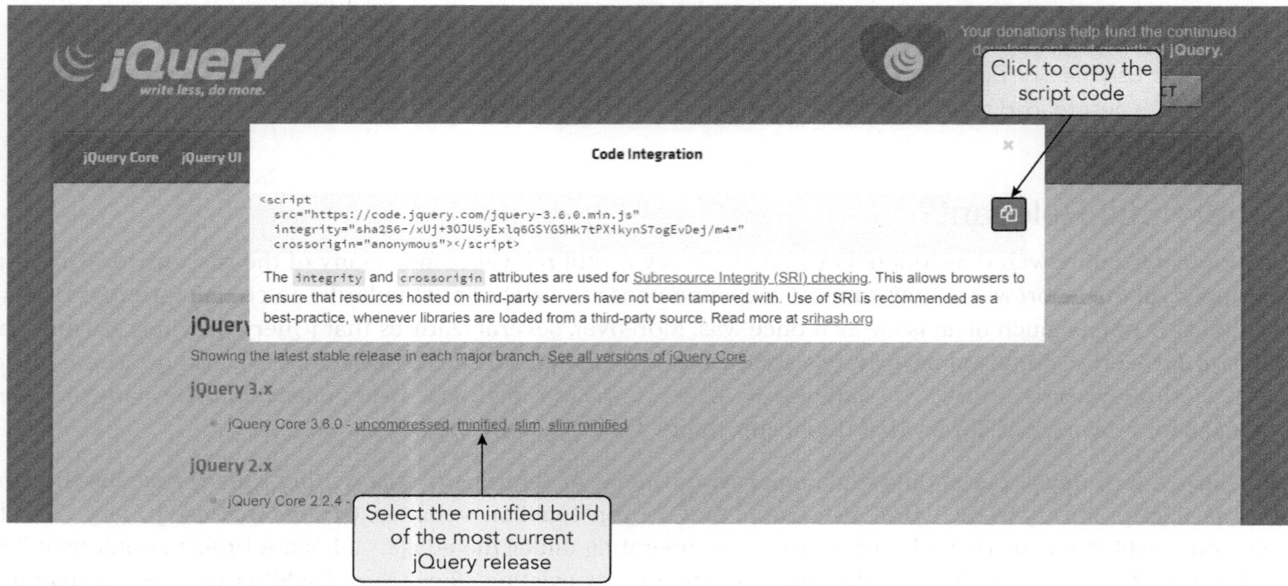

Figure 12-3 Copying the link to the minified jQuery build

5. Click the **Copy** button to copy the code.
6. Return to the **js12.html** file in your code editor.
7. Directly above the closing `</head>` insert the copied script.
8. Add the following `script` element to link the page to the js12.js file. (You do not need to include the `defer` attribute.) **Figure 12-4** shows the code in the file.

```
<script src="js12.js"></script>
```

```
   <meta charset="utf-8" />
   <meta name="viewport" content="width=device-wi          ale=1.0">
   <title>Bonsai Expressions FAQ</title>
   <link rel="stylesheet" href="styles.css" />
   <script src="https://code.jquery.com/jquery-3.6.0.min.js"
           integrity="sha256-/xUj+3OJU5yExlq6GSYGSHk7tPXikynS7ogEvDej/m4="
           crossorigin="anonymous">
   </script>
   <script src="js12.js"></script>
</head>
```

Link to the minified version of the core jQuery file

The integrity and crossorigin attributes ensure that the CDN has not been tampered with

Figure 12-4 Script elements in the document head

Always place any scripts for the web app after the `script` element that loads or links jQuery, thus ensuring that the browser has loaded the jQuery library before attempting to use its commands.

9. Study the code for the page body to become familiar with its contents and structure and then close the file, saving your changes.

Now that you have linked the page to the jQuery library, you can use the library to code the FAQ page.

Note | Because jQuery is used throughout the web, many users will have the linked jQuery file already saved in their browser's cache, speeding up the time it takes to load and execute the library.

Working with jQuery Selectors

All jQuery commands begin with a $ symbol indicating any code following should be interpreted as part of the jQuery library. jQuery commands follow the general syntax:

```
$(selector).action(parameters)
```

where *selector* references a selection of elements from the web page document, *action* is an action performed on that object, and *parameters* are parameter values associated within that action. Parameters can be values, but they can also reference callback functions that are run in response to the action.

For example, the following statement applies the `ready()` action to the web document, telling the browser to wait until the web document is completely loaded, and once it is loaded and read, the anonymous callback function will be run in response:

```
$(document).ready(function() {
    jQuery statements
    })
```

Later versions of jQuery also support the following more concise command to accomplish the same task:

```
$(function() {
    jQuery statements
});
```

This code can also be written even more concisely in arrow function syntax as:

```
$( () => {
    jQuery statements
});
```

Note | The expression `$()` is a concise alias for `jQuery()`. If you are using another JavaScript library that employs the `$` symbol, use `jQuery()` to avoid naming conflicts.

Use the `$(function() { })` syntax now to create a function that will not be loaded until the document is ready.

To run jQuery commands only after the page is loaded and read:

1. Return to the **js12.js** file in your code editor.
2. Directly below the comment section add the following statements:

```
// Run once the page is loaded and ready
$( () => {
});
```

   See **Figure 12-5**.

3. Save your changes to the file and then open **js12.html** in your browser.
4. Check the browser developer tools to verify that no mistakes have been introduced in writing the initial code or in linking to jQuery. Close the Developer pane after you have verified that the code is free of syntax errors.

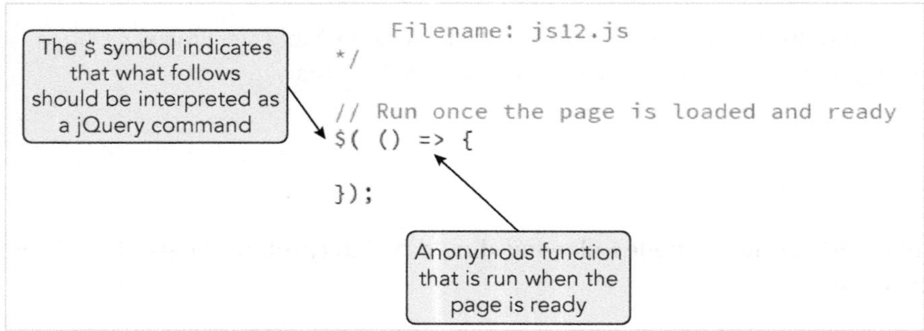

Figure 12-5 Running a function when the document is ready

Before writing the code to display and hide the FAQ answers, you must first review how to manage elements and events using jQuery.

Selecting Elements from the DOM

Like the `querySelector()` and `querySelectorAll()` methods, the jQuery `$(selector)` expression references a selection of elements based on CSS selector patterns. Any selector pattern supported by CSS can be used in a `$(selector)` expression. The following expression returns an array of all paragraphs nested as direct children of the `dd` element.

```
$("dd > p")
```

To select paragraphs that are direct children of either a `dt` or `dd` element, use:

```
$("dd > p, dt > p")
```

To select all paragraphs nested within `article` elements belonging to the story class, use:

```
$("article.story p")
```

The selected elements can be treated as items within an array. To reference the first and second paragraphs within an `article` element, apply the following expressions:

```
$("article.story p")[0]
$("article.story p")[1]
```

As with all JavaScript arrays, jQuery array indexes start with zero up to one less than the number of items in the array.

Note | Always enter a CSS selector pattern as a text string, placed within quotation marks.

jQuery selectors can be saved as variables as in the following code that stores a reference to the paragraphs nested within the main `h1` heading under the variable name `mainPara`.

```
let mainPara = $("h1#main p");
$(mainPara) // references paragraphs of the main h1 heading
```

Notice that variable is also placed with the `$()` expression to indicate that it should be treated as a jQuery selector. Once a selector has been stored as a variable, the array of selected elements generated by that expression is available to the JavaScript parser without requiring a rescan of the DOM.

Best Practices | Optimizing jQuery Selectors

Because jQuery selectors are based on CSS selector patterns, you can speed up your processing time by optimizing your use of selectors. This is especially important for large documents in which searching through the node tree would involve investigating several branches. Here are some tips to keep in mind to optimize jQuery selectors:

- The `id` attribute is unique for every page element. The fastest way to retrieve a specific element is by its `id` value.
- Be specific in your selectors. Instead of referencing all `article` elements, use a selector like `$("article.news")` so that JavaScript limits its search to `article` elements of the `news` class.
- Include a context for the selectors whenever possible to reduce the size of the node tree that the parser will search. For example, instead of using `$("p")` to search for any paragraph, use `$("article.news > p")` to limit the search only for paragraphs that are direct children of `article` elements belong to the `news` class.
- Cache your selectors by storing them within variables. By storing the selector as a variable, JavaScript does not have to rescan the DOM to recreate the node collection.
- Avoid pseudo-selectors. A selector like `$("div:first")` takes up valuable processing time as the JavaScript parser needs to parse the entire node tree to evaluate which **`div`** element is first in the list. Instead use `id` attributes if you need to reference specific nodes.

A little bit goes a long way with code optimization. Speed up your jQuery apps by writing selectors that are efficient and specific.

Traversing the DOM with jQuery

Just as JavaScript includes properties and methods for traversing the document node tree, jQuery provides tools to navigate through the node tree from parent elements through sibling and child elements. **Figure 12-6** describes some of the methods supported by jQuery for traversing the DOM.

METHOD	DESCRIPTION
`children(`*`filter`*`)`	Returns all direct children of the selected elements, where *`filter`* is an optional selector expression or jQuery expression that narrows down the search
`closest(`*`filter`*`)`	Returns the closest ancestor of the selected elements
`contents(`*`filter`*`)`	Returns all children (including text and comment nodes) of the selected elements
`find(`*`filter`*`)`	Returns descendant elements that match a filter
`first()`	Returns the first element from a list of selected elements
`has(`*`element`*`)`	Returns all elements which contain a specified *`element`*
`last()`	Returns the last element from a list of selected elements
`next(`*`filter`*`)`	Returns the next sibling of the selected elements
`nextAll(`*`filter`*`)`	Returns all next siblings of the selected elements
`parent(`*`filter`*`)`	Returns the parent of the selected elements
`parents(`*`filter`*`)`	Returns all ancestors of the selected elements
`prev(`*`filter`*`)`	Returns the previous sibling of the selected elements
`prevAll(`*`filter`*`)`	Returns all previous siblings of the selected elements
`siblings(`*`filter`*`)`	Returns all siblings of the selected elements

Figure 12-6 jQuery methods to traverse the node tree

jQuery can traverse the node tree in any direction and includes optional filters to narrow the search. For example, the following expression returns an array of all sibling elements of the main article, which themselves are also articles:

```
$("article#main").siblings("article")
```

The process by which a jQuery selector is appended with jQuery methods that extends or redirects the selected elements is known as object chaining.

Object chains can be extended indefinitely to create even more specific element arrays. The following expression extends the object chain to include only those sibling articles that also contained unordered lists:

```
$("article#main").siblings("article").has("ul")
```

The jQuery methods are often more versatile than their JavaScript counterparts so that if an app needs to navigate a complex path through the node tree it may be more efficient and easier to use jQuery's object chaining in place of standard JavaScript node methods.

Note | If a method does not include a filter, it selects all elements from the specified direction in the node tree.

Working with Attributes and CSS Properties

jQuery also provides methods to work with element attributes and CSS properties. Using these methods, you can narrow a search based on element or CSS property values or you can create new attributes and CSS properties. **Figure 12-7** describes some of the jQuery methods for attributes and properties.

METHOD	DESCRIPTION
`addClass(class)`	Adds one or more class names to selected elements
`attr(att, value)`	Returns or sets attribute values to selected elements
`css(prop)`	Returns or sets CSS properties for the selected elements
`hasClass(class)`	Returns a Boolean value indicating whether the selected elements have a specified class attribute
`prop(prop)`	Returns or sets properties of the selected elements
`removeAtt(attr)`	Removes one or more attributes from the selected elements
`removeClass(class)`	Removes one or more classes from the selected elements
`removeProp(prop)`	Removes a property set by the `prop()` method
`toggleClass(class)`	Toggles between adding and removing one or more classes from the selected elements.

Figure 12-7 jQuery methods for classes and attributes

Using jQuery methods, you can get or set the attributes and CSS properties of selected elements. The following expression gets the value of the `width` attribute for the first inline image of the `slides` class:

```
$("img.slides").first().attr("width")
```

To set an attribute value, include the value within the `attr()` method as in the following expression that sets the width to 500 pixels:

```
$("img.slides").first().attr("width", "500px")
```

Multiple attributes can be provided in JSON format. The following expression sets both the width and the height of the inline image:

```
$("img.slides").first().({"width": "500px", "height": "300px"})
```

CSS properties, whether placed as inline styles or in external style sheets, are also accessible to jQuery. The following expression gets the CSS `font-size` property of the main `h1` heading. Note that hyphenated property names like `font-size` are written in camel case.

```
$("h1#main").css("fontSize")
```

Note | If several items are returned by the jQuery selector, the `css()` and `attr()` methods will return values for the first matched element in the array.

As with element attributes, the value of multiple CSS properties can be set in JSON format. The following expression sets both the color and the font size of the main `h1` heading:

```
$("h1#main").css({
   fontSize: "2em",
   color: "blue"
})
```

jQuery returns the computed values of CSS styles, which is not necessarily the value defined in the style sheet. For example, the following style rule defines the font size and color of article text in an `em` unit and a color name:

```
article {
   font-size: 2em;
   color: green;
}
```

The value of those properties returned by jQuery would be expressed in pixels and the `rgb` color value.

```
$("article").css("fontSize") // 32px
$("article").css("color")    // rgb(0, 128, 0)
```

If an app needs to access the CSS value as defined in the style sheet, it will have to be done using JavaScript. It cannot be done under jQuery.

Changing the DOM Structure

jQuery contains a large library of methods to edit and replace elements existing in the DOM or to create and add new elements. **Figure 12-8** describes a few of the jQuery methods for manipulating the DOM structure.

METHOD	DESCRIPTION
`add(`*`content`*`)`	Adds new content after the selected elements
`after(`*`content`*`)`	Inserts new content before the selected elements
`append(`*`content`*`)`	Appends new content at the end of the selected elements
`before(`*`content`*`)`	Inserts new content before the selected elements
`clone()`	Makes a copy of the selected elements (including event handlers)
`detach(`*`elems`*`)`	Detaches elements from the selected elements
`empty()`	Removes all child nodes and content from selected elements
`html(`*`content`*`)`	Gets or sets the HTML content of the selected elements
`prepend(`*`content`*`)`	Inserts new content at the beginning of the selected elements

Figure 12-8 jQuery methods to modify the DOM

(Continues)

METHOD	DESCRIPTION
`remove(elems)`	Removes elements from the selected elements
`replace(old, new)`	Replaces an old string with a new text string within the selected elements
`replaceAll(selector)`	Applies a new HTML structure to the selected elements.
`replaceWith(html)`	Replaces selected elements with new HTML content
`text(str)`	Gets or sets the text content of selected elements
`val(value)`	Gets or sets the value of selected form elements
`unwrap()`	Removes the parent element surrounding the selected elements, leaving the selected elements within the DOM
`wrap(html)`	Wraps HTML structure around the selected elements

Figure 12-8 **jQuery methods to modify the DOM—(Continued)**

jQuery methods act as both getters and setters. A getter is a method that gets a value, while a setter is a method that sets a value. The following statement acts as a getter by getting the value stored in the username input box:

```
$("input#username").val()
```

while this statement acts as a setter to set the value stored in the input box:

```
$("input#username".val("dawson4815")
```

In the same fashion, the `text()` and `html()` methods can act as both getters and setters.

The other methods listed in Figure 12-8 are used to change the structure of the DOM but can do so more efficiently with few lines of code than would be required in standard JavaScript. For example, the following HTML fragment

```
<h1 class="old">Main Heading</h1>
<h1 class="old">Main Heading</h1>
<h1 class="old">Main Heading</h1>
```

can be changed to

```
<h2 class="new">Minor Heading</h2>
<h2 class="new">Minor Heading</h2>
<h2 class="new">Minor Heading</h2>
```

by applying the single jQuery statement:

```
$("<h2 class='new'>Minor Heading</h2>").replaceAll("h1.old");
```

Note The jQuery `replaceAll()` and `replaceWith()` methods accomplish the same task except that the order of the arguments is reversed. In the `replaceWith()` method, the selected elements are listed first followed by the replacement HTML code.

The `wrap()` method encloses elements within a specified HTML structure, creating a new parent for the elements. To enclose the following `h1` headings:

```
<h1 class="story">Main Heading</h1>
<h1 class="story">Second Heading</h1>
```

within the following `article` elements:

```
<article>
   <h1 class="story">Main Heading</h1>
</article>
```

```
<article>
   <h1 class="story">Second Heading</h1>
</article>
```

and apply the jQuery `wrap()` method to the selected elements:

```
$("h1.story").wrap("<article></article>")
```

To remove the `article` elements but keep the `h1` headings within the DOM, apply the `unwrap()` method:

```
$("h1.story").unwrap()
```

The unwrapped content will take as its new parent, the parents of the `article` elements that were removed.

Handling Events with jQuery

jQuery uses the same syntax for managing events as it does for applying methods to selected elements. The general format is:

```
$(selector).event(handler)
```

where *`selector`* are the elements that experience the event, *`event`* is the name of the event, and *`handler`* is the function that handles the event. jQuery responds to events during the bubbling phase. If you need to respond to events during the capture phase, use JavaScript's `addEventListener()` method.

Note | If an event method is supplied without a handler function, jQuery triggers the event instead of responding to it.

Figure 12-9 describes the most common of the many jQuery event methods.

METHOD	DESCRIPTION
`blur(`*`handler`*`)`	The focus leaves a form element, running the *`handler`* function. If no *`handler`* is specified, the event is triggered rather than responded to.
`change(`*`handler`*`)`	An input field value changes
`click(`*`handler`*`)`	Selected elements are clicked
`dblclick(`*`handler`*`)`	Selected elements are double-clicked
`focus(`*`handler`*`)`	The focus is applied to a form element
`hover(`*`handlerIn, handlerOut`*`)`	Mouse pointer enters the element to initiate the *`handlerIn`* function, leaves the element to initiate the *`handlerOut`* function.
`mousenter(`*`handler`*`)`	The mouse pointer enters the selected elements
`mouseover(`*`handler`*`)`	The mouse pointer moves over the selected elements
`mouseout(`*`handler`*`)`	The mouse pointer leaves the selected elements
`ready(`*`handler`*`)`	The DOM is ready and loaded by the browser
`submit(`*`handler`*`)`	The web form is submitted by the browser

Figure 12-9 Common jQuery event methods

As with the JavaScript event model, jQuery supports an event object that is passed as an object of the handler function. **Figure 12-10** describes some of the properties associated with the jQuery event object.

PROPERTY OR METHOD	DESCRIPTION
event.currentTarget	Returns the current element experiencing the event during the bubbling phase
event.preventDefault()	Prevents the default browser action associated with the event
event.stopPropagation()	Stops the propagation of the event from the current element to its parents
event.target	Returns the DOM element which triggered the event
event.type	Returns the type of event which was triggered

Figure 12-10 Properties and methods of the jQuery event object

The following code demonstrates how to apply the `click()` event to every `h1` element in the document to display the text of the element that follows the heading. In this handler function, the heading clicked by the user is stored in the `e.target` property. The `next()` method selects the next sibling element in the DOM, and the `text()` method displays the text stored within that sibling.

```
$("h1").click(e => {
   console.log($(e.target).next().text());
});
```

Notice that the event object property, `e.target`, has to be placed within the jQuery selector, `$()`, so that jQuery handles the methods associated with the event target.

You now have enough information to begin creating the app that displays answers to the question on the Bonsai Expressions FAQ page. Questions on the page are enclosed within a definition list (`dl`) element. Each question is marked with a `dt` element and the answer to each question immediately follows, marked with a `dd` element. Add a `click` event method for every `dt` element within the FAQ, running a function that will alternately hide and unhide the answers.

To add a `click` event for every question:

1. Return to the **js12.js** file in your code editor.
2. Within the function that runs when the page is loaded and ready, add the following code that runs an anonymous function each time a `dt` element is clicked:

```
// Add click events to each question in the FAQ
$("dl#faq dt").click( e => {
});
```

Indent the code to make it easier to read as shown in **Figure 12-11**.

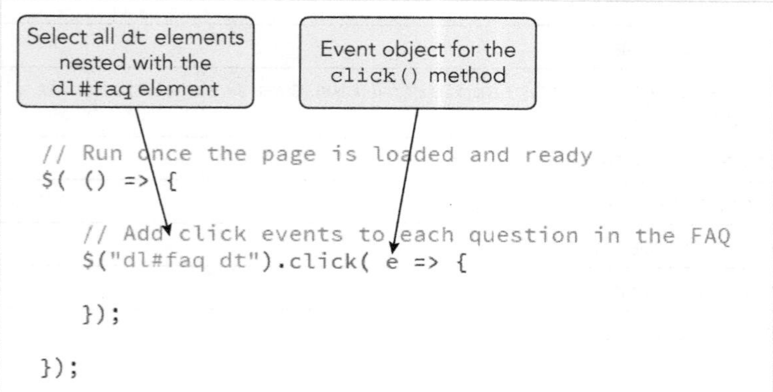

Figure 12-11 Apply the jQuery `click()` method

When answers are hidden, the question is prefaced with the + symbol. When answers are displayed the symbol changes to a – symbol. The + and – symbols are graphical elements displayed as part of the background image of the question text. The background image is determined by the value of the `class` attribute assigned to the `dt` element. If the class attribute value is "hiddenAnswer" then the + image is displayed. If there is no class attribute, the – image is used as the background.

Switch between the two symbols by using the jQuery toggleClass() method to alternate between turning the class attribute on and off.

To apply the toggleClass() method:

1. Within the anonymous function for the click event add the following code:

```
// Alternate between hiding and showing the answer
let question = $(e.target);
let answer = $(question.next());
$(question).toggleClass("hiddenAnswer");
```

   Figure 12-12 shows the newly added code in the function.

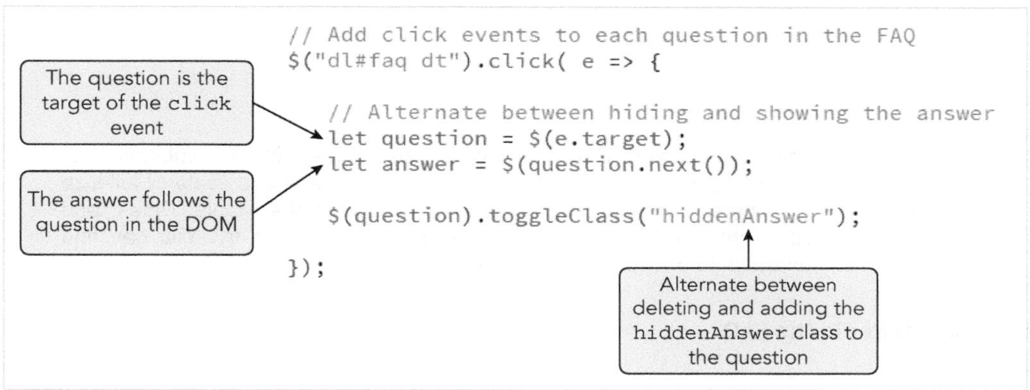

Figure 12-12 Toggling the class attribute on and off

2. Save your changes to the file and then reload **js12.html** in your browser.
3. Click each of the questions in the FAQ, verifying that the symbol switches between a + and a –.

Next you will alternately show and hide the answer to the clicked question. Elements can be shown and hidden using the following jQuery methods:

```
$(selector).show()
$(selector).hide()
```

Hiding does not remove the selected elements from the DOM, it merely hides them from view. Use these two methods now to show and hide the question answers depending on the value of the question's class attribute.

To alternate between shown and hidden answers:

1. Return to the **js12.js** file in your code editor.
2. Within the anonymous function for the click event, add the following:

```
if ($(question).hasClass("hiddenAnswer")) {
   $(answer).hide();
} else {
   $(answer).show();
}
```

   See **Figure 12-13**.
3. Save your changes to the file and reload **js12.html** in your browser.
4. Click each of the questions in the FAQ, verifying that the answers alternate between being hidden and being shown. See **Figure 12-14**.

```
// Alternate between hiding and showing the answer
let question = $(e.target);
let answer = $(question.next());

$(question).toggleClass("hiddenAnswer");

if ($(question).hasClass("hiddenAnswer")) {
    $(answer).hide();
} else {
    $(answer).show();
}
```

Hide the answer on the page

Display the answer on the page

Figure 12-13 Displaying and hiding an FAQ answer

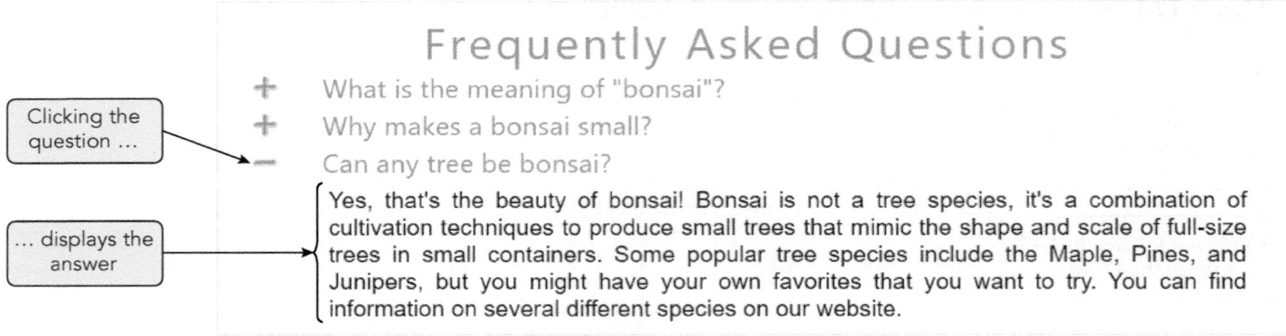

Frequently Asked Questions
What is the meaning of "bonsai"?
Why makes a bonsai small?
Can any tree be bonsai?
Yes, that's the beauty of bonsai! Bonsai is not a tree species, it's a combination of cultivation techniques to produce small trees that mimic the shape and scale of full-size trees in small containers. Some popular tree species include the Maple, Pines, and Junipers, but you might have your own favorites that you want to try. You can find information on several different species on our website.
Clicking the question ...
... displays the answer

Figure 12-14 Displaying an answer in the FAQ

You have completed the initial work on the FAQ page. In the next section you will learn how to apply jQuery effects and animations to objects on the page.

Common Mistakes

Managing jQuery Efficiently

jQuery is a great supplement to standard JavaScript. However, like all JavaScript libraries it can be used well or poorly. Here are some common mistakes to avoid when using jQuery with your projects.

- **Not using a minified version of jQuery**. Unless you have a real need to view the underlying jQuery code, there is no reason to not use the compressed version. You will save bandwidth and increase the speed and responsiveness of your apps.
- **Not using a CDN**. Using a CDN reduces the load on your own server and with browser caching, jQuery may actually load quicker. Unless you need to work offline, there is little reason not to use a CDN.
- **Using selectors inefficiently**. jQuery's $(*selector*) method is a great and simple tool for referencing arrays of elements. However, do not overuse it. Chain your methods together so that jQuery only scans the DOM once.
- **Mixing jQuery and JavaScript methods**. jQuery integrates so well with standard JavaScript that it is easy to forget when jQuery ends, and JavaScript begins. A common mistake is trying to apply a JavaScript method to a jQuery object and vice versa.

Another common mistake is using jQuery when you do not have to. Before committing to jQuery make sure you have exhausted everything that can be done with HTML, CSS, and JavaScript. There may be solutions you have overlooked.

Quick Check 1

1. What is a Content Delivery Network (CDN)?
2. Provide a jQuery selector that selects all articles of the `story` class that are descendants of the `aside` element.
3. Provide a jQuery expression that selects the sibling elements prior to the `aside` element with the id "sidebar".
4. What jQuery method can be used to enclose selected elements within a specified HTML code string?
5. Provide jQuery code to run a handler function to respond to the mouse pointer entering an inline image belonging to the "photos" class.

Working with Effects and Animations

The `show()` and `hide()` methods used in the last section are examples of a jQuery effect, which is a method that applies a visual effect to an element selection. The complete syntax of the two methods is as follows:

```
show(speed, easing, callback)
hide(speed, easing, callback)
```

where *`speed`* is `slow`, `fast`, or the length of the effect in milliseconds, *`easing`* specifies the speed of the effect at different points in the animation, and *`callback`* is a callback function that is run after the effect is completed. The *`easing`* parameter has two possible values:

- **swing** The default easing in which the changes are slower at the beginning and at the end, but faster in the middle
- **linear** An easing in which the changes occur at a constant rate

You could not see any special effects in the last section because the duration was set to 0 milliseconds by default. To experience the transitions used by the `show()` and `hide()` methods, increase to duration to 0.6 seconds or 600 milliseconds.

To set the duration of the `show()` and `hide()` effects:

1. Return to the **js12.js** file in your code editor.
2. Change the `hide()` and `show()` methods to **`hide(600)`** and **`show(600)`**, respectively. See **Figure 12-15**.

```
if ($(question).hasClass("hiddenAnswer")) {
   $(answer).hide(600);
} else {
   $(answer).show(600);
}
```

Set the duration of the effects to 0.6 seconds

Figure 12-15 Setting the duration of a jQuery effect

3. Save your changes to the file and reload **js12.html** in your browser.
4. Click each of the questions and note that the effect is applied over a longer interval.

The `hide()` method works by reducing the size of the selected elements to 0 pixels and their opacity to 0 (making the elements completely transparent.) The `show()` methods works just the opposite: increasing the size of elements from 0 pixels to its default size and increasing their opacity to 1 (making the elements completely opaque.) Other effects are also supported by jQuery as described in **Figure 12-16**.

METHOD	DESCRIPTION
`fadeIn()`	Changes the opacity of the selected elements from 0 to 1 as the elements fade into view
`fadeOut()`	Changes the opacity of the selected elements from 1 to 0 as the elements fade out of view
`fadeTo()`	Fades to a specified opacity value
`fadeToggle()`	Toggles between fading in and fading out depending on the current state of the selected elements
`hide()`	Hides the selected elements by reducing their size and their opacity
`show()`	Reveals the selected elements by increasing their size and their opacity
`slideDown()`	Reveals the selected elements with a vertical sliding motion
`slideToggle()`	Toggles between sliding down and sliding up based on the current state of the selected elements
`slideUp()`	Hides the selected elements with a vertical sliding motion
`toggle()`	Toggles between `hide()` and `show()` methods depending on the current state of the selected elements

Figure 12-16 jQuery effect methods

Each of the methods described in Figure 12-16 also support the *`speed`*, *`easing`*, and *`callback`* parameters. The `fadeTo()` method includes an additional parameter specifying the opacity value that the selected elements should fade to.

You will modify the code for the FAQ page so that the questions are revealed and hidden using the `slideDown()` and `slideUp()` effects.

To apply the `slideDown()` and `slideUp()` effects:

1. Return to the **js12.js** file in your code editor.
2. Change the `hide(6000)` and `show(600)` methods to **`slideUp(600)`** and **`slideDown(600)`**, respectively. See **Figure 12-17**.

```
if ($(question).hasClass("hiddenAnswer")) {
    $(answer).slideUp(600);
} else {
    $(answer).slideDown(600);
}
```

Hide the answer by sliding up
Reveal the answer by sliding down

Figure 12-17 Using the **`slideUp()`** and **`slideDown()`** methods

3. Save your changes to the file and reload **js12.html** in your browser.
4. Click each of the questions, verifying that the answers are revealed by sliding down and hidden by sliding up.

Chaining Effects

jQuery effects can be chained in a queue so that one effect quickly follows another. The following code creates a queue in which the selected elements are initially revealed with the `slideDown()` effect over a 0.5-second interval, followed by several fade-ins and fade-outs over 0.1-second intervals.

```
$(selector).slideDown(500)
.fadeOut(100).fadeIn(100).fadeOut(100).fadeIn(100)
.fadeOut(100).fadeIn(100).fadeOut(100).fadeIn(100);
```

The overall effect is one in which the element is revealed and then flashes by, quickly fading out and in.

Callback functions can be interspersed within a chain of effects so that the function is run as soon as one effect in the chain concludes but before the next effect begins. With this approach you can time actions to occur within the middle of an effects queue. The following code applies a 1-second fadeout to the `div#caption` element and then changes the text to "New caption". After the callback function is finished, the next effect that fades in the element is run.

```
$("div#caption")
.fadeOut(1000, () => {
   $("div#caption").text("New caption");
})
.fadeIn(1000);
```

When this chain of effects is applied, the old caption text will fade out, followed by the fading in of an entirely new caption.

> **Note** | A common syntax error with callback functions within jQuery effects is to forget to properly close the function's command block or the effect parenthesis.

Creating Custom Effects with Animate

In addition to the jQuery effect methods, you can create custom effects using animations. A jQuery animation is a visual effect accomplished by gradually changing the values of a collection of CSS properties over a specified time interval. Animations are created using the following `animate()` method:

```
$(selector).animate({properties}, duration, callback)
```

where *`properties`* is an object literal of CSS properties and their values, *`duration`* is `slow`, `fast`, or the time interval in milliseconds, and *`callback`* is a function that is run once the animation is concluded.

Every animation needs to have a starting condition to build upon, entered either in the style sheet or within the jQuery code. The following example application applies an animation to the `h1.caption` elements. Each heading starts within an initial font size, width, and opacity of 0. Over a span of 0.5 seconds, the font size increases to 2em, the width to 800 pixels, and the opacity to 1.

```
$("h1.caption").css({
   fontSize: 0,
   width: 0,
   opacity: 0
})
.animate({
   fontSize: "2em",
   width: "800px",
   opacity: 1
}, 500)
```

The effect will be a heading that appears to grow with increasing font size, width, and opacity. Notice that property values that include units such as the "px" unit for length, need to be quoted. Property values that are numeric do not need quotes.

> **Note** | Not all CSS properties can be animated. In general, only those CSS properties whose value can be expressed in numbers, lengths, or percentages can be animated.

A CSS property can be changed relative to its current value using the += and -= operators. In the following code, the font size of the h1.caption elements is increased by 1em relative to their initial font size when the animation starts:

```
$("h1.caption").animate({
    fontSize: "+=1em"
}, 500);
```

Finally, property values can be entered using the following keywords:

- hide Changes the CSS property value to zero.
- show Restores the CSS property value to its initial condition.
- toggle Switches the CSS property value between zero and its initial condition.

For example, the following code toggles the font size and opacity of the h1.caption elements between zero and their initial conditions. The effect alternately hides and reveals the headings each time the animation is applied.

```
$("h1").animate({
    fontSize: "toggle"
    opacity: "toggle"
}, 500);
```

You will use the animate() method to animate the main heading of the FAQ page when it is initially opened by the browser.

To apply the animate() method:

1. Return to the **js12.js** file in your code editor.
2. Directly above the click() method for the $("dl#faq dt") selector, add the following code to set the initial font size and opacity of the h1 heading:

```
// Animate the h1 heading
$("section > h1").css({
    fontSize: 0,
    opacity: 0
})
```

3. Add the following animate() method to increase the font size and opacity of the h1 heading over a 0.6-second interval:

```
.animate({
    fontSize: "2.3em",
    opacity: 1
}, 600);
```

   Figure 12-18 shows the completed code in the file.

4. Save your changes and then reload **js12.html** in your browser. Verify that when the page is opened, an animation effect revealing the h1 heading is applied to the page.

If the animation fails, check the debugger console for errors. Common mistakes are not closing off the parenthesis within the css() and animate() methods and not separating CSS properties with a comma.

```
// Run once the page is loaded and ready
$( () => {

   // Animate the h1 heading
   $("section > h1").css({
      fontSize: 0,
      opacity: 0
   })
   .animate({
      fontSize: "2.3em",
      opacity: 1
   }, 600);

   // Add click events to each question in the FAQ
   $("dl#faq dt").click( e => {
```

Set the initial font size and opacity of the heading to zero
Increase the font size and the opacity over a 0.6-second interval

Figure 12-18 Applying an `animate()` method

Controlling the Animation Queue

Animation effects placed within a queue are run in order with each animation starting as soon as the preceding animation finishes. Once an animation has started, it will continue to the end of its duration value. jQuery provides methods to control the queue by delaying an animation, halting a current animation, or removing animations from the queue. **Figure 12-19** describes the jQuery methods for controlling the animation queue.

METHOD	DESCRIPTION
clearQueue(*queue*)	Removes all items from the queue which have not yet been run, where *queue* is an optional parameter that references the name of the animation queue. The default queue name is "fx".
delay(*duration*, *queue*)	Sets a timer to delay execution of subsequent items in the queue where *duration* is the delay time in milliseconds
dequeue(*queue*)	Executes the next function in the queue and then removes that function
finish(*queue*)	Stops the current animation and removes all queued animations, setting the selected elements to their end state
queue(*queue*)	Returns information about the named queue associated with the selected elements
stop(*clearQueue*, *jumpToEnd*)	Stops the current animation running in the queue, where *clearQueue* is an optional parameter indicating whether to remove queued animation as well, and *jumpToEnd* is an optional parameter whether go to the end state of the current animation

Figure 12-19 Methods to control the animation queue

In the following code, moving a mouse pointer over the `div.box` element will shift the box 20 pixels to the right over a duration of 1 second. The animation will continue even if the mouse pointer is no longer over the box.

```
$("div.box").mouseenter( e => {
   $(e.target).animate({
      left: "+=20px"
   }, 1000)
});
```

To stop the animation when the pointer leaves the box, add the following `stop()` method, which leaves the box in its current position in the animation:

```
$("div.box").mouseout( e => {
   $(e.target).stop()
}
```

The overall effect will be that as the pointer enters the box, the box moves to the right and as the pointer leaves the box, that movement stops.

Because an app might have several jQuery animations, all running simultaneously, the queue for each animation can be given a unique name that can be referenced in the `clearQueue()`, `delay()`, `dequeue()`, `finish()`, `queue()`, and `stop()` methods.

Programming Concepts | Libraries vs. Frameworks

Libraries and frameworks often get mistaken for one other and while they have a lot in common, there are important differences. A JavaScript library, like jQuery, is a reusable collection of code that is often directed toward one use or purpose. The developer "calls" on the library to perform tasks or get information. When you use jQuery, you are calling on the jQuery library to do those tasks that you could have done in JavaScript, but that are done much easier using the tools jQuery provides.

On the other hand, a framework like React.js, Vue.js, or Angular.js encompasses all the tools you need in application development. A framework might contain a collection of several libraries and scripts and whatever other tools are necessary to deliver a final project. The framework organizes those tools for the developer and the developer provides the code. Unlike libraries, frameworks call on your code to complete a task; your code does not call on the framework. It is part of the framework.

Exploring jQuery Plugins

You can create interesting visual effects with the jQuery effects and animation methods. For more advanced effects and other tasks, you can download one of the many jQuery plugins available on the web. There are hundreds of plugins for creating web page objects such as photo slideshows, calendars, and form widgets. You can find a searchable list of plugins in the jQuery Plugin Registry at *https://plugins.jquery.com*. To use a jQuery plugin, you need to:

1. Read the documentation for the plugin and view demos to understand what the plugin can do and how to integrate it with your website.
2. Either download the plugin files to your site or create a link to a CDN hosting the plugin. For some plugins you may need to download or link to several files, including CSS style sheets and image files.
3. Edit the HTML and CSS code for your website to load the required files for the plugin. The script element for plugins must always be placed *after* the script element for the jQuery library.
4. Edit the JavaScript code to take full advantage of the plugin's capabilities.

Because you are using a third-party library in your website, the first step is crucial. You will not be able to easily debug your code if you are not using the plugin in the correct way.

Note | With some plugins you might need an *older* version of jQuery because more recent jQuery releases might have removed some features required by an older plugin.

The most popular jQuery plugin is the jQuery UI, which expands the functionality of jQuery with a large collection of functions and methods for creating specialized user interfaces. As with jQuery, the jQuery UI is available either as a downloadable .js file or via a link to a CDN. You will use the jQueryUI to add one more visual effect to the FAQ page.

To access the jQuery UI library from a CDN:

1. Go to **code.jquery.com/ui** in your browser.
2. Click the link for the minified build of the last jQuery UI library. Copy the link from the Code Integration overlay shown in **Figure 12-20**.

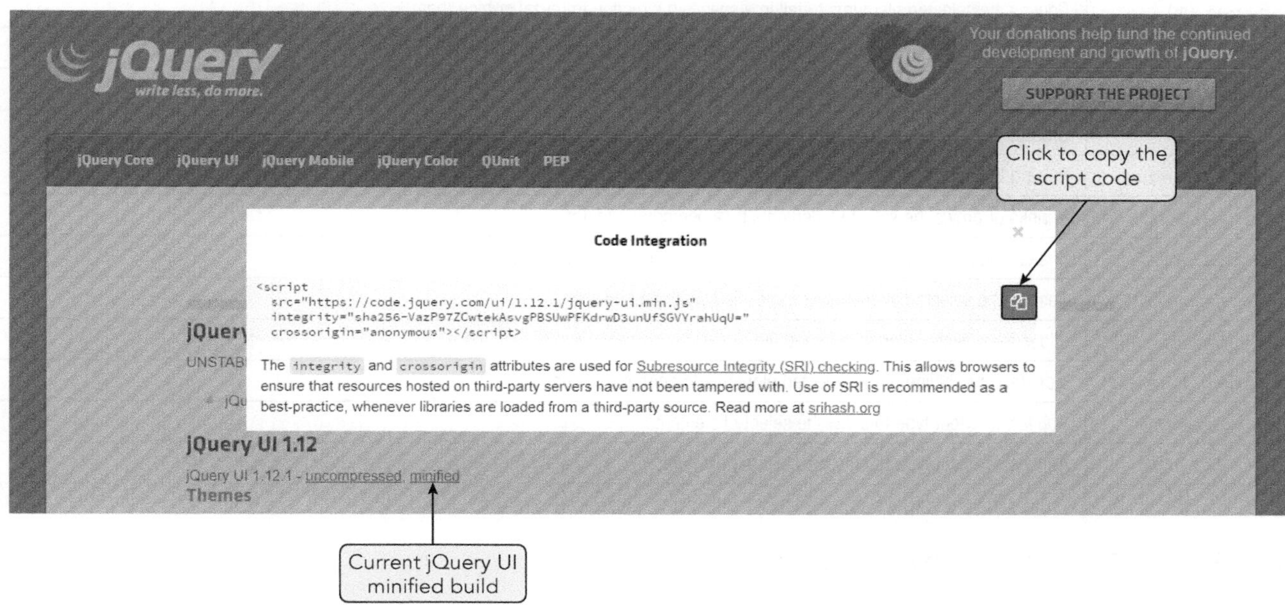

Figure 12-20 Copying the link to the minified jQuery UI build

3. Click the **Copy** button to copy the code.
4. Return to the **js12.html** file in your code editor.
5. After the script element for the jQuery library, paste the copied script element for the jQuery UI library as shown in **Figure 12-21**.

```
   <title>Bonsai Expressions FAQ</title>
   <link rel="stylesheet" href="styles.css" />
   <script src="https://code.jquery.com/jquery-3.6.0.min.js"
           integrity="sha256-/xUj+3OJU5yExlq6GSYGSHk7tPXikynS7ogEvDej/m4="
           crossorigin="anonymous">
   </script>
   <script src="https://code.jquery.com/ui/1.12.1/jquery-ui.min.js"
           integrity="sha256-VazP97ZCwtekAsvgPBSUwPFKdrwD3unUfSGVYrahUqU="
           crossorigin="anonymous">
   </script>
   <script src="js12.js"></script>
</head>
```

Link to the minified version of the jQuery UI library

Figure 12-21 Linking to the minified jQuery UI build

6. Close the js12.html file, saving your changes.

To add other visual effects to selected elements, the jQuery UI library provides the following `effect()` method:

```
effect(type, options, speed, callback)
```

where *`type`* is the type of effect, *`options`* is an object containing parameter values for the effect type, *`speed`* is the speed of the effect, and *`callback`* is a function that will be run once the effect is over. **Figure 12-22** describes some of the effect types supported by the `effect()` method.

EFFECT METHOD	DESCRIPTION
`blind(param)`	Pulls a "blind" over the element content in the horizontal or vertical direction, where *param* are the parameters associated with the method
`bound(param)`	Bounces the element with the first bounce either fading the element in or the last bounce fading the element out
`clip(param)`	Hides or shows the selected elements by clipping them horizontally or vertically
`drop(param)`	Causes the selected elements to fall in a specified direction to reveal or hide them
`explode(param)`	Splits the selected elements into several pieces to reveal or hide them
`fold(param)`	Folds the selected elements to reveal them or hide them
`puff(param)`	Creates a puff effect by scaling the selected elements up and hiding them at the same time
`pulsate(param)`	Pulsing the selected elements in and out to reveal or hide them
`scale(param)`	Shrinks or grows the selected elements by a percentage factor
`shake(param)`	Shakes the selected elements several times in the vertical or horizontal direction
`size(param)`	Resizes the selected elements to a specified width and height
`slide(param)`	Slides the selected elements in and out of the viewport to reveal or hide them
`transfer(param)`	Transfers the outline of the selected elements to another element
`show(effect)`	Applies an effect type to show the selected elements
`hide(effect)`	Applies an effect type to hide the selected elements
`toggle(effect)`	Toggles the effect type between showing and hiding the selected elements

Figure 12-22 Effect types from jQuery UI

You will use the `clip()` method to display the list of questions onto the FAQ page when the page is initially opened by the browser. The general syntax of the method is:

```
effect("clip", {
   mode: mode,
   direction: direction,
}, speed, callback)
```

where *mode* is either `hide` or `show` and *direction* is `vertical` (the default) or `horizontal`. Add this method the `dl#faq` selector.

To add a clip effect:

1. Go to **js12.js** file in your code editor.
2. Directly below the `animate()` method, add the following code to initially hide the list of frequently asked questions when the page is loaded by the browser:

```
// Reveal the questions when the page opens
$("dl#faq")
.hide()
```

3. Add the following `effect()` method to "unclip" the list of questions horizontally over a 0.6-second time interval:

```
.effect("clip", {
   mode: "show",
   direction: "horizontal"
}, 600);
```

Figure 12-23 describes the code added to the file.

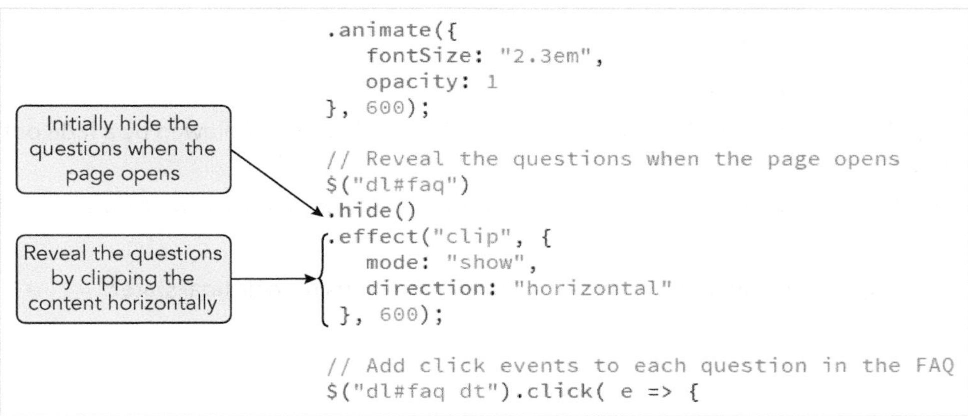

Figure 12-23 Adding the clip effect from the jQuery UI

4. Close the file, saving your changes.
5. Reload **js12.html** in your browser. Verify that when the FAQ page loads, the list of questions is revealed, unclipping in the horizontal direction.

You have concluded your work on the Bonsai Expressions FAQ page. You can continue to explore jQuery and jQuery UI for other methods and objects that can be useful to you in your work. jQuery provides an easy way to add special features to your website that will be supported across all browsers.

Skills at Work | Becoming a Professional

Web developers are important professionals in this age of information. There is hardly an aspect of life that has not been profoundly affected by the web. There is a lot of opportunity for the professional web developer to find meaningful and varied work across a wide range of disciplines. As you consider entering this field, consider the following:

- **Choose an area of specialization.** The tools, languages, and techniques in creating and maintaining a website is vast and few people can do it all. Find the area that interests you most from web design to server security and focus your attentions and mastering that field.
- **Learn the technical skills.** Even if you are specializing in a specific area you need to have a broad understanding of the field. Employers want employees well versed in three main areas: HTML, CSS, and JavaScript. Beyond that you should have some knowledge of CSS frameworks like Bootstrap and Foundation as well as backend languages like Ruby, PHP, and SQL Server.
- **Practice Practice Practice.** The web provides several sites where you can hone your coding skills. Set up a GitHub account and submit code samples to that site. An active Github profile can help you get noticed and will demonstrate your problem-solving ability and your ability to work in a group dynamic.
- **Create a portfolio.** Getting certified in a wide range of languages and software tools is very important, but employers want to see what you have done and what you can do. Maintain a portfolio of your coding projects and place it online where prospective employers can easily access it.

Finally, *never stop learning*. This is an actively changing field. New languages, software, and approaches are constantly being developed, and established methods can become quickly outdated. The way you interact with the web today will not be the same way you interact with it four years hence. A professional is always a student.

Quick Check 2

1. What are two easing values used by jQuery effects?
2. Provide jQuery code to slide up the `article#main` element over a half-second interval, followed by a fade out over another half-second interval.
3. Provide jQuery code to change the font size of the `article#main` element from an initial value of 1em to a final value of 1.4em over a 2-second interval.
4. What jQuery method is used to stop an animation and move all queued animations to their final state?
5. What is jQuery UI?

Summary

- jQuery is a JavaScript library built on JavaScript and providing objects, properties, and methods that simplify common coding challenges.
- jQuery can be downloaded from the jQuery website and linked to on a Content Delivery Network (CDN).
- jQuery commands are marked with $ symbol and elements are selected using the `$(`*`selector`*`)` where *`selector`* is a CSS selector.
- jQuery methods are connected to the `$(`*`selector`*`)` to traverse the DOM, create new elements, and modify element content and style.
- Events are managed in jQuery by connecting event methods to the `$(`*`selector`*`)`.
- The jQuery `show()` method is used to reveal selected elements; the `hide()` method is used to hide those elements.
- jQuery supports several methods to apply effects and animations to selected elements.
- The jQuery UI plugin contains a library of expanded effects and user interfaces that can be used in conjunction with jQuery.

Key Terms

Content Delivery Network (CDN)
getter
JavaScript library
jQuery
jQuery animation
jQuery effect
jQuery plugin
jQuery UI
normal jQuery build
object chaining
setter
slim jQuery build
Subresource Integrity checking (SRI)

Review Questions

1. What language is jQuery written in?
   a. CSS
   b. JavaScript
   c. HTML
   d. Java

2. Instead of hosting your own copy of the jQuery library, you can link to a copy of the jQuery file ______________.
   a. on the W3C website
   b. on the WHATWG website
   c. in a stylesheet
   d. on a CDN

3. Every jQuery statement begins with which character?
   a. #
   b. $
   c. .
   d. (

4. Which of the following jQuery statements selects all h1 headings of the intro class?
   a. `$(h1.intro)`
   b. `getElementByClassName("intro")`
   c. `$("h1.intro")`
   d. `"h1.intro"`

5. What is accomplished by the following code?

```
$(()=> {
   jQuery statements
});
```

   a. An anonymous function is attached to an empty element.
   b. An anonymous function is run when the DOM is ready.
   c. An anonymous function is applied to every element in the DOM.
   d. An anonymous function is applied to none of the elements in the DOM.

6. Provide code to select all siblings of the `nav#links` element.
   a. `$(nav#links).siblings()`
   b. `$(nav#links.siblings)`
   c. `$("nav#links").siblings`
   d. `$("nav#links").siblings()`

7. What jQuery method can be used to get or set the HTML content of an element?
   a. `innerHTML`
   b. `html()`
   c. `innerHTML()`
   d. `text()`

8. To enclose selected elements within specified HTML content, which jQuery method should be used?
   a. `wrap()`
   b. `outerHTML()`
   c. `enclose()`
   d. `replaceOuter()`

9. Provide jQuery code that runs when the `input#user` element changes value.
   a. `$("input#user").onchange()`
   b. `$(input#user).onchange()`
   c. `$("input#user").change()`
   d. `$("input#user").addChange()`

10. Which of the following objects could reference the event object from a jQuery event method that initiated the event?
    a. `$(e.target)`
    b. `e.target`
    c. `$("e.target")`
    d. `($e.target)`

11. Provide code to apply the `show()` method to every `article` element in the document over a 2-second time interval.
    a. `$(article.show(2))`
    b. `$(article).show(2)`
    c. `$("article").show(2000)`
    d. `$(article).show(2000)`

12. How does the browser handle jQuery effects that are chained?
    a. The effects are run asynchronously.
    b. The effects are run synchronously.
    c. Only the effect that finishes first is run.
    d. Only the last effect in the chain is run.

13. The `animate()` method is used for which action?
    a. It applies changes in the CSS properties of the selected elements over time.
    b. It runs an animation from the jQuery UI.
    c. It places effects within a quue.
    d. It is used only for animated text.

14. What jQuery method is used to halt all effects in a queue?
    a. `halt()`
    b. `stop()`
    c. `cancel()`
    d. `finish()`
15. Which effect type from jQuery UI causes the selected elements to fall in a specified direction?
    a. `fall`
    b. `clip`
    c. `puff`
    d. `drop`
16. Why should you load the minified version of jQuery?
17. What is the difference between applying a jQuery method that includes a parameter value and method that is empty of a parameter value?
18. Where should the `script` element that links or loads the jQuery library be placed relative to the script for the app's code?
19. Why should jQuery methods be chained to a selector rather than placing the methods within separate commands?
20. Why is jQuery still relevant to web developers despite advances in the standard JavaScript language?

Hands-On Projects

Hands-On Project 12-1

In this project you will use jQuery on the *Wildlife Sea Cruises* website. Most of the content and styles have been completed for you. Your task will be to finish the project by creating a dropdown menu containing links to other pages on the website. A preview of the completed project is shown in **Figure 12-24**.

Figure 12-24 Completed Project 12-1

Do the following:

1. Use your code editor to open the **project12-01_txt.html** and **project12-01_txt.js** files from the js12 ▶ project01 folder. Enter your name and the date in the comment section of each file and save them as **project12-01.html** and **project12-01.js**, respectively.
2. Go to the **project12-01.html** file in your code editor. Add a `script` element to load the latest minified build of the jQuery library from the CDN on the jQuery website. Add another `script` element loading the contents of the project12-01.js file. Take some time to study the contents and structure of the document and then close the file, saving your changes.
3. Go to the **project12-01.js** file in your code editor. Below the comment section insert jQuery code that runs an anonymous function when the page is loaded and ready. Within the anonymous function do the tasks described in Steps 4 and 5.
4. Create a jQuery selector for the `li.submenu` element. Attach the `mouseover()` method to the selector that runs an anonymous function. Within the anonymous function apply the `show()` method to `$(e.currentTarget).children("ul")` selector to show the contents of the dropdown menu during the mouseover event.
5. Chain the `mouseout()` method to the `li.submenu` selector. Within the anonymous function apply the `hide()` method to `$(e.currentTarget).children("ul")` selector to hide the contents of the dropdown menu during the mouseout event.
6. Save your changes to the file and the open the **project12-01.html** file in your browser.
7. Verify that when you move the mouse pointer over any of the three menu headings, a submenu appears below the heading and that when you move the pointer off, the submenu disappears.

Hands-On Project 12-2

In this project you will complete a Fahrenheit-to-Celsius calculator using jQuery methods. **Figure 12-25** shows a preview of the page.

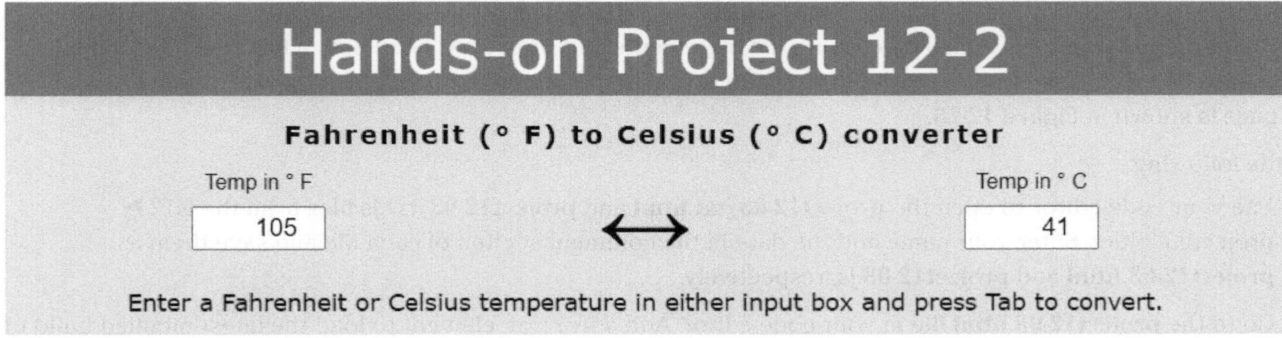

Figure 12-25 Completed Project 12-2

When users change the value of either the Fahrenheit or Celsius input box, the value of other input box will automatically update to reflect the change. To create this calculator, the app will use the jQuery `change()` method to respond to each change in the input boxes and the `val()` method to either get or set the temperature values.

Do the following:

1. Use your code editor to open the **project12-02_txt.html** and **project12-02_txt.js** files from the js12 ▶ project02 folder. Enter your name and the date in the comment section of each file and save them as **project12-02.html** and **project12-02.js**, respectively.

2. Go to the **project12-02.html** file in your code editor. Add a `script` element to load the latest minified build of the jQuery library from the CDN on the jQuery website. Add another `script` element to load the contents of the project12-02.js file and defer that script until after the page is completely loaded. Study the contents and structure of the document and then close the file, saving your changes.
3. Go to the **project12-02.js** file in your code editor. Below the comment section apply the `change()` method to the `input#cValue` element, responding to changes in the Celsius input box. Within the `change()` method create an anonymous function that does the following:
    a. Declare the **`celsius`** variable, setting its value equal to the value of the event target. Use the `val()` method to get the event target's value.
    b. Declare the **`fahrenheit`** variable with a value equal to 1.8 times the `celsius` variable's value plus 32.
    c. Apply the `val()` method to the `input#fValue` element, displaying the value of the `fahrenheit` variable. Apply the `toFixed(0)` method to that variable, displaying the calculate value as an integer.
4. Apply `change()` method to the `input#fValue` element, responding to changes to the fahrenheit input box. Add the following commands to the anonymous function for the `change()` method:
    a. Declare the **`fahrenheit`** variable, setting its value equal to the value of the event target. Once again, use the `val()` method to get the event target value.
    b. Declare the **`celsius`** variable with a value equal to the value of the `fahrenheit` variable minus 32 and then divided by 1.8.
    c. Apply the `val()` method to the `input#cValue` element, displaying the value of the `celsius` variable. Once again, use the `toFixed(0)` method to display the temperature value as an integer. </EOCAL>
5. Save your changes to the file and then open **project12-02.html** in your browser. Verify that when you change the value of one temperature input box, the value of the other temperature automatically updates to show the corresponding Celsius or Fahrenheit value.

Hands-On Project 12-3

In this project you will use jQuery to add visual effects to a recipe page for the dessert website *Save your Fork*. Each recipe has an ingredients list and a list of directions. To save page space, both lists are initially hidden, but their contents can be revealed by clicking the Ingredients and Directions headings. When those headings are clicked, the lists toggle between sliding down to reveal their content and sliding up to hide it. A preview of the page is shown in **Figure 12-26**.

Do the following:

1. Use your code editor to open the **project12-03_txt.html** and **project12-03_txt.js** files from the js12 ▶ project03 folder. Enter your name and the date in the comment section of each file and save them as **project12-03.html** and **project12-03.js**, respectively.
2. Go to the **project12-03.html** file in your code editor. Add a `script` element to load the latest minified build of the jQuery library from the CDN on the jQuery website. Add another `script` element to load the contents of the project12-03.js file, deferring the script until after the page loads. Review the contents and structure of the document and then close the file, saving your changes.
3. Go to the **project12-03.js** file in your code editor. Below the comment section apply the `click()` method to the `article > h2` selector. Within the anonymous function inserted into the `click()` method, do the tasks described in Steps 4 through 6.
4. Declare the following variables using jQuery.
    a. Declare the **`heading`** variable referencing the target of the click event.
    b. Declare the **`list`** variable referencing the next sibling element of the heading variable.
    c. Declare the **`headingImage`** variable referencing the children of the heading variable whose tag name is "img".

Hands-on Project 12-3
Save your Fork
Apple Bavarian Torte
A classic European torte baked in a springform pan. Cream cheese, sliced almonds, and apples make this the perfect holiday treat (12 servings).

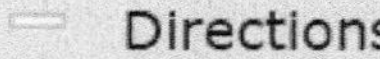

Directions
1. Preheat oven to 450° F (230° C).
2. Cream together butter, sugar, vanilla, and flour.
3. Press crust mixture into the flat bottom of a 9-inch springform pan. Set aside.
4. In a medium bowl, blend cream cheese and sugar. Beat in egg and vanilla. Pour cheese mixture over crust.
5. Toss apples with sugar and cinnamon. Spread apple mixture over all.
6. Bake for 10 minutes. Reduce heat to 400° F (200° C) and continue baking for 25 minutes.
7. Sprinkle almonds over top of torte. Continue baking until lightly browned. Cool before removing from pan.

Figure 12-26 Completed Project 12-3

5. Alternate between hiding and showing the content of the lists by applying the `slideToggle()` method to the `list` variable over a half-second interval.
6. Change the symbol displayed in the headings by applying the `attr()` method to `headingImage` variable to get the value of the `src` attribute. If `src` attribute value is equal to "plus.pg", apply the `attr()` method to `headingImage` to set the `src` attribute value to "minus.png"; otherwise set the `src` attribute value to "plus.png".
7. Save your changes to the file and then load **project12-03.html** in your web browser.
8. Click the Ingredients and Directions headings and verify that the contents of each list are displayed using a sliding effect and that the symbol within each heading alternates between a plus and a minus.

Hands-On Project 12-4

In this project you will use jQuery to add visual effects to interactive slideshow. The user progresses through the slides by clicking the left and right arrow buttons located on either side of the slide box. Twelve images are stored within the slide box, but only one image is displayed at a time. The other images are brought into view by moving the image list to the left or right within the box. A caption for each image is displayed below the box. **Figure 12-27** shows a preview of the slideshow page.

Figure 12-27 Completed Project 12-4

The images are moved by changing the value of the CSS `left` property for each image using the `animate()` method. The image caption is changed by using the blind effect from the jQuery UI. The syntax of the blind effect is as follows:

```
$(selector).effect("blind", {
   mode: mode,
   direction: direction,
}, speed, callback)
```

where *mode* is either `show` or `hide` and *direction* is `up`, `down`, `left`, `right`, `vertical`, or `horizontal`. The callback function will change the image caption text.

Do the following:

1. Use your code editor to open the **project12-04_txt.html** and **project12-04_txt.js** files from the js12 ► project04 folder. Enter your name and the date in the comment section of each file and save them as **project12-04.html** and **project12-04.js**, respectively.
2. Go to the **project12-03.html** file in your code editor.
   a. Add a `script` element to load the latest minified build of the jQuery library from the CDN on the jQuery website.
   b. Following this `script` element with another `script` element that loads the latest minified build of the jQuery UI plugin from the jQuery CDN.
   c. Finally, add another `script` element that loads the contents of the project12-04.js file, deferring the script until after the page loads.
   d. Review the contents and structure of the document and then close the file, saving your changes.

3. Go to the **project12-04.js** file in your code editor. Below the comment section declare the **`slideNumber`** variable and set its initial value to 0.
4. Apply the `click()` method to the `img#leftbutton` selector. When this button is clicked, images will be moved to the right through the slide box.
5. Within the anonymous function for the `click()` method insert an `if` statement that tests whether `slideNumber` is greater than 0. If true, do the following:
   a. Apply the `animate()` method to the `img.slideImages` selector. Within the animate method, set the value of the `left` property to `"+=401px"`. Apply the animate method over a 1-second interval.
   b. Decrease the value of `slideImage` by 1.
   c. Declare the **`currentSlide`** variable, referencing the selector `$("img.slidesImages")[slideNumber]`.
   d. Declare the **`slideCaption`** variable, setting its value equal to `$(currentSlide).attr("alt")`.
   e. Call the `changeCaption()` function using `slideCaption` as the parameter value.
6. Copy and paste the code from Steps 4 and 5 at the end of the file. Make the following changes to the pasted code.
   a. Change `click()` method so that it is applied to the `img#rightbutton` selector, which moves images to the left through the slide box.
   b. Change the `if` statement to test whether `slidenumber` is less than 11.
   c. Change the statement that sets the value of the `left` property within the animate method to `"-=401px"`.
   d. Change the statement that decreases the value of the `slideImage` variable by 1 to increase the value of that variable by 1.
7. Create the `changeCaption()` function with a single parameter named **`captionText`**. The purpose of this function is to change the image caption using the `blind` effect from the jQuery UI plugin. Add the following commands to the function:
   a. Apply the blind effect method to the `div#caption` selector. Set the `mode` parameter to "hide" and the `direction` parameter to "left". Set the speed to 500 milliseconds. Add an anonymous callback function that contains the single statement: `$("div#caption").text(captionText);`
   b. Chain another blind effect method to the `div#caption` selector. Set the `mode` parameter to "show", the `direction` parameter to "left", and the speed to 500 milliseconds.
8. Save your changes to the file and then load **project12-04.html** in your browser.
9. Verify that you can scroll back and forth through the slide images by clicking the right and left buttons. Also verify that the caption changes with each new image and is revealed using the blind effect. Note that the slideshow cannot go past the last image or go before the first image.

Hands-On Project 12-5

Debugging Challenge

You have been given a web form in which users supply their username, email address, and password. The validation for the form has been written in jQuery. However, the validation is not working because of errors in the code. You have been asked to fix the code so that the form validates the user data and submits that data for processing. A preview of the form is shown in **Figure 12-28**.

Do the following:

1. Use your code editor to open the **project12-05.html** and **project12-05.js** files from the js12 ▶ project05 folder. Enter your name and the date in the comment section of each file and save them as **project12-05.html** and **project12-05.js**, respectively.

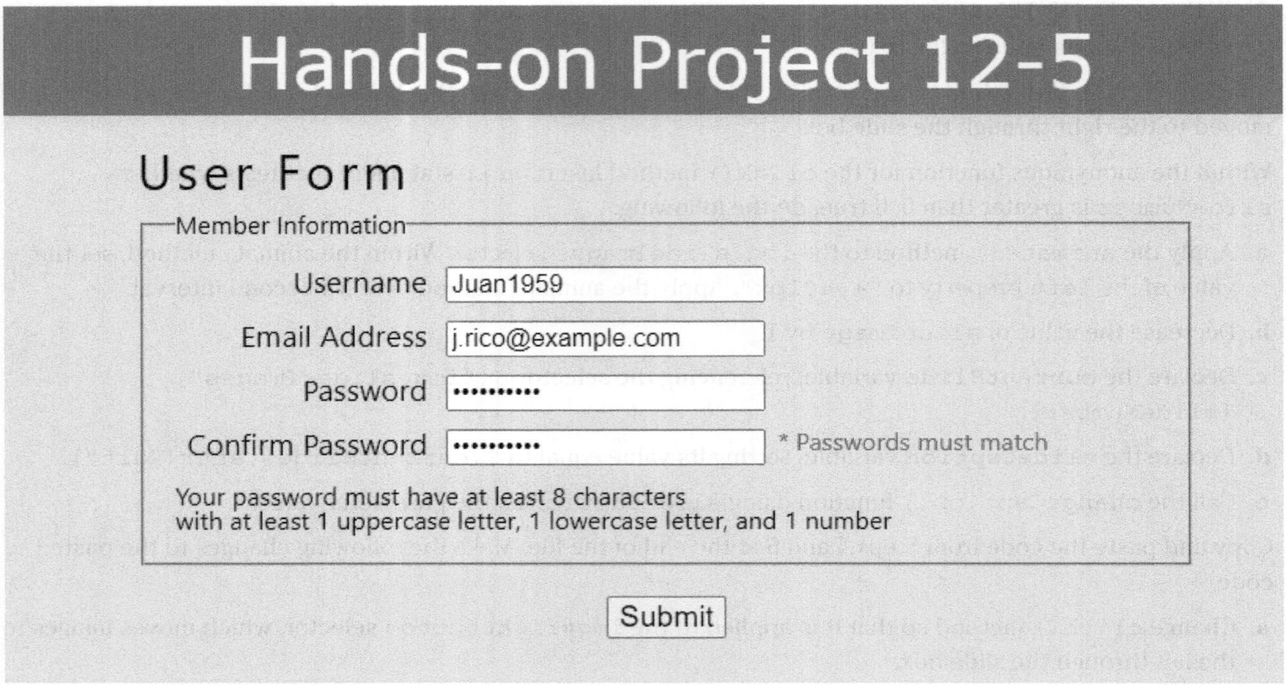

Figure 12-28 Completed Project 12-5

2. Go to the **project12-05.html** file in your code editor. Add a `script` element to load the latest minified build of the jQuery library from the CDN on the jQuery website. Add another `script` element to load the contents of the project12-05.js file, deferring the script until after the page loads. Take some time to study the contents of the file and then close the file, saving your changes.
3. Go to the **project12-05.js** file in your code editor. Fix the following mistakes in the file:
   a. The first statement selects the web form from the page, but there is an error in the selector.
   b. To methods are chained to the selector, applying the `attr()` and `submit()` methods. But there is an error that breaks the chain.
   c. The code tests whether the value in the `username` input box is equal to an empty text string, but there is a mistake in the `if` statement.
   d. The `email` variable stores the reference to the email input box. Correct the mistake in the statement.
   e. The `mailRE` variable stores a regular expression literal to match email addresses. There is an error in creating the regular expression literal.
   f. The code applies a chain of methods to the `$(pwd).next()` selector to display an error message. There is a mistake in constructing the chain.
   g. If the passwords are not equal, the app will display an error message to the user after a 0.5-second interval. However, there is a mistake in specifying the interval for the `$(pwd2).next()` selector.
   h. If the `isValid` variable is equal to `false`, the form will not be submitted. There is a mistake in the `if` statement that tests this condition.
4. Save your changes to the file and then load **project12-05.html** in your web browser.

5. Verify the following in the completed form:
   a. Verify that if you do not enter a username, an error is displayed on the form.
   b. Verify that if you do not enter a proper email address, the form displays an error message.
   c. Verify that if you do not enter a password consisting of at least characters with at least one uppercase letter, at least one lowercase letter, and at least one number, an error is reported.
   d. Verify that if the two passwords do not match, an error is reported.
   e. Verify that if the form is properly completed and submitted, the browser displays a web containing the form values you entered.

Case Projects

Individual Case Project

In your individual website, revise a function to use jQuery selectors and methods. Identify a function that contains at least three selectors that you can replace with jQuery selectors, and that performs at least one DOM traversal or CSS change that you can replace with a jQuery method. Comment out the code you replace rather than deleting it. Be sure to link to the jQuery library in all HTML documents that link to the .js file you have updated. When your revisions are done, test all pages that use the function to ensure they still perform as they did when the function was written in standard JavaScript.

Team Case Project

Examine the documentation of jQuery methods and properties at api.jquery.com. As a group, pick a jQuery method that would enhance the appearance or function of one or more pages of your group website. As a group, agree on which sections of your code need to be changed to implement this method. Make the changes as a group and continue to save and test your changes until the feature works as you expect.

APPENDIX A

Installing and Configuring a Testing Server

For frontend development with HTML, CSS, and JavaScript, you do most of your testing on your own laptop or desktop computer. However, some web app functionality can be tested only by moving the code to a web server and opening it in your browser using an HTTP connection. A web server used privately for testing purposes is known as a testing server. Applications published on a testing server are available only to the developers working on them, and not to other users of the Internet or a local intranet. When testing is complete and your application is ready to be released, you move your app to a production server accessible to your target audience.

It is common for web developers to install a testing server on the same computer they use to code. Having both the server and client on the same machine enables quick testing of changes while coding or debugging, without needing to be connected to a network or to first transfer files to another machine.

Like any web server, a testing server consists of server software and interpreters. The server software listens for and processes HTTP requests. When necessary, it passes requests along to interpreters of specific languages for parsing and processing and then forwards the results to the client. Most web servers on the web today are running either Apache, nginx, or Internet Information Services for server software.

This appendix provides instructions the XAMPP server software, which is free and available for computers running Windows or Mac OS X. XAMPP installs the Apache web server along with the MySQL database and interpreters for the PHP and Perl languages.

Installing XAMPP for Windows

The following instructions detail installing XAMPP for Windows. These steps are followed by a separate set of instructions for installing XAMPP for Mac OS X.

To install XAMPP for Windows:

1. In your browser, open **apachefriends.org**. As **Figure A-1** shows, the Download page provides links for multiple versions of XAMPP for each operating system at the time of this writing. Your page may appear different.

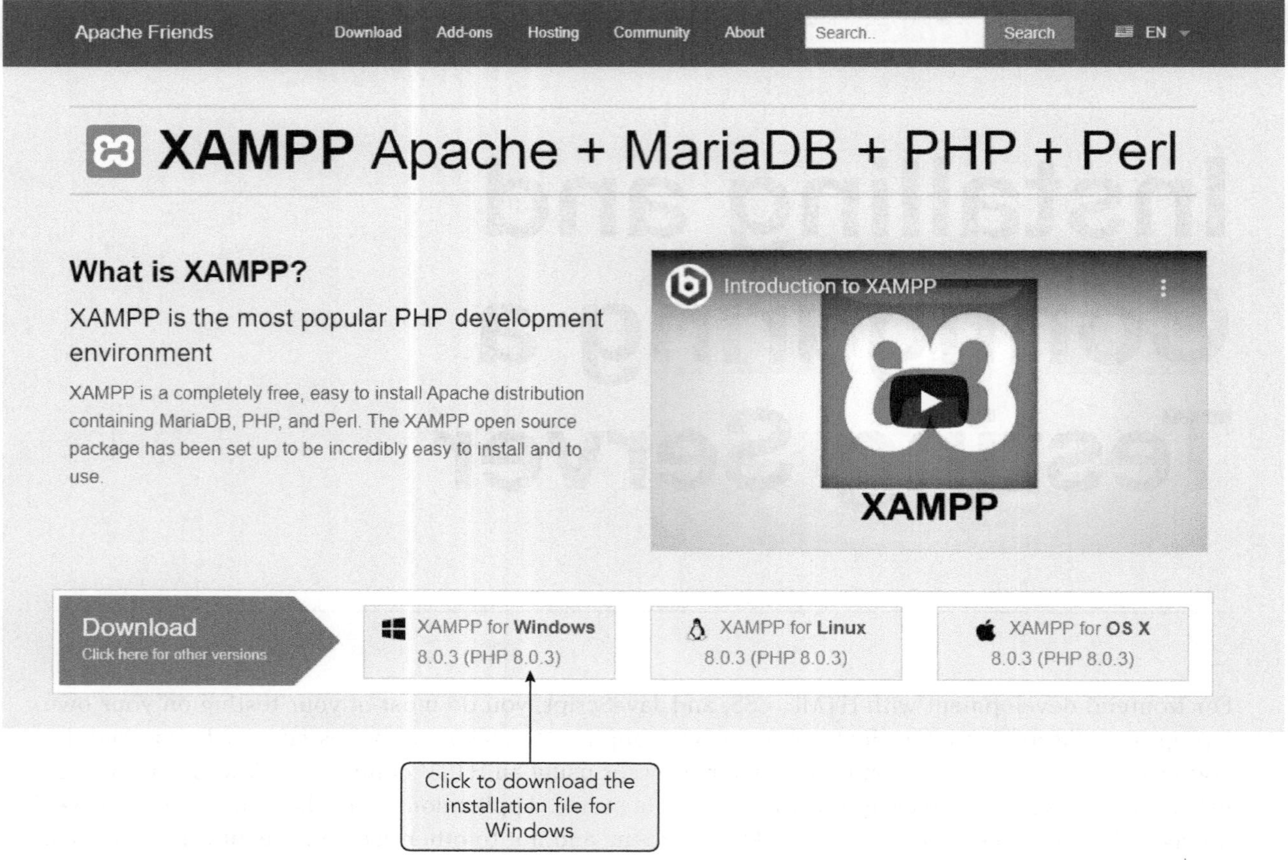

Figure A-1 XAMPP download page for Windows

2. Click the download link for the Windows edition of XAMPP to save the executable installation file to your computer.
3. When the download is completed, if your browser offers you the option to run the downloaded file, follow the browser instructions to do so. Otherwise, open the folder to which the file was downloaded, locate the downloaded file, and double-click it to start the installer.
4. If Windows asks for confirmation that you wish to install the file, follow the instructions shown to authorize the installation.
5. If a warning is displayed about the interaction of the XAMPP installer with antivirus, click Yes to continue with the installation. The installer may also display a window discussing the interaction between XAMPP and Windows User Account Control. Click **OK**. The Setup window is displayed, as shown in **Figure A-2**.
6. Click Next. The Select Components window is displayed. Ensure that all boxes are checked, as shown in **Figure A-3**, and then click **Next**.
7. The Installation folder window is displayed. Choose the location in which you want XAMPP installed as shown in **Figure A-4**. Click **Next**.
8. The language configuration window is displayed. Choose your language and click **Next**.
9. The Bitnami for XAMPP window is displayed, which offers more information about enhancing an XAMPP installation with other open-source apps. Uncheck the Learn more about Bitnami for XAMPP box to specify a basic installation and then click **Next**.
10. The Ready to Install window is displayed. Click **Next**. A progress bar is displayed while the installer downloads required files and installs the XAMPP server software.

Figure A-2 Setup window

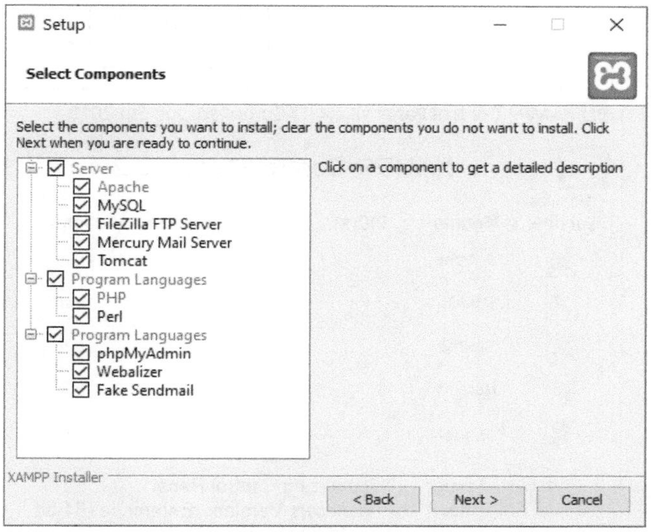

Figure A-3 Selected components window

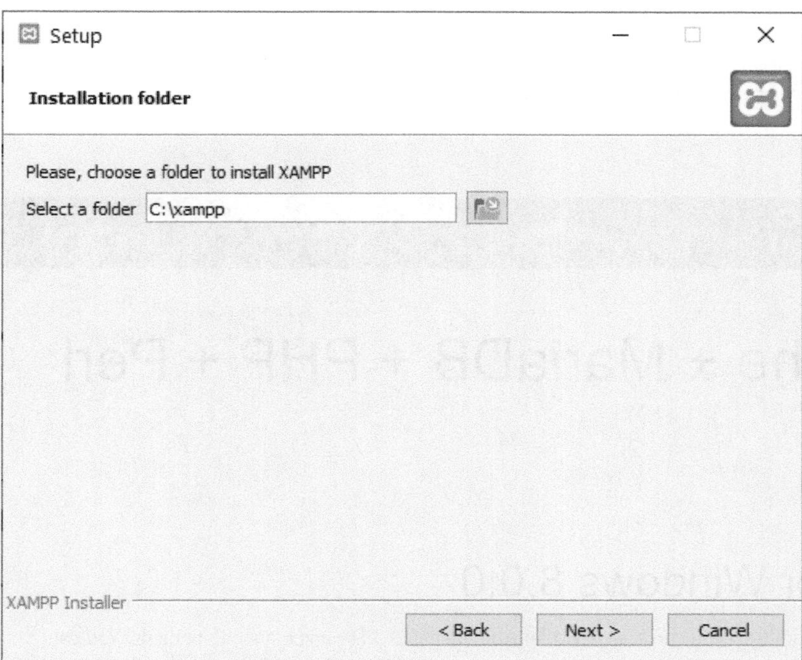

Figure A-4 Installation folder window

11. When setup is completed, you will be able to open the XAMPP control panel shown in **Figure A-5**.

12. The Control Panel lists several modules. In the line for the Apache module, click the **Start** button to start the Apache service. If Windows displays a security alert dialog box, click Allow access to continue. (Note: If you see a Stop button instead of a Start button, the Apache service is already started, so you can skip this step.)

13. To test your XAMPP installation, open your browser, then in the address bar, type **localhost** and press **Enter**. Your browser should display a default web document for XAMPP, as shown in **Figure A-6** (your page may differ.) This confirms that your Apache web server is working correctly.

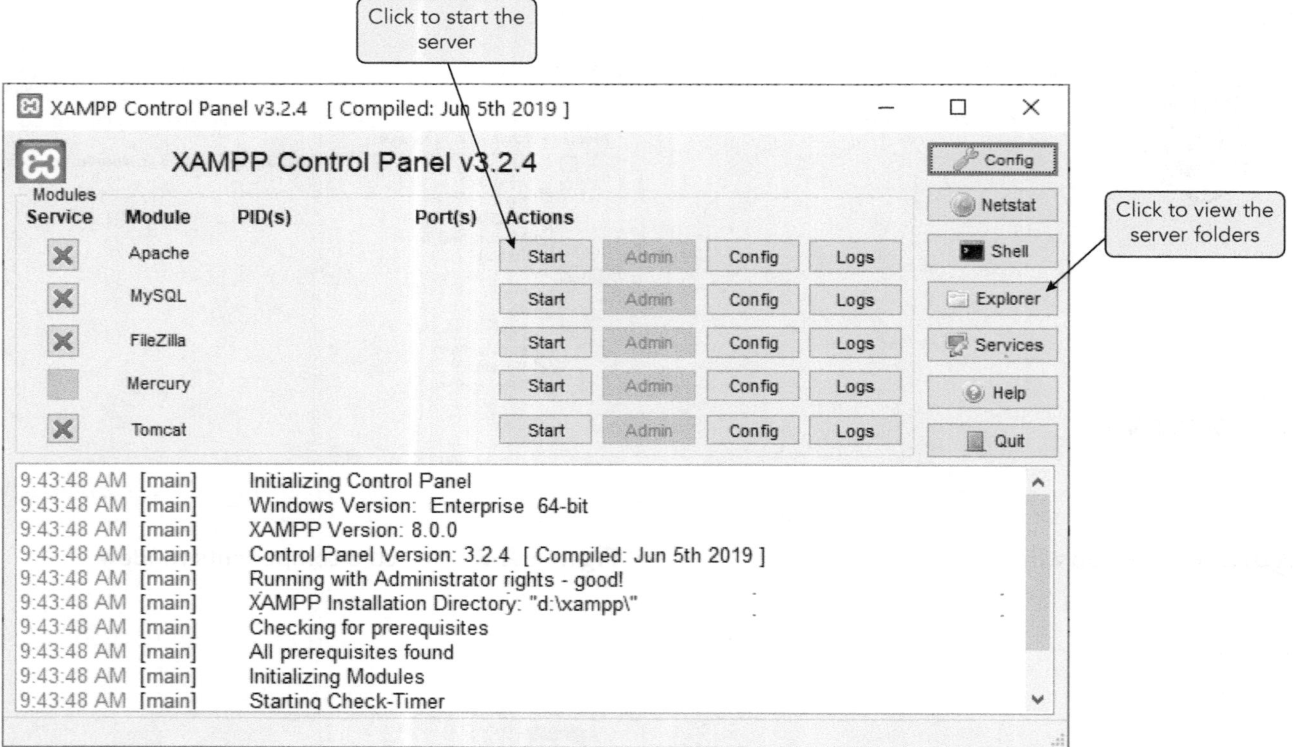

Figure A-5 XAMPP control panel

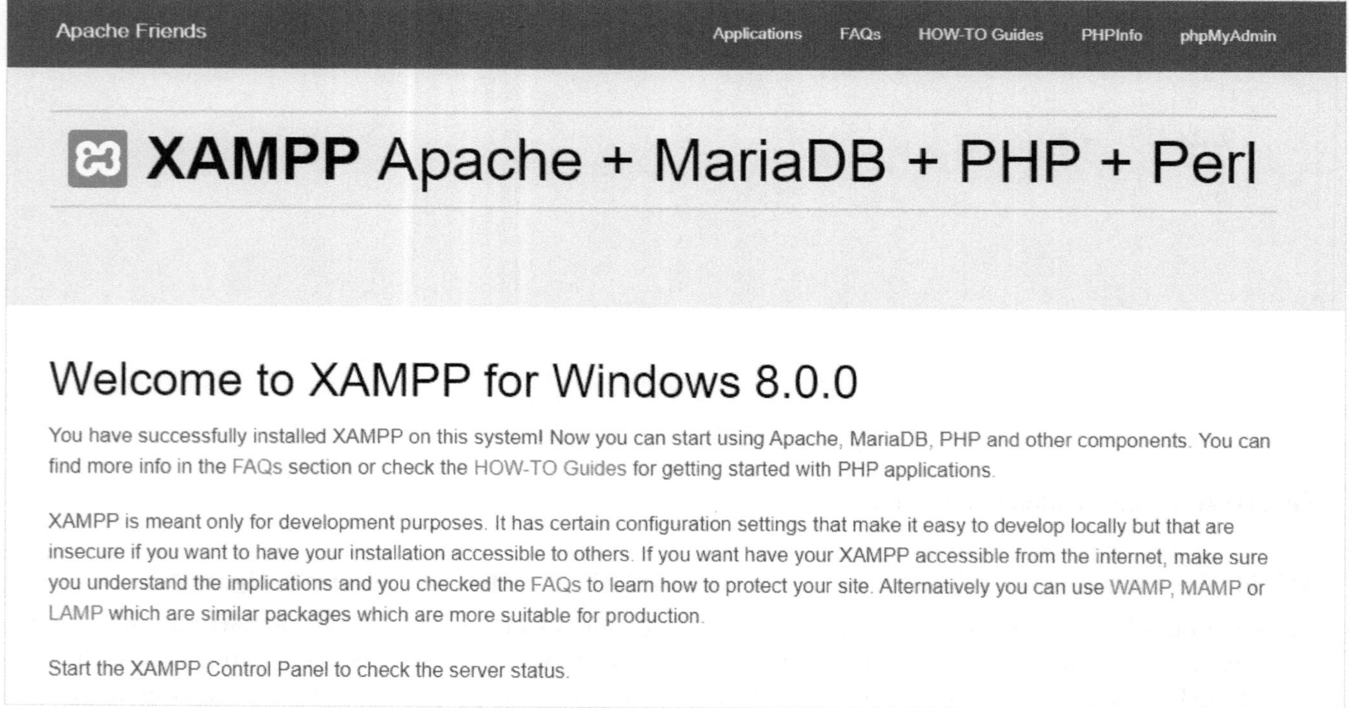

Figure A-6 Default XAMPP for the local server

Once the server is installed and running, you can move files and folders into the XAMPP folder structure so they can be viewed through the server connection at localhost.

To move your own files to the Apache installation so you can open them with an HTTP connection, open File Explorer, navigate to the location of your files, copy and paste one or more files or folders to the clipboard, navigate to *xampp*/`htdocs` where *xampp* is the installation folder for your version of XAMPP specified during the Install routine, and then paste your copied files or folders.

For instance, if you copied a file called register.html to the `htdocs` folder, you would open this file in a browser by entering `localhost/register.html`. If you copied a folder called website containing a file called info.html, you would open this file in a browser by entering `localhost/website/info.html`.

If your website needs to use Perl, you will have to edit your server script so that it accesses the perl.exe file, which is located at the following address:

```
xampp\perl\bin\perl.exe
```

where *xampp* is the installation folder for XAMPP. You can reference XAPP's extensive list of online documentation to configure other aspects of your local server.

Installing XAMPP for Mac OS X

The following instructions detail installing XAMPP for Mac OS X.

To install XAMPP for Mac OS X:

1. In your browser, open **apachefriends.org** and then scroll down to the XAMPP for Apple section. As **Figure A-7** shows, the Download page provides links for multiple versions of XAMPP for each operating system.

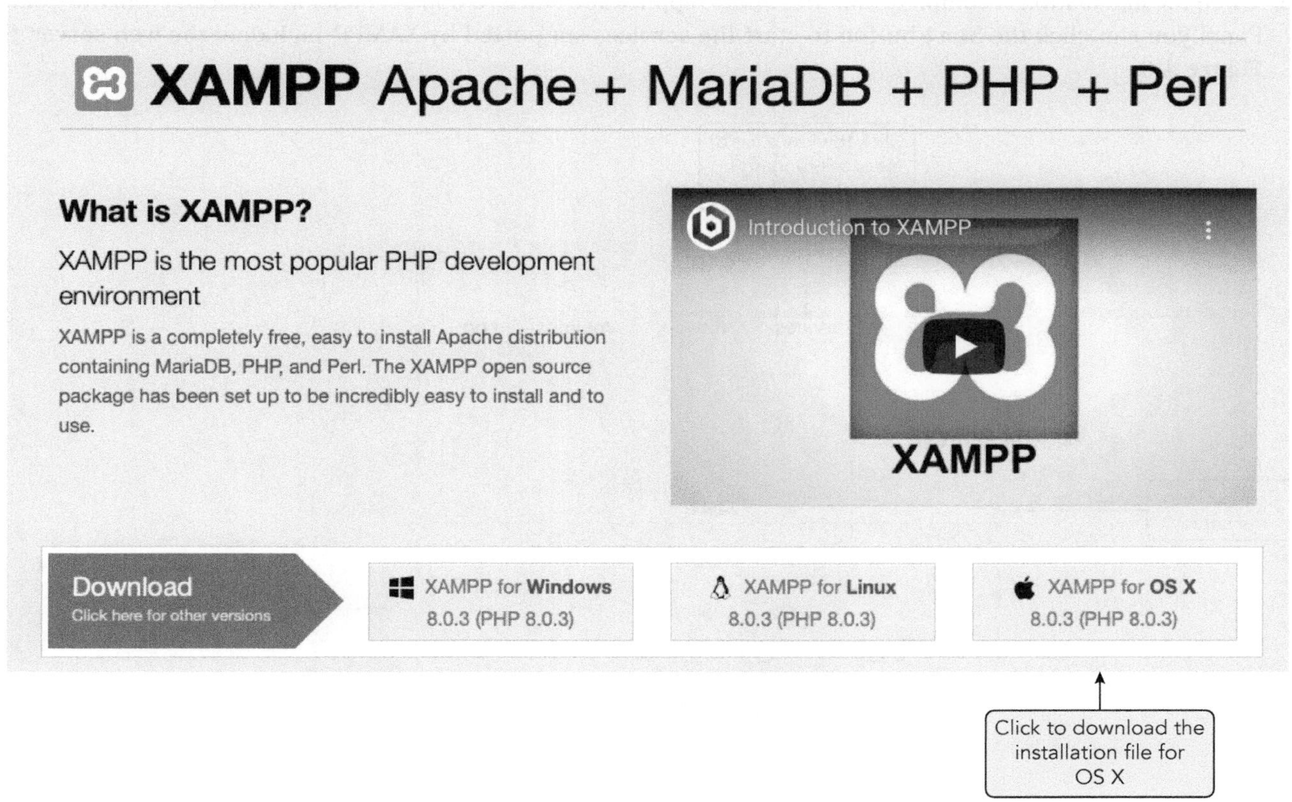

Figure A-7 XAMPP download page for Mac OS X

2. Click the download link for the Windows edition of XAMPP to save the executable installation file to your computer.
3. When the download is completed, run the executable installation file.

4. After the installation file has run, move the XAMPP application into the Applications folder (see **Figure A-8**).

Figure A-8 Installing XAMPP in the Applications folder

5. If your computer asks for confirmation that you wish to run the application, provide your administrator credentials (username and password.)
6. When the installation is complete and the XAMPP application starts, a Control Panel will appear. From the Control Panel you can click the **Start** button to start the services supported by XAMPP, including the web server. See **Figure A-9**.

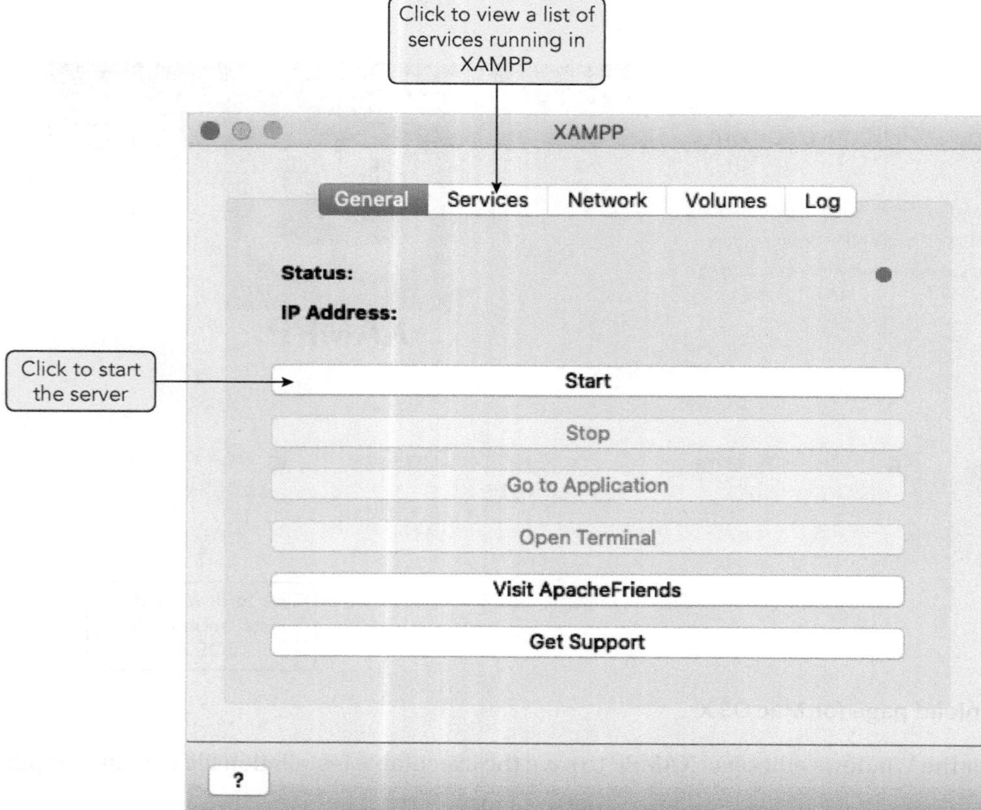

Figure A-9 Starting the XAMPP services

7. To access folders on the server, you must first mount the server volumes. Go to the **Volumes** tab in the Control Panel and click the **Mount** button as shown in **Figure A-10**.

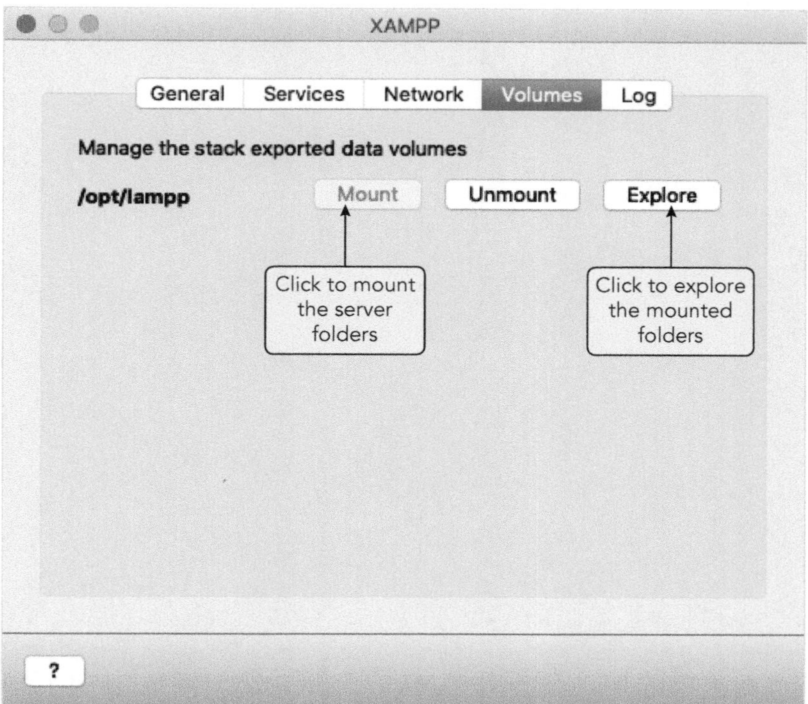

Figure A-10 Mounting volumes from the server

8. To view the contents of the server volumes, create new folders, or upload files, click the **Explore** button and then use the Mac's file tools to modify the contents of the server volumes.
9. To test your XAMPP installation, open your browser, then in the address bar, type **localhost** and press **Enter**. Your browser should display the default web document for XAMPP.

Files that will appear on the local server, should be moved into the htdocs folder of the mounted server volumes. For instance, if you copied a file called register.html to the `htdocs` folder, you would open this file in a browser by entering `localhost/register.html`. If you copied a folder called website containing a file called info.html, you would open this file in a browser by entering `localhost/website/info.html`.

If your website needs to use Perl, you will have to edit your server script so that it accesses the perl.exe file, which is located at the following address:

```
xampp\perl\bin\perl.exe
```

where *xampp* is the installation folder for XAMPP. You can reference XAPP's extensive list of online documentation to configure other aspects of your local server.

APPENDIX B

Working with HTML and CSS

Writing HTML5

Compared to many other markup languages, HTML5 is not very strict in the elements it requires to be present in a document, or the syntax it requires. However, to ensure that parsers interpret your HTML5 code as you intended, it's advisable to follow some guidelines for the documents you create.

Defining the Document Type

The **DOCTYPE declaration** in the first line of an HTML document specifies the Document Type Definition with which the document complies. A **Document Type Definition**, or **DTD**, defines the elements and attributes that can be used in a document, along with the rules that a document must follow for its structure. Although many DOCTYPE declarations exist for different versions of HTML and other markup languages, HTML5 uses the following simple DOCTYPE:

```
<!DOCTYPE html>
```

This DOCTYPE declaration should come first in your HTML document, before the opening `<html>` tag that starts the page content.

Specifying the Character Encoding

Every text document, including an HTML5 file, has a **character encoding**, which is the system used to encode the human-readable characters that make up the page in a machine-readable format. Many character encoding systems exist, including ASCII and ISO-8859-1. The standard encoding used across the web today is UTF-8. To specify that your document uses this encoding, you include the following `meta` element in your document's head section:

```
<meta charset="utf-8" />
```

Using Semantic Elements

The `div` element is a useful tool for applying styles to element or groups of elements that don't fit semantically into common HTML tags. However, the added semantic value of more specific tags can enhance the interpretation of your web pages by user agents and increase the value of the information indexed by search engines. To bridge this gap, HTML5 defines a set of elements that serve the same function as the `div` element, but that include semantic value. **Figure B-1** describes some of these elements.

SEMANTIC ELEMENT	INTENDED USE
`article`	Standalone piece of work, such as a single entry in a blog
`aside`	Part of a page that's tangential to the main page content; in a book, this might lend itself to a sidebar or pull quote
`footer`	Information about a section or document that usually appears at the end, such as attributions and/or footnotes
`header`	Information about a section or document that usually appears at the beginning, such as a heading, logo, and/or table of contents
`nav`	A list of navigational links to other pages in the website or in external websites
`section`	Section of content focused on a common theme, such as a chapter of a larger work

Figure B-1 HTML5 Semantic Elements

Writing XHTML

XHTML is a version of HTML that's written to conform to the rules of XML. Because XML is a relatively strict language, XHTML documents must include several elements and must conform to a specific syntax.

XHTML Document Type Definitions (DTDs)

When a document conforms to the rules and requirements of XHTML, it is said to be **well formed**. Among other things, a well-formed document must include a DOCTYPE declaration and the `html`, `head`, and `body` elements. As in an HTML5 document, the DOCTYPE declaration belongs in the first line of an XHTML document and determines the Document Type Definition with which the document complies. You can use three types of DTDs with XHTML documents: transitional, strict, and frameset. To understand the differences among the three types of DTDs, you need to understand the concept of deprecated HTML elements. One of the goals of XHTML is to separate the way HTML is structured from the way the parsed web page is displayed in the browser. To accomplish this goal, the W3C decided that several commonly used HTML elements and attributes for display and formatting would not be used in XHTML 1.0. Instead of using HTML elements and attributes for displaying and formatting web pages, the W3C recommends you use the Cascading Style Sheets (CSS) language, which is discussed later in this appendix.

Elements and attributes that are considered obsolete and that will eventually be eliminated are said to be **deprecated**. **Figure B-2** lists the HTML elements that are deprecated in XHTML 1.0.

ELEMENT	DESCRIPTION
`applet`	Executes Java applets
`basefont`	Specifies the base font size
`center`	Centers text
`dir`	Defines a directory list
`font`	Specifies a font name, size, and color
`isindex`	Creates automatic document indexing forms
`menu`	Defines a menu list
`s` or `strike`	Formats strikethrough text
`u`	Formats underlined text

Figure B-2 HTML elements that are deprecated in XHTML 1.0

The three DTDs are distinguished in part by the degree to which they accept or do not accept deprecated HTML elements. This is explained in more detail in the following sections.

The Transitional, Frameset, and Strict DTDs

The **transitional DTD** allows you to use deprecated style elements in your XHTML documents. The DOCTYPE declaration for the transitional DTD is as follows:

```
<!DOCTYPE html PUBLIC
   "-//W3C//DTD XHTML 1.0 Transitional//EN"
   "http://www.w3.org/TR/xhtml1/DTD/xhtml1-transitional.dtd">
```

The **frameset DTD** is identical to the transitional DTD, except that it includes the `frameset` and `frame` elements, which allow you to split the browser window into two or more frames.

The !DOCTYPE declaration for the frameset DTD is as follows:

```
<!DOCTYPE html PUBLIC
   "-//W3C//DTD XHTML 1.0 Frameset//EN"
   "http://www.w3.org/TR/xhtml1/DTD/xhtml1-frameset.dtd">
```

Because frames have been deprecated in favor of layouts using CSS, frameset documents are rarely used. However, you may encounter them if you need to modify an existing web page that was created with frames.

The **strict DTD** eliminates the elements that were deprecated in the transitional DTD and frameset DTD. The !DOCTYPE declaration for the strict DTD is as follows:

```
<!DOCTYPE html PUBLIC
   "-//W3C//DTD XHTML 1.0 Strict//EN"
   "http://www.w3.org/TR/xhtml1/DTD/xhtml1-strict.dtd">
```

Using the strict DTD ensures that your web pages conform to the most current web page authoring techniques.

Writing Well-Formed XHTML Documents

As you learned earlier, a well-formed document must include a !DOCTYPE declaration and the `html`, `head`, and `body` elements. The following list describes some other important components of a well-formed document:

- All XHTML documents must use `html` as the root element. The `xmlns` attribute is required in the `html` element and must be assigned the `http://www.w3.org/1999/xhtml` URI.
- XHTML is case sensitive.
- All XHTML elements must have a closing tag.
- Attribute values must appear within quotation marks.
- Empty elements must be closed.
- XHTML elements must be properly nested.

Most of the preceding rules are self-explanatory. However, the last rule requires further explanation. **Nesting** refers to how elements are placed inside other elements. For example, in the following code, the `a` element is nested within the `span` element, while the `span` element is nested within an `li` element.

```
<li><span><a>Contact</a></span></li>
```

HTML parsers can be somewhat forgiving if elements are not closed in the order in which they are opened. For instance, examine the following modified version of the preceding statement:

```
<li><span><a>Contact</span></a></li>
```

In this version, the opening a element is nested within the span element, which, in turn, is nested within the li element. Notice, however, that the closing </a> tag is outside the closing </span> tag. The a is the innermost element. In XHTML, the innermost element in a statement must be closed before another element is closed. In the preceding statement, the span element is closed before the a element. Although the order in which elements are closed generally does not prevent an HTML parser from interpreting the content, the preceding code would prevent an XHTML document from being well formed.

The second-to-last rule in the list ("Empty elements must be closed.") also requires further explanation. One of the most common empty elements in HTML is the img element, which adds an image to the document. You close an empty element in XHTML by adding a space and a slash before the element's closing bracket. For example, the following code shows how to use the img element in an XHTML document.

```
<header>
    <h1>
       <img src="images/logo.png" alt="" title="" />
    </h1>
    <p>Ducks in a Row Organizing Service</p>
</header>
```

Working with Cascading Style Sheets (CSS)

Once you have marked up the content of a web document with HTML, you can specify how it should be presented to users by using CSS, a standard set by the W3C for managing the visual design and formatting of HTML documents. A single piece of CSS formatting information, such as text alignment or font size, is referred to as a **style**. Some of the style capabilities of CSS include the ability to change fonts, backgrounds, and colors, and to modify the layout of elements as they appear in a web browser.

CSS information can be added directly to documents or stored in separate documents and shared among multiple web pages. The term "cascading" refers to the ability of web pages to use CSS information from more than one source. When a web page has access to multiple CSS sources, the styles "cascade," or "fall together." Keep in mind that CSS design and formatting techniques are truly independent of the content of a web page. CSS allows you to provide design and formatting specifications for well-formed documents that are compatible with all user agents.

CSS Properties

CSS styles are created with two parts separated by a colon: the **property**, which refers to a specific CSS style, and the value assigned to it, which determines the style's visual characteristics. Together, a CSS property and the value assigned to it are referred to as a **declaration** or **style declaration**. The following code creates a simple style declaration for the color property that changes the color of an element's text to blue:

```
color: blue;
```

CSS Selectors

To apply a style declaration to an HTML document, you need to specify the element or elements to which it applies. You do this using **selectors**. When you associate a selector with one or more style declarations, you create a **style rule**, which has the following general format:

```
selector {
   property: value;
   property: value;
   ...
}
```

Some of the simplest selectors simply specify an element name and result in applying associated styles to every occurrence of that element. For instance, the selector p selects all p elements in an HTML document to which it is applied. The following selector applies the foreground color blue to all p elements:

```
p {
   color: blue;
}
```

In addition to selecting all occurrences of an element, you can specify an element id value by preceding its name with the pound symbol (#). Likewise, you can specify a class value by preceding its name with a period (.). **Figure B-3** describes some basic CSS selectors.

NAME	FORMAT	SELECTS
Element	*element*	All occurrences of the specified element
ID	#*id*	The element with the id value *id*
Class	.*class*	All elements with the class value *class*
Attribute	[*attribute*]	All elements containing the attribute *attribute*
Attribute value	[*attribute*=*value*]	All elements containing the attribute *attribute* with a value of *value*

Figure B-3 Basic CSS selectors

You can also create style rules using combined selectors to specify multiple types of elements, or to choose elements with specific relationships to other elements. **Figure B-4** describes common selector combinations.

TYPE	FORMAT	SELECTS
Child	*selector1* > *selector2*	Every occurrence of *selector2* that is a child element of *selector1*
Descendant	*selector1 selector2*	Every occurrence of *selector2* that is a descendant (child, grandchild, etc.) of *selector1*
Multiple	*selector1, selector2*	All elements that match *selector1* and all elements that match *selector2*

Figure B-4 Common CSS selector combinations

Inline Styles

You can apply styles to a single element in a document using **inline styles**, which uses the style attribute to assign inline style information to the element. For instance, the following code assigns the value Verdana to the font-family property for a p element:

```
<p style="font-family: Verdana">
   Ducks in a Row Organizing Service
</p>
```

You can include multiple style declarations in an inline style by separating each declaration with a semicolon.

When you change the style property of an element using JavaScript, you are adding an inline style.

Internal Style Sheets

You use an **internal style sheet** to create styles within an HTML document that apply to that entire document. You create an internal style sheet within a `style` element placed within the document head, as follows:

```
<style>
   p {
      color: blue;
   }
</style>
```

Within the `style` element, you create any style instructions for a specific element that are applied to all instances of that element contained in the body of the document.

Inline styles and internal style sheets are rarely written in HTML documents. Instead, web developers generally limit HTML documents to HTML code, and they keep CSS code separate in a CSS document.

External Style Sheets

An **external style sheet** is a separate text document containing style declarations that can be used by multiple documents on a website. You create an external style sheet in a text editor, just as you create HTML and JavaScript documents, and you save it with an extension of .css. A style sheet document should not contain HTML elements, only style declarations.

To link the styles in an external style sheet to a web document, you add a `link` element to the head section of the HTML document. You include two attributes in the `link` element: an `href` attribute that is assigned the URL of the style sheet and the `rel` attribute that is assigned a value of `stylesheet` to specify that the referenced file is a style sheet. For example, to link a document to a style sheet named corpstyles.css, you include the following `link` element in the document head:

```
<link rel="stylesheet" href="corpstyles.css">
```

One of the advantages of putting styles in an external file is that it separates page content from page design. One team of developers can work on keeping the website content current, while another team can focus on the presentation of that content.

GLOSSARY

A

accelerometer Hardware in a mobile device that detects changes in speed.

actual parameter *See* argument.

AJAX *See* Asynchronous JavaScript and XML.

anchors The regular expression characters ^ and $ that mark the beginning and ending of a text string.

anonymous function A function with no name assigned to it.

API key A string of characters passed from the application to an API platform, verifying that the application has access to the tools built into the API.

Application Programming Interface (API) A set of procedures that access an application such as a web page or a web browser.

argument Values supplied to a method or function call statement.

arithmetic operators Operators used to perform mathematical calculations, such as addition, subtraction, multiplication, and division.

array A set of data represented by a single variable name.

array literal A single statement that declares an array variable and its content.

arrow function A terse representation of a function that removes all extraneous characters from the function definition.

assignment operator The operator (=) used to assign the value on the right side of an expression to the variable on the left side of the expression.

associative array A data structure with data values defined using `key:value` pairs.

associativity The order in which operators of equal precedence execute.

asynchronous Type of client-server connection in which client activity continues in the background while waiting for a server response.

asynchronous callback A callback function that accomplishes its task working in parallel with the caller.

Asynchronous JavaScript and XML A technology for transferring asynchronous HTTP messages between a client and server with particular support for XML documents.

B

back end *See* server.

back-end developer A developer who works mainly with server-side languages and libraries, such as PHP, SQL, and Node.js.

backtracking An operation of a regular expression in which the regular expression contains quantifiers such as the * or + characters, which force the parser to examine each possible substring within a larger text string.

base object The fundamental JavaScript object whose properties and methods are shared with all custom and native objects.

Binary Large Object (Blob) An object used for data storage in which the data is stored as a chunk of bytes.

binary operator An operator that requires an operand before and after it.

Blob *See* Binary Large Object.

block comment A comment that contains multiple lines of code; created by enclosing the multiple lines within the /* and */ characters.

block scoped The scope in which a variable can only be referenced within the command block in which it is declared using the `let` keyword.

BOM *See* Browser Object Model (BOM).

Boolean value A logical value of `true` or `false`.

bracket notation The `object["property"]` notation that connects an object name with an object property.

break mode The temporary suspension of program execution in a browser so the programmer can monitor values and trace program execution.

breakpoint A designation added to a specific statement in a program that causes program execution to pause when it reaches that statement.

browser console A browser pane that displays error messages.

Browser Object Model (BOM) The aspect of JavaScript that describes how to access the features and behaviors of the browser itself.

browser test A conditional statement that tests whether a feature of the JavaScript language is supported by the browser.

browser-based validation Validation tasks performed by browsers themselves without any extra JavaScript, enabled by recent enhancements to HTML and to modern browsers; also known as native validation.

bubbling phase The propagation of an event moving up the object hierarchy from the most specific object to the most general or from the innermost object to the browser window.

bug Any error in a program that causes it to function incorrectly, whether because of incorrect syntax or flaws in logic.

bulletproofing Writing code that anticipates and handles potential problems.

C

caching Temporary storage for data on a local device to enable faster access to that data.

call A statement that invokes a function to perform a task or calculate a value.

call stack The ordered list maintained by a JavaScript processor containing all the procedures, such as functions, methods, or event handlers, that have been called but have not yet finished processing.

callback Executable code that is called to complete a task or return value.

callback function A function that is passed as a parameter to another function or method.

callback hell A programming challenge in which callbacks involving multiple asynchronous requests are organized in a large and unwieldy nested structure.

camel case A method of capitalization that uses a lowercase letter for the first letter of the first word in a variable name, with subsequent words starting with an initial cap, as in `myVariableName`.

capture phase The propagation of an event moving down the object hierarchy from the most general object to the most specific or from the browser window to the innermost object.

Cascading Style Sheets (CSS) A complementary language to HTML, developed for specifying the appearance of web page elements on a specified device.

CDATA *See* character data.

CDN *See* content delivery network.

character class A collection of regular expression characters that limits characters to a select group.

character data A section of an HTML document that is not interpreted as markup.

checksum algorithm A mathematical algorithm used with the digits within numeric ids to verify that such ids are legitimate.

client In a two-tier system, the tier that presents an interface to the user.

client-side scripting Programming written in a scripting language that runs on a local browser (on the client tier) instead of on a web server (on the processing tier).

client-side validation Validation of web form data that takes place on the user's browser.

closure A copy of a function and the lexical environment of the function's variables.

code editor An app used for writing and managing program code such as the code for HTML, CSS, and JavaScript.

code injection attack A security threat in which a program or user enters JavaScript code that changes the function of the web page.

command block Multiple JavaScript statements enclosed within a set of opening and closing curly braces.

commenting out A debugging technique in which program errors are located by changing potentially incorrect program code to comments.

comments Lines of code that are not processed by browsers and which serve as notes about the meaning and purpose of program statements.

compare function A function called by the `sort()` method to specify how array items should be sorted.

comparison operator An operator to compare two operands and determine their relative value.

compiled A process by which instructions from a programming language are transformed into machine code.

compiler A program that transforms programming code into machine code that can be understood by the computer or computer device.

compound assignment operators Assignment operators other than the equal sign, which perform mathematical calculations on variables and literal values in an expression, and then assign a new value to the left operand.

concatenation operator The plus symbol (+) use to either add numeric values or to combine text strings.

conditional operator The `?:` operator, which executes one of two expressions based on the results of a conditional expression.

conditional statement *See* decision-making statement.

confirmation window A system dialog box created with the `confirm()` method that displays an OK and Cancel button, returning a value of true or false depending on which button the user clicks.

console *See* browser console.

Constraint Validation API The set of properties and methods that enables developers to customize the validation of web forms.

constructor function A function used to define an object class.

content delivery network (CDN) A server that maintains web servers optimized for fast delivery of content.

controlling flow Changing the order in which JavaScript code is executed.

cookie A small piece of information stored as a text string that is exchanged between a web server and client device with every HTTP request.

CORS *See* Cross Origin Resource Sharing.

counter A variable that is incremented or decremented with each iteration of a program loop.

Cross Origin Resource Sharing A method of bypassing the same origin policy by including a special HTTP request header in the message from the client to the server.

CSS *See* Cascading Style Sheets (CSS).

custom object Object created by the user for a specific programming task.

D

data interchange format A data format that is a common standard for information exchange.

data transparency The process of making it clear to users what information an app needs to collect and how it will be used.

data type The specific category of information that a variable contains, such as numeric, Boolean, or string.

`dataTransfer` object An object used to transfer data collected during a drag and drop action.

`Date` object A JavaScript object that stores date and time values and provides methods and properties for managing dates and times.

debugging The act of tracing and resolving program errors.

decision making The process of choosing which code to execute at a given point in an application.

decision-making statement A special type of JavaScript statement used for making decisions.

decision-making structure *See* decision-making statement.

declare The process by which a variable is defined using the `var`, `let`, or `const` keywords.

deep copy A copy of a node that includes all the node's descendants.

defensive coding *See* secure coding.

dependencies The relationships that exist when statements depend on the successful execution of other statements or functions.

Device Orientation API An API providing access to data from specialized hardware in many mobile devices for detecting changes in position and speed.

`DirectionsRenderer` object An object that draws a route on a map or writes turn-by-turn directions given results queried from a Google Maps `DirectionsService` object.

`DirectionsService` object An object that queries the Google Maps Directions service to find the most efficient route between two locations for a given mode of travel.

DnD API *See* Drag and Drop API.

document fragment A set of connected nodes that are not part of a document.

Document Object Model (DOM) The aspect of JavaScript that describes how to access the contents of the web page and user actions within that page.

DOM *See* Document Object Model (DOM).

dot operator The *`object.property`* notation that connects an object name with an object property.

Drag and Drop API A JavaScript API that manages all parts of a drag and drop operation.

driver program A simplified, temporary program that is used for testing functions and other code.

drop zone An element that is enabled to receive items dropped from a drag and drop action.

duck typed *See* loosely typed.

dynamically typed *See* loosely typed.

E

ECMA *See* European Computer Manufacturers Association (ECMA).

ECMA-262 *See* EMCAScript.

ECMAScript An international, standardized version of JavaScript.

element An individual value contained in an array or a page object marked within an HTML file.

empty string A zero-length string value.

encapsulation The process by which all code (primarily properties and methods) and data needed for the object are completely contained within the object itself.

encoding The process of converting each special character in a text string to its corresponding hexadecimal ASCII value, preceded by a percent sign.

endpoint The point of contact between the client and server resource, often specified as the URL that receives the client request.

enumerable The property of being countable.

escape To convert characters to their character code equivalents, similar to encoding.

escape character The backslash character (\), which tells JavaScript compilers and interpreters that the character that follows it has a special purpose.

escape sequence The combination of the escape character (\) with one of several other characters, which inserts a special character into a string; for example, the `\b` escape sequence inserts a backspace character.

European Computer Manufacturers Association (ECMA) A non-profit organization that develops standards in computer hardware, communications, and programming languages, including ECMAScript.

event A specific occurrence within a web page or browser that is initiated either by the user or the browser itself.

event handler Code that tells a browser how to respond to an event within the web page or browser.

event listener A method that listens for events that propagate through the object hierarchy either in the capture phase or the bubbling phase.

event listener breakpoint A breakpoint that is activated when an event occurs within the web page or browser.

event model A model that describes how objects and events interact within the web page and web browser.

event object An object that contains information about events captured by an event handler or event listener.

exception An error that occurs in the execution of a program.

exception handling A method of bulletproofing code that allows a program to handle errors as they occur in the execution of the program.

executor The command block contained within a promise.

exponential notation A shortened format for writing very large numbers or numbers with many decimal places, in which numbers are represented by a value between and multiplied by raised to some power.

expression A literal value or variable or a combination of literal values, variables, operators, and other expressions that can be evaluated by a JavaScript interpreter to produce a result.

Extensible Markup Language (XML) A document language to create structure documents using markup tags.

F

fallthrough A situation in which execution of a `switch` statement does not stop after the statements for a particular `case` label are executed, but continues evaluating the rest of the `case` labels in the list.

falsy values Values or expressions that are treated in comparison operations as the Boolean value `false`.

fat arrow The `=>` symbol that replaces the function keyword in an arrow function.

Fetch API A JavaScript API replacement for AJAX that uses promises to manage server requests and responses.

File API A JavaScript API that allows for the retrieval of the contents of selected files on the local computer or network.

`file` object A single file within the `files` collection.

File Reader API A JavaScript API used for reading the contents of an external file and created with the `new FileReader()` object constructor.

`files` collection A collection of files retrieved using the `file` data type of the `input` element.

first-in-first-out (FIFO) A principle of data structures in which the first items added to the queue are the first ones removed.

flag A regular expression character that modifies the global behavior of the regular expression.

floating point number A number that contains decimal places or that is written in exponential notation.

focus The state where a web form control is active, either by clicking it or moving the cursor into it.

freemium service A service in which there are no costs to the web developer if server requests are few.

front end *See* client.

front-end developer A developer who works primarily with HTML, CSS, and client-side JavaScript.

full stack developer A developer who has skills to manage both client-side and server-side code.

fully qualified domain A domain that can receive data from a service resource without hindrance from the browser.

function A related group of JavaScript statements that are executed as a single unit.

function braces The set of curly braces that contain the statements used within a function.

function call A statement that runs a named function and passes argument values to that function.

function expression A statement that stores a function as a variable.

function scope Scope in which a variable can only be referenced within the function in which it is declared by the `var` keyword.

G

geolocation A process that determines the position of the client device using either a built-in GPS receiver or information drawn from the client's network IP address.

Geolocation API An API that provides information on the global position of the client device.

`get` method A method of sending data to the server that appends the data as part of a query string added to the URL of a web page address.

getter A method that gets a value from selected elements.

global object A term for the `window` object, based on the fact that all other objects in the browser object model are contained within it.

global scope Scope in which a function or variable is defined outside of any command block or function and thus is accessible throughout the program.

global variable A variable that is accessible to all functions and statements within a program.

Google Maps API An API developed by Google to provide interactive global maps.

gyroscope Hardware in a mobile device that detects its spatial orientation.

H

history list The internal list maintained by the `history` object of all the documents that have been opened during the current web browser session.

`history` object The child object of the `window` object that maintains an internal list of all the documents that have been opened during the current web browser session.

host object An object provided by the browser for use in interacting with the web document and browser.

HTML *See* Hypertext Markup Language (HTML).

HTML Collection Object A group of HTML elements within the Document Object Model.

HTTP *See* Hypertext Transfer Protocol (HTTP).

HTTP client An application, usually a web browser, that makes a request from a server.

HTTP message A message transferred between a server and client via the HTTP protocol.

HTTP request Part of the HTTP protocol that is generated each time the web server and client exchange data, consisting of a header containing data about the browser and its capabilities and a body containing information necessary to process the request.

HTTP server A web server or computer that receives HTTP request and returns a response to HTTP clients.

Hypertext Markup Language (HTML) A markup language used to define the content and structure of web pages.

Hypertext Transfer Protocol (HTTP) A communication standard used on the web to exchange information between servers and client devices.

I

IDE *See* Integrated Development Environment (IDE).

identifier The name assigned to a variable.

immutable A property of objects that cannot be modified.

index A number associated with an element in an array, which represents the element's position within the array.

infinite loop A program loop than repeats without end.

initialize The process by which a variable is defined and given an initial value.

instantiating Creating an object from an object class.

integer A positive or negative number with no decimal places.

Integrated Development Environment (IDE) An application that manages all of the facets of website development, including the writing and testing of JavaScript code.

interface The programmatic elements that make the inner workings of an object accessible to other programs and scripts.

interpreter A program that scans scripting language code for errors and executes it.

invalid event An event that is fired when the browser encounters invalid data within a web form control.

iteration Each repetition of a program loop.

J

JavaScript A client-side scripting language that allows web page authors to develop interactive web pages and sites.

JavaScript library A set of JavaScript code that can be organized and shared with other programmers to reduce time and effort in developing an app.

JavaScript Object Notation (JSON) A text data structure organized in a format similar to JavaScript objects.

JavaScript source file An external file containing JavaScript code, which can be referenced in a web document.

jQuery A free public JavaScript library that enables developers to implement many common tasks with minimal code.

jQuery animation A jQuery visual effect accomplished by gradually changing the values of a collection of CSS properties over a specified time interval.

jQuery effect A jQuery method that applies a visual effect to a selection of elements.

jQuery plugin A jQuery add-on package that extends the capabilities of jQuery with new effects, methods, objects, and properties.

jQuery UI A jQuery plugin that expands the functionality of jQuery with a large collection of functions and methods for creating specialized user interfaces.

JScript An early version of JavaScript used by Microsoft Internet Explorer in the 1990s.

JSON *See* JavaScript Object Notation

JSON with Padding (JSONP) A technique for requesting data from a server on a different origin in which the request is folded within a `script` element rather than as a request object or a Fetch promise.

JSONP *See* JSON with Padding.

K

keywords *See* reserved words.

L

last-in-first-out (LIFO) A principle of data structures in which the last items added to the stack are the first ones removed.

lexical environment The programming environment that encompasses a function and its variables and their values.

lexical scope The scope of variables, functions, and other objects is based on their physical location within the source code.

lexicographical order An ordering of the characters within a language.

library A JavaScript source file that contains generic scripts that can be applied to different web apps.

lightbox A web app that displays multiple images in a scrolling gallery with the capability to enlarge single images.

line comment A comment that occupies only a single line or part of a line; created by adding two slashes (//) before the comment text.

linting The process of running code through a program that flags common issues that may affect code quality and performance.

literal A value such as a literal string or a number.

literal string *See* text string.

load-time error An error that occurs when the program is initially loaded by the browser.

local scope Scope in which a function or variable is available only to a command block or a function but not outside those contexts.

local storage object Web storage in which the data is permanently stored by the browser and can be accessed anytime by the user running that browser on that client device.

local variable A variable that is declared inside a function and is available only within the function in which it is declared, because it has local scope.

`location` object The child object of the `window` object that contains properties and methods associated with the address of the current web page.

logging A debugging technique that involves writing values directly to the browser console.

logic The order in which various parts of a program run, or execute.

logic error A flaw in a program's design that prevents the program from running as anticipated.

logical operators The Or (||), And (`&&`), and Not (`!`) operators, which are used to modify Boolean values or specify the relationship between operands in an expression that results in a Boolean value.

loosely typed A programming language that does require variable data types to be explicitly declared.

Luhn algorithm A checksum algorithm used with credit card numbers.

M

machine code Binary code that can be understood by a computer or computer device.

man-in-the-middle attack An attack in which data being exchanged between two parties is read and potentially changed in transit.

markup language A language that defines the content, structure, and appearance of a document.

`Math` object A built-in JavaScript object used for performing mathematical operations and storing mathematical constants.

matrix Numbers stored in a rectangular grid of rows and columns.

method A procedure associated with an object.

middle tier *See* processing tier.

MIME type A property of a file that indicates the type of content that file contains.

minifying A method of reducing the size of a file by removing comments, indents, and line breaks, and tweaking the code in other ways to make it smaller.

mod 10 algorithm *See* Luhn algorithm.

modal a window that takes control of an application and must be closed before the user can continue using the app.

modal window *See* modal.

modifier keys The Alt, Ctrl, Shift, and Command keys.

modulus Operator represented by the `%` character that returns the remainder after division.

multidimensional array A data structure in which two or more arrays are nested within one another.

multitier client/server system *See* three-tier client/server system.

N

n-tier client/server system *See* three-tier client/server system.

named function A function that is identified by an assigned name.

native object An object that is part of the JavaScript language.

native validation *See* browser-based validation.

`navigator` object The child object of the `window` object that is used to obtain information about the current browser.

nested decision-making structure The type of structure created by nesting one decision-making statement within another decision-making statement.

node Each item in the DOM tree.

node list An indexed collection of nodes.

node tree Nodes organized into a hierarchical structure.

normal jQuery build The build of jQuery that includes the full features of the jQuery library.

O

object Programming code and data that can be treated as an individual unit or component.

object chaining The process by which a jQuery selector is appended with jQuery methods that extends or redirects the selected elements.

object class A template or blueprint for the creation of new objects all sharing a common collection of properties and methods.

object constructor A command in the form `new Class(parameters)` used to create new objects from an object class.

object instance A specific object created from an object class.

object literal A standalone object used once for a single purpose.

object-oriented programming (OOP) Programming technique involving the creation of reusable software objects that can be easily incorporated into multiple programs.

OOP *See* Object Oriented Programming.

operand A variable or a literal contained in an expression.

operator A symbol such as + or * used in an expression to manipulate operands.

operator precedence The system that determines the order in which operations in an expression are evaluated.

origin The location of a web resource indicated by its protocol, port, and host.

overlay An element that lays on top of web page content, partially obscuring the page.

P

parameter A variable that is used within a function.

parsed character data A section of an HTML document that is interpreted as markup.

passing arguments Providing one or more arguments for a method or called function.

path A storage folder on the server.

PCDATA *See* parsed character data.

Perl A popular server-side scripting language often used to generate and manipulate text strings.

persistent cookie A cookie that remains available beyond the current browser session and is stored in a text file on a client computer.

pointer event Any action that involves using a device to point at an object on the screen.

popup window An external window to be opened and displayed on top of or adjacent to the application content.

`position` object An object that contains data on the device's position.

`post` method A method of submitting web forms that appends the form data to the body of the HTTP request.

postfix operator An operator that is placed after a variable name.

posttest loop A program loop in which the stopping condition is evaluated after the command block has been executed at least once.

prefix operator An operator that is placed before a variable name.

pretest loop A program loop in which the stopping condition is evaluated before each iteration of the command block.

primitive types Data types that can be assigned only a single value.

private method A method created within the constructor function and thus accessible only within the constructor.

privileged method A method that accesses private variables and methods but is also accessible to the public.

procedure In a computer program, a logical unit composed of individual statements, which is used to perform a specific task.

processing tier The part of a three-tier client/server system that handles the interaction between the web browser client and the data storage tier.

program loop A command block that is executed repeatedly until a stopping condition is met.

programming language A set of instructions directing the actions of the computer or computer device

promise An object that does not have a value currently but might have one in the future once certain conditions are met.

promise chain A sequence of promises in which each promise relies on the successful resolution of the prior promise.

prompt window A system dialog box created with the `prompt()` method that displays a input box, returning the text entered by the user into the box.

property A piece of data, such as a color or a name, that is associated with an object.

prototypal inheritance The process by which the properties and methods of an object class at one level are shared with an object class within a nested level.

prototype A template for all the properties and methods associated with the object's class.

prototype chain A hierarchy of objects from a base object class down to lower classes or subclasses.

proxy server A server that handles an HTTP request for the client rather than relying on the client's own server.

public method A method defined for the object prototype which can be called outside of the object.

Q

query string Text appended to a URL containing data field names and data field values; a set of name-value pairs appended to a target URL.

queue A data structure in which new items are added to the bottom or beginning of the array.

R

regular expression Code that concisely describes the general pattern and content of characters within a text string

regular expression literal A regular expression pattern entered in JavaScript as `/pattern/`.

relational operator *See* comparison operator.

request A query sent to a server resource asking for content.

reserved words Special words that are part of the JavaScript language syntax.

response A reply from a server resource when data is requested.

root node The `html` node in a web document, which is also the parent of all other nodes in the node tree.

RSS newsfeed A technology that uses XML to transmit current news stories to media outlets and podcasts.

runtime error An error that occurs when a JavaScript interpreter encounters a problem while a program is executing.

S

same-origin policy A JavaScript security feature that restricts how JavaScript code in one window, tab, or frame accesses a web page in another window, tab, or frame on a client computer.

scientific notation *See* exponential notation.

scope A characteristic of a function or variable that indicates where it can be referenced within the program code.

Scope window A section of the browser debugger pane that lists all local and global variables and objects available to the program and their current values.

`screen` object The child object of the `window` object that is used to obtain information about the display screen's size, resolution, and color depth.

script A JavaScript program contained within a web page.

scripting language A subcategory of programming languages that are interpreted rather than compiled and run directly from a program or script, often used to control a web page or return some sort of response to a web browser.

secure coding The process of writing code to minimize any intentional or accidental security issues.

Secure Sockets Layer (SSL) The main protocol used to encrypt data on websites.

server A device or application from which a client requests information; a server fulfills a request for information by managing the request or serving the requested information to the client.

server-side scripting Programming written in a scripting language that is executed from a web server.

server-side validation Validation of web form data that takes place on the web server.

session The interaction that occurs each time the client device connects to the web server within a browser window or tab.

session cookie Cookie that remains available only for the current browser session.

session storage object Web storage in which the data is accessible only during the current session.

setter A method that sets the value within selected elements.

slim jQuery build The build of jQuery that removes features such as AJAX and animation effect tools.

spaghetti code A pejorative programming term that refers to convoluted or poorly written code.

sparse array An array in which some array elements are left undefined so that the length of the array is not the same as the number of defined values.

spread operator A JavaScript operator written as an ellipsis of three dots (`...`), which spreads out the items within an array into a comma-separated list of values.

SRI *See* Subresource Integrity checking.

SSL *See* Secure Sockets Layer.

stack A data structure in which new items are added to the top or end of the array.

state information Information about individual visits to a website.

stateless A communication protocol that does not accommodate the storage of data beyond the current session.

statement An individual line of code in a JavaScript program.

static Description of a web page that can't change after a browser renders it.

static scope *See* lexical scope.

statically typed *See* strongly typed.

step in The stepping option that executes an individual line of code and then pauses until instructed to continue; also known as *step into*.

step into *See* step in.

step out The stepping option that executes all remaining code in the current function.

step over The stepping option to skip function calls; the program still executes each function stepped over, but appearing in the debugger as if a single statement executes.

stepping options Options in browser debugging tools to continue program execution after program breaks.

stop words Words that are not normally included within a word cloud.

strict mode A JavaScript processing mode in which adherence to JavaScript syntax is strictly enforced.

strongly typed Description of a programming language that requires the declaration of variable data types.

subarray A section of an array.

subclass An object class at the lower levels of a prototype chain.

Subresource Integrity checking (SRI) A software check that ensures that the resources on the CDN have not been tampered with.

substring A portion of a larger text string.

superclass An object class at the higher levels of a prototype chain.

synchronous The halting of program operation pending a response from a callback function or other code currently being run.

synchronous callback A callback function that accomplishes its task before returning control to the caller.

syntax The rules for a programming language.

syntax error An error that occurs when an interpreter fails to recognize code, such as a statement that is not recognized by a browser's scripting engine.

T

target phase The phase during event propagation in which the event reaches the event target.

template literal A text string enclosed with the backtick character (`) which allows the string to be written across several lines and be made available to JavaScript tools for handling text characters.

ternary operator An operator that takes three operands.

text string Text passed as an argument, contained within double or single quotation marks.

third-party scripts Scripts from other domains.

`this` object The object that references the owner of a currently running segment of JavaScript code.

three-tier client/server system A system that consists of three distinct pieces: the client tier, the processing tier, and the data storage tier.

throw A JavaScript statement used to trigger an error event.

timed command A command or function that is run at a specified time or repeated at set intervals.

TLS *See* Transport Layer Security.

token A string of random characters used to verify a user's identity in a system that supports persistent logins.

touch cascade A sequence of touch and mouse events triggered during interaction with a touch surface.

Touch interface An interface with a touchscreen that involves a single point of contact.

TouchEvent interface An interface with a touchscreen that involves changing the state of touchpoints on the touch surface.

TouchList interface An interface with a touchscreen that involves multiple simultaneous points of contact.

touchpoint A single point of contact on a touch surface.

tracing A debugging technique that involves examining individual statements in an executing program.

Transport Layer Security (TLS) The encryption standard planned to eventually replace SSL.

truthy values A value or expression that is treated as the Boolean value `true`.

two-tier system A system consisting of a client and a server.

U

unary operator An operator that requires just a single operand either before or after it.

URI-encoded character A character that is replaced with its URI character code.

user error An error initiated by the user through operating the program in a way not intended by the developer.

user-defined object *See* custom object.

V

validating parser A program that checks whether a web page is well formed and whether the document conforms to a specific DTD.

validation The process of checking that information provided by users conforms to rules to ensure that it appropriately answers the form's questions and is provided in a format that the site's back-end programs can work with.

`ValidityState` object A text string appended to a URL containing field names and values.

variables The values a program stores in computer memory.

W

W3C *See* World Wide Web Consortium (W3C)

Watch window A section of the debugger pane used for tracking the changing values of a variable or expression.

web *See* World Wide Web.

web application A program that is executed on a server but is accessed through a web page loaded in a client browser.

Web Storage API A JavaScript specification that enables browsers to store data as text strings within an associative array that can be read by the client device using the browser interface.

well formed A document that conforms to the rules and requirements of a markup language such as HTML or XHTML.

whitespace character Any blank or nonprintable character such as a space, tab, or line break.

word A regular expression pattern consisting solely of word characters.

word characters Characters that are alphabetical characters, digits, or the underscore character (_).

word cloud A graphical representation of the words and phrases used within a document in which the size and style of each word indicates its frequency and importance.

World Wide Web A system for easily accessing cross-referenced documents using the Internet.

World Wide Web Consortium (W3C) An organization established to oversee the development of web technology standards.

X

XHR object *See* `XMLHttpRequest` object.

XML *See* Extensible Markup Language.

`XMLHttpRequest` object A request object used to send requests from the client to the server over the HTTP communication protocol.

INDEX

F